2016
The Supreme Court Review

2016
The

"Judges as persons, or courts as institutions, are entitled to no greater immunity from criticism than other persons or institutions . . . [J]udges must be kept mindful of their limitations and of their ultimate public responsibility by a vigorous stream of criticism expressed with candor however blunt."

—*Felix Frankfurter*

". . . while it is proper that people should find fault when their judges fail, it is only reasonable that they should recognize the difficulties. . . . Let them be severely brought to book, when they go wrong, but by those who will take the trouble to understand them."

—*Learned Hand*

THE LAW SCHOOL

THE UNIVERSITY OF CHICAGO

Supreme Court Review

EDITED BY

DENNIS J. HUTCHINSON

DAVID A. STRAUSS

AND GEOFFREY R. STONE

THE UNIVERSITY OF CHICAGO PRESS

CHICAGO AND LONDON

INTERNATIONAL STANDARD BOOK NUMBER: 978-0-226-49084-7

LIBRARY OF CONGRESS CATALOG CARD NUMBER: 60-14353

THE UNIVERSITY OF CHICAGO PRESS, CHICAGO 60637

THE UNIVERSITY OF CHICAGO PRESS, LTD., LONDON

PRINTED IN THE UNITED STATES OF AMERICA

The paper used in this publication meets the minimum requirements of American National Standard for Information Sciences–Permanence of Paper for Printed Library Materials, ANSI Z39.48-1984. ♾

TO

DEAN MARTHA MINOW

Educational leader, teacher, scholar,
and citizen, deeply committed to social justice

CONTENTS

DAVID A. STRAUSS

FISHER v UNIVERSITY OF TEXAS AND THE CONSERVATIVE CASE FOR AFFIRMATIVE ACTION

Fisher v University of Texas at Austin[1] had a long, strange trip at the Supreme Court. *Fisher* was the Court's latest encounter with affirmative action in higher education. In 2012, the Court granted certiorari in the case to review a decision by the Fifth Circuit that upheld the university's affirmative action plan.[2] Aspects of the case arguably made it inappropriate for the Court's review, so the decision to intervene suggested that the Justices were eager to issue a significant ruling on affirmative action. The Court then spent a long time deliberating: it heard argument in October 2012, then did not issue its decision until almost the last day of the Term, in June 2013. But that decision, surprisingly, was narrow and nearly unanimous. The Court

David A. Strauss is Gerald Ratner Distinguished Service Professor of Law, The University of Chicago.

AUTHOR'S NOTE: I am grateful to William Baude, Justin Driver, Hannah Solomon-Strauss, and Geoffrey Stone for very helpful conversations, for comments on an earlier draft, and for sharing their work with me. I also thank the Burton and Adrienne Glazov Faculty Fund at the University of Chicago Law School for financial support.

[1] 136 S Ct 2198 (2016).

[2] *Fisher v University of Texas at Austin*, 631 F3d 213 (5th Cir 2011), cert granted, 132 S Ct 1536 (2012). Seven judges on the court of appeals dissented from the denial of rehearing en banc. See 644 F3d 301, 303 (5th Cir 2011).

978-0-226-49084-7/2017/2016-0001$10.00

merely corrected the standard that the court of appeals had used and remanded the case for further proceedings.[3]

On remand, the Fifth Circuit again held that the university's plan was constitutional.[4] The Supreme Court again granted certiorari.[5] The second grant, one might have thought, was a signal that the Court was sure to restrict, in a significant way, state universities' ability to engage in affirmative action; why else would it have taken the case again?[6] But the Court did nothing of the kind. Its decision was, again, narrow; in fact, it was explicitly limited to the University of Texas's unusual situation. And it affirmed the Fifth Circuit's decision upholding the constitutionality of the university's plan. After two plenary hearings and deliberations spread over two Terms, the Court essentially left the status quo intact, raising the question why the Court had not just denied review in the first place. When it was all over, Justice Ginsburg commented, in an interview with the *New York Times*, "I don't expect we're going to see another affirmative action case, at least in education."[7]

What happened in *Fisher*? One possibility is that the Court finally recognized a tension that has been present since its first decision about an affirmative action program, forty years ago, in *Regents of University of California v Bakke*.[8] The Court has held that affirmative action is subject to "strict scrutiny"—meaning that the Court will insist that the university, or other government entity, demonstrate that its affirmative action measures are no more extensive than necessary to advance a compelling interest. The Court has said that achieving educational diversity is a compelling interest. But educational diversity is an objective that resists the kind of clear definition that strict scrutiny requires. If the end cannot be clearly defined, then

---

[3] *Fisher v University of Texas at Austin (Fisher I)*, 133 S Ct 2411 (2013).

[4] *Fisher v University of Texas at Austin*, 758 F3d 633 (5th Cir 2014).

[5] *Fisher v University of Texas at Austin*, cert granted, 135 S Ct 2888 (2015).

[6] The inference that the Court was prepared to do something significant is especially strong because the petition was granted by an eight-Justice Court. (Justice Kagan did not participate, see id, apparently because she had been involved in the case when she was Solicitor General.) The Court had already deliberated about the case once. Had the Justices anticipated a 4–4 division, there would have been no point in granting certiorari a second time.

[7] Adam Liptak, *Ruth Bader Ginsburg, No Fan of Donald Trump, Critiques Latest Term* (NY Times, July 10, 2016), archived at https://perma.cc/4NXK-RA5B.

[8] 438 US 265 (1978). See also note 11 and accompanying text.

a court cannot decide, as strict scrutiny requires, whether the means are closely adapted to achieving it.

Besides that, one central principle in the Court's cases since *Bakke* has been that affirmative action measures must not be too transparent. It must not be too clear just how much affirmative action a state university, for example, is engaging in. As a result, the law governing affirmative action, as it has developed in the Court's decisions, demands a rigorous showing of a close means-ends fit between ends that cannot be clearly defined and means that cannot be too openly avowed. It's hard to explain why you're doing just the right amount of something when you aren't supposed to be clear about how much of it you're doing and no one can really say what the right amount is. *Fisher* presented this conundrum vividly, and that might explain the Court's struggle with the case.

It does not, however, explain the Court's surrender—its decision to uphold the university's affirmative action plan after all. The Court might have resolved the tension by declaring that affirmative action is unconstitutional in all, or most, circumstances, or at least by repudiating the idea that educational diversity is a compelling interest. A reason for the Court's decision not to do that—to allow the university to continue doing what it was doing under the muddled standard that the Court had developed—reflects, perhaps paradoxically, an important strand of conservative thought, one that has been beneath the surface of its opinions from the beginning.

A conservative tradition identified with Edmund Burke, Friedrich Hayek, and Michael Oakeshott holds that abstract principles, however theoretically appealing, are less reliable than the specific, often unarticulated knowledge of people going about their ordinary day-to-day work in society. At least by the time of *Fisher*, and probably long before, it had become clear that affirmative action is deeply embedded in American society. Institutions throughout the nation—universities, corporations, governments—engage in affirmative action.[9] The people responsible for those institutions may not have a well-developed theoretical rationale for affirmative action, but they have concluded that the best way for their institutions to operate is to

[9] See, for example, Randall Kennedy, *For Discrimination: Race, Affirmative Action, and the Law* 15 (Pantheon, 2013) ("The affirmative action ethos has become deeply rooted. The social forces that created it, combined with the changes it has wrought, have made racial homogeneity unacceptable in most key public forums.").

engage in some degree of race-conscious action favoring minorities. If people in those positions have consistently adopted a practice, that is a good reason to think the practice is sound. Affirmative action, the Court has perhaps realized, has passed that test.

Affirmative Action in the Court

Regents of University of California v Bakke[10] was the Court's first full-dress encounter with affirmative action.[11] The medical school of the University of California, Davis, set aside sixteen places in its 100-student entering class for members of certain specified minority groups. A nonminority applicant who had been rejected challenged that plan. Four Justices would have upheld the university's plan.[12] Four determined that it violated Title VI of the Civil Rights Act of 1964, which forbids racial discrimination in programs that receive federal financial aid.[13] The ninth Justice, Justice Powell, concluded that the Davis program was unconstitutional, but his opinion described how affirmative action in higher education could, in his view, be upheld.[14]

Justice Powell's opinion stated three principles that ultimately came to govern the area.[15] First, all racial classifications, whether or not they purport to benefit minorities, are subject to strict scrutiny—"the most exacting judicial examination."[16] That means that an affirmative action measure has to promote a "compelling" interest and that the

---

[10] 438 US 265 (1978).

[11] In fact, the Court had earlier dealt with—and upheld—the constitutionality of race-conscious measures designed to aid desegregation. See, for example, *McDaniel v Barresi*, 402 US 39 (1971). See also note 84. In *DeFunis v Odegaard*, 416 US 312 (1974), the Court considered a challenge to an affirmative action program at the University of Washington Law School but ruled that the case was moot.

[12] See 438 US at 324–79 (Brennan, White, Marshall, and Blackmun, JJ, concurring in judgment in part and dissenting in part).

[13] See id at 408–21 (Stevens, J, concurring in judgment in part and dissenting in part).

[14] See id at 269–320 (1978) (opinion of Powell, J).

[15] John C. Jeffries, Jr., *Bakke Revisited*, 2003 Supreme Court Review 1, tells, very well, the remarkable story of how Justice Powell, who "had lived most of his life, uncomplainingly, in racial segregation and educational apartheid," id at 1, came to write the opinion that not only sustained the legality of affirmative action at the time of *Bakke* but has provided the template for upholding affirmative action in education to this day. See also John C. Jeffries, Jr., *Justice Lewis F. Powell, Jr.* 469–95 (Maxwell Macmillan, 1994).

[16] 438 US at 291.

measure must be "necessary" (or, as the Court later came to say, "narrowly tailored") to promote that interest.[17]

Second, Justice Powell concluded that a university's interest in having a racially diverse student body is such a compelling interest. "[T]he interest of diversity is compelling in the context of a university's admissions program"[18] because "the attainment of a diverse student body" is a "goal that is of paramount importance in the fulfillment of [a university's] mission."[19] Crucially, "[e]thnic diversity" was "one element"—although, Justice Powell said, "only one element"—in "a range of factors a university properly may consider in attaining the goal of a heterogeneous student body."[20]

The third element of Justice Powell's approach was that an affirmative action program may not simply set aside a certain number of places for minority applicants, as Davis's did. The compelling interest, as Justice Powell saw it, "is not an interest in simple ethnic diversity" but instead "encompasses a far broader array of qualifications and characteristics of which racial and ethnic origin is but a single though important element."[21] An admissions program must be "flexible enough to consider all pertinent elements of diversity in light of the particular qualifications of each applicant."[22] In practice, this meant that "race or ethnic background may be deemed a 'plus' in a particular applicant's file" as long as the university does not "insulate the individual from comparison with all other candidates for the available seats"[23] and as long as the admissions committee considers other qualities "likely to promote beneficial educational pluralism."[24] Justice Powell cited Harvard College's description of its affirmative action program as an example of an approach that met his standard.[25]

---

[17] Justice Powell initially formulated the standard as requiring that the government interest be "substantial," id at 305 (internal quotation marks and citation omitted), but elsewhere he used the term "compelling," see id at 314. See also id at 315 (affirmative action program must be "necessary to promote this [compelling] interest.").

[18] Id at 314.

[19] Id at 311, 313.

[20] Id at 314.

[21] Id at 315.

[22] Id at 317.

[23] Id.

[24] Id.

[25] See id at 316–17.

After *Bakke*, the Court did not decide a case about affirmative action in higher education for twenty-five years. During that time, though, in *City of Richmond v J. A. Croson Company*[26]—a case involving affirmative action in a local government's award of construction contracts—a majority of the Court ruled, in agreement with Justice Powell's *Bakke* opinion, that a state or local affirmative action plan is subject to strict scrutiny.[27] The Court also emphasized that, in order to satisfy strict scrutiny, a measure had to be "narrowly tailored," and that one element of narrow tailoring was whether the government had considered "race-neutral" alternatives to affirmative action.[28] The Court in *Croson*, again echoing Justice Powell's opinion in *Bakke*, suggested that the affirmative action plan in *Croson* was deficient because it used a "rigid numerical quota."[29]

In 2003, when the Court returned to affirmative action in higher education, a majority of the Court, in an opinion by Justice O'Connor, explicitly adopted Justice Powell's approach across the board.[30] In *Grutter v Bollinger*,[31] the Court upheld the University of Michigan Law School's affirmative action program. Notably, the Court did not begin its analysis with a discussion of the principles behind the Equal Protection Clause, or with its own post-*Bakke* precedents. Instead, the Court began by invoking the practice that had developed in higher education in the quarter century since *Bakke*. That practice, the Court said—citing amicus curiae briefs—essentially followed Justice Powell's opinion. "Since this Court's splintered decision in *Bakke*, Justice Powell's opinion . . . has served as the touchstone for constitutional analysis of race-conscious admissions policies. Public and private universities across the Nation have modeled their own admissions programs on Justice Powell's views on permissible race-conscious policies."[32]

---

[26] 488 US 469 (1989).

[27] Id at 493–94 (opinion of O'Connor, J); id at 520 (Scalia, J, concurring in judgment).

[28] Id at 507 (opinion of the Court). See also *Adarand Constructors, Inc. v Pena*, 515 US 200, 235 (1995) (ruling that the same standard applied to the federal government).

[29] *Croson*, 488 US at 508.

[30] See *Grutter v Bollinger*, 539 US 306, 325 (2003). Justice Kennedy, in dissent, agreed: "The opinion by Justice Powell [in *Bakke*], in my view, states the correct rule for resolving this case." 539 US at 387 (Kennedy, J, dissenting).

[31] 539 US 306 (2003).

[32] Id at 323.

The Court in *Grutter* then "endorse[d] Justice Powell's view that student body diversity"—the only interest that the law school asserted in defense of its affirmative action plan—"is a compelling state interest that can justify the use of race in university admissions."[33] The Court said that the "narrow tailor[ing]" component of strict scrutiny required "truly individualized consideration" and precluded the use of a quota.[34] The law school's program satisfied these requirements, because it consisted of "a highly individualized, holistic review of each applicant's file, giving serious consideration to all the ways an applicant might contribute to a diverse educational environment."[35]

In addition to endorsing Justice Powell's view, *Grutter* and its companion case, *Gratz v Bollinger*,[36] revealed something important about what the Court meant by "individualized" review: the crucial element was not avoiding quotas, as Justice Powell's opinion seemed to say, but avoiding transparency. If a university made it clear just how much affirmative action it was engaging in, by an explicit quota or otherwise, that would violate the Constitution. But the hidden use even of a quota was less of a problem. The Court did not say this, but it follows from the way the Court approached the two cases.

Gratz declared unconstitutional the affirmative action program used by the University of Michigan's undergraduate College of Literature, Science, and the Arts. The college used a numerical index to determine whether applicants would be admitted. The maximum score was 150 points; applicants who scored over 100 were, with rare exceptions, automatically admitted.[37] Below that threshold, applicants' chances of admission declined linearly. Applicants who scored above seventy points could, however, be "flagged" for review by a committee and might be admitted irrespective of their score.[38] The Court described the numerical system this way:

> Each application received points based on high school grade point average, standardized test scores, academic quality of an applicant's high

---

[33] Id at 325.

[34] Id at 334.

[35] Id at 337.

[36] 539 US 244 (2003).

[37] Id at 255.

[38] Id at 256, 274.

> school, strength or weakness of high school curriculum, in-state residency, alumni relationship, personal essay, and personal achievement or leadership. Of particular significance here, under a "miscellaneous" category, an applicant was entitled to 20 points based upon his or her membership in an underrepresented racial or ethnic minority group.[39]

The college explained that it used a numerical system because it received a large number of applications. It could not review each one in the way the law school did.[40]

The Court held that this program did not "provide [the] individualized consideration" that *Bakke* and the Court's other decisions required.[41] The Court noted that nearly every qualified applicant from a minority group had been admitted, but the Court did not otherwise explain why the system was deficient.[42] There was no finding of fact, for example, that the college had chosen twenty points instead of some other quantity because that would produce a certain number of minority admissions; the district court's findings, which the Court did not overturn, were to the contrary.[43] Instead, the ma-

---

[39] Id at 255.

[40] Id at 275.

[41] Id at 271.

[42] Id at 273. The Court also emphasized that "extraordinary talent" could gain an applicant only five points. Id. Justice Souter, in dissent, responded that "[n]onminority students may receive 20 points for athletic ability, socioeconomic disadvantage, attendance at a socioeconomically disadvantaged or predominantly minority high school, or at the Provost's discretion; they may also receive 10 points for being residents of Michigan, 6 for residence in an underrepresented Michigan county, 5 for leadership and service, and so on." Id at 294–95 (Souter, J, dissenting).

[43] The Supreme Court summarized the district court's findings as follows:

> The court emphasized that the [college's] current program does not utilize rigid quotas or seek to admit a predetermined number of minority students. The award of 20 points for membership in an underrepresented minority group, in the District Court's view, was not the functional equivalent of a quota because minority candidates were not insulated from review by virtue of those points. Likewise, the court rejected the assertion that the . . . program operates like the two-track system Justice Powell found objectionable in *Bakke* on the grounds that [the] applicants are not competing for different groups of seats. . . . The court also dismissed [plaintiffs'] assertion that the [college's] current system is nothing more than a means by which to achieve racial balancing. The court explained that the [college] does not seek to achieve a certain proportion of minority students, let alone a proportion that represents the community.

539 US at 258–59 (citations omitted). The Court granted certiorari before judgment, so the district court's findings were not reviewed by the court of appeals. See id at 259–60.

jority emphasized the "automatic[ ]" and "mechanical" nature of the college's process.[44]

If the key feature of an impermissible affirmative action plan is that it uses a quota, then both *Grutter* and *Gratz* were, arguably, wrongly decided. At the very least, the Court should have been more skeptical of the law school's program, and more receptive to the college's. A "holistic" approach like the law school's—in which every aspect of the applicant's background can be considered, with no clear criteria about the weight given to each—lends itself to the covert, possibly even unconscious, use of a quota. If the number of minority admissions in a particular year seems to be unusually low, it would be only natural for an admissions officer, reviewing applications "holistically," to begin to give greater weight to an applicant's minority status. In that way, the system could, in practice, impose a quota. In fact, in Michigan's case, the law school's admissions officers made periodic reports to the Director of Admissions that kept track of the demographic characteristics (such as race and ethnicity) of the students who had been admitted.[45] And the dissenters in *Grutter* argued that the law school had, in fact, been using a covert quota system.[46]

By contrast, specifying a fixed number of points for minority applicants to receive, as the college did, makes it less likely that the admissions office will covertly use a quota. Minority applicants who, with the added points, meet the admissions threshold, are admitted; those who do not, are not. If the admissions office departs from the numerical ranking in order to admit a predetermined number of minority applicants, its action will be obvious. The Court never acknowledged this anti-quota feature of the college's system.

The Court may have believed, contrary to the district court's findings, that the college chose the twenty-point allocation specifically to guarantee the admission of all qualified minority applicants. But if that was the basis for the Court's decision, it could have identified

[44] See id at 271, 272; id at 280 (O'Connor, J, concurring).

[45] *Grutter*, 539 US at 318. The director of admissions said that he used these reports "to ensure that a critical mass of underrepresented minority students would be reached so as to realize the educational benefits of a diverse student body" but that "he did not seek to admit any particular number or percentage of underrepresented minority students." Id. The putative distinction between a critical mass and a quota became one of the main issues in *Fisher*. See text at note 83.

[46] *Grutter*, 539 US at 378–88 (Rehnquist, CJ, dissenting); id at 389–94 (Kennedy, J, dissenting).

that as a particular failing of the college's program, while signaling that in general a system like the college's is better than the law school's. As it is, however, the combined effect of *Grutter* and *Gratz* was, if anything, to make the covert use of quotas more likely. The lesson of those two cases is that an admissions office is well advised to adopt a "holistic" process that keeps the reasons for its decisions opaque, even though such an approach can become, in practice, a hard-to-detect quota. And after *Gratz*, it would be a mistake for an admissions office to adopt a numerical system that assigns a specific weight to minority status and then lets the chips fall where they may, even though such a system presents much less of a risk of becoming a covert quota.

A Court that was concerned about quotas would have encouraged exactly the opposite outcome. It would have said that the college's system was preferable in principle, whatever its specific flaws, and that the law school's approach was inherently suspect. Instead, what the Court did in *Grutter* and *Gratz* suggests that the problem is not quotas per se but transparency. Quotas are not so problematic if they are not obvious. But a system that makes it clear what weight is assigned to race is likely to be unconstitutional even if it effectively precludes the use of a quota. Admissions processes that benefit members of minority groups are more likely to be upheld if they obscure the extent to which race plays a role.

This impression—that the Court values nontransparency in affirmative action—was reinforced by *Parents Involved in Community Schools v Seattle School District No. 1*.[47] In *Parents Involved*, two school districts, in Seattle and Louisville, took students' race into account in assigning them to elementary and secondary schools. The school districts used a number of criteria in making assignments, but in some circumstances, they would assign a student to a school in which that student's racial group was in the minority, in order to maintain racial integration at the school. The Court, by a vote of 5–4, held that the school districts' policies were unconstitutional. Justice Kennedy, whose vote was necessary to the majority, wrote a separate concurrence that criticized the other members of the majority for being too unequivocally hostile to the use of race.[48]

---

[47] 551 US 701 (2007).

[48] See id at 787–88 (Kennedy, J, concurring in part and concurring in judgment).

Justice Kennedy agreed with the plurality that "the state-mandated racial classifications at issue, official labels proclaiming the race of all persons in a broad class of citizens . . . are unconstitutional."[49] But he said that school boards should be free to adopt "race-conscious measures" to promote integration as long as they did not "treat each student in different fashion solely on the basis of a systematic, individual typing by race."[50] He explained:

> School boards may pursue the goal of bringing together students of diverse backgrounds and races through other means, including strategic site selection of new schools; drawing attendance zones with general recognition of the demographics of neighborhoods; allocating resources for special programs; recruiting students and faculty in a targeted fashion; and tracking enrollments, performance, and other statistics by race. These mechanisms are race conscious but do not lead to different treatment based on a classification that tells each student he or she is to be defined by race, so it is unlikely any of them would demand strict scrutiny to be found permissible.[51]

This seems to be an explicit requirement of nontransparency. Justice Kennedy objected to "individual typing by race," but a school board cannot do the things Justice Kennedy describes without identifying the race of the students in the school district.[52] A school board cannot site schools or draw attendance zones in a way that promotes integration unless it knows the race of students living in various places in the district and causes the students' race to determine, at least sometimes, which school they will go to. The difference seems to be that the measures Justice Kennedy describes do not require that the race of individual students be stated openly, and it might not be obvious to observers that the school board took race into account in making its decision, even though it did. Justice Kennedy spoke for only himself, but his approach—making nontransparency central to the constitutionality of affirmative action—followed from *Grutter* and *Gratz* and Justice Powell's opinion in *Bakke*.

---

[49] Id at 782.

[50] Id at 788–89.

[51] Id at 789.

[52] See, on the contrast between Justice Kennedy's aversion to individual racial classifications and his willingness to allow race to be used as a criterion in other ways, Justin Driver, *The Schoolhouse Gate: Public Education, the Supreme Court, and the Shaping of America's Constitutional Rights* ch 5 (Pantheon, forthcoming 2018). See also *Parents Involved*, 551 US at 723 n 11.

Fisher

The University of Texas at Austin engaged in affirmative action in undergraduate admissions. Its program was shaped by litigation. Before 1997, the university considered an applicant's "Academic Index" (AI)—a numerical composite of high school grades and academic performance—and the applicant's race.[53] In 1996, in *Hopwood v Texas*,[54] the Fifth Circuit held unconstitutional a similar system used by the university's law school. The university then stopped considering race in undergraduate admissions. It continued to use the AI, but it also devised a "Personal Achievement Index" (PAI). The PAI "measure[d] a student's leadership and work experience, awards, extracurricular activities, community service, and other special circumstances" such as whether the student came from a disadvantaged background.[55] The Texas state legislature also responded to *Hopwood*: it enacted what came to be known as the Top Ten Percent law.[56] That statute provided that any student who graduated in the top 10 percent of his or her high school class in Texas (and who met certain other standards) would be guaranteed admission to any public state college in the state, including the university.[57]

Grutter effectively abrogated *Hopwood*, and in 2004 the university began explicitly including race in the PAI, without assigning race a specific value. The admissions decision was then a function of the AI and PAI.[58] Abigail Fisher, a white woman who had been rejected by the university, sued to challenge the constitutionality of the program. The Fifth Circuit upheld summary judgment in favor of the university.[59] Fisher petitioned for certiorari.

In its Brief in Opposition, the university identified several reasons for the Court to deny the petition.[60] After she had been rejected at Texas, Fisher was accepted at Louisiana State University, and she was scheduled to graduate before the Court could decide her case on the

[53] *Fisher v University of Texas (Fisher I)*, 133 S Ct 2411, 2415 (2013).

[54] 78 F3d 932 (5th Cir 1996).

[55] *Fisher I*, 133 S Ct at 2415–16.

[56] Id at 2416.

[57] Id.

[58] Id.

[59] *Fisher v University of Texas at Austin*, 631 F3d 215 (5th Cir 2011).

[60] See Brief in Opposition, *Fisher v University of Texas at Austin*, No 11-345 (October Term, 2011).

merits. She had not sued as a class representative. So her claim for injunctive relief would be moot. The issues in the case were closely tied to the specific situation in Texas, with its Top Ten Percent statute. The petition did not assert that there was a conflict among the courts of appeals and did not ask the Supreme Court to overrule *Grutter*.[61] And the university argued that Fisher would not have been admitted no matter what her race.[62]

The Court nonetheless granted the petition. The Court took an unusually long time to decide the case—the argument was in the second week of the Term, but the case was not decided until two days before the end of the Term—and reports afterward suggested that there was heated disagreement among the Justices.[63] But the decision was nearly unanimous—only Justice Ginsburg dissented[64]—and very narrow. The Court reaffirmed that *Grutter*, and Justice Powell's *Bakke* opinion, stated the governing law.[65] But the Court ruled that the Fifth Circuit had misapplied strict scrutiny by being too deferential to the university.

The Court said that the decision to pursue diversity as an educational objective "is, in substantial measure, an academic judgment to which some, but not complete, judicial deference is proper."[66] But the university "must prove that the means [it] chose[] . . . to attain diversity are narrowly tailored to that goal," and on that issue, "the University receives no deference."[67] Specifically, the Court said, the university had to show that it evaluated "'each applicant . . . as an individual'" and that "available, workable race-neutral alternatives do not suffice."[68]

---

[61] See id. Fisher did not contest these points but did assert that she could recover damages, so the case was not moot, and that the issues raised were of sufficient importance to warrant the Court's review. See Reply Brief for Petitioner, *Fisher v University of Texas at Austin*, No 11-345 (October Term, 2011).

[62] See Transcript of Oral Argument, *Fisher v University of Texas at Austin*, No 11-345 (October 10, 2012) at 54–55.

[63] See Joan Biskupic, *Breaking In: The Rise of Sonia Sotomayor and the Politics of Justice* 200–12 (Farrar, Straus and Giroux, 2014).

[64] Justices Scalia and Thomas each filed a concurring opinion. Justice Kagan did not participate. See *Fisher I*, 133 S Ct at 2422.

[65] Id at 2417–19.

[66] Id at 2419.

[67] Id at 2420.

[68] Id, quoting *Grutter*, 539 US at 337.

On remand, the court of appeals reevaluated the evidence and reinstated its prior judgment, affirming the district court's grant of summary judgment in favor of the university.[69] The Court granted certiorari again, but its opinion left one wondering why it had done so. "The University's program is *sui generis*," the Court announced, at the beginning of its analysis.[70] The reason was that the Top Ten Percent plan filled 75 percent of the places in the entering class.[71] The part of the university's admissions process that Fisher challenged used what the Court acknowledged was "an approach similar to the one in *Grutter*" for the remaining 25 percent.[72] A *sui generis* state action, indistinguishable in relevant respects from an unchallenged precedent, is an unlikely candidate for one grant of certiorari, let alone two.

In addition, Fisher had not challenged the Top Ten Percent plan, and, the Court said, the university did not have the power to change that plan, so as a result the "record . . . [wa]s almost devoid of information about the students" who were admitted through that plan.[73] That made it difficult to evaluate the university's assertion that its use of a race-conscious PAI was needed to add an element of diversity beyond that provided by the plan. "That this case has been litigated on a somewhat artificial basis," the Court remarked, "may limit its value for prospective guidance."[74] All of these aspects of the case—in addition to others, such as Fisher's limited interest in the outcome—had been apparent from the start.

The Court went on to say that the university's plan did satisfy strict scrutiny. It "articulated concrete and precise goals";[75] it provided "both statistical and anecdotal evidence" that its affirmative action plan was needed;[76] it used race-neutral alternatives to the extent it could; and it engaged in an ongoing process of deliberation about its

---

[69] *Fisher v University of Texas at Austin*, 758 F3d 633 (5th Cir 2014). Judge Garza dissented, as he had from the first court of appeals decision. Id at 661–76. Five judges voted in favor of granting rehearing en banc. *Fisher v University of Texas at Austin*, 771 F3d 274 (5th Cir 2014).

[70] *Fisher II*, 136 S Ct at 2208.

[71] Id at 2206.

[72] Id.

[73] Id at 2209.

[74] Id.

[75] Id at 2211.

[76] Id at 2212.

admissions procedures.[77] The Court concluded by suggesting that Texas and other universities could serve as "'laboratories for experimentation'" to help determine whether and when affirmative action programs were appropriate.[78]

Justice Alito wrote a long and strongly worded dissent.[79] He began, reasonably enough, by remarking: "Something strange has happened since our prior decision in this case."[80] He criticized the university, and the Court, for failing to define the interest in diversity with specificity: "[I]n order for us to assess whether UT's program is narrowly tailored, the university must identify *some sort of concrete interest.*"[81] Justice Alito quoted the goals that the majority had identified—"'the destruction of stereotypes, the promot[ion of] cross-racial understanding, the preparation of a student body for an increasingly diverse workforce and society, and the cultivat[ion of] a set of leaders with legitimacy in the eyes of the citizenry'"[82]—and argued that those goals were so imprecise that there was no way to tell whether the university engaged in more affirmative action than was needed to promote them, or even whether affirmative action promoted those objectives at all. Justice Alito then reviewed some more specific objectives that the university had identified at various points—achieving a "critical mass," increasing minority representation in classes where minority groups were underrepresented, and having minority students with different characteristics from those admitted through the Top Ten Percent program—and dismissed all of those justifications. "Critical mass" was either undefined or was a numerical quota and therefore strictly forbidden by the Court's decisions; the record did not show that the affirmative action plan increased classroom diversity; and the "diversity within diversity" argument relied on unsupported and pernicious stereotypes about the minority students admitted under the Top Ten Percent plan.[83]

---

[77] Id at 2214–15.

[78] Id at 2214, quoting *United States v Lopez*, 514 US 549, 581 (1995) (Kennedy, J, concurring).

[79] 136 S Ct at 2215–43 (Alito, J, dissenting). The Chief Justice and Justice Thomas joined the dissent; Justice Thomas wrote a separate dissent. Id at 2215.

[80] Id at 2215 (Alito, J, dissenting).

[81] Id at 2222–23 (emphasis in original).

[82] Id at 2223, quoting id at 2211 (majority opinion) (brackets in original; internal quotation marks omitted in original).

[83] Id at 2224–36 (Alito, J, dissenting).

The Problem with Strict Scrutiny

Justice Alito's dissent was, on its own terms, convincing. Texas, and the Court, did not reduce "educational diversity" to a criterion that was specific enough to allow a court to judge, one way or another, whether the affirmative action plan was "necessary." To the extent the university tried to define a specific objective—like, for example, a "critical mass"—it risked establishing a quota. Justice Alito also criticized the university for considering only African-Americans and Hispanics in the affirmative action plan and paying no attention to the possible underrepresentation of Asian-Americans, which, he asserted, was by some measures even greater than the underrepresentation of other minority groups.

In a sense, though, the dissent was too convincing. *Any* affirmative action plan that is justified as a means of achieving educational diversity will be vulnerable to the kinds of criticisms that Justice Alito made. The dissent conspicuously did not explain how educational diversity might be reduced to a set of objectives that were concrete enough to allow a reviewing court to decide whether an admissions policy promoted them, but not so concrete that they amounted to a quota. In *Grutter*, where a majority of the Court for the first time endorsed Justice Powell's view that educational diversity was a compelling interest, the dissenters made just that objection: that educational diversity was such an amorphous objective that a court simply could not, with any confidence, determine whether a particular admissions policy promoted it. *Fisher* proved their point. The synthesis that Justice Powell advocated in *Bakke*, and that became the law—treating educational diversity as a compelling interest, insisting on nontransparency, but enforcing strict scrutiny—is untenable.

The central problem is that judgments about the kind and degree of diversity that a student body should have—like countless other judgments that university administrators make—are simply not susceptible to precise metrics. That is the nature of those judgments. Asking the university why it wanted just the number of minority students that it admitted, or why it wanted those minority groups and not other groups, or why it wanted minority students besides those admitted through the Top Ten Percent program would be like asking admissions officers why they wanted a certain mix of students interested in particular academic majors, or students interested in particular extracurricular activities. It would certainly be possible for a university to give some reasons. But those reasons would often be vague and abstract—like the reasons the University of Texas gave about encouraging cross-cultural understandings and preparing students for a diverse society—and admissions officers would necessarily have to rely on their own judgments about what was best for the university.

The point is not limited to university administrators. People responsible for institutions routinely make judgments of that kind about the attributes they want among the people involved in their institutions. If you are assembling a police force, or a corporate board, or a team of engineers in a technology company, you will have to make the same kinds of judgments. You will be able to give some reasons for your decisions, but if pressed about why exactly you wanted a certain number of people with certain characteristics, at some point you will have to acknowledge that it was just a matter of judgment. Of course some qualifications are essential, and some are more important than others; the University of Texas insisted on a certain level of academic achievement, and considered academic qualifications beyond that level in conjunction with everything else. And some claims about the proper composition of a student body or a workforce might be so obviously contrived, or so poorly thought through, that they can be rejected. But ultimately the people making judgments about the right degree and kind of diversity will have to rely on considerations that cannot be specified with precision and that therefore cannot be reviewed with the kind of rigor that strict scrutiny envisions.

In *Fisher I*, the Court remanded the case because it thought the Fifth Circuit gave too much deference to the university. Then when the case came before the Court again, the Court—as Justice Alito pointed out—ended up taking the university officials' word, to a large degree, on how much diversity the university needed, and of what kind. But the Court really had no alternative, if it was going to continue to accept educational diversity as one of the objectives that can justify affirmative action.

There may have been a way to make these judgments measurable in affirmative action cases, but it is foreclosed by the approach the Court has taken. The Court could, in theory, have said that it would establish numerical criteria as a rough-and-ready proxy for educational diversity. The Court might, for example, say that the interest in educational diversity is satisfied if the percentage of minorities in the entering class approximated that in the applicant pool, or in the cohort that graduated from high school in the previous year, or in the general population. That would have provided a definite benchmark against which the university's policies could be judged. The numerical criteria would be an imperfect measure of the value of educational diversity, but that might be the price of making it possible to apply strict scrutiny to affirmative action measures.

This would not have been an outlandish way to proceed. It is somewhat comparable to what courts did when they enforced school desegregation orders, and similar to remedies that courts enforced against recalcitrant discriminatory employers: in those instances, numerical goals were used as an admittedly crude way to approximate what nondiscriminatory conduct would achieve.[84] By analogy, a court might use numerical criteria to determine whether a university was approximating what a diverse student body would be. Ever since *Bakke*, though, the use of numerical criteria has been anathema in affirmative action cases. That left the Court with an imprecisely defined criterion against which to measure the affirmative action program.

There is another aspect of the opinions in *Fisher II*—both the majority opinion and Justice Alito's dissent—that showed how strict scrutiny cannot be coherently applied to a university's claim that it is pursuing racial diversity in education. The Court has repeatedly said, in affirmative action cases, that "narrow tailoring" requires the government to show that it could not have accomplished its objectives by race-neutral means: if there were nonracial means of promoting the compelling interest, then it was not necessary to use race. The majority in *Fisher II* asserted that the university had shown that race-neutral measures were ineffective; Justice Alito disagreed. But the supposedly race-neutral alternatives that both opinions identified in *Fisher*—and that the Court identified in *Grutter*, the other case in which educational diversity was the objective—were not actually race-

[84] See, for example, *Local 28, Sheet Metal Workers v EEOC*, 478 US 421, 448–49 (1986) (citing cases): "Where an employer or union has engaged in particularly longstanding or egregious discrimination, an injunction simply reiterating Title VII's prohibition against discrimination will often prove useless. . . . In such cases, requiring recalcitrant employers or unions to hire and to admit qualified minorities roughly in proportion to the number of qualified minorities in the work force may be the only effective way to ensure the full enjoyment of the rights protected by Title VII." See also *Parents Involved*, 551 US at 823–24 (Breyer, J, dissenting) (discussing *Swann v Charlotte-Mecklenburg Board of Ed.*, 402 US 1, 16 (1971) and *North Carolina Board of Ed. v Swann*, 402 US 43, 45 (1971)); *Parents Involved*, 551 US at 847 (Breyer, J, dissenting) (discussing *United States v Montgomery County Board of Ed.*, 395 US 225, 232 (1969)).

neutral. They just used race covertly. They were race-neutral on their face, but they were chosen because of their racial effects.

The Top Ten Percent plan is the most conspicuous example. Justice Alito treated the Top Ten Percent plan as if it were racially neutral. But as Justice Ginsburg and Justice Souter had repeatedly said in earlier cases, and the majority in *Fisher II* finally acknowledged,[85] the Top Ten Percent plan was adopted, in response to the Fifth Circuit's decision in *Hopwood*, specifically to increase minority representation in state universities. The Top Ten Percent plan was a kind of gerrymander: the state deliberately drew a line to accomplish a racial effect without admitting it was doing so. If a state had adopted a similar plan to keep minorities out of its universities, no one would have called it "race-neutral." Recruiting efforts designed to increase minority applications—the other supposedly race-neutral alternative suggested in the *Fisher* opinions—are also not race-neutral, any more than recruiting efforts deliberately designed to avoid minority applicants would be. These measures are non-transparent, at least compared to the acknowledged consideration of race in the university's admissions program, but they are not race-neutral.

In fact, there are no race-neutral means of pursuing the kind of diversity that the Court treats as a compelling interest. Educational diversity, as the Court understands it, includes a racial component: as Justice Powell said, and as the Court repeated in *Grutter* and in *Fisher II*, "racial and ethnic origin is but a single though important element" of the compelling objective of educational diversity.[86] If seeking racial diversity is a permissible objective, then it makes no sense to say that a university must try to use nonracial means to achieve that objective. Seeking racial diversity means deliberately trying to enroll more minority students than the university would otherwise enroll. That is true even if racial diversity is just one component of a broader concern with diversity, even if the university does not have a specific number of minority enrollments in mind, and even if the university would be hard-pressed to identify the particular students who benefited from affirmative action: seeking racial diversity means seeking more minority students. If a university is going

[85] See *Fisher II*, 136 S Ct at 2213, citing *Fisher I*, 133 S Ct at 2433 (Ginsburg, J, dissenting); *Gratz*, 539 US at 297–98 (Souter, J, dissenting).

[86] *Bakke*, 438 US at 315.

to do that, it has to consider race—if not overtly, then covertly. If it cannot consider race, then it cannot seek racial diversity; all it can do is hope to achieve racial diversity by accident.

If the objective of an affirmative action plan were defined in nonracial terms—for example, if the objective were to have different points of view expressed in classrooms, or to have students who would go to work among different communities in the state—then it would be possible to say that the university can look at race only as a last resort, after it has used all other criteria that might achieve the student body it wanted. But, since *Bakke*, that is not how diversity has been understood. Those nonracial objectives are reasons, among others, why a university might value racial diversity. But under Justice Powell's approach in *Bakke*, adopted by the Court in *Grutter* and *Fisher*, a university has a compelling interest in pursuing racial diversity, in particular, as one component of a broader diversity program. So a core requirement of strict scrutiny—that the government try nonracial means before considering race—becomes logically impossible to meet in affirmative action cases when racial diversity is the state's objective.

The Conservative Solution

It is easy to criticize the Court's approach to affirmative action as incoherent. When *Bakke* was decided, Justice Powell's opinion was widely attacked on that ground.[87] One obvious criticism is that the Court, following Justice Powell, has tried to identify a middle ground where none exists. If, as the Court has said in justifying its use of strict scrutiny, affirmative action is no different in principle from discrimination against minorities, then it should be unconstitutional in nearly all instances: that is what strict scrutiny means when it is applied to discrimination against minorities. Alternatively, the Court might recognize that affirmative action is radically different from discrimination against minorities and seldom warrants judicial intervention. But the first approach—treating affirmative action as nearly always unconstitutional—has never been accepted by the Court, even though some Justices embrace it. And the second approach—subjecting affirmative action measures only to rational basis review—has never

[87] See, for example, Jeffries, 2003 Supreme Court Review at 9–10 (cited in note 15) (summarizing the criticisms).

been endorsed by any Justice. Justice Powell's seemingly incoherent middle ground has become dominant.

But there may be a justification for that middle ground. It is a way for Justices who are uneasy about affirmative action to acknowledge that race-conscious decisions have become such an entrenched practice in many important American institutions that it would be unwise for them to try uproot it. This kind of justification—recognizing that established practices might deserve to be maintained even if, in principle, they are questionable—is derived from an important current of conservative thought. The idea is that, in dealing with complex political issues, abstract principles are not as good a guide as the actual practice, over time, of people engaged day to day in operating institutions. People in that position have to respond to the specific problems they encounter. They do that by exercising their judgment about what those problems require. When people in that position act in roughly the same way, and for an extended time, that is evidence that their course of action is the best anyone can do.

The locus classicus for this way of thinking is some well-known passages from Edmund Burke's *Reflections on the Revolution in France*. Burke said, for example, that "[t]he science of constructing a commonwealth, or renovating it, or reforming it, is, like every other experimental science, not to be taught a priori."[88] Instead, it "requires experience, and even more experience than any person can gain in his whole life, however sagacious and observing he may be."[89] It follows that "it is with infinite caution that any man ought to venture upon pulling down an edifice which has answered in any tolerable degree for ages the common purposes of society."[90] In the case of affirmative action, of course, it is not a matter of an approach that has lasted "for ages." But the point is to choose experience over a priori theories, and to accept that the question is not whether an approach is theoretically optimal but whether it serves the public interest to a "tolerable degree."

Similar themes—a distrust of abstract reasoning in favor of the lessons of experience, and especially the experience of individuals dealing with matters that they are particularly familiar with—are in

---

[88] Edmund Burke, *Reflections on the Revolution in France* 220 (J. C. D. Clark, ed) (Stanford, 2001).

[89] Id.

[90] Id.

Friedrich Hayek's *The Constitution of Liberty*.[91] Michael Oakeshott's *Rationalism in Politics* is a similar celebration of the unsystematic knowledge that comes from practice—"knowledge . . . [that] exists only in use" and "cannot be formulated in rules."[92] That kind of "practical knowledge" is found in "a customary or traditional way of doing things, or, simply, in practice."[93]

Whether the Supreme Court is aware of it or not, that seems to be how it has been dealing with affirmative action.[94] Justice Powell's opinion in *Bakke* relied on the practices of Harvard College and other colleges and universities.[95] Those institutions' amicus brief explained that Harvard had pursued diversity in admissions for many years by taking into account extracurricular interests, the place where an applicant grew up, or "a life spent on a farm" because "a farm boy from Idaho can bring something to Harvard College that a Bostonian cannot offer."[96] Taking race or ethnicity into account was just an extension of that long-standing admissions practice. But the Harvard admissions committee did not "set[] a minimum number of blacks or

---

[91] Friedrich Hayek, *The Constitution of Liberty* (Chicago, 1960). See, for example, id at 25 ("Not all knowledge of the ever changing particular facts that man continually uses lends itself to organization or systematic exposition"); id at 26 ("Our habits and skills, our emotions and attitudes, our tools, and our institutions—all are in [a] sense adaptations to past experience which have grown up by selective elimination of less suitable conduct."); id at 27 ("The [] 'tools' which man has evolved and which constitute such an important part of his adaptation to his environment . . . consist in large measure of forms of conduct which he habitually follows without knowing why; they consist of what we call 'traditions' and 'institutions,' which he uses because they are available to him as a product of cumulative growth without ever having been designed by one mind."); id ("Concurrent with the growth of conscious knowledge there always takes place an equally important accumulation of tools in this wider sense, of tested and generally adopted ways of doing things."). See generally id at 22–30.

[92] Michael Oakeshott, *Rationalism in Politics*, in *Rationalism in Politics and Other Essays* 12 (Liberty, 1991).

[93] Id at 15. If affirmative action is understood in this way, then measures forbidding race-conscious decisions that are adopted by popular vote—like California's Proposition 209, Cal Const, Art I, § 31(a), or Michigan's Proposal 2, see *Schuette v Coalition to Defend Affirmative Action*, 134 S Ct 1623 (2014)—might be seen as the kind of actions that Burkean conservatives warn against: measures based on abstract theoretical arguments, in this instance in favor of "colorblindness," that are appealing to the population at large but that underestimate the complexity of the problems they address and that fail to take advantage of the lessons of experience, particularly the experience of people who have been dealing with those problems for some time.

[94] See also the account in Jeffries, 2003 Supreme Court Review at 23 (cited in note 15), describing Justice Powell's *Bakke* opinion as "a particularly telling example of constitutional adjudication as an appeal to the future."

[95] See *Bakke*, 438 US at 316–17 (Powell, J, concurring).

[96] Id at 316 (internal quotation marks and citations omitted).

of people from west of the Mississippi who are to be admitted"; it just "pa[id] some attention to distribution among many types and categories of students."[97] Justice Powell was obviously troubled by affirmative action as a matter of principle—he emphasized that all "racial and ethnic distinctions" were suspect[98]—but he endorsed a practice that important institutions thought was valuable and that was in keeping with their traditional ways of making admissions decisions.

When the Court, in *Grutter*, adopted Justice Powell's approach, Justice O'Connor's majority opinion similarly relied on the established practices of educational, and other, institutions: "Public and private universities across the Nation have modeled their own admissions programs on Justice Powell's views on permissible race-conscious policies."[99] The Court cited amicus briefs from law schools, colleges, and universities to support its conclusion.[100] The Court said the University of Michigan Law School's "educational judgment that [racial] diversity is essential to its educational mission is one to which we defer."[101] And the Court relied on statements emphasizing the value of racial diversity in amicus briefs filed by major U.S. corporations and by retired officers and civilian leaders of the U.S. military.[102] The Court—or crucial Justices, in any event—were unwilling to impose a revolutionary change that would require so many institutions to abandon a practice that they found so valuable.[103]

Needless to say, this kind of conservatism, to the extent it is valid at all, has its limits. Not every traditional practice should be maintained, and dramatic changes are sometimes warranted. Or perhaps affirmative action should be regarded as constitutionally unproblematic, so that it does not need a Burkean justification. But for Justices whose views fall somewhere between those poles—who see affirmative action as troubling but not wholly indefensible—it would be reasonable to treat the weight of accumulated practice as decisive.

---

[97] Id at 316–17 (internal quotation marks and citations omitted).

[98] See id at 290–91.

[99] *Grutter*, 539 US at 323.

[100] Id.

[101] Id at 328.

[102] Id at 330–31.

[103] See also *Parents Involved*, 551 US at 828–29 (Breyer, J, dissenting) (discussing numerous race-conscious measures adopted by Congress, state legislatures, and executive orders).

This way of understanding the Court's affirmative action cases can help make sense of what might be the most puzzling aspect of them, the Court's insistence on nontransparency. That feature of the cases might just be a reflection of some Justices' ambivalence about affirmative action: it is easier to accept that race-conscious decisions are permitted if you do not know just how often they are made or what effect they have.[104] But nontransparency might be justified as a way of imposing a limit on the extent to which a university can engage in affirmative action.[105] The more aggressively a university engages in affirmative action, the more likely it is that its actions will be obvious, or will resemble quotas. The Court can then intervene to limit the extent of race-conscious action. If the Court's view is that affirmative action is problematic but is, at this point, too deeply entrenched to be rejected entirely, that is a plausible way to proceed.

It is commonly said that affirmative action is a divisive issue, and in some ways it certainly seems to be.[106] There are also obvious difficulties in the Supreme Court's approach to the issue, possibly reflecting the ambivalence in society generally: the Court purports to apply strict scrutiny, but does not, really; it has identified no principle for determining what counts as a compelling interest; it insists that the extent of race-conscious action be kept hidden, without ever explaining why. But in the forty years since the Supreme Court decided *Bakke*, many significant institutions in American society have made up their own minds about affirmative action. *Fisher*, for all its oddities, may reflect that the Court is finally willing to face both the tensions in its doctrine and the fact that large and important parts of U.S. society have reached their own conclusion about affirmative action, and that that conclusion should be respected.

---

[104] See generally Paul J. Mishkin, *The Uses of Ambivalence: Reflections on the Supreme Court and the Constitutionality of Affirmative Action*, 131 U Pa L Rev 907, 917 (1983).

[105] See Jeffries, 2003 Supreme Court Review at 20–21 (cited in note 15).

[106] In a Gallup poll conducted after *Fisher II* was decided, 65 percent of those surveyed disagreed with the decision, and 63 percent believed that race should play no role in college admissions. See Scott Jaschik, *Poll: Public Opposes Affirmative Action*, Inside Higher Ed (July 8, 2016), archived at https://perma.cc/F8HK-8ALR. But a poll conducted two years earlier by Pew, after the Court's decision in *Schuette v Coalition to Defend Affirmative Action*, 134 S Ct 1623 (2014) (upholding Michigan's Proposal 2, which forbade the use of race in admissions), found the opposite: 63 percent of those surveyed said that "affirmative action programs designed to increase the number of black and minority students on college campuses are a 'good thing.'" That was consistent with the finding of a Pew survey taken in 2003. See Bruce Drake, *Public Strongly Backs Affirmative Action Programs on Campus* (Pew Research Center, Apr 22, 2014), archived at https://perma.cc/Z8GV-D2C9.

EMILY BUSS

THE DIVISIVE SUPREME COURT

Obergefell v Hodges,[1] the Supreme Court's decision invalidating state same-sex marriage bans, was widely perceived as the work of a partisan elite imposing its policy preferences on the American people. Two aspects of the decision support this conclusion. First, the case was decided by the narrowest possible margin, with Justices splitting along ideological lines. Second, the majority opinion is not well reasoned, suggesting that the Justices' decision was weakly supported by law. This perception of *Obergefell* as an elitist, partisan power grab to resolve a controversial social issue reflects broader concerns about intensifying divisions in our society, and their harmful effects on our political discourse.

I agree with these criticisms, but I argue that the fault lies, not in the recognition of a federal constitutional right to same-sex marriage, but in the Supreme Court's intervention. Before the Supreme Court took over, the federal right to same-sex marriage was protected by a growing patchwork of cases decided by a politically diverse group of federal judges who were deeply connected to the states whose laws they were reviewing and who applied constitutional doctrine with

Emily Buss is Mark and Barbara Fried Professor of Law, The University of Chicago.

Author's note: My thanks to William Baude, William Buss, Anthony Casey, Rosalind Dixon, Alison Lacroix, Lior Strahilevitz, and Laura Weinrib for their helpful comments on earlier drafts, and to Viviana Aldous, Haley Barton, William Brumfield, Rachel Bukberg, Brittany Ellenberg, Jeremy Green, Jimmy Lin, and Paige Scheckla for their excellent research assistance. I am also grateful for the financial support of the Arnold and Frieda Shure Research Fund.

[1] 135 S Ct 2584 (2015).

978-0-226-49084-7/2017/2016-0002$10.00

considerable care. Taken together, the nineteen federal district court decisions that struck down same-sex marriage bans on federal constitutional grounds in the two years leading up to the *Obergefell* ruling manifested the ongoing emergence of a national consensus in favor not only of same-sex marriage but of a federal constitutional right protecting those marriages. But when the Supreme Court stepped in, it transformed this emerging, bipartisan, locally grounded legal consensus into a legally questionable political act of a coastal elite who barely outvoted their colleagues who passionately disagreed.

In Part I, I set out the majority's analysis, with a focus on the objections raised by the *Obergefell* dissenters and echoed by its political critics. In their view, a partisan majority on the Court effectively enacted its own policy preferences, in violation of principles of federalism and democratic self-rule. I endorse many of the critics' objections, but not their disagreement with the outcome of the case. In Part II, I consider the federal district court decisions in which the federal right to same-sex marriage was originally developed and the extent to which the *Obergefell* critics' objections could be applied to this aggregation of cases. I conclude that the challenges of elitism and partisanship have no application to the patchwork of lower court decisions authored by judges of all political stripes whose life histories are those of local rather than national prominence. These judges oversaw the same-sex litigation as federal representatives of the people of their states, sharing not only a common background but also an ongoing connection to these constituencies. As a result, the dissenters' worries about federalism and even democratic governance are blunted when applied to this aggregation of lower court decisions.

The doctrinal analysis is far more disciplined and thorough in these lower court decisions, producing a series of well-reasoned opinions that follow a variety of doctrinal paths. In my view, we were better off when the law was controlled by multiple, well- (if variously) reasoned opinions, than when the Supreme Court finalized these legal developments in a doctrinally weak opinion likely required to secure its bare majority of five votes. In deciding the case itself, the Court obscured the emerging consensus, and rendered the law, and the Court that declared it, more vulnerable to attack.

In Part III, I address some likely objections to my suggestion that the Supreme Court should have left the law in the hands of the lower courts rather than deciding *Obergefell*. The first is that the federal district court decisions did not truly reflect the emergence of a noteworthy consensus; if those courts thought they were following the clear direction of the Supreme Court set out in *United States v Windsor*,[2] they should not be credited with discerning or developing a local consensus. The many backgrounds, politics, and local connections of the deciding judges are immaterial if those judges were simply doing what the Supreme Court had already told them they must do. But in fact there is ample evidence of the district courts' independence—particularly in their rejection of *Windsor*'s analysis, in their willingness to treat their own circuit precedents as obsolete, and in their resistance to issuing stays pending appeal—that they perceived their role as interpreters, rather than simple implementers, of the law.

A second objection is that whatever value came from state-level decision making in the district courts was already significantly attenuated when the cases were affirmed in the federal courts of appeals, courts much closer to the Supreme Court in their makeup and national orientation. But the tone of the court of appeals decisions that affirmed the district court rulings, and the fact that the court of appeals decisions were also diverse and were subject to further review, preserved the relevance of the district court decisions in the appellate decisions and in the press coverage of those decisions. The effect of the appellate court decisions was more additive than preemptive, an effect *Obergefell* did not, and probably could not, preserve.

A third objection is that, once a circuit conflict emerged, the Court had no choice but to take the case. But the Court always has a choice, and that choice should take into account what will be gained and lost through Supreme Court intervention, a balance tipped heavily against intervention in this case. A fourth objection is that the Supreme Court's decision could be understood to be built upon and to preserve the consensus reflected in the lower court opinions: after all, Justice Kennedy's majority opinion in *Obergefell* not only mentions the lower court developments but catalogs all of the relevant lower court decisions in an appendix.[3] The crucial point, though, is that the displacement of lower court antecedents is an inevitable aspect of a Supreme Court decision. This displacement of multiple lower court decisions with a single final decision by the Supreme Court is often

[2] 133 S Ct 2675 (2013).

[3] 135 S Ct at 2608–10.

beneficial, providing clarity and certainty in the law. But in *Obergefell*, the Court failed to deliver that.

I. Obergefell's Failings

A. obergefell's doctrinal failings

The majority opinion in *Obergefell* was widely criticized, by supporters as well as opponents of same-sex marriage rights, as a poorly reasoned opinion.[4] This did not come as a surprise, as it followed *Windsor*, another weakly reasoned opinion, with the same five Justices in the majority, and the same incentives among them to join a single opinion authored by swing and senior Justice Kennedy.[5] The doctrinal issues raised in the same-sex marriage litigation were difficult and contested. Even among champions of same-sex marriage, there was considerable disagreement about the best doctrinal path to that end. The value of solidarity the Justices in the majority could achieve by signing on to Justice Kennedy's opinion may have given them some comfort that the issue would be favorably resolved without forcing difficult and contentious doctrinal development among them. But, I will argue, that exaggerates the value of a Supreme Court ruling and underestimates the harm it can cause.

The doctrinal issues pressed in *Obergefell* were, to simplify, whether a right to same-sex marriage was protected under the Due Process Clause, the Equal Protection Clause, or both and, depending on how that threshold question was answered, how those two clauses should

---

[4] See, for example, Andrew Koppelman, *The Supreme Court Made the Right Call on Marriage Equality, but They Did it the Wrong Way*, Salon (June 29, 2015), http://www.salon.com/2015/06/29/the_supreme_court_made_the_right_call_on_marriage_equality_%e2%80%94_but_they_did_it_the_wrong_way/; Ilya Somin, *A Great Decision on Same-Sex Marriage—but Based on Dubious Reasoning*, Washington Post (June 26, 2015); Carrie Severino, *Obergefell v. Hodges: Lots of Noise; Not Much Law*, National Review (2015), http://www.nationalreview.com/bench-memos/420403/obergefell-v-hodges-lots-noise-not-much-law-carrie-severino; David Upham, *A Tremendous Defeat for "We the People" and Our Posterity*, SCOTUS Blog (June 26, 2015), http://www.scotusblog.com/2015/06/symposium-a-tremendous-defeat-for-we-the-people-and-our-posterity/.

[5] See Ruthann Robson, *Justice Ginsburg's Obergefell v. Hodges*, 84 UMKC L Rev (2016) (noting that Justice Kennedy had authored all of the Supreme Court's most important cases addressing LGBT rights, that he had been "rightly . . . criticized for the lack of doctrinal rigor," and that Justice Ginsburg, in public remarks, had intimated that the decision to all join a single majority opinion was a strategic one, aimed at producing a "more powerful" ruling); Robert C. Farrell, *Justice Kennedy's Idiosyncratic Understanding of Equal Protection and Due Process, and Its Costs*, 32 Quinnipiac L Rev 439 (2014) ("though Kennedy's opinions in [*Romer v Evans, Lawrence v Texas, and United States v Windsor*] had very dramatic results, the legal reasoning he used to reach those results was anything but clear").

be applied. The due process analysis required an account of "substantive due process" rights that included same-sex marriage within the "fundamental liberties" afforded special protection. Precedents suggested, somewhat murkily, that marriage was a fundamental right, but did not answer the difficult question of how "marriage" that qualified for constitutional protection was to be defined. Any definition that broadened the scope of the definition beyond the long-held, traditional definition of marriage as the union between one man and one woman raised questions about whether the arguments for that expansion to same-sex couples might equally support an expansion to other aspects of that definition (e.g., why one and not two?). Equal protection doctrine, for its part, called for a determination, first, of the level of scrutiny to be applied to the same-sex marriage ban (heightened scrutiny or rational basis?), and then the application of a specific standard, tied to the level of scrutiny required.

In his majority opinion, Justice Kennedy engaged none of these doctrinal questions, even leaving ambiguity about the constitutional clause his opinion rested upon.[6] That said, it is fairly clear that the core of his opinion qualifies as substantive due process analysis, manifesting all of the hazardous potential for ill-reasoned invocations of liberty warned against by the doctrine's opponents.

> The nature of injustice is that we may not always see it in our own times. The generations that wrote and ratified the Bill of Rights and the Fourteenth Amendment did not presume to know the extent of freedom in all its dimensions, and so they entrusted to future generations a charter protecting the right of all persons to enjoy liberty as we learn its meaning. . . . The right to marry is fundamental as a matter of history and tradition, but rights come not from ancient sources alone. They rise, too from a better informed understanding of how constitutional imperatives define a liberty that remains urgent in our own era.[7]

In issuing a decision that avoided engagement with the doctrine, the Court left the ruling vulnerable to the suggestion that the conclusion

[6] 135 S Ct at 2602–03 ("the Due Process Clause and the Equal Protection Clause are connected in a profound way, though they set forth independent principles. Rights implicit in liberty and rights secured by equal protection may rest on different precepts and are not always co-extensive, yet in some instances each may be instructive as to the meaning and reach of the other. In any particular case one Clause may be thought to capture the essence of the right in a more accurate and comprehensive way, even as the two Clauses may converge in the identification and definition of the right. This interrelation of the two principles furthers our understanding of what freedom is and must become.").

[7] Id at 2598–2602.

it reached was not merely unsupported, but also unsupportable, a suggestion effectively exploited by the Justices who opposed the recognition of the right.

In his criticism of the majority's analysis, Chief Justice Roberts remained polite, though he did not mince words in suggesting that the majority's opinion lacked any legal foundation. On the substantive due process analysis, Justice Roberts noted that the majority opinion articulated four principles and traditions weakly tied to precedent; the majority relied, he said, on the "driving themes that marriage is desirable and petitioners desire it."[8] The Chief Justice noted that, "although the majority randomly inserts the adjective 'two' in various places, the majority offered no reason at all why the two-person element of the core definition of marriage may be preserved, while the man-woman element may not."[9] On the majority's equal protection analysis, Justice Roberts noted that it "does not seriously engage" the equal protection claim, and that its discussion of the Equal Protection Clause was "quite frankly, difficult to follow."[10] He further noted the absence in the opinion of "anything resembling our usual framework for deciding equal protection cases," the sort of complex "means-ends"[11] analysis applied so exhaustively in the lower courts.

Justice Scalia was far less polite. The majority's was "an opinion lacking even a thin veneer of law"[12] that was "profoundly incoherent."[13] "The Supreme Court of the United States has descended from the disciplined legal reasoning of John Marshall and Joseph Story to the mystical aphorisms of the fortune cookie."[14] While this was characteristic Scalia acerbity, less usual, perhaps, is the extent to which many, including many who supported the majority's outcome, shared his harsh view of the opinion's incoherence.[15] And among same-sex

---

[8] Id at 2619 (Roberts, CJ, dissenting).

[9] Id at 2621 (Roberts, CJ, dissenting).

[10] Id at 2623 (Roberts, CJ, dissenting).

[11] Id.

[12] Id at 2628 (Scalia, J, dissenting).

[13] Id at 2630 (Scalia, J, dissenting).

[14] Id at 2630 n 22 (Scalia, J, dissenting).

[15] See, for example, Koppelman, Salon (June 29, 2015) (cited in note 4) ("The fundamental problem is that Kennedy's opinion does not explain what business the Court has addressing the marriage question in the first place. . . . If this is all the explanation they are going to get, then conservatives are right to feel bullied by judicial oligarchs."); Somin, Washington Post (June 26, 2015) (cited in note 4) ("Overall, I can't avoid the conclusion that much of Ken-

marriage opponents, that was strong evidence that the granting of same-sex marriage rights was a raw exercise of power.[16]

B. OBERGEFELL'S REPRESENTATIONAL FAILINGS

While the four *Obergefell* dissenters focused on different doctrinal details, they shared a common central complaint: The *Obergefell* majority opinion reflected nothing more than the policy preferences of five Justices. "Five lawyers have closed the debate and enacted their own vision of marriage as a matter of constitutional law,"[17] Chief Justice Roberts lamented, calling the majority's decision "an act of will, not legal judgment."[18] Justice Scalia, too, recast the Justices as partisan advocates, or "lawyers," and announced that "[t]oday's decree says that my Ruler, and the Ruler of 320 million Americans coast-to-coast, is a majority of the nine lawyers on the Supreme Court."[19] Justice Thomas argued that the majority opinion "roa[med] at large in the constitutional field, guided only by their personal views."[20] And Justice Alito warned against "five unelected Justices" "invent[ing] a

nedy's reasoning is dubious and flawed."); Ariel Schneller, *How Justice Kennedy Could Have Baked a Better Fortune Cookie*, Los Angeles Times (June 29, 2015), http://www.latimes.com/nation/la-oe-0629-schneller-kennedy-20150629-story.html (criticizing Justice Kennedy's "flimsy fundamental rights analysis," and arguing that he should have focused his analysis on equal protection).

[16] See, for example, Richard F. Duncan, *Justice Scalia and the Rule of Law: Originalism vs. the Living Constitution*, 29 Regent U L Rev 9, 30 (2017) (questions whether Justice Kennedy's opinion in *Obergefell* was a valid application of the written Constitution, or instead, an illegitimate exercise of raw judicial power); Michael Stokes Paulsen, *The Wreckage of Obergefell*, First Things (Oct 2015), https://www.firstthings.com/article/2015/10/the-wreckage-of-obergefell ("All four dissents go beyond refuting the majority opinion; they condemn it as illegitimate. The Court is not just wrong, but has become a renegade institution that needs to be reined in by democratic forces outside of itself."); *Santorum Compares Supreme Court Ruling on Gay Marriage to Dred Scott*, FoxNews.com (Aug 6, 2015) (reporting that Senator Rick Santorum described *Obergefell* as a "rogue" decision with "no constitutional basis" and comparing the decision to the Supreme Court's infamous proslavery decision in *Dred Scott v Sandford*); Mike Schutt, *The Illegal Trouble with Obergefell*, Relay: The Journal of Worldview Academy (Aug 1, 2015), http://www.worldview.org/relay/the-illegal-trouble-with-obergefell/ (arguing that *Obergefell* "was not based on law—in fact it had nothing to do with law. The case was decided, instead, on pure will: the political and social preferences of five justices of the Supreme Court.").

[17] 135 S Ct at 2612 (Roberts, CJ, dissenting).

[18] Id.

[19] Id at 2627 (Scalia, J, dissenting).

[20] Id at 2631 (Thomas, J, dissenting) (quoting *Planned Parenthood of Southeastern Pennsylvania v Casey*, 505 US 833, 953, 965 (1992) (Rehnquist, CJ, concurring in judgment in part and dissenting in part)).

new right"[21] and "imposing their personal vision of liberty upon the American people."[22]

The dissenters suggested that the imposition of the Justices' views on the American people was particularly problematic because the decision came as close as a Supreme Court case can come, with nine sitting Justices, to a tie.[23] But Justice Scalia went further in making the case that the Justices as a group were particularly unqualified to decide the issue, arguing that the elitism and lack of connection between the Justices and the American people made the Justices' control of marriage policy especially disturbing:

> This Court . . . consists of only nine men and women, all of them successful lawyers, who studied at Harvard or Yale Law School. Four of the nine are natives of New York City. Eight of them grew up in east- and west-coast States. Only one hails from the vast expanse in-between. Not a single South-westerner or even, to tell the truth, a genuine Westerner (California does not count). Not a single evangelical Christian (a group that comprises about one quarter of Americans), or even a Protestant of any denomination. . . . [T]o allow the policy question of same-sex marriage to be considered and resolved by a select, patrician, highly unrepresentative panel of nine is to violate a principle even more fundamental than no taxation without representation: no social transformation without representation.[24]

The dissenters' objection to what Justice Scalia called a judicial "putsch" focused on the decision's interference with both the democratic process and the balance of authority between nation and state. Notably, the interference with the democratic process, and the control of law making by "the people," got higher billing in all four dissents, despite the fact that the federalism issue was more directly at stake. Absent a federal constitutional right, state courts could, and often already had, rejected state legislative bans on state constitutional grounds.

---

[21] Id at 2643 (Alito, J, dissenting).

[22] Id at 2640 (Alito, J, dissenting).

[23] See, for example, id at 2631 (Scalia, J, dissenting) ("with each decision that is unabashedly based not on law, but on the 'reasoned judgment' of a bare majority of this Court . . ."); id at 2632 (Thomas, J, dissenting) ("That a 'bare majority' of this Court . . . is able to grant this wish, wiping out with a stroke of the keyboard the results of the political process in over 30 States, based on a provision that guarantees only 'due process' is but further evidence of the danger of substantive due process") (footnote omitted).

[24] Id at 2629 (Scalia, J, dissenting).

This failure to protect the state lawmaking process was especially problematic, the dissenters suggested, when that process had been so productive and dynamic. Justice Scalia noted:

> Until the courts put a stop to it, public debate over same-sex marriage displayed American democracy at its best. Individuals on both sides of the issue passionately, but respectfully, attempted to persuade their fellow citizens to accept their view. Americans considered the arguments and put the question to a vote. The electorates of 11 States, either directly or through their representatives, chose to expand the traditional definition of marriage. Many more decided not to. Win or lose, advocates for both sides continued pressing their cases, secure in the knowledge that an electoral loss can be negated by a later electoral win. That is exactly how our system of government is supposed to work.[25]

Chief Justice Roberts noted the special problem of the Supreme Court "seiz[ing] for itself a question the Constitution leaves to the people, at a time when the people are engaged in a vibrant debate on that question,"[26] and added to the eleven states that legalized gay marriage by majority vote the five states whose highest courts "decreed that same result under their own Constitutions."[27]

The state-level developments in same-sex marriage law preceding *Obergefell* were, indeed, a remarkable display of democratic engagement and state experimentation and learning. And all signs suggested that the trend was shifting in favor of same-sex marriage, though the enactment of constitutional amendments banning same-sex marriage in a number of states prevented simple majorities from reversing policy there. The dissenters noted the loss, to people's perception of legitimacy, of a law imposed by the Court, rather than worked out over time in the states, a loss marriage equality advocates would not have had to incur, some of the dissenters hinted, in order to vindicate their views:

> [H]owever heartened the proponents of same-sex marriage might be on this day, it is worth acknowledging what they have lost, and lost forever: the opportunity to win the true acceptance that comes from persuading their fellow citizens of the justice of their cause. And they lose this just when the winds of change were freshening at their backs.[28]

---

[25] Id at 2627 (Scalia, J, dissenting).

[26] Id at 2612 (Roberts, CJ, dissenting).

[27] Id at 2615 (Roberts, CJ, dissenting); see also id at 2631 (Thomas, J, dissenting) (lamenting that the majority had "enshrine[d] their definition of marriage and put it beyond the reach of the normal democratic processes.").

[28] Id at 2625 (Roberts, CJ, dissenting).

We should be particularly worried, Chief Justice Roberts suggested, about the impact the decision would have on the attitudes of those who disagreed with its conclusion. "Stealing this issue from the people will for many cast a cloud over same-sex marriage, making a dramatic social change that much more difficult to accept."[29] Justice Alito shared this concern about the divisive effect of the decision, forecasting the "marginalization" of many Americans and the infliction of "bitter and lasting wounds,"[30] a theme that is routinely invoked today, in a broader political context, as a source of serious concern.[31]

Even worse, the dissenters argued, the majority opinion disparaged same-sex marriage opponents, many of whose positions are grounded in religious belief. "Perhaps the most discouraging aspect of today's decision," Chief Justice Roberts wrote toward the end of his dissent, "is the extent to which the majority feels compelled to sully those on the other side of the debate."[32] "These apparent assaults on the character of fair minded people will have an effect in society and in court," he warned.[33]

---

[29] Id at 2612 (Roberts, CJ, dissenting).

[30] Id at 2643 (Alito, J, dissenting).

[31] See generally John Moretta, *The End of the Liberal Experiment*, The Poleax (Feb 22, 2017), https://thepoleax.com/the-end-of-the-liberal-experiment-3eadef46e82c#.17qkap2nr ("Trump has energized an angry yet somewhat amorphous working class claiming to be fed up with the defamation of all they believed about American greatness and exceptionalism—as well as their place in it with their bitter feelings about being economically discounted and culturally marginalized by liberal elites."); Bill Connor, *Media Elite Still Doesn't Get Why Trump Won the Election*, Canada Free Press (Nov 15, 2016), http://canadafreepress.com/article/media-elite-still-doesnt-get-why-trump-won-the-election (explaining how the elite national media and Democratic Party have increasingly marginalized and demeaned the views and concerns of conservatives, leading to Trump's election); *What Drives Trump Supporters?: Sociologist Arlie Russell Hochschild on Anger & Mourning of the Right*, Democracy Now (Sept 28, 2016), https://www.democracynow.org/2016/9/28/what_drives_trump_supporters_sociologist_arlie (summarizing an interview with Ms. Hochschild in which she discussed her book, *Strangers in Their Own Land: Anger and Mourning on the American Right* (New Press, 2016), and the insight it provides into Trump's supporters' experience of marginalization); Rod Dreher, *Trump: Tribune of Poor White People*, American Conservative (July 22, 2016), http://www.theamericanconservative.com/dreher/trump-us-politics-poor-whites/ (summarizing an interview with J. D. Vance, author of *Hillbilly Elegy* [*A Memoir of a Family and Culture in Crisis* (Harper Collins, 2016)] acknowledging the hurt of working-class voters and explaining their support for candidate Trump).

[32] 135 S Ct at 2626 (Roberts, CJ, dissenting). For a repetition of this idea in the popular press, see, for example, Tom Garrett, *What Was Lost*, The Axis of Ego, posted on Breitbart (June 28, 2015), at http://www.breitbart.com/big-government/2015/06/28/just-how-crazy-is-the-cultural-change-that-culminated-in-obergefell-v-hodges/ (decrying gay rights activists' achievement, in *Obergefell*, of, among other things "[s]uccessfully brand[ing] opponents as simple 'bigots' for daring to hold a different view").

[33] See also id at 2642 (Alito, J, dissenting) (warning against the "vilif[ication]" of "Americans who are unwilling to assent to the new orthodoxy").

There is much to be said for this set of objections, pressed in the dissents and echoed by critics in the popular press and our political discourse. A small group of liberal judges who are out of touch with the country's " vast expanse in between" the coasts ruled that the Constitution protects the right of same-sex marriage, without engaging in any disciplined legal analysis, thereby putting to an immediate stop the vibrant debate and development of the issue in the states. But what the *Obergefell* dissents obscured is the fact that leading up to that elitist and ill-reasoned decision of five partisans were nineteen carefully reasoned decisions of federal judges from all parts of the country, party affiliations, and walks of life that lined up, one after the other, in favor of a right to same-sex marriage.

In the following part, I will suggest that the federal litigation, particularly in the district courts, played an important bridging role between the emergence of same-sex marriage law in a growing number of states and the recognition of a federal right protecting those marriages. That remarkable aggregation of lower court rulings offered a better grounding for the right than the *Obergefell* decision that displaced it. In a sense, of course, the lower courts will always be better situated to represent the people in whose states they sit than the small Ivy League educated group in Washington, but it was the broad uniformity of the district courts' rulings that made the Supreme Court's intervention particularly unnecessary, and the foreseeability of a weak Supreme Court opinion that made the intervention reckless.

II. The Right to Same-Sex Marriage in the Federal District Courts

A. Windsor and the Justices' Anticipation of Lower Federal Court Litigation

Two years prior to its decision in *Obergefell*, the Supreme Court decided *United States v Windsor*,[34] the case in which the Justices, by the same bare majority, struck down the Defense of Marriage Act (DOMA), which limited federal marriage benefits to opposite-sex couples. In his dissent in *Windsor*, Justice Scalia warned that it would lead to *Obergefell*'s result:

[34] 133 S Ct 2675 (2013).

> It takes real cheek for today's majority to assure us, as it is going out the door, that a constitutional requirement to give formal recognition to same-sex marriage is not at issue here—when what has preceded that assurance is a lecture on how superior the majority's moral judgment in favor of same-sex marriage is. . . . I promise you this: The only thing that will "confine" the Court's holding is its sense of what it can get away with.[35]

Scalia made a point of distinguishing "*this* Court,"[36] and potential "panel(s) of like-minded federal judges," that is, other appellate judges, from the federal district courts and state courts, whom he called upon to exercise independence in assessing the constitutional challenges to state same-sex marriage bans that were headed their way:

> I do not mean to suggest disagreement with the Chief Justice's view . . . that lower federal courts and state courts can distinguish today's case when the issue before them is state denial of marital status to same-sex couples. . . . Lord, an opinion with such scatter-shot rationales as this one (federalism noises among them) can be distinguished in many ways. And deserves to be. State and lower federal courts should take the Court at its word and distinguish away.[37]

In separate dissents, Chief Justice Roberts and Justice Alito both offered the district courts doctrinal ammunition for their resistance. For his part, Chief Justice Roberts emphasized that the *Windsor* majority opinion depended upon a finding that the authority to define marriage rested with the states, not the national government.[38] And Justice Alito plotted a course through the doctrine that led to the conclusion that neither the Due Process Clause nor the Equal Protection Clause of the Constitution prevented states from prohibiting same-sex marriage.[39] Endorsing the majority's declaration that the *Windsor* decision only protected the marriages authorized by state law, the dissenting Justices reminded the district court judges that the constitutionality of same-sex marriage bans was an open question.

The district court (and state court) judges did—in one sense—take up Justice Scalia's call. In a rapid and steady stream of decisions, they exercised independent judgment, giving the attention to the "argu-

---

[35] Id at 2709 (Scalia, J, dissenting).

[36] Id (emphasis in original).

[37] Id.

[38] Id at 2697 (Roberts, CJ, dissenting) ("I think the majority goes off course, as I have said, but it is undeniable that its judgment is based on federalism").

[39] Id at 2714 (Alito, J, dissenting) (" Same-sex marriage presents a highly emotional and important question of public policy—but not a difficult question of constitutional law").

ments put forward" by the defenders of state bans, which Justice Scalia complained had been ignored by the *Windsor* majority.[40] Those courts also substituted careful doctrinal analysis for what Justice Scalia called the "disappearing trail of legalistic argle-bargle"[41] set out by the *Windsor* majority. But the independent, careful work of this large, far-flung, locally grounded set of lower court judges led them to the result that Justice Scalia feared would be imposed upon them by five Justices in Washington, D.C. These judges agreed with the Chief Justice that *Windsor* did not decide the issue, and they agreed with Justice Scalia that it was their job to carefully analyze and decide it for themselves. But with near unanimity they rejected Justice Alito's constitutional analysis, not because they thought *Windsor* required them to reject it, but because they concluded that his analysis was wrong.

Justice Scalia's dissent in *Windsor* ended on an eloquent note. He lauded the evolution of society's debate over same-sex marriage, with it "victories in one place for some . . . offset by victories in other places for others,"[42] and he worried that the *Windsor* decision would "rob the winners of an honest victory, and the losers of the peace that comes from a fair defeat,"[43] a worry echoed by some marriage equality proponents in the period leading up to *Windsor*.[44] The explosion of district court decisions striking down state same-sex marriage bans

[40] Id at 2707 (Scalia, J, dissenting) (the majority opinion "makes only a passing mention of the 'arguments put forward' by the Act's defenders, and does not even trouble to paraphrase or describe them").

[41] Id at 2709 (Scalia, J, dissenting).

[42] Id at 2710 (Scalia, J, dissenting).

[43] Id at 2711 (Scalia, J, dissenting).

[44] See, for example, Emily Bazelon, *Backlash Whiplash*, SLATE (May 14, 2013), http://www.slate.com/articles/news_and_politics/jurisprudence/2013/05/justice_ginsburg_and_roe_v_wade_caution_for_gay_marriage.html ("I still worry that too much, too soon from the Supreme Court could become fodder for another wave of states' rights anger"); William Eskridge, *Marriage Equality State by State*, SCOTUSblog (Aug 15th, 2011), http://www.scotusblog.com/2011/08/marriage-equality-state-by-state/ ("Add same-sex marriage as an issue that now divides the country both 'intensely and evenly' and is therefore an issue that ought not be resolved one way or the other until public preferences become more settled" to avoid political backlash); Robin Wilson, *Same-Sex Marriage Symposium: The Overlooked Benefit of Leaving Perry in Place*, SCOTUSblog (Sept 18th, 2012), http://www.scotusblog.com/2012/09/same-sex-marriage-symposium-the-overlooked-benefit-of-leaving-perryin-place/ ("Whatever else may be said of the Supreme Court's [potential] decision not to consider the constitutionality of same-sex marriage bans in *Perry*, leaving the Ninth Circuit's opinion in *Perry* intact will allow legislators in Delaware, Illinois, New Jersey, Rhode Island, and California to build on this burgeoning story of compromise—and that is a good thing for same-sex marriage supporters and opponents alike").

that followed, while certainly a shift in the direction of national control over the issue, should be understood as another chapter in the progress toward an "honest victory." From the beginning, state courts were active players in those victories and defeats, and the emerging consensus reflected a complicated interaction between state court decisions and legislative and popular voting. While the federal district judges shifted the analysis to federal law, they did so in a role firmly grounded in local politics and culture. In an area of law in which popular attitudes were shifting, not only about whether same-sex marriage should be permitted, but also whether it should be understood as a civil right, the federal district judges played an important role as state-affiliated interpreters of the federal Constitution. In this way, they manifested a sort of federalism within the federal courts.

After setting the scene with a somewhat detailed account of the judges and their decisions that started things off in Utah,[45] I consider in the aggregate the federal district court decisions striking down same-sex marriage bans between the Supreme Court's decisions in *Windsor* and *Obergefell*. I conclude that those decisions were not vulnerable to the same charges of partisan elitism and lawless decision making that have been legitimately aimed at the Supreme Court's decision in *Obergefell*.

B. UTAH, OF ALL PLACES

In March, 2013, three months before *Windsor* was decided, three gay and lesbian couples filed suit in the United States District Court for the District of Utah alleging that Utah's statutory and constitutional ban on same-sex marriage violated their due process and equal protection rights under the Fourteenth Amendment of the United States Constitution. The case, *Kitchen v Herbert*,[46] was assigned to Judge Robert Shelby, an assignment that might have provoked a mixed reaction from litigants on both sides. Judge Shelby was a recent Obama appointment, but he was also a Republican who had been heralded by Utah's two Republican senators Lee and Hatch as

---

[45] Prior to the Utah ruling, a judge in Ohio had granted a temporary restraining order in the early days of *Obergefell*, compelling an Ohio state official to recognize the out-of-state marriage of a same-sex couple on a death certificate. *Obergefell v Kasich* (July 23, 2013, TRO). While Judge Black's initial ruling focused only on the question of out-of-state marriage recognition and his order only required one act by one government official, this case ultimately addressed the broader question of the states' power to ban same-sex marriage and became the captioned case of the Supreme Court's ruling.

[46] 961 F Supp 2d 1181 (D Utah 2013).

"pre-eminently qualified,"[47] with an "unwavering commitment to the law."[48] Judge Shelby had moved to Utah to attend college, and then made it his permanent home. At eighteen, he joined the Utah National Guard, later serving as a combat engineer in Operation Desert Storm alongside his fellow Utah guardsmen.[49] After attending the University of Virginia Law School, he returned to Utah to pursue his legal career, a career that consisted of a strong but unremarkable private practice in Salt Lake City.

On December 20, 2013, Judge Shelby issued his decision, striking down Utah's statutory and state constitutional bans on same-sex marriage and declaring that Utah's bans "deny its gay and lesbian citizens their fundamental right to marry." This declaration was significant, not only because it legalized gay marriage in Utah, but also because it announced the opinion's analytic independence from *Windsor*. While *Windsor* was a doctrinally opaque opinion, its emphasis on DOMA's problematic "discrimination of an unusual character"[50] tied its analysis more closely to equal protection than to substantive due process. Judge Shelby's opinion, in contrast, clearly focused on due process and the fundamental right to marry, an analysis that looked to other decisions, rather than *Windsor*, for support.

Kitchen was decided on cross-motions for summary judgment, focused on a legal question. That said, the judge's analysis depended upon findings of fact that were based on the undisputed testimony of the plaintiffs that plaintiffs' sexual orientation was "an inherent characteristic of their identities."[51] From this adjudicative fact, he drew the conclusion that the state's prohibition of same-sex marriage constituted a complete denial of the right to marry for those who could only develop "feelings of deep intimacy" with persons of the same sex.[52]

---

[47] *Confirmation Hearings on Judicial Appointments, Hearing Before the Committee on the Judiciary, United States Senate*, 112th Cong, 2d Sess 323 (2012) (Statement of Senator Mike Lee), http://www.gpo.gov/fdsys/pkg/CHRG-112shrg76131/html/CHRG-112shrg76131.htm.

[48] Id (Statement of Senator Orrin Hatch), http://www.judiciary.senate.gov/imo/media/doc/12-3-28HatchStatement.pdf.

[49] Id.

[50] *Windsor*, 133 S Ct at 2692–93. This equal protection focus is consistent with the approach taken by all the circuits that considered DOMA challenges before the Court decided *Windsor*, and most of the scholarship addressing the issues presented in the case.

[51] *Kitchen*, 961 F Supp 2d at 1200 ("The State accepts without contest the Plaintiffs' testimony that they cannot develop the type of intimate bond necessary to sustain a marriage with a person of the opposite sex. . . . The Plaintiffs' testimony supports their assertions that their sexual orientation is an inherent characteristic of their identities").

[52] Id at 1201.

Judge Shelby's opinion considered the source and scope of the fundamental right to marry at considerable length and went on to consider, and reject, the defendants' several arguments against the plaintiffs' fundamental rights claims.[53] Judge Shelby then turned to the Equal Protection Clause, concluding that it, too, prohibited the same-sex marriage ban. His consideration of equal protection doctrine included some discussion of fundamental rights[54] and heightened scrutiny,[55] but he concluded that the laws could not even survive rational basis review.[56]

Judge Shelby's opinion is notable for how he wrote both about the plaintiffs and about the people who voted for the laws he struck down. His detailed and personal descriptions of the plaintiff couples is unremarkable, the typical humanization of those whose rights an opinion goes on to protect. What is somewhat striking, however, is how frequently the judge tied the plaintiffs, in those descriptions, to Utah, and communities and institutions within Utah.[57] More notably, he went to some pains to avoid ascribing animus to the Utah voters (at least some of them) who supported the laws, and while he emphasized the lack of guidance on defining and identifying animus from the Supreme Court in *Windsor* or its earlier decision in *Romer v Evans*,[58] his conclusion that "it is impossible to determine what was in the mind of each individual voter"[59] went further, saying, in effect, that even the most well-intentioned, unhateful Utah citizens had enacted an unconstitutional law. Judge Shelby very intentionally avoided the polemical language Justice Kennedy adopted in *Windsor*, where he characterized the Congress that enacted DOMA as having the "avowed purpose . . . [of] impos[ing] a disadvantage, a separate status, and so a stigma."[60] *Kitchen v Herbert*, in contrast, is an opinion written by a Utah judge, for the citizens of Utah, of which he is one.

---

[53] Id at 1196–1205.

[54] Id at 1205.

[55] Id at 1206–10 (finding that the marriage bans should be subject to heightened scrutiny as discrimination on the basis of sex, but not on the basis of sexual orientation, which issue had been ruled out by prior Tenth Circuit precedent).

[56] Id at 1210–15.

[57] See, for example, id at 1190 ("[plaintiff] Laurie Wood has lived in Utah since she was three years old. She grew up in American Fork, received a B.A. from the University of Utah, and received her Master's degree from BYU. She spent over eleven years teaching in the public school system in Utah County and is now employed by Utah Valley University.").

[58] 517 US 620 (1996).

[59] Id at 1209.

[60] *Windsor*, 133 S Ct at 2693.

As important as this first crack in what would soon become an explosion of district court decisions were the developments in Utah that followed. There was, to no one's surprise, a considerable outcry against the decision. The Mormon Church released a statement expressing its disappointment and endorsing the views of the Utah citizens who had voted to amend the Utah constitution to forbid same-sex marriage.[61] The Utah attorney general and governor immediately criticized the opinion, noting, apparently accurately, that there was no direct Tenth Circuit precedent to support Judge Shelby's fundamental rights analysis.[62] They filed a notice of appeal and requested a stay pending a decision in that appeal.

Judge Shelby declined to stay his ruling, and within days more than 1,300 same-sex couples applied for marriage licenses. The remarkable number of applications filed so quickly after the decision opened people's eyes, across the country: even in Utah, a state that had banned same-sex unions three times over and was home to a large religious institution strongly opposed not only to same-sex marriage but to homosexuality in general, there were over a thousand same-sex couples ready and waiting to get married. The Utah couples' response to the decision had its own effect within the state and nationwide on popular perceptions of the issue and the scope of its reach.[63]

The Tenth Circuit also refused, multiple times, to enter a stay of Judge Shelby's ruling pending its decision on appeal, concluding that appellants had failed to show irreparable harm and a significant likelihood of prevailing on appeal.[64] The stay was ultimately granted by

---

[61] *Federal Judge Strikes Down Utah's Ban on Same-Sex Marriage*, http://fox13now.com/2013/12/20/federal-judge-strikes-down-utahs-ban-on-same-sex-marriage/.

[62] See http://archive.sltrib.com/article.phi?id=29291928&itype=storyID; http://www.ksl.com/?sid=28099570.

[63] See William N. Eskridge, *Backlash Politics: How Constitutional Litigation Has Advanced Marriage Equality in the United States*, 93 B U L Rev 275, 305 (2013) (noting that the growing number and visibility of same-sex marriages has "sparked a revolution in American understandings about LGBT people, family law, and marriage itself"); Michael J. Klarman, *From the Closet to the Altar: Courts, Backlash, and the Struggle for Same-Sex Marriage* xi (Oxford, 2013) (noting the effect the legalization of same-sex marriage in first states had on public perception of the issue and the people affected).

[64] The Tenth Circuit denied requests for stays on three consecutive days. See Order filed by Judges Holmes and Bacharach denying motion for stay filed by Appellants, *Kitchen v Herbert*, No 13-04178 (10th Cir, filed Dec 22, 2013); Order filed by Judges Holmes and Bacharach denying appellants' renewed motion for stay filed by Appellants, *Kitchen* (Dec 23, 2013); Order filed by Judges Holmes and Bacharach denying motion for stay pending appeal and for temporary stay filed by Appellants, *Kitchen* (Dec 24, 2013). While these stay orders are extremely brief, the Tenth Circuit's third order denying the stay on December 24, 2013 explains that "[h]aving considered the district court's decision and the parties' arguments

the Supreme Court sixteen days after Judge Shelby entered his initial ruling. During this sixteen-day gap, over 1,000 couples had been married,[65] and when Utah refused to recognize the marriages in certain contexts,[66] new plaintiffs sought a preliminary injunction in state court. In a noteworthy twist, the state defendants removed the case, *Evans v Utah*, to federal court, where it was assigned to Judge Dale Kimball.

If Judge Shelby might have been seen as an uncertain draw in *Kitchen*, the assignment of *Evans* to Judge Kimball must have surely given the plaintiffs pause. Like Judge Shelby, Judge Kimball's Utah roots ran deep: he was a seventy-five-year-old Utah native who grew up on a Utah dairy farm, attended BYU for college and the University of Utah for law school, and lived in Utah his entire life. His career consisted primarily of commercial litigation, with a two-year term as a professor at BYU's law school. Perhaps most notably, Judge Kimball also was (and is) a member of the Mormon Church, where he has served as a bishop, High Councilor, Stake President, and Regional Representative of the Twelve.

Noting that a preliminary injunction is an extraordinary remedy which should only be ordered when the "right to relief is 'clear and unequivocal,'"[67] Judge Kimball nevertheless entered an injunction compelling Utah to recognize the marriages conducted between Judge Shelby's ruling and the Supreme Court's stay. He ruled that a divestiture of already vested marriage rights would violate the plaintiffs' due process rights under the U.S. Constitution. Judge Kimball cited to federal cases, ending with *Windsor*, that have found inherent in the Due Process Clause of the Fourteenth Amendment a protected liberty interest in "freedom of personal choice in matters of marriage and family life." He also cited state cases that recognized due process

concerning the stay factors [with particular attention to] the likelihood of success on appeal [and] the threat of irreparable harm if the stay is not granted . . . we conclude that a stay is not warranted." Id at 2.

[65] *Evans v Utah*, 21 F Supp 3d 1192, 1197 (D Utah 2014) ("While it is not known how many of those [over 1,300] couples granted licenses solemnized their marriages before January 6, 2014, news reports put the number at over 1,000.").

[66] Id at 1200 ("The State continues to recognize Plaintiffs' marriages for purposes of joint state tax filings for 2013 and already issues state documents with marriage-related name changes. However, for all other purposes [including adoption, next-of-kin status for medical care and insurance benefits pressed by plaintiffs] the State is applying its marriage bans retroactively to Plaintiffs' marriages.").

[67] Id.

protection for vested interests including interests in a marriage validly solemnized. While Judge Kimball was clear that the case before him did not require him to assess whether the decision in *Kitchen* was correct,[68] he based his decision on similar substantive due process analysis.

Judge Kimball went on to determine that plaintiffs faced irreparable harm. He noted that this conclusion was near automatic when a constitutional right was at stake, and he focused on the fact that these particular plaintiffs would face legal limbo "with respect to adoptions, child care and custody, medical decisions, employment and health benefits, future tax implications, and inheritance,"[69] among other things. The judge also found that the balance of harm tipped "decidedly in Plaintiffs' favor," as did the public's interest, as "it is always in the public interest to prevent the violation of a party's constitutional rights."[70] All told, Judge Kimball concluded that the case for enjoining retroactive enforcement of the marriage ban against couples legally married while the ban was lifted was an easy one. Based on similar analysis, Judge Kimball determined that the "state ha[d] not met its burden of establishing the factors required for a stay pending appeal," but nevertheless "in [the court's] discretion . . . grant[ed] the State a limited 21-day stay during which it may pursue an emergency motion to stay with the Tenth Circuit."[71] The Tenth Circuit continued that temporary stay, which was displaced by another Supreme Court order staying the preliminary injunction entered in *Evans*. The story of these Utah stays, in sum, is the story of two confident district court judges underlining the strength of the plaintiffs' claims on the merits and the significance of the constitutional harm they faced, and sending a strong message that they did not expect their merits rulings to be overturned on appeal.

All of this considerable detail on the two Utah cases and the judges behind them would not be justified if it were an isolated tale of two federal district judges in one state far from Washington, D.C. who happened to preside over two among a small group of cases that raised

---

[68] Id at 1207–08 ("Whether or not *Kitchen* is ultimately upheld, the district court's injunction was controlling law and Utah's marriage bans were a legal nullity until the Supreme Court issued the Stay Order on January 6, 2014").

[69] Id at 1210.

[70] Id at 1211.

[71] Id at 1212.

a constitutional issue on its way to the Supreme Court. But *Kitchen* was followed swiftly by many others,[72] and it is through the aggregation of the many district court decisions striking down their states' same-sex marriage bans that the country's constitutional right to same-sex marriage emerged. In this patchwork of federal district court decisions, issued by a large group of judges in near total agreement across geographical region and politics, we see a sort of federalism hybrid: Federal judges acted as their states' representatives in interpreting the federal Constitution and interacted with state political actors who continued to play a role in shaping the development of the law.

C. THE JUDGES FROM THE VAST EXPANSE IN BETWEEN

Unlike the Supreme Court Justices, whose common elitist pedigrees and lack of geographical diversity were cataloged by Justice Scalia, the federal district court judges who struck down their states' same-sex marriage bans after *Windsor* in advance of any controlling appellate precedent hailed from nineteen different states and had distinctly local pedigrees as well. Many of these judges were born in the states in which they served, most attended college or law school (often both) in those states, and all pursued their legal careers ex-

[72] A total of nineteen federal district courts ruled, between the Supreme Court's decision in *United States v Windsor* and the entry of a binding appellate precedent, that their states' same-sex marriage bans violated the United States Constitution. *Searcy v Strange*, No 1:14-cv-00208-CG-N, 2015 US Dist LEXIS 7776 (SD Ala, Jan 23, 2015); *Rosenbrahn v Daugaard*, 61 F Supp 3d 862 (D SD, Jan 12, 2015); *Campaign for Southern Equality v Bryant*, 64 F Supp 3d 906 (SD Miss, Nov 25, 2014); *Jernigan v Crane*, 64 F Supp 3d 1260 (ED Ark, Nov 25, 2014); *Lawson v Kelly*, 58 F Supp 3d 923 (WD Mo, Nov 7, 2014); *Brenner v Scott*, 999 F Supp 2d 1278 (ND Fla, Aug 21, 2014); *Love v Beshear*, 989 F Supp 2d 536 (WD Ky, July 1, 2014); *Baskin v Bogan*, 12 F Supp 3d 1144 (SD Ind, June 25, 2014); *Wolf v Walker*, 986 F Supp 2d 982 (WD Wis, June 6, 2014); *Whitewood v Wolf*, 992 F Supp 2d 410 (MD Pa, May 20, 2014); *Geiger v Kitzhaber*, 994 F Supp 2d 1128 (D Or, May 19, 2014); *Latta v Otter*, 19 F Supp 3d 1054 (D Idaho, May 13, 2014); *DeBoer v Snyder*, 973 F Supp 2d 757 (ED Mich, March 21, 2014); *Tanco v Haslam*, 7 F Supp 3d 759 (MD Tenn, Mar 14, 2014); *Lee v Orr*, 2014 WL 683680 (ND Ill, Feb 21, 2014); *DeLeon v Perry*, 975 F Supp 2d 632 (WD Tex, Feb 26, 2014); *Bostic v Rainey*, 970 F Supp 2d 456 (ED Va, Feb 13, 2014); *Bishop v Oklahoma*, 962 F Supp 2d 1252 (ND Okla, Jan 14, 2014); and *Kitchen v Herbert*, 961 F Supp 2d 1181 (D Utah, Dec 20, 2013). In two other cases, federal district courts held that their state's nonrecognition laws (forbidding recognition of same-sex marriages validly celebrated in other states) violated the United States Constitution, *Obergefell v Wymyslo*, 962 F Supp 2d 968 (SD Ohio, Dec 23, 2013); *Bourke v Beshear*, 996 F Supp 2d 542 (WD Ky, Feb 12, 2014), adding Ohio (number 20) to the list of federal district courts which held that the Constitution afforded protection to same-sex marriages. And while this article focuses on the cases decided after *Windsor*, a federal district court had struck down California's same-sex marriage ban in advance of that decision, *Perry v Schwarzenegger*, 704 F Supp 921 (ND Cal 2010), bringing the total number of states in which federal district court cases protected same-sex marriage ahead of an appellate directive to twenty-one.

clusively, or nearly exclusively, in those states. Moreover, many of the state educational institutions they attended and practices they pursued were more local than national in their orientation. Judge Terrence Kern of the Northern District Court of Oklahoma, for example, who was the next district judge to strike down his state's same-sex marriage ban,[73] was born and educated in Oklahoma and practiced law in an Oklahoma town of 25,000 for twenty-five years before he was appointed to the bench. Judge John E. Jones, who struck down Pennsylvania's ban,[74] was born in Pottsville, Pennsylvania, a town of 14,000, attended Dickinson College and Law School, and then entered private practice in Pottsville, eventually starting his own firm. Judge Bernard A. Friedman, who struck down Michigan's ban,[75] was born in Detroit, attended Michigan State University and the Detroit College of Law, and then practiced law in Detroit and in one of its suburbs. He left the state only when serving on active duty in the army. Judge Ortie Smith, who struck down Missouri's same-sex marriage ban,[76] attended college and law school in Missouri and then practiced law in Nevada, a Missouri town of 8,000, located two hours away from a city of any significant size.

The judges striking down their states' same-sex marriage bans reflected remarkable political as well as geographic diversity. These judges, themselves, came from both parties, and were appointed by Presidents Carter,[77] Reagan,[78] Bush,[79] Clinton,[80] Bush II,[81] and Obama.[82] While the majority of the judges were appointed by Obama

---

[73] *Bishop v US ex rel Holder*, 962 F Supp 2d 1252 (ND Okla 2014).

[74] *Whitewood v Wolf*, 992 F Supp 2d 410 (MD Pa 2014).

[75] *DeBoer v Snyder*, 973 F Supp 2d 757 (ED Mich 2014).

[76] *Lawson v Kelly*, 58 F Supp 3d 923 (WD Mo 2014).

[77] Judge Barbara Crabb of the Western District of Wisconsin.

[78] Judge Bernard A. Friedman of the Eastern District of Michigan.

[79] Judge John G. Heyburn of the Western District of Kentucky.

[80] Judge Terrence C. Kern of the Northern District of Oklahoma; Judge Orlando Garcia of Western District of Texas; Judge Aleta Trauger of the Middle District of Tennessee; Judge Richard Young of the Southern District of Indiana; Judge Robert L. Hinkle of the Northern District of Florida; Judge Ortie Smith of the Western District of Missouri; Judge Karen Schreier of the District of South Dakota.

[81] Judge John E. Jones of the Middle District of Pennsylvania; Judge Callie Virginia Smith Granade of the Southern District of Alabama.

[82] Judge Robert Shelby of the District of Utah; Judge Arenda L. Wright of the Eastern District of Virginia; Michael J. McShane of the District of Oregon; Judge Kristine Baker of the Eastern District of Arkansas; Judge Timothy S. Black of the Southern District of Ohio;

or Clinton, the party of the appointing president in no way predicted the outcome. Unlike the *Obergefell* decision, in which five Justices on one side of the political spectrum barely beat out the dissenting Justices on the other, a heavy majority of the judges appointed by all six of these presidents all lined up on one side. And of the two judges, one in Louisiana and one in Puerto Rico, that ruled the other way, one was appointed by Reagan,[83] and one by Carter.[84] Thus, the constitutional rulings protecting same-sex marriage in the federal district courts were neither elitist and geographically isolated, nor fractured and partisan.

D. THE FEDERAL DISTRICT JUDGES AS STATE REPRESENTATIVES

The importance of this geographical and political diversity of judges, as Justice Scalia suggested in decrying the absence of such diversity in his colleagues, lies in the judges' ability to represent the American people as a whole. In fact, the district judges' role as state representatives runs much deeper than their geographic and political credentials.

1. *The judges' state affiliations.* In the early years of the Republic, aligning federal district courts' names and boundaries with those of individual states was seen as a means of preserving state power.[85] The very creation of inferior federal courts concerned the antifederalists,[86] and while much of their concern focused on the scope of these courts' authority, they were also troubled by proposals to assign new federal names and boundaries to these courts.[87] One critic of a bill in Congress proposing this independent federal geographic organization described the bill as "a very broad stroke to draw all the powers

Judge Sharon Johnson Coleman of the Northern District of Illinois; and Judge Carlton Wayne Reeves of the Southern District of Mississippi.

[83] Judge Martin Feldman of the Eastern District of Louisiana, *Robicheaux v Caldwell*, 2 F Supp 3d 910 (ED La 2014).

[84] Judge Juan Manuel Pérez-Giménez of the District of Puerto Rico, *Conde-Vidal v Garcia-Padilla*, 54 F Supp 3d 157 (D PR 2014).

[85] Alison L. LaCroix, *The New Wheel in the Federal Machine: From Sovereignty to Jurisdiction in the Early Republic*, 2007 Supreme Court Review 345.

[86] Id at 374.

[87] Id at 378 ("an amendment to breach state boundaries by creating a multistate district covering portions of Maryland, Virginia, and Delaware failed in the House, suggesting that maintaining the states' territorial integrity—rather than drawing entirely new political boundaries solely for federal purposes—was important to members"), and at 384–85 (describing opposition to the new names and boundaries proposed in the Harper Bill).

to the general government and to do away as far as possible not only [with] state powers but even boundaries."[88] The debate over the proper reach of the inferior federal courts' jurisdiction continued for decades, but the alignment of federal district courts with state names, boundaries, and, through these, identities, has been fixed since their creation.[89]

The significance of this state affiliation has engendered, and, in turn, been reinforced by, a distinct judicial appointment process for federal district judges. Although the details of the process have varied over time, appointing presidents have long shown substantial deference to the views of the senators from the state in which the district court judge would sit.[90] What has come to be known as the "Blue Slip" process has ensured that judicial nominees have the support of at least one, and usually both, of the state's senators. The value of this local senatorial support has been especially high in administrations that have faced the strongest resistance to their appointments from the Senate as a whole—administrations that include those of Presidents Clinton and Obama.[91] The selection process produced in our nineteen judges a group of judges who, though diverse in many ways including their politics and appointing presidents, were alike in their deep connections—personal, professional, and political—to the states in which they served.

These local connections were frequently celebrated when the judges were appointed. In his endorsement of Utah Judge Kimball, Senator Orrin Hatch highlighted not only the "respect Dale Kimball has earned from the Utah legal community," but also his "dedication to serving his community" as a "member of the Board of Pioneers Theatre Company, Alta View Hospital, the Deseret News Publish-

---

[88] Statement of Senator Abraham Baldwin, cited in LaCroix, 2007 Supreme Court Review at 385 (cited in note 85).

[89] The first set of thirteen District Court judges were assigned, one each, to the thirteen original states. Kevin L. Lyles, *The Gatekeepers: Federal District Courts in the Political Process* (1997). As their numbers grew, some states were assigned multiple judges and states were subdivided into regions, but those regions continued to be named and organized by state.

[90] Id at 44; Brannon P. Denning, *The "Blue Slip": Enforcing the Norms of the Judicial Confirmation Process*, 10 Wm & Mary Bill of Rights J 75 (2001).

[91] See, for example, Sheldon Goldman, Elliot Slotnick, and Sara Schiavoni, *Obama's First Term Judiciary: Picking Judges in the Minefield of Obstructionism*, 97 Judicare 7 (2013); Sheldon Golman and Elliot Slotnick, *Clinton's Judicial Legacy: Picking Judges Under Fire*, 84 Judicature 265 (2001) ("In the face of a hostile political environment, moderation, compromise, and accommodation were paramount in making judicial appointments").

ing Company [a company, affiliated with the Mormon church, that produced an influential paper], the Jordan Education Foundation [which supports a school district in the Salt Lake City area], and the J. Reuben Clark Law Society [whose primarily Mormon membership champions bringing together religious belief and legal service]."[92] Judge Richard Young, the Clinton appointment who struck down Indiana's marriage ban, was praised by Republican Senator Coats for his "sound, solid hoosier values" and for community service in Indiana's civic and arts organizations that was as extensive and diverse as Judge Kimball's in Utah.[93] And in Mississippi, when Judge Carlton Wayne Reeves, the judge who struck down Mississippi's ban, was nominated by President Obama, he had the endorsement of both of the state's Republican senators as well as both houses of the Mississippi state legislature. In a Concurrent Resolution, that legislature lauded Reeves as "a native of Yazoo County [who] never forgot about his home."[94]

A special form of local connection prevalent among the nineteen judges is their history of service in state politics and government. Judge Orlando Garcia, who struck down Texas's same-sex marriage ban,[95] lived his entire life in Texas, attended the University of Texas for college and law school, and served for a decade in the Texas legislature before becoming first a state and then a federal judge. Judge Friedman served for six years on the Michigan state court, and Judge Michael McShane, who struck down Oregon's ban,[96] served on Oregon's state court for sixteen years. Judger Trauger, who struck down Tennessee's ban,[97] served as chief of staff for the mayor of Nashville, and Judge Heyburn, who struck down Kentucky's ban,[98] served as special counsel to then Jefferson County judge/executive Mitch McConnell. Judge Jones of Pennsylvania ran unsuccessfully for the U.S.

---

[92] 143 Cong Rec S 10996 (Oct 22, 1997).

[93] 144 Cong Rec S 1293 (1998).

[94] Mississippi Senate Concurrent Resolution No 536 (adopted by the Mississippi Senate, Jan 13, 2011; adopted by the Mississippi House of Representatives, Jan 19, 2011), http://mdah.state.ms.us/arrec/digital_archives/governmentrecords/files/sos/sosenrolled/sos-enrolled-2011/senate-resolutions/SC536.pdf.

[95] *DeLeon v Perry*, 975 F Supp 2d 632 (WD Tex 2014).

[96] *Geiger v Kitzhaber*, 994 F Supp 2d 1128 (D Or 2014).

[97] *Tanco v Haslam*, 7 F Supp 3d 759 (MD Tenn 2014).

[98] *Love v Beshear*, 989 F Supp 2d 536 (WD Ky 2014).

House of Representatives and co-chaired Republican Governor Tom Ridge's transition committee.

Even after assuming their federal role, these judges maintained their connection to their local communities and constituencies in their work and private lives. At work, their interaction with local staff, litigants, witnesses, and juries and their engagement in fact-finding and adjudication of locally based disputes reinforced this connection.[99] While federal judges can hire clerks from any law school in the country, federal district court judges often hire locally. Among the judges who decided the same-sex marriage cases, several employed long-term "career clerks" from their communities,[100] or short-term clerks from in-state law schools.[101] Even those who hired from out-of-state law schools appeared to seek out students who came from their states.[102] Moreover, these judges continued to live where they had lived before they assumed their federal role, maintaining connections with local schools, churches, and organizations. In other contexts, scholars have noted the ongoing significance of district judges' local civic and social relationships that have sometimes led federal district courts to resist even clear direction on the Constitution's meaning.[103]

---

[99] Ori Aronson, *Inferiorizing Judicial Review: Popular Constitutionalism in Trial Courts*, 43 U Mich J L Ref 971, 995, 1012–13 (2010) (characterizing the work of federal district judges as "street-level bureaucratic" work done in contact with "real-life constituents" and local juries).

[100] For example, during the period when these judges were issuing same-sex marriage rulings, Judge Dale A. Kimball (D Utah) had only career clerks, both of whom received their law degrees from the University of Utah Law School, and Judge Bernard Friedman (ED Mich), Judge John E. Jones III (MD Pa), Judge Terence Kern (ND Okla), and Judge Richard L. Young (SD Ind) were among the judges who had at least one career clerk in chambers. 20 (1) *Judicial Yellow Book* at 259, 310, 427, 449.

[101] See, for example, Judge Orlando L. Garcia (WD Tex), who had one career law clerk, and one shorter-term law clerk who had formerly served as a "briefing attorney" for a Justice on the Texas Fourth Court of Appeals, earned his J.D. from St. Mary's University School of Law in San Antonio, Texas and an L.L.M. from the University of Texas Law School. Id at 497; Justice Marialyn Barnard, Lorien Whyte, and Emmanuel Garcia, *Is My Case Mandamusable?: A Guide to the Current State of Texas Mandamus Law* 45 St Mary's L J 143, 182 (author profiles).

[102] For example, Judge John G. Heyburn II (WD Ky) had three clerks in chambers during the relevant period, two of whom received their law degrees from the University of Kentucky, and the third of whom received her law degree from Harvard Law School, but who hailed from Louisville, Kentucky. *Judicial Yellow Book* (2014) at 276; *Wedding Celebrations*, New York Times (August 18, 2013).

[103] Robert A. Carp and C. K. Rowland, *Policymaking and Politics in the Federal District Courts* (Tennessee, 1983) (noting evidence that there is state-to-state variation in how district courts administer justice, and suggesting that differences are caused by district judges' close political, social, and cultural links to their states); J. W. Peltason, *58 Lonely Men: Southern Federal Judges and School Desegregation* (Harcourt, Brace & World, 1961) (describing the influence of local

2. *The judges' attention to their state constituencies.* The strength of the district judges' state affiliations was also demonstrated in their opinions, through their characterization of the plaintiffs and the voters who enacted the laws the plaintiffs challenged, and through their attempts to communicate a message to the citizens of their states. The plaintiffs were identified, first and foremost, as citizens of the state, leading productive lives, owning homes and businesses, and otherwise contributing to their communities.[104] They were also lauded for the role they played in their litigation, as local heroes for the cause. "No court record of this proceeding," Michigan Judge Friedman wrote in his conclusion, "could ever fully convey the personal sacrifice of these two plaintiffs who seek to ensure that the state may no longer impair the rights of their children and the thousands of others now being raised by same-sex couples."[105] And in announcing her reluctant issuance of a stay of her injunction blocking enforcement of Wisconsin's same-sex marriage ban, Judge Barbara Crabb of the Western District of Wisconsin explained that "[a]fter seeing the expressions of joy on the faces of so many newly wedded couples featured in media reports, I find it difficult to impose a stay on the event that is responsible for eliciting that emotion."[106]

Clearly, these judges were closer to the plaintiffs whose lives had been affected by the marriage bans than appellate courts are likely to be. More significantly, they were also closer to the people who voted for and continued to support the bans. And for all the judges' willingness to wax truly hyperbolic in their praise of the plaintiffs and in their sermon-like calls for justice,[107] they were repeatedly unwilling to cast aspersions on the voters who enacted the unjust laws. "Today's Court decision is not made," Judge Garcia assured his readers, "in defiance of the great people of Texas or the Texas Legislature, but in

---

social life and culture on the implementation of *Brown v Board of Education* by federal district court judges).

[104] *Bishop v Oklahoma*, 962 F Supp 2d at 1262 ("Plaintiffs Susan Barton and Gay Phillips have resided in Oklahoma for over fifty years and currently own a home in Tulsa, Oklahoma. They also own Barton, Phillips, and Associates, Inc., a company that provides training to agencies serving homeless teens. Ms. Phillips has a doctorate degree in sociology, and Ms. Barton is an adjunct professor at Tulsa Community College").

[105] *DeBoer v Synder*, 973 F Supp 2d at 775 (ED Mich 2014).

[106] *Judge Halts Same-Sex Marriages in Wisconsin*, CNN.com (June 14, 2014), http://www.cnn.com/2014/06/13/us/wisconsin-same-sex-marriage/.

[107] *Geiger v Kitzhaber*, 994 F Supp 2d at 1147 (Ore 2014) ("Let us look less to the sky to see what might fall; rather, let us look to each other . . . and rise").

compliance with the U.S. Constitution and Supreme Court precedent."[108] This hesitancy to ascribe hateful motives was surely born, at least in part, of the judges' proximity, in place, in life circumstances, in relationships, to those whose laws they were striking down. In an interview with the *Indiana Economic Digest* after he invalidated Indiana's same-sex marriage ban, Judge Richard Young acknowledged that many Indiana citizens were upset about his ruling and had been calling his chambers and speaking with chambers staff. "[W]e're here to serve the public and we can't ignore the calls. We have to answer them, talk to them and listen," he explained.[109]

Perhaps the most striking example of a judge's effort to reach citizens opposed to his ruling was Judge Heyburn's kindly (and lengthy) civics lesson, attached to the end of his first ruling, in which he concluded that Kentucky's refusal to recognize out-of-state marriages was unconstitutional:

> For many, a case involving these issues prompts some sincere questions and concerns. After all, recognizing same-sex marriage clashes with many accepted norms in Kentucky—both in society and faith. To the extent courts clash with what likely remains that majority opinion here, they risk some of the public's acceptance. For these reasons, the Court feels a special obligation to answer some of those concerns.[110]

Judge Heyburn went on to discuss religious liberty, the lack of any effect on opposite-sex marriages, and the nature of constitutional interpretation. Some portions of this section of the opinion read like an FAQ fact sheet for concerned Kentucky citizens. ("Many others may wonder about the future of marriage generally and the right of a religion to set its own rules. Must churches now marry same-sex couples? How will this decision change or affect my marriage?").[111] In one passage, Judge Heyburn explained the reach of the Fourteenth Amendment, and noted: "In fact, the first Justice to articulate this view was one of Kentucky's most famous sons, Justice John Marshall

[108] *DeLeon v Perry*, 975 F Supp 2d at 665 (WD Tex 2014) ("In reaching [the] decision [that a same-sex marriage ban is unconstitutional, there is no need] to disparage the legislators and citizens who voted in good conscience for the marriage amendment.").

[109] Thomas B. Langhorne, *Federal Judge Knows of the Furor Created by His Decision Striking Down Same-Sex Ban*, Indiana Economic Digest (June 29, 2014), http://indianaeconomicdigest.com/main.asp?SectionID=31&subsectionID=235&articleID=75256.

[110] *Bourke v Beshear*, 996 F Supp 2d at 554.

[111] Id at 555.

Harlan."[112] While Judge Heyburn's approach was unusual, he shared with many of the other district judges a sense of connection with, and accountability to, all the citizens of their states, perhaps in some ways most particularly those whose political will they had thwarted.

In sum, both the district judges themselves, and the opinions they wrote finding a federal constitutional right to same-sex marriage, reflect the judges' conception of themselves as state representatives to the federal bench serving the citizens of their state through their efforts to faithfully interpret the Constitution.[113] They are not the elites at a distance, decried by *Obergefell*'s critics, but local insiders taking responsibility for a legal determination that will make a significant portion of their fellow citizens unhappy.

E. THE FEDERAL DISTRICT JUDGES AS CONTRIBUTORS TO THE STATE POLITICAL PROCESS

State political actors also interacted with the federal district court litigation in ways that blurred the lines between state and federal, and the judicial and the political. In many instances, elected officials reacted to the litigation in a manner that at least demonstrated a political position and often had the effect of shaping, or at least potentially shaping, their states' laws.

Mark Herring, as attorney general of Virginia, was one of the first elected officials to use his role in same-sex marriage litigation to take a political position. As a state senator, Herring had voted in 2006 for the state constitutional amendment prohibiting same-sex marriage. But thirteen days after he began his four-year term as attorney general in January 2014, and a month after Judge Shelby entered his order in *Kitchen*, Herring announced that he would not defend Virginia's same-sex marriage ban in federal court and filed a brief asking the court to strike down the law. While he was attacked by his opponents for not doing his duty to defend Virginia's laws for political gain, his justification focused on his obligation to Virginia's citizens. He explained that his decision to challenge rather than defend the ban was based, not only on his need to protect the rights of those the ban unlawfully discriminated against, but also, more strikingly, "be-

[112] Id.

[113] Consider Katie Eyer, *Lower Court Popular Constitutionalism*, 123 Yale L J Online 197 (2013) (suggesting that federal district courts can be "entry points for popular constitutional understandings").

cause of our unique history in Virginia when it comes to civil rights." He cited Virginia's poor track record, reflected in earlier federal litigation on school desegregation and interracial marriage, and concluded that it was time for Virginia to finally come down on "the right side of history."[114] While "being on the right side" presumably meant at least taking the right position in the litigation, Herring's filing of a brief opposing Virginia's law increased the chances that the law would be struck down.

Two weeks later, Nevada's attorney general, Catherine Cortez Masto, withdrew the state's brief defending Nevada's same-sex marriage ban before the Ninth Circuit after the Ninth Circuit ruled, in another context, that distinctions based on sexual orientation were entitled to heightened scrutiny under the Equal Protection Clause.[115] Nevada Governor Sandoval announced that "it has become clear that this case is no longer defensible in court"[116] and supported Masto's withdrawal from the case. In this case, it appears that the officials' actions had no effect on the ultimate outcome of the case, but the shift in position altered the significance of the court's ultimate rejection of the Nevada law, which now conformed with the position of its chief executive.

In Pennsylvania, the interrelated decisions of the state's attorney general and governor produced a legal result that at least hastened the end of Pennsylvania's same-sex marriage ban. When Attorney General Kathleen Kane, a democrat and a named defendant, withdrew from the litigation and announced that the ban was "wholly unconstitutional,"[117] the governor, Tom Corbett, a Republican running for reelection, stepped in to defend the law. But after district Judge John Jones struck down Pennsylvania's ban, Corbett announced that he would not appeal the decision.[118] For Corbett, the court's decision

[114] Markus Schmidt, *Herring's 1st Year as Attorney General Defined by Gay Marriage Case*, Richmond Times-Dispatch (Dec 27, 2013), http://www.richmond.com/news/virginia/government-politics/article_b71eebb6-847c-5213-affa-830b4aa2da93.html.

[115] *SmithKline Beecham Corp. v Abbott Laboratories*, 740 F3d 471 (9th Cir 2014).

[116] Steve Benen, *Nevada Moves Away from Gay-Marriage Ban* (February 11, 2014), The Maddow Blog, http://www.msnbc.com/rachel-maddow-show/nevada-moves-away-gay-marriage-ban.

[117] PennLive, *AG Kathleen Kane Says She Won't Defend Pa.'s Same-Sex Marriage Ban* (July 11, 2013), http://www.pennlive.com/midstate/index.ssf/2013/07/ag_kathleen_kane_says_she_wont.html.

[118] Trip Gabriel, *Pennsylvania Governor Won't Fight Ruling That Allows Gay Marriage*, New York Times (May 21, 2014).

gave him perfect political cover. He could maintain that he personally opposed same-sex marriage, but that he could not justify a likely unsuccessful appeal. The lack of any coherent account of how he determined his odds on appeal underscores the likelihood that Judge Jones's decision allowed Corbett to secure a legal outcome he was willing to accept, perhaps even preferred, if he could avoid political accountability for that outcome.

In other states, the litigation did not offer any needed cover; it just helped political actors achieve their desired ends. As far back as 2004, a single Oregon county began issuing marriage licenses to same-sex couples. These actions inspired litigation and then a referendum banning same-sex marriage. This ban was eventually challenged in a federal lawsuit, *Geiger v Kitzhaber*,[119] one of the cases considered here. Before scheduled argument in *Geiger*, Oregon Attorney General Ellen Rosenblum withdrew from the case, stating that "performing same-sex marriages in Oregon would have no adverse effect on existing marriages."[120] Judge Michael McShane subsequently struck down the Oregon ban, leading proponents of a referendum calling for the legalization of same-sex marriage to drop their efforts (despite having obtained enough signatures to put the referendum on the ballot) and announce that they were "confident that the freedom to marry is secure in Oregon."[121]

In Illinois, state political actors contributed more directly to the reach of the federal judge's decision. The Illinois litigation was unusual, because it was filed after the Illinois legislature had voted to legalize same-sex marriage. Pursuant to the state constitution, however, the law was not scheduled to go into effect for several months. Plaintiffs in Cook County sued the Cook County clerk, seeking an order compelling him to issue marriage licenses to same-sex couples prior to the effective date of the Illinois law. The clerk was happy to be sued, because he supported the plaintiffs' wish to get married immediately. Finding that the plaintiffs had a constitutional right to marry, Judge Sharon Johnson Coleman entered the requested order. Because the suit was filed only against the Cook County clerk, the judge

---

[119] 994 F Supp 2d 1128 (D Or 2014).

[120] Defendant's answer in *Rummel v Kitzhaber* (consolidated with *Geiger*) (February 20, 2014).

[121] Reuters, *After Gay Marriage Legalized in Oregon, Advocates Abandon Ballot Push* (May 23, 2014).

determined that her ruling applied only in Cook County. After her decision was entered, however, Illinois Attorney General Lisa Madigan published an opinion informing clerks in other counties that "they should find Judge Coleman's decision persuasive as they evaluate whether to issue marriage licenses to same-sex couples."[122] Governor Pat Quinn in turn announced that the Illinois Department of Public Health would record same-sex marriages issued by any county clerk. Thus state political action bolstered officials' willingness to cooperate with the federal litigation, and, ultimately, to stretch its disposition beyond the borders established by the judge.

In Missouri, county clerks relied on the federal district court ruling striking down the ban in St. Louis County, but ignored the same judge's order staying its ruling pending appeal and began issuing marriage licenses to same-sex couples the next day. And, paralleling the approach taken in Illinois, a county executive from Jackson County (Kansas City) relied on the single-county ruling in St. Louis to extend the right to same-sex marriage to other parts of the state. "Courts are ruling that marriage is a fundamental right of every citizen," a Jackson county executive announced. "Sound public policy dictates that right to be applied uniformly across the state."[123]

These last accounts likely reflect influence in both directions: Most obviously, state officials built upon the federal district court decisions to move same-sex marriage recognition ahead. It is also likely that evolving state attitudes, reflected in the expressed views of executive branch leadership as well as the county clerks charged with issuing the marriage licenses,[124] had some effect on the district courts' perceptions of the issues. These judges were clearly operating in the midst of state law making, law enforcing, and politicking. And without attempting to identify what effects that immersion in the local political and legal environment had on federal district courts' analysis and decision making, it is indisputable that the district court judges took an awareness of the local scene with them to work. Even if that awareness had no effect on their decisions, it inevitably shaped their

---

[122] Letter of Attorney General Lisa Madigan to Macon County Clerk Stephen M. Bean (Mar 4, 2014).

[123] Kansas City Star (Nov 7, 2014), www.kansascity.com/news/government-politics/article 3619714.html.

[124] See, for example, Oakland County Clerk Lisa Brown, who was named as a defendant in *DeBoer v Snyder*, but adopted plaintiffs' legal position challenging the Michigan ban and testified on behalf of the plaintiffs at trial. 973 F Supp 2d at 757 n 1, 764–65.

understanding of what they were doing and whom it would effect. This grounding of their decisions upon a local landscape, and the delivery of their decisions to a local constituency, itself had some bearing on the building of a national consensus. Just as state court decisions and bare-majority votes advanced that consensus, if messily, so, too, did decisions of state-affiliated federal judges in striking down their own states' laws.

The district courts' role in developing and manifesting the growing consensus was also in line with an emerging shift in the focus of that consensus. Where earlier polls showed rapidly growing popular support for same-sex marriage, even while a majority of Americans favored resolution of the issues in the states, polls taken as these district court decisions began to be issued showed growing popular support for the recognition of a federal constitutional right.[125]

This shift paralleled a shift in state court decisions as well. In the period leading up to *Obergefell*, state courts began striking down marriage bans on federal constitutional grounds sometimes ahead of,[126] sometimes in lieu of,[127] and sometimes after but apparently inde-

[125] Scott Clement and Robert Barnes, *Poll: Gay-Marriage Support at Record High*, Washington Post (April 23, 2015), http://www.washingtonpost.com/politics/courts_law/poll-gay-marriage-support-at-record-high/2015/04/22/f6548332-e92a-11e4-aae1-d642717d8afa_story.html ("A record-high 6 in 10 Americans support same-sex marriage and a similar share say individual states should not be allowed to define marriage as only between a man and a woman, according to a new Washington Post–ABC News poll.").

[126] *Wright v Arkansas*, 2014 WL 1908815 (Ark Cir) (Trial Order, May 9, 2014) (striking down Arkansas's same-sex marriage ban on federal (as well as state) constitutional grounds six months prior to the district court's holding in *Jernigan v Crane*, 64 F Supp 3d 1260 (ED Ark, Nov 25, 2014); *State of Missouri v Florida*, 2014 WL 5654040 (Mo Cir) (Trial Order, Nov 5, 2014) (striking down Missouri's same-sex marriage ban on federal constitutional grounds two days before the district court's ruling in *Lawson v Kelly*, 58 F Supp 3d 923 (WD Mo, Nov 7, 2014)); *Brinkman v Long*, 2014 WL 3408024 (Colo Dist) (Trial Order, July 9, 2014) (ruling that Colorado's same-sex marriage ban was unconstitutional three months prior to the federal district court's decision in *Burns v Hickenlooper*, 2014 WL 5312541 (Oct 17, 2014), but after the Tenth Circuit's affirmance of the Utah district court's ruling in *Kitchen v Herbert*, 755 F3d 1193 (10th Cir, June 25, 2014). The Colorado state trial court ruling, apparently drafted prior to the Tenth Circuit's ruling in *Kitchen*, makes no mention of that decision, though it cites frequently to the district court's decision in *Kitchen* as well as several other federal district court decisions striking down same-sex marriage bans); *Huntsman v Heavilin*, 21 Fla L Weekly Supp 916a (Fla 16th Cir, July 17, 2014) (holding Florida's same-sex marriage bans unconstitutional a month before the federal district court's ruling in *Brenner v Scott*, 999 F Supp 2d 1278 (Aug 21, 2014).

[127] *Costanza v Caldwell* (Minute Entry Ruling, Sept 22, 2014, Parish of LaFayette) (holding Louisiana's same-sex marriage ban and nonrecognition law violated the federal Constitution, despite the federal district court's previous ruling three weeks earlier in *Robicheaux v Caldwell*, 2 F Supp 3d 910 (ED La, Sept 3, 2014), upholding the bans); see also *Garden State Equality v Dow*, 434 NJ Super 163; 82 A3d 336 (2013) (applying *Windsor* to conclude that, because New

pendent of[128] a federal district court decision. Some of these state courts cited extensively to federal district court cases that had struck down same-sex marriage bans in other states prior to their rulings.[129] Others charted their own way through Supreme Court equal protection and due process doctrine.[130] Like federal district court judges, these state court judges, too, answered Justice Scalia's call to give their independent assessment of the constitutional question, and they, too, concluded with near unanimity[131] that their states' same-sex marriage bans violated the United States Constitution.

Ironically, the reaction of state government officials in one state *against* its federal district court's ruling likely served to strengthen national support for a federal constitutional right. In Alabama, the day after Judge Callie Virginia Smith Granade became the last district judge to strike down a same-sex marriage ban ahead of a binding appellate ruling, Chief Justice Roy S. Moore of the Alabama Supreme Court wrote an open letter to Alabama Governor Robert Bentley, decrying Judge Granade's ruling and declaring that it did not bind the Alabama courts:

> The recent ruling of Judge Callie Granade of the United States District Court for the Southern District of Alabama has raised serious, legitimate concerns about the propriety of federal court jurisdiction over the Alabama Sanctity of Marriage Amendment. . . . The laws of this state have always recognized the Biblical admonition stated by our Lord:
>
>> But from the beginning of the creation God made them male and female. For this cause shall a man leave father and mother, and cleave to his wife. And the twain shall be one flesh. . . .
>
> I am encouraged by the Alabama Probate Judges Association which has advised probate judges to follow Alabama law in refusing to license mar-

---

Jersey civil unions did not qualify couples for federal marriage benefits as same-sex marriages would, these civil unions no longer afforded couples rights equal to those of married opposite-sex couples, and therefore violated the New Jersey Constitution).

[128] *In the matter of A.L.F.L. and K.L.L.*, No 2014-CI-02421 (Tex Dist, June 30, 2014) (ruling that Texas's marriage law was unconstitutional in the context of adjudicating a same-sex divorce).

[129] *Wright v Arkansas*, 2014 WL 1908815 (Ark Cir, May 9, 2014); *Brinkman v Long*, 2014 WL 3408024 (Colo Dist, July 9, 2014).

[130] *Costanza v Caldwell*, No 2013-0052 D2 (La Dist, Sept 22, 2014, Parish of LaFayette); *Missouri v Florida*, 2014 WL 5654040 (Mo Cir) (Trial Order, Nov 5, 2014).

[131] The one exception is the state court in Tennessee, which concluded that Tennessee's nonrecognition law was constitutional after the district court had ruled, in *Tanco v Haslam*, 7 Supp 3d 759, that it was unconstitutional. See *Borman v Pyles-Borman*, 2014 WL 4251133 (Aug 5, 2014).

> riages between two members of the same sex. However, I am dismayed by those judges in our state who have stated they will recognize and unilaterally enforce a federal court decision which does not bind them.[132]

Chief Justice Moore is the same judge who in 2003 was removed from his position as Chief Justice (a position he later regained) when he refused to remove a monument to the Ten Commandments despite a federal order to do so.[133] And while Judge Granade's relationship to the federal judge who wrote the majority opinion in the decision striking down Alabama's bus segregation[134] law in 1956 is coincidental (she is his granddaughter), her place in her grandfather's role in conflict with a state official who was notorious for his lawless disregard for federal authority created a certain sense of political and legal déjà vu. When some of Alabama's probate judges refused to issue marriage licenses to couples not included in Judge Granade's order for a preliminary injunction, the plaintiffs compared these judges to "George Wallace at the school house door staring defiantly upon this Court's order" and likened the need for clarification of the scope of Judge Granade's order to the parallel need, during the civil rights era, for a second, broader opinion striking down Alabama's anti-miscegenation statute, after a first order was only narrowly enforced.[135]

The reaction of Chief Justice Moore, some of the probate judges, and then, in a similar vein, the Alabama governor[136] served to underline the parallel between the civil rights movement and the marriage equality movement in the eyes of the nation. By the time the nation was watching Alabama's reaction to Judge Granade's ruling in January, 2015, what it saw was not a sympathetic state citizenry pushed around by a national elite, but rather a specific and familiar subset of Alabama citizens who needed to be brought into line once

---

[132] Letter from Chief Justice Roy S. Moore to Governor Robert Bentley (Jan 27, 2015), http://media.al.com/news_impact/other/Read%20Chief%20Justice%20Moore%20letter.pdf.

[133] CNN.com, *Ten Commandments Judge Removed from Office* (Nov 14, 2003), http://www.cnn.com/2003/LAW/11/13/moore.tencommandments/.

[134] *Browder v Gayle*, 142 F Supp 707 (MD Ala 1956) (Judge Richard Rives, Judge Granade's grandfather, wrote the opinion for a three-judge court).

[135] Plaintiffs' Objection and Response to Defendants' Motion to Stay, *Searcy v Strange*, No 1:14-cv-00208-CG-N, 6 (SD Ala, filed Jan 24, 2015).

[136] Justin Snow, *Alabama Chief Justice Vows to Fight Marriage-Equality Ruling*, Metro Weekly (Jan 27, 2015), http://www.metroweekly.com/2015/01/alabama-chief-justice-vows-to-fight-marriage-equality-ruling/.

again.[137] In this way, the federal judge was also replaying a familiar local role, the role of those "58 Lonely Men"[138] called upon to bring some of their own recalcitrant citizens into line when they refused to desegregate their schools. By framing its state's rights resistance in such unpalatable terms, Alabama's reaction served to advance the federal constitutional cause.

The district court litigation engendered an interplay with political action precisely because it was state specific and subject to continuing development. The political influences began before litigation was filed (shaping the district courts' perceptions of the issues) and continued through the course of the litigation (shaping the positions taken by litigants and by others in reference to the litigation) and after the cases were decided (reflected in decisions about compliance, enforcement beyond that required to comply, and decisions on appeal). In this important sense, the rich debate among the American people on the issue of same-sex marriage celebrated by the *Obergefell* dissenters continued to occur through the federal litigation in the district courts.[139] It was not silenced until *Obergefell* declared a final, nationwide resolution.[140]

F. DOCTRINAL ANALYSIS IN THE FEDERAL DISTRICT COURTS

1. *The judges' substantive analysis.* Another benefit of the locally limited nature of the district court rulings was the freedom it gave

---

[137] This specter made visible what Judge Reeves had emphasized again and again in his opinion striking down Mississippi's same-sex marriage ban. Unlike most of the rest of the district court judges who took pains to avoid casting aspersions on the citizens who supported the same-sex marriage bans in their states, Judge Reeves announced that his state's discrimination against gays and lesbians was a clear echo of its shameful Jim Crow past. *Campaign for Southern Equality v Bryant*, 64 F Supp 3d at 929–41.

[138] Peltason, *58 Lonely Men* (cited in note 103).

[139] Amy Davidson captured the participatory nature of litigation in her Comment, *Southern Honeymoon*, New Yorker (Jan 5, 2015), http://www.newyorker.com/magazine/2015/01/05/southern-honeymoon:

> The courts are not simply a check on the democratic process but a part of it. Across the country, men and women have filed declarations, testified, gone to trial, and appealed. If voting is an act of participatory democracy, so are those actions. Southerners with cases pending include a widow in Georgia, who doesn't want her wife's death certificate to bear a box checked "never married," and two female Atlanta police officers, who want to be sure that each is recognized as a spouse and a parent in case one is killed in the line of duty.

[140] While some resistance continued, even after *Obergefell* was decided, that resistance was isolated and minimal. See Alan Blinder and Tamar Lewin, *Clerk in Kentucky Chooses Jail Over Deal on Same-Sex Marriage*, New York Times (Sept 3, 2015).

the judges to explore the relevant constitutional doctrine. What this produced was a set of district court opinions that share the conclusion that the Constitution protected the right to same-sex marriage, but that explored a variety of different doctrinal paths to reach that common conclusion. Some judges focused on substantive due process, some on equal protection, and many on both. Within their equal protection analysis, various judges reached different conclusions on whether the marriage bans were subject to heightened scrutiny, and, if so, based on what form of classification.[141] The state defendants offered a variety of different justifications for their bans, and each judge addressed those particular justifications at considerable length, adding additional variation to the opinions.

The district courts' decisions manifest the care and comprehensiveness that can be expected of such important rulings, sure to be reviewed on appeal, and likely scrutinized by opponents and advocates alike.[142] Each judge was deciding the case for one state, with no need to gain the votes of other judges who might take another analytic approach. This encouraged the judges to pursue clean lines of analysis exhaustively. What mattered was internal coherence, not the achievement of cross-judge consensus. That said, as the number of cases grew, the district courts drew increasingly on the previously decided cases, picking preferred approaches among them, and pointing to the consistency of the results to underline the certainty of their own decisions.[143] To the extent an analytic consensus began to emerge, however, it was more like a consensus that emerges among lawmaking states, reflecting the cross-learning derived from their fifty-state laboratory, than the strategic consensus that inspired four Jus-

---

[141] Compare, for example, *Kitchen v Herbert*, 961 F Supp 2d at 1206–07 (finding that same-sex marriage ban discriminated on the basis of sex, which required the application of heightened scrutiny), with *Whitewood v Wolf*, 992 F Supp 2d 425–30 (finding that sexual orientation qualified as a quasi-suspect class and therefore distinctions based on sexual orientation were subject to heightened scrutiny).

[142] See Richard A. Posner, *The Supreme Court 2004 Term—Foreword: A Political Court*, 119 Harv L Rev 32, 34–35, 43 (2005) (comparing lower federal courts, who are "bound by Supreme Court precedent and so are better able to exhibit a certain respect for the conventional materials of decisions," with the Supreme Court, a "lawless judicial institution" with "an ocean of discretion"); see also Eyer, 123 Yale L J Online at 197 (cited in note 113) (suggesting, in the period leading up to *Windsor*, that "it is in the lower courts that the important details of gay equality claims have been worked out.").

[143] See, for example, *Tanco v Haslam*, 7 F Supp 3d at 768 (relying on a "rising tide of persuasive post-*Windsor* federal case law" to support the court's assessment of the merits of plaintiffs' claim on a motion for preliminary injunction).

tices to set aside their likely doctrinal scruples to sign on to Justice Kennedy's ill-reasoned opinion in *Obergefell.*

Of course, the very individuality of district court decisions will commonly create a pattern of conflict that prevents any emergence of clear law at the district court level. What was distinctive about the district court same-sex marriage decisions was that, for all their doctrinal diversity, and with no obligation to coordinate or follow one another's lead, the district judges repeatedly reached the same result. What the district court judges produced, together, was an increasingly widespread constitutional protection of the right to same-sex marriage, supported by a range of doctrinal justifications, explored with discipline. Because none of them bound the others, the law could comfortably tolerate the analytic diversity, allowing the protection of the right to precede the resolution of the difficult, and more contested, doctrinal questions. Moreover, that doctrinal diversity created opportunities for jurisdictional variation in the development of antidiscrimination and marriage law in other contexts, variation that could have benefited the Supreme Court's ultimate resolution of the doctrinal questions pressed in the same-sex marriage context.

While a single, well-reasoned declaration of constitutional law from the Supreme Court is the best way, ultimately, to advance the development of constitutional law, that option does not appear to have been available to the Supreme Court when it decided *Obergefell.* The lower court decisions make clear that the Supreme Court's inability to formulate such a declaration did not stem from any dearth of doctrinal grounding on which the ruling could have been based. Rather, it stemmed from the composition of the Supreme Court itself. In such circumstances, it surely would have been better to forestall final resolution of the issue until the court was prepared to support it with a well-reasoned opinion. In rushing to declare the right in an ill-reasoned opinion, the Court opened itself up to the critics, who have exploited its lawlessness to attack the legitimacy of the ruling and the Court itself. The harm caused by the rush is particularly troubling because it was not needed to protect same-sex couples' federal constitutional right to marry in most parts of the country. As I will argue in Part III, even after the Sixth Circuit's ruling produced a circuit split in legal outcome, the Supreme Court paid too big a price to achieve immediate national uniformity.

2. *The judges' findings of fact.* Another relevant dimension along which the district court decisions differed was procedural. Most com-

mon were decisions, like *Kitchen*, granting and denying the parties' cross-motions for summary judgment that focused on issues of law. Some of these rulings, however, included findings of fact, whether based on an undisputed record presented in the motions, or on factual concessions offered at oral argument. Judge Shelby relied on such conceded facts in concluding that sexual orientation was an inherent trait, for example.[144]

In other litigation, one side or the other submitted substantial evidentiary support that was taken into account in the judge's ruling. In his consideration of the plaintiffs' request for a permanent injunction and a declaratory judgment in *Obergefell*, Ohio Judge Black relied extensively on the expert reports submitted by plaintiffs in concluding that gays and lesbians had faced historical discrimination, lacked political power, and were discriminated against on the basis of a "a core trait or condition that one cannot or should not be required to abandon," all supporting his conclusion that discrimination based on sexual orientation was entitled to heightened scrutiny.[145] He also relied on an expert's report to find that children raised by same-sex couples did as well as children raised by opposite-sex couples.[146] Conversely, in *Bishop*, Oklahoma Judge Kern reported that the defendants provided "twenty-five exhibits consisting primarily of articles and scholarly writings on marriage, child-rearing and homosexuality, ranging in date from the early twentieth century to 2008, all of which this Court has carefully reviewed,"[147] although in his case he apparently decided to disregard their conclusions. In both of these cases, any findings of fact tied to the evidentiary submissions or otherwise derived by the judges can best be understood as legislative rather than adjudicative facts.[148]

In *DeBoer*, in contrast, Judge Friedman held a nine-day trial. The trial came after he determined that there were genuine disputes of

---

[144] *Kitchen*, 961 F Supp 2d at 1200–1201.

[145] *Obergefell v Wymsylo*, 962 F Supp 2d at 987–91, 998–99 (citing plaintiffs' experts' reports to support findings that factors requiring heightened scrutiny apply to discrimination on the basis of sexual orientation).

[146] Id at 994 n 20 (citing plaintiffs' experts to support its conclusion that "the overwhelming scientific consensus, based on decades of peer-reviewed scientific research, shows unequivocally that children raised by same-sex couples are just as well adjusted as those raised by heterosexual couples").

[147] 962 F Supp 2d at 1290.

[148] For a general discussion of the difference between legislative and adjudicative facts, see Kenneth S. Broun, *McCormick on Evidence* § 328 (West, 7th ed 2014).

material fact, particularly surrounding child-rearing practices and the relative risks and benefits of being raised by an opposite- or same-sex couple. Judge Friedman concluded that he needed to engage in conventional adjudicative fact-finding to sort through the defendant's rational basis claims. The commitment to conducting a lengthy trial suggested considerable openness to the defendant's justifications for Michigan's same-sex marriage ban, and both sides presented the judge with a long line of experts supporting their arguments for and against the rationality of the ban. In the end, however, the court's assessment of the various experts and related findings of fact were devastating to defendants. He refused to qualify one of defendant's experts altogether, concluded that a second had skewed his results to satisfy a funder, and generally found every other expert offered by the defendant "unbelievable and not worthy of serious consideration."[149] In contrast, he found every expert witness offered by the plaintiff "highly credible" and gave their testimony "great weight,"[150] relying on that testimony to conclude, among other things, that same-sex couples were successful parents and that children fared better with two parents, regardless of their sex, than one. While a single judge's adjudicative fact-finding regarding same-sex parenting should not drive the ultimate determination of whether a state's concerns for children's upbringing could justify a same-sex marriage ban under rational basis review, Judge Friedman's ability, and willingness, to test the parties' claims in court captures the district court's special proximity to the litigants and the issues they pressed.

It is this special connection to the citizens of their states, citizens who are voters as well as litigants, that gave the district court judges' decisions special integrity,[151] and the near unanimity of their conclusion, across region and across politics, a special significance. The nineteen opinions of these judges, often interacting with state political activity, manifested a groundswell of support across the nation for the constitutional protection of same-sex couples' right to marry. But in displacing those decisions with *Obergefell*, the Supreme Court cut off the ruling from its origins prematurely, obscuring the breadth of support for the ruling from view. The conclusion that the United

---

[149] *DeBoer v Snyder*, 973 F Supp at 766.

[150] Id at 762, 764.

[151] Ori Aronson notes the value of federal district judges' "direct contact with real-life constituents." Aronson, 43 U Mich J L Reform at 995 (cited in note 99).

States Constitution protected a right of same-sex marriage did not begin with a partisan elite, but it ended with one, and when the Supreme Court decides a case, it is only this ending that people see. Supreme Court decisions always shift control to a small elite in Washington, and controversial cases always give that control to a potentially partisan majority, but in *Obergefell* that shift in control came at a special cost and without any justifying benefits. Where the Supreme Court's involvement will sacrifice a law's connection to the people living in the "vast expanse in between," without introducing doctrinal clarity, the Court should have the wisdom and humility to stay out.

III. Can the Supreme Court's Intervention Be Defended?

There are a number of reasons to doubt the wisdom, or feasibility, of leaving the law in the hands of the lower courts. Perhaps the district courts were merely trying to implement their understanding of the Supreme Court's direction in *Windsor*, in which case it would be wrong to suggest that their decisions told us anything about an emerging consensus or the breadth of the support for the law. Moreover, even conceding a distinct contribution from these lower court decisions, we might doubt the staying power of that contribution. By the time the Supreme Court granted certiorari in *Obergefell*, five courts of appeals had ruled on the constitutionality of same-sex marriage, and cases were pending in other circuits. And once the Sixth Circuit produced a circuit split, it was broadly assumed that the Supreme Court had to take the case. And perhaps the *Obergefell* decision preserved, or could have preserved, the relevance of the lower court decisions.

None of these objections is sound. There is abundant evidence of the district courts' independence in the substance of their opinions and their procedural control of the litigation. And while many of these rulings were affirmed on appeal, the court of appeals' decisions did not eclipse the district court decisions, as *Obergefell* did (and Supreme Court decisions inevitably do). When the Sixth Circuit ruled the other way, it increased the value of Supreme Court intervention, but not enough to justify the cost of that eclipse.

A. The Federal District Judges as Leaders Not Followers

In *Windsor*, Justice Scalia called on the federal district court judges to "distinguish away," because he feared they would interpret *Wind-*

sor as a mandate to recognize a right to same-sex marriage. If the district courts, in striking down same-sex marriage bans, were merely reading the "writing on the wall," the volume and near unanimity of their decisions would tell us little about the breadth of support for federal same-sex marriage rights. There is ample evidence, however, that the district court judges were acting as independent constitutional interpreters rather than dutiful implementers.[152] We see this evidence in their declarations that *Windsor* does not control, and, more significantly, in their analytic independence both from the Supreme Court's previous cases addressing sexual orientation and from their own circuits' refusal to recognize sexual orientation as a suspect classification. And we see it in the judges' approach to attempts to stay their rulings pending appeal.

1. *Substantive independence.* A number of the district court opinions expressly stated that they did not view *Windsor* as controlling.[153] There is ample support for this view in the *Windsor* majority's own opinion as well as the *Windsor* dissents, though, of course, Justice Scalia's dissent makes clear that he doesn't believe the majority means what it says. More telling is the analytic separation between the district courts' opinions and the majority opinion in *Windsor*. Not one district judge tries to duplicate the *Windsor* majority's analysis.

As I have noted, many district judges were unwilling to disparage the citizens who enacted the bans; this led most of the judges to avoid, and many to expressly reject, any version of the argument that those bans were based on animus,[154] despite the centrality of that argument

[152] Others have acknowledged some interpretive role in the lower federal courts, but have suggested that role was heavily controlled by *United States v Windsor*. See Neil Siegel, *Reciprocal Legitimation in the Federal Courts System*, 70 Vand L Rev (forthcoming 2017) (arguing that the Supreme Court may have intentionally left the question of the constitutionality of same-sex marriage bans open in *Windsor* to give lower courts an opportunity to legitimize the Court's ultimate ruling on the subject); Craig Green, *Turning the Kaleidoscope: Toward a Theory of Interpreting Precedents*, 94 NC L Rev 379, 465 (2016) (characterizing the federal district court opinions banning same-sex marriage as interpretations of *United State v Windsor*).

[153] See, for example, *Lawson v Kelly*, 58 F Supp 3d 923, 927 ("The State is wrong when it contends *Windsor* holds that state statutes forbidding same-sex marriage are constitutional. Plaintiffs are wrong when they contend *Windsor* holds that states are constitutionally required to allow same-sex marriages. Thus, both parties are incorrect when they contend *Windsor* dictates a favorable outcome for their positions.").

[154] See *Kitchen v Herbert*, 961 F Supp 2d at 1209; *Love v Beshear*, 989 F Supp 2d at 547; *Wolf v Walker*, 986 F Supp 2d at 1017–19; *Whitewood v Wolf*, 992 F Supp 2d at 430–31; *Geiger v Kitzhaber*, 994 F Supp 2d at 1146–47; *Latta v Otter*, 12 F Supp 3d at 1142–43; *Baskin v Bogan*, 7 F Supp 3d at 768–69; *DeBoer v Snyder*, 973 F Supp 2d at 775; *Bostic v Rainey*, 970 F Supp 2d at 482; *Bourke v Beshear*, 996 F Supp 2d at 549–52.

in *Windsor* and in Justice Kennedy's earlier opinions addressing gay and lesbian rights.[155]

On the other hand, many of the district court judges were eager to press for the recognition of sexual orientation as a suspect classification, despite the Supreme Court's avoidance of the question in *Windsor* and, in many cases, their own circuits' contrary precedents.[156] In the majority of the six circuits in which there was a precedent rejecting sexual orientation as a suspect classification,[157] the district court judges made clear that they thought the circuit precedent was likely or certainly wrong and called for its reconsideration. Judges Black (Ohio) and Heyburn (Kentucky) directly challenged the Sixth Circuit's precedent, despite the fact that the case establishing the precedent was just decided in 2012. The justification for ignoring that precedent, which was first set out by Judge Black, and then echoed by Judge Heyburn, was that the relevant Sixth Circuit case had erroneously relied on a line of cases based on *Bowers v Hardwick*, "which," Judge Black noted, "was *overruled by Lawrence in 2003*."[158] The italics are in the original, presumably to punctuate the error of the Sixth Circuit's ways. Judge Heyburn made the same point in a gentler, more roundabout way. Noting, as did Judge Black, that the precedential case relied on *Bowers*, the judge optimistically predicted that

---

[155] *Romer v Evans*, 517 US 620 (1996) (holding that a law that singled out sexual orientation for exclusion from antidiscrimination protections was motivated only by animus, which could not qualify as a rational basis). While *Lawrence v Texas*, which struck down Texas's sodomy laws, was grounded on substantive due process rather than equal protection analysis, and therefore did not invoke the animus doctrine, the Court in *Lawrence* invoked a common tone when it declared that its holding would prevent the state from "demean[ing gay couples'] existence." *Lawrence v Texas*, 539 US 558, 578 (2003).

[156] Katie Eyer has suggested that the district court's openness, prior to the Supreme Court's decision in *United States v Windsor*, to arguing that sexual orientation qualified as a suspect classification may have been inspired by the Obama Administration's endorsement of that position in the *Windsor* litigation. Eyer, 123 Yale L J Online at 197 (cited in note 113). However influential the Obama Administration's position may have been in the district courts prior to the Court's decision in *Windsor*, it is still notable that these courts continued to press the issue against the contrary precedent of their circuit courts after the Supreme Court declined to embrace the Obama Administration's analysis. See id at 216 (noting, shortly after the Supreme Court decided *Windsor*, that "it is certainly possible that the Supreme Court's decision . . . may be read by the lower courts as a signal to halt the incipient move" in the direction of recognizing sexual orientation as a suspect classification).

[157] *Davis v Prison Health Servs*, 679 F3d 433, 438 (6th Cir 2012); *Price-Cornelison v Brooks*, 524 F3d 1103, 1105 (10th Cir 2008); *Citizens for Equal Protection v Bruning*, 455 F3d 859 (8th Cir 2006); *Lofton v Sec'y of Dep't of Children & Family Servs*, 358 F3d 804 (11th Cir 2004); *Schroeder v Hamilton School Dist.*, 282 F3d 946, 950–51 (7th Cir 2002); *Baker v Wade*, 769 F2d 289, 292 (5th Cir 1985).

[158] *Obergefell v Wymsylo*, 962 F Supp 2d at 986.

"it would be no surprise, however, were the Sixth Circuit to reconsider its view."[159] Judge Crabb, too, faced some precedential obstacles in the Seventh Circuit, which she suggested she could work around without the direct challenge that Judges Black and Heyburn contemplated. In the same Seventh Circuit, Judge Young of Indiana concluded he was barred from treating sexual orientation as a suspect class, but "agree[d] with plaintiffs that it is likely time to reconsider this issue, especially in light of the Ninth Circuit's decision in *SmithKline*."[160] Florida Judge Hinkle delivered a challenge to the Eleventh Circuit much like Judge Black's to the Sixth, noting that he could not treat sexual orientation as a suspect classification "at least for now," and that the Eleventh Circuit precedent was inconsistent with *Lawrence*, *Romer*, and *Windsor*, two of which preceded the Eleventh Circuit decision.[161]

Perhaps most starkly, Judge Reeves in Mississippi declared, after an extensive comparison of the history of discrimination on the basis of race and sexual orientation:

> Intermediate scrutiny is most appropriate. If this court had the authority, it would apply intermediate scrutiny to government sexual orientation classifications. . . . Although circuit precedent forecloses this finding "it is safe to say that there is some doctrinal instability in this area" [citing the First Circuit decision in *Windsor*, 699 F3d at 181] which merits renewed consideration by the en banc Fifth Circuit or the Supreme Court.[162]

This repeated insistence by many district courts that their own circuits take a fresh look at a question the Supreme Court majority seemed determined to duck, along with their rejection of the premise that same-sex marriage bans were the product of animus—a premise that the Supreme Court, and particularly Justice Kennedy, clearly embraced—well captures the leadership role the district courts were eager to take in considering the constitutionality of same-sex marriage.[163]

---

[159] *Bourke v Beshear*, 996 F Supp 2d at 548.

[160] *Baskin v Bogan*, 12 F Supp 3d at 1160.

[161] *Brenner v Scott*, 999 F Supp 2d at 1291.

[162] *Campaign for Southern Equality v Bryant*, 64 F Supp 3d at 941.

[163] These manifestations of independence run counter to common accounts of the constraints imposed on lower federal courts by the appellate hierarchy. See Aronson, 43 U Mich J L Reform at 991 (cited in note 99) ("Conscientious trial court judges, who practice within a system that conceives of the Supreme Court as the only legitimate source for constitutional meaning, are bound to submit to a jurisprudence of deference"); Ashutosh Bhagwat, *Separate*

2. *Procedural independence.* The district judges' responses to efforts to stay their rulings favoring same-sex marriage pending appeal also suggest that they did not see themselves as simply following the Supreme Court's lead. In Utah, Judge Shelby refused to enter a stay and Judge Kimball suggested that his brief stay was more a matter of courtesy than legal requirement. The Supreme Court ultimately stayed the injunction against Utah's same-sex marriage ban, and that affected decisions made, sometimes grudgingly, by other district judges thereafter. Most of the district judges whose decisions followed the Supreme Court's order in *Kitchen* concluded that they were compelled to enter a stay to conform to the Supreme Court's "unusual intervention"[164] in *Kitchen*. But Judge Friedman, despite the entry of the *Kitchen* order and the request of defendants for a comparable stay pending appeal, nevertheless refused to enter a stay, giving over 300 couples an opportunity to get married before the Sixth Circuit entered its own stay the next day.[165] Like Judge Friedman, Judge Crabb of Wisconsin initially refused to grant a stay and several clerks issued marriage licenses to same-sex couples. When she later determined that a stay was required, she explained her decision in these terms:

> If I were considering these [stay] factors as a matter of first impression, I would be inclined to agree with plaintiffs that defendants have not shown that they are entitled to a stay [which requires a showing that defendants will "likely succeed on appeal" and that their irreparable harm, if a stay is denied, will outweigh any irreparable harm imposed on plaintiffs by the entry of the stay]. However, I cannot ignore the Supreme Court's order in *Herbert v. Kitchen*, in which the Court stayed a district court's order enjoining state officials in Utah from enforcing its ban on same-sex marriage. It is impossible to know the Court's reasoning for issuing the stay because the Court did not accompany the order with an opinion, but, since *Herbert*, every statewide order enjoining the enforcement of a ban on same-sex marriage has been stayed, either by the district court or the court of

---

But Equal?: The Supreme Court, the Lower Federal Courts, and the Nature of the "Judicial Power," 80 B U L Rev 967, 967 (2000) ("the judges of the lower, or 'inferior,' federal courts are viewed by the [Supreme] Court, and even view themselves, as subordinates who must defer to 'judicial superiors'"). Perhaps the district courts' same-sex marriage cases call this account into question, or perhaps they are all the more significant because they represent an unusual departure from federal district court norms. Either way, they show the federal district court playing an important, independent role in the development of the law.

[164] *Bourke v Beshear*, 996 F Supp 2d at 558.

[165] *Michigan Clerks Marry Gay Couples After Judge Strikes Down Ban*, Chicago Tribune (March 22, 2014).

> appeals. . . . In following *Herbert*, other courts have stated that, despite the lack of any reasoning in *Herbert*, they did not see any grounds for distinguishing the Supreme Court's order.[166]

The lower courts' chafing at the Supreme Court's unexplained stay in *Kitchen* reflects a tension between the stay standard in the Supreme Court and that in district and appellate courts. While the Supreme Court's decision to grant a stay rests on a range of factors, some unique to that Court,[167] the justification for a district or appellate court stay rests much more heavily on the courts' assessment of the merits. In determining the appropriateness of the requested stays after the Supreme Court entered the stay in *Kitchen*, the district courts (and to a large extent the courts of appeals as well) found themselves caught between their own confidence in the correctness of their decisions and their obligation to show deference to the Supreme Court's action, whether merits driven or not.

In asserting their authority, rather than couching their decisions in deferential anticipation of appellate review, the district courts conveyed a state-like, federalist independence. Of course, in the end, their decisions would be reviewed, and the final word on the constitutionality of same-sex marriage bans would come from higher courts, but the authoritative independence with which they undertook their task produced its own version of a fifty-state laboratory, a laboratory experimenting with multiple doctrinal formulas, pumping out remarkably consistent results.

B. EXPANSION MORE THAN DISPLACEMENT IN THE CIRCUIT COURTS

As the district courts continued to strike down their state bans, some of the earliest decisions began to be reviewed on appeal. There were early indications of appellate support in the form of denied and reluctantly granted stays.[168] And on June 25, 2014, a year after the

---

[166] Order granting stay in *Wolf v Walker*, 3:14-cv-00064-bbc, Document #134, filed June 13, 2014.

[167] See Stephen M. Shapiro, Kenneth S. Geller, Timonthy S. Bishop, Edward A. Hartnett, and Dan Himmelfarm, *Supreme Court Practice* at 872–910 (10th ed, 2013).

[168] The Tenth Circuit thrice denied the request to stay the effect of Judge Shelby's ruling in the Utah district court pending appeal in *Kitchen v Herbert*, No 13-04178 (10th Cir, filed Dec 22, 2013) (discussed in note 64). See also *Latta v Otter*, Order granting stay of Idaho district court's order pending appeal, No 14-35420 (9th Cir, May 20, 2014) (Hurwitz, J, concurring) ("I concur in the order granting the stay pending appeal . . . solely because I believe that the Supreme Court, in *Herbert v Kitchen*, has virtually instructed courts of appeals to grant stays in [these] circumstances").

Supreme Court decided *Windsor*, the Tenth Circuit affirmed the Utah district court's ruling in *Kitchen*,[169] and three weeks later, it affirmed the Oklahoma district court's ruling in *Bishop*.[170] The Fourth Circuit followed soon thereafter, affirming the Virginia district court's ruling,[171] which was, in turn, followed by the Seventh Circuit, affirming rulings in Indiana and Wisconsin.[172] Court of appeals judges arguably have more in common with Supreme Court Justices than with locally connected district court judges, so it might be said that these affirmances already effected the displacement I blame on the Supreme Court's decision in *Obergefell*.

But, to a large extent, the analysis in the court of appeals decisions, and the media coverage of those cases, served to preserve the significance of the long and continuing run of district court cases. This preservation is most evident in the Tenth Circuit's affirmance of *Kitchen*. In *Kitchen*, the Tenth Circuit closely followed Judge Shelby's analysis and quoted language from his opinion with glowing approval.[173] More notably, the Tenth Circuit's opinion cited repeatedly to many of the other district court decisions, at several different points in the opinion, to support most aspects of its analysis.[174] The overall tone of the decision suggested that the Tenth Circuit was adding to the many decisions that had come before it, rather than initiating their displacement.

We see the same attention to these decisions in Judge Holmes's concurring opinion in *Bishop v Smith*,[175] the second Tenth Circuit de-

---

[169] *Kitchen v Herbert*, 755 F3d 1193 (10th Cir 2014).

[170] *Bishop v Smith*, 760 F3d 1070 (10th Cir 2014).

[171] *Bostic v Schaefer*, 760 F3d 352 (4th Cir 2014).

[172] *Baskin v Bogan*, 766 F3d 648 (7th Cir 2014).

[173] 755 F3d at 1218 ("As the district court eloquently explained, 'it is not the Constitution that has changed, but the knowledge of what it means to be gay or lesbian.'").

[174] See, for example, 755 F3d at 1215–16 (citing to *DeLeon* for support of its contention that liberty interests must be defined in a manner to protect freedom of personal choice); id at 1216 (citing the district court's decision in *Bostic* for support of its contention that "gay and lesbian individuals share the same capacity as heterosexual individuals to form, preserve and celebrate loving, intimate and lasting relationships"); id at 1216 (citing "several recent district court decisions" including *Geiger*, *Latta*, *DeBoer*, *DeLeon*, and *Bostic* that have rejected state claims, like the one it rejects, based on "procreative concerns"); id at 1223 ("emphatically agree[ing] with the numerous cases decided since *Windsor*" including *Kitchen*, *Geiger*, *DeBoer*, *DeLeon*, *Bostic*, and *Bishop*, "that it is wholly illogical to believe that state recognition of the love and commitment between same-sex couples" will alter the relationships of opposite-sex couples) among other examples.

[175] 760 F3d at 1097 (Holmes, J, concurring) (praising the district court in *Bishop* for declining to rely on animus analysis and noting that "[m]ost of the other recent judicial decisions

cision by the same panel, which endorsed the lower court's—and other district courts'—refusal to suggest that same-sex marriage bans were the product of animus. In *Bostic v Bogan*, the Fourth Circuit relied on multiple district court decisions in addressing the place of federalism in their constitutional analysis[176] and the court's authority to reach the constitutional question.[177] The Fourth Circuit also borrowed from Judge Friedman's fact-finding in *DeBoer*, noting that it provided evidentiary support for the findings on same-sex parenting reported by the American Psychological Association in its amicus brief.[178]

The press coverage of these court of appeals decisions also treated them as a continuation of previous decisions, rather than dramatic new developments—a notable contrast with the subsequent coverage of the Supreme Court's decision in *Obergefell*. While some of the news coverage attempted to explain to a nonlawyer readership that a court of appeals decision reached further, and had greater authority, than a district court decision, much of the coverage described the circuit court rulings as "expanding the streak of legal victories,"[179] or adding to the "stream of gay marriage suits"[180] that began in the district courts. Again, the message was more that of accumulation and reinforcement than displacement, a message likely derived in part from the ongoing fragmentation of the authority across regions as well as the potentially temporary nature of their rulings.

C. THE SUPREME COURT'S INEVITABLE DISPLACING EFFECT

Perhaps the Supreme Court, like the courts of appeals, should be understood as building upon, rather than displacing, the federal district court decisions. Justice Kennedy does give a nod to this idea with his reference to "extensive litigation in state and federal courts [in which j]udicial opinions addressing the issue have been informed by

---

invalidating same-sex marriage laws have exercised the same forbearance," citing *Kitchen*, *Love*, *Wolf*, *Whitehood*, *Geiger*, *Latta*, *Baskin*, *DeBoer*, *Bostic*, and *Bourke*).

[176] 760 F3d at 378 n 8.

[177] Id at 373.

[178] Id at 383.

[179] Jack Healy, *Appeals Court Rejects Utah's Ban on Gay Marriage, Prodding the Supreme Court*, New York Times (June 25, 2014).

[180] Erik Larson, *Virginia Gay Wedding Ban Third Tossed by Appeals Courts*, Bloomberg Business (July 28, 2014), http://www.bloomberg.com/news/articles/2014-07-28/virginia-gay-marriage-ban-unconstitutional-court-affirms.

the contentions of parties and counsel, which, in turn, reflect the more general, societal discussion of same-sex marriage and its meaning that has occurred over the past decades."[181] Professor Neil Siegel suggests that the reference to lower federal court decisions, cataloged in Appendix A,[182] had a legitimizing effect on the Supreme Court's decision in *Obergefell*, and that the Court might have purposefully cultivated this legitimizing effect by leaving the lawfulness of same-sex marriage bans open in *Windsor*.[183]

But Justice Kennedy's invocation of the lower court rulings fails to preserve their legitimizing effect. His reference to these cases, going back to the 1980s and blending together acceptance and rejection of same-sex couples' claims of a constitutional right, obscures the striking unity of the decisions leading up to the Supreme Court's *Obergefell* decision. And his long list of bare case citations fails to give any sense of the political and geographic diversity of the opinions, let alone the doctrinal rigor of their analysis. And unlike the courts of appeals, the *Obergefell* majority did nothing to suggest it was joining, rather than displacing, the opinions that came before it. In the end, the catalog of cases served to demonstrate only that the issue had been well vetted.

Most important, though, while Justice Kennedy could have done a better job of capturing this striking development in the lower courts, it would not have made much of a difference. Supreme Court rulings inevitably displace the patchwork of lower court developments on a legal question with a single final decision. This is a central aspect of our judicial design, reinforced by the special attention given by scholars and the press to Supreme Court rulings.[184] For that reason, the Court should be sensitive to what will be gained and what will be lost with that displacement. In *Obergefell*, the Court paid a big price in lost representative grounding, for a decision that declares an outcome without developing the law.

---

[181] 135 S Ct at 2605.

[182] Id at 2608–10.

[183] Siegel, *Reciprocal Legitimation*, 70 Vand L Rev (cited in note 152).

[184] Some scholars have commented critically on this so-called "supreme court capture." See, for example, Aronson, 43 U Mich J L Reform at 985–93 (cited in note 99) (critically describing scholars' exclusive focus on the Supreme Court in their analysis of judicial review as "supreme court capture"); Frederick Schauer, *The Occasions of Constitutional Interpretation*, 72 B U L Rev 729, 729 (1992) (noting an "odd preoccupation with the Supreme Court" in discussions of constitutional interpretation).

D. THE SUPREME COURT'S OPTION TO STAY OUT

On October 6, 2014, the Supreme Court denied certiorari without opinion in all the cases from the Tenth, Fourth, and Seventh Circuits and lifted the stays on the district court orders in Utah, Oklahoma, Virginia, Indiana, and Wisconsin, directing states to recognize and celebrate same-sex marriages. The Court's actions had the immediate effect of legalizing same-sex marriage in the five states with cases before the Court and precipitated the issuance of district court orders legalizing same-sex marriage in the seven remaining states in those circuits that had not yet addressed the issue. The day after the Supreme Court denied certiorari, the Ninth Circuit also expanded its earlier ruling in *Perry v Brown*,[185] striking down bans on same-sex marriage in Idaho and Nevada.[186] In the view of many, the battle against same-sex marriage was over, and would be controlled by law developed in the district and circuit courts.[187]

But a month later, On November 6, 2014, the Sixth Circuit created a circuit split by reversing the district court rulings in Kentucky, Ohio, Tennessee, and Michigan. In *DeBoer v Snyder*,[188] the Sixth Circuit ruled in a 2–1 decision that it was bound by the Supreme Court's 1971 summary dismissal of a same-sex couple's claim in *Baker v Nelson*,[189] before going on to reject the underlying constitutional claims of the same-sex couples. The Supreme Court granted certiorari in the case, presumably to resolve the conflict that did not exist when it earlier denied review. But the Supreme Court did not need to decide whether there was a right to same-sex marriage to resolve, or at least forestall, the circuit conflict. Moreover, the Court should have tolerated some interjudicial conflict in order to extend the time for political and judicial developments, federal and state, to occur. This was an occasion for the Court to display the "passive virtues"—to recognize that sometimes the Court's best course is to temporize.[190]

---

[185] 671 F3d 1052 (9th Cir 2012).

[186] *Latta v Otter*, 779 F3d 902 (9th Cir 2015).

[187] Consider Justice Thomas's objection to the denial of certiorari, set out in his dissent from a denial of a stay in an unrelated case, *Maricopa County v Lopez-Valenzuela*, 135 S Ct 428 (2014) (noting that "we often review decisions striking down state laws, even in the absence of a disagreement among lower courts," and lamenting the court's failure to do so "with any consistency in recent months," citing the denials of certiorari in the same-sex marriage cases).

[188] 772 F3d 388 (6th Cir 2014).

[189] 409 US 810 (1971).

[190] Alexander M. Bickel, *The Least Dangerous Branch: The Supreme Court at the Bar of Politics* (Yale, 2d ed 1986).

To address the split between the Sixth Circuit and the Fourth, Seventh, Ninth, and Tenth, the Supreme Court could have granted certiorari and then vacated the Sixth Circuit's decision on the ground that *Baker* no longer controlled (a view clearly held by at least five Justices). The Court could then have sent the case back to the Sixth Circuit, to reconsider the merits of the constitutional claim, in light of that holding.[191] This approach would have extended the period for legal development, which would have given the states in the Sixth Circuit an opportunity to pursue reforms through the legislative process in response to the swelling national consensus. Efforts in Ohio, for example, to put a state constitutional amendment in favor of same-sex marriage on the ballot might well have resumed in the face of this Sixth Circuit reprieve, and continued to collect important support from Republican state politicians.[192] And Michigan efforts to repeal its constitutional ban on same-sex marriage through a ballot initiative would surely have continued.[193]

Extending the time before the Supreme Court took up the issue would also, of course, allow for further developments in other parts of the country. Cases were pending in the Fifth, Eighth, and Eleventh Circuits, and in all of those circuits, there was the possibility of reform through the democratic process as well as state litigation. The value of this ongoing development might have justified the Court's holding off, even if it did not clear up the conflict with the Sixth Circuit.

Resolving the circuit conflict was, in the minds of some, particularly critical to secure the cross-border stability of marriages. This concern was exacerbated by a broadly accepted understanding of the Full Faith and Credit Clause that I have argued, elsewhere, is flawed.[194]

---

[191] Thanks to my colleague Will Baude for this insight.

[192] Nick Wing, *Jim Petro, Former Ohio GOP Attorney General Backs Campaign to Overturn State Gay Marriage Ban*, Huffington Post (July 8, 2013), http://www.huffingtonpost.com/2013/07/08/jim-petro-ohio-gay-marriage_n_3563112.html (noting that "the campaign to overturn Ohio's gay marriage ban now has support from two high-profile Republicans," a senator and a former attorney general, who both changed their position based on family experiences).

[193] See https://ballotpedia.org/Michigan_Same-Sex_Marriage_Amendment_ (2016) (describing the ballot initiative to reverse the same-sex marriage ban in the Michigan constitution, which ended with the Supreme Court's ruling in *Obergefell*).

[194] See Emily Buss and William Buss, *Escaping the American Blot: A Comparative Look at Federalism in Australia and the United States Through the Lens of Family Law*, 48 Cornell Intl L J 105 (2015) (arguing that the conventional categorization of marriage certificates as "Acts" was mistaken, and that, properly understood as "Records," the text and subsequent judicial interpretation of the Full Faith and Credit Clause readily applied to official records of specific marriages validly celebrated).

If states were constitutionally required to recognize out-of-state marriages, validly celebrated and recorded, then the law could have more readily tolerated extending the period of jurisdictional diversity to reap the benefits clearly associated with the passage of time.

But the Court did not wait, and we got *Obergefell*, a decision that transformed the groundswell of support for a constitutional right to same-sex marriage into a decision reached by a "patrician, highly unrepresentative" group of five Justices. A power grab, indeed, but one that took the decision away not from "the people" but from their own judicial colleagues from up and down the coasts and from the "vast expanse in between."

MARY ZIEGLER

SUBSTANTIAL UNCERTAINTY: WHOLE WOMAN'S HEALTH v HELLERSTEDT AND THE FUTURE OF ABORTION LAW

Commentators have heralded the Supreme Court's most recent abortion decision as the most significant in decades.[1] By a vote of five to three in *Whole Woman's Health v Hellerstedt*, the Court struck down two key provisions of a Texas statute known as HB2.[2] One of the disputed provisions required physicians performing abortions to have admitting privileges at a hospital within thirty miles. Another mandated that all abortion clinics comply with state regulations governing ambulatory surgical centers (ASCs). HB2 promised to revolutionize abortion access in Texas, because compliance with the law was expensive or even impossible for most providers in the state. After

Mary Ziegler is the Stearns Weaver Miller Professor at Florida State University College of Law.

AUTHOR'S NOTE: Thanks to Maya Manian, Johanna Schoen, David Strauss, and Daniel Williams for helpful comments.

[1] For examples of commentators expressing these views, see Amanda Hollis-Bruskey and Rachel VanSickle-Ward, *Here Are Two Ways that Breyer's Wonky Opinion in Whole Woman's Health Could Transform Abortion Politics*, Wash Post (July 13, 2016) (available at https://www.washingtonpost.com/news/monkey-cage/wp/2016/07/03/here-are-2-ways-that-breyers-wonky-opinion-in-whole-womens-health-could-transform-abortion-politics/); Deanna A. Rohlinger, *Turning the Anti-Abortion Tide*, American Prospect (July 5, 2016) (available at http://prospect.org/article/turning-anti-abortion-tide); Erik Eckholm, *Anti-Abortion Group Presses Ahead Despite Recent Supreme Court Ruling*, NY Times (July 9, 2016) (available at http://www.nytimes.com/2016/07/10/us/anti-abortion-group-supreme-court-ruling.html?_r=0).

[2] 136 S Ct 2292 (2016).

978-0-226-49084-7/2017/2016-0003$10.00

it was allowed to go into effect, the admitting-privileges provision had forced nearly twenty clinics to close. Had Texas enforced the ASC provision, at least another ten seemed likely to shutter.[3]

By striking down the law, the Court's decision will likely expand abortion access in Texas and set the stage for the invalidation of laws like HB2 in other states. Perhaps more importantly, *Whole Woman's Health* also put teeth in the undue-burden test first announced in *Planned Parenthood v Casey*.[4] The Court held that *Casey* required consideration of both the benefits and the burdens created by a law regulating abortion and demanded meaningful proof that a law claiming to protect women's health actually did so.[5]

Whole Woman's Health defied the expectations of those who believed that the Court would further narrow abortion rights. After the 2007 decision in *Gonzales v Carhart*,[6] many in the antiabortion movement believed that the Court would look favorably on additional restrictions and might even clarify that all abortion laws should receive only rational-basis review. For these activists, *Whole Woman's Health* was obviously a profound disappointment.[7] But *Whole Woman's Health* could provide far less reliable protection for abortion rights than might appear, especially when one considers the strategies that abortion opponents have used. While refusing to take at face value the claim that abortion procedures, providers, and clinics hurt women, *Whole Woman's Health* set the stage for fact-intensive litigation about the benefits and burdens of measures restricting access to abortion.

This is not the first time that the Court, intentionally or not, has invited a war about the facts. Over the past three decades, antiabortion

---

[3] See id at 2301. For the admitted-privilege provision, see Tex Health & Safety Code Ann § 171.0031(a)(1); 25 Tex Admin Code §§ 139.53(c)–56(a). For the ASC provision, see Tex Health & Safety Code Ann § 245.010(a); 25 Tex Admin Code § 139.40.

[4] 505 US 833 (1992) (plurality decision).

[5] See 136 S Ct at 2310.

[6] 550 US 124 (2007).

[7] For antiabortion expressions of disappointment in *Whole Woman's Health*, see Stephanie H. To, *Breaking Down Whole Woman's Health: A Critical Abortion Ruling*, Catholic Stand (June 28, 2016) (available at http://www.catholicstand.com/breaking-whole-womans-health-critical-abortion-ruling/); Focus on the Family, *Whole Woman's Health v. Hellerstedt* (June 29, 2016) (available at https://www.focusonthefamily.com/socialissues/promos/whole-womans-health-v-hellerstedt); Jay Sekulow, *Supreme Court Puts Big Abortion's Profits Over Women's Health in Striking Down Commonsense Abortion Regulations*, American Center for Law and Justice (June 30, 2016) (available at http://aclj.org/pro-life/supreme-court-places-big-abortions-profits-over-womens-health-in-striking-down-common-sense-abortion-restrictions).

activists have developed a strategy based on the idea that abortion harms women psychologically and physically. When this argument debuted in the Court in the early 1980s, pro-lifers failed because they did not have credible enough evidence for their assertions. Over time, movement leaders turned to a different tactic. Rather than trying to establish that women did in fact suffer trauma as a result of abortion, pro-lifers argued that research on the issue was inconclusive. Given the potential risks women faced, scientific uncertainty became a key political and even constitutional justification for abortion restrictions. In *Gonzales v Carhart*, this strategy paid off, notwithstanding the fact that the evidence supporting postabortion trauma was no stronger than it had been in previous decades.

This history shows that *Whole Woman's Health* may promise less than it seems. The Court's decision requires more convincing evidence to justify abortion restrictions but offers little guidance about how much (or how good) the proof must be before lawmakers can regulate. *Whole Woman's Health* also gives courts little guidance on how to deal with claims of scientific uncertainty, which have been a warrant for abortion restrictions in the past. The influence of *Whole Woman's Health* on politics or constitutional litigation will be anything but easy to foresee.

Part I of this article traces the evolution of antiabortion arguments involving women's health. Part II uses this history to put the *Whole Woman's Health* litigation in broader context, exploring the origins and tactical value of the regulations at issue in the case. Part III returns to the reasoning of *Whole Woman's Health*, and, drawing on the development of arguments about scientific uncertainty, suggests that the influence of the decision may not be as sweeping or as certain as many commentators have proclaimed. Part IV briefly concludes.

I. Evolution of Arguments

Whole Woman's Health in some ways became a referendum on a constitutional strategy antiabortion attorneys have honed for decades, one centered on the idea that abortion hurts women. As early as the 1970s, abortion opponents wove this idea into several independent legislative campaigns. In particular, movement members lobbied for mandated-consent laws and waiting periods as well as onerous targeted regulation of abortion providers ("TRAP" laws).

At first, antiabortion organizations used these trauma arguments to claim that some abortion restrictions passed muster under *Roe v*

Wade[8] because they benefited, rather than burdened, women. But in 1983, in *City of Akron v Akron Center for Reproductive Health* (*Akron I*),[9] the Court struck down an informed-consent law on which activists had pinned their hopes. The law had required women to hear information about the physical and psychological consequences of abortion. In invalidating the disputed provision, the Court emphasized that there was little or no evidence for the harms to women detailed in the statute.

But instead of putting an end to woman-protective arguments, *Akron I* intensified the movement's efforts. If pro-lifers could not prove that abortion hurt women, activists planned to create enough doubt to convince the legislatures and the courts.

Initially—as early as the 1960s—activists in organizations like National Right to Life Committee (NRLC) and Americans United for Life (AUL) had prioritized a right to life and equal treatment for fetal life that advocates identified with the Declaration of Independence and the Fourteenth Amendment. Abortion opponents argued that the unborn child was a person within the meaning of the Constitution. If unborn children were persons, abortion represented a deprivation of life without due process of law. Movement members also insisted that abortion constituted an act of discrimination against the unborn child under the Equal Protection Clause. When making these claims, pro-lifers explicitly identified their agenda with other efforts to protect embattled minorities, including people of color, women, and the poor. In the early 1970s, AUL's Declaration of Purpose repeated the movement's claims about equal treatment, committing "to impress upon all the dignity and worth of each individual life, whatever the state or circumstance, especially the innocent, the incompetent, the impaired, the impoverished, the aged, and all others who are weak and disadvantaged."[10]

Roe devastated the pro-life movement. Many activists had hoped that the Court might recognize a right to life rather than a right to

---

[8] 410 US 113 (1973).

[9] 416 US 462 (1983).

[10] Declaration of Purpose from Americans United for Life (1971) (Americans United for Life Collection, Executive File, the Concordia Seminary, Lutheran Church–Missouri Synod, St. Louis, Missouri). For more arguments of this kind, see Robert M. Byrn, *Abortion in Perspective*, 5 Duquesne L Rev 125, 134–35 (1966); Thomas L. Schafer, *Abortion, the Law, and Human Life*, 3 Valp U L Rev 94, 106 (1967–68); David Louisell, *The Practice of Medicine and the Due Process of Law*, 16 UCLA L Rev 233, 234 (1969).

abortion. In spite of their dismay, most movement members did not discard the arguments promoted before 1973. Instead, immediately after *Roe*, antiabortion organizations campaigned for a federal constitutional amendment that would restore what abortion opponents believed were the protections that the Court had destroyed. In February 1973, for example, NRLC hosted a strategy meeting to craft a response to *Roe*. By the time of the gathering, most states had held local meetings about how to draft an ideal constitutional amendment. While activists at the strategy meeting discussed statutes that would restrict abortion access, these incremental attacks seemed at most to be "a back pocket option."[11]

In 1975–76, two congressional subcommittees held hearings on antiabortion amendments. In 1976, Senator Jesse Helms (R-NC) moved for the full Senate to consider a personhood amendment, but the Senate tabled his motion. In 1977, after a full week of hearings, no serious step was taken to bring any amendment up for a vote.[12]

Convinced that it would be impossible to change the text of the Constitution, abortion opponents became desperate for an alternative. First, many considered the idea of a constitutional convention. By 1977, nine states had passed legislation calling for a convention, but many believed that there was no longer any chance for formal constitutional change. Even NRLC no longer seemed convinced that a federal constitutional solution was possible. The group's board of directors unanimously passed a resolution rejecting the call for a constitutional convention. Later, after the election of Ronald Reagan, some believed that a constitutional amendment might be within reach. But divisions within the movement doomed both a proposed statute and a constitutional amendment that would have gutted *Roe*. Forced to give up on a constitutional solution for the time being, movement leaders developed the pieces of an incremental litigation strategy that would later come together in *Whole Woman's Health*.[13]

---

[11] Meeting Minutes, National Right to Life Committee Ad Hoc Strategy Meeting (Feb 11, 1973), 6 (National Right to Life Committee Records, Box 4, Gerald Ford Memorial Library, University of Michigan); see also National Right to Life Committee Memorandum, "Progress" (Sept 21, 1973) (National Right to Life Committee Records, Box 6, Gerald Ford Memorial Library, University of Michigan).

[12] See National Committee for a Human Life Amendment, Human Life Amendment: Major Texts 1 (available at http://www.nchla.org/datasource/idocuments/HLAmajortexts.pdf).

[13] On opposition to the "con-con" strategy within the movement, see "National Right to Life Committee Rejects Constitutional Convention Call" (Jan 31, 1977), 2–3 (Edward Golden

These strategists argued that the movement should focus on introducing legislation that the Supreme Court might uphold. If prolifers could successfully defend these laws in the courts, then *Roe* would mean very little, even if the Supreme Court never overruled it. The best-known triumph of early pro-life incrementalism was the Hyde Amendment, a federal ban on the use of Medicaid funds for abortion. The decisions handed down by the Court in the mid-1970s also fueled antiabortion interest in both mandatory-consent laws and undue-burden reasoning.[14]

The movement had reason to focus on mandated-consent laws after the Court's 1976 decision in *Planned Parenthood of Central Missouri v Danforth*.[15] That case involved a multirestriction Missouri statute requiring everything from informed consent to parental involvement. When *Danforth* came down, the Court defied expectations by upholding part of the Missouri law—a provision that required a woman to certify in writing that her decision to terminate a pregnancy had been informed. The Court upheld the regulation even though Missouri did not require similar consent for any other surgical procedure. "The decision to abort, indeed, is an important and often a stressful one, and it is desirable and imperative that it be made with full knowledge of its nature and consequences," Justice Blackmun wrote.[16] "The woman is the one primarily concerned, and her awareness of the decision and its significance may be assured, constitutionally, by the State to the extent of requiring her prior written consent."[17]

The Court's early decisions on abortion funding also gave prolifers a potential vehicle for their constitutional claims. In *Maher v Roe*,[18] *Poelker v Doe*,[19] and *Beal v Doe*,[20] the Court upheld a variety of

Papers, Box 3, Folder 1, College of the Holy Cross Archives and Inventory Collection). For more on the "con-con" strategy, see William Robbins, *Abortion Foes Look to Ultimate Victory*, NY Times (June 19, 1977) at 24; *Massachusetts Is the Ninth State to Seek a Convention on the Issue of Abortion*, NY Times (June 9, 1977) at 88.

[14] On the importance of the funding cases to antiabortion incrementalism, see Mary Ziegler, *After Roe: The Lost History of the Abortion Debate* 66–68, 131–41 (Harvard, 2015); Scott Ainsworth and Thad E. Hall, *Abortion Politics in Congress: Strategic Incrementalism and Policy Change* 80–87 (Cambridge, 2010).

[15] 428 US 52 (1976).

[16] Id at 67.

[17] Id.

[18] 432 US 464 (1977).

[19] 432 US 519 (1977).

[20] 432 US 438 (1977).

local laws on the use of public facilities and funding for abortion, but the language of *Maher* particularly intrigued abortion opponents. The *Maher* Court distinguished the challenged Connecticut statute, which denied Medicaid funding for abortion, from the Texas abortion ban struck down in *Roe v Wade*, explaining that there was no absolute constitutional bar to abortion regulations. "[T]he right protects the woman from unduly burdensome interference with her freedom to decide whether to terminate her pregnancy," the *Maher* Court explained.[21] "It implies no limitation on the authority of a State to make a value judgment favoring childbirth over abortion, and to implement that judgment by the allocation of public funds."[22] In the context of poor women, the Court held that poverty stemmed not from anything that the government had done but from broader political, economic, and legal forces, and the government had no obligation to fund abortions.

For abortion opponents, *Maher* raised interesting new constitutional possibilities. The Court suggested that some abortion restrictions would be constitutional. Movement lawyers also saw the seeds of an alternative to strict scrutiny. *Maher* had singled out only those abortion regulations that were "unduly burdensome."[23] Two years later, in a case involving minors' abortion rights, the Court held that parental-involvement laws would be unconstitutional only if they created an undue burden on minors' rights.[24] These decisions convinced some abortion opponents that the undue-burden test protected abortion far less than whatever standard applied in *Roe*. In the years to come, movement leaders set out to convince the Court to apply undue-burden analysis to every case.

A. EXPERIMENTS WITH WOMAN-PROTECTIVE ARGUMENTS BEGIN

The first major political use of woman-protective arguments came as pro-lifers promoted the undue-burden analysis. After an initial failed attempt, local antiabortion activists again asked the Akron, Ohio, city council to pass a comprehensive antiabortion ordinance. Local organizers created an independent group, Citizens for Informed

---

[21] *Maher*, 432 US at 473–74.

[22] Id at 474.

[23] Id.

[24] See *Bellotti v Baird*, 443 US 622, 642–45 (1979) (*Bellotti II*).

Consent, to promote a new strategy that would take advantage of the opening created by *Danforth* and *Maher*. Movement members hoped that the ordinance would provide information geared toward discouraging women from having abortions. Better yet, the law would create a platform for pro-lifers to try the same arguments before the courts and the nation. Jane Hubbard, the president of Akron Right to Life, insisted that the law's aim was "to ensure that a woman who decides to abort her child will have . . . scientifically and medically accurate information: that the child she aborts is alive and growing, and the procedure may cause her physical or psychological harm."[25] Martin Weinberger, the leader of Citizens for Informed Consent, reinforced this point. "All we are giving them is the biological facts," he asserted.[26]

The woman-protective strategy used in Akron reached back to the years before the *Roe* decision and continued to circulate in pro-life organizations in the early 1980s. In the 1960s, when Colorado and other states introduced reform laws based on the American Law Institute (ALI) model, groups like Planned Parenthood insisted that forcing a woman to carry an unwanted pregnancy to term would cause psychological distress, mental illness, and even suicidal ideation. Physicians opposed to abortion responded that abortion itself caused regret, distress, and depression. In an AUL brief submitted on behalf of antiabortion medical professionals, similar arguments featured prominently. In 1981, Vincent Rue, a psychologist and the director of the Sir Thomas More Clinics of Southern California, testified before Congress on the psychological consequences of abortion. "It is superfluous to ask whether patients experience guilt," he stated. "[I]t is axiomatic that they will."[27]

---

[25] Jane Hubbard, Letter to Editor, *Should Akron Monitor Abortions*, Akron Beacon Journal (Nov 21, 1977) at A6.

[26] Reginald Stuart, *Akron Divided by Heated Abortion Debate*, NY Times (Feb 1, 1978) at A10.

[27] Constitutional Amendments Relating to Abortion: Hearings on SJ Res 18, SJ Res 19, and SJ Res 110 Before the Subcommittee on the Constitution of the Committee on the Judiciary, 97th Cong 329–39 (1981) (testimony of Vincent Rue). For an overview of abortion-rights arguments about the connection between abortion and mental illness, see Mary Ziegler, *Beyond Backlash: Legal History, Polarization, and Roe v. Wade*, 71 Wash & Lee L Rev 969, 984–85 (2014). For a sample of the antiabortion response, see Dennis Mahoney, *Therapeutic Abortions—The Psychiatric Indication—A Double-Edged Sword*, 72 Dickinson L Rev 270, 288–89 (1968); John G. Herbert, *Is Legalized Abortion the Solution to Criminal Abortion?*, 37 U Colo L Rev 291, 291 (1964). For the brief in *Roe* making these arguments, see Motion and Brief

The Akron ordinance presented arguments about the negative effect of abortion on women as scientific fact. The law required physicians to recite the following statement:

> [A]bortion is a major surgical procedure which can result in serious complications, including hemorrhage, perforated uterus, infection, menstrual disturbances, sterility and miscarriage and prematurity in subsequent pregnancies; and . . . abortion may leave essentially unaffected or may worsen any existing psychological problems [a woman] may have, and can result in severe emotional disturbances.[28]

Abortion-rights supporters recognized that a different kind of strategy would be needed to defuse the threat posed by the ordinance. Instead of emphasizing women's rights to autonomy or equal treatment, Cheryl Swain, a feminist from Akron, suggested that the evidentiary foundation for the statute was flimsy at best. She told the national media that abortion opponents quite simply failed "to accept certain facts."[29]

Just as would be the case years later in the lead-up to *Whole Woman's Health*, the Akron ordinance prompted a major fact-gathering effort on the part of abortion-rights supporters. Recognizing that pro-lifers planned to use the statute as a "national precedent," Swain told Jane Hodgson, a Minnesota obstetrician-gynecologist and leading figure in the movement, that the ordinance would "severely limit the availability of abortion as well as psychologically intimidate women."[30]

Hodgson played a prominent part in building the record used to challenge the Akron law. In her testimony before the city council, she focused on the inaccuracy of the information women had to hear, labeling the proposed ordinance "medically unnecessary."[31] Item by item, she tried to refute the factual arguments supporting the ordinance. "Psychological studies have failed to show any more effects from abortion such as depression and suicide than would occur from compulsory child bearing," she asserted.[32] Hodgson also offered ad-

---

Amicus Curiae of Certain Physicians, Professors, and Fellows of the American College of Obstetricians and Gynecologists, *Roe v Wade*, 410 US 113 (1973) (Nos 70-18, 70-40).

[28] Akron Ordinance No 60-1978 § 1870.06.

[29] Stuart, *Akron Divided* (cited in note 26) at A10.

[30] Cheryl Swain to Jane Hodgson (Nov 23, 1977) (Jane Hodgson Papers, Box 15, Akron Folder).

[31] Jane Hodgson, Testimony Presented to the Akron City Council Re: Proposed Regulations Governing Abortion Clinics (Feb 1978), 4 (Jane Hodgson Papers, Box 15, Akron Folder).

[32] Id at 4–5.

vice to lawmakers on how to separate real from phony evidence. She advised council members to rely on organizations of experts, like the American Public Health Association, in determining where the truth lay.[33]

The city council nevertheless passed the ordinance, and other cities and states rushed to pass similar ordinances. By 1979, eleven states had done so. Faye Wattleton of the Planned Parenthood Federation of America branded these laws "an attempt to promote political ideology in the guise of a health regulation."[34]

The threat to abortion access posed by the Akron ordinance and others like it was clear. The ordinance required not only the recitation of certain supposed facts but also mandated that all abortions during or after the second trimester had to be performed in hospitals. If widely adopted, hospital restrictions promised to eliminate most abortion access, much like the law considered in *Whole Woman's Health* would have forced the closure of most clinics in Texas. In 1973, more than half of all abortions took place in hospitals, but with the advent of new techniques, most abortions could be safely performed in freestanding clinics, and political pressure discouraged hospitals from offering abortion services. By 1980, only 22 percent of abortions happened in hospitals, and the number continued to decline. Roy Lucas, one of the attorneys to litigate *Roe*, wrote his colleagues that "[t]he worst outcome in 1983 could be a decision allowing extensive overregulation of abortion clinics and banning second trimester abortions except in a few hospitals."[35]

Pro-lifers used the Akron case to push the undue-burden standard as an alternative to heightened scrutiny. Working with the Reagan administration and AUL attorneys, the city of Akron offered the Court a different way of thinking about abortion doctrine. "The initial question posed on review before this Court," the city's brief explained, "is whether the state's interest in maternal health and wellbeing is such that it may regulate abortion in a reasonable manner

[33] See id.

[34] *Akron Council Passes Abortion Law*, Ellensburg City Record (March 1, 1978) at 6. On the passage of the Akron ordinance, see William Hershey, *Council Passes Abortion Control Bill: Opponents Vow Challenge in Court*, Akron Beacon Journal (Feb 28, 1978) at A1.

[35] Roy Lucas to Robert McCoy (June 30, 1982) (Jane Hodgson Papers, Box 15, Akron Folder). On the changing role of abortion clinics and hospitals, see Stanley K. Henshaw, Jacqueline Darroch Forrest, and Elaine Blaine, *Abortion Services in the United States, 1981 and 1982*, 16 Family Planning Perspectives 119, 119–27 (1984).

which is not unduly burdensome, even during the first trimester of pregnancy."[36] Movement lawyers argued that the undue-burden test applied to any abortion restriction, not just those involving minors or funding. As importantly, pro-lifers hoped that the undue-burden test would be a vehicle for claims about the facts, particularly those concerning women and abortion. "In *Roe v. Wade* and *Doe v. Bolton*, the Court prohibited the state from regulating doctors only in ways which burden the woman's fundamental right to decide," explained AUL attorney Dolores Horan in a brief for Feminists for Life.[37] "It is impossible for the state to burden the woman's right to decide by requiring that she be given factual information which, in fact, enhances her ability to decide."[38]

Antiabortion briefs spotlighted the woman-protective factual arguments that would become a staple of movement advocacy in the years to come. At trial, movement attorneys tried to establish the "unborn child's sensitivity to pain"[39] and emphasized that women did not understand what abortion involved or how much an unborn child had developed. In making this argument, Feminists for Life highlighted affidavits collected from individual women who regretted their abortions. According to the brief, "[w]omen could be spared the severe guilt and trauma [that] they will later experience upon discovering [the] information" detailed in the statute.[40] By relying on these factual assertions, AUL and other pro-life groups insisted that the Court could find an undue burden only if an abortion restriction harmed women.[41]

During trial and in amicus briefs, pro-choice groups built a convincing factual case against the ordinance. Expert witnesses testified that abortion involved few serious risks, particularly in the first trimester, which was when most women terminated their pregnancies. Briefs highlighted peer-reviewed studies, data from the Centers for

[36] Brief for Petitioner City of Akron, 16–17, *Akron v Akron Center for Reproductive Health*, 462 US 416 (1983) (Nos 81-463, 81-1643).

[37] See Brief Amicus Curiae for Feminists for Life, 7, *Akron v Akron Center for Reproductive Health*, 462 US 416 (1983) (Nos 81-463, 81-1643).

[38] Id.

[39] Id.

[40] Id.

[41] See id.; see also Brief of Americans United for Life, 16–18, *Akron v Akron Center for Reproductive Health*, 462 US 416 (1983) (Nos 81-463, 81-1643); Brief for the Petitioner, 54–55, *Akron v Akron Center for Reproductive Health*, 462 US 416 (1983) (Nos 81-463, 81-1643).

Disease Control, and expert testimony on the limited risk of complications following abortion. According to pro-choice amici, emotional trauma following abortion was rare and often resulted from preexisting personal or psychological difficulties. These briefs insisted that the state had no legitimate interest in forcing women to listen to information that was "medically irrelevant, false, and/or harmful to the patient."[42] An amicus curiae brief submitted by NARAL and the American Public Health Association similarly pointed to statistics from the Centers for Disease Control, physician testimony, and peer-reviewed scholarship to establish that the mandated-consent provision was "especially burdensome."[43]

As would be the case later in *Whole Woman's Health*, the pro-choice effort to prove the inaccuracy and impact of the Akron ordinance paid dividends. The Supreme Court in *Akron I* struck down the entire ordinance by a vote of six to three. While holding that Akron could not prove that abortion was dangerous, the majority also rejected any suggestion that the undue-burden standard differed from heightened scrutiny.[44]

The Court's analysis of the mandated-consent provision was particularly revealing. After expressing concern about the "straitjacket" the law forced on physicians, the Court concluded that women could not benefit from hearing highly questionable information. Parts of the law, like a measure stating that human life began at conception, struck the Court as a way of deterring women from terminating their pregnancies. Mostly, however, the law troubled the Court because the information it detailed was "speculative" and factually "dubious."[45] The Court particularly took issue with the description of abortion's impact on women. The law's list of complications struck the Court as nothing more than a "'parade of horribles' intended to suggest that abortion is a particularly dangerous procedure."[46]

---

[42] Brief of Amici Curiae Planned Parenthood Federation of America et al, 31, *City of Akron v Akron Center for Reproductive Health*, 462 US 416 (1983) (Nos 81-463, 81-1643); see also Brief for Respondents and Cross-Petitioners, 45–52, *City of Akron v Akron Center for Reproductive Health*, 462 US 416 (1983) (Nos 81-463, 81-1643).

[43] Summary of Akron Amicus Curiae Brief (1983), 4–5 (Jane Hodgson Papers, Box 15, Akron Folder).

[44] *City of Akron v Akron Center for Reproductive Health*, 462 US 416, 442–46 (1983).

[45] See id at 444.

[46] Id at 444–45.

Justice O'Connor, in her dissenting opinion, framed the undue-burden test—and the potential risk of abortion for women—in a very different light. Because Justice O'Connor was President Ronald Reagan's first nominee to the Court, commentators closely read her dissent to see if she, like Reagan, believed that *Roe* was not good law. Writing for three other Justices, Justice O'Connor rejected *Roe*'s trimester framework as factually flawed because it depended on medical technology and best practices that would change over time. As an alternative, she urged that all regulations be subject to a less protective undue-burden test. She suggested that courts would find an undue burden "for the most part in situations involving absolute obstacles or severe limitations on the abortion decision."[47] Justice O'Connor also seemed open to arguments involving women's health. "[J]ust because the State has a compelling interest in ensuring maternal safety once an abortion may be more dangerous," Justice O'Connor wrote, "it simply does not follow that the State has *no* interest before that point that justifies state regulation to ensure that first-trimester abortions are performed as safely as possible."[48]

B. PRO-LIFERS RETHINK THEIR STRATEGY IN THE WAKE OF AKRON I

Because *Akron I* had undone what seemed to be the most promising model antiabortion ordinance, it would have been no surprise for pro-lifers to abandon the woman-protective strategy that the Court had so firmly rejected. And at least at first, it seemed that movement members had scaled back their expectations considerably. At the NRLC convention in August 1983, General Counsel James Bopp, Jr. and Maura Quinlan of AUL held a closed-door meeting with state lawmakers to discuss the possibilities that remained open after the Court's decision. Rather than discussing woman-protective strategies, attendees discussed legislation barring suits for wrongful life or wrongful birth and laws that would bar insurance coverage for abortion or deny hospital admitting privileges to any doctor performing abortions.[49]

Nonetheless, *Akron I* created a platform for AUL attorneys convinced that woman-protective strategies could still be used to limit

---

47 Id at 464 (O'Connor, J, dissenting).

48 Id at 461 (O'Connor, J, dissenting).

49 See National Right to Life Committee Statehouse Update (Aug 12, 1983), 1–4 (Galebach Files, OA 9106, Ronald Reagan Presidential Library).

abortion access. The winter following *Akron I*, the organization held a conference "to unite the movement around the relatively uncontroversial proposition . . . that the Court should reverse itself."[50] Those assembled saw the most immediate promise in destabilizing the idea of fetal viability. Justice O'Connor's dissent had flagged the issue as one of the weaknesses of *Roe*'s trimester framework, and those at the AUL conference hoped to capitalize on it.[51]

AUL attorneys also hoped, however, to revive the woman-protective arguments that the *Akron I* majority had found unconvincing. Movement leaders argued for the creation of research organizations that could collect proof that abortion hurt women and convince key decision makers, particularly politicians, that legal abortion did more harm than good. Victor Rosenblum and Thomas Marzen of AUL claimed that the movement might have more success promoting laws that supposedly benefited women if pro-lifers could popularize enough "[f]avorable statistical data."[52] As the two explained:

> "Accepted medical practices" must change before barriers to reversal can be broken down; whether or not abortion is "acceptable" is determined by the view and customary practices of the very people who perform abortions. They are unwilling to increase the state's authority to regulate abortion. A possible long-term approach to meeting this dilemma is the development of new sources for abortion data.[53]

Creating new research organizations would allow abortion opponents to more confidently make claims about the facts. As importantly, even if the courts did not buy the movement's factual claims, abortion opponents could work through politics to create enough scientific uncertainty about what "accepted medical practices" should involve.

At first, supporters of abortion rights did not always understand the threat posed by the factual claims abortion opponents continued to make. Indeed, some believed that the undue-burden standard embraced by the *Akron I* majority had put questionable factual claims off

---

[50] Steven Baer, Report of the Education Division of Americans United for Life (1984), 1–3 (Mildred F. Jefferson Papers, Box 13, Folder 5, Schlesinger Library, Harvard University).

[51] See Victor Rosenblum and Thomas J. Marzen, "Strategies for Reversing Roe v. Wade Through the Courts," in Dennis Horan et al, eds, *Abortion and the Constitution: Reversing Roe v. Wade Through the Courts* 198–200 (Georgetown, 1987).

[52] See id at 201.

[53] Id.

limits. Janet Benshoof of the ACLU Reproductive Freedom Project believed that the Court's idea of an undue burden required heightened scrutiny. She said that under *Akron I*, "a state may enact some regulations 'touching' on a woman's abortion right in the first trimester so long as the regulations have 'no significant impact' and so long as they are justified by important health objectives."[54]

Benshoof suggested that the movement could work with the majority's idea of an undue burden by bringing forward more evidence of the real-world impact of restrictions on abortion access. After all, the Court had been receptive to pro-choice testimony on medical realities and access. Benshoof concluded that "[a]ny first trimester regulation which can be shown to impose a burden on the exercise of the abortion right [should be] invalid."[55]

By contrast, NARAL leaders believed that if the Court focused on the facts, abortion rights would not be safe unless Republicans were no longer putting Justices on the Court. *Akron I* only solidified this strategy, inspiring a campaign called "40 More Years?." NARAL lawyers wrote Executive Director Nanette Falkenberg that *Roe* had required strict judicial scrutiny for abortion regulations, whereas the undue-burden standard would allow laws that would create "substantial delay, cost, and/or emotional suffering."[56] NARAL members concluded that the only way for the movement to protect abortion rights was to ensure that another O'Connor never joined the Supreme Court.[57]

The events of the next several years legitimized NARAL's concerns about what could go wrong in a war about the facts. Abortion opponents experimented with questionable factual claims in promoting a film, *The Silent Scream*, supposedly depicting fetal suffering during an abortion. Produced by Crusade for Life, an antiabortion group, the film narrated the suction abortion of a twelve-week-old fetus. With a voiceover by former NARAL leader Bernard Nathanson,

---

[54] Memorandum, Janet Benshoof, ACLU Reproductive Freedom Project, "The New Supreme Court Abortion Decision: A Legal Analysis with Questions and Answers" (July 18, 1983), 1–12 (Pauli Murray Papers, Box 114, Folder 2040, Schlesinger Library, Harvard University).

[55] Id.

[56] Gail Harmon and William S. Jordan to Nanette Falkenberg (June 1984), 1–3 (NARAL Papers, Second Accession, Box 218, Folder 18, Schlesinger Library, Harvard University).

[57] See Emily Tynes to NARAL Affiliates (Sept 6, 1984), 2 (NARAL Papers, Second Accession, Box 218, Folder 18, Schlesinger Library, Harvard University).

the film claimed to depict "a child's mouth open in a silent scream"—evidence that unborn children supposedly felt pain early in pregnancy.[58]

While *The Silent Scream* traded in familiar pro-life images and arguments, the film attracted unprecedented attention, with screenings on high school and college campuses across the nation and an endorsement from President Reagan. The waves made by the film seemed puzzling to those aware that the factual premises of the film had come into question. Dr. James Hobbins of Yale Medical School told viewers of the CBS Morning Show that unborn children at twelve weeks could not feel pain or move with purpose, and any description to the contrary was inaccurate. Indeed, the American Medical Association's Council on Scientific Affairs condemned the film and a pro-choice response to it as "designed to solicit emotional reactions rather than to clarify scientific issues."[59] Feminists echoed these arguments about the facts. Judy Goldsmith of the National Organization for Women (NOW) emphasized that while *The Silent Scream* suggested that an unborn child suffered pain and fought abortion, "embryologists say that neural pathways are not developed until the 24th week."[60]

Pro-lifers responded to questions about the film's accuracy by arguing for fetal-protective policies in the face of scientific uncertainty. Movement leaders cited a 1980 article in the *British Medical Journal* and a handful of other sources suggesting that the fetus might feel pain. Bernard Nathanson, the narrator of *The Silent Scream*, insisted that Americans responded to the film because "the accumulating scientific evidence . . . finally won them over."[61] Even if the movement could not eliminate any doubt about the accuracy of the film, uncertainty militated in favor of protecting life. As one op-ed put it, "[w]e can't know what the fetus feels because it can't tell us."[62]

The Silent Scream forced feminists to recognize that they could lose a war about the facts even if medical evidence seemed to be on their

---

[58] Sandy Johnson, *"Graphic in the Extreme": Anti-Abortion Doctor Plans Follow-Up Film*, LA Times (Dec 5, 1985) at 24; see also Stephen Chapman, *Abortion and the Silent Scream*, Chicago Tribune (March 17, 1985) at D3.

[59] Elizabeth Mehren, *Medical Group Cites Flaws in "Silent Scream,"* LA Times (Dec 3, 1985) at 1.

[60] Paul Houston, *"Silent Scream" Called Testament for Pro-Life*, LA Times (Feb 13, 1985) at B6.

[61] Elizabeth Mehren and Betty Cuniberti, *He's the Force Behind Silent Scream*, LA Times (Aug 8, 1985) at 1.

[62] Chapman, *Abortion* at D3 (cited in note 58).

side. In a February letter to Judy Goldsmith, Nanette Falkenberg wondered how activists could overcome the "sense of powerlessness and frustration among our supporters and other pro-choice individuals."[63] Falkenberg recognized that *The Silent Scream* had relied on factual claims to connect emotionally with viewers, many of whom did not seem concerned with the accuracy of the film. As Falkenberg explained, the pro-choice movement could make progress only if it "recapture[d] the emotional side of the issue."[64]

Feminists faced a similar problem when dealing with increasingly prominent arguments about postabortion trauma. New support groups, including Project Rachel, a Catholic organization, and Women Exploited by Abortion (WEBA), spread this reasoning, sharing the experiences of women who believed their abortions to be a mistake.[65]

C. UNCERTAINTY EMERGES AS PART OF A PLAN OF ATTACK

In the mid-1980s, psychologist David Reardon collected the stories of WEBA veterans and published *Aborted Women: Silent No More* (1987). Although his strategy initially received a mixed reception from mainstream antiabortion groups, Reardon's plan closely resembled the one described by AUL lawyers earlier in the 1980s: movement leaders tried to collect enough evidence to generate scientific uncertainty. Reardon made the emotional case for limiting abortion: if abortion might hurt women, then states should have the power to regulate it until researchers could rule out a serious risk to women's health. "[T]he American 'experiment' with abortion has yet to gain any comprehensive data," Reardon argued. "The abortion industry has everything to gain by withholding data, and nothing to lose."[66]

As Reardon's arguments spread more widely within the antiabortion movement, his idea of uncertainty soon received a hearing at the

---

[63] Letter from Nanette Falkenberg to Judy Goldsmith (Feb 1, 1985) (NOW Papers, Box 8, Folder 8, Schlesinger Library, Harvard University).

[64] Id.

[65] On the founding and early years of Project Rachel, see Ellie Lee, *Abortion, Motherhood, and Mental Health: Medicalizing Reproduction in the United States and Great Britain* 24 (De Gruyter, 2003); Cynthia Burack, *Tough Love: Sexuality, Compassion, and the Christian Right* 76 (State University of New York, 2014). On the founding and early years of WEBA, see Sara Diamond, *Spiritual Warfare: The Politics of the Christian Right* 97–98 (Black Rose, 1990).

[66] David Reardon, *Aborted Women: Silent No More* 103 (Loyola, 1987).

highest political levels. Reagan's advisors Dinesh D'Souza and Gary Bauer asked C. Everett Koop, the surgeon general, to issue a report concluding that abortion traumatized women. As early as 1987, Reardon wrote to Koop, presenting his upcoming report as an opportunity to "launch [the] nation into a new era of debate, one based not on fetus versus woman rhetoric, but rather on the facts of what abortion does to women alone."[67] Reardon also reassured Koop that the state of the evidence should be no obstacle to his plan of attack. What mattered was that abortion opponents created enough uncertainty to make a "prima facie case for restricting abortion on public health grounds."[68]

By July 1988, Reardon had heard that Koop was worried that there was not enough proof of postabortion trauma for any firm conclusions to be drawn. In correspondence with Koop, Reardon emphasized that pro-lifers needed only to show a lack of certainty, not to establish convincing proof themselves. Reardon acknowledged: "there is insufficient data to project any sort of figure as to how many women are suffering from Post-Abortion Syndrome."[69] However, as Reardon saw it, "[t]he mere potential for such a problem . . . is a potent argument for expanding our efforts to understand the aftereffects of abortion."[70]

Reardon's arguments ultimately failed to convince Koop. In a 1989 letter that leaked to the press, Koop told Reagan that "the available scientific evidence about the psychological sequelae of abortion simply cannot support the pre-conceived beliefs of those who are pro-life or pro-choice."[71] By the time Koop had made his statement, both allies in the White House and members of the Court had found the evidence of postabortion harm wanting.[72]

Any celebration for pro-choice groups was, however, premature. Reardon's focus on uncertainty increasingly caught the broader movement's attention. Still primarily committed to arguments involving fetal rights, organizations like AUL and NRLC did not initially spon-

[67] David Reardon to C. Everett Koop (Sept 14, 1987), on file with the author.

[68] Id.

[69] Id.

[70] Id.

[71] Letter from C. Everett Koop, US Surgeon General, to President Ronald Reagan (Jan 9, 1989), on file with the author.

[72] See Reva B. Siegel, *The Right's Reasons: Constitutional Conflict and the Spread of Woman-Protective Antiabortion Argument*, 57 Duke L J 1641, 1663–64 (2008).

sor the kind of research that Reardon recommended. Instead of gathering evidence, movement members relied on testimonials like those that Reardon had gathered. Meanwhile, researchers affiliated with the movement published studies suggesting that abortion caused trauma, stress, breast cancer, and suicidal ideation. Antiabortion activists contended that even if the risks of abortion could not be conclusively proven, women's personal experiences made abortion restrictions a necessary precaution.

Abortion opponents in the late 1980s and early 1990s faced a series of difficulties: the election of Bill Clinton, a pro-choice president, the radicalization of the clinic-blockade movement, and the murder of several abortion providers and clinic staff. While these circumstances convinced abortion opponents to change their argumentative strategy, movement leaders initially focused more on sharpening woman-protective arguments than on gathering evidence of the effects of abortion. Emphasizing woman-protective arguments made sense at a time when the movement wanted to rehabilitate its image. At an AUL conference for state legislators, Laurie Ann Ramsey summarized the results of market research on the image of the antiabortion movement: "[W]e are also seen as extremist . . . , violent, intolerant, and unconcerned about women, the homeless, and the poor."[73] "The [movement's] focus on the unborn child neglects . . . the mother," Mary Ellen Jensen, a public-relations specialist at AUL, explained at the time.[74] "Communicating greater concern for the woman . . . must be one of the objectives."[75]

Between 1990 and 1997, pro-life groups also began sponsoring research on the supposed risks of abortion. Starting in 1986, Marquette began hosting annual conferences on postabortion trauma. By the 1990s, pro-life groups also promoted published studies purportedly documenting a link to suicidal ideation, postabortion trauma, or breast cancer. Nevertheless, antiabortion organizations did not try to match the evidence-gathering capabilities of major pro-choice organizations like the Guttmacher Institute. Nor did antiabortion groups court donors as effectively. Pro-choice research organizations attracted

---

[73] Laurie Ann Ramsey, "How Public Opinion Polls Should Guide Pro-Life Strategy," Americans United for Life Legislative Conference (1991), 3–4 (Mildred Jefferson Papers, Box 13, Folder 6, Schlesinger Library, Harvard University).

[74] Mary Ellen Jensen, "How Public Opinion Polls Should Guide Pro-Life Strategy" (1991), 5 (Mildred F. Jefferson Papers, Box 13, Folder 6, Schlesinger Library, Harvard University).

[75] Id.

major support from the Buffett, Hewlett, and Packard Foundations, among others. Until the founding of the Charlotte Lozier Institute in 2011, pro-life organizers did not channel significant resources to research initiatives of their own.[76]

Instead, for the most part, antiabortion organizations emphasized that existing research was incomplete, biased, or open to interpretation. When the American Psychological Association commissioned a study on the subject and found that postabortion trauma was rare, Vincent Rue argued that the study was incomplete and biased. "People who are in favor of abortion in this country are very uninclined to acknowledge [the] existence" of postabortion trauma, he stated.[77] In 1997, when another study replicated these results, antiabortion researchers like Reardon and Wanda Franz questioned the methodology and factual foundation of the research. Reardon maintained that researchers had ignored the unique symptomatology of postabortion trauma. Franz faulted the study for missing "a large body of data on post-abortion trauma."[78] The two repeated what had become common movement arguments that existing studies were incomplete.[79]

When the Court heard *Planned Parenthood v Casey*, pro-life amici relied on a similar claim. Rather than arguing that the facts of the matter were beyond question, amici presented the very possibility of postabortion trauma as a justification for abortion restrictions. Whereas the *Akron I* petitioners had presented abortion risks and complications as facts, the *Casey* briefs suggested that the questions remained too open to expose women to the risk of harm. The Rutherford Foundation described Pennsylvania's spousal-notification provision as a necessary protection for women against the possibility of postabortion regret. The conservative National Legal Foundation also drew on Rue's testimony at trial to claim that the Pennsylvania informed-consent law would prevent postabortion regret.[80]

---

[76] See Nina Martin, *How One Abortion Megadonor Forced the Supreme Court's Hand*, Mother Jones (July 14, 2016) (available at http://www.motherjones.com/politics/2016/07/abortion-research-buffett). On the annual postabortion trauma conference, see Barbara Brotman, *Both Sides in Abortion Issue Also Remain Divided Over Post-Abortion Stress*, Chicago Tribune (April 15, 1990) at E4.

[77] Brotman, *Both Sides* at 4 (cited in note 76).

[78] Jane E. Brody, *Study Disputes Abortion Trauma*, NY Times (Feb 12, 1997) at C8.

[79] See id.

[80] See Brief Amicus Curiae of the National Legal Foundation, 13–14, *Planned Parenthood of Southeastern Pennsylvania v Casey*, 505 US 833 (1992) (Nos 91-744, 91-902); Brief Amici

The evidentiary foundation for these arguments was no stronger than it had been when Akron passed its ordinance. Pennsylvania had relied almost exclusively on Dr. Rue's testimony in supporting several provisions of the statute, but the trial court had not found Rue to be credible, citing his potential bias, his lack of experience with informed-consent procedures, and his "lack . . . of academic qualifications and scientific credentials."[81] Nevertheless, the *Casey* plurality responded to the *possibility* that women could suffer regret after an abortion:

> It cannot be questioned that psychological well-being is a facet of health. Nor can it be doubted that most women considering an abortion would deem the impact on the fetus relevant, if not dispositive, to the decision. In attempting to ensure that a woman apprehend the full consequences of her decision, the State furthers the legitimate purpose of reducing the risk that a woman may elect an abortion, only to discover later, with devastating psychological consequences, that her decision was not fully informed.[82]

The Court reacted to perceived uncertainty about postabortion regret. By raising the possibility that women suffered trauma after an abortion, abortion opponents provided a sufficient justification for informed-consent restrictions. The government could act to "reduc[e] the risk" of "devastating psychological consequences."[83]

Casey energized abortion opponents who hoped to use the same scientific-uncertainty argument to convince state legislators. Paige Cunningham of AUL announced "a major rhetorical shift" in the organization's agenda, one focused on "right to know laws" patterned on *Casey*.[84] "We must help people understand that abortion hurts women too," she insisted.[85] By the fall of 1993, the organization had announced a major fifteen-year plan. "Our first goal is to shatter the myth that abortion helps women," the framers of the plan explained.[86]

Curiae of the Rutherford Institute et al, 8, *Planned Parenthood of Southeastern Pennsylvania v Casey*, 505 US 833 (1992) (Nos 91-744, 91-902).

[81] *Planned Parenthood of Southeastern Pennsylvania v Casey*, 744 F Supp 1323, 1332–33 (E D Pa 1990).

[82] *Planned Parenthood of Southeastern Pennsylvania v Casey*, 505 US 833, 882–83 (1992) (plurality opinion).

[83] Id.

[84] AUL Board Meeting Minutes (April 24, 1993) (Mildred F. Jefferson Papers, Box 13, Folder 5, Schlesinger Library, Harvard University).

[85] Id at 3.

[86] Id.

Right-to-know laws were a stirring success. By 2013, twenty-two states had introduced such statutes. The questionable evidence of post-abortion regret did nothing to slow the momentum of related laws in the courts or the legislatures.[87]

By 2007, the potential impact of uncertainty claims on the Supreme Court was obvious. In *Gonzales v Carhart*, the Court, in upholding the so-called Partial Birth Abortion Ban Act of 2003, relied heavily on a brief emphasizing affidavits collected by Operation Outcry, a group closely associated with WEBA and Reardon.[88] That brief stressed the testimony of women who believed that they had experienced postabortion trauma, state legislative findings, and expert testimony by Dr. Rue.[89] *Carhart* acknowledged that the evidentiary foundation for postabortion trauma syndrome was weak,[90] but anecdotal evidence or even common sense was enough to persuade the Court that women regretted abortions, regardless of convincing medical proof to the contrary. "It is self-evident," the Court reasoned, "that a mother who comes to regret her choice to abort must struggle with grief more anguished and sorrow more profound when she learns . . . that she allowed a doctor to pierce the skull and vacuum the fast-developing brain of her unborn child."[91]

II. Broader Context

The activists behind Texas's HB2, like the lawyers involved in the litigation of *Carhart* and *Casey*, relied on claims that abortion hurt women and tried to turn scientific uncertainty to their advantage. The regulations at issue in *Whole Woman's Health* themselves had a long history. In the 1970s, movement leaders had first called for laws requiring all later-term abortions to be performed in hospitals. By the early 1980s, as facilities responded to individual practitioners or committees afraid that hospitals performing abortions

---

[87] *Counseling and Waiting Periods for Abortion*, Guttmacher Institute (Dec 29, 2016) (available at https://www.guttmacher.org/state-policy/explore/counseling-and-waiting-periods-abortion).

[88] *Carhart*, 550 US at 159 (citing Brief for Sandra Cano et al as Amici Curiae at 22–24, *Gonzales v Carhart*, 550 US 124 (2007) (No 05-380)).

[89] See Brief for Sandra Cano et al as Amici Curiae at 18–25 (cited in note 88).

[90] See, for example, 550 US at 159 ("While we find no reliable data to measure the phenomenon, it seems unexceptionable to conclude some women come to regret their choice to abort the infant life they once created and sustained.").

[91] Id.

would damage their reputations, few hospitals performed abortions. As hospitals began to merge and Catholic hospitals took over a larger share of the market, the difficulty of finding a hospital willing to perform the procedure grew. Requiring women to have abortions in hospitals seemed likely to put the procedure off limits for many women.[92]

In the same period, movement members experimented with laws that would indirectly achieve the same result as the hospital requirements. In 1977, in Cocoa Beach, Florida, James Bopp, Jr. of the NRLC represented a city council that had passed a law requiring the only abortion clinic in town to comply with state regulations governing ambulatory surgical centers. Pro-lifers contended that these regulations advanced the state's interest in protecting women's health—a governmental purpose explicitly recognized by *Roe*. Although the courts often struck down these laws, emphasizing that they singled out abortion clinics, incrementalists refused to give up on a court-centered strategy. "We must not . . . consider ignoring the courts in our effort to seek protection for the unborn," AUL explained in 1978.[93] "To do so would disenfranchise the pro-life voter because all significant legislation is, and will continue to be, challenged by our opponents in the courts."[94]

In the mid-1980s, AUL introduced a major initiative to pass TRAP laws like the one at issue in *Whole Woman's Health*. After a 1978 exposé by the *Chicago Sun Times* on the state's abortion industry, the organization focused its efforts on Illinois. The *Sun Times* had reported on unsterile, dangerous, dishonest, and unprincipled practices at four Chicagoland clinics, and in 1982, at the urging of the pro-life movement, the state introduced a TRAP law. In the decades to come, pro-lifers would renew the push for similar laws when clinic scandals emerged in other states and cities.[95]

---

[92] On the history of hospital access in the early 1980s, see Faye D. Ginsburg, *Contested Lives: The Abortion Debate in an American Community* 55 (California, 1998). On the impact of hospital mergers, see Barbara Mann Wall, *American Catholic Hospitals: A Century of Changing Markets and Missions* 12, 21 (Rutgers, 2011).

[93] "AUL Perspective," *Lex Vitae* (Feb 1, 1978) 12 (Wilcox Collection, Lex Vitae Folder, University of Kansas).

[94] Id. On Bopp's push in Cocoa Beach, see Americans United for Life, "Legislation," *Lex Vitae* (June 29, 1978) at 2 (Wilcox Collection, Lex Vitae Folder, University of Kansas).

[95] For examples of this strategy, see Donna O'Neal, *Martinez to HRS: Shut Clinics*, Orlando Sentinel (Sept 23, 1989) at G1; Ed Anderson, *Bill That Would Regulate Abortions in La. Is Filed*, New Orleans Times Picayune (April 18, 1991) at 1A. On the *Sun Times* exposé, see Johanna

When providers challenged the Illinois regulations in 1989, pro-life incrementalists celebrated. The leader of the Illinois Right to Life Committee, a NRLC state affiliate, explained: "We want the Court to have as many opportunities as possible to look at *Roe vs. Wade* to overturn it or chip away at it some more."[96] Paige Cunningham, a leader of AUL, presented the state's regulations as a necessary means of protecting women from abortion. Not only did the law not create an undue burden; the Illinois measure was needed to keep women safe from "unqualified physicians, unsanitary conditions or debilitating injury."[97]

The Illinois litigation was settled and never reached the Supreme Court, but pro-lifers continued to make regulation of clinics a part of a broader woman-protective strategy. In 1999, for example, South Carolina adopted a law requiring the licensure of clinics that performed more than a threshold number of abortions and mandated that the state health department promulgate regulations to govern abortion clinics. Regulators later issued a complex set of rules, requiring among other things that all clinics (but no other freestanding medical facilities) undertake extensive physical plant changes, test all patients for both pregnancy and sexually transmitted diseases, and ensure that only a registered nurse, rather than a physician, supervise nursing staff. The state emphasized that these measures would protect women's health:

> This Regulation does not look to strike at a woman's right to choose whether to have an abortion; rather, these regulations look to protect the health of women who seek abortions by ensuring, among many other things, that women will be offered medical tests to determine whether they have venereal diseases which could complicate abortions and cause other health problems; that abortion providers are housed in facilities which are properly equipped to handle the complications associated with abortions; and that women are treated by medical providers who possess the skills required to perform the abortion procedure safely.[98]

Schoen, *Abortion After Roe: Abortion After Legalization* 96–118 (North Carolina, 2015); Brooke Kroeger, *Undercover Reporting: The Truth About Deception* 248 (Northwestern, 2012).

[96] Lynn Sweet, *Abortion Foes Fight Deal on Key Case*, Chicago Sun Times (Aug 31, 1989) at 14.

[97] Jim Merriner, *Another Group Opposes Settling of Abortion Case*, Chicago Sun Times (Sept 1, 1989) at 8.

[98] See Brief of Appellants, 57, *Greenville Women's Clinic v Bryant*, 222 F3d 157 (4th Cir 2000) (Nos 99-1319, 99-1710, 99-1725).

The state mustered relatively little evidence for these assertions. With respect to the physical-plant requirements, for example, South Carolina relied on a single expert witness with experience constructing ambulatory surgical centers, who testified that the regulations would make for safer clinics.[99] From South Carolina's standpoint, the undue-burden test required nothing more. Given that the state's regulations simply made abortion more expensive and shuttered only a handful of clinics, the undue-burden test was satisfied, the state claimed, regardless of whether the law actually advanced its stated end. For the providers challenging the regulations, the undue-burden test had a very different meaning. As they explained: "The Supreme Court's abortion jurisprudence demonstrates that the state may not burden access to abortion with alleged health regulations unless those regulations actually promote maternal health."[100]

Pro-life activists continued to see TRAP laws as the perfect way to push both woman-protective reasoning and a new understanding of the undue-burden test. Clarke Forsythe told other AUL members: "In most states, veterinary clinics face more regulations than abortion clinics, which result in the deaths of numerous women (the second victims of abortion)."[101] If the movement could convince the Supreme Court that such laws did not fail the undue-burden test, Forsythe predicted that the movement would "be in a position to regulate abortion clinics in all fifty states."[102] After Barack Obama's election in 2008, laws regulating clinics took on new importance. Without an ally in the White House, pro-lifers refocused on state legislation. In January 2009, NRLC Executive Director David N. O'Steen insisted that "affiliates can still be effective in passing state legislation," maintaining that such laws had "saved 7 million babies since 1973, a victory that the Obama administration cannot take away."[103]

---

[99] See id at 16.

[100] Brief of Appellees, 27, *Greenville Women's Clinic v Bryant*, 222 F3d 157 (4th Cir 2000) (Nos 99-1319, 99-1710, 99-1725).

[101] Americans United for Life, Fundraising Letter (Oct 18, 2000), 1–2 (Mildred F. Jefferson Papers, Box 13, Folder 6, Schlesinger Library, Harvard University).

[102] Id.

[103] National Right to Life Committee Board of Directors Meeting Minutes (Jan 24–25, 2009), 1–3 (Mildred F. Jefferson Papers, Box 5, Folder 7, Schlesinger Library, Harvard University).

A. TEXAS INTRODUCES MODEL ANTIABORTION LEGISLATION

In 2013, to advance this agenda, AUL encouraged Texas lawmakers to adopt two pieces of model legislation, the Women's Health Protection Act and the Abortion Providers Privileging Act. The AUL proposal required that all abortion providers have admitting privileges at a hospital within thirty miles and mandated detailed regulations on everything from the size of clinics to the training of staff. "[T]he [vast majority] of all abortions in this State are performed in clinics devoted solely to providing abortions and family planning services," stated the legislative findings proposed for each law.[104] "In most instances, the woman's only actual contact with the abortion provider occurs simultaneously with the abortion procedure, with little opportunity to ask questions about the procedure, potential complications, and proper follow-up care."[105] After quoting several Supreme Court opinions on the importance of protecting women's health, the findings further explained:

> Abortion is an invasive, surgical procedure that can lead to numerous and serious (both short- and long-term) medical complications. Potential complications for abortion include, among others, bleeding, hemorrhage, infection, uterine perforation, uterine scarring, blood clots, cervical tears, incomplete abortion (retained tissue), failure to actually terminate the pregnancy, free fluid in the abdomen, organ damage, missed ectopic pregnancies, cardiac arrest, sepsis, respiratory arrest, reactions to anesthesia, and even death.[106]

At a time when state legislators pushed a variety of abortion restrictions, Texas lawmakers considered a proposal patterned on the AUL model law. Legislators also considered a ban on abortions after twenty weeks and a requirement that Planned Parenthood be last in line for state funding for family planning. Democratic Senator Wendy Davis gained national attention by filibustering the abortion restrictions, but by July 2013, Governor Rick Perry had signed HB2 into law. The following September, a group of abortion pro-

---

[104] *Women's Health Protection Act*, 2013 Model Law and Policy Guide (available at http://www.aul.org/wp-content/uploads/2012/11/Womens-Health-Protection-Act-Abortion-Clinic-Regulations-2013-LG.pdf); *Abortion Providers Admitting Privileges Act*, Americans United for Life Model Legislation and Policy Guide for the 2015 Legislative Year (available at http://www.aul.org/downloads/2015-Legislative-Guides/Abortion/Abortion_Providers_Admitting_Privileges_Act_-_2015_LG.pdf).

[105] Id at 5.

[106] Id at 5–6.

viders sought the facial invalidation of the admitting-privileges measure. The district court enjoined the law, but the Fifth Circuit vacated the injunction only days later, ensuring that the Texas measure would go into effect.[107] The Fifth Circuit subsequently issued an opinion upholding the law.[108]

At the trial, Texas put forward several expert witnesses arguing that the admitting-privileges requirement improved patients' continuity of care and providers' credentialing. These experts claimed that patients faced risks either because of a miscommunication during a transfer to a hospital or because of a lack of proper care available at emergency rooms. The Fifth Circuit reasoned that if women faced longer travel distances as a result of the law, that alone did not constitute an undue burden under *Casey*. The court also did not find enough support in the record for the district court's findings that abortion clinics had closed because of the admitting-privileges requirement or that providers were unable to comply with the law. The court emphasized that abortion access might have declined for other reasons, including the aging of abortion providers and concerns about low pay and antiabortion violence.[109]

The providers did not seek review of the Fifth Circuit's decision but instead, a week later, an overlapping group of providers filed another suit, this time challenging the ambulatory-surgical center (ASC) provision as applied anywhere in the state and the admitting-privileges provision as applied to facilities in McAllen and El Paso. At trial, the parties stipulated that only seven facilities in major cities would be able to comply with the ASC provision. Texas again offered several expert witnesses. As to the ASC requirement, state witnesses claimed that any abortion required entry into the uterus, a matter best performed in sterile facilities like hospitals. State witnesses also repeated claims that an admitting-privilege requirement would im-

---

[107] On the proposals considered by Texas in 2013, see Matthew Waller, *Texas Legislature: Abortion Continues to Divide 40 Years After Legal Ruling*, San Angelo Standard Times (Jan 22, 2013). On the filibuster and the signing of the law, see Jayme Fraser and Kolten Parker, *Perry Signs Abortion Bill; Opponents Vow to Fight On*, Houston Chronicle (July 18, 2013) at A1. For the district court's decision enjoining the admitting-privilege requirement, see *Planned Parenthood of Greater Texas Surgical Health Services v Abbott*, 951 F Supp 891 (W D Tex 2013). For the Fifth Circuit's order vacating the injunction, see *Planned Parenthood of Greater Texas Surgical Health Services v Abbott*, 734 F3d 406 (5th Cir 2013).

[108] *Planned Parenthood of Greater Texas Surgical Services v Abbott*, 748 F3d 583 (5th Cir 2014).

[109] See id at 593–601.

prove the credentialing of abortion providers and guarantee women better continuity of care.[110] Although Vincent Rue did not testify, he played an important role behind the scenes: The district court stated that Rue exercised "considerable editorial and discretionary control over the contents of the [State] experts' reports and declarations. . . . [T]he level of input exerted by Rue undermines the appearance of objectivity and reliability of the experts' opinions[, and] the court is dismayed by the considerable efforts the State took to obscure Rue's level of involvement with the experts' contributions."[111]

The district court enjoined enforcement of both provisions throughout the state.[112] The court emphasized that compliance with the ASC provision would cost existing clinics over $1 million and require new facilities to pay three times as much. The district court concluded that if HB2 went into effect, the number of clinics offering abortions in the state would drop, resulting in dramatically higher travel times that would particularly affect poor, rural, and minority women.[113]

The Fifth Circuit again reversed.[114] As to the admitting-privileges requirement, the court held both that the district court had granted broader relief than abortion providers had requested and that the Fifth Circuit's earlier ruling on the admitting-privileges requirement precluded the challenge to that requirement. Texas also argued that *res judicata* barred the challenge to the ASC requirement because the providers could have challenged this measure in 2013 and failed to do so. The court of appeals agreed but nevertheless reached the merits. The court concluded that the law ensured that women received the best medical care and rejected the suggestion that the stated purpose of the law was mere pretext because the ASC provision applied only to abortion providers, had no demonstrable health benefits, and would result in the closure of a majority of abortion clinics.[115]

Nor, according to the Fifth Circuit, did the ASC measure have an impermissible effect under *Casey*. The court found that even if the law

[110] See *Whole Woman's Health v Lakey*, 46 F Supp 3d 673, 680–84 (W D Tex 2014).

[111] Id at 680 n 3. On Rue's role in the litigation of *Whole Woman's Health*, see Mary Tuma, *Roe's End?*, Austin Chronicle (Jan 29, 2016) (available at http://www.austinchronicle.com/news/2016-01-29/roes-end/).

[112] Id at 687–88.

[113] See *Lakey*, 46 F Supp 3d at 680–84.

[114] *Whole Woman's Health v Cole*, 790 F3d 563, modified, 790 F3d 598 (5th Cir 2015).

[115] See *Cole*, 790 F3d at 582–83.

would require 17 percent of women in the state to travel 150 miles or more, that number was not high enough to satisfy the "large fraction" test set out in *Casey*. If poor, young, or minority women would have a harder time accessing abortion, the court blamed that fact on women's preexisting circumstances, not on HB2. When it came to the small number of ASCs currently operating in the state, the Fifth Circuit faulted the plaintiffs for failing to prove that existing facilities could not expand their capacity and perform more procedures.[116]

The Supreme Court's intervention in the case was a source of optimism for abortion opponents. AUL called the case "the most significant . . . before the Supreme Court in decades."[117] Charmaine Yoest, the former president of AUL, presented *Whole Woman's Health* as a potential vindication of the woman-protective strategy that the movement had refined for decades. "After more than four decades of the abortion industry's recalcitrant opposition to meaningful oversight," she stated, "the Supreme Court must unequivocally affirm that it meant what it has said as far back as *Roe*: states may regulate abortion to protect a mother's health."[118]

III. Influence of the Decision

Whole Woman's Health represented a stunning reversal of fortune for activists who expected the Court to equate the undue-burden test with rational-basis review. The scale of the defeat suffered by the antiabortion movement comes through clearly by a comparison of the Court's decision and the arguments in AUL's amicus brief in the case. "[T]he State is not required to *prove* the positive impact of HB2 in order for a court to determine that the requirement has a rational basis (and is, thus, not an undue burden)," AUL argued in its brief.[119] "The burden is on the Plaintiffs challenging to prove that the State has absolutely no rational justification for enacting the regulation."[120]

---

[116] See id at 584–89.

[117] Press Release, *AUL Represents State Legislators in Historical Supreme Court Case, Fights to Protect Health and Safety Standards for Women Vulnerable to Abortion Industry Abuses* (Feb 3, 2016) (available at http://www.aul.org/2016/02/aul-represents-state-legislators-in-historic-supreme-court-case-fights-to-protect-health-and-safety-standards-for-women-vulnerable-to-abortion-industry-abuses/).

[118] Id.

[119] Amici Curiae Brief of Forty-Four State Legislators in Support of Defendants-Appellants, 15, *Whole Woman's Health v Cole*, 2014 WL 6647162 (CA 5) (2016) (No 14-50928).

[120] Id.

For AUL, *Whole Woman's Health* represented the culmination of decades of dialogue about the meaning of an undue burden on the abortion right. Expanding on that decades-long effort, AUL attorneys defined the undue-burden test as the functional equivalent of rational-basis review. While recognizing that some laws would have a sufficiently burdensome effect to trigger heightened scrutiny under *Casey*, AUL insisted that the undue-burden test required no analysis of the relationship between the means and ends of a law as long as a rational legislature could conclude that such a relationship existed.

The Court not only declined the invitation to apply rational-basis review to abortion restrictions but also strengthened the protection of abortion rights. Abortion opponents' disappointment was palpable. AUL vowed to continue the fight for woman-protective legislation. NRLC seemed even more dismayed, saying nothing about woman-centered strategies and emphasizing primarily that the Court had not touched a twenty-week abortion ban also on the books in Texas (which had not been challenged in the litigation).[121]

Like abortion opponents, commentators predicted that the decision would have a major impact. Sociologist Deanna Rohlinger emphasized that for the first time in years, "pro-life advocates [found] themselves squarely on the losing side of a watershed legal decision."[122] Planned Parenthood leader Cecile Richards cited the Court's decision in announcing plans to challenge TRAP laws throughout the nation. Writing in the *New Yorker*, Margot Talbot summarized the view of many, claiming that *Whole Woman's Health* had "reinvigorated the undue-burden test, and with it the fundamental right of abortion."[123]

---

[121] For AUL's response, see Press Release, *Supreme Court Rejects Texas Health and Safety Standards for Abortion Clinics* (June 27, 2016) (http://www.aul.org/2016/06/supreme-court-rejects-texas-health-and-safety-standards-for-abortion-clinics-aul-says-fight-to-protect-women-from-predatory-abortion-industry-continues/). On the NRLC's response, see Press Release, *NRLC Responds to Supreme Court Decision in Whole Woman's Health v Hellerstedt* (June 27, 2016) (available at http://www.nrlc.org/communications/releases/2016/release062716/).

[122] Rohlinger, *Turning the Anti-Abortion Tide* (cited in note 1).

[123] Margot Talbot, *The Supreme Court's Just Application of the Undue Burden Test*, New Yorker (June 27, 2016) (available at http://www.newyorker.com/news/news-desk/the-supreme-courts-just-application-of-the-undue-burden-standard-for-abortion). For Richards's statement, see Cecile Richards, *On Abortion Access: The Supreme Court's Signal Is Clear*, Houston Chronicle (July 2, 2016) (available at http://www.houstonchronicle.com/opinion/outlook/article/Richards-On-abortion-access-the-Supreme-Court-s-8338537.php).

But *Whole Woman's Health* may not begin the new era so many have predicted. Writing for a five-to-three majority, Justice Stephen Breyer, after rejecting the argument that *res judicata* barred the providers' claims, explained why the Fifth Circuit had misunderstood *Casey*. "The rule announced in *Casey* . . . requires that courts consider the burdens a law imposes on abortion access together with the benefits those laws confer," he said.[124] Although the court of appeals understood *Carhart* to require deferential review of legislative fact-finding, Justice Breyer asserted that *Carhart* did nothing to change the "Court's constitutional duty to review factual findings when constitutional rights are at stake."[125] In Justice Breyer's reading, *Carhart* had weighed Congress's findings against record evidence that conflicted with lawmakers' conclusions. Thoughtful analysis, not "uncritical deference," was the hallmark of *Carhart*.[126]

According to Justice Breyer, *Casey* had also balanced the burdens and benefits of a spousal-notification and parental-involvement law, relying "heavily on the District Court's factual findings and the research-based findings of amici in declaring a portion of the law at issue unconstitutional."[127] As Justice Breyer described it, the undue-burden test required a similarly thorough consideration of any legislative findings, as well as evidence in the record, particularly expert testimony.[128]

In applying this revamped version of the undue-burden test, the Court seemed to attach more significance to some dimensions of the record than to others. Distinguishing *Whole Woman's Health* from *Carhart*, Justice Breyer noted that Texas lawmakers had made no legislative findings. Concluding that the record contained enough evidence to support the district court's ruling, the Court further emphasized peer-reviewed studies, arguments made in amicus briefs, and other record evidence. Breyer relied on "direct testimony and [the] reasonable inferences" drawn from the record.[129]

---

[124] *Whole Woman's Health*, 135 S Ct at 2309.

[125] Id at 2310 (citing *Carhart*, 550 US at 165).

[126] Id (citation omitted).

[127] Id.

[128] See id.

[129] Id at 2310–17.

The Court's thorough rejection of HB2 seemed to represent a resounding defeat for AUL and others who had embraced a woman-protective strategy. Justice Thomas believed that the Court had undone decades of prior abortion jurisprudence.[130] He suggested that while *Casey* and *Carhart* had applied something like rational-basis review, *Whole Woman's Health* replaced that analysis "with something much more akin to strict scrutiny."[131] Justice Thomas took the Court's decision as an example of the problems with the "'made-up tests'" and "'randomness'" plaguing the use of tiers of scrutiny.[132]

Justice Thomas also asserted that the Court's decision had ignored *Carhart*'s reasoning about scientific uncertainty. According to Justice Thomas, *Carhart* stood for the proposition that legislatures had wide discretion to regulate abortion "[w]henever medical justifications for an abortion restriction are debatable."[133] *Whole Woman's Health* had refused to "leave disputed medical science to the legislature."[134] As long as there were "conflicting [medical] positions," legislators should have the latitude to regulate. Any balancing in earlier cases involved *Casey*'s spousal-notification provision, a measure that had "nothing to do with disputed medical science."[135]

While Justice Thomas strongly denounced the Court's ruling, no other Justices joined his opinion. Although the other dissenters might well have shared Justice Thomas's dismay about the majority opinion, Justice Alito's dissent was still telling. At a minimum, the dissent reveals what Justice Alito and Chief Justice Roberts might have believed was necessary to win another vote. After a lengthy discussion of *res judicata*, Justice Alito addressed the majority's reworking of the undue-burden test. While taking the majority to task for failing to acknowledge that "[t]he proper standard for facial challenges is unsettled in the abortion context," Justice Alito said nothing about the balancing analysis detailed by the Court. Nevertheless, Justice Alito did not identify any obvious conflict between the majority opinion and *Carhart* when it came to the idea of scientific uncertainty or to the

---

[130] Id at 2321–30 (Thomas, J, dissenting).

[131] Id at 2324 (Thomas, J, dissenting).

[132] Id at 2327 (Thomas, J, dissenting) (citations omitted).

[133] Id at 2325 (Thomas, J, dissenting).

[134] Id.

[135] Id.

reworking of the undue-burden test as a whole. Instead, Justice Alito primarily faulted the Court for not requiring real proof of whether HB2 had forced clinics to close or whether existing ASCs could expand to meet women's demands after the law went into effect.[136]

Justice Alito may have had strategic reasons for keeping the more significant parts of the majority decision out of the spotlight. Nevertheless, the impact of *Whole Woman's Health* seems far more ambiguous than Justice Thomas suggested. The Court did clarify that *Casey* required courts to weigh the benefits and burdens of law. At least when applying this balancing analysis to HB2, *Whole Woman's Health* applied a standard that would lead courts to strike down many more abortion regulations. However, in illustrating what *Casey* demanded, the Court presented *Carhart* as an example of balancing analysis rather than a misapplication of it. Indeed, the majority said nothing explicit about *Carhart*'s understanding of scientific uncertainty.

The medical impact of *Whole Woman's Health* may be considerable. The Court's decision will affect abortion access in Texas, and similar laws in other states may soon be invalidated. The political and constitutional impact of the decision, however, remains far less clear. *Whole Woman's Health* does not foreclose the use of scientific uncertainty as a justification for restricting abortion, the strategy relied on so successfully by abortion opponents for decades.

IV. Conclusion

Even after the decision, antiabortion groups remain committed to that strategy in calling for new, far-reaching restrictions. AUL's 2016 handbook on model state legislation lays out several approaches that hinge on questionable scientific claims. Many still highlight the risks of abortion for women. "Progress toward overturning *Roe v. Wade* will depend, in large part, on raising public awareness of the negative impact of abortion on women through targeted legislation," the handbook contends.[137]

The organization has proposed several laws that draw on the supposed uncertainty surrounding the safety of abortion for women. The

---

[136] Id at 2330–52 (Alito, J, dissenting).

[137] AUL, *Defending Life: 2016 Edition* (2016), 20 (available at http://www.aul.org/defendinglife/2016/AUL_DL2016.pdf).

Women's Health Defense Act would impose a ban on abortion after twenty weeks for two reasons: the supposed "pain felt by an unborn child during a late-term abortion" and the higher mortality risks that the organization links to abortion after the twentieth week of pregnancy.[138] Although *Whole Woman's Health* recognized the safety of abortions, AUL seeks to profit from medical literature on the increasing risks of abortion beyond the first trimester.[139]

The idea of uncertainty also animates AUL's proposed expansion of informed-consent restrictions. One model statute stresses the claim that medication abortions can be reversed. Another proposal recommends that lawmakers "enhance their informed consent laws by requiring information on fetal pain, the availability of ultrasounds, [and] the link between abortion and breast cancer ("ABC link")."[140] Although AUL admits that the connection between breast cancer and abortion is not "undisputed," the organization maintains that enough studies "reveal an . . . increased risk of breast cancer as a result of the loss of a protective effect of a first full-term pregnancy."[141]

Whole Woman's Health seems unlikely to deter antiabortion groups from using some understanding of scientific uncertainty to advance fetal-protective laws. NRLC has invested in what members of the organization call the "Unborn Child Protection from Dismemberment Act," a law that would ban dilation and evacuation (D&E), the most common second-trimester abortion procedure. In talking points issued in support of the law, NRLC emphasizes that D&E procedures—the most widely used method that is commonly believed to be safe—do not "have wide support in the medical community" and are "never necessary to preserve the life of the mother in an acute . . .

[138] AUL, *Women's Health Defense Act: Model Legislation and Policy Guide for the 2016 Legislative Year* (2016) (available at http://aul.org/downloads/2016-Legislative-Guides/WPP/Womens_Health_Defense_Act_-_2016_LG.pdf).

[139] On the comparably higher rates of complications in the second trimester, see Daniel Grossman, Kelly Blanchard, and Paul Blumenthal, *Complications After Second Trimester Medical and Surgical Abortions*, 16 Reproductive Health Matters 173, 173–82 (2008).

[140] AUL, *Women's Right to Know Act: Model Legislation and Policy Guide for the 2016 Legislative Year* (2016) (available at http://www.aul.org/downloads/2016-Legislative-Guides/WPP/Womens_Right_to_Know_Act_(Informed_Consent)_-_2016_LG.pdf).

[141] Id. On the AUL model showcasing the supposed dangers of medication abortions, see AUL, *Abortion-Inducing Drugs Safety Act: Model Legislation and Policy Guide for the 2016 Legislative Year* (2016) (available at http://www.aul.org/downloads/2016-Legislative-Guides/WPP/Abortion-Inducing_Drugs_Safety_Act_-_2016_LG.pdf).

emergency."[142] NRLC also claims that the law protects fetal life from "feeling the pain of being ripped apart."[143]

The factual premises of dismemberment bans are contested at best. In its description of D&E, the American College of Obstetricians and Gynecologists (ACOG) states that "[a]bortion is a low-risk procedure," even later in pregnancy.[144] The American Medical Association (AMA) acknowledges that D&E is the procedure most "commonly used to induce abortion after the first trimester."[145] Arguing that the medical community as a whole rejects D&E seems implausible, but movement members have less trouble arguing that the legitimacy of D&E is disputed, given the position of organizations that oppose use of the procedure like the American Association of Pro-Life Obstetricians and Gynecologists (AAPLOG).[146]

Nor is the argument that D&E (or any abortion procedure) is always unnecessary to save a pregnant woman's life universally accepted. ACOG has taken the position that abortion is required to save a woman's life under limited circumstances, including in cases of heart failure, severe infections, and grave cases of preeclampsia. NRLC has included a life-of-the-mother exception in many of its legislative proposals. Again, however, pro-life physicians and medical professionals challenge the conclusion that women would ever die if they did not terminate their pregnancies. Identifying supposed uncertainty remains an easier task than collecting proof.[147]

---

[142] National Right to Life Committee, *Talking Points: Unborn Child Protection from Dismemberment Abortion Act* (2015), 3 (available at http://www.nrlc.org/uploads/stateleg/Dismemberment FAQJan15.pdf).

[143] Id at 1.

[144] American College of Obstetricians and Gynecologists, *Induced Abortion* (May 2015) (available at http://www.acog.org/Patients/FAQs/Induced-Abortion).

[145] American Medical Association, "H. 5.982: Late-Term Pregnancy Termination Techniques," *Health and Ethics Policies of the AMA House of Delegates* (available at http://www.ama-assn.org/ad-com/polfind/Hlth-Ethics.pdf).

[146] On the founding of AAPLOG, see American Association of Pro-Life Obstetricians and Gynecologists, *About Us* (available at http://www.aaplog.org/about-2/).

[147] On the debate about whether abortions are ever needed to save a woman's life, see Kim Painter, *Doctors Say Abortions Sometimes Do Save Women's Lives*, USA Today (Oct 22, 2012) (available at http://www.usatoday.com/story/news/nation/2012/10/19/abortion-mother-life-walsh/1644839/). NRLC has drawn criticism from other antiabortion organizations for supporting legislation with exceptions for abortions in cases of rape, incest, or a threat to the woman's life. The most recent involves the federal Pain-Capable Unborn Child Protection Act, a law opposed by some House Republicans and activists because of the exceptions made in the law. See *U.S. House Passes Bill to Protect Children in the Sixth Month of Pregnancy and*

The fetal-pain laws sponsored by NRLC also rely on the claim of scientific uncertainty. At the state and federal level, the organization sponsors laws that ban abortion after twenty weeks, the time that NRLC argues that "unborn children are capable of experiencing pain."[148] Together with Doctors on Fetal Pain, an antiabortion organization focused on the issue, NRLC relies on a variety of peer-reviewed studies, but several of the authors of these articles have dismissed antiabortion leaders' interpretation of their work. NRLC leaders hope to use these disputed scientific conclusions to establish what is in effect a moral or legal proposition. Mary Spaulding Balch of the NRLC stated: "the unborn child's capacity to experience pain is a significant developmental milepost, making the unborn child at that point sufficiently akin to an infant or older child to trigger a compelling state interest."[149]

Constitutionally, the defense of fetal-pain and dismemberment laws also relies heavily on *Carhart* and its idea of uncertainty. *Whole Woman's Health* did not involve the government's interest in protecting fetal life, and the Court's opinion did not criticize *Carhart*'s call to protect fetal dignity as well as fetal life. Perhaps unsurprisingly, then, *Carhart* stands at the heart of the movement's defense of dismemberment and fetal-pain laws.

In promoting dismemberment laws, the NRLC extensively quotes from *Carhart*, characterizing D&E as a procedure "laden with the potential to devalue human life."[150] NRLC also relies on *Carhart* in assuaging those concerned that dismemberment laws will be little more than "just another doomed attempt to reverse *Roe v. Wade*."[151] The organization claims that states passing such legislation simply advance the interests that "the Court recognized in [*Carhart*], that states have a separate and independent compelling interest in 'fos-

---

Later, Christian Newswire (June 18, 2013) (available at http://www.christiannewswire.com/news/8865172295.html).

[148] *Pain Capable Unborn Child Protection Act* (May 31, 2016) (available at http://www.nrlc.org/uploads/stateleg/PCUCPAfactsheet.pdf).

[149] Mary Spaulding Balch, JD, Director State Development Department, *To Whom It May Concern, Re: Constitutionality of the Model Pain-Capable Unborn Child Protection Act* (July 2013) (available at http://www.nrlc.org/uploads/stateleg/PCUCPAConstitutionality.pdf). On the arguments made by Doctors on Fetal Pain, see *Doctors on Fetal Pain: The Evidence* (2016) (available at http://www.doctorsonfetalpain.com/).

[150] National Right to Life Committee, *Talking Points* at 2 (cited in note 142) (quoting *Carhart*, 550 US at 158).

[151] Id at 3.

tering respect for life by protecting the unborn child from death by dismemberment abortion' and 'in protecting the integrity of the medical profession with passage of this law.'"[152]

Similar reasoning runs through NRLC's constitutional case for fetal-pain laws. According to NRLC, *Carhart* made apparent that "the interests states may assert are not limited to those previously recognized in prior abortion cases."[153] Defending fetal-pain laws will afford abortion opponents the opportunity to identify yet another state interest involving the prevention of fetal suffering. Uncertainty makes an even bigger difference to NRLC's constitutional strategy. "While some dispute the capacity of the 20-week unborn child to experience pain," the organization asserts, "Justice Kennedy's opinion for the Court in [*Carhart*] makes clear that medical unanimity is not required in order for legislatures to make and act on determinations of medical fact."[154]

What of the woman-protective legislation sponsored by AUL? The organization might take hope from the distinctions drawn between *Carhart* and *Whole Woman's Health*, particularly the lack of legislative findings supporting HB2. *Whole Woman's Health* certainly cast doubt on the Court's openness to any woman-protective legislation. As AUL's handbook suggests, the best chance of defending such laws before the Court after *Whole Woman's Health* depends on *Carhart*. AUL explains: "[T]he Court has held that legislative bodies enjoy wide discretion to enact regulations where there is medical uncertainty as to the safety of abortion procedures, both surgical and chemical."[155]

The history of uncertainty arguments suggests that antiabortion activists may not be wrong to believe that *Carhart* will still advance their cause even after *Whole Woman's Health* dealt the movement a significant blow. In the past, activists like David Reardon have stressed the severe psychological consequences of abortion. Reardon and his allies persisted in making these claims even after leading medical organizations refuted them. Rather than abandoning his strategy, Reardon argued that even anecdotal evidence of great harm

[152] Id at 4.

[153] Balch, *To Whom It May Concern* at 1 (cited in note 149).

[154] Id at 4.

[155] AUL, *Women's Protection Project* (2013), 2 (available at http://www.aul.org/wp-content/uploads/2014/01/WWP-full.pdf).

justified abortion restrictions. In spite of the questionable evidence supporting Reardon's claims, antiabortion activists successfully persuaded the *Casey* and *Carhart* Courts to make them a significant part of abortion jurisprudence.

Nothing in the Court's most recent decision rules out such a strategy. *Whole Woman's Health* establishes that Texas failed to prove the benefits achieved by HB2, but the Court tailored most of its analysis to the specific statute at issue in the case. If anything, Justice Breyer's opinion suggested that trial courts should enjoy considerable deference in making the findings required by *Casey*'s balancing test. If one takes the opinion in *Whole Woman's Health* at face value, there is little stopping lower courts from upholding abortion restrictions whenever they can make factual findings that are not clearly erroneous and that support the conclusion that the balance of benefits and burdens supports the restriction.

Similarly, because *Carhart*'s approach to scientific uncertainty was not squarely rejected by *Whole Woman's Health*, that aspect of *Carhart* may still leave legislators considerable latitude in regulating abortion. The Court in *Carhart* acknowledged that the evidentiary foundation for postabortion trauma syndrome was weak but still relied on evidence of postabortion harm.[156] This idea of uncertainty may be even more politically compelling when pro-lifers emphasize the potential of injury, pain, or death. In *Carhart*, the Court seemed open to the argument that *Casey*'s balancing would favor whoever invokes a real possibility of grave harm.

Allowing abortion restrictions whenever there is a chance that new evidence could change the scientific status quo could permit far more regulation than those who have celebrated *Whole Woman's Health* might expect. *Whole Woman's Health* does suggest that abortion opponents will have to work much harder to make a case for abortion restrictions before the courts, but the decision still seems likely to reignite a war about the facts. Because the Court in *Whole Woman's Health* made a point of deferring to the district court's finding of fact, trial courts will have considerable discretion in making findings about the purpose or effect of an abortion regulation.

Claims about uncertainty underlie the effort to introduce bans on D&E and on any abortion after twenty weeks. Arguments relying on

---

[156] *Carhart*, 550 US at 159.

Carhart represent the best hope for reviving woman-protective legislation that closely resembles HB2 in its logic or rationale. Until the Court does more to explain what lower courts should do in the face of claims of scientific uncertainty when reproductive rights are at stake, pro-lifers have no obvious cause to abandon these tactics.

So while *Whole Woman's Health* was certainly a victory for abortion rights, the game in other ways remains unchanged. Both sides depend heavily on the outcome of presidential elections and the replacement of one or more of the Justices currently sitting on the Court. Pro-choice organizations will continue to pursue a broader agenda that includes access to contraception. Long committed to avoiding any mention of birth control, mainstream pro-life organizations will continue drawing on claims about conscience and the free exercise of religion in seeking exemptions for those providing any form of medical care, including abortion.[157] In the meantime, pro-life activists have no real reason to deviate from a strategy that plays to their strengths: targeting later-term abortions and seeking to stigmatize and discredit abortion providers. Indeed, even before the decision in *Whole Woman's Health*, there were signs that the movement had begun again to put more emphasis on the fetal-protective strategies that had inspired the movement at its founding and that continue to motivate most of its members. In the summer of 2015, for example, when the pro-life Center for Medical Progress's series leaked edited videos supposedly showing Planned Parenthood employees selling fetal tissue for profit, the attention paid to the strategy was a reminder that some in the movement felt it was time for a change of focus: they already believed that activists had waited too long to return to an emphasis on fetal rights.[158]

[157] On the importance that pro-choice and pro-life groups have attached to presidential elections, see Suzanne Staggenborg, *The Pro-Choice Movement: Organization and Activism in the Abortion Conflict* 133–37 (Oxford, 1991); Daniel K. Williams, *Defenders of the Unborn: The Pro-Life Movement Before Roe v. Wade* 239–42 (Oxford, 2015). For examples of the broader agenda adopted by pro-choice organizations, see NARAL Pro-Choice America, *What Is Choice?* (2016) (available at http://www.prochoiceamerica.org/what-is-choice/); Planned Parenthood Federation of America, *Who We Are* (2016) (available at https://www.plannedparenthood.org/about-us/who-we-are). On the importance of antiabortion conscience claims, see Elizabeth Deutsch, Note, *Expanding Conscience, Shrinking Care: The Crisis in Access to Reproductive Health Care and the Affordable Care Act's Nondiscrimination Mandate*, 124 Yale L J 2470 (2015). On the broader history and politics of conscience, see Reva B. Siegel and Douglas NeJaime, *Conscience Wars: Complicity-Based Conscience Claims in Religion and Politics*, 124 Yale L J 2516, 2542–89 (2015).

[158] On the Planned Parenthood videos put out by the Center for Medical Progress, see Manny Fernandez, *2 Abortion Foes Behind Planned Parenthood Videos Are Indicted*, NY Times

If *Whole Woman's Health* did not on its own push abortion opponents toward a renewed emphasis on fetal life, the Court's decision also did not begin a conflict about the facts of abortion. The basic dynamics of debate about the effects of abortion on women and unborn children have been in place for decades. It has always been a war waged not just with concrete proof but also with emotion and ideology. At least in the context of abortion, the degree to which factual claims convince people, including judges, has never depended entirely on the quality of evidence gathered by either side. As long as the abortion conflict rages on, the line between facts and ideology will be hard to draw.

(Jan 25, 2016) (available at http://www.nytimes.com/2016/01/26/us/2-abortion-foes-behind-planned-parenthood-videos-are-indicted.html?_r = 0).

JOHN RAPPAPORT

THE STRUCTURAL FUNCTION OF THE SIXTH AMENDMENT RIGHT TO COUNSEL OF CHOICE

The Sixth Amendment guarantees "the accused," "[i]n all criminal prosecutions," "the Assistance of Counsel for his defence."[1] The right to court-appointed, publicly funded counsel this language calls to mind today is a recent invention.[2] The "root meaning" of the Sixth Amendment's Counsel Clause, the Supreme Court has stressed—the one with ties to the founding tradition—is the right to retain counsel of one's choice.[3] Yet until just last Term, no criminal defendant had ever persuaded the Court to reverse a conviction solely on counsel-of-choice grounds; many had tried in vain. I consider in this article whether there is any satisfying, functional account that can explain the disjuncture between what the Court *says* about the

John Rappaport is Assistant Professor of Law, The University of Chicago Law School.

Author's note: The article benefited from excellent comments from Will Baude, Rich Chen, Andrew Crespo, Richard McAdams, Michael Morley, and Geof Stone, as well as presentation at the Loyola Constitutional Law Colloquium. Thanks to Matt Enloe, Jorgen Rehn, and especially Hannah Gelbort for helpful research assistance and to the Darelyn A. & Richard C. Reed Memorial Fund for financial support.

[1] US Const, Amend VI.

[2] See *Gideon v Wainwright*, 372 US 335 (1963).

[3] *United States v Gonzalez-Lopez*, 548 US 140, 147–48 (2006). See also *Kaley v United States*, 134 S Ct 1090, 1102 (2014).

978-0-226-49084-7/2017/2016-0004$10.00

right to counsel of choice and what it *does* when presented with an asserted violation of that right.

The leading academic and judicial theories justify the right to counsel of choice either as securing the effective assistance of counsel, and thus a fair trial, or as a facet of the defendant's prerogative to control his own defense. These theories, however—grounded in majestic-sounding notions of fairness and autonomy, respectively—struggle to explain counsel-of-choice doctrine. For one thing, indigent defendants—who number more than four out of every five—simply have no right to choose their counsel at all. And while criminal procedure rights are seldom absolute, balancing the defendant's fairness and autonomy interests against the government's countervailing needs cannot explain the pattern of Court decisions in anything but the most ad hoc manner. Seemingly unremarkable governmental interests prevail while a stronger one faltered this past Term.

My claim is that something very different makes sense of the Supreme Court's counsel-of-choice decisions. The failure of the leading theories, therefore, does not condemn the doctrine to incoherence. The right to counsel of choice, I argue, functions not as a powerful individual entitlement, as much of the judicial and scholarly writing suggests, but rather as a weak, system-level safeguard against socialization of the criminal defense bar. I use "socialization" here to refer to "the action or process of bringing" an institution "under state ownership or public control"—that is, not in the sense of social psychology but rather the political theory of socialism.[4] Only when the government advances a theory for restraining defendant choice that, if accepted, would allow it to strangle the private defense bar and socialize criminal defense does this antisocialization principle require that the right to counsel of choice prevail. This means that even a weak governmental interest—like a judge's desire to push a case to trial quickly—can overcome the right as long as that interest is meaningfully bounded in its reach across the criminal docket. But it also means that a law requiring all defendants to use court-appointed counsel—mandating a socialized defense bar—would violate the Sixth Amendment despite its equality-promoting effects.

An antisocialization principle explains, in particular—far better than a theory grounded in individual fairness or autonomy—last

[4] *Oxford English Dictionary* (Oxford, 3d ed 2009), archived at https://perma.cc/Q2LJ-UESL.

Term's counsel-of-choice decision, *Luis v United States*,[5] in which the Court for the first time found a stand-alone counsel-of-choice violation. The defendant in *Luis* was charged with health care fraud of around $45 million, almost all of which she had already spent. Seeking to preserve the $2 million remaining in the defendant's possession, which would be necessary to pay restitution and criminal penalties if the defendant were convicted, the government obtained a pretrial order prohibiting the defendant from dissipating her assets. This included the defendant's "untainted" assets—assets not traceable to her alleged crimes—which the defendant wished to spend to mount her criminal defense.[6]

Reversing the Eleventh Circuit Court of Appeals, a fractured Supreme Court held that the trial court's order violated the defendant's Sixth Amendment right to counsel of choice. Justice Breyer announced the Court's judgment in a four-Justice plurality opinion, joined by Chief Justice Roberts and Justices Ginsburg and Sotomayor. Justice Thomas concurred in the judgment, resting on a textual and historical analysis. Justice Kennedy, joined by Justice Alito, dissented, finding the case indistinguishable from precedent that had rebuffed similar counsel-of-choice claims. Justice Kagan also dissented, questioning whether that same precedent had been correctly decided.

An antisocialization theory—but neither fairness nor autonomy—cogently distinguishes *Luis* from all of the cases in which the Court rejected counsel-of-choice claims. That includes the two famous and closely related precedents the Justices in the majority strained to differentiate in *Luis*,[7] ultimately relying on unpersuasive statutory and historical formalisms that I will examine. Antisocialization can also begin to explain (though not necessarily justify) the complete denial of the counsel-of-choice right to indigent criminal defendants, a disquieting feature of the doctrine in light of equal-protection principles.

I explore these issues below. Part I introduces the leading theories courts and commentators have developed to justify the right to counsel of choice. It then exposes the inability of these theories to

---

[5] 136 S Ct 1083 (2016).

[6] Id at 1087–88 (Breyer, J) (plurality).

[7] *Caplin & Drysdale, Chartered v United States*, 491 US 617 (1989); *United States v Monsanto*, 491 US 600 (1989).

explain the doctrine. Part II demonstrates how an antisocialization theory better describes the law. In the tradition of criminal procedure scholarship seeking theories that reconcile the Court's decisions,[8] I do not argue that antisocialization *ought to* drive the doctrine; my project is positive, not normative. I seek to explain the law, not to justify it. Nevertheless, I do develop in Part II a *plausible* normative defense for the antisocialization theory in order to bolster my descriptive claim. The defense is sufficient to persuade me that *Luis* was correctly decided. Were I to craft my own justification for the counsel-of-choice right, however, it might well be markedly more robust.

My argument is not that antisocialization is the only fathomable theory that explains the doctrine. It is possible, for example, that counsel-of-choice doctrine tracks historical understandings of the right. Yet neither the Justices nor commentators have shown this to be generally true, leaving the burden of proof, for the time being, on the historical theory's would-be proponents. I am skeptical, though, I will add, that a historical theory would be as useful as the functional theory I explicate here, confronting, as it must, the familiar problem of what to do when formal materials (i.e., historical understandings) run out.[9]

In Part III, in lieu of a traditional conclusion, I step outside the Sixth Amendment to critique counsel-of-choice doctrine from an external perspective. The doctrine itself is young and undertheorized, and much remains to be worked out in due course. But regardless of how the Court resolves any outstanding Sixth Amendment questions, I argue in Part III that several of its counsel-of-choice precedents may run aground on other, settled constitutional protections. These are conflicts the Court should consider alongside Sixth Amendment principles as it continues to elaborate the right to counsel of choice.

---

[8] See, for example, William J. Stuntz, *Self-Incrimination and Excuse*, 88 Colum L Rev 1227, 1231–32 (1988) (arguing that "a great deal of the doctrine is consistent with what the Justices would have done had they . . . viewed the privilege" against self-incrimination in light of the author's excuse theory); Peter Westen and Richard Drubel, *Toward a General Theory of Double Jeopardy*, 1978 Supreme Court Review 81, 155 (offering a descriptive theory of double-jeopardy law and arguing that "[t]he measure of a theory is its usefulness in explaining the data—in this case the decisions of the Supreme Court").

[9] See Michael W. McConnell, *Time, Institutions, and Interpretation*, 95 BU L Rev 1745, 1761 (2015) (acknowledging, as an originalist, that "[w]hen history runs out, we have to use other methods of interpretation").

I. Difficulties with the Leading Descriptive Theories

Two principal theories—what I call fairness and autonomy—dominate judicial and scholarly thinking on the right to counsel of choice. Yet however well these theories might justify the right as a philosophical matter, they cannot explain counsel-of-choice doctrine. In this part, I describe the fairness and autonomy theories and illustrate the limits of their descriptive power. In particular, I show how these theories are unable cogently to distinguish *Luis*, in which the Court found a stand-alone violation of the defendant's right to counsel of choice, from the many cases in which it did not.[10]

A. Fairness

Probably the most popular theory of counsel of choice describes the right as helping the defendant secure a fair trial. This fairness theory is outcome-oriented and instrumental—it regards the right as a means to the ultimate end of fair adjudication in an adversary system. Perhaps more precisely, the fairness theory views the right to counsel of choice as securing the right to effective assistance of counsel, which itself ensures a fair adjudicatory process.

The plurality opinion in *Luis* (to the extent it is theorized at all) seems to rest upon this understanding. Although it acknowledges that the entitlement at stake is that to "counsel of choice," the plurality elides that right with the more "fundamental" right to counsel itself, without which the defendant, "though he be not guilty, . . . faces the

---

[10] There are several well-known decisions my analysis does not cover. In *Gonzalez-Lopez v United States*, 548 US 140 (2006), the case in which the Court first called the right to counsel of choice the "root meaning" of the Counsel Clause, the government had conceded a counsel-of-choice violation; the Court did not consider whether one had occurred. Id at 144. There are also two cases in which the Court is sometimes said to have found a violation of the right to counsel of choice, but which in fact involved deprivation of the right to counsel itself. See *Glasser v United States*, 315 US 60, 76 (1942) (holding that the trial court had denied the defendant "his right to have the effective assistance of counsel" by appointing the defendant's attorney to represent another defendant simultaneously); *Powell v Alabama*, 287 US 45, 58 (1932) (holding that defendants charged with rape "were not accorded the right of counsel in any substantial sense"). On *Powell*, see also *United States v Cronic*, 466 US 648, 660–61 (1984) (characterizing *Powell* as a case in which "the likelihood that counsel could have performed as an effective adversary was so remote as to have made the trial inherently unfair"); Lawrence M. Friedman, *Crime and Punishment in American History* 299, 376 (Basic, 1993) (describing the rape charge as "a complete fabrication" and the trial as "a scandal . . . thick with race prejudice" and asserting that "the defendants, practically speaking, had no help at all from their lawyers"); Janet C. Hoeffel, *Toward a More Robust Right to Counsel of Choice*, 44 San Diego L Rev 525, 529 (2007) ("*Powell* was not a case about right to counsel of choice.").

danger of conviction because he does not know how to establish his innocence."[11] Elsewhere the Court has "recognized that the purpose of providing assistance of counsel 'is simply to ensure that criminal defendants receive a fair trial,'" and thus, "while the right to select and be represented by one's preferred attorney is comprehended by the Sixth Amendment, the essential aim of the Amendment is to guarantee an effective advocate for each criminal defendant."[12]

There is a related position, which is sometimes portrayed as independent from the fairness theory, but which seems to me sufficiently related to warrant common treatment. That view regards the right to counsel of choice as facilitating a "meaningful relationship" between counsel and her client. The idea is that a criminal defendant will place greater trust in, and form a better relationship with, a lawyer he has selected rather than one the court has thrust upon him.[13] Upon inspection, however, most formulations of the "meaningful relationship" position are grounded in the belief that a better attorney-client relationship will enable a stronger defense.[14] The relationship is typically not thought to be valuable in its own right.

Some argue that good attorney-client relationships help legitimize case outcomes—that defendants will accept their fate more readily if they believe they received zealous representation from counsel they

[11] *Luis*, 136 S Ct at 1088–89 (Breyer, J) (plurality) (quotation mark omitted), quoting *Gideon v Wainwright*, 372 US 335, 345 (1963), quoting *Powell*, 287 US at 69.

[12] *Wheat v United States*, 486 US 153, 159 (1988), quoting *Strickland v Washington*, 466 US 668, 689 (1984). See also, for example, Bruce A. Green, *Lethal Fiction: The Meaning of "Counsel" in the Sixth Amendment*, 78 Iowa L Rev 433, 441 (1993) ("The right to choose counsel promotes the fairness and reliability of criminal proceedings. . . .").

[13] See, for example, *Luis*, 136 S Ct at 1089 (Breyer, J) (plurality); Green, 78 Iowa L Rev at 441 (cited in note 12); Hoeffel, 44 San Diego L Rev at 527, 542 (cited in note 10); Wayne D. Holly, *Rethinking the Sixth Amendment for the Indigent Criminal Defendant: Do Reimbursement Statutes Support Recognition of a Right to Counsel of Choice for the Indigent?*, 64 Brooklyn L Rev 181, 187–88, 207 (1998); Bruce J. Winick, *Forfeiture of Attorneys' Fees Under RICO and CCE and the Right to Counsel of Choice: The Constitutional Dilemma and How to Avoid It*, 43 U Miami L Rev 765, 802 (1989).

[14] See, for example, *Caplin & Drysdale, Chartered v United States*, 491 US 617, 645 (1989) (Blackmun, J, dissenting) (referring to "the trust between attorney and client that is necessary for the attorney to be a truly effective advocate"); *Morris v Slappy*, 461 US 1, 21 (1983) (Brennan, J, concurring in result) (asserting that "crucial decisions" of trial strategy "can best be made, and counsel's duties most effectively discharged, if the attorney and the defendant have a relationship characterized by trust and confidence"); Alfredo Garcia, *The Right to Counsel Under Siege: Requiem for an Endangered Right?*, 29 Am Crim L Rev 35, 95 (1991) ("An inextricable link exists between the confidence and trust a criminal defendant has in his lawyer and the effectiveness of the defense attorney."); Hoeffel, 44 San Diego L Rev at 541 (cited in note 10); Holly, 64 Brooklyn L Rev at 188 (cited in note 13); Winick, 43 U Miami L Rev at 802–04 (cited in note 13).

selected.[15] To the extent the outcomes being legitimized are substantively fair, this seems reasonable to me, though not meaningfully distinct from the fairness theory itself. To the extent that *unfair* outcomes will appear legitimate, it is far less clear that this plausibly justifies the right.

B. AUTONOMY

A second strand of legal thought—absent in *Luis*—maintains that the right to counsel of choice has intrinsic value as an aspect of the criminal defendant's individual autonomy and control over his own defense. Unlike the fairness theory, this autonomy theory is not outcome-oriented; it does not depend on an assumption or prediction about how counsel will affect the fairness or result of the defendant's proceedings. The right to counsel of choice, on this view, is valuable for its own sake, not because of the results it's thought to produce.[16]

The Supreme Court's opinion in *Gonzalez-Lopez v United States*[17] exemplifies the autonomy position. The Sixth Amendment "commands," the Court admonished in *Gonzalez-Lopez*, "not that a trial be fair, but that a particular guarantee of fairness be provided—to wit, that the accused be defended by the counsel he believes to be best."[18] This "right to select counsel of one's choice," the Court continued, "has never been derived from the Sixth Amendment's purpose of ensuring a fair trial" and should not be confused with the "right to effective counsel."[19] It "reflects constitutional protection of the defendant's free choice independent of concern for the objective fairness of the proceeding."[20]

---

[15] See, for example, *Caplin & Drysdale*, 491 US at 645 (Blackmun, J, dissenting) ("[T]he defendant's perception of the fairness of the process, and his willingness to acquiesce in its results, depend upon his confidence in his counsel's dedication, loyalty, and ability."); Garcia, 29 Am Crim L Rev at 96–97 (cited in note 14); Winick, 43 U Miami L Rev at 802 (cited in note 13).

[16] For a thorough normative defense of the criminal defendant's autonomy interest, see Erica J. Hashimoto, *Resurrecting Autonomy: The Criminal Defendant's Right to Control the Case*, 90 BU L Rev 1147 (2010). For a skeptical take, see Robert E. Toone, *The Incoherence of Defendant Autonomy*, 83 NC L Rev 621 (2005).

[17] 548 US 140 (2006).

[18] Id at 146.

[19] Id at 147, 148.

[20] *Flanagan v United States*, 465 US 259, 268 (1984). Of course, some jurists subscribe to both the fairness and autonomy views. See, for example, *Wheat*, 486 US at 165–66 (Marshall, J, dissenting) (arguing that "a primary purpose of the Sixth Amendment is to grant a

Much scholarly commentary on the right to counsel of choice accords with this view, agreeing that "the most important decision a defendant makes in shaping his defense is his selection of an attorney."[21] The attorney acts, among other things, as conduit for the defendant's "communicative activity in the public forum of the courtroom"; respect for the defendant's choice of counsel is thus "'respect for the individual'" himself.[22] One commentator, analogizing to the right to self-representation, aptly quoted the Court's sharp language from that context: "An unwanted counsel 'represents' the defendant only through a tenuous and unacceptable legal fiction. Unless the accused has acquiesced in such representation, the defense presented is not the defense guaranteed by the Constitution, for, in a very real sense, it is not his defense."[23]

C. THE THEORIES' DESCRIPTIVE SHORTCOMINGS

The fairness and autonomy theories for the right to counsel of choice are perfectly lucid as a philosophical matter. What they lack, however, is any real explanatory power. If the theories did explain the doctrine, they would be able to distinguish *Luis*, in which the Court found a counsel-of-choice violation, from the many cases in which it did not. Yet as I show in this section, neither theory is up to this task. Specifically, neither theory is able persuasively to differ-

---

criminal defendant effective control over the conduct of his defense" because "'it is he who suffers the consequences if the defense fails,'" but also that "lodging the selection of counsel with the defendant generally will promote the fairness and integrity of criminal trials"), quoting *Faretta v California*, 422 US 806, 819–20 (1975).

[21] Winick, 43 U Miami L Rev at 803 (cited in note 13), quoting *United States v Laura*, 607 F2d 52, 56 (3d Cir 1979); Holly, 64 Brooklyn L Rev at 189 (cited in note 13).

[22] Winick, 43 U Miami L Rev at 803 (cited in note 13), quoting *Wilson v Mintzes*, 761 F2d 275, 286 (6th Cir 1985). Public defense reformers, by developing a "client-centered" model of representation, have worked to effectuate defendant autonomy even when defendants cannot choose their counsel. See, for example, Robin Steinberg and David Feige, *Cultural Revolution: Transforming the Public Defender's Office*, 29 NYU Rev L & Soc Change 123 (2004).

[23] Winick, 43 U Miami L Rev at 804 (cited in note 13) (quotation marks omitted), quoting *Faretta*, 422 US at 821. For additional academic commentary supporting the autonomy theory, see Garcia, 29 Am Crim L Rev at 92–98 (cited in note 14); Green, 78 Iowa L Rev at 442 (cited in note 12); Hoeffel, 44 San Diego L Rev at 543–44 (cited in note 10); Eugene L. Shapiro, *The Sixth Amendment Right to Counsel of Choice: An Exercise in the Weighing of Unarticulated Values*, 43 SC L Rev 345, 385 (1992); Note, *Rethinking the Boundaries of the Sixth Amendment Right to Choice of Counsel*, 124 Harv L Rev 1550, 1571 (2011).

entiate *Luis* from three sets of counsel-of-choice precedents that capture most, if not all, of the Supreme Court's work in this domain: (1) cases involving the inherent powers of the trial court to control litigation; (2) fee-forfeiture cases involving "tainted" (rather than "untainted") assets; and (3) cases involving indigent criminal defendants.

1. *Inherent powers.* Mundane decisions courts make in the course of criminal litigation, or even antecedent choices regarding judicial administration, can have the effect of denying a criminal defendant his first-choice aide. Consider three examples. In one case, the court denies a midtrial continuance necessary to accommodate the desired attorney's schedule. In another, it prohibits counsel from representing the defendant alongside two of his codefendants, notwithstanding conflict-of-interest waivers from all of the defendants concerned. And in the third, it simply enforces court rules barring practice by nonlawyers, disbarred lawyers, and lawyers from out of state.

In none of these cases, the Court has said, does the trial court violate the defendant's right to counsel of choice.[24] But the trial court's actions in each instance certainly implicate the defendant's fairness and autonomy interests. The defendant who was denied a continuance, for example, argued that the lawyer assigned to him had not zealously represented his interests.[25] Disagreeing, the Court denied his claim and expressly rejected the lower court's position, rooted in the fairness theory, that the right to counsel of choice safeguards a "meaningful relationship" between the defendant and his attorney.[26] Likewise, deciding to roll the dice with a lay representative[27] or

[24] See *Wheat*, 486 US at 159 (conflict of interest); *Slappy*, 461 US at 13 (continuance); Note, 124 Harv L Rev at 1554 (cited in note 23) ("No Supreme Court case has turned directly on the question of whether choice of counsel may be limited entirely to current members of the bar, but the Court has clearly asserted this much in dicta."). But see, for example, *United States v Whitesel*, 543 F2d 1176, 1179 (6th Cir 1976) (rejecting strict equation of "counsel" with "attorneys at law").

[25] *Slappy*, 461 US at 8.

[26] Id at 13–14.

[27] See, for example, Green, 78 Iowa L Rev at 470–71 (cited in note 12); Mindy D. Block, Comment, *The Criminal Defendant's Sixth Amendment Right to Lay Representation*, 52 U Chi L Rev 460, 470 (1985). See also *Faretta*, 422 US at 820 n 16 (observing that "[t]he first lawyers were personal friends of the litigant, brought into court by him so that he might 'take "counsel" with them' before pleading," and "the first 'attorneys' were personal agents, often lacking any professional training"), quoting Frederick Pollock and Frederic William Maitland, 1 *The History of English Law Before the Time of Edward I* 211 (Cambridge, 2d ed 1898).

one subject to a potential conflict of interest[28] would seem to fall squarely within the autonomy-premised right to control one's defense. This is the same interest, notably, that supports the right to self-representation, which requires the trial court to let an uneducated defendant represent himself.[29] At the very least, these outcomes are difficult to reconcile with the type of robust individual protection the Court's "root meaning" language implies.

Of course, observing that the right fails in some cases to protect the defendant's interests—whether rooted in fairness or autonomy—may suggest nothing more than that those interests were outweighed by the government's countervailing needs through a process of interest-balancing. Yet if counsel-of-choice doctrine reflects a weighing of fairness or autonomy interests, on the one hand, and government need, on the other, we would expect the government to prevail when it matters most and lose when it matters least—especially as the defendants' interests seem roughly equivalent across the cases.[30]

The doctrine does not line up this way, however. This is a point that was harder to see before *Luis*, because the government's interests had prevailed in *every* case. That they fell short in *Luis* suggests—if the doctrine indeed reflects a balance of the defendant's fairness or autonomy interests against state prerogatives—that the government interest in *Luis* was weaker than in all the prior cases. But that is a difficult position to maintain. In the earlier cases, the government won by asserting interests such as the "great deal of latitude" necessary "in scheduling trials,"[31] the desire to ensure that "legal proceedings appear fair to all who observe them,"[32] and "the legitimate wish of district courts that their judgments remain intact on appeal."[33] In *Luis*, it had what the Court has elsewhere characterized as a "strong governmental interest in obtaining full recovery of all for-

---

[28] See Bruce A. Green, *"Through a Glass, Darkly": How the Court Sees Motions to Disqualify Criminal Defense Lawyers*, 89 Colum L Rev 1201, 1233–38 (1989) (criticizing the Court's conflict-of-interest precedent on autonomy grounds).

[29] *Faretta*, 422 US at 833.

[30] See Stuntz, 88 Colum L Rev at 1236 (cited in note 8) (making the point for self-incrimination doctrine).

[31] *Slappy*, 461 US at 11.

[32] *Wheat*, 486 US at 160.

[33] Id at 161. See Green, 89 Colum L Rev at 1239–48 (cited in note 28) (arguing that the Court's reliance on the institutional interests of the judiciary is misguided).

feitable assets,"[34] which aims to punish and deter serious crimes.[35] If there is a theory as to why that "strong governmental interest" is actually weaker than the trial court's interest in controlling litigation by, say, denying a continuance, the Court has never disclosed it.

The point is not that balancing is irrelevant, or in no way enhances the explanatory power of the leading theories. Rather, the point is that, to transcend simplistic, ad hoc explanations, balancing—to borrow from Professor William Stuntz—"must reflect some underlying theoretical structure."[36] Where, as here, the interests on each side of the balance are neither trivial nor overwhelming, "balancing without structure explains all results equally well; it is not so much a positive theory as a confession that no positive theory exists."[37] "The real challenge," I agree with Stuntz, "is to explain why the balances are struck as they are in particular cases, and to do so in a way that allows one to assess, at least in broad terms, whether the doctrine is internally coherent."[38] Proponents of the fairness and autonomy theories have produced no such explanation, and I am doubtful that they can.

2. *Fee forfeiture.* A pair of fee-forfeiture cases the Court decided in 1989 framed the issues it considered in *Luis*. In *Caplin & Drysdale, Chartered v United States*,[39] the Court held that the Sixth Amendment permits Congress to authorize postconviction forfeiture of so-called "tainted" assets, traceable to criminal activity, even when the defendant seeks to spend the assets to pay the lawyers who defended him.[40] The same thing goes, the Court said in *United States v Monsanto*,[41] for a *pretrial* order freezing assets the government alleges are tainted and therefore forfeitable.[42]

---

[34] *Caplin & Drysdale, Chartered v United States*, 491 US 617, 631 (1989). The plurality in *Luis* characterized this governmental interest as lying fairly far from the "heart of a fair, effective criminal justice system." 136 S Ct at 1093 (Breyer, J) (plurality). Of course, the same can be said, probably more strongly, of the government interests asserted in the prior cases.

[35] On the forfeiture statute's aims, see Winick, 43 U Miami L Rev at 833–34 (cited in note 13).

[36] Stuntz, 88 Colum L Rev at 1237 (cited in note 8).

[37] Id (citation omitted).

[38] Id.

[39] 491 US 617 (1989).

[40] Id at 632–33.

[41] 491 US 600 (1989).

[42] Id at 616.

The Court's reasoning went like this: (1) tainted assets, though in the defendant's possession, are "not rightfully his," and (2) the defendant has "no Sixth Amendment right to spend another person's money for services rendered by an attorney, even if those funds are the only way that that defendant will be able to retain the attorney of his choice."[43] Put another way, "impecunious defendants have [no] Sixth Amendment right to choose their counsel," and a defendant whose assets are tainted properly counts as "impecunious."[44]

Any tainted assets, it bears noting, will not be *proven* forfeitable until conviction, by which time the defense attorneys, having rendered services, will have established an interest in them. Yet through a statutory relation-back provision, title in the tainted assets vests in the United States at the time of the criminal act triggering forfeiture, giving the government a claim to the assets superior to the lawyers'.[45] And the pretrial order in *Monsanto*—entered, of course, long before conviction—is analogous to pretrial detention of the defendant himself. It is, in other words, a restraint on the defendant's property "to protect its 'appearance' at trial and protect the community's interest in full recovery of any ill-gotten gains."[46]

It seems uncontroversial to say that the restraint of assets with which a criminal defendant wishes to pay his attorney intrudes on the fairness and autonomy interests the right to counsel of choice is said to protect. Rendered indigent, or at least less wealthy, the defendant may be forced to proceed with less-qualified counsel and fewer total defense resources, weakening his ability to compete with the prosecution in an adversarial setting and depriving him of some control over his own defense. If the fairness and autonomy theories are to explain these cases, therefore, it must be because the "strong governmental interest in obtaining full recovery of all forfeitable assets" outweighs the defendants' interests.[47] And indeed, considered in isolation, this does not seem like a far-fetched proposition. The principal difficulty is how to reconcile these earlier cases with the defendant's victory in *Luis*. Neither the fairness nor the autonomy theory explains why the Court reached the opposite result in that case.

---

[43] *Caplin & Drysdale*, 491 US at 626.

[44] Id at 624.

[45] Id at 626–28.

[46] *Monsanto*, 491 US at 615–16.

[47] *Caplin & Drysdale*, 491 US at 631.

The key distinction between *Monsanto* and *Luis*—to focus on the closest cousins—is that *Monsanto* involved the restraint of allegedly tainted assets, but in *Luis* the money was concededly clean.[48] How does that affect the Sixth Amendment analysis under the fairness and autonomy theories? As an initial matter, whether the assets are tainted does not affect the defendant's fairness and autonomy interests. Her interests in controlling her defense and obtaining a fair adjudication are the same regardless of what kind of money she seeks to spend. The explanation, if there is one, must instead be that the government's argument for recovering tainted assets is stronger than for untainted assets. The *Luis* plurality can be read to take this position. Its formalistic reasoning, however, is unpersuasive—at least to one in search of a functional theory.

The plurality characterized the distinction between tainted and untainted assets as "the difference between what is yours and what is mine."[49] Under the statutory relation-back provision, the plurality reminded, title to tainted assets passes to the government at the time the crime is committed.[50] The same is not true, it implied,[51] of untainted assets: "regarding her untainted assets," the defendant can, before trial, "reasonably claim that the property is still 'mine,' free and clear."[52] This move allowed the plurality to characterize the government's interest in "obtaining payment of a criminal forfeiture or restitution order" using untainted assets as "contingent," lacking in "constitutional protection," and, compared to the right to counsel of choice, "further from the heart of a fair, effective criminal justice system."[53]

The distinction between tainted and untainted assets cannot bear the weight the plurality puts upon it.[54] First, while it is true that the government does not own forfeitable untainted assets before con-

[48] The government went after the defendant's "substitute" assets in *Luis* because, it alleged, the defendant had already spent the proceeds of her crime—the kind of "tainted" assets held forfeitable in *Caplin & Drysdale* and *Monsanto*. See *Luis*, 136 S Ct at 1087–88 (Breyer, J) (plurality).

[49] Id at 1091.

[50] Id at 1092, citing 21 USC § 853(c).

[51] But see, for example, *United States v McHan*, 345 F3d 262, 270–72 (4th Cir 2003).

[52] *Luis*, 136 S Ct at 1092 (Breyer, J) (plurality).

[53] Id at 1093.

[54] This is not to deny that the distinction mattered at common law, or that it retains significance in certain legal contexts today.

viction, the same is true of forfeitable *tainted* assets. What the Court consistently calls "tainted" assets are, after all, only *allegedly* tainted assets.[55] Until conviction, "[t]he defendant maintains ownership of either type, with the Government holding only a contingent interest."[56] What made the pretrial order constitutionally permissible in *Monsanto* is that the defendant's assets were (prima facie) *forfeitable*, not that they were *tainted*.[57] The assets in that case happened to be forfeitable *because* they were tainted, but that does not mean that assets Congress deems forfeitable for some other reason—such as to substitute for tainted assets already dissipated—are of a different constitutional order.

Put another way, to say the government can freeze tainted but not untainted assets is to beg the question. The purpose of the trial—in either case—is to *determine whether* the assets are the defendant's or are instead forfeitable because the defendant committed a crime. Before trial, when the assets are restrained, the answer to this question is unknown. The reason the *Monsanto* Court thought tainted assets aren't "the defendant's" up until conviction was simply that Congress said so—Congress said they could be frozen upon a showing of probable cause.[58] Congress said the exact same thing here, with respect to untainted, substitute assets.[59]

Second, the relation-back doctrine—which the *Luis* plurality seemed to think applies to tainted but not untainted assets—is beside the point. "The doctrine's purpose is to prevent defendants from avoiding forfeiture by transferring their property to third parties"; it does not, however, "alter the time at which title to forfeitable property passes to the Government."[60] Nor is it clear why Congress's statutory treatment of property is relevant to a Sixth Amendment

[55] See id at 1112 (Kagan, J, dissenting) ("[T]he plurality's use of the word 'tainted,' to describe assets at the pre-conviction stage, makes an unwarranted assumption about the defendant's guilt. Because the Government has not yet shown that the defendant committed the crime charged, it also has not shown that allegedly tainted assets are actually so.") (citation omitted).

[56] Id; id at 1106–07 (Kennedy, J, dissenting).

[57] See *Monsanto*, 491 US at 615; *United States v Wingerter*, 369 F Supp 2d 799, 810 (ED Va 2005).

[58] *Monsanto*, 491 US at 611–14, discussing 21 USC § 853(e).

[59] See *Luis*, 136 S Ct at 1108 (Kennedy, J, dissenting), discussing 18 USC § 1345.

[60] *Luis*, 136 S Ct at 1107 (Kennedy, J, dissenting). See also Winick, 43 U Miami L Rev at 835 (cited in note 13) (discussing legislative history).

analysis. If relation-back applies only to tainted assets, that fact is simply a matter of "congressional whim[ ]."[61] It is hard to imagine that, if Congress extended relation-back to untainted, substitute assets, the plurality would change its tune. But that is what the logic of its analysis implies.

Finally, because money is fungible, "the plurality's approach leads to utterly arbitrary distinctions as among criminal defendants who are in fact guilty."[62] To borrow an example from Justice Kennedy's dissent, imagine a thief who steals $1 million and wins another $1 million in a lottery. If he spends his lottery winnings on fancy cars and meals, and then needs money for defense counsel, he's out of luck; the government can restrain the stolen funds. But if he spends the stolen money first, he can use the lottery winnings to pay an attorney.[63] This is senseless: "the Government's and the defendant's respective legal interests" in the two pots of money—tainted and untainted—"are exactly the same."[64]

Justice Thomas's concurring opinion, I should add, fares no better. Thomas argued, essentially, that the original understanding of the Counsel Clause protects the defendant's right to spend his money to employ a defense attorney; that that right necessarily implies some limit on the government's ability to restrain the defendant's assets before trial; and that the common-law practice permitting pretrial restraint of tainted but not untainted assets supplies that necessary limit.[65]

There are several problems with Justice Thomas's position for my purposes. First, Thomas expressly eschews any interest in an analysis that demands functional reasons for the distinctions it draws.[66] Historical practice is Thomas's lodestone, however much (or little) sense it makes. Second, it is far from clear that Justice Thomas advances a theory of the *Sixth Amendment* at all, as opposed to a theory about the due process prerequisites to the restraint of any individual's untainted assets. Thomas argues that a defendant's untainted assets

[61] *Luis*, 136 S Ct at 1108 (Kennedy, J, dissenting).

[62] Id at 1113 (Kagan, J, dissenting), citing id at 1108–09 (Kennedy, J, dissenting).

[63] Id at 1103 (Kennedy, J, dissenting).

[64] Id at 1112 (Kagan, J, dissenting).

[65] Id at 1096–97 (Thomas, J, concurring in judgment).

[66] Id at 1101.

may not be restrained before trial whether he wishes to spend them on a defense attorney or something else entirely.[67] This suggests that the Sixth Amendment itself is actually doing precious little work. Finally, even if historical practice does adequately reconcile *Luis* with the prior forfeiture cases, Justice Thomas makes no attempt to show that it also explains the Court's other counsel-of-choice precedents, declining to engage that body of law at all. As I acknowledged at the outset, it remains theoretically possible that all of the Court's decisions happen to align with historical understandings, but I am doubtful, and neither the Court nor commentators have done the work to prove it.

* * *

In sum, because the *defendant's* interest in counsel of choice is the same regardless whether he wishes to pay his attorney with tainted or untainted assets, the fairness and autonomy theories can explain the forfeiture cases only if the *government's* side of the balance is weightier in the former case than in the latter. There is, however, no good functional account of why *that* would be so. The forfeiture cases thus detract significantly from the explanatory power of these leading theories of the right.

3. *Indigence.* The notion that indigent criminal defendants might retain a Sixth Amendment right to counsel of choice has been, to the Court, a nonstarter.[68] "It is hornbook law," one commentator wrote, "that indigent defendants have no right to counsel of choice."[69] If the dominant theories are correct, this must be because (for reasons absent in *Luis*) assigning counsel to these defendants is not unfair, does not intrude on autonomy interests, or is justified by overriding governmental interests—or some combination of the three. All of these arguments, however, are weaker than they may at first seem. I address each one in turn.

---

[67] Id at 1099.

[68] See, for example, *Gonzalez-Lopez*, 548 US at 151 ("[T]he right to counsel of choice does not extend to defendants who require counsel to be appointed for them."); *Caplin & Drysdale*, 491 US at 624 ("Petitioner does not, nor could it defensibly do so, assert that impecunious defendants have a Sixth Amendment right to choose their counsel."); *Wheat*, 486 US at 159 ("[A] defendant may not insist on representation by an attorney he cannot afford. . . .); *Slappy*, 461 US at 23 n 5 (Brennan, J, concurring in result) (calling the defendant's "right to choose his own counsel" a "right that indigent defendants do not enjoy").

[69] Vivian O. Berger, *The Supreme Court and Defense Counsel: Old Roads, New Paths—A Dead End?*, 86 Colum L Rev 9, 49 n 207 (1986).

a) *Fairness.*—Consider what would have happened to the defendant in *Luis* had the Court ruled against her and deemed her untainted assets unavailable to pay counsel. There is no suggestion that she would have been forced through trial unaided by "the guiding hand of counsel."[70] Of course not. Instead, the court would have appointed an attorney to represent her—either a public defender or a private attorney funded under the Criminal Justice Act.[71] Such an appointment could have threatened to injure the defendant (under a fairness theory) only if there were an unacceptable risk that appointed counsel would fail to provide the effective assistance of counsel necessary to make the trial fair.

One of two conclusions follows. First, it may be that forcing the defendant to proceed with appointed counsel would *not* have jeopardized her right to a fair trial, and thus should not have been deemed to violate her right to counsel of choice. Indeed, the Court has repeatedly rejected any presumption that appointed counsel are categorically ineffective or less effective than retained counsel.[72] Effectiveness must be judged, the Court has instructed, after the fact, on a case-by-case basis.[73]

As an empirical matter, this is not an unreasonable conclusion. One federal government study, for example, found that conviction rates and average sentences were similar for defendants represented by publicly financed and private attorneys.[74] And federal judges rate public defenders as superior to (and court-appointed counsel as equal

[70] *Powell*, 287 US at 69.

[71] See 18 USC § 3006A.

[72] See, for example, *Cronic*, 466 US at 658 (holding, in a case of appointed counsel, that "we presume that the lawyer is competent to provide the guiding hand that the defendant needs"); *Cuyler v Sullivan*, 446 US 335, 344 (1980) ("We may assume with confidence that most counsel, whether retained or appointed, will protect the rights of an accused.").

[73] See, for example, *Strickland v Washington*, 466 US 668 (1984); *Cronic*, 466 US at 666. But see Lauren Sudeall Lucas, *Reclaiming Equality to Reframe Indigent Defense Reform*, 97 Minn L Rev 1197, 1216–20 (2013) (discussing preconviction ineffective-assistance-of-counsel claims).

[74] Caroline Wolf Harlow, *Special Report: Defense Counsel in Criminal Cases* *1 (US Dept of Justice, Bureau of Justice Statistics, Nov 2000), archived at https://perma.cc/8XRU-48RX. See also Richard D. Hartley, Holly Ventura Miller, and Cassia Spohn, *Do You Get What You Pay For? Type of Counsel and Its Effect on Criminal Court Outcomes*, 38 J Crim Just 1063, 1067 (2010) (determining, based on data from Cook County, Illinois, that type of counsel—public defender versus private attorney—has no statistically significant impact on the court's decision to incarcerate or the defendant's sentence length). For a helpful review of the literature comparing outcomes among different criminal attorney types, as well as an original analysis, see Thomas H. Cohen, *Who Is Better at Defending Criminals? Does Type of Defense Attorney Matter in Terms of Producing Favorable Case Outcomes?*, 25 Crim Just Pol Rev 29, 32–33 (2014).

to) private criminal defense lawyers.[75] But such a conclusion—that public and private attorneys are equally effective—would mean that the fairness theory fails to explain the *Luis* decision.

There is, however, an alternate conclusion one might draw. Perhaps forcing the defendant in *Luis* to use a public attorney would indeed have exposed her to an unacceptable risk of deficient representation and jeopardized her fair-trial right. After all, crushing resource constraints plague public defense nationwide.[76] Appointed counsel often work under conditions no paying client would tolerate, and ethical rules discourage.[77] Some data suggest that results may suffer.[78] The Court in *Luis*, on this assumption, narrowly rescued the defendant from "injury by public defender."[79]

On this view, the outcome in *Luis* was correct. But consider the implications. Appointed counsel is the norm, not the exception, in criminal defense. Roughly 80 percent of all criminal defendants—and probably a higher share of capital defendants—rely on court-appointed lawyers to defend them.[80] If forcing the defendant in

---

[75] See Richard A. Posner and Albert H. Yoon, *What Judges Think of the Quality of Legal Representation*, 63 Stan L Rev 317, 319, 325–26 & nn 30–31 (2011).

[76] See, for example, *Justice Denied: America's Continuing Neglect of Our Constitutional Right to Counsel* *50 (The Constitution Project, National Right to Counsel Committee, Apr 2009), archived at https://perma.cc/N33T-L95J.

[77] See Donald J. Farole Jr. and Lynn Langton, *Special Report: County-Based and Local Public Defender Offices, 2007* *1 (US Dept of Justice, Bureau of Justice Statistics, Sept 2010), archived at https://perma.cc/6X3B-6QYD ("About three-quarters (73%) of county-based public defender offices exceeded the maximum recommended limit of cases received per attorney in 2007."). See also Preeti Lala, *Notes from the Field: Challenges of Indigent Criminal Defense*, 12 NY City L Rev 203, 224–26 (2008).

[78] See Harlow, *Special Report* at *1 (cited in note 74) (reporting that, "of those found guilty, higher percentages of defendants with publicly financed counsel were sentenced to incarceration"); Morris B. Hoffman, Paul H. Rubin, and Joanna M. Shepherd, *An Empirical Study of Public Defender Effectiveness: Self-Selection by the "Marginally Indigent,"* 3 Ohio St J Crim L 223 (2005) (finding, based on Colorado data, that public defenders achieved poorer outcomes than their privately retained counterparts); Marian R. Williams, *The Effectiveness of Public Defenders in Four Florida Counties*, 41 J Crim Just 205, 211 (2013) (demonstrating that, even with an "above-average public defender system," private attorneys in Florida obtain better outcomes than public defenders), citing Marian R. Williams, *A Comparison of Sentencing Outcomes for Defendants with Public Defenders versus Retained Counsel in a Florida Circuit Court*, 23 Just Sys J 249 (2002).

[79] Consider Judith Resnik, *Trial as Error, Jurisdiction as Injury: Transforming the Meaning of Article III*, 113 Harv L Rev 924 (2000).

[80] See Harlow, *Special Report* at *1 (cited in note 74); *Slamming the Courthouse Doors: Denial of Access to Justice and Remedy in America* *7 (ACLU, Dec 2010), archived at https://perma.cc/G5B7-6TWL ("With rare exceptions, defendants facing capital charges cannot afford a lawyer, and therefore rely on the state to appoint an attorney to provide an adequate defense.").

Luis to rely on a public defender would have been unfair, then what of all these other defendants? To explain *Luis* on a fairness theory, in other words, is to destabilize the whole regime of indigent defense, cracking the very foundation of our contemporary criminal justice system.[81]

The Court can't have it both ways. Either appointed counsel are presumptively effective notwithstanding the constraints under which they operate—in which case the fairness theory cannot explain the outcome in *Luis*—or they're not, in which case *Luis* is correct but implicitly acknowledges a constitutional crisis.

b) *Autonomy*.—If the fairness theory fails to explain the outcome in *Luis*, perhaps autonomy can fare better. The challenge here is to explain why the assignment of counsel would violate the autonomy interests of the defendant in *Luis* but not of the myriad indigent defendants. This task is not as easy as it might first seem. After all, at the moment she needed to pay counsel, the defendant in *Luis was* effectively indigent, her assets having been frozen.[82] She prevailed by persuading the Court to focus on an earlier time, immediately before the asset freeze, when she still had cash to spend. Yet certainly some other indigent defendants could also point to a previous moment at which they were not indigent, and to the intervening events that led them into poverty. Why is this particular intervention—a pretrial order freezing untainted assets—the only one thought to intrude impermissibly on the defendant's autonomy interests?

The explanation must be that it matters *why* the defendant is indigent: In *Luis*, the government reached out and restrained the defendant's money, whereas restraints on the typical indigent defendant's finances (and thus his autonomy) are exogenously determined. This explanation, though, however plausible on the surface, can be sustained only by resort to notoriously slippery conceptual distinctions and arbitrary framing devices.

---

[81] See *Luis*, 136 S Ct at 1110 (Kennedy, J, dissenting) ("Given the large volume of defendants in the criminal justice system who rely on public representation, it would be troubling to suggest that a defendant who might be represented by a public defender will receive inadequate representation."). Consider also *Kaley v United States*, 134 S Ct 1090, 1102 n 13 (2014) (observing that, if forcing defendants to proceed with appointed counsel—by freezing their assets pretrial—jeopardizes the trial's fairness, "the right way to start correcting the problem is not" by according more procedural protections before the asset restraint, "but by ensuring that the right to effective counsel is fully vindicated" by appointed counsel).

[82] See *Luis*, 136 S Ct at 1110 (Kennedy, J, dissenting) (describing the defendant as someone who "simply cannot afford the legal team she desires").

Consider first some of the ways an indigent criminal defendant may have ended up indigent. Perhaps he was born into poverty, his employer paid him too little, or the bank foreclosed on his home. In each instance, one might argue, some private party, not the government, bears responsibility. In *Luis*, by contrast, *the government*, not any private actor, took the defendant's money. But why look at things this way? As an initial matter, if the defendant in *Luis* had simply been wealthier—if she had had $100 million in her accounts instead of $2 million—she could have afforded private counsel even after the asset freeze.[83] Why not attribute her inability to retain counsel to her (very relative) impecuniousness—which, of course, may well have resulted from private action—rather than focus on the trial court's order?[84]

More fundamentally, the public/private distinction—which supplies the intuition that *the government* taking a defendant's money is different from a *private party* doing so—is, at least in contemporary society, a porous one. Our indigent defendant was born into poverty partly because estate law allows wealthy individuals to bequeath their fortunes to heirs rather than redistributing them widely; his wages were too low partly because labor and employment law required no more; and he lost his home partly because financial regulations permitted subprime lending to unqualified buyers. In a well-regulated society, in other words, private parties always act on the permission or forbearance of the government; the government's fingerprints are everywhere.[85]

Still, one might respond, in none of these examples did the government actually *do* anything to the now-indigent defendant.[86] The grievance is that the government didn't help him enough, or that it

---

[83] See *Caplin & Drysdale*, 491 US at 625 ("The forfeiture statute does not prevent a defendant who has nonforfeitable assets from retaining any attorney of his choosing.").

[84] Consider generally Mark Kelman, *Interpretive Construction in the Substantive Criminal Law*, 33 Stan L Rev 591 (1981) (arguing that answers to legal controversies in criminal law often follow from nonrational, interpretive constructs that frame up the controversies out of factual scenarios).

[85] For arguments developing this "baselines" critique, see, for example, Louis Michael Seidman and Mark V. Tushnet, *Remnants of Belief: Contemporary Constitutional Issues* 49–71 (Oxford, 1996); Cass Sunstein, *The Partial Constitution* (Harvard, 1993).

[86] Consider, for example, *Flagg Brothers, Inc. v Brooks*, 436 US 149, 160 n 10 (1978) ("It would intolerably broaden, beyond the scope of any of our previous cases, the notion of state action under the Fourteenth Amendment to hold that the mere existence of a body of property law in a State, whether decisional or statutory, itself amounted to 'state action' even though no process or state officials were ever involved in enforcing that body of law.").

should have structured society differently. In *Luis*, by contrast, the government's involvement was not limited to framing the background conditions in which private parties compete for wealth. In *Luis*, the government *took* the defendant's money—it reached out and literally "rendered [the defendant] indigent."[87] And while "a State need not equalize economic conditions" among criminal defendants, prejudice "resulting from a money hurdle erected by a State" is nonetheless unconstitutional.[88]

For essentially the same reasons that the public/private distinction falters in this context, though, this act/omission distinction fails to hold up as well. It is wholly arbitrary to describe the government as having (passively) "allowed" wealthy individuals to bequeath their wealth, having "allowed" private employers to pay low wages or prohibit collective bargaining, or having "allowed" banks to issue irresponsible loans. One could just as readily say that the government, having considered the alternatives, *selected* (i.e., *acted to adopt*) rules that favored powerful testators, employers, and banks.[89] So the government may have "acted" in *Luis* in a way that reduced the defendant's wealth, but the same can be said in the case of many indigent defendants.[90]

The conceptual problems don't stop there. Suppose we put these academic quibbles to the side and posit that the government really did, in some meaningful sense, take the defendant's money in *Luis*. One might be tempted to respond, "What else is new?" The government takes money from individuals all the time, without regard for whether they're facing criminal charges, and it's never thought to raise a Sixth Amendment issue. Taxation is only the most salient example. All sorts of agencies—say, the Securities and Exchange Commission or Customs and Border Protection—are empowered to restrain assets in pursuit of their regulatory objectives. They can

---

[87] *Luis*, 136 S Ct at 1095 (Breyer, J) (plurality).

[88] *Griffin v Illinois*, 351 US 12, 23 (1956) (Frankfurter, J, concurring in judgment).

[89] There are numerous sophisticated critiques of the act/omission distinction with respect to the government. See, for example, Susan Bandes, *The Negative Constitution: A Critique*, 88 Mich L Rev 2271, 2312–13 (1990); Christopher Serkin, *Passive Takings: The State's Affirmative Duty to Protect Property*, 113 Mich L Rev 345, 372–77 (2014); David A. Strauss, *Discriminatory Intent and the Taming of Brown*, 56 U Chi L Rev 935, 968 (1989); Cass R. Sunstein and Adrian Vermeule, *Is Capital Punishment Morally Required? Acts, Omissions, and Life-Life Tradeoffs*, 58 Stan L Rev 703, 719–28 (2005).

[90] See *United States v Brodson*, 241 F2d 107, 111 (7th Cir 1957) ("[T]he manner in which the defendant is rendered indigent is immaterial.").

also file civil suit, creating obligations to pay judgments or settlements.[91] Any of these could be the cause-in-fact of a criminal defendant's indigence. How do we know which government money-seizures matter for Sixth Amendment purposes?

There has to be some theory akin to proximate cause to sort the constitutionally relevant causes from the irrelevant ones. Yet proximate cause itself is famously circular—there is no reliable way to decide, in a nonarbitrary fashion, which causes are proximate.[92] Temporal proximity doesn't work. True, the government froze the defendant's assets in *Luis* the same day it filed criminal charges.[93] But a large tax bill might have come due the following day,[94] or the IRS might have filed a jeopardy assessment to restrain the very same assets.[95] Neither of these occurrences would have sounded Sixth Amendment alarms.[96] And even if the asset freeze *were* the closest-in-time occurrence, money is constantly flowing between the government and would-be defendants' hands. Why focus only on the very last exchange rather than letting the government offset the money it froze by pointing to benefits it had conferred upon the defendant, say in the recent past?[97]

Nor does it help to point out that a pretrial asset freeze, unlike the tax examples, is internal to the criminal justice system. For one

[91] See Kathleen F. Brickey, *Attorneys' Fee Forfeitures: On Defining "What" and "When" and Distinguishing "Ought" from "Is,"* 36 Emory L J 761, 769–72 (1987) (giving these and other examples).

[92] See Kelman, 33 Stan L Rev at 642 n 126 (cited in note 84) ("The logic [of proximate cause] says a defendant must cause a harm to be justly punished, and a defendant causes a harm when it is not so accidental as to make it unjust to punish him."). See also Daryl J. Levinson, *Framing Transactions in Constitutional Law*, 111 Yale L J 1311, 1373 (2002) ("Absent some explanation of why proximate harms and benefits are especially relevant to one another, nexus and germaneness limitations . . . seem to be recommended by little more than the understanding that constitutional law is impossible if transactional frames may be expanded indefinitely.").

[93] *Luis*, 136 S Ct at 1104 (Kennedy, J, dissenting).

[94] See 26 USC § 6851, setting forth a "termination of taxable year" procedure that allows the IRS to demand immediate payment of taxes and levy property under certain conditions.

[95] See 26 USC § 6861, establishing a "jeopardy assessment" procedure that permits the IRS, in certain circumstances, to assess a tax immediately, creating a lien on the taxpayer's property and allowing the IRS to levy summarily upon it.

[96] See *Caplin & Drysdale*, 491 US at 631–32 & n 8 (citing cases upholding jeopardy assessments "against constitutional attack" and observing that "[c]riminal defendants [ ] are not exempted from federal, state, and local taxation simply because these financial levies may deprive them of resources that could be used to hire an attorney"); Kathleen F. Brickey, *Forfeiture of Attorneys' Fees: The Impact of RICO and CCE Forfeitures on the Right to Counsel*, 72 U Va L Rev 493, 526–27 (1986) (collecting cases).

[97] See Levinson, 111 Yale L J at 1337 (cited in note 92).

thing, as a formal matter, that's not necessarily true—the government obtained the pretrial order in *Luis* in a separate, civil case, not in the criminal case.[98] But that aside, no one would think collection of a fine imposed in an unrelated criminal matter would violate a defendant's right to counsel of choice in a new prosecution. A transactional approach also fails. What if the government had sued the defendant civilly for the very same set of business transactions in *Luis*—would the Sixth Amendment block it from collecting on a resulting judgment? I doubt it.

For similar reasons, the distinction between *direct* and *incidental* burdens on the right to counsel of choice—most familiar from First Amendment jurisprudence, which typically directs closer judicial scrutiny to the former than the latter[99]—does not help to identify Sixth Amendment violations, at least without substantially more theorization.[100] For one thing, it can be awfully difficult to tell the difference—indeed, the Justices disagreed in *Luis* itself about whether the trial court's order directly or only incidentally burdened the defendant's Sixth Amendment interests.[101] It is also not clear that direct burdens always raise the same degree of suspicion under the Sixth Amendment as under the First, at least if I am correct that the Sixth Amendment would not block the government from collecting on a judgment awarded against a criminal defendant in a related civil case.[102]

---

[98] *Luis*, 136 S Ct at 1104 (Kennedy, J, dissenting).

[99] See Geoffrey R. Stone, *Content-Neutral Restrictions*, 54 U Chi L Rev 46, 105–14 (1987).

[100] There is reason to question whether the distinction between direct and incidental burdens on constitutional rights translates straightforwardly from the context of "primary conduct rights" (like free speech) to "litigation rights" (like the right to counsel of choice), see Michael C. Dorf, *Incidental Burdens on Fundamental Rights*, 109 Harv L Rev 1175, 1246–51 (1996); Michael C. Dorf, *Facial Challenges to State and Federal Statutes*, 46 Stan L Rev 235, 265–66 (1994), or even from one right to another within each of these categories, see Joseph Blocher and Darrell A. H. Miller, *What Is Gun Control? Direct Burdens, Incidental Burdens, and the Boundaries of the Second Amendment*, 83 U Chi L Rev 295 (2016) (developing a framework specifically to evaluate incidental burdens on Second Amendment rights).

[101] Contrast *Luis*, 136 S Ct at 1102 (Thomas, J, concurring in judgment) ("The asset freeze here is not merely an incidental burden on the right to counsel of choice; it targets a defendant's assets, which are necessary to exercise that right, simply to secure forfeiture upon conviction."), with id at 1105 (Kennedy, J, dissenting) ("To be sure, a pretrial restraint may make it difficult for a defendant to secure counsel who insists that high defense costs be paid in advance. That difficulty, however, does not result in a Sixth Amendment violation any more than high taxes or other government exactions that impose a similar burden.").

[102] Some have argued that, when it restrains a defendant's assets pretrial, the government acts with the impermissible *purpose* of disabling the defense. See, for example, *Caplin & Drysdale*, 491 US at 635 (Blackmun, J, dissenting) ("[I]t is unseemly and unjust for the Government to beggar those it prosecutes in order to disable their defense at trial."). This accusation seems unwarranted in general; Congress likely did not legislate with this agenda in mind. See Winick, 43 U

Only, then, by relying on multiple, dubious conceptual distinctions and arbitrary framing choices can we explain why freezing the defendant's assets in *Luis* and forcing her to accept appointed counsel would violate her autonomy interests, yet foisting appointed counsel on an indigent criminal defendant leaves his autonomy undisturbed. And if we cannot explain that, then autonomy fails as a general descriptive theory of the right to counsel of choice.

To venture normative briefly, it is worth observing that, in addition to courting incoherence, distinguishing *Luis* from the indigence cases on autonomy grounds requires a deeply conservative view of the Sixth Amendment's protections. The position entrenches the status quo by shielding (untainted) assets the defendant possesses immediately before the government moves on them, without regard for how or why the defendant has those assets, while offering no solicitude to the defendant who is indigent when first pursued, without regard for how or why he lacks the assets his wealthier counterpart possesses. It distributes autonomy unequally according to wealth, and regards that wealth as natural rather than as what it is—the product of a lifetime of give-and-take between the individual and his government as well as other private actors on terms the government sets.[103]

c) Countervailing interests.—Many readers, I suspect, will at this point have the impulse to explain the indigence cases by pointing to the government's strong, systemic, countervailing interests. To be sure, the argument goes, choosing lawyers for indigent defendants

---

Miami L Rev at 833–38 (cited in note 13) (reviewing statutory purposes). Still, the prosecutor in a particular case may indeed act with this purpose by, say, targeting for restraint the assets of defendants who retain certain disfavored defense attorneys. See Morgan Cloud, *Government Intrusions into the Attorney-Client Relationship: The Impact of Fee Forfeitures on the Balance of Power in the Adversary System of Criminal Justice*, 36 Emory L J 817, 829–30 (1987). My tentative view is that such targeting may be prosecutorial misconduct, but that it does not affect the Sixth Amendment calculus under the dominant theories, as any infringement on the defendant's fairness or autonomy interests is the same regardless of the prosecutor's purpose. Consider, for example, *United States v Marshall*, 526 F2d 1349, 1355 (9th Cir 1975) (rejecting, absent a showing of prosecutorial misconduct, argument that alternative funds be made available when the defendant's assets were under a tax levy).

[103] See Levinson, 111 Yale L J at 1361 (cited in note 92) (describing wealth as "largely dependent on a network of government subsidies and structures ranging from corporate law to government-supported property rights"); Cass R. Sunstein, *The Limits of Compensatory Justice*, in John W. Chapman, ed, *Nomos XXXIII: Compensatory Justice* 281, 286, 294, 298–99 (NYU, 1991).

intrudes on those defendants' fairness and autonomy interests, just as in *Luis*. But it's the only way to run the system. If we let indigent defendants pick, they'll all want Johnnie Cochran. He couldn't possibly take on all that work (even were he alive) and, even if he could, it seems terribly unfair to punish his success with appointed counsel's wages (and implausible for the state to pay his regular rate). The indigence cases, on this view, simply bow to practicality. Fairness and autonomy interests are indeed at stake, but they're overcome by administrative realities.[104]

There is a doctrinal clue supporting this explanation: while indigent defendants do not enjoy the right to counsel of choice, they do retain various fair-trial protections as well as other aspects of the right to control their defense. Indigent defendants, like all others, have the right to effective assistance of counsel, a fair judge, and a prosecutor who toes the line.[105] "It is also recognized that the accused has the ultimate authority to make certain fundamental decisions regarding the case, as to whether to plead guilty, waive a jury, testify in his or her own behalf, or take an appeal."[106] The point is that granting indigent defendants these rights furthers the same fairness and autonomy objectives thought to motivate the right to counsel of choice but without the concomitant disruption. This suggests that concern about that disruption indeed may have informed the Court's decision to withhold the counsel-of-choice right from indigent defendants.

The concern, however, is likely overblown. Effectuating an indigent defendant's right to counsel of choice could mean something as simple as letting him choose a public defender or panel attorney who is available and willing to represent him—perhaps an attorney with whom he is familiar from a prior case, or one a friend has recom-

---

[104] See *Slappy*, 461 US at 23 n 5 (Brennan, J, concurring in result) (listing "the State's interest in economy and efficiency" as "considerations that may preclude recognition of an indigent defendant's right to choose his own counsel"); *United States v Ely*, 719 F2d 902, 905 (7th Cir 1983) (arguing that "indigent defendants cannot be allowed to paralyze the system by all flocking to one lawyer"); Stephen J. Schulhofer, *Client Choice for Indigent Criminal Defendants: Theory and Implementation*, 12 Ohio St J Crim L 505, 528–29 (2015) (describing cases "assuming that client choice would place unmanageable strains on the management of the criminal docket"). Alternatively, one might argue that "indigent" merely describes the class of individuals who cannot afford *any* lawyer, and whom the right to counsel of choice, if formally accorded, would not benefit in any way.

[105] *Strickland v Washington*, 466 US 668, 686 (1984); *Bracy v Gramley*, 520 US 899, 904–05 (1997); *Brady v Maryland*, 373 US 83, 87 (1963).

[106] *Jones v Barnes*, 463 US 745, 751 (1983).

mended.[107] The military, for example, affords an accused the right to representation "by military counsel of his own selection if that counsel is reasonably available."[108] England, Scotland, Wales, and Ontario, Canada give indigent defendants the right to select their attorney,[109] and both the Judicial Conference of the United States and the American Bar Association at one time suggested the same domestically.[110] Professors Stephen Schulhofer and David Friedman have outlined the structure of a workable voucher system.[111] In short, to recognize the indigent defendant's right to counsel of choice, the government need not conscript the bar or foot the bill for Johnnie Cochran.[112] Administrative concerns, in other words, may explain why the right to counsel of choice must be *cabined* for indigent defendants, but they cannot explain the current doctrine, which withholds that right altogether.

* * *

[107] See, for example, *Slappy*, 461 US at 22–23 & n 5 (Brennan, J, concurring in result) (arguing that recognizing "an indigent defendant's interest in continued representation by an appointed attorney with whom he has developed a relationship of trust and confidence" is not impractical); *Drumgo v Superior Court of Marin County*, 506 P2d 1007, 1013–14 (Cal 1973) (in bank) (Mosk dissenting) (contending that the state should minimize interference with the defendant's choice, particularly where the defendant desires qualified counsel who is ready and willing to serve). For academic arguments supporting a right to counsel of choice for indigent defendants, including refutation or accommodation of the government's presumed interests in efficient administration of the justice system, see Hoeffel, 44 San Diego L Rev at 549 (cited in note 10); Holly, 64 Brooklyn L Rev at 205–17, 224–29 (cited in note 13); Norman Lefstein, *In Search of Gideon's Promise: Lessons from England and the Need for Federal Help*, 55 Hastings L J 835, 918–19 (2004); Stephen J. Schulhofer and David D. Friedman, *Rethinking Indigent Defense: Promoting Effective Representation Through Consumer Sovereignty and Freedom of Choice for All Criminal Defendants*, 31 Am Crim L Rev 73 (1993); Peter W. Tague, *An Indigent's Right to the Attorney of His Choice*, 27 Stan L Rev 73, 80–84, 89–97 (1974); Kenneth P. Troccoli, *"I Want a Black Lawyer to Represent Me": Addressing a Black Defendant's Concerns with Being Assigned a White Court-Appointed Lawyer*, 20 Law & Ineq 1, 48–51 (2002).

[108] 10 USC § 838(b)(3)(B).

[109] See Schulhofer, 12 Ohio St J Crim L at 508 n 17 (cited in note 104) (collecting sources).

[110] See Judicial Conference of the United States, Committee to Review the Criminal Justice Act, *Interim Report* (1992), reprinted in 51 Crim L Rep 2335, 2337 (1992); 1 ABA Standards for Criminal Justice, Providing Defense Services § 5-2.3 (2d ed 1980).

[111] See Schulhofer and Friedman, 31 Am Crim L Rev at 112–22 (cited in note 107). See also Norman Lefstein, *Securing Reasonable Caseloads: Ethics and Law in Public Defense* 241–49 (ABA, 2011). Inspired by Schulhofer and Friedman's work, Comal County, Texas now permits indigent defendants to choose the publicly funded attorney who will represent them. Schulhofer, 12 Ohio St J Crim L at 509 (cited in note 104).

[112] See *Douglas v California*, 372 US 353, 357 (1963) ("Absolute equality is not required; lines can be and are drawn and we often sustain them.").

Insurmountable problems plague the fairness and autonomy theories of the right to counsel of choice and, indeed, I suspect, any theory of the right premised on individual interests. There is simply too much doctrine that is irreconcilable with a model that straightforwardly balances individual against government interests. In the next part, I offer a system-focused theory that, I argue, better explains the law.

II. The Antisocialization Alternative

I begin this part by describing the antisocialization theory and showing how it explains the outcome in *Luis*. I then illustrate how, unlike the fairness and autonomy theories, an antisocialization theory can also distinguish *Luis* from all of the prior decisions in which the Court found no counsel-of-choice violation. I conclude by sketching out a plausible normative case for the theory, though I do not attempt a full-throated normative defense (nor am I sure I would want to). Under the antisocialization theory I propose, the right to counsel of choice is plausibly justified not by the advantages it provides to the individuals who invoke it, but by the benefits it confers on other defendants.

A. Illustrating the Theory

An antisocialization theory conceives of the right to counsel of choice not as a powerful individual protection but rather as a weak, system-oriented safeguard against socialization of the criminal defense bar.[113] On this view, only when the government advances a theory for restricting the defendant's right to counsel of choice that, if accepted, would allow it to socialize criminal defense by shrinking the private defense bar below some minimal threshold does the counsel-of-choice right prevail over the government's interest. Illustrating how the antisocialization principle can explain the outcome in *Luis* will make the concept more concrete.

---

[113] Consider Richard H. Fallon Jr. and Daniel J. Meltzer, *New Law, Non-Retroactivity, and Constitutional Remedies*, 104 Harv L Rev 1731, 1777–91 (1991) (arguing that individual remedies for rights violations are often, but not always, required, so long as the overall system of remedies is "effective in maintaining a regime of lawful government").

The plurality's opinion in *Luis* actually contains the seeds of an antisocialization theory. The plurality observed, correctly, that a contrary outcome in the case would have "unleash[ed] a constitutional principle that would have no obvious stopping place."[114] That principle would permit Congress to "write more statutes authorizing pretrial restraints in cases involving other illegal behavior—after all," the plurality pointed out, "a broad range of such behavior can lead to postconviction forfeiture of untainted assets."[115] And "[e]ven beyond the forfeiture itself, criminal fines can be high, and restitution orders expensive."[116]

The *Luis* plurality may, if anything, have undersold its point. For one thing, Congress has already authorized pretrial restraints more widely than the plurality's language might be read to suggest; it has also, as the plurality notes, widely permitted postconviction forfeiture of substitute assets.[117] It's only the combination of the two—*pretrial* restraint of *substitute* assets—that remains rare. Congress could change that with the flick of a pen, adjusting a statutory cross-reference or two. It need not "write more statutes," as the plurality suggested, only make the tiniest amendment to some existing ones. The machinery is already in place—Congress just needs to power it on. Restitution, moreover, is *mandatory* in a huge array of federal cases, including both violent and property crimes.[118] While the broad federal restitution statute does not presently authorize pretrial restraint of assets, that, of course, is simply a matter of "congressional whim[ ]" that could change at any moment.[119] Indeed, both Houses of Congress have considered bills that would amend the federal res-

---

[114] *Luis*, 136 S Ct at 1094 (Breyer, J) (plurality). Justice Thomas, too, stressed this point. Id at 1098 (Thomas, J, concurring in judgment).

[115] Id at 1094 (Breyer, J) (plurality).

[116] Id.

[117] For example, the Racketeer Influenced and Corrupt Organizations Act (RICO) authorizes both pretrial restraint of tainted assets and postconviction forfeiture of substitute assets. 18 USC § 1963(e), (m). So does the Controlled Substances Act, 21 USC § 853(e), (p). See also 18 USC § 982 (authorizing forfeiture for a large number of federal offenses and incorporating the procedures in 21 USC § 853). Drug cases alone make up roughly a third of the federal criminal docket. See US Sentencing Commission, *Overview of Federal Criminal Cases Fiscal Year 2015* *2 (June 2016), archived at https://perma.cc/M2JX-3UQ9 (reporting figure of 31.8 percent).

[118] See 18 USC § 3663A.

[119] *Luis*, 136 S Ct at 1108 (Kennedy, J, dissenting).

titution statute to do exactly that.[120] Restitution is also mandated, or at least authorized, in every state-court system.[121] And all that's before we get to criminal fines.[122]

A contrary result in *Luis* would have allowed the government (federal or state) to attach substantial monetary penalties to any offense—murder, arson, forgery, whatever—and then freeze pretrial assets the defendant may need to pay those penalties. Indeed, given how close we already are to such a regime (as just explained), a contrary result in *Luis* may well have encouraged this development. One need not imagine improper legislative motives, I should add. Particularly in an age of heightened, bipartisan awareness about the financial and social costs of mass incarceration, the increasing use of monetary penalty schemes as a supplement to or substitute for imprisonment does not seem far-fetched.[123] Such a development would prevent the vast majority of defendants from retaining counsel and make appointed counsel the norm in all but the most aberrant case (e.g., the super-wealthy defendant). It exaggerates little, then, to conclude that a contrary outcome may have socialized the criminal defense bar.[124] This is what it means to say that an antisocialization theory explains the outcome in *Luis*.

---

[120] Restitution for Crime Victims Act of 2007, S 973, 110th Cong, 1st Sess (Mar 22, 2007); Restitution for Crime Victims Act of 2007, HR 4110, 110th Cong, 1st Sess (Nov 7, 2007).

[121] US Dept of Justice, Office for Victims of Crime, *Legal Series Bulletin No. 6: Ordering Restitution to the Crime Victim* *1 (Nov 2002), archived at https://perma.cc/XJE4-MAPG.

[122] Justice Kennedy, dissenting in *Luis*, argued that fines present a "separate and distinct" issue from forfeiture, but did not explain why. *Luis*, 136 S Ct at 1108 (Kennedy, J, dissenting). Indeed, at oral argument, Justice Kennedy acknowledged that, "if the government prevails in this case, every State in the union, every locality could say that in the event of . . . any crime involving a bodily injury, that the government is entitled to restrain disposition of assets that might be used for medical care, for pain and suffering." Transcript of Oral Argument at *32, *Luis v United States* (US Nov 10, 2015) (No 14-419) (available on Westlaw at 2015 WL 8491825). He added, in language resonant with an antisocialization theory, that "this would, in effect, prevent the private bar from—from practicing law unless it does so on a contingent basis." Id at *32–33.

[123] Indeed, aside from the judgment-proof problem, monetary penalties are economically superior to incarceration as a mode of criminal punishment even when the economy is strong. See Frank H. Easterbrook, *Criminal Procedure as a Market System*, 12 J Legal Stud 289, 293 (1983). See generally David Dagan and Steven Teles, *Prison Break: Why Conservatives Turned Against Mass Incarceration* (Oxford, 2016).

[124] Writing before *Luis*, one commentator criticized the Supreme Court's fee-forfeiture decisions for facilitating "socialization of the criminal defense bar." See Matthew R. Lasky, Comment, *Imposing Indigence: Reclaiming the Qualified Right to Counsel of Choice in Criminal Asset Forfeiture Cases*, 104 J Crim L & Criminol 165, 180–82 (2014). My argument is that the Court's doctrine *prevents* socialization of the defense bar, a point that became clear only after *Luis*.

B. BROADER EXPLANATORY POWER

More important, unlike the fairness and autonomy theories, an antisocialization theory explains what is unique about *Luis*; it distinguishes *Luis* from all of the cases before it. Consider first the disputes concerning the trial court's inherent powers to control litigation. Recall that the trial court has broad discretion to deny a continuance, disqualify an attorney for conflict of interest (even in the face of conflict waivers), and exclude nonlawyers, disbarred lawyers, and out-of-state lawyers from practice—all regardless whether its decision has the effect of depriving the defendant of counsel of choice. What explains these cases (juxtaposed with *Luis*) is not the relative weakness of the defendant's fairness or autonomy interests, or the strength of the government's need—it's that these are one-off disputes. There's no danger that trial courts will exercise their discretion under these precedents to suffocate the private defense bar. This is because most prosecutions will not present the issues these precedents resolve, and because, even if they did, the trial court's powers enable it to preclude particular attorneys, one at a time, rather than all attorneys the defendant might retain. Nor is there any way for the legislature to amend the law, as it could under a contrary holding in *Luis*, to give the government the opportunity to exploit the Court's holdings.

The same antisocialization principle explains the distinction between tainted and untainted assets the Court drew in *Luis* to distinguish *Monsanto*. The individual-rights theories failed to explain the distinction because "the Government's and the defendant's respective legal interests in those two kinds of property, prior to a judgment of guilt, are exactly the same."[125] Under an antisocialization theory, the explanation is that limiting pretrial asset restraint to tainted assets prevents the government from restraining the defendant's assets in *every* case, and therefore ensures that *some* defendants will retain the use of funds to spend on private counsel. The decision in *Luis*, that is, has the rough-and-ready effect of cabining the government's use of pretrial asset restraint to the subset of crimes that generate monetary proceeds.[126] Only in these cases—not in most cases of

---

[125] *Luis*, 136 S Ct at 1112 (Kagan, J, dissenting).

[126] See id at 1113 (referring to the plurality's "effort to cabin *Monsanto*").

murder, arson, and so forth—will there be any tainted assets to freeze. And in this way, the doctrine guarantees the continued vitality of the private criminal defense bar.[127]

Finally, the leading theories could not persuasively explain why appointing counsel in *Luis* would have violated the defendant's right to counsel of choice, but assigning counsel for indigent defendants is unobjectionable. The explanation under an antisocialization theory is straightforward: denying indigent defendants the right to counsel of choice will not starve the private criminal defense bar because indigent defendants, by definition, lack the resources to pay a lawyer and thus to support the bar. The doctrine upholds the right to counsel of choice only when doing so is necessary to prevent socialization of the defense bar; affording the right to indigent defendants is, on this view, a luxury, not a necessity.

C. NORMATIVE PLAUSIBILITY

My argument has been that an antisocialization theory explains counsel-of-choice doctrine and that the leading descriptive theories, grounded in the individual defendant's fairness and autonomy interests, do not. My aim is *not* to defend the antisocialization theory as a normative matter, and I doubt that I would want to. It is, however, worth considering whether there is even a plausible normative justification for antisocialization, "for a theory that seems preposterous as a matter of policy or values does not explain persuasively—at least not unless one assumes that those who make the law have preposterous values or policy goals."[128]

It's not completely obvious that the answer is yes. Efforts to articulate the individualized harm that befalls a defendant who is denied the right to counsel of choice—the project of Part I—have failed. And if we cannot articulate the harm, then why should we mind if

---

[127] It is tempting to speculate that defendants charged with these money-making crimes are the only ones with funds to spend on counsel; in other words, that the only defendants with the financial wherewithal to hire counsel are precisely the ones who'll be disabled from spending. The data, however, appear not to substantiate this supposition. See Harlow, *Special Report* at *5 (cited in note 74) (reporting that in 1996 rates of appointed counsel were roughly similar across different crime types, with those accused of public-order crimes hiring private attorneys somewhat more frequently than defendants accused of violent, property, or drug crimes).

[128] Stuntz, 88 Colum L Rev at 1292 (cited in note 8).

additional defendants—that last one out of every five—are also denied the choice?[129]

The plurality in *Luis* does offer one argument on this point. If the government had its way, the plurality observes, all of the newly affected defendants—the defendants who could have afforded counsel previously, but now cannot because the government has frozen their substitute assets—would "fall back upon publicly paid counsel, including overworked and underpaid public defenders."[130] This would "increas[e] the government-paid-defender workload" even further, "render[ing] less effective the basic right the Sixth Amendment seeks to protect."[131]

The plurality's basic position seems sound—the last thing publicly funded attorneys need is more work. But to make the plurality's point more than merely rhetorical, and more than marginally relevant to the constitutional calculus, everything must be just so: (1) current resource constraints must not be so severe as to subject indigent defendants to a present and undue risk of ineffective assistance of counsel; (2) the addition of a relatively small number of newly impoverished defendants must then strain the indigent defense system to its breaking point; (3) indigent defense funding levels must not adjust upward in response; and (4) the Court must be willing in the future (as it so far has not been) to hold that funding deficiencies, if severe enough, can violate the Constitution. This strikes me as a dubious set of assumptions.

A better justification would identify reasons to resist socialized criminal defense *even assuming the constitutional adequacy of government-funded counsel* in a socialized world. If public defenders are good enough for the indigent, in other words, are there nevertheless reasons not to have all defendants use them? Or, to frame the issue

---

[129] Similarly, several commentators suggest that it would be dangerous if all criminal defense lawyers were (financially) beholden to the government. See, for example, William J. Genego, *The Legal and Practical Implications of Forfeiture of Attorneys' Fees*, 36 Emory L J 837, 852 (1987); David Rudovsky, *The Right to Counsel Under Attack*, 136 U Pa L Rev 1965, 1971 n 24 (1988); Winick, 43 U Miami L Rev at 779–80 & n 64 (cited in note 13). But if it is acceptable for the state to pay four of every five defense lawyers, what is the problem with having it pay the fifth? These commentators do not say. One possibility is that the private defense bar serves as a bulwark against authoritarianism because it's difficult for the government to control—the government cannot, for example, condition its funding on acquiescence in regulation that dulls its power to challenge government action.

[130] *Luis*, 136 S Ct at 1095 (Breyer, J) (plurality).

[131] Id.

slightly differently, does the existence of a private criminal defense bar that services only one in five defendants benefit the other four in any way?[132] Does privately funded criminal defense create positive externalities?

There are several reasons to think the answer might be yes. I should caution that my discussion of these reasons generalizes about the qualities of the "public" and "private" defense bars. In fact, there is wide variation in experience and skill within both bars alike. The point here is only that *some* aspects of the private defense bar *may* redound to the benefit of at least *some* indigent defendants.

First, the existence of a private criminal defense bar may help attract legal talent to the field. Many public defenders, to be sure, are "cause lawyers" for whom law practice is not primarily an economic enterprise. But some promising young lawyers may be more likely to begin their careers in public defense if they know they can "cash in" down the road at a job in the private defense bar.[133] One com-

---

[132] Consider the analogy to First Amendment overbreadth, discussed in Richard H. Fallon Jr., *Making Sense of Overbreadth*, 100 Yale L J 853, 867–70 (1991). Note that a contrary result in *Luis* would not prevent volunteer counsel—from, say, a public interest organization or law firm—from appearing on a defendant's behalf. A system that precluded even volunteer representation, by requiring defendants to proceed with the lawyer the court appointed to their case, would raise additional difficulties. I will not discuss these problems except to observe that history is replete with examples of locally disfavored defendants relying upon out-of-town, volunteer counsel when local lawyers were too biased, or captured by local interests, to represent them zealously. *Powell v Alabama* was such a case—after the defendants were denied effective representation at trial, the International Labor Defense organization volunteered to litigate the appeal. Michael J. Klarman, *Powell v. Alabama: The Supreme Court Confronts "Legal Lynchings,"* in Carol S. Steiker, ed, *Criminal Procedure Stories* 4, 6–7 (Foundation, 2006). See also, for example, Michael Meltsner, *Cruel and Unusual: The Supreme Court and Capital Punishment* 97 (Random House, 1973) (discussing NAACP involvement in *Maxwell v Bishop*, 398 US 262 (1970) (per curiam)). See generally David S. Mann, *Not for Lucre or Malice: The Southern Negro's Right to Out-of-State Counsel*, 64 Nw U L Rev 143, 147 (1969) (asserting that "out-of-state attorneys participated in an average of 68.69% of the cases, federal and state, involving civil rights and arising in the states of the Fifth Circuit from 1965 to 1968"). Consider also *Sanders v Russell*, 401 F2d 241 (5th Cir 1968) (invalidating federal district court's restrictions on practice by out-of-state attorneys in civil rights cases).

[133] See Matt Kaiser, *4 Ways to Break into White-Collar Criminal Defense Work* (Above the Law, Dec 5, 2013), archived at https://perma.cc/N2VL-LKSN (advising young lawyers seeking private, white-collar defense work to consider federal public defense as a stepping stone); *White Collar Defense/Internal Investigations* (Ballard Spahr LLP), archived at https://perma.cc/9JUC-QTUN (advertising "seasoned veterans" including "former public defenders"); *Criminal Defense* (Loyola U Chi Law Sch), archived at https://perma.cc/X6Z4-2E9K (advising law students that "private defense attorneys . . . often gain experience in criminal litigation by working as public defenders"). See also Kenneth Mann, *Defending White-Collar Crime: A Portrait of Attorneys at Work* 21–22 (Yale, 1985) (describing the high demand across the country for white-collar defense attorneys, which initially targeted federal prosecutors and, later, "a number of attorneys without prosecutorial experience who had worked with leading litigators and received their basic training on the defense side"); William J. Genego,

mentator claims exactly this effect: "If the financial top of the criminal defense market is destroyed by fee forfeiture, fewer and less capable lawyers will enter the field."[134] Eliminating the prospect of lucrative private defense work in the future may deter some "young lawyers from working in the comparatively low paying public jobs in state public defender . . . offices,"[135] especially because these jobs, unlike stints on the prosecutor's side, are not reliable stepping-stones to politics or private civil firms.

Second, and related, both human and knowledge capital may spill over from the private to the public side. Many new attorneys—especially from elite law schools—head from law school to large law firms, where they can sock away money and learn to practice criminal defense "the right way," typically in a corporate or white-collar setting. As these lawyers tire of law-firm practice, fail to make partner, or simply desire a different course, some pursue careers in public interest work, including public defense.[136] These transitioning attorneys import into public defender offices the knowledge, skills, and habits they acquired at the firm, and attempt to adapt them to the constraints of their new practice. It is difficult to tell how often this happens, and it may be more common in some public-defense domains than others. But it's not hard to find examples.[137]

The New Adversary, 54 Brooklyn L Rev 781, 787 (1988) (asserting that "rich defendants" who retain counsel affect "the criminal defense bar in general" by bringing "many new attorneys and firms into the market place" who "compete on the basis of their reputations for vigorous and successful defenses to government prosecutions").

[134] Winick, 43 U Miami L Rev at 782 (cited in note 13).

[135] Id. See also Morgan Cloud, *Forfeiting Defense Attorneys' Fees: Applying an Institutional Role Theory to Define Individual Constitutional Rights*, 1987 Wis L Rev 1, 35 (arguing that, by "driving [the most capable lawyers] from the market, the government would weaken the collective strength of the defense bar" and skew "the balance of power in favor of the government in these—and perhaps most—criminal prosecutions"); Pamela S. Karlan, *Discrete and Relational Criminal Representation: The Changing Vision of the Right to Counsel*, 105 Harv L Rev 670, 723 (1992) (discussing the "systemic interest in ensuring that skilled lawyers are attracted to and remain in criminal defense practice," which is disserved by permitting the government to disable a defendant's chosen counsel too readily).

[136] Scott L. Cummings, *The Politics of Pro Bono*, 52 UCLA L Rev 1, 102, 138 (2004) (describing how young lawyers "cycle through the private sector for a short stint in order to pay off debt, build skills, or develop professional relationships," and then "leave the firm, entering other practice sites that provide more supportive environments for their commitments"); Jane E. Tewksbury, *The Changing Face of Public Sector Practice: Apprenticeships as a Recruitment Tool*, 40 Boston Bar J 12 (Nov–Dec 1996) (reporting that, due to downsizing and attorney interest in work-life balance, "public sector agencies now find that they are the beneficiaries of an increasing number of applications from private sector attorneys with five to seven years legal experience").

[137] See, for example, Parker Douglas and Megan Green, *How I Got My Job as a Public Defense Attorney* (SJ Quinney College of Law, May 15, 2012), archived at https://perma.cc

Similarly, well-funded private defense attorneys may develop novel strategies or technologies that, after presentation in open court, publicly funded counsel can emulate. (Consider Barry Scheck's influential cross-examination of the police officer who headed evidence collection as part of O. J. Simpson's defense team, for example.[138]) Innovation in defense strategy demands at least two ingredients. The first is the flexibility to experiment.[139] While socialization may cut against experimentation, it's not fatal—even in a "socialized" world, our decentralized system of public defense permits variation across public defender offices or among appointed counsel. But the second ingredient—resources—would undoubtedly dry up in a socialized system.[140] The point is that, when wealthy defendants spend huge sums to innovate, in some cases they produce public goods from which indigent defendants also benefit. Likewise, the private market likely breeds subject-matter experts who subsist primarily on high fees from paying clients but who devote a small portion of their practice to pro bono or reduced-rate work on behalf of indigent defendants.

/GAJ8-RX36 (describing federal public defense attorneys "who work their way up through the ranks . . . at law firms doing criminal work"); *Kenneth P. Troccoli* (Am U Wash College of Law), archived at https://perma.cc/B6E5-TYC6 (listing experience practicing "primarily white-collar criminal defense at three law firms" before becoming a state, and then federal, public defender); *President Obama Nominates Four to Serve on the U.S. District Court* (White House, Apr 25, 2012), archived at https://perma.cc/AEN5-UH39 (describing now-Judge Jesus G. Bernal, who worked as a litigation associate at a major law firm before joining a federal public defender office). A search of the speakers list at one recent federal public defender conference turned up numerous additional examples. See, for example, *Hector Dopico* (Bizzabo), archived at https://perma.cc/T52Z-2P37; *Mark Drozdowski* (Bizzabo), archived at https://perma.cc/W74Q-XB3S; *Michael Novara* (Bizzabo), archived at https://perma.cc/3V5L-QDES.

[138] Patt Morrison, *Barry Scheck on the O.J. Trial, DNA Evidence and the Innocence Project*, LA Times (June 17, 2014), archived at https://perma.cc/ZKS2-K4AC; David Margolick, *A Simpson Lawyer Makes New York Style Play in Judge Ito's Courtroom*, NY Times (Apr 17, 1995), archived at https://perma.cc/TKF9-NHND.

[139] See *Caplin & Drysdale*, 491 US at 647 (Blackmun, J, dissenting) (contending that socialization of criminal defense work "too readily would standardize the provision of criminal-defense services," and stressing the social importance of "the maverick and the risk taker and [of] approaches that might not fit into the structured environment of a public defender's office"). Consider, by analogy, the argument that nationalized health care stifles innovation. See, for example, James G. Barlow, *Changing the Innovation Landscape in the UK's National Health Service to Meet Its Future Challenges*, 2 Innovation and Entrepreneurship in Health 59 (2015).

[140] Lala, 12 NY City L Rev at 258 (cited in note 77) (encouraging public defenders to "continue to experiment with innovative ways to provide more effective representation to [their] clients," but cautioning that "bold measures are difficult to take" due to financial constraints).

Third, if we assume that law enforcement authorities regard private defense counsel as more formidable foes than publicly funded lawyers—even maintaining the prior assumption that government-paid counsel are minimally adequate—then the existence of a private defense bar may help deter the type of police and prosecutorial misconduct that defense lawyers frequently litigate.[141] This would be true to the extent that the authorities may be unsure, at the time the misconduct would occur, which kind of lawyer they will face.

Finally, private defense counsel may affect the content of the law, tending to push it in a defendant-friendly direction. The idea here would be that superior resources enable private counsel to outperform government-paid lawyers in persuading courts that legal doctrine should accommodate defendants' interests, or even just in persuading courts to rule for their clients in ways that end up benefiting future defendants as legal authority.[142]

I have not proved these normative claims, or even close. One or more of them might be wrong. But as a group, they strike me as plausible enough to conclude that justifying the right to counsel of choice on antisocialization grounds would not be "preposterous."[143] That is good enough not to disqualify antisocialization as a descriptive theory.

III. External Normative Complications

Scholarly analysis of the Sixth Amendment right to counsel of choice is largely critical. Motivating the criticism is a sense that the Court has been getting the cases wrong. Until *Luis*, the Court consistently rejected defendants' counsel-of-choice claims, even when the balance of individual and government interests did not clearly

---

[141] See Nancy Leong, *Making Rights*, 92 BU L Rev 405, 421–29 (2012) (reporting the types of Fourth Amendment claims that are litigated in criminal cases and civil rights lawsuits, respectively).

[142] Lasky, 104 J Crim L & Criminol at 181–82 (cited in note 124); Andrew Manuel Crespo, *Regaining Perspective: Constitutional Criminal Adjudication in the U.S. Supreme Court*, 100 Minn L Rev 1985, 2001–05 (2016) (reviewing evidence that quality of advocacy affects case outcomes and opinion content). See also Einer R. Elhauge, *Does Interest Group Theory Justify More Intrusive Judicial Review?*, 101 Yale L J 31, 66–87 (1991) (arguing that the litigation process is susceptible to the same disproportionate influence of those who can organize, mobilize resources, and overcome free-rider problems as is the political process).

[143] Stuntz, 88 Colum L Rev at 1292 (cited in note 8).

favor the state.[144] My claim is that the Court's decisions are explicable upon the realization that the doctrine treats counsel of choice not as an individual right at all, but instead as a system-level safeguard against a socialized criminal defense bar. Were I asked to predict the Court's next counsel-of-choice decision, I would—on the admittedly controversial assumption that most Justices, in most cases, make some effort to decide disputes consistently with the pattern of preceding decisions[145]—look to this explanation before the fairness and autonomy theories commentators have assumed the Court has been ineptly attempting to implement. And were I to critique the doctrine on normative grounds, I would consider whether antisocialization ought to delineate its bounds.

I want here, however, to turn to a different normative point: There are reasonable arguments, based on separate constitutional principles, independent from the right to counsel of choice, that several of the precedents discussed above are incorrect. The first is *Monsanto*. Justice Kagan, dissenting in *Luis*, characterized *Monsanto* as "a troubling decision," and I agree.[146] The reason is that, as Justice Kagan points out, at the moment the government freezes the defendant's assets pretrial—based on a showing of probable cause to believe the assets will be proved forfeitable—"the presumption of innocence still applies."[147] And while it's true, as the *Monsanto* Court reasoned, that the government may sometimes restrain *persons* pretrial "where there is a finding of probable cause to believe that the accused has committed a serious offense,"[148] the analogy is less persuasive than it appears.

---

[144] See, for example, Garcia, 29 Am Crim L Rev at 86 (cited in note 14) ("The Court's jurisprudence in this sphere is seriously flawed, reflecting its strong preference for crime control and efficiency imperatives and its corresponding depreciation of the critical role of the defense attorney in the criminal process."); Note, 124 Harv L Rev at 1558 (cited in note 23) (criticizing the doctrine for doing "almost no work whatsoever").

[145] See Ronald Dworkin, *Law's Empire* 228–32, 397–99 (Harvard, 1986) (comparing judges to authors of a "chain novel"); David A. Strauss, *Common Law Constitutional Interpretation*, 63 U Chi L Rev 877, 883 (1996) ("Mostly the courts decide cases by looking to what the precedents say.").

[146] *Luis*, 136 S Ct at 1112 (Kagan, J, dissenting).

[147] Id, quoting *Kaley v United States*, 134 S Ct 1090, 1096 (2014). See also *United States v Al Sharaf*, 2015 WL 4238784, *2–3 (DDC) (citing the defendant's presumption of innocence in rejecting the government's request for pretrial restraint of assets the defendant might need to pay restitution if convicted).

[148] *Monsanto*, 491 US at 615–16.

First, while a criminal indictment may issue based on probable cause, pretrial restraint of the accused "cannot be justified by the fact of the indictment alone."[149] The government must also show, by clear and convincing evidence at an adversarial hearing, that "no condition or combination of conditions will reasonably assure the appearance of the person [for trial] and the safety of any other person and the community."[150] Second, it would not be difficult to ensure that the defendant's assets be used only for their intended purpose. The assets could be placed in escrow and released to the defendant's attorney upon submission of a reasonable request for fees. Upon resolution of the case, the balance would be returned to the defendant or forfeited, as appropriate.[151] Such an arrangement would advance the legislative aims of punishing crime and disgorging its proceeds but not the impermissible aim of hobbling the accused's ability to defend himself.[152]

Yet simply rolling back *Monsanto* may not be satisfactory either. There is the nagging problem of the hypothetical robbery suspect, first raised by the Court in *Caplin & Drysdale*. "A robbery suspect," the Court there pointed out, "has no Sixth Amendment right to use funds he has stolen from a bank to retain an attorney to defend him if he is apprehended. The money, though in his possession, is not rightfully his," the Court continued, and so "the Government does not violate the Sixth Amendment if it seizes the robbery proceeds and refuses to permit the defendant to use them to pay for his defense."[153]

---

[149] *Caplin & Drysdale*, 491 US at 654 (Blackmun, J, dissenting).

[150] 18 USC § 3142(e)–(f). See also *Kaley*, 134 S Ct at 1111 (Roberts, CJ, dissenting) ("Retaining one's counsel of choice ensures the fundamental fairness of the actual trial, and thus may be far more valuable to a criminal defendant than pretrial release.").

[151] See Cloud, 36 Emory L J at 832 (cited in note 102) ("Methods exist to ensure that a rule exempting fees from forfeiture would not be abused by defendants and unscrupulous attorneys.").

[152] See *Caplin & Drysdale*, 491 US at 652 (Blackmun, J, dissenting) ("[W]eakening the ability of an accused to defend himself at trial . . . is not a legitimate government interest that can be used to justify invasion of a constitutional right."), quoting *United States v Monsanto*, 852 F2d 1400, 1403 (2d Cir 1988) (Feinberg concurring) (quotation marks omitted); Winick, 43 U Miami L Rev at 835–37 (cited in note 13) (discussing the government's various interests in forfeiture and arguing that none is substantially weakened by allowing defendants to pay bona fide attorney fees); Lisa F. Rackner, Note, *Against Forfeiture of Attorneys' Fees Under RICO: Protecting the Constitutional Rights of Criminal Defendants*, 61 NYU L Rev 124, 140 (1986). But see *Caplin & Drysdale*, 491 US at 630 (questioning but ultimately agreeing with "[t]he notion that the Government has a legitimate interest in depriving criminals of economic power, even insofar as that power is used to retain counsel of choice").

[153] *Caplin & Drysdale*, 491 US at 626.

One might respond, of course, that the robbery suspect is only that—a *suspect*—and the funds he wishes to spend, only *alleged* robbery proceeds.[154] It is not difficult, though, to conjure factual scenarios in which this position would become untenable. To reach a solution that accommodates not only the defendant's right to counsel of choice (whatever it means) and the government's interest in forfeitable assets, but also the presumption of innocence, the Court must surface all of these competing interests. It must resist the temptation to rely on a false binary in which money is either "stolen" or wholly "innocent." Probably some heightened burden of proof for pretrial asset restraint, beyond probable cause, is in order.[155]

The second precedent—or principle, really—that appears to contravene separate constitutional values, apart from what counsel-of-choice doctrine ought to require, is the principle that indigent defendants enjoy no control whatsoever over who represents them (apart from the option to eschew counsel altogether). Even when the Constitution does not require the state to furnish criminal defendants a particular right, when the state voluntarily undertakes to do so, the Equal Protection Clause demands that it afford the right to wealthy and poor alike.[156] The mandate is not that all defendants be put on equal footing, ignoring, for example, "the harsh reality that the quality of a criminal defendant's representation frequently may turn on his ability to retain the best counsel money can buy."[157] The discriminatory effects of wealth disparities are not unconstitutional, in other words. But "discrimination against 'indigents' by name" is another matter.[158]

The principle denying indigent defendants *any* right to counsel of choice is of this latter, more pernicious sort. The Court in these cases does more than nod to the "harsh reality" that wealthy crim-

---

[154] See Lasky, 104 J Crim L & Criminol at 183–85 (cited in note 124) (attacking the bank robber analogy).

[155] See Terrance G. Reed and Joseph P. Gill, *RICO Forfeitures, Forfeitable "Interests," and Procedural Due Process*, 62 NC L Rev 57, 91–92 (1983) (advocating a clear-and-convincing-evidence standard for pretrial asset restraint).

[156] The canonical cases are *Douglas v California*, 372 US 353 (1963), which concerned the provision of appellate counsel in felony cases, and *Griffin v Illinois*, 351 US 12 (1956), about access to a trial transcript or other record adequate to afford effective appellate review.

[157] *Caplin & Drysdale*, 491 US at 630, quoting *Slappy*, 461 US at 23 (Brennan, J, concurring in result).

[158] *Griffin*, 351 US at 35 (Harlan, J, dissenting).

inal defendants can afford fancier lawyers than poor ones. It withholds the right to counsel of choice from indigent defendants altogether. Perhaps the thinking is that affording indigent defendants a say in the matter is impracticable. Yet there are ways to structure the appointment of counsel, discussed above, that accommodate administrative realities while according indigent defendants a measure of choice.[159] This is an accommodation we ought to pursue and, indeed, the Fourteenth Amendment would seem to impel us to do so.[160]

* * *

If one can say nothing else, it is that the right to counsel of choice is grossly undertheorized, particularly for an entitlement said to embody the "root meaning" of the "mo[st] essential" criminal procedure right.[161] Perhaps the Court's decision in *Luis* deserves the praise it has received.[162] But it looks to me a lot like selective empathy that is, at bottom, difficult to justify by notions of individual desert. Seeing the doctrine now for what it really does, we are positioned to consider whether the right is best limited, as it is today, to effectuating system architecture, or whether it ought to be given wider compass to benefit all defendants more directly.

---

[159] See text accompanying notes 107–11.

[160] For a similar argument, see Tague, 27 Stan L Rev at 88–89 (cited in note 107).

[161] *Lakeside v Oregon*, 435 US 333, 341 (1978) ("In an adversary system of criminal justice, there is no right more essential than the right to the assistance of counsel.").

[162] See, for example, Mark Joseph Stern, *The Supreme Court Affirms Your Right to Hire a Lawyer of Your Choosing* (Slate, Mar 30, 2016), archived at https://perma.cc/84Y7-MW64.

ALLEGRA M. McLEOD

POLICE VIOLENCE, CONSTITUTIONAL COMPLICITY, AND ANOTHER VANTAGE

What role has the U.S. Supreme Court played in perpetuating police violence? In a series of remarkable dissenting opinions, Justice Sonia Sotomayor has underscored the Supreme Court's complicity in police abuse.

Dissenting in *Mullenix v Luna*, Justice Sotomayor warned that the Court has sanctioned "a 'shoot first, think later' approach to policing."[1] As Sotomayor explained: "When Mullenix"—an officer who had just shot and killed a motorist despite receiving instructions not to do so—"confronted his superior officer after the shooting . . . [Mullenix's] first words were, 'How's that for proactive?'" This comment "was apparently referencing an earlier counseling session" in which his superior officer noted Mullenix "was not enterprising enough." Sotomayor observed that the "glib comment does not impact our legal analysis; an officer's actual intentions are irrelevant to the Fourth Amendment's 'objectively reasonable' inquiry." She suggested, however, that "the comment seems . . . revealing of the culture this Court's decision supports when it calls it reasonable—or even reasonably

Allegra M. McLeod is Professor of Law at Georgetown University Law Center.

Author's note: I am grateful to Amna Akbar, Paul Butler, Didier Fassin, Sherally Munshi, Louis Michael Seidman, Abbe Smith, and Geof Stone for their generous engagement of the ideas in this essay.

[1] 136 S Ct 305, 316 (2015) (Sotomayor, J, dissenting).

978-0-226-49084-7/2017/2016-0005$10.00

reasonable—to use deadly force for no discernible gain and over a supervisor's express order to 'stand by.'"[2]

At oral argument in *Heien v North Carolina*, as Justice Sotomayor questioned the senior deputy attorney general representing North Carolina, she pointed out that the traffic stop in question was purely pretextual: "There is a problem, however, I'm sorry," Sotomayor interjected.[3] "The police officer wasn't stopping him because of the brake light. The police officer was involved in criminal interdictions and admitted that this was a pretext, a lawful pretext, he thought. . . . So how many citizens have been stopped for one brake light who are asked to have their car searched? And is that something we as a society should be encouraging?"[4] Ultimately, in her dissent in *Heien*, Sotomayor wondered "how a citizen seeking to be law-abiding and to structure his or her behavior to avoid these invasive, frightening, and humiliating encounters could do so."[5]

In her dissent in *Utah v Strieff*, addressing the reader directly, Justice Sotomayor described how "this Court has allowed an officer to stop you for whatever reason he wants—so long as he can point to a pretextual justification after the fact."[6] The majority opinion in *Strieff*, authored by Justice Clarence Thomas, held only that the discovery of an outstanding warrant following an initial illegal stop may permit the entry into evidence of subsequently identified contraband. Yet, Sotomayor's dissent in *Strieff* assailed both the majority's holding and the pernicious contours and effects of the Court's Fourth Amendment jurisprudence more generally.[7] Sotomayor described how the "Court has given officers an array of instruments to probe and examine" without adequate cause, to target "pedestrians in an arbitrary manner," and to treat "members of our communities as second class citizens."[8] Citing the writings of W. E. B. Du Bois, James Baldwin, Marie Gottschalk, and Gabriel Chin, among others, Sotomayor analyzed the legal question in *Strieff* in connection with the relevant findings of federal investigations of local police departments,

---

[2] Id.

[3] Transcript of Oral Argument in *Heien v North Carolina*, Oct 6, 2014, at 33.

[4] Id at 33–34.

[5] 135 S Ct 530, 544 (Sotomayor, J, dissenting).

[6] 136 S Ct 2056, 2069 (2016) (Sotomayor, J, dissenting) (citing *Whren v United States*, 517 US 806, 813 (1996)).

[7] See id at 2059 (majority).

[8] See id.

and concluded that until our constitutional discourse meaningfully attends to the experiences and voices of marginalized peoples, "our justice system will continue to be anything but."[9]

Sotomayor's dissenting opinions in these cases importantly reconceptualize the relationship of constitutional law to the persistent legacies of racialized violence in the United States. While recognizing that constitutional law is not the primary cause of police violence nor the most direct or effective means of redressing it, Sotomayor intimates that for the United States to break from these brutal histories and continuing practices will require, among other things, a transformation of our constitutional discourse and imagination. Moreover, while noting in her dissent in *Strieff* that she is writing "only for herself" and relying in part on her own "professional experience"—perhaps suggesting a departure from a more conventional form of judicial analysis—Sotomayor gestures toward what a more just constitutional discourse might entail.[10] In so doing, she offers both a vision of what ails constitutional criminal procedure—its permission to police to engage in needless violence, its empty formalism, its ahistorical originalism—and an account of how constitutional discourse might one day be transformed to more fully recognize the voices of those too seldom heard.

This article unfolds in two parts. Part I explores the parameters of the Supreme Court's complicity in police violence, engaging further Justice Sotomayor's critique of constitutional criminal procedure with particular attention to her dissent in *Strieff*. More specifically, Part I reveals how the Court has fashioned a body of doctrine that countenances what Paul Butler calls "police super powers" to engage in racialized abuse at the same time that the Court elides the reality of the violence of policing through a vacuous formalism and amnesiac originalism.[11] Part II considers the gesture implicit in Sotomayor's dissents toward an alternative constitutional future, however distant that future might be.

I. "No One Can Breathe in This Atmosphere"

According to the Department of Justice, police departments across the United States—from Baltimore to Los Angeles—have

---

[9] See id at 2071, 2064–71 (Sotomayor, J, dissenting).

[10] See id at 2069.

[11] See Paul Butler, *The System Is Working the Way It Is Supposed To: The Limits of Criminal Justice Reform*, 104 Georgetown L J 1419 (2016).

routinely conducted pretextual stops, and engaged in profiling, harassment, and the use of excessive force.[12] The names Philando Castile, Sandra Bland, Eric Garner, and numerous others now widely call to mind the horrific scenes:[13] a young man stopped by police for a trivial violation and shot dead at point-blank range in his car in front of his girlfriend and her small child;[14] a young woman detained and assaulted following a minor traffic infraction, dead in custody shortly after;[15] a father choked to death on the sidewalk in the course of an arrest for allegedly selling loose cigarettes.[16]

Many others are less well known. The Justice Department's investigation of the Baltimore City Police Department, for instance, recounts the experience of one young woman strip searched on the side of the street, her anal cavity inspected, in the course of a routine traffic stop for a broken headlight, and then released with a repair order for her vehicle after no weapons or contraband were found.[17] In another incident, while responding to a call to assist in transporting an unarmed woman in mental health crisis for evaluation, police repeatedly deployed a taser on her in drive-stun mode, causing painful electric shocks to course through her body, despite the fact that she posed no serious threat to the officers or others and was being transported for a psychiatric evaluation rather than arrested for a crime.[18]

Although the facts of individual cases may be disputed and no one example demonstrates necessarily that something is seriously amiss, there is an undeniable pattern of case after case of police violence. These incidents often begin with a police stop for a trivial offense and

---

[12] See Department of Justice, Investigations of Law Enforcement Agencies, Cases and Matters, at https://www.justice.gov/crt/special-litigation-section-cases-and-matters0#police (providing links to investigation reports on more than twenty law enforcement agencies finding a pattern and practice of rights violations).

[13] See Damien Cave and Rochelle Oliver, *The Raw Videos That Have Sparked Outrage Over Police Treatment of Blacks*, NY Times (Oct 4, 2016) (last updated), at http://www.nytimes.com/interactive/2015/07/30/us/police-videos-race.html.

[14] See, for example, Matt Furber and Richard Pérez-Peña, *After Philando Castile's Killing, Obama Calls Police Killings "an American Issue,"* NY Times (July 7, 2016).

[15] See Abby Ohlheiser and Abby Phillip, *"I will light you up!": Texas Officer Threatened Sandra Bland with Taser During Traffic Stop*, Wash Post (July 22, 2015).

[16] See Joseph Goldstein and Nate Schweber, *Man's Death After Chokehold Raises Old Issue for the Police*, NY Times (July 18, 2014).

[17] See U.S. Department of Justice, Civil Rights Division, Investigation of the Baltimore City Police Department, August 10, 2016, at 32.

[18] See id at 78.

end with extraordinary brutality. In her dissent in *Strieff*, Justice Sotomayor calls attention to this broader context and to the connections between these brutal acts, insisting that we "not pretend the countless people who are routinely targeted by police are 'isolated.'" Instead, she observes, "[t]hey are the canaries in the coal mine, whose deaths, civil and literal, warn us that no one can breathe in this atmosphere"—evoking Eric Garner's dying plea that has become a protest cry for the Black Lives Matter movement, "I can't breathe."[19] As Lani Guinier and Gerald Torres proposed in *The Miner's Canary*, which Sotomayor references, these acts of racialized violence, like the ailing canary in the coal mine, point to the existence of a toxic environment. And one part of that toxic environment, which Sotomayor's dissents elucidate, is a body of constitutional law that demands transformation.[20]

A. DOCTRINAL COMPLICITY

The Supreme Court's constitutional criminal procedure doctrine sanctions much of the policing activity that led to the deaths of Philando Castile, Sandra Bland, and Eric Garner, as well as to the roadside strip search and tasing of the two women in Baltimore whose ordeals are recounted in the Department of Justice's report.

1. *Profiling and the routine use of pretextual stops.* The Supreme Court in *Whren v United States* unanimously authorized police to engage in pretextual policing consistent with the Fourth Amendment, targeting people on racial grounds so long as there is a traffic violation or other minor criminal offense to support the stop.[21] Given the vast criminalization of so much harmless conduct, pretexts are readily available.

Philando Castile was pulled over in a traffic stop, as the officer explained over the police radio, because Castile looked "suspicious"

[19] See 136 S Ct at 2071; *"I can't breathe": Eric Garner Put in Chokehold by NYPD Officer*, Guardian (Dec 4, 2014), at https://www.theguardian.com/us-news/video/2014/dec/04/i-cant-breathe-eric-garner-chokehold-death-video.

[20] See Lani Guinier and Gerald Torres, *The Miner's Canary: Enlisting Race, Resisting Power* (2002).

[21] See 517 US 806, 809–10 (1996). Although the Court has said only that pretextual stops do not violate the Fourth Amendment, and has acknowledged that such stops could violate the Equal Protection Clause, any redress for profiling and the use of pretextual stops is unlikely under the Equal Protection Clause. There is no exclusionary rule for the Equal Protection Clause, equal protection violations are difficult to prove, and many pretextual stops do not satisfy the Court's onerous criteria for equal protection violations.

to the officer.[22] "The two occupants just look like people that were involved in a robbery," the officer maintained as he commenced the stop.[23] "The driver looks more like one of our suspects, just because of the wide-set nose. I couldn't get a good look at the passenger."[24] Castile was an African-American male driving with a female passenger and her young child.[25] The suspects in a robbery committed earlier that week were reportedly two African-American males.[26] No other information suggested any similarities in appearance or otherwise between the suspects and Castile.

Castile's partner, Diamond Reynolds, who was in the car and witnessed Castile being killed, reported that the officers pulled over the vehicle for a broken taillight.[27] During the decade before his death, Castile was pulled over by police almost fifty times for minor infractions like driving with his license plate improperly illuminated or turning into a parking lot without signaling.[28] In the course of what would be his final stop, Castile informed the officer that he had a lawful license to carry a firearm and that he would provide his identification and registration as requested. Within 103 seconds of the initial stop, one of the officers had shot and killed Castile.[29]

Increased exposure to stops increases the risk that encounters will escalate to the sort of violence that led to Castile's death. And these are precisely the kind of unnecessary pretextual stops the Supreme Court has authorized. As Justice Sotomayor points out in her dissent in *Strieff*, the Supreme Court has countenanced the use of minor pretexts and profiles so long as there is some basis to support a stop, such as a broken taillight.[30] The basis for the stop, Sotomayor cautions, may "factor in your ethnicity,"[31] and it may also take into ac-

---

[22] See Andy Mannix, *Police Audio: Officer Stopped Castile on Robbery Suspicion*, Star Tribune (July 12, 2016).

[23] Id.

[24] Id.

[25] Id.

[26] See id.

[27] See id.

[28] See Sharon LaFraniere and Mitch Smith, *Philando Castile Was Pulled Over 49 Times in 13 Years, Often for Minor Infractions*, NY Times (July 16, 2016).

[29] See Mannix, *Police Audio: Officer Stopped Castile on Robbery Suspicion* (cited in note 22).

[30] See 136 S Ct at 2069.

[31] See *United States v Brignoni-Ponce*, 422 US 873, 886–87 (1975) (permitting the consideration of "Hispanic appearance" with regard to Mexican border violations).

count one's place of residence,[32] attire,[33] and even quite possibly such innocent behavior as jogging or running, especially if the target is in a "lower-income, high-crime" neighborhood.[34] Echoing her dissent in *Heien*, Sotomayor added that "[t]he officer does not even need to know which law you might have broken so long as he can later point to any possible infraction—even one that is minor, unrelated, or ambiguous."[35]

The Court's recent decision in *Strieff* compounds the problems posed by routine stops for trivial infractions by effectively enabling police to stop anyone they suspect may have an outstanding warrant. Immediately before his arrest, Edward Strieff was leaving a home suspected to be a "drug house."[36] Officer Frackrell had received an anonymous tip that drug activity was ongoing at this particular residence and the officer had conducted surveillance on the residence over several days. Officer Frackrell was suspicious because he had noticed more people than he thought would be typical coming and leaving the house. Although he did not see Edward Strieff enter the home, and though he had no other information about Strieff, Officer Frackrell decided to stop Strieff as he was leaving the residence. He approached Strieff and demanded his name and identification. The State of Utah conceded that Officer Frackrell did not have any lawful justification or reasonable suspicion to stop Strieff, and the Supreme Court likewise assumed there was no lawful justification for the stop. But the officer stopped Strieff nonetheless. Then, when Officer Frackrell ran Strieff's identification he discovered an unpaid traffic warrant and proceeded to arrest Strieff. In the course of the arrest, Officer Frackrell discovered narcotics and drug paraphernalia in Strieff's pocket. The majority in *Strieff* allowed this material to be entered into evidence notwithstanding the illegal stop and warrant check.[37] By eliminating the remedy of exclusion following such illegal stops, *Utah v Strieff* effectively extends the authority for a stop, arrest, and search to those circumstances in which there was no lawful ba-

[32] See *Adams v Williams*, 407 US 143, 147 (1972).

[33] See *United States v Sokolow*, 490 US 1, 4–5 (1989).

[34] See *Illinois v Wardlow*, 528 US 119, 124–25 (2000).

[35] See *Devenpeck v Alford*, 543 US 146, 154–55 (2004); *Heien v North Carolina*, 135 S Ct 530 (2014).

[36] See 136 S Ct at 2059–60 (majority).

[37] See id at 2059.

sis for the stop but where the officer later identifies an outstanding warrant.

As Justice Sotomayor and Justice Kagan both emphasize in their separate dissents, millions of Americans have outstanding warrants for minor traffic-related offenses or unpaid tickets.[38] Utah alone lists 180,000 outstanding misdemeanor warrants, and at the time of Strieff's arrest "Salt Lake County had a 'backlog of outstanding warrants' so large that it faced the 'potential for civil liability.'"[39]

Strieff thus encourages officers to stop those persons they suspect may have minor outstanding warrants, even without any justification whatsoever. If no warrant is discovered, the aggrieved citizen is unlikely to seek or obtain any recompense or redress. But often, the officer will get lucky, discover a warrant, make an arrest, and, as in Strieff's case, the officer may even locate some drug-related or other evidence to support additional charges.

The Supreme Court could instead have forbidden the use of unnecessary pretextual stops as unreasonable searches and seizures violative of the Fourth Amendment. More generally, police departments could concentrate resources on addressing more serious harms, instructing line law enforcement officers to refrain from pretextual policing or stopping people, like Strieff, who might be suspected of having outstanding warrants for minor infractions. But instead, the Supreme Court has encouraged law enforcement practices that tend to exacerbate the dynamics of predatory policing.

2. *The degrading ordeal of searches and arrests.* Once a stop has taken place, the Supreme Court has approved invasive procedures to search and has upheld as consistent with the Fourth Amendment a full custodial arrest and intrusive body-cavity inspection even for the most trivial offenses. In *Atwater v City of Lago Vista*, a mother driving with her two young children was subject to a full custodial arrest for failure to fasten her seatbelt. In 2001, the Court held this to be a constitutionally reasonable seizure, permitting a full custodial arrest when the violation in question is as minor as a simple traffic infraction.[40]

---

[38] See id at 2068 (Sotomayor, J, dissenting), 2073 (Kagan, J, dissenting).

[39] See id at 2066 (Sotomayor, J, dissenting) (citing Dept of Justice, Bureau of Justice Statistics, Survey of State Criminal History Information Systems, 2014 (2015) (Systems Survey) (Table 5a), at https://www.ncjrs.gov/pdffiles1/bjs/grants/249799.pdf; Inst for Law and Policy Planning, Salt Lake County Criminal Justice System Assessment 6.7 (2004), at http://www.slco.org/cjac/resources/SaltLakeCJSAfinal.pdf.

[40] 532 US 318, 354 (2001).

As a consequence, after Sandra Bland was stopped purportedly for a failure to signal when changing lanes, the officer, "fearing for his safety," could constitutionally order her from her vehicle, arrest her for the traffic violation, and subject her to a search of her body. Eric Garner was likewise subject to a full custodial arrest for selling loose cigarettes, a course of action also countenanced by the Court's Fourth Amendment jurisprudence. Like unnecessary, pretextual stops, such searches and arrests for non-serious offenses increase the risk of exposure to physical abuse and are too often associated with lethal violence.

Even absent any cause or decision to arrest, the Supreme Court has authorized invasive and humiliating roadside and pedestrian searches for minor infractions, as Justice Sotomayor noted in her dissent in *Strieff*:

> The indignity of the stop is not limited to an officer telling you that you look like a criminal. The officer may next ask for your "consent" to inspect your bag or purse without telling you that you can decline. Regardless of your answer, he may order you to stand, "helpless, perhaps facing a wall with [your] hands raised." If the officer thinks you might be dangerous, he may then "frisk" you for weapons. This involves more than just a pat down. As onlookers pass by, the officer may "feel with sensitive fingers every potion of [your] body. A thorough search [may] be made of [your] arms and armpits, waistline and back, the groin and area about the testicles, and entire surface of the legs down to the feet."[41]

An individual who is subject to arrest, even for a minor traffic violation, may then be subjected to a close visual inspection of his or her naked body without any individualized suspicion under *Florence v Board of Chosen Freeholders of the County of Burlington*.[42] As Justice Breyer explained in his dissent in *Florence*, for the individual so inspected this includes "spreading and/or lifting his testicles to expose the area behind them and bending over and/or spreading the cheeks of his buttocks to expose his anus. For females, the procedures are similar except females must in addition, squat to expose the vagina."[43] Furthermore, in the course of effectuating such an arrest and bringing the individual into custody, the Court has authorized the use of such

[41] 136 S Ct at 2070 (extensive internal citations omitted) (citing *Florida v Bostick*, 501 US 429, 438 (1991), *Terry v Ohio*, 392 US 1, 17 (1968)).

[42] 132 S Ct 1510, 1518 (2012).

[43] Id at 1525 (Breyer, J, dissenting).

force as the officer deems "reasonably necessary" in his or her "split-second judgment" to bring the arrestee under law enforcement control.[44]

The Court is complicit in these acts of physical and sexual violation, in which the arrestee may be forced to strip naked and submit to a close inspection of his or her genitals and anus. Such a search may be conducted in the absence of any individualized suspicion and at the threat of force should the arrestee not comply. In any context other than in jail or prison, where the Supreme Court has held that such invasions are constitutionally reasonable, a forced encounter of this sort would be understood as a profoundly violative assault.[45]

3. *"Shoot first, think later" policing.* In addition to the rules governing the early stages of police-citizen encounters and arrests, the Supreme Court has authorized the use of deadly force under circumstances that expose certain citizens to undue risks of serious injury and even death. The Court's opinions on the use of lethal force, together with its qualified immunity doctrine, exacerbate these risks. In *Scott v Harris*, decided in 2007, the Court considered a civil suit brought by Victor Harris.[46] Harris, a college student, fled police when they tried to apprehend him for a traffic violation as he drove home from a long day at work and school.[47] As Harris led officers on a high-speed chase, the police decided to use a potentially lethal "pit stop" maneuver to end the pursuit.[48] After an officer executed the maneuver, Harris's car flipped over several times.[49] Harris was severely injured and rendered quadriplegic.[50]

As is often the case, it was not necessary for the officers in that situation to use deadly force. To end the pursuit, the officers could simply have taken down Harris's license plate number and later apprehended him for the traffic violation and his flight, or they could have used tire spikes to end the chase, among other alternatives.[51]

---

[44] See *Graham v Connor*, 490 US 386, 397 (1989).

[45] See Gabriel Arkles, *Regulating Prison Sexual Violence*, 7 Northeastern U L J 71 (2015).

[46] See 550 US 372.

[47] See *Why I Ran*, video, at https://www.youtube.com/watch?v=JATVLUOjzvM (documenting Victor Harris and Officer Scott's respective experiences of the events in *Scott v Harris*).

[48] See 550 US at 375.

[49] See id.

[50] See id.

[51] See, for example, id at 393 (Stevens, J, dissenting) ("What would have happened if the police had decided to abandon the chase? We now know that they could have apprehended

Nonetheless, the Court—in an eight-to-one decision authored by Justice Scalia with only Justice Stevens dissenting—held that summary judgment should have been granted to the officer on the basis of qualified immunity. The Court thus made clear from that point forward that the police may use deadly force consistent with the Fourth Amendment, even when death or severe injury could be readily avoided. Although the Court had previously held that deadly force could not be used to arrest an individual unless that person posed a risk of significant bodily harm, *Harris* determined that the suspect's flight itself posed such a risk.[52]

Subsequently, in *Mullenix v Luna*, the Court explained that Israel Leija fled the police in his car after an officer attempted to serve a warrant on him.[53] In order to end the chase, other officers set up tire spikes in three locations some distance ahead of Leija's vehicle.[54] But just before Leija approached the tire spikes, Officer Mullenix, against his supervisor's instructions, fired repeated shots at Leija, four of which hit Leija's upper body, killing him.[55] In a per curiam opinion, decided without the benefit of full briefing or oral argument, the Court held that Officer Mullenix was entitled to qualified immunity, because no clearly established law required him to desist from using lethal force until other avenues of terminating the encounter had been exhausted. The Court reiterated its earlier decisions to the effect that the Fourth Amendment does not require police officers to attempt to de-escalate an encounter before using deadly force.[56] By failing to hold that the Fourth Amendment forbids the use of unnecessary and unreasonable force in such circumstances, the Court ensured that police officers will continue to invoke qualified immunity in similar cases in the future.

Justice Sotomayor was the lone dissenter *Mullenix*.[57] In her dissent, she decried the "shoot first, think later" model of policing that the

respondent later because they had his license plate number. Even if that were not true, and even if he would have escaped any punishment at all, the use of deadly force in this case was no[t] . . . appropriate. . . .").

[52] See id at 383–84.

[53] See 136 S Ct at 306.

[54] See id.

[55] See id at 307.

[56] See *Scott v Harris*, 550 US 372 (2007).

[57] See 136 S Ct at 313–16.

Court has consistently tolerated.[58] As a consequence of these and other precedents, in *Fenwick v Pudimott*, after officers opened fire on a sixteen-year-old unarmed boy for failing to stop his car in a parking lot when ordered, Judge David Tatel—writing for a unanimous panel of the D.C. Circuit—held that the officers violated no clearly established law and were therefore entitled to qualified immunity.[59]

Even when officers are called to assist a person in mental health crisis, the Court has upheld a grant of qualified immunity to officers who unnecessarily shot at a mentally impaired individual in order to take her to the hospital. In *City and County of San Francisco v Sheehan*, a social worker at a group home for the mentally ill called for assistance to transport Teresa Sheehan—a woman with a schizoaffective disorder who was suffering an acute mental health crisis—to a hospital facility for secure evaluation and treatment.[60] A social worker at the group home reported to police that Sheehan had been refusing medication for days and had not been eating or changing her clothes.[61] When confronted by the social worker in her private room, Sheehan issued verbal threats, but had not left her bed. Staff described her to the police as "gravely disabled."[62]

After arriving on the scene, two police officers contacted the psychiatric emergency services department at San Francisco General Hospital to confirm that the staff there would be prepared to admit Sheehan.[63] The officers then attempted to enter Sheehan's room using the social worker's key. Sheehan responded by verbally threatening the officers and grabbing a knife from her kitchen area, stating that she did not need any help. The officers retreated and phoned for backup.[64]

Within minutes, the officers heard sirens indicating that backup was nearing the scene, but before the backup arrived, and reportedly fearing Sheehan might escape through a window, the officers reentered Sheehan's room.[65] Sheehan again wielded the kitchen knife

[58] See id at 316.

[59] See 778 F3d 133, 138–40 (2015).

[60] 135 S Ct 1765, 1769–70 (2015).

[61] See id.

[62] See id.

[63] Id at 1770.

[64] See id.

[65] See id at 1771.

and the officers pepper sprayed her in her face. When Sheehan did not drop the knife, both officers opened fire, shooting Sheehan multiple times.[66] The Supreme Court held that the officers were entitled to qualified immunity because, under established law, they had no obligation to alter their conduct to accommodate Sheehan's known disability.[67]

In these and other opinions, the Supreme Court has authorized the police to act with relatively little restraint, approving expansive police discretion or police "super powers." In the process, the Court has normalized and constitutionalized a set of practices that consign the most vulnerable citizens, especially those in low-income communities of color, to a condition of virtual statelessness, characterized by the simultaneous over-enforcement and under-protection of the law.[68] And while the Court's decisions were not the only or even the primary cause of these brutal events and circumstances, they have contributed to their occurrence and served to legitimate the unconscionable use of police violence.

B. THE FORMALIST ABYSS AND VOICES UNHEARD

Apart from these specific doctrines, there are other features of constitutional criminal procedure jurisprudence that tend to countenance and legitimate police abuse. Particularly notable is the Court's formalist and hypertechnical approach, which accompanies a pervasive inattention to other perspectives and accounts of relevant harms. Justice Sotomayor cautions the reader at the outset of her dissent in *Strieff*: "Do not be soothed by the opinion's technical language."[69] And it is, indeed, often the technical language and reasoning associated with the Court's formalist approach in this area of the law that has facilitated the Court's neglect of the actual state of police-citizen encounters.

This formalist approach obscures the actual meaning and effect of this body of law both by neglecting the voices and experiences of

---

[66] See id.

[67] See id at 1774.

[68] See Butler, 104 Georgetown L J (cited in note 11); see also Monica C. Bell, *Police Reform and the Dismantling of Legal Cynicism*, 126 Yale L J (forthcoming 2017); Lisa L. Miller, *What's Violence Got to Do With It? Inequality, Punishment, and State Failure in U.S. Politics*, 17 Punishment & Society 184, 185 (2015).

[69] See 136 S Ct at 2064.

those most directly concerned and by centering attention instead on a highly technical analysis of existing doctrinal terms and exceptions. The Court's Fourth Amendment jurisprudence consistently takes this form, focusing on narrow terminological questions and time frames. The doctrine generally requires that a wrong be identified in peculiarly formalist and abstract procedural language that references specific doctrinal subcategories developed in prior decisions. Rather than focus on the actual circumstances at issue in a case—the effects of a particular course of law enforcement conduct on a particular person—the Court concentrates on a narrow subset of judicially created categories and exceptions without considering the reasonableness, fairness, or justice of the conditions it confronts. In short, this body of law has become mired in internal and highly formalistic disputes, while losing sight of the actual experiences and realities it purports to address.

The Court's opinion in *Utah v Strieff* perfectly illustrates this formalist approach and its far remove from the most pressing questions posed by the case. The majority's opinion begins by reciting the convoluted morass of exceptions to the exclusionary rule and specifically those associated with the "fruit of the poisonous tree" doctrine. As Justice Thomas explains, although the Court has held that in certain circumstances an illegal search or seizure will require the exclusion of subsequently discovered evidence, it has developed a tripartite framework to determine whether evidence discovered following an illegal stop or search should be considered contaminated by the initial illegality—as fruit of the poisonous tree—and excluded, or whether it should be admitted under one of several exceptions to the fruit of the poisonous tree doctrine.[70]

Of the various exceptions to the exclusionary rule, three relate specifically to the fruit of the poisonous tree doctrine and to "the causal relationship between an unconstitutional act and the discovery of evidence."[71] These three exceptions include the "independent source doctrine," which asks whether the police had independent lawful access to the evidence in question through a separate source; the "inevitable discovery doctrine," which asks whether an already commenced investigation would invariably have identified the evidence in question; and the "attenuation doctrine," which is the primary focus of

[70] See id at 2061 (majority).

[71] Id.

the analysis in *Strieff*.[72] The attenuation doctrine assesses the "causal link between the government's unlawful acts and the discovery of evidence."[73] Justice Thomas characterizes the central question in *Strieff* as "whether this attenuation doctrine applies when an officer makes an unconstitutional investigatory stop; learns during that stop that the suspect is subject to a valid arrest warrant; and proceeds to arrest the suspect and seize incriminating evidence during a search incident to that arrest."[74]

Whether this attenuation doctrine applies depends on another multipart test, which evaluates three factors articulated in *Brown v Illinois*.[75] First, a court is to consider the temporal proximity of the government's unlawful acts to the discovery of the evidence.[76] Second, a court is to consider whether there were intervening circumstances that led to the discovery of the evidence apart from the government's unlawful acts.[77] Third, a court is to assess the flagrancy and purpose of the official misconduct.[78] The relevant benchmarks in this analysis are primarily previous decisions in which these terms—temporal proximity, intervening circumstance, and flagrancy—have been defined. The broader context of the law enforcement practice in question and the likely effects of the practice on the lives of real people and real communities figure nowhere in this analysis.

Predictably, then, the majority in *Strieff* mechanically applied the three *Brown* factors to find that exclusion was not warranted.[79] More specifically, the majority reasoned that although the state lost on the first factor—temporal proximity—because the unlawful stop of Strieff was very close in time to the discovery of the outstanding warrant, it won on the other two factors.[80] With respect to the second factor, the majority treated the discovery of the warrant as an intervening circumstance independent of the unlawful stop because the warrant pre-

---

[72] See id.

[73] See id.

[74] Id at 2059.

[75] See 422 US 590 (1975).

[76] See 136 S Ct at 2061–62.

[77] See id.

[78] See id.

[79] See id at 2062–64.

[80] See id.

existed the stop.[81] With respect to the third factor, the majority suggested there was no evidence in this case that the unlawful stop was especially "flagrant" or purposefully orchestrated as part of a practice of conducting such illegal stops, but instead merely reflected "negligence" on the part of the officer.[82] The majority thus held that because the state prevailed on factors two and three, the evidence was admissible.[83]

Notwithstanding increased public attention to questions of policing, the majority's opinion did not move beyond this highly abstract, formalistic application of the attenuation doctrine. The majority treated the rigid attenuation framework as exhausting the interpretive and analytic possibilities available to resolve the case. The extensive evidence of illegal warrant checks cited by Justice Sotomayor in dissent and also referenced in Justice Kagan's dissent—as well as by the Utah Supreme Court—did not figure anywhere in the majority's analysis. Justice Thomas also failed to explain why we have reached a juncture where this is how the question in the case should be framed and answered, rather than by addressing more generally the reasonableness of a suspicionless seizure that leads to the discovery of an outstanding warrant for a petty offense.

It bears noting that there is nothing necessarily wrong with using fine-tuned predetermined rules to guide legal analysis. Problems arise, though, when a predetermined formal framework precludes any analysis of the relevant implications of the decision either for the parties or for other affected individuals and communities. Just as the Court in *Katz v United States* revisited the meaning of "search" to adapt the application of the Fourth Amendment to new circumstances and understandings, so too should the Court today revisit the meaning of "unreasonable" in light of current realities.[84] In short, the Court should ask whether the current practices of law enforcement conduct are "reasonable," as the text of the Fourth Amendment plainly requires. Is it "reasonable" for police officers to conduct suspicionless stops, demand identification, and then run that information to determine whether an individual has an outstanding warrant for which he or she might be arrested, searched, and detained? For those steeped in current doctrine and accustomed to its formal conventions, the

[81] See id.

[82] See id.

[83] See id.

[84] 389 US 347 (1967).

narrow terminological points of emphasis in the Court's analysis will seem natural, perhaps even inevitable, but this is only because we have become inured to this mode of narrowly formalist legal discourse. This approach to constitutional decision making simply ignores or countenances criminal law enforcement's violent excesses.

Of course, this is not a new phenomenon. Nearly a century ago, realist critics identified the terminological circularity and nearsightedness of the pervasive formalism in American law.[85] More recently, Michael Klarman and Naomi Murakawa have identified how legal actors in the middle of the twentieth century invoked formal procedural approaches to avoid addressing racial injustice in criminal law enforcement in a more meaningful manner.[86] This capture of constitutional criminal procedure by narrow formalism and empty proceduralism has only worsened in recent years.

The late William Stuntz pointed to a related paradox or contradiction that defines the U.S. criminal process. On the one hand, the Constitution establishes extensive criminal procedure protections, and, on the other hand, the United States maintains an excessively harsh, unconscionably violent, racially and class skewed criminal process.[87] Stuntz believed this paradox could be explained in part by the fact that the Supreme Court has focused almost exclusively on procedural rather than substantive justice in its constitutional decisions.[88] But what the development of constitutional law in this realm over the last two decades demonstrates is that the Court is no longer meaningfully attending to procedural justice. The perverse consequence of the Warren Court's turn to more formal procedural rules to replace vague often-violated standards in criminal law enforcement is that the Warren Court's rule-bound jurisprudence has over time distracted attention from a fact-specific, context-sensitive analysis of police-citizen encounters.[89] Instead, the Court has lost its way in a formalist abyss.

---

[85] See, for example, Felix S. Cohen, *Transcendental Nonsense and the Functional Approach*, 35 Colum L Rev 809, 811 (1935) ("Strange as this manner of argument will seem to laymen, lawyers trained by long practice in believing what is impossible, will accept this reasoning as relevant, material, and competent.").

[86] See, for example, Michael Klarman, *The Racial Origins of Modern Criminal Procedure*, 99 Mich L Rev 48 (2000); Naomi Murakawa, *The First Civil Right: How Liberals Built Prison America* (2014).

[87] See, for example, William J. Stuntz, *The Collapse of American Criminal Justice* (2011); William J. Stuntz, *The Pathological Politics of Criminal Law*, 100 Mich L Rev 505, 509; William J. Stuntz, *The Political Constitution of Criminal Justice*, 119 Harv L Rev 780, 792 (2006).

[88] See id.

[89] See, for example, Charles D. Weisselberg, *Mourning Miranda*, 96 Cal L Rev 1519 (2008).

A further distorting effect of the prevailing approach to constitutional criminal procedure is that this formalist understanding also shapes public perceptions of the relevant metrics by which we should assess pressing social concerns. After Sandra Bland's death, for example, the public discussion of what occurred focused overwhelmingly on the constitutionality of the events leading up to Bland's arrest within these narrow formalist terms.[90] CNN's Danny Cevallos's discussion of the constitutional implications of Bland's case provides a succinct illustration:

> In the sometimes nebulous law of car stops, there are a few bright-line rules. One of these rules will inform how this video will be scrutinized over the next few days, and it is this: If your motor vehicle is lawfully stopped for a traffic violation, police can order you out of the car. Period. Texas State Trooper Brian Encinia stopped Bland on July 10, supposedly for not signaling a turn. After Trooper Encinia decided to issue only a warning, but before Bland knew she was free to leave, he asked her why she was upset. Then he ordered her to extinguish her cigarette. Bland refused. Trooper Encinia then ordered her to step out of the car. When she refused that, Encinia told her she was under arrest, saying, "I am giving you a lawful order" and pulling a weapon that looks to be a Taser. In an instant, this escalated from a mere warning to the Trooper shouting, "Get out of the car!" and threatening to ". . . light you up! Get out! Now!" Like the vast majority of citizens, Sandra Bland appeared to be just unaware of the rule; as evidenced by her audible objection to the idea that you could be ordered out of your car after failing to signal a turn. Bland says, "Wow, really, for a failure to signal? You're doing all of this for a failure to signal?" The officer certainly was aware that he had this power. . . . Surely he had been trained to know the moment she refused his "exit order," she unwittingly committed a technical violation that would ultimately form the basis of an arrest. But like most citizens, Bland was shocked at the notion that we can be ordered from our cars during a routine stop. It just feels wrong, doesn't it? Not to the U.S. Supreme Court it doesn't.[91]

---

[90] See, for example, Orin Kerr, *The Law of the Sandra Bland Traffic Stop*, Wash Post (July 23, 2015), at https://www.washingtonpost.com/news/volokh-conspiracy/wp/2015/07/23/the-law-of-the-sandra-bland-traffic-stop/?utm_term=.e3ba76c4ea46; Mark Joseph Stern, *Sandra Bland Arrest: Her Detention Was Legal, but Encina Used Excessive Force*, Slate (July 22, 2015), at http://www.slate.com/blogs/the_slatest/2015/07/22/sandra_bland_arrest_her_detention_was_legal_but_encinia_used_excessive_force.html; Rachel Kleinman, *What the Supreme Court Would Say About Sandra Bland's Arrest*, MSNBC (July 22, 2015), at http://www.msnbc.com/msnbc/what-scotus-would-say-sandra-bland-arrest; K. K. Rebecca Lai et al, *Assessing the Legality of Sandra Bland's Arrest*, NY Times (July 22, 2015), at http://www.nytimes.com/interactive/2015/07/20/us/sandra-bland-arrest-death-videos-maps.html?_r=0.

[91] Danny Cevallos, *Was Sandra Bland's Traffic Stop Legal and Fair?*, CNN (July 23, 2015), at http://www.cnn.com/2015/07/23/opinions/cevallos-sandra-bland-traffic-stop/; see also *Pennsylvania v Mimms*, 434 US 106 (1977) (holding an officer may order a passenger out of a car if concerned for his or her safety).

Cevallos concluded that even though the existing rules of criminal procedure may authorize law enforcement conduct that seems altogether unfair or wrong, the wise choice when stopped by the police is to remain quiet and deliver the requisite number of obsequious "yes sirs" in order to escape the situation as quickly as possible.[92] After all, Cevallos reminds us, this is our law.[93]

It is along these lines, then, that this formalist constitutional framework captures the popular imagination to the extent that public discussion even after these acts of police brutality tends to center on their constitutionality in the narrow and artificial terms supplied by misguided doctrine rather than addressing police beatings or killings with reference to other values or concerns—and rather than questioning the legitimacy of the constitutional doctrine itself. A related cost of these formalist interpretive practices is that they tend to legitimize the exclusion of other perspectives and voices from the public reckoning with police violence.

C. ORIGINALISM AND CREEDAL DELUSIONS

An alternative to the Court's formalist analysis illustrated in *Strieff* is to address contemporary controversies by returning to the Constitution's original meaning. Like the formalist approach, though, the originalist project also neglects the perspectives and experiences of those most impacted by contemporary policing practices. In *California v Hodari D*, for example, the Court considered the constitutionality of a police chase of a group of African-American youths in a "high-crime area of Oakland, California"—a chase that commenced without any substantial justification.[94] As Justice Scalia wrote for the Court, late on the night in question two plain-clothes officers in an unmarked police vehicle drove toward a group of young people standing around a car at the curbside. When the youths saw the unmarked vehicle approach, they "apparently panicked, and took flight."[95] The officers decided to pursue and detain as many of the youths as possible. Hodari D ran into an alley and Officer Petroso pursued him on foot. When Officer Petroso was "almost upon him," Hodari D threw away "what appeared

[92] See id.

[93] See id.

[94] See 499 US 621, 622 (1991).

[95] See id at 623.

to be a small rock."[96] Officer Petroso tackled Hodari D and handcuffed him. Hodari D was charged in juvenile proceedings with possession of crack cocaine. He moved to suppress the drug evidence on the ground that there was no suspicion to support the chase, a circumstance that the prosecution conceded. Hodari D therefore contended that he had been unconstitutionally seized by the officers when they chased him down without justification. Accordingly, he argued, the drug evidence in question should be excluded.[97]

Justice Scalia, however, invoked what he described as "the original understanding" of a seizure, based in founding-era common law, which requires a "taking possession."[98] The Constitution's protections do not apply, he concluded, unless there has been submission to a show of authority or a "taking possession" by a "laying on of hands."[99] In other words, an officer does not seize a suspect by chasing him, even with the officer's weapon drawn, but only when the suspect has been subdued.[100]

Justices Stevens and Marshall dissented, rejecting the majority's turn to a version of the founding-era common law in order to resolve the case, pointing out that the Court had turned its back on a long line of precedent which had understood a seizure to have occurred when a reasonable person would feel his liberty was constricted.[101] Justices Stevens and Marshall also noted that as a consequence of the Court's opinion "a police officer may now fire his weapon at an innocent citizen and not implicate the Fourth Amendment—as long as he misses his target."[102]

As Justice Scalia's reasoning in *Hodari D* illustrates, originalist analysis ignores these relevant contemporary considerations invoked by Justices Stevens and Marshall—perhaps most notably the serious risks of abuse and harm set in motion by this ruling—and looks instead to the past, to dictionary definitions of constitutional text, and to the eighteenth-century common law. As Justice Scalia wrote for

---

[96] Id at 623.

[97] See id at 623–24.

[98] See id at 624–25.

[99] See id.

[100] See id.

[101] See id at 629–31 (Stevens, J, dissenting).

[102] See id at 630.

the Court in another decision, Fourth Amendment analysis should consider the general reasonableness of law enforcement conduct only when eighteenth-century common law fails to provide an answer.[103] According to this approach, which the Court has increasingly embraced over the years, the real-world consequences of a decision, which logically should inform the determination of whether any particular search or seizure is "unreasonable," receive short shrift.

Moreover, as in *Hodari D*, the originalist project defines constitutional criminal procedure protections principally in terms of possessory property rights as they were defined and understood by the common law in the eighteenth century. Thus, the originalist account of the Fourth Amendment, which Justice Scalia reintroduced to constitutional criminal procedure discourse, defines a Fourth Amendment "search" with reference to whether there has been a trespass on private property or a trespass to chattels—the Court's characterization of the eighteenth-century common law rule.[104] As Justice Scalia explained in *United States v Jones*, citing *Entick v Carrington*: "[O]ur law holds the property of every man so sacred, that no man can set his foot upon his neighbour's close without his leave; if he does he is a trespasser, though he does no damage at all; if he will tread upon his neighbour's ground, he must justify it by law."[105] According to Justice Scalia, the Fourth Amendment must be understood in terms of its "close connection to property."[106]

Other commentators have noted how this private property-based conception of constitutional criminal procedure privileges the wealthy and the landholding and places at a relative disadvantage those who spend more of their lives in public, on a bus, or in the street.[107] But more fundamentally, this property-based conception of constitutional rights holds at its center an earlier world in which property holders

---

[103] See *Wyoming v Houghton*, 526 US 295 (1999).

[104] See *United States v Jones*, 132 S Ct 945 (2012).

[105] Id at 949 (citing 95 Eng Rep 807 (C. P. 1765)).

[106] See id.

[107] See, for example, Michelle Estrin Gilman, *The Class Differential in Privacy Law*, 77 Brooklyn L Rev 1389, 1444–45 (2012); Kami Chavis Simmons, *Future of the Fourth Amendment: The Problem with Privacy, Poverty, and Policing*, 14 U Md L J Race Religion Gender & Class 240 (2015); David Sklansky, *The Fourth Amendment and Common Law*, 100 Colum L Rev 1739, 1745–46 (2000) ("[T]he eighteenth-century law of search and seizure systematically and intentionally protected class privilege."); William J. Stuntz, *The Distribution of Fourth Amendment Privacy*, 67 Geo Wash L Rev 1265, 1272 (1999).

wielded exclusive political power and influence, and many of the dispossessed were treated and even traded as property.[108]

The characterization of eighteenth-century property law that animates the originalist interpretive project should not be imagined as distinct from this fuller historical context. The fact is that originalist interpretation builds upon a historical context that was profoundly exclusionary, violent, and unjust. It privileges a historically distant period in which African-American people were forced into slavery, women were largely relegated to the home and politically disenfranchised, Native Americans were dispossessed and subject to genocide, and the only fully participating citizens were property-holding white men. As Mark Graber has shown, these unequal conditions, and especially slavery, "unambiguously pervaded the antebellum constitutional order."[109] Quite apart from the substance of any particular rule arrived at through originalist analysis, in neglecting these entailments of the legal and political sources animating the originalist project, this approach remains decidedly ahistorical and amnesiac.

The originalist project is also decidedly undemocratic as it is predicated on the notion that a highly unrepresentative subset of people no longer living should determine for today and all time the most fundamental questions of our public life. In this regard, this framework is at odds with a democratic project that seeks to realize shared contemporary interests through collective processes of transparent reasoned deliberation.

Even those originalists who suggest that the Reconstruction amendments somehow redeemed the original Constitution neglect the fact that the Reconstruction amendments themselves were profoundly com-

---

[108] Edward Baptist, *The Half Has Never Been Told: Slavery and the Making of American Capitalism* (2014); Saidiya V. Hartman, *Scenes of Subjection: Terror, Slavery, and Self-Making in Nineteenth Century America* (1997); Aziz Rana, *The Two Faces of American Freedom* (2010).

[109] Mark A. Graber, *Dred Scott and the Problem of Constitutional Evil* 12 (2006). In this regard, the common law and the language of human capture—the "taking possession" of another human being that was Justice Scalia's focus in *Hodari D*—should call to mind the hunting of fugitive slaves. See Stanley W. Campbell, *The Slave Catchers: Enforcement of the Fugitive Slave Law, 1850–1860* (2011); Sally E. Haden, *Slave Patrols: Law and Violence in the Carolinas* (2003). In fact, early police forces in the United States were commissioned to capture enslaved people who had escaped, and to repossess them and return them to their masters. In contrast to the rule established by *Hodari D*, however, those subject to capture were stripped of any constitutional rights or dignified regard, not only prior to capture but also after. See Baptist, *The Half Has Never Been Told* (cited in note 108); Manisha Sinha, *The Slave's Cause: A History of Abolition* (2016).

promised.[110] The Reconstruction amendments offered meager redress for centuries of injustice, and were drafted and ratified by the same highly unrepresentative demographic as the original Constitution.[111] The Thirteenth Amendment, which is widely understood to have abolished slavery, continued to permit involuntary servitude as punishment for a crime.[112] Many people freed from slavery were arrested for petty crimes and forced to return to labor on plantations throughout the South,[113] and the Fourteenth Amendment explicitly contemplated the disenfranchisement of people with criminal convictions.[114]

It is also illuminating to recall that originalism gained prominence in its contemporary formulation in the second half of the twentieth century in significant part as a component of the conservatives' "Declaration of Constitutional Principles" and "Southern Strategy."[115] In

[110] See Guyora Binder, *The Slavery of Emancipation*, 17 Cardozo L Rev 2063, 2063 (1996) ("[T]he Thirteenth Amendment secured little more than the manumission of slaves already practically freed by the friction of war. It guaranteed, in Confederate General Robert Richardson's now well-known phrase, 'nothing but freedom.'").

[111] See Stephen Best and Saidiya Hartman, *Fugitive Justice*, 92 Representations 1, 2 (2005) ("How does one compensate for centuries of violence that have as their consequence the impossibility of restoring a prior existence, of giving back what was taken, of repairing what was broken?").

[112] See US Const, Amend XIII, § 1 ("Neither slavery nor involuntary servitude, *except as a punishment for crime whereof the party shall have been duly convicted*, shall exist within the United States, or any place subject to their jurisdiction.") (emphasis added).

[113] See, for example, Douglas A. Blackmon, *Slavery by Another Name: The Re-Enslavement of Black Americans from the Civil War to World War II* (2008); Alex Lichtenstein, *Twice the Work of Free Labor: The Political Economy of Convict Labor in the New South* (1996); David Oshinsky, *Worse Than Slavery: Parchman Farm and the Ordeal of Jim Crow Justice* (1996).

[114] See US Const, Amend XIV, § 2 (Section 2 of the Fourteenth Amendment provides that states would not suffer reduced political representation if they denied or abridged voting rights of citizens "who participat[ed] in rebellion, or other crime.").

[115] See *Declaration of Constitutional Principles*, 102 Cong Rec 4515–16 (1956); see also *The Southern Manifesto of 1956*, US House of Representatives: History, Art & Archives, Highlights Mar 12, 1956, at http://history.house.gov/Historical-Highlights/1951-2000/The-Southern-Manifesto-of-1956/ ("On this date, Howard Smith of Virginia, chairman of the House Rules Committee, introduced the Southern Manifesto in a speech on the House Floor. Formally titled the 'Declaration of Constitutional Principles,' it was signed by 82 Representatives and 19 Senators—roughly one-fifth of the membership of Congress and all from states that had once composed the Confederacy. It marked a moment of southern defiance against the Supreme Court's 1954 landmark *Brown v. the Board of Education of Topeka (KS)* decision. . . ."); *The Southern Manifesto*, Time (March 26, 1956) ("On the floor of the U.S. Senate last week, Georgia's Walter F. George read a manifesto signed by 82 Southern Representatives and 19 Southern Senators. It pledged the signers to exert 'all lawful means' toward reversing the Supreme Court's desegregation decision. . . .").

an interview in 1981, conservative strategist Lee Atwater described the evolution of the GOP's Southern Strategy in these terms:

> You start out in 1954 by saying "N***er, n***er, n***er." By 1968 you can't say "n***er"—that hurts you. Backfires. So you say stuff like forced busing, states' rights and all that stuff. You're getting so abstract now [that] you're talking about cutting taxes, and all these things that you're talking about are totally economic things and a byproduct of them is [that] blacks get hurt worse than whites. And subconsciously maybe that is part of it. I'm not saying that. But I'm saying that if it is getting that abstract, and that coded, that we are doing away with the racial problem one way or the other. You follow me—because obviously sitting around saying, "We want to cut this," is much more abstract than even the busing thing, and a hell of a lot more abstract than "N***er, n***er."[116]

In legal discourse, fidelity to the original Constitution or originalism served as the corollary of these other abstractions associated with the Southern Strategy. Originalism functioned as a more abstract means of invoking opposition to egalitarian projects associated with the civil rights movement like desegregation. Senator Sam J. Ervin Jr. of North Carolina, a leading opponent of the Court's decision in *Brown v Board of Education* who helped to draft the Declaration of Constitutional Principles, noted in that document that the "original Constitution does not mention education" and nor "does the Fourteenth Amendment nor any other amendment. The debates preceding the submission of the Fourteenth Amendment clearly show that there was no intent that it should affect the system of education maintained by the States."[117] When Senator Ervin questioned soon-to-be-Justice Thurgood Marshall at his Supreme Court confirmation hearings in July 1967, he asked Marshall: "Is not the role of the Supreme Court simply to ascertain and give effect to the intent of the framers of this Constitution and the people who ratified the Constitution?" Marshall handled the question adeptly, responding "Yes, Senator, with the understanding that the Constitution was meant to be a living docu-

[116] See Rick Perlstein, *Exclusive: Lee Atwater's Infamous 1981 Interview on the Southern Strategy*, Nation (Nov 13, 2012), at https://www.thenation.com/article/exclusive-lee-atwaters-infamous-1981-interview-southern-strategy/ (within the text of this article is a link to the full 42-minute interview from which the Atwater quote is excerpted); see also Bob Herbert, *Impossible, Ridiculous, Repugnant*, NY Times (Oct 6, 2005).

[117] See Nomination of Thurgood Marshall: Hearing Before the S Comm on the Judiciary, 90th Cong 49 (1967) (statements of Sam J. Ervin Jr., U.S. Senator, and Thurgood Marshall, U.S. Solicitor General).

ment."[118] In the intervening years, however, the deference to the legitimacy of the originalist project may have conceded too much.

As Jamal Greene writes, "as an African-American, a narrative of restoration is deeply alienating; what America has been is hostile to my personhood and denies my membership in its political community. The only way I can call this Constitution my own is to view it through a lens of redemption, the lens that originalism rejects."[119] According to Justice Scalia, after all, the "whole purpose" of the Constitution is to "obstruct modernity" and to preserve the values of the past.[120] Greene remarks, in partial response to Scalia's conception of constitutional originalism, that a "racially-sensitive constitutionalism must always, therefore, hold out the possibility of legitimate dissent from history. Originalism denies that possibility, and so for me, as I suspect for many African-Americans, it speaks in a foreign tongue."[121] So too for many non-African-American women, immigrants of color and their children and grandchildren, poor and working people, queer people, Native Americans—for all, or at least many of us, I imagine, originalism likewise speaks in a foreign tongue.

My point is not that originalist or hyperformalist approaches necessarily tend toward regressive outcomes. There are prominent adherents of originalism across the political spectrum.[122] Furthermore, in her dissent in *Strieff*, Justice Kagan takes on the majority's analysis in its own hyperformalist terms, as does Justice Sotomayor at the outset of her dissent, and both persuasively argue in those terms for the opposite, more rights-protective result.[123] But these interpretive frameworks—whether hyperformalist or originalist—necessarily turn away from the sources, histories, and experiences that could rescue our democracy and shed new light on the just resolution of contemporary controversies. Recourse to eighteenth-century common law and historical dictionary definitions of constitutional terms, or to an inward-focused, hypertechnical doctrinal formalism, necessarily elides

---

[118] See id; see also Justin Driver, *Ignoble Specificities*, New Republic (March 15, 2012).

[119] See Jamal Greene, *Originalism's Race Problem*, 88 Denver U L Rev 517, 521 (2011).

[120] See Antonin Scalia, *Modernity and the Constitution*, in Constitutional Justice Under Old Constitutions 313, 315 (1995).

[121] See Greene, 88 Denver U L Rev at 517, 522 (cited in note 119).

[122] See, for example, Jack Balkin, *Living Originalism* (2011); Laura Donohue, *The Original Fourth Amendment*, 83 U Chi L Rev 1181 (2016).

[123] *Strieff*, 136 S Ct at 2068 (Sotomayor, J, dissenting), 2073 (Kagan, J, dissenting).

or gives minimal attention to contemporary and historical social contexts and to the real-world implications of the most important cases the Court confronts.

Aziz Rana identifies a further problem associated with contemporary constitutionalism, one that is particularly pronounced in an originalist framework.[124] As Rana explains, Americans have come to imagine their nation in civic rather than white-settler terms, even though the history of this country is one of a white-settler and slave-trading nation. Rana shows how "[t]he country's identitarian shift from settler to civic nation has meant that Americans have never properly confronted the country's colonial infrastructure or the living legacy of its settler history."[125] Rana describes further how "[a]s a consequence, today's vision of the country as intrinsically—if incompletely—liberal systematically deemphasizes those forms of economic and political subordination that continue to mark the experience of historically marginalized communities."[126] Rana refers to this attachment to a vision of the Constitution and American history as essentially anticolonial, liberatory, and egalitarian as Americans' *creedal* narrative—our creedal account of our own history—a concept he develops from the work of the Swedish sociologist Gunnar Myrdal.[127]

Given originalism's attachment to a sanitized version of history to guide us in the present, originalist constitutionalism is particularly susceptible to this problem—what we might characterize as a *creedal delusion*. In originalism's partial understanding of American history—and in particular in its failure to attend to the white-settler, colonial, slave-trading origins of the United States and to the persistent legacies of that history—the originalist approach deprives us of the ability to more fully break from this past in order to embrace a different future. Originalism prevents the sort of reckoning with the past and its persistent legacies that might actually allow us to move beyond it.

So how can we confront the insularity of originalist and formalist paradigms in criminal constitutional discourse, and specifically their disregard of and inattention to their own limitations and effects? The following part returns to Justice Sotomayor's dissenting opinions in

---

[124] See Rana, *The Two Faces of American Freedom* (cited in note 108).

[125] Aziz Rana, *Colonialism and Constitutional Memory*, 5 UC Irvine L Rev 263, 268 (2015).

[126] Id.

[127] See id at 266.

order to suggest a different vantage from which to imagine alternative constitutional futures.

II. Toward a New Constitutionalism

In the end, the hope for meaningful change probably lies less in revised Supreme Court doctrine than in political mobilization to confront long-standing racial, economic, and social inequalities. Nonetheless, constitutional jurisprudence could be reoriented to reduce rather than to exacerbate the violence of policing. Justice Sotomayor's recent dissents offer both a critique of constitutional law's complicity in racial injustice and a gesture toward such alternative constitutional possibilities.

A. A Critique of Constitutional Complicity

Justice Sotomayor's critique of constitutional complicity opens the door to reimagining the parameters of constitutional doctrine by laying bare the consequences of the current doctrinal landscape. Once we understand how the Court's jurisprudence immunizes the unnecessary use of force against society's most vulnerable citizens and authorizes countless pretextual, racially motivated stops and senseless chases of young men and women, we are better able to envision what an alternative regime might entail.

The direct, passionate, and critical tone that Justice Sotomayor adopts in her dissent in *Strieff* impels the reader to rethink the precise rules in question:

> The Court today holds that the discovery of a warrant for an unpaid parking ticket will forgive a police officer's violation of your Fourth Amendment rights. . . . This case allows the police to stop you on the street, demand your identification, and check it for outstanding traffic warrants—even if you are doing nothing wrong. . . .[128]

Justice Sotomayor goes on to make vivid the "severe consequences" of "unlawful 'stops,'" which are, she explains, "much greater than the inconvenience suggested by the name."[129] Citing the relevant Supreme Court decisions, Sotomayor exposes the line of precedents complicit in such "degrading" and "arbitrary" treatment:

---

[128] *Strieff*, 136 S Ct at 2064 (Sotomayor, J, dissenting).

[129] See id at 2069.

> Although many Americans have been stopped for speeding or jaywalking, few may realize how degrading a stop can be when the officer is looking for more. . . . The officer's control over you does not end with the stop. If the officer chooses, he may handcuff you and take you to jail for doing nothing more than speeding, jaywalking, or driving your pickup truck . . . with your 3-year-old son and 5-year-old daughter . . . without your seatbelt fastened. Even if you are innocent, you will now join the 65 million Americans with an arrest record and experience the "civil death" of discrimination by employers, landlords, and whoever else conducts a background check. And, of course, if you fail to pay bail or appear for court, a judge will issue a warrant to render you "arrestable on sight" in the future. . . .[130]

Justice Sotomayor makes clear that the Court should reach different results in many of its criminal procedure cases. The Court could and should hold, for example, that it is constitutionally unreasonable to subject a person to a full custodial arrest for a nonjailable offense, such as a seatbelt violation, reversing *Atwater*, even if that person has an outstanding warrant for a minor infraction. The Court also could and should extend the exclusionary rule to discourage illegal stops and searches, even those that lead to the discovery of an outstanding warrant, as in *Strieff*. This may decrease in some small measure the payment of tickets and minor fines because people could no longer be jailed for such infractions. It should be possible to develop less oppressive means of encouraging social cooperation.

The other jarring examples of Court-approved pat-down and body-cavity strip searches, discussed earlier in this essay and noted by Sotomayor in her dissent in *Strieff*, make plain that the Court could and should hold that a search of a person's genitals and anal cavity without any individualized justification likewise violates the Constitution, reversing *Florence*. And Justice Sotomayor's critique in *Mullenix* helps us see that the Court could and should hold that the use of force is constitutionally reasonable only when necessary and not when there are readily available alternative means to de-escalate a situation. But reconfiguring these doctrinal rules is only the beginning.

Sotomayor's critical perspective serves also to loosen the hold of the past on the present. By weakening the appeal of stare decisis in the face of changed circumstances and understandings, she enables our constitutional vision to evolve in as yet unanticipated directions. In her concurrence in *United States v Jones*, for example, Sotomayor

---

[130] Id at 2069–70.

wrote separately to call attention to important considerations neglected by the Court's originalist and formalist analyses.[131] In *Jones*, Antoine Jones faced a life sentence for his involvement in a cocaine conspiracy.[132] Police had placed a GPS monitoring device on his vehicle, outside the scope of a valid warrant, and used the device to track all of his movements for nearly one month.[133] Jones sought to suppress the GPS evidence, and Justice Scalia wrote for the Court that the surveillance was unconstitutional because it amounted to a "trespass" on the vehicle to which the GPS was attached.[134] Justice Alito wrote a separate opinion, which reached the same result, but on the basis of the Court's "reasonable expectations of privacy" doctrine, rather than on the basis of Justice Scalia's property-based approach.[135]

Although joining the Court's majority opinion, Justice Sotomayor in her own concurring opinion discussed other factors that, in her view, ought to inform the Court's analysis:

> Awareness that the Government may be watching chills associational and expressive freedoms. And the Government's unrestrained power to assemble data that reveal private aspects of identity is susceptible to abuse. The net result is that GPS monitoring—by making available at a relatively low cost such a substantial quantum of intimate information about any person whom the Government, in its unfettered discretion, chooses to track—may "alter the relationship between citizen and government in a way that is inimical to democratic society."[136]

Sotomayor went on to note that she would "take these attributes of GPS monitoring into account"[137] and would consider further "the appropriateness of entrusting to the Executive, in the absence of any oversight from a coordinate branch, a tool so amenable to misuse, especially in light of the Fourth Amendment's goal to curb arbitrary exercises of police power and [to] prevent 'a too permeating police surveillance.'"[138]

---

131 132 S Ct 945, 956 (2012).

132 See id at 949.

133 See id.

134 Id at 949–53.

135 See id at 957–59.

136 Id at 956 (Sotomayor, J, concurring) (citing *United States v Cuevas-Perez*, 640 F3d 272, 285 (7th Cir 2011)).

137 132 S Ct at 956.

138 Id (quoting *United States v Di Re*, 332 US 581, 595 (1948)).

Sotomayor's perspective not only introduced new insights about the possible abuses of GPS surveillance, it also recognized that these insights might make it necessary to revisit and reverse long-standing precedent. At the end of her concurring opinion, for example, she expressly called into question the continuing wisdom of the "third party doctrine":

> [I]t may be necessary to reconsider the premise that an individual has no reasonable expectation of privacy in information voluntarily disclosed to third parties. . . . This approach is ill suited to the digital age, in which people reveal a great deal of information about themselves to third parties in the course of carrying out mundane tasks. . . . I for one doubt that people would accept without complaint the warrantless disclosure to the Government of a list of every Web site they had visited in the last week, or month, or year. But whatever the societal expectations, they can attain constitutionally protected status only if our Fourth Amendment jurisprudence ceases to treat secrecy as a prerequisite for privacy. I would not assume that all information voluntarily disclosed to some member of the public for a limited purpose is, for that reason alone, disentitled to Fourth Amendment protection.[139]

The critical disposition reflected here and elsewhere in Sotomayor's opinions—particularly her distance from hyperformalist doctrinal and originalist preoccupations—models a welcome willingness to question stare decisis, especially when, as in *Jones*, the world has changed in ways that make it necessary to reevaluate earlier decisions. Sotomayor's bold strides in this direction have not been without influence. When the Court later decided to extend Fourth Amendment protection to prohibit warrantless cell phone searches in *Riley v California*, Chief Justice Roberts, writing for the Court, cited Justice Sotomayor's concurrence and reflections in *Jones*, rather than the positions set out in that case by Justices Scalia and Alito.[140]

Justice Sotomayor's opinions in these cases also invite a more honest understanding of both American history and contemporary practices—an understanding that is more accurate and open, and one that invites new and better ways of addressing pressing questions. In her dissenting opinion in *Schuette v Coalition to Defend Affirmative Action*, for example, Sotomayor identifies plainly the United States' history of racial exclusion, domination, and violence, and she does so

[139] Id at 957 (internal citations omitted).

[140] See *Riley v California*, 134 S Ct 2473, 2490 (2014).

with a forthrightness rarely exhibited in either judicial opinions or American public discourse: "to know the history of our Nation is to understand its long and lamentable record of stymieing the right of racial minorities to participate in the political process."[141] This, she adds, "is a history we strive to put behind us. But it is a history that still informs the society we live in, and so it is one we must address with candor."[142]

Justice Sotomayor writes of the severe limitations of the Reconstruction amendments in remedying past racial injustice, offering a corrective to creedal delusions about the nation's past: "The Fifteenth Amendment, ratified after the Civil War, promised to racial minorities the right to vote. But many States ignored this promise. In addition to outright tactics of fraud, intimidation, and violence, there are countless examples of States categorically denying to racial minorities access to the political process."[143] She then recounts the systematic racial exclusion and domination over many decades experienced by racial minorities in housing, education, and other spheres of public life, continuing in numerous contexts to the present.

She therefore rejects the view—dominant in Supreme Court jurisprudence and elsewhere—that it is through purported colorblindness that this history will be overcome. Sotomayor argues forcefully that instead of closing its eyes to the past and to the present, the Court would do better to admit that "[r]ace matters," conjuring Cornel West's book by the same name.[144] Race matters, she contends, because of our "long history" of racial subordination and because of "persistent racial inequality in society—inequality that cannot be ignored and that has produced stark socioeconomic disparities."[145] Toward the end of her lengthy dissent in *Schuette*, Sotomayor puts the matter in these pointed terms:

> In my colleagues' view, examining the racial impact of legislation only perpetuates racial discrimination. This refusal to accept the stark reality that race matters is regrettable. The way to stop discrimination on the basis of race is to speak openly and candidly on the subject of race, and to apply

---

[141] *Schuette v Coalition to Defend Affirmative Action*, 134 S Ct 1623, 1651 (2014) (Sotomayor, J, dissenting).

[142] Id at 1654.

[143] Id.

[144] Id at 1676; Cornel West, *Race Matters* (1994).

[145] 134 S Ct at 1676.

> the Constitution with eyes open to the unfortunate effects of centuries of racial discrimination. As members of the judiciary tasked with intervening to carry out the guarantee of equal protection, we ought not sit back and wish away, rather than confront, the racial inequality that exists in our society. It is this view that works harm, by perpetuating the facile notion that what makes race matter is acknowledging the simple truth that race *does* matter.[146]

In this dissent, Justice Sotomayor herself serves as a guide to the project she commends of directly addressing race and inequality with openness and candor.

In the course of these dissenting opinions, Justice Sotomayor also works to incorporate the perspectives of those citizens whose voices are typically absent from the Court's consideration. In her dissenting opinion in *Schuette*, for instance, she elaborated some of the ways in which race matters:

> Race matters to a young man's view of society when he spends his teenage years watching others tense up as he passes, no matter the neighborhood where he grows up. Race matters to a young woman's sense of self when she states her hometown, and then is pressed, "No, where are you *really* from," regardless of how many generations her family has been in the country. . . . Race matters because of the slights, the snickers, the silent judgments that reinforce that most crippling of thoughts: "I do not belong here."[147]

Even if Justice Sotomayor's critical perspectives fall for now on deaf ears among her colleagues on the Court, she has introduced into constitutional discourse a more substantial, more historically informed, and more powerfully egalitarian constitutional vision. Her honest, critical appraisal of the profound problems in constitutional discourse makes it possible to fundamentally reimagine ingrained doctrinal rules, patterns of thought, and persistently troubled practices as their actual implications are laid bare. Her direct and frank critical analysis loosens the hold of the past on the present in ways that enable new and more honest understandings, positive transformation, and new forms of constitutional interpretation. And her more critical disposition toward hyperformalist doctrinal analysis and originalist and creedal delusions creates more space for other perspectives and voices to enter.

---

[146] Id.

[147] Id.

B. REIMAGINING THE CONSTITUTIONAL CANON

With her dissent in *Strieff*, Justice Sotomayor also begins to reimagine the resources that may be called upon in constitutional adjudication. Sotomayor's jurisprudence is empirically informed, and rigorously so. She frames her critical intervention in *Strieff*, for example, in significant part around the available empirical evidence relating to contemporary policing practices. These data guide Sotomayor's serious effort to understand and then to forthrightly address the consequences of suspicionless warrant checks. Whereas the majority limits its analysis to the application of formalist doctrines, Sotomayor takes careful notice of the available empirical evidence. She looks to the Department of Justice's Bureau of Justice Statistics reports on outstanding warrants and notes that Utah lists over 180,000 misdemeanor warrants in its database.[148] From these and other data, as well as careful attention to the facts of the case, Sotomayor rightly concludes that "[t]he officer's discovery of a warrant was not some intervening surprise he could not have anticipated."[149]

Moreover, Sotomayor relies upon extensive empirical evidence to decimate the majority's suggestion that suspicionless warrant checks like the one at issue in *Strieff* represent "isolated" and "negligent" conduct rather than purposeful violations.[150] To the contrary, she demonstrates that "[o]utstanding warrants are surprisingly common."[151] And invoking the Brennan Center for Justice's study *Criminal Justice Debt* and Human Rights Watch's investigation of for-profit probation, she offers a persuasive account of how "a person with a traffic ticket [who] misses a fine payment or court appearance" will become subject to a court-issued warrant.[152] As she makes clear, state and federal government databases contain "over 7.8 million outstanding warrants, the vast majority of which appear to be for minor offenses."[153] These databases may not even include the "'staggering' number of warrants, 'drawers and drawers full' that many cities issue for traffic violations and ordinance infractions."[154]

---

[148] See 136 S Ct at 2066.

[149] Id.

[150] See id at 2067–68.

[151] Id at 2068.

[152] Id.

[153] Id.

[154] Id.

In addition to her reliance on rigorous empirical evidence to inform her analysis and her understanding of the legal questions before her, Justice Sotomayor also returns to the legal realists' project of incorporating a more general account of the relevant sociological context. She explains in her dissent in *Strieff*, for example, that "Justice Department investigations across the country have illustrated how these astounding numbers of warrants can be used by police to stop people without cause."[155] In New Orleans, she notes, in one year officers "made nearly 60,000 arrests, of which about 20,000 were of people with outstanding traffic or misdemeanor warrants from neighboring parishes for such infractions as unpaid tickets."[156] Drawing on the Department of Justice's Ferguson Report, Sotomayor describes how officers in the St. Louis metropolitan area "'routinely' stop people—on the street, at bus stops, or even in court—for no reason other than 'an officer's desire to check whether the subject had a municipal arrest warrant pending.'"[157] Thoroughly debunking the notion that suspicionless warrant checks are "isolated instance[s] of negligence," Justice Sotomayor addresses the evidence of institutionalized training procedures in police departments around the country, which in fact encourage such suspicionless stops.[158] And she highlights the Utah Supreme Court's own description of such suspicionless warrant checks as "routine procedure" and "common practice."[159]

Justice Sotomayor concludes her discussion of these various investigations and studies by warning that "it should not take a federal investigation of Salt Lake County before the Court would protect someone in Strieff's position." As Sotomayor's analyses in *Strieff* and *Schuette* make clear, intelligent and informed constitutional jurisprudence will require an expansion of the resources available in constitutional adjudication to include relevant empirical studies, government investigations, and sociolegal scholarship.

Significantly, Sotomayor also expands the constitutional canon in her dissent in *Strieff* to encourage greater attention to the voices and

[155] Id.

[156] See id (quoting Dept of Justice, Civil Rights Div, Investigation of the New Orleans Police Department 29 (2011)).

[157] Id at 2068 (quoting Dept of Justice, Civil Rights Div, Investigation of the Ferguson Police Department 49, 57).

[158] See id at 2069.

[159] Id at 2073.

experiences of those who are often invisible in constitutional discourse, but whose perspectives and insights ought to inform such analyses. She notes that the suspicionless stop of the white defendant in *Strieff* reveals that "anyone's dignity can be violated in this manner," but she observes—citing political scientist Marie Gottschalk's *Caught: The Prison State and the Lockdown of American Politics* and Michelle Alexander's *The New Jim Crow*—that it is "no secret that people of color are disproportionate victims of this type of scrutiny."[160]

Considering the implications of the Court's holding in *Strieff*, Justice Sotomayor focuses in particular on the experience of generations of black and brown parents who have given their children "the talk"—warning their little ones to never "run down the street; always keep your hands where they can be seen; do not even think of talking back to a stranger—all out of fear of how an officer with a gun will react to them."[161] And in this discussion, Sotomayor incorporates the work of W. E. B. Du Bois and James Baldwin—major American cultural figures whose writings shed light on these and other experiences of African-Americans forged in part through abusive and sometimes brutal experiences with criminal law enforcement. Du Bois and Baldwin serve in Sotomayor's analysis as alternative sources of authority regarding our national past. Rather than invoking the founding fathers or the eighteenth-century common law in order to glean the original meaning of the Constitution, Sotomayor expands the cultural and historical material that may serve to fill in the content of constitutional ideals like justice, liberty, reasonableness—and make those ideals more meaningful. She also cites Ta-Nehisi Coates's *Between the World and Me*, which consists of a public letter to Coates's son, as James Baldwin's *The Fire Next Time* consisted in part of a letter to his young nephew, and both of which include a version of "the talk."[162]

Sotomayor explores how the law enforcement conduct that is the focus of "the talk" contributes to producing a certain "double consciousness," of which W. E. B. Du Bois wrote so powerfully:

> It is a peculiar sensation, this double-consciousness, this sense of always looking at one's self through the eyes of others, of measuring one's soul

---

[160] Id at 2070.

[161] Id.

[162] See id.

> by the tape of a world that looks on in amused contempt and pity. One ever feels his two-ness—an American, a Negro; two souls, two thoughts, two unreconciled strivings; two warring ideals in one dark body, whose dogged strength alone keeps it from being torn asunder.[163]

Sotomayor concludes that it is in part Supreme Court opinions, illustrated by the majority's opinion in *Strieff*, that "legitimiz[e] the conduct that produces this double consciousness."[164]

Strieff and other decisions in the long line of precedent Sotomayor assails in her dissent "tell[] everyone, white and black, guilty and innocent, that an officer can verify your legal status at any time."[165] She declares that *Strieff* stands for the proposition that "your body is subject to invasion while courts excuse the violation of your rights."[166] In the end, these decisions imply "that you are not the citizen of a democracy but the subject of a carceral state, just waiting to be catalogued."[167] As Justice Sotomayor reminds us, in an attempt perhaps to summon the voices of those subject to police brutality: "no one can breathe in this atmosphere" in which "unlawful police stops corrode all of our civil liberties and threaten all of our lives."[168]

Ultimately, it is only through this process of recognizing the voices and experiences of those too seldom heard that constitutional and public discourse might begin to more closely approximate justice: "Until their voices matter too," Sotomayor concludes, "our justice system will continue to be anything but."[169] Justice Sotomayor's dissent aims to open a space within which other voices might enter, though it remains only an initial foray in that direction.

C. "BEYOND ANY BORDERS VISIBLE FROM THIS VANTAGE"

Although these gestures toward a new constitutionalism in Justice Sotomayor's dissents remain incipient and partial works in process, this feature may be among the greatest strengths of this emergent

---

[163] W. E. B. Du Bois, *The Souls of Black Folk* 38 (1903).

[164] 136 S Ct at 2070.

[165] See id.

[166] Id.

[167] Id at 2071.

[168] Id.

[169] Id.

jurisprudence. Sotomayor seems to recognize that a new, more just constitutional discourse, one that takes us considerably beyond where we currently stand, can only be developed incrementally over time. In her autobiography, *My Beloved World*, Sotomayor writes:

> Almost daily, people ask me what I hope my legacy will be, as if the story were winding down, when really it has just begun. I can only reply that if I were to determine in advance the character of my jurisprudence, mine would be a far more blinkered and unworthy legacy than I hope. My highest aspiration for my work on the Court is to grow in understanding beyond what I can foresee, beyond any borders visible from this vantage.[170]

A truly alternative constitutionalism cannot be fully explicated from our current vantage; nor can a complete program to end police brutality be fully elaborated from where we now stand. For now, it is apparent that a more just engagement with criminal law enforcement will not likely occur without a more general reckoning with other dimensions of public life that are similarly affected by racial, social, and economic inequality. As Justice Sotomayor's dissenting opinion in *Strieff* suggests, law enforcement excesses are connected to the marginalization, criminalization, and poverty of affected communities. So, too, the youth movements that have arisen over the last several years in response to police abuse call attention to the interrelationships between injustice in the criminal process and other forms of economic, racial, and social injustice.

As Janae Bonsu, an organizer with Black Youth Project 100, wrote in the *Hill*, leading up to a week of lobbying in Washington on the part of black youth activists associated with Black Lives Matter and the Movement for Black Lives: "While our movement has been sparked by the very visible and persistent instances of police violence against black people, our agenda for policy intervention is far more expansive. . . . [T]his movement thematically calls for a divestment from institutions that harm people—ranging from police to jails—and for that money to be reallocated to our communities so that we can invest in the education, employment, and healing of black people."[171] The detailed policy statements of the Black Youth Project—

---

[170] See Justice Sonia Sotomayor, *My Beloved World* 382 (2013).

[171] See Janae Bonsu, *Black Lives Matter Is Much More Than the Protests*, The Hill (Sept 12, 2016).

their *Agenda to Build Black Futures*—and the Movement for Black Lives' *Platform* call for "bold shifts in economic policy in order to acquire the resources needed to build healthy lives, strong families, and communities"[172] and focus on the importance of "investments in the education, health and safety of black people, instead of investments in . . . criminalizing, caging, and harming. . . ."[173] The Constitution and the Supreme Court's constitutional doctrine are, of course, implicated in all of these matters, from access to education, to the parameters of approved surveillance, to permitting or foreclosing regulatory interventions that aim to promote greater economic and social justice.

What it will entail in the end to reconfigure constitutional discourse, to render it more responsive to these issues and less complicit in the persistent legacies of past violence, will become more fully apparent only as alternative understandings and coalitions emerge in changing times. Our capacity to foresee and articulate alternative visions in response to these concerns, whether constitutional or otherwise, is limited by the intellectual, institutional, legal, and material conditions of our present.[174] If we allow this project to remain emergent and in process, we may remain open to genuine alternatives.

CONCLUSION

In certain countries emerging from regimes of state-imposed and privately enforced racial inequality and social injustice, citizens have explicitly broken from the past in part by adopting a new constitution.[175] Perhaps the United States, too, will require a new constitution or at least a recognized rupture from the past in order to properly acknowledge and break from our own often violent history and present reality.[176] In South Africa and elsewhere, a new constitutional discourse did not by itself eliminate the vast and persistent problems

---

[172] See Black Youth Project, Agenda to Build Black Futures (2016), at http://agendatobuildblackfutures.org.

[173] See Movement for Black Lives, Platform (2016), at https://policy.m4bl.org/platform/.

[174] See, for example, Allegra M. McLeod, *Confronting Criminal Law's Violence: The Possibilities of the Unfinished*, 8 Harv Unbound 109 (2013).

[175] See, for example, Lauren Segal and Sharon Cort, *One Law, One Nation: The Making of the South African Constitution* (2012); Heinz Klug, *The Constitution of South Africa: A Contextual Analysis* (2010).

[176] See Rana, 5 UC Irvine L Rev (cited in note 125).

of racial and economic inequality.[177] But at least these processes of reconstitutive rupture from a racist and otherwise unequal past placed constitutional jurisprudence on the side of progress and justice, and helped to shape a revitalized public and legal discourse informed more explicitly by values of equality, dignity, justice, and fairness.

---

[177] See Kristina Bentley, Laurie Nathan, and Richard Calland, eds, *Falls the Shadow: Between the Promise and the Reality of the South African Constitution* (2013).

WILLIAM BAUDE

STANDING IN THE SHADOW OF CONGRESS

In *Spokeo v Robins*,[1] the Supreme Court confronted one of the harder questions of its intricate law of standing to sue. The question is whether Article III of the Constitution limits Congress's ability to create legal rights that can be vindicated in federal court—and, if so, what those limits are. The Court's cases had provided two contradictory approaches to answering it.

Boxed in by these conflicting precedents, *Spokeo* failed to resolve the problem. The violation of a legal right can support standing, said the Court, only if it represents an injury that is "concrete"—a term that simultaneously includes some "intangible" injuries, but requires that they be "real."[2] These terms, and the Court's explanation of them, do little work to answer the core question. And to the extent that they do point to a general approach, that approach is a wrong turn.

But *Spokeo* also produced a glimmer of hope for approaching standing in the future: a concurring opinion by Justice Thomas,

William Baude is Neubauer Family Assistant Professor of Law, University of Chicago Law School.

AUTHOR'S NOTE: Thanks to Sam Bray, Justin Driver, Zach Price, John Rappaport, Richard Re, Steve Sachs, and David Strauss for helpful advice and to Craig Fligov, Layne Novak, and Margo Uhrman for excellent research assistance. The Alumni Faculty Fund and SNR Denton Fund provided research support.

[1] 136 S Ct 1540 (2016).

[2] Id at 1548–49.

978-0-226-49084-7/2017/2016-0006$10.00

building off of an important line of scholarship on the long-standing difference between public rights and private rights. While Justice Thomas's proposal is not yet fully developed, it may provide a theoretically satisfying way to make sense of the Court's approach to statutory standing. Even if his answers are not perfect, they are answers to the right questions, which will reframe the problem of standing in a helpful way. Justice Thomas's concurrence may be one of the most fruitful things to happen to standing at the Supreme Court in many years.

The rest of this article explains the problem of standing in the face of Congress's creation of statutory rights. Part I describes the basic problem and the prior cases that address it. Part II describes the Court's attempted answer in *Spokeo*. Part III argues that *Spokeo*'s answer is unhelpful and even problematic, and could have ominous implications for the law of privacy and other areas of substantive law. Part IV shows why Justice Thomas may have provided a better way forward.

I. The Problem of Standing to Enforce Statutory Rights

The Constitution gives federal courts the "judicial" power to decide "cases" or "controversies."[3] It is black letter law that these terms require the case to be between the proper sorts of parties, ones who have some legal dispute that the court can resolve. A key part of this requirement is that the plaintiff have "standing" to sue, which means—says the Court—that the plaintiff must have suffered (or be likely to suffer) a "concrete, particularized" "injury" (or sometimes "injury in fact"); that the injury must be "fairly traceable to the challenged action"; and that the injury must be "redressable by a favorable ruling."[4]

To be sure, even these propositions have had their critics, Raoul Berger[5] and Laurence Tribe[6] among them. And there are further complexities as well, such as the questions of whether standing should

[3] US Const, Art III, §§ 1, 2.

[4] *Clapper v Amnesty International*, 133 S Ct 1138, 1147 (2013). There are many similar but subtly different formulations in the case law.

[5] See, for example, Raoul Berger, *Standing to Sue in Public Actions: Is It a Constitutional Requirement?*, 78 Yale L J 816 (1969).

[6] Laurence H. Tribe, *American Constitutional Law* § 3-27, at 110–12 (1st ed, 1978); 1 Laurence H. Tribe, *American Constitutional Law* § 3-14, at 391–92 (3d ed, 2000).

be seen as jurisdictional or part of the merits of the claim,[7] and of whether "standing" and "injury in fact" are novel concepts or old ones in new language.[8] But these requirements of standing doctrine have grown relatively settled despite the debates.

Beyond this settlement, however, the Court's standing cases have equivocated about an important question lying behind those requirements. What relationship do *statutes* have to the injury needed for standing? Is the violation of a statutory right an injury? To ask these questions is not to doubt that injury is a requirement—it is now taken as a given that injury is required.[9] Rather the question is what law *defines* that injury. To what extent is it shaped by ordinary law, and therefore by Congress, and to what extent is it instead hard-coded in Article III?

In two mostly separate lines of reasoning, the Court has said on the one hand that the content of an injury is shaped by law, and therefore by Congress; and said on the other hand that some congressional attempts to do so are unconstitutional. The two lines of reasoning—which I will, unoriginally, call Proposition A and Proposition B[10]—have coexisted for some time, but they are in tension.

A. "CONGRESS MAY ENACT STATUTES CREATING LEGAL RIGHTS, THE INVASION OF WHICH CREATES STANDING"

This first branch of the Court's cases reflects a seemingly simple intuition: Legislatures create rights. Invasions of those rights are injuries. To consider an obvious example, it might be that no private person has standing to sue over misuse of a piece of public property,

---

[7] For example, Lee A. Albert, *Standing to Challenge Administrative Action: An Inadequate Surrogate for Claim for Relief*, 83 Yale L J 425, 450–56 (1974); William A. Fletcher, *The Structure of Standing*, 98 Yale L J 221, 223 (1988).

[8] Compare Cass R. Sunstein, *What's Standing After Lujan? Of Citizen Suits, "Injuries," and Article III*, 91 Mich L Rev 163, 166 (1992), and Steven L. Winter, *The Metaphor of Standing and the Problem of Self-Governance*, 40 Stan L Rev 1371 (1988), with Ann Woolhandler and Caleb Nelson, *Does History Defeat Standing Doctrine?*, 102 Mich L Rev 689 (2004).

[9] Cf. John G. Roberts, Jr., *Article III Limits on Statutory Standing*, 42 Duke L J 1219, 1219 (1993) (criticizing critics of *Lujan* for failing to "grant the artist . . . his donee"—*viz* "that injury in fact is required for standing under Article III").

[10] Cf. Paul M. Bator, Daniel J. Meltzer, Paul J. Mishkin, and David L. Shapiro, *Hart and Wechsler's The Federal Courts and the Federal System* 995 (3d ed 1988) (dividing federal question cases into "Proposition A" and "Proposition B"); Thomas W. Merrill, *Anticipatory Remedies for Takings*, 128 Harv L Rev 1630, 1634 (2015) (ascertaining "two separate lines of authority about takings remedies, which I will call the A line and the B line").

owned in common by the public. But if the legislature parcels up that property into private plots, each new owner has standing to litigate their own private property rights against intruders.[11]

Various early cases in England and America featured this basic intuition that invasion of legal rights was necessarily an injury. As early as the fourteenth and fifteenth centuries, English courts had allowed suits for trespass (to persons and to property) even when there had been no damage and no injury in fact apart from the *legal* injury of the trespass itself.[12] And in America, Joseph Story affirmed an expanded version of this principle when allowing downstream mill owners to sue an upstream mill owner for illegal diversion of water.[13] Surveying the precedents, he concluded: "whenever there is a clear violation of a right, it is not necessary in an action of this sort to show actual damage; that every violation imports damage; and if no other be proved, the plaintiff is entitled to a verdict for nominal damages."[14]

It took longer for this principle to appear explicitly in Supreme Court cases about standing, perhaps in part because the language of modern standing doctrine did not appear until the twentieth century. In any event, in the twentieth century, the Court reaffirmed that legal rights are sufficient to ground standing. Moreover, they were sufficient to do so even in the case of rights unknown to the common law.

For instance, in *Trafficante v Metropolitan Life Insurance*, the Court found standing for two tenants of an apartment building to challenge their landlord's illegally discriminatory rental practices.[15] The tenants had obviously not themselves been denied the ability to rent there (that is why they were tenants), but they wanted to live in a more racially mixed apartment building and thought the law gave them a right to do so. Even though such a right would not have existed at the common law, it was enough for standing.

To be sure, it is not clear that the statutory right was the only source of standing, since the plaintiffs had also named other injuries, such as the loss of "social benefits," "missed business and professional advantages," and the "embarrassment and economic damage . . . from

[11] See Woolhandler and Nelson, 102 Mich L Rev at 693–94 (cited in note 8).

[12] F. Andrew Hessick, *Standing, Injury in Fact, and Private Rights*, 93 Cornell L Rev 275, 281 (2008) (discussing *I de S et ux v W de S* (1348), and *Hulle v Orynge* (1466)).

[13] *Webb v Portland Manufacturing Co.*, 29 F Cas 506 (CCD Me 1838) (opinion of Story, Circuit Justice) (cited in Hessick, 93 Cornell L Rev at 285 (cited in note 12)).

[14] Id.

[15] 409 US 205, 207 (1972).

being 'stigmatized' as residents of a 'white ghetto.'"[16] But the majority did not spend time substantiating these consequences. And four Justices wrote separately to emphasize their reliance on the statutory right: "Absent the Civil Rights Act of 1968, I would have great difficulty in concluding that petitioners' complaint in this case presented a case or controversy within the jurisdiction of the District Court under Art. III of the Constitution. But with that statute purporting to give all those who are authorized to complain to the agency the right also to sue in court, I would sustain the statute."[17]

The Court relied on this proposition most explicitly in *Havens Realty v Coleman*, where it considered (among other things) the rights of Sylvia Coleman, a black Fair Housing Act "tester."[18] Coleman had been told, apparently falsely and because of her race, that there were no apartments available to rent, and she sued for the violation of the Fair Housing Act's "steering" provisions. Even though she had no intent to actually rent from the defendants, the Court found that she had standing to sue. The key was the injury to her statutory rights to truthful and nondiscriminatory information.

As the Court put it:

> Congress has thus conferred on all "persons" a legal right to truthful information about available housing. This congressional intention cannot be overlooked in determining whether testers have standing to sue. As we have previously recognized, the actual or threatened injury required by Art. III may exist solely by virtue of "statutes creating legal rights, the invasion of which creates standing." . . . In the instant case, respondent Coleman—the black tester—alleged injury to her statutorily created right to truthful housing information. . . . If the facts are as alleged, then respondent has suffered "specific injury" from the challenged acts of petitioners, and the Art. III requirement of injury in fact is satisfied.[19]

The holding in *Havens* relied on similar statements the Court had repeatedly made in dicta: For instance, it had said that "Congress may enact statutes creating legal rights, the invasion of which creates standing, even though no injury would exist without the statute"[20] or

[16] Id at 208.

[17] Id at 212 (White, J, concurring).

[18] 455 US 363 (1982).

[19] Id at 373–74 (citations omitted).

[20] *Linda RS v Richard D*, 410 US 614, 617 n 3 (1972), subsequently quoted in *O'Shea v Littleton*, 414 US 488, 493 n 2 (1973).

that "[t]he actual or threatened injury required by Art. III may exist solely by virtue of 'statutes creating legal rights, the invasion of which creates standing.'"[21] Similarly, in denying standing to challenge potential conflicts of interest under the Constitution's Incompatibility Clause[22] the Court expressed "no doubt that if the Congress enacted a statute creating such a legal right, the requisite injury for standing would be found in an invasion of that right."[23]

Not all applications of the principle are dicta, either. For instance, in *Hardin v Kentucky Utilities*, the Court noted that it had "repeatedly held that the economic injury which results from lawful competition cannot, in and of itself, confer standing on the injured business."[24] But the Court also pointed to a different line of cases that recognized standing for injured competitors "when the particular statutory provision invoked does reflect a legislative purpose to protect a competitive interest."[25] *Hardin* found standing on that basis, which works only because Congress can create rights against competitive injuries that support standing.

Similarly, in *FEC v Akins*, the Court held that a group of voters had standing to challenge the Federal Election Commission's refusal to subject the American Israel Public Affairs Committee to various disclosure requirements.[26] The Court concluded that the voters' "inability to obtain information . . . that, on respondents' view of the law, the statute requires that AIPAC make public" was enough to satisfy Article III's standing requirements. It admitted that a similar injury had *not* been enough for standing in *United States v Richardson*, where the Court had rejected a taxpayer's demand for information about CIA expenditures.[27] But in *Akins*, by contrast, "there [was] a statute which . . . does seek to protect individuals such as respondents

---

[21] *Warth v Seldin*, 422 US 490, 500 (1975) (quoting *Linda RS v Richard D*).

[22] US Const, Art I, § 6, cl 2 ("no person holding any office under the United States, shall be a member of either House during his continuance in office").

[23] *Schlesinger v Reservists to Stop the War*, 418 US 208, 224 n 14 (1973).

[24] *Hardin v Kentucky Utilities*, 390 US 1, 5–6 (1967) (citing *Railroad Co. v Ellerman*, 105 US 166 (1882); *Alabama Power v Ickes*, 302 US 464 (1938); *Tennessee Power v TVA*, 306 US 118 (1939); *Perkins v Lukens Steel*, 310 US 113 (1940)).

[25] *Hardin*, 390 US at 6 (citing *Chicago Junction Case*, 264 US 258 (1924); *Alton Railroad v United States*, 315 US 15, 19 (1942); *Chicago v Atchison, Topeka & Santa Fe Railroad*, 357 US 77, 83 (1958)).

[26] 524 US 11 (1998).

[27] *United States v Richardson*, 418 US 166 (1974) (discussed by *Akins*, 524 US at 21–22).

from the kind of harm they say they have suffered, *i.e.*, failing to receive particular information about campaign-related activities."[28] While the Court noted other differences between the cases, the statute seemed to be the crux of it:[29] "failing to receive particular information" was itself a constitutionally sufficient injury in *Akins*, but not in *Richardson*, because of the right created by Congress.

Similar logic presumably supports standing in cases under the Freedom of Information Act (FOIA), where individuals may request information from the government and sue if it is denied.[30] The only injury in such cases is the denial of information, as in *Akins* and *Richardson*, but the Court has said in dictum that FOIA plaintiffs need show only "that they sought and were denied specific agency records,"[31] and it continues to decide FOIA cases without demanding any more.[32]

As we will see, these and other cases led many lower courts to think of Proposition A as presenting the general rule of standing: that a statutory cause of action created by Congress necessarily creates a right, the invasion of which satisfied Article III's requirement of injury.[33]

B. "A HARD FLOOR OF ARTICLE III JURISDICTION THAT CANNOT BE REMOVED BY STATUTE"

Despite the Court's widespread use of statutory rights as a basis for Article III standing, the Court has also sometimes adverted to Article III limits on those rights. That is, it has found that federal courts

[28] *Akins*, 524 US at 22.

[29] Id (observing "[t]he fact that the Court in *Richardson* focused upon taxpayer standing, not voter standing, places that case at still a greater distance from the case before us." But adding "[w]e are not suggesting ... that *Richardson* would have come out differently if only the plaintiff had asserted his standing to sue as a voter, rather than as a taxpayer.").

[30] See generally 5 USC § 552. See also David Pozen, *Freedom of Information Beyond the Freedom of Information Act*, 165 U Pa L Rev (forthcoming 2017), at https://ssrn.com/abstract=2907719 (describing individual-centered FOIA regime).

[31] *Public Citizen v U.S. Department of Justice*, 491 US 440, 449 (1989). See also Roberts, 42 Duke L J at 1228 n 60 (cited in note 9) ("When an agency wrongfully denies an individual's FOIA request, that particular individual has suffered injury in fact under Article III and has standing to sue in federal court to redress that injury.").

[32] See Seth F. Kreimer, *"Spooky Action at a Distance": Intangible Injury in Fact in the Information Age*, 18 U Pa J Const L 745, 771 (2016) (citing cases).

[33] See, for example, *Beaudry v TeleCheck Services, Inc.*, 579 F3d 702, 707 (6th Cir 2009); *Hammer v Sam's East, Inc.*, 754 F3d 492 (8th Cir 2014); *Edwards v First American*, 610 F3d 514 (9th Cir 2010); *Robey v Shapiro, Marianos & Cejda, LLC*, 434 F3d 1208, 1211 (10th Cir 2006); *Zivotofsky ex rel Ari Z v Secretary of State*, 444 F3d 614, 617–19 (DC Cir 2006).

lack constitutional power to hear certain lawsuits, even when Congress has tried to create an enforceable legal right and that legal right has been violated.

The most famous case in this second line is *Lujan v Defenders of Wildlife*, an opinion written by the late Justice Scalia that denied standing to an environmental group whose members wished to challenge a regulation under the Endangered Species Act.[34] (The regulation had interpreted Section 7(a)(2) of the Act,[35] which required interagency consultation to avoid harm to endangered and threatened species, to apply only to actions taken in the United States or on the high seas.[36])

Some of the group's theories of standing turned on claims that the regulation would injure their ability to see or study various animals. The Court rejected these as "pure speculation and fantasy."[37] This required the Court to turn to the more lasting issue: whether Congress had created a right to those procedures, the invasion of which could support standing.

The argument had persuaded the D.C. Circuit, and the Court summarized it as follows:

> that, because § 7(a)(2) requires interagency consultation, the citizen-suit provision [16 USC § 1540(g)] creates a procedural right to consultation in all persons—so that anyone can file suit in federal court to challenge the Secretary's (or presumably any other official's) failure to follow the assertedly correct consultative procedure, notwithstanding his or her inability to allege any discrete injury flowing from that failure.[38]

The Court seemed to assume for purposes of the case that the statute had indeed created such a right (though the opinion cast some aspersions by describing it as "an abstract, self-contained, noninstrumental 'right' to have the Executive observe the procedures required by law").[39] But the Court denied that the invasion of such a congressionally created right was sufficient to support standing, holding that "there is absolutely no basis for making the Article III

[34] *Lujan v Defenders of Wildlife*, 504 US 555 (1992)

[35] 16 USC § 1536(a)(2).

[36] 51 Fed Reg 19926 (1986).

[37] *Lujan*, 504 US at 567.

[38] Id at 572.

[39] Id.

inquiry turn on the source of the asserted right."[40] It would violate the separation of powers, the Court concluded, "[t]o permit Congress to convert the undifferentiated public interest in executive officers' compliance with the law into an 'individual right' vindicable in the courts."[41]

Lujan has been subject to extensive academic criticism,[42] but it was neither the last case in this line nor the first. Sixteen years later, the Court said the same thing in another case quite like *Lujan*, *Summers v Earth Island Institute*.[43]

Summers was another environmental group's challenge to another procedural defect in another environmental regulation—this one concerning fire rehabilitation and timber salvage sales. Once again, in an opinion by Justice Scalia, the Court rejected various theories of standing including one premised on Proposition A. The Court acknowledged that the challengers claimed to "have suffered procedural injury, namely that they have been denied the ability to file comments on some Forest Service actions," but concluded that "deprivation of a procedural right without some concrete interest that is affected by the deprivation—a procedural right in vacuo—is insufficient to create Article III standing."[44]

Then the Court explicitly denied Proposition A:

> *It makes no difference that the procedural right has been accorded by Congress.* That can loosen the strictures of the redressability prong of our standing inquiry. . . . Unlike redressability, however, the requirement of injury in fact is a hard floor of Article III jurisdiction that cannot be removed by statute.[45]

The Court has also found standing limits on Congress's ability to create enforceable rights in other cases, including in opinions not written by Justice Scalia. In *Raines v Byrd* the Court expanded Proposition B to create limits on congressional standing. In *Raines*

---

[40] Id at 576.

[41] Id at 577. Justice Kennedy wrote a concurring opinion, which I discuss below.

[42] For example, Sunstein, 91 Mich L Rev at 163 (cited in note 8); Gene R. Nichol, Jr., *Justice Scalia, Standing, and Public Law Litigation*, 42 Duke L J 1141 (1993); Richard J. Pierce, Jr., *Lujan v Defenders of Wildlife: Standing as a Judicially Imposed Limit on Legislative Power*, 42 Duke L J 1170 (1993).

[43] 555 US 488 (2009).

[44] Id at 496

[45] Id at 497 (emphasis added).

several legislators wished to challenge the so-called Line Item Veto Act, which authorized the President to decline to spend money they had voted to appropriate.[46] As a prestatutory matter, it was somewhat debatable whether legislators had been personally injured when the consequence of their votes was illegally ignored.[47] But in *Byrd* there was once again an express statutory right to sue, specifically vested in "any Member of Congress" to enjoin the act as unconstitutional.[48] The Court was unimpressed, declaring it "settled that Congress cannot erase Article III's standing requirements by statutorily granting the right to sue to a plaintiff who would not otherwise have standing."[49] Not even Justices Breyer and Stevens, who wrote dissents, relied heavily on Proposition A.[50]

And indeed this skeptical line of cases has early roots. The Supreme Court had rejected, on Article III grounds, a congressionally created right to sue as early as 1911, in a confusing opinion in *Muskrat v United States*.[51] That case arose after Congress had passed a series of statutes altering various allotments of property from the Cherokee tribe.[52] Four people—David Muskrat, J. Henry Dick, William Brown, and Levi B. Gritts—wanted to bring various suits challenging some of the statutes, and Congress wanted to help them do so. In 1907 Congress had passed a statute providing:

> That William Brown and Levi B. Gritts . . . and David Muskrat and J. Henry Dick . . . be, and they are hereby, authorized and empowered to institute their suits in the court of claims to determine the validity of any

[46] *Raines v Byrd*, 521 US 811 (1997).

[47] Id at 820–29 & n 4 (discussing precedents).

[48] Line Item Veto Act, § 3(a)(1), Pub Law No 104-130, 110 Stat 1200, 1211 (1996).

[49] *Raines*, 521 US at 820.

[50] Id at 835 (Stevens, J, dissenting); id at 838–39 (Breyer, J, dissenting) ("As the majority points out, Congress has enacted a specific statute (signed by the President) granting the plaintiffs authority to bring this case. That statutory authorization eliminates any prudential standing limitations and significantly lessens the risk of unwanted conflict with the Legislative Branch. Congress, however, cannot grant the federal courts more power than the Constitution itself authorizes us to exercise.").

[51] 219 US 346 (1911).

[52] For the original allotment, see An Act to provide for the allotment of the lands of the Cherokee Nation, for the disposition of town sites therein, and for other purposes, ch 1375, 32 Stat 716 (1902); for the amendments, see An Act to provide for the final disposition of the affairs of the Five Civilized Tribes in the Indian Territory, and for other purposes, ch 1867, 34 Stat 137 (1906), amended by 1907 Indian Appropriations Bill, ch 3504, 34 Stat 325 (1906); and also An Act Authorizing the Secretary of the Interior to grant right of way for pipe lines through Indian lands, ch 505, 33 Stat 65 (1904).

> acts of Congress passed since the said act of July first, nineteen hundred and two, in so far as said acts, or any of them, attempt to increase or extend the restrictions upon alienation, encumbrance, or the right to lease the allotments of lands of Cherokee citizens, or to increase the number of persons entitled to share in the final distribution of lands and funds of the Cherokees beyond those enrolled for allotment as of September first, nineteen hundred and two, and provided for in the said act of July first, nineteen hundred and two.[53]

When Muskrat's case got to the Supreme Court, the Court acknowledged that "[t]his act is the authority for the maintenance of these two suits."[54] But it found that act, and its authority, unconstitutional under Article III.

The Court's reasoning was famously obscure.[55] It mentioned several earlier cases that had invalidated claims legislation where the adjudications would not be enforced without exercise of political discretion.[56] But the Muskrat statute made the Supreme Court's decision final[57] and so it did not raise this problem. Instead, the Court seemed to have two related complaints, both of which echo modern standing requirements. One was that the plaintiffs had been wrong to sue the United States, when their goal was "not to assert a property right as against the government, or to demand compensation for alleged wrongs because of action upon its part."[58] The other was that their suit was effectively a request for an advisory opinion about the constitutionality of the allotment statutes.[59]

---

[53] 1908 Indian Appropriations Bill, ch 2285, 34 Stat 1015, 1028.

[54] *Muskrat*, 219 US at 351.

[55] David P. Currie, *The Constitution in the Supreme Court: The Second Century, 1888–1986*, at 92 (1990); Henry M. Hart, Jr. and Herbert Wechsler, *The Federal Courts and the Federal System* 130 (1st ed 1953) ("Complete the following sentence: 'The Supreme Court held that no justiciable controversy was presented in the Muskrat case because . . .'"); see also 3 Kenneth Culp Davis, *Administrative Law Treatise* § 21.01, at 120–24 (1958) ("The Court gave seven reasons for the decision, not one of which will withstand close examination.").

[56] *Muskrat*, 219 US at 353–54 (citing *Gordon v United States*, 117 US 697, 702 (1885); *United States v Ferreira*, 54 US (13 How) 40, 47 (1852)).

[57] *Muskrat*, 219 US at 351, 361.

[58] Id.

[59] Id ("It is therefore evident that there is neither more nor less in this procedure than an attempt to provide for a judicial determination, final in this court, of the constitutional validity of an act of Congress"); id at 361–62 ("The whole purpose of the law is to determine the constitutional validity of this class of legislation, in a suit not arising between parties concerning a property right necessarily involved in the decision in question, but in a proceeding against the government in its sovereign capacity, and concerning which the only judgment required is to settle the doubtful character of the legislation in question").

In the end, even though Congress had attempted to give the plaintiffs a right to that adjudication, the Court found it violated Article III: "This attempt to obtain a judicial declaration of the validity of the act of Congress is not presented in a 'case' or 'controversy,' to which, under the Constitution of the United States, the judicial power alone extends," and hence "exceeded the limitations of legislative authority."[60] *Muskrat* thus shows that the Court's skepticism about the full force of Proposition A has deep roots. It may be tempting to distinguish both *Raines* and *Muskrat* as reflecting special separation-of-powers concerns, and therefore as not strictly relevant to the question of statutory rights and Article III standing. But this distinction is artificial. The Court has described its Article III standing doctrine generally as a doctrine of separation of powers.[61] To quote *Raines* itself: "'The law of Article III standing is built on a single basic idea—the idea of separation of powers.'"[62]

The Court has not expounded the two propositions about statutory rights in complete isolation from one another. Some of the Proposition B cases attempt to reconcile themselves with Proposition A. For instance, in *Lujan*, the Court stressed that "Nothing in this contradicts the principle that "[t]he . . . injury required by Art. III may exist solely by virtue of 'statutes creating legal rights, the invasion of which creates standing.'"[63] That principle, *Lujan* suggested, "involved Congress' elevating to the status of legally cognizable injuries concrete, de facto injuries that were previously inadequate in law."[64]

Similarly, Justice Kennedy, who provided one of the five votes for the majority opinion in *Lujan*, added in a separate concurrence that: "As Government programs and policies become more complex and far reaching, we must be sensitive to the articulation of new rights of action that do not have clear analogs in our common-law tradition. . . . In my view, Congress has the power to define injuries and articulate chains of causation that will give rise to a case or controversy where none existed before, and I do not read the Court's opinion to suggest

---

[60] Id at 361–62.

[61] See, for example, *Susan B. Anthony List v Driehaus*, 134 S Ct 2334, 2341 (2014); *Arizona Christian School Tuition Org. v Winn*, 563 US 125, 132, 135 (2011); *Lujan*, 504 US at 560. See also Antonin Scalia, *The Doctrine of Standing as an Essential Element of the Separation of Powers*, 17 Suffolk U L Rev 881 (1983).

[62] *Raines*, 521 US at 820 (quoting *Allen v Wright*, 468 US 737, 752 (1984)).

[63] *Lujan*, 504 US at 578 (quoting *Warth* and *Linda RS*).

[64] *Lujan*, 504 US at 578.

a contrary view."[65] He added that "[i]n exercising this power, however, Congress must at the very least identify the injury it seeks to vindicate and relate the injury to the class of persons entitled to bring suit," and he did not think that Congress had done so in *Lujan*.[66] Still, as we will see, such acknowledgments have not prevented a conflict from arising between the two propositions.

C. THE GROWING TENSION

While these two propositions have coexisted in standing case law for decades, the tension between them makes a simple question very hard to answer: *When* does a right created by Congress nonetheless fall below the "hard floor" of Article III jurisdiction? In the years leading up to *Spokeo*, the difficulty of that question became apparent.

That difficulty became salient in *First American Financial Corp. v Edwards*,[67] a case brought under the Real Estate Settlement Procedures Act, which forbids kickbacks and revenue splits for those who settle regulated mortgage transactions.[68] These restrictions are designed to eliminate conflicts of interest among, for example, one's lender, one's real estate lawyer, and one's title insurer. The restrictions are backed by criminal penalties,[69] and also a civil cause of action that awards statutory damages "equal to three times the amount of any charge paid for such settlement service."[70]

Denise Edwards bought a house in Cleveland with title insurance provided by First American, and then complained that First American had been the beneficiary of a referral agreement banned by the act. As a matter of law, her damages seemed to be $2,186.55, three times the amount that she and her settlement agent paid for the insurance.[71] But as a matter of reality, her damages seemed to be zero: Ohio law regulates the price and terms of title insurance,[72] so Edwards got exactly what she would have gotten in any event. First American might

---

[65] Id at 580 (Kennedy, J, concurring in part and concurring in the judgment).

[66] Id.

[67] 567 US 756 (2012).

[68] 12 USC § 1607 (a), (b).

[69] 12 USC § 1607 (d)(1).

[70] 12 USC § 1607 (d)(2).

[71] See *Edwards v First American Corp.*, 610 F3d 514, 516 (9th Cir 2010) for these numbers, though I did the math myself.

[72] Ohio Rev Code Ann §§ 3935.04, 3935.07.

have profited from an illegal referral agreement, but Edwards did not suffer from it; the victims, if any, were First American's competitors.

Under established standing doctrine, the case presented a puzzle. On one hand, black letter law requires Edwards to have suffered an actual or imminent injury, and she was not in fact overcharged. So the case seems to fall below the "hard floor" of Article III. On the other hand, perhaps we can see her injury as being not her out-of-pocket costs, but the conflict of interest itself: Congress gave Edwards "a right to a conflict-free transaction,"[73] and that right can be vindicated even if it is not an economic one, just as the right to live in legally integrated housing can be vindicated even if it is not an economic one either. And yet if Congress can define such an injury, what remains of Article III's "hard floor"?

The Ninth Circuit did not fully confront the problem, instead writing its opinion as if only the Proposition A cases existed:

> "The injury required by Article III can exist solely by virtue of 'statutes creating legal rights, the invasion of which creates standing.'" "Essentially, the standing question in such cases is whether the constitutional or statutory provision on which the claim rests properly can be understood as granting persons in the plaintiff's position a right to judicial relief." Thus, we must look to the text of RESPA to determine whether it prohibited Defendants' conduct; if it did, then Plaintiff has demonstrated an injury sufficient to satisfy Article III.[74]

The first two quotations are true enough, but the last sentence does not quite follow. For as we have seen, while the Court has said that Congress can create legal rights that support standing, it has also sometimes said that it cannot—otherwise *Summers* and *Lujan* and *Raines* and even *Muskrat* would all be wrongly decided. The Ninth Circuit gave no explanation for invoking Proposition A while ignoring Proposition B.

Perhaps it is not surprising, then, that the Supreme Court took an interest in the case. And at oral argument, it looked as if the Court was poised to continue expanding Proposition B beyond *Lujan* and *Summers*. For instance, the Chief Justice seemed to deny the existence of Proposition A altogether:

---

[73] This was one of her counsel's formulations in the Supreme Court oral argument. *First American Financial Corp. v Edwards*, No 10-708, Supreme Court Oral Argument Transcript at 28, 39.

[74] *Edwards v First American Corp.*, 610 F3d 514, 517 (9th Cir 2010) (quoting *Fulfillment Services v UPS*, 528 F3d 614, 618 (9th Cir 2008), and *Warth v Seldin*, 422 US 490, 500 (1975)).

> You said violation of a statute is injury in fact. I would have thought that would be called injury in law. And when we say, as all our standing cases have, is that what is required is injury in fact, I understand that to be in contradistinction to injury in law. And when you tell me all that you've got or all that you want to plead is violation of the statute, that doesn't sound like injury in fact.[75]

So too did Justice Alito: "[W]e are looking for whether there is an injury in fact. Put aside the question of whether there is a breach of the duty in law. There is allegedly here. I just don't see where there is an injury in fact."[76] And Justice Scalia described the plaintiff's injury as "the vague notion of—of buying it from—from—I don't know, a white knight? Is—is that the kind of injury-in-fact that our cases talk about? . . . It seems to me purely—I don't know—philosophical."[77]

Meanwhile, Justice Kennedy described Proposition A as "circular": "For you to say he was entitled to it and, therefore, it's an injury, that's just—that's just circular. That gives no substance at all to the—to the meaning of the term 'injury.'"[78] And he later expressed skepticism specifically "that Congress can say that you have a right to buy a conflict-free title insurance policy."[79] It looked to observers as if the Court would reject a thorough endorsement of Proposition A, "under which no showing of injury is required simply because Congress has provided for statutory damages."[80]

Then came an unexpected reprieve: on the last day of the Term, seven months after oral argument, the Court dismissed the case as improvidently granted. As is typical, the Court issued no explanation for the late abandonment of the case. The timing makes it unlikely that the Court had suddenly discovered a "vehicle problem"[81]—a procedural wrinkle or faulty premise that made it hard to reach the question presented. Rather, it seems that the Court had some difficulty *answering* the question. Perhaps a Justice changed his or her

[75] *First American Financial Corp. v Edwards*, No 10-708, Supreme Court Oral Argument Transcript at 32–33.

[76] Id at 29.

[77] Id at 44.

[78] Id at 47.

[79] Id at 57.

[80] Christopher Wright, *Argument Recap: First American Financial Corp. v. Edwards*, SCOTUSBlog, Nov 29 (2011), at http://www.scotusblog.com/2011/11/argument-recap-first-american-financial-corp-v-edwards/.

[81] Pamela S. Karlan, *Foreword: Democracy and Disdain*, 126 Harv L Rev 1, 62 (2012).

mind at the last minute; perhaps the Court's resources were stretched thin by the massive drafting exercise in *NFIB v Sebelius* (decided that day);[82] or perhaps the Justices simply regretted confronting one of the hardest questions in modern federal courts doctrine. Later that year, Pam Karlan suggested that "[a]s with . . . the significance of the French Revolution for western civilization—it may be too soon to tell."[83] As it happens, we did not have to wait long for the next sortie.

II. Spokeo's Attempted Answer

Last Term, the Court tried once again to make progress on the doctrinal problem it had created for itself. The vehicle was *Spokeo v Robins*, another consumer protection case arising out of the Ninth Circuit.[84] This time the consumer protection statute was the Fair Credit Reporting Act, which contains a range of substantive and procedural requirements for consumer reporting agencies, including the requirement that they "follow reasonable procedures to assure maximum possible accuracy of the information concerning the individual about whom the report relates."[85] It also gives a cause of action to consumers "with respect to [whom]" these requirements are violated, for $100–$1,000 in statutory damages.[86]

The plaintiff was Thomas Robins, an unemployed, unmarried man living in Virginia. Like many of us, Mr. Robins was the subject of a consumer report on www.spokeo.com. And as with many of us, not all of that information was accurate.[87] But as in *First American*, even if these inaccuracies reflected a violation of the Fair Credit Reporting Act, it was a little hard to say how they had actually injured Mr. Robins. Spokeo described him as richer and more educated than

[82] 132 S Ct 2566 (2012).

[83] Karlan, 126 Harv L Rev at 62 (cited in note 81).

[84] 136 S Ct 1540 (2016).

[85] 15 USC § 1681(e).

[86] 15 USC § 1681(n).

[87] For instance, while writing this article I signed up at www.spokeo.com to look up my own information, and discovered that pieces of it seemed to be associated with at least nine different identities, which variously contained the wrong age, http://www.spokeo.com/William-Baude/Illinois/Chicago/p40004472993, wrong address, http://www.spokeo.com/William-Baude/Indiana/Bloomington/p30715587001, wrong marital status, http://www.spokeo.com/William-Baude/Illinois/Chicago/p40024907275, and even the wrong surname, http://www.spokeo.com/William-Bavde/Connecticut/New-Haven/p40001834445 and http://www.spokeo.com/William-Daude/California/San-Diego/p11151218031. I did not sue.

he really was, with a spouse and children that he did not have. To the extent these facts have a valence, they might seem like good things. At a minimum, they do not obviously seem like bad things.

That is how the district court saw the case, and it held that despite the statutory violation, Robins lacked standing to sue. It thought, per Proposition B, that Robins had to show a concrete and imminent injury beyond the statutory violation.[88] In principle, this could be something like showing that the inaccuracies had caused him to lose or miss out on a job, which Robins tried to allege,[89] but the court thought the allegation was "speculative, attenuated and implausible" and that Robins had "fail[ed] to allege facts sufficient to trace his alleged harm to Spokeo's alleged violations."[90]

The Ninth Circuit, however, found standing because of the statutory violation, as it had in *First American*.[91] This time its reasoning was slightly more careful. It concluded (citing *First American*)[92] that "the violation of a statutory right is *usually* a sufficient injury in fact to confer standing,"[93] in accordance with Proposition A. But it also recognized, in accordance with Proposition B, that "[o]f course, the Constitution limits the power of Congress to confer standing."[94] The Ninth Circuit concluded that those limits did not apply to Robins, because his injury was personal (i.e., his rather than somebody else's) and individual (i.e., not collective).[95] Hence, it thought, Robins's statutory injuries were "concrete, de facto injuries" that Congress could "elevat[e] to the status of legally cognizable injuries."[96]

---

[88] See Order Correcting Prior Ruling and Finding Moot Motion for Certification, No CV10-05306 ODW (AGRx) (CD Cal, Sept 19, 2011) ("Mere violation of the Fair Credit Reporting Act does not confer Article III standing, moreover, where no injury in fact is properly pled. Otherwise, federal courts will be inundated by web surfers' endless complaints.").

[89] First Amended Complaint, *Robins v Spokeo, Inc.*, No CV10-05306 7–8.

[90] Spokeo Order (cited in note 88).

[91] *Robins v Spokeo, Inc.*, 742 F3d 409, 412 (9th Cir 2014), vacated and remanded, 136 S Ct 1540 (2016).

[92] *First American* remained good law in the Ninth Circuit because of the dismissal of certiorari two years earlier. Unlike the Ninth Circuit's en banc rules, see Ninth Circuit Advisory Committee Note to Rules 35-1 to 35-3 (3), nothing automatically vacates or suspends an opinion that is up for review by the Supreme Court.

[93] *Robins*, 742 F3d at 412.

[94] Id at 413.

[95] Id at 413–14.

[96] Id (quoting *Lujan* at 578).

Once again, however, the Supreme Court was not satisfied. Justice Alito wrote an opinion for the Court reversing the Ninth Circuit and ordering a remand. It was joined by five other Justices, one of whom—Justice Thomas—also wrote a separate opinion to which we will return. Justices Ginsburg and Sotomayor dissented. (The new lineup shed little light on what had gone wrong in *First American*; and it is also possible that the case was reoriented when Justice Scalia died a few months after argument and (presumably) the drafting assignment.)[97]

The fundamental tension between Proposition A and Proposition B was evident in the Court's opinion in *Spokeo*. From Proposition B cases, the Court repeated that "Congress cannot erase Article III's standing requirements by statutorily granting the right to sue to a plaintiff who would not otherwise have standing,"[98] and that "[i]n no event may Congress abrogate the Art. III minima."[99] And it denied that "a plaintiff automatically satisfies the injury-in-fact requirement whenever a statute grants a person a statutory right and purports to authorize that person to sue to vindicate that right."[100]

But in a nod to the Proposition A cases, the Court also acknowledged that "both history and the judgment of Congress play important roles. . . . because Congress is well positioned to identify intangible harms that meet minimum Article III requirements,"[101] that "Congress may 'elevate to the status of legally cognizable injuries concrete, de facto injuries that were previously inadequate in law,'"[102] and that "'Congress has the power to define injuries and articulate chains of causation that will give rise to a case or controversy where none existed before.'"[103]

---

[97] Cf. Richard M. Re, *Explaining SCOTUS Repeaters*, 69 Vand L Rev En Banc 297, 317 (2016) (suggesting this).

[98] *Spokeo*, 136 S Ct at 1547–48 (quoting *Raines*, 521 US at 820 n 3).

[99] Id at 1548 (quoting *Gladstone, Realtors v Village of Bellwood*, 441 US 91, 100 (1979)).

[100] Id at 1549.

[101] Id.

[102] Id (quoting *Lujan*, 504 US at 578).

[103] Id (quoting *Lujan*, 504 US at 580 (Kennedy, J, concurring in part and concurring in the judgment)). See also Judith Resnik, *Revising Our "Common Intellectual Heritage": Federal and State Courts in Our Federal System*, 91 Notre Dame L Rev 1831, 1899 (2016) ("Two competing common heritages can now be drawn upon, one counseling hospitality and the other committed to limiting both judicial and congressional authority to provide remedies in courts.").

To attempt to ease that tension, the Court's opinion made a narrow doctrinal innovation, though in the service of a broader, implicit theme of narrowing Proposition A. The narrow doctrinal innovation was to focus on asking whether the statutory injury was "concrete." The word "concrete" had appeared in the Court's standing cases before. For instance, *Lujan* had described an "injury in fact" as being "an invasion of a legally protected interest which is (*a*) *concrete* and particularized, and (*b*) actual or imminent, not conjectural or hypothetical."[104] But the word had not before been given any independent definition or meaning in the Court's standing doctrine.

Prior to *Spokeo*, in the context of statutory rights, the requirement that the injury be "concrete" might have seemed to be effectively the same as the requirement of particularization. This had been Judge O'Scannlain's reasoning in the Ninth Circuit opinion below. He concluded that an injury is "concrete" so long as it is (1) an invasion of a legal right created by Congress, (2) personal, and (3) individualized.[105]

The Supreme Court's opinion in *Spokeo* disagreed, concluding that "[c]oncreteness . . . is quite different from particularization."[106] The Court also concluded that not all legal injuries, and not all injuries to defined statutory rights, were concrete.[107] A statutory right required something more.

But as to what more, exactly, was required, the Court was somewhat mysterious. Citing dictionaries, it said that to be concrete an injury "must actually exist," and be "'real,' and not 'abstract.'"[108] And yet the harm could also nonetheless be "intangible" or based only on the "risk of real harm."[109] The Court did not explain, however, why some statutory rights are not "real," especially when some intangible harms apparently can be. After providing a few sentences of guidance for how to apply this new requirement to the Fair Credit Reporting

[104] *Lujan*, 504 US 555, 560 (1992) (emphasis added; citations and quotation marks omitted).

[105] *Robins*, 742 F3d at 413–14.

[106] *Spokeo*, 136 S Ct at 1548.

[107] Id at 1549 ("Congress' role in identifying and elevating intangible harms does not mean that a plaintiff automatically satisfies the injury-in-fact requirement whenever a statute grants a person a statutory right and purports to authorize that person to sue to vindicate that right").

[108] Id at 1548 (quoting dictionaries).

[109] Id at 1549.

Act itself, the Court remanded the case to the lower courts for further consideration.[110]

As noted above, the broader message of the Court's opinion seemed to be a certain measure of skepticism about Proposition A, and a search for some additional rule for limiting Congress's ability to create private rights, the invasion of which supports standing. As I will discuss in a moment, that skepticism, and the Court's attempt to implement it, are understandable, but problematic.

There were two other opinions in *Spokeo*: Justice Ginsburg, joined by Justice Sotomayor, dissented, while largely following the majority's framework. Her dissent emphasized the Court's Proposition A cases[111] but also acknowledged the Proposition B cases.[112] She also read the concreteness requirement more narrowly and thought that Robins's complaint had already satisfied that requirement.[113] Justice Thomas, meanwhile, wrote a concurring opinion attempting to ground the Court's standing doctrine in historical principles differentiating public rights and private rights.[114] I will return to his view in Part IV.

III. The Problems with Spokeo's Answer

Taken seriously, both the larger and smaller implications of *Spokeo* are problematic. They cast doubt on standing in several different cases where standing seemed to be widely presumed. That is not to say that the majority's approach is obviously wrong. It may reflect just how difficult it is to find a principled way of reconciling the two long-standing propositions of the Court's case law.

A. Nominal Damages

The first problem with the Court's ruling in *Spokeo* is that it creates a tension with the basic notion of nominal damages. Nominal damages are damages in a trivial amount—a nominal sum—that allow a plaintiff to litigate important legal rights without seeking or litigating damages issues. As we have seen, nominal damages were available at common

---

[110] The Ninth Circuit called for supplemental briefing and argument, and heard argument again on December 13, 2016. Docket No 108, *Robins v Spokeo*, No 11-56843 (9th Cir). As of now, the case remains outstanding.

[111] 136 S Ct at 1554–55 (Ginsburg, J, dissenting).

[112] See, for example, id at 1555 (quoting *Lujan*).

[113] Id at 1555–56 (Ginsburg, J, dissenting).

[114] Id at 1551–53 (Thomas, J, concurring).

law for trespass claims, where the plaintiff mostly cared about establishing a property right,[115] or in libel cases where the plaintiff cared most about "brand[ing] the defamatory publication as false."[116] Nominal damages have been called "in many respects an early precursor to the declaratory judgment proceeding."[117]

"[I]t has long been settled that a claimant may waive or forgo claims for compensatory and punitive damages and pursue nominal damages alone."[118] In more modern cases, the Court has specifically affirmed that nominal damages are available to compensate for the violation of legal rights. In *Carey v Piphus*, the Court concluded that "the denial of procedural due process should be actionable for nominal damages without proof of actual injury."[119] And in a later case the Court even went on to hold that an award of nominal damages is a sufficient victory to make a plaintiff eligible for attorneys fees (though they might not actually be awarded in all cases).[120]

But it is hard to see how nominal damages are fully consistent with the logic of *Spokeo*. The very premise of nominal damages is that one cannot show any "actual injury" apart from the violation of the legal right itself.[121] *Spokeo* seems to require something more than just the violation of a legal right. The *Spokeo* opinion is ambiguous on this score, given its reference to concrete but "intangible" injuries,[122] but it is nonetheless at odds with the basic idea of nominal damages, whose very point is that nothing more concrete need be shown.

B. ZIVOTOFSKY

Spokeo is also inconsistent with other causes of action that the Court has taken for granted as constitutional up until now. Consider, for instance, the statutory cause of action that the Court confronted the

---

[115] *Webb v Portland Manufacturing Co.*, 29 F Cas 506 (CCD Me 1838).

[116] *Gertz v Robert Welch, Inc.*, 418 US 323, 372 (1974).

[117] James E. Pfander, *Resolving the Qualified Immunity Dilemma: Constitutional Tort Claims for Nominal Damages*, 111 Colum L Rev 1601, 1620 (2011). There are some who argue that nominal damages should not be available in circumstances where a declaratory judgment would not be. See generally *Utah Animal Rights Coalition v Salt Lake City*, 371 F3d 1248, 1262–67 (10th Cir 2004) (McConnell, J, concurring).

[118] Pfander, 111 Colum L Rev at 1620 (cited in note 117).

[119] *Carey v Piphus*, 435 US 247, 266 (1978).

[120] *Farrar v Hobby*, 506 US 103, 113 (1992).

[121] *Carey*, 435 US at 266.

[122] 136 S Ct at 1549.

previous year in *Zivotofsky v Kerry*.[123] *Zivotofsky* presented a separation-of-powers issue that arose under Section 214(d) of the Foreign Relations Authorization Act, Fiscal Year 2003. Section 214(d) stated that "[f]or purposes of the registration of birth, certification of nationality, or issuance of a passport of a United States citizen born in the city of Jerusalem, the Secretary shall, upon the request of the citizen or the citizen's legal guardian, record the place of birth as Israel."[124] The suit was brought in the name of a child, Menachem Binyamin Zivotofsky, to vindicate his statutory right to a passport that said "Israel."

The Court ultimately concluded that the statute was unconstitutional, at least as applied to passports, because it infringed on the executive's power over foreign affairs.[125] But under the logic of *Spokeo*, it is not clear whether the Court should have gotten that far. Before the case reached the Supreme Court, the D.C. Circuit had been forced to confront the question of Zivotofsky's standing, and it had relied expressly on the broad form of Proposition A. It wrote:

> The Supreme Court has recognized that "Congress may enact statutes creating legal rights, the invasion of which creates standing, even though no injury would exist without the statute." Or stated differently, "Congress may create a statutory right or entitlement the alleged deprivation of which can confer standing to sue even where the plaintiff would have suffered no judicially cognizable injury in the absence of statute."[126]

As for the Proposition B cases, the D.C. Circuit understood them to be limited to having "qualified statutory standing in one respect," namely, the exclusion of "a generalized interest shared by all citizens in the proper administration of the law."[127] In other words, the D.C. Circuit's theory of standing in *Zivotofsky* tracked almost exactly the Ninth Circuit's theory of standing in *Spokeo*. If *Spokeo* is right, then it seems that *Zivotofsky* was wrong to reach the merits.

To be sure, the Supreme Court may not have focused on the standing question in *Zivotofsky*. By 2015 the parties had stopped

---

[123] 135 S Ct 2076 (2015).

[124] Foreign Relations Authorization Act, Fiscal Year 2003, Pub L No 107-228, 116 Stat 1350, 1366 (2002).

[125] 135 S Ct at 2081, 2096. For evaluation of the merits, see Jack Goldsmith, *Zivotofsky II as Precedent in the Executive Branch*, 129 Harv L Rev 112, 115–32 (2015); Saikrishna Bangalore Prakash, *Zivotofsky and the Separation of Powers*, 2015 Supreme Court Review 1 (2015).

[126] *Zivotofsky ex rel Ari Z v Secretary of State*, 444 F3d 614, 617 (DC Cir 2006) (quoting *Linda RS v Richard D*, 410 US 614, 617 n 3 (1973) and *Warth v Seldin*, 422 US 490, 514 (1975)).

[127] *Zivotofsky ex rel Ari Z*, 444 F3d at 618.

contesting the issue of standing, though the government had contested it before losing on the issue in the D.C. Circuit. But courts have an obligation to consider standing questions on their own, and both an amicus brief[128] and some public commentary[129] pointed out the standing problems in *Zivotofsky* while it was pending in the Supreme Court. And the Supreme Court granted certiorari in *Spokeo* just six weeks before deciding *Zivotofsky*.[130] Nonetheless, none of the Justices in *Zivotofsky* acknowledged the standing problem, even though three of them joined the majority opinion in both that case and *Spokeo*.

Perhaps some members of the Court thought that standing in *Zivotofsky* was permissible because there was a concrete injury apart from the statutory right. But it is hard to see what that would be. One could perhaps imagine that some Section 214(d) claimants would suffer psychological harm from the treatment of their passports, and one can read *Spokeo* to treat psychological harms as sufficiently "concrete."[131] But, as the D.C. Circuit pointed out, at the time of its standing decision Menachem Zivotofsky was "only three years old" and any psychological harm seemed "conjectural."[132] What is more, standing is supposed to exist *when the complaint is filed*.[133] When the complaint in *Zivotofsky* was filed, Menachem was eleven months old.[134] It seems implausible that he had any psychological harm from the contents of his passport at that time.

---

[128] Brief of True Torah Jews as amicus curiae in support of respondent, *Zivotofsky v Kerry*, No 13-628 (US Supreme Court, filed Sept 29, 2014).

[129] William Baude, *The Standing Problem in Zivotofsky, Revisited*, Washington Post, Volokh Conspiracy (Dec 4, 2014), at https://www.washingtonpost.com/news/volokh-conspiracy/wp/2014/12/04/the-standing-problem-in-zivotofsky-revisited/; William Baude, *The Legal Power of "Standing,"* NY Times (May 14, 2015), at http://www.nytimes.com/2015/05/14/opinion/the-legal-power-of-standing.html. But see Andy Hessick, *Zivotofsky and Spokeo*, Notice & Comment: A Blog from the Yale J on Reg (May 18, 2015), at http://www.yalejreg.com/blog/zivotofsky-and-spokeo-by-andy-hessick.

[130] 135 S Ct 1892 (2015) (granting certiorari).

[131] Rachel Bayefsky, *Psychological Harm and Constitutional Standing*, 81 Brooklyn L Rev 1555, 1568–69, 1597–98 (2016).

[132] *Zivotofsky ex rel Ari Z*, 444 F3d at 617.

[133] See *Newman-Green v Alfonzo-Larrain*, 490 US 826, 830 (1989) ("The existence of federal jurisdiction ordinarily depends on the facts as they exist when the complaint is filed."); *Lujan*, 504 US at 569 n 4 (plurality); see also *Campbell-Ewald v Gomez*, 136 S Ct 663, 669 (2016) (Article III "demand[s] that an actual controversy be extant at *all* stages of review, not *merely* at the time the complaint is filed.") (emphasis added, internal quotation marks and alterations omitted).

[134] Complaint, *Zivotofsky v Secretary of State*, No 03-1921 (DDC, filed Sept 16, 2003) (noting Menachem Zivotofsky's birthdate as October 17, 2002).

Or perhaps one could characterize *Zivotofsky*'s injury as expressive. *Spokeo* gave as examples of permissible "intangible injuries" violations of free speech and free exercise rights,[135] and one could see the right to put one's country of origin on one's passport as an expressive right. But that seems like a strained interpretation of the passport (and one that the majority in *Zivotofsky* indeed rejected).[136] Moreover, it simply raises the question why the abstract rights to engage in free speech and free exercise are "concrete" but the right to reasonable accuracy in *Spokeo* might not be.

One might dismiss the question of standing in *Zivotofsky* as a moot point. The Justices did not discuss the standing question, and therefore the case establishes no precedent on standing.[137] But the contrary treatment of standing in *Zivotofsky* and *Spokeo* suggests that there is something confused about the Court's intuitions in this area. Moreover, the question of standing in cases like *Zivotofsky* may well arise again, even under the very same statute. That is because Section 214(d) applies not only to passports but to consular reports of birth abroad. Justice Thomas expressly distinguished the two and argued that Congress has greater power to regulate the latter in light of its naturalization power.[138] And the majority expressly reserved the question because it had been waived.[139] Hence, if Jersusalem-born U.S. citizens wish to litigate the issue of consular birth reports, the courts will have to confront the standing question in light of *Spokeo*.

C. PRIVACY

Finally, *Spokeo* has also raised questions about the enforcement of privacy statutes throughout the lower courts. In these cases, plaintiffs sue somebody who has illegally disclosed information about them;

---

[135] *Spokeo*, 136 S Ct at 1549.

[136] For example, *Zivotofsky*, 135 S Ct at 2095 (describing "a passport's place-of-birth section as an official executive statement").

[137] *Arizona Christian School Tuition Org. v Winn*, 563 US 125, 144 (2011) ("When a potential jurisdictional defect is neither noted nor discussed in a federal decision, the decision does not stand for the proposition that no defect existed.").

[138] 135 S Ct at 2109–11 (Thomas, J, concurring in the judgment in part and dissenting in part).

[139] Id at 2083 ("The arguments in Zivotofsky's brief center on his passport claim, as opposed to the consular report of birth abroad. . . . He has . . . waived the issue here by failing to differentiate between the two documents. As a result, the Court addresses Zivotofsky's passport arguments and need not engage in a separate analysis of the validity of § 214(d) as applied to consular reports of birth abroad.").

they are then confronted with the question of whether illegal disclosure of information, without more, is a concrete injury under *Spokeo*. Remarkably, most courts have said "no." Taken seriously, this would imply constitutional limits on federal enforcement of privacy rights. This further demonstrates the implausibility of *Spokeo*.

For instance, last summer the D.C. Circuit confronted a lawsuit by two D.C. shoppers who complained that local clothing stores had demanded their zip codes in violation of local law. Without disputing that the information was illegally demanded, D.C. Circuit dismissed the case for lack of standing.[140] The forced disclosure of one's zip code, it held, was not a concrete injury after *Spokeo*. In *Spokeo* the Court had offered a coincidentally similar example, writing: "not all inaccuracies cause harm or present any material risk of harm. An example that comes readily to mind is an incorrect zip code. It is difficult to imagine how the dissemination of an incorrect zip code, without more, could work any concrete harm."[141]

The D.C. Circuit found the dictum apt, writing, "If, as the Supreme Court advised, disclosure of an incorrect zip code is not a concrete Article III injury, then even less so is [the plaintiffs'] naked assertion that a zip code was requested and recorded without any concrete consequence. [The plaintiffs] do not allege, for example, any invasion of privacy, increased risk of fraud or identity theft, or pecuniary or emotional injury."[142]

This is probably the correct conclusion to draw from *Spokeo*'s somewhat gratuitous discussion of zip codes, but at a more fundamental level it again suggests that something is wrong with *Spokeo*. Why must the plaintiffs show something like a risk of identity theft or emotional injury to demonstrate a concrete injury? Why can't an illegal disclosure *itself* be a concrete injury? As to a zip code, this may seem strange. But imagine that the illegal disclosure was something else—an unflattering photograph or email, perhaps. Surely this ought to be actionable without showing a subsequent consequence, like the loss of one's job or social standing. Or, more modestly, imagine somebody who is embarrassed by their middle name and does not wish to see it disclosed. If that person has a legal right against disclosure, why should they need anything more?

---

[140] *Hancock v Urban Outfitters*, 830 F3d 511 (DC Cir 2016) (Millett, J).

[141] *Spokeo*, 135 S Ct at 1550.

[142] *Hancock*, 830 F3d at 514.

There are two possible ways to resolve the scope of privacy laws in light of the courts' position on zip codes. One possibility, the more aggressive one, is to conclude that illegal disclosure of facts about oneself is never itself a concrete injury. To sue over the disclosure of one's address, photos, name, or anything else, one would have to demonstrate some sort of downstream consequences from these disclosures. In other words, privacy itself would not be a protectable interest under Article III. This position has a certain logical purity, but one hopes that it is too implausible even for today's courts to adopt. It would mean that even injuries recognized under longstanding common law principles would not be enough to satisfy the "injury in fact" requirement.[143]

The alternative possibility, a more modest one, is that some illegal disclosures are injurious in themselves, and others are not. For instance, perhaps the disclosure of photographs is different in kind from the disclosure of zip codes, even if both are protected by legal right. (The D.C. Circuit's attempt to distinguish "invasion of privacy" as an actionable "concrete consequence" might point to this possibility.)[144] There is some common sense intuition behind this approach, but it is not entirely principled. If the legislature has made the judgment to protect both kinds of information, it is not at all clear why judges may decide that one is "concrete," that is, "real," and the other is not.[145] This saves some of privacy law from *Spokeo* only by creating a constitutional common law of privacy interests.

Other post-*Spokeo* decisions in the lower courts reveal more ambiguity and troubling possibilities. For instance, in *Braitberg v Charter Communications*, the Eighth Circuit dismissed a lawsuit brought by a former customer complaining that his cable company had illegally retained some of his personal information in violation of federal law.[146]

---

[143] See Samuel D. Warren and Louis D. Brandeis, *The Right to Privacy*, 4 Harv L Rev 193, 206–13 (1890) (suggesting that under "the existing law" the "invasion of privacy" is "a legal *injuria*"); see also Restatement (Second) of Torts § 652D (1977) (collecting cases).

[144] *Hancock*, 830 F3d at 514 ("Hancock and White do not allege, for example, any invasion of privacy, increased risk of fraud or identity theft, or pecuniary or emotional injury.").

[145] See *Leading Case, Spokeo, Inc. v Robins*, 130 Harv L Rev 437, 444–45 (2016) ("For example, even incorrect zip codes assuredly cause harm of some degree, since insurance and marketing companies often segment by zip code, and individuals are prone to make generalizations about race, religion, or ethnicity based on where somebody lives. The pertinent question is not exactly how much harm is caused, but why is it not harm enough?").

[146] 836 F3d 925 (8th Cir 2016).

The court concluded that illegally retaining personal information was not itself a harm for which Congress could authorize suit, suggesting once again that Article III might impose limits on federal privacy law.

Like the D.C. Circuit, the Eighth Circuit tried to salvage some privacy law, by noting that in this case the defendant had not "disclosed the information to a third party" nor "used the information in any way during the disputed period."[147] This was relevant, said the court, because at common law, "the retention of information lawfully obtained, without further disclosure, traditionally has not provided the basis for a lawsuit in American courts."[148] This is somewhat reassuring for privacy law, but not entirely. In rejecting Congress's attempts to modestly expand the scope of personal informational rights in the Cable Communications Policy Act, the Eighth Circuit cast doubt on whether Congress can expand privacy rights beyond their common law scope at all. It is unclear why, in this area, Congress should not be allowed to protect interests beyond those protected by the common law, as it has been allowed in other cases.

On the other hand, the Third Circuit has taken the opposite lesson from *Spokeo*. In *In re Nickelodeon Consumer Privacy Litigation*,[149] the court concluded that statutory privacy claims automatically supply standing. Dealing with a class of consumers who alleged that Viacom had illegally disclosed children's web-browsing data to Google, the court wrote that while their harms were "perhaps 'intangible,'" they nonetheless presented "a clear *de facto* injury, *i.e.*, the unlawful disclosure of legally protected information."[150] While the D.C. Circuit in *Hancock* thought the unlawful disclosure of legally protected information was not an injury without more—without some consequences flowing from that unlawful disclosure—the Third Circuit thought that the disclosure was itself the harm.

D. SUBSTANTIVE DUE PROCESS ALL OVER AGAIN?

The purpose of reciting these problematic implications of *Spokeo* is not to show that Article III limits on statutory standing are obvi-

---

[147] Id at 930.

[148] Id.

[149] 827 F3d 262 (2016).

[150] Id at 274. See also *In re Horizon Healthcare Services Inc. Data Breach Litigation*, 846 F3d 625 (3d Cir 2017) (reaffirming this holding).

ously wrong. While there may once have been widespread academic skepticism of restrictions on Congress's plenary power to confer standing through statutory rights,[151] that power has been limited in several cases that seem well entrenched. But even accepting those limits, the conflict between the Court's two lines of standing doctrine raises tricky problems, and *Spokeo* does not do much to solve them.

Indeed, the Court's so far unsuccessful quest to define the limits of statutory standing is reminiscent of the path of another doctrine—that of substantive due process. This analogy has been made before by some critics of Proposition B's limits on statutory standing[152] who have said that it "uses highly contestable ideas about political theory to invalidate congressional enactments, even though the relevant constitutional text and history do not call for invalidation at all"[153]—an analogy intended as "particular anathema to those members of the Court most anxious to tell us that there are Article III limitations on statutory grants of standing."[154] The analogy between standing limitations and substantive due process is an apt one, but in a more nuanced and sympathetic way than those critics may intend. The vagueness of Proposition B, illustrated by *Spokeo*, invites courts either to fashion constitutional limits out of nothing, or to say that only interests protected by the common law satisfy Article III requirements—both paths that have proven unworkable in the substantive due process context.

In a nutshell, one story of substantive due process's early rise is this: The Due Process Clause forbids deprivations of "life, liberty, or property without due process of law."[155] This was paradigmatically understood as a rule regulating the executive and judicial branches, requiring them to obey the positive law when their actions might injure a private person.[156] It might have been satisfying to conclude

[151] Richard B. Stewart, *The Reformation of American Administrative Law*, 88 Harv L Rev 1669, 1734–42 (1975); David P. Currie, *Misunderstanding Standing*, 1981 Supreme Court Review 41, 42–43, 47; Fletcher, 98 Yale L J at 253–54 (cited in note 7); Sunstein, 91 Mich L Rev at 191–92, 236 (cited in note 8).

[152] Fletcher, 98 Yale L J at 233 (cited in note 7); Sunstein, 91 Mich L Rev at 205–06, 234–35 (cited in note 8).

[153] Sunstein, 91 Mich L Rev at 167 (cited in note 8).

[154] Fletcher, 98 Yale L J at 233 (cited in note 7).

[155] US Const, Art V. See also id Art XIV.

[156] John Harrison, *Substantive Due Process and the Constitutional Text*, 83 Va L Rev 493, 504–05 (1997).

that the clause does not apply to the legislature at all—and seemingly consistent with due process's forebearer, the requirement that the government conform to "the law of the land."[157] But the clause could not easily ignore the legislature, for what if the legislature passed a statute saying that the executive branch could do whatever it wished and dispense with the courts? Or what if the legislature itself directly effected the deprivation? In order to prevent what seem like obvious evasions of the clause, it was logical to characterize those legislative actions, too, as deprivations of due process.[158]

Perhaps one could still hold the line by insisting that the requirement as applied to the legislature be strictly procedural: The legislature could create whatever substantive rules or liabilities it wished so long as they were adjudicated by a court and through "due" procedures. But regulations of substance can circumvent the requirements of process. What if, for example, the legislature passes a statute making it a crime to be on an officially maintained list of enemy combatants? One can have all of the process one likes, limited to the single element of the offense: whether one is on the list. The hypothetical is troubling because its substance makes procedure irrelevant.

And while courts did not confront exactly that hypothetical, they confronted other substantive regulations that seemed similar to them, such as a law providing for the one-time election of county clerks,[159] or a law prohibiting the sale of liquor,[160] and found them to violate due process principles.[161] These substantive rules came so close to evading the constitutionally required process that it seemed natural to invalidate them too. Thus due process expanded to include certain substantive constraints that supplement procedural due process, such as

---

[157] Ryan C. Williams, *The One and Only Substantive Due Process Clause*, 120 Yale L J 408, 428–35 (2010).

[158] Harrison, 83 Va L Rev at 506–20 (cited in note 156) (describing, though not endorsing, this move); Nathan S. Chapman and Michael W. McConnell, *Due Process as Separation of Powers*, 121 Yale L J 1672, 1713–17 (2012) (describing Alexander Hamilton's view); id at 1724 ("Most American courts and jurists in the early Republic agreed, at a minimum, that legislative enactments that authorized other branches to deprive persons of life, liberty, or property without traditional procedural protections or their equivalent violated due process.").

[159] *Hoke v Henderson*, 15 NC (4 Dev) 1 (1833).

[160] *Wynehamer v People*, 13 NY 378 (1856).

[161] See Chapman and McConnell, 121 Yale L J at 1751–54, 1768–70 (cited in note 158) and Williams, 120 Yale L J at 461, 465, 468–70 (cited in note 157) for discussion.

the requirements that legislation authorizing deprivations be "general" or "prospective."[162]

But once one has started invalidating substantive regulations, it is easy to see how one slips into even more "substantive" applications of due process—whether a right to freedom of contract or a right to intimate decision making or what have you. Having abandoned the most formally stark principles, like the rule that due process does not apply to the legislature, or applies only to process and never to substance, the doctrinal category has tended to drift out into more open territory. And in this open sea, courts looking for landmarks instead drift to things like common-law tradition or their own ethical intuitions.

This is not to say that this evolution from formally procedural to broadly substantive due process is inevitable—on the contrary! Many jurists and scholars have put forward plausible theories about how and where the stopping line should have been drawn. But it is to say that it is easier than one might think to slip from formal procedural rules to quite substantive judge-made ones. And it is hard to draw a coherent, stable line in such an area by proceeding only in intuitive, case-by-case fashion.

Congressionally created standing has much the same character. It might have been satisfying to conclude that standing limitations do not apply to the legislature at all—but that would suggest that Congress could even go so far as to authorize federal courts to issue advisory opinions, whose illegality is supposedly one of the paradigm rules of Article III. It seemed natural enough, perhaps even necessary, to describe the legal right to an advisory opinion as violating the requirement of a "judicial" "case" or "controversy." This gives us *Muskrat*, the first of the standing cases supporting today's Proposition B.[163]

Even once standing doctrine has extended to limit legislatively created rights, one might attempt to limit that doctrine to a ban on advisory opinions. But courts saw in some procedural legal rights the

[162] Chapman and McConnell, 121 Yale L J at 1717, 1738 (cited in note 158); Williams, 120 Yale L J at 423–25 (cited in note 157).

[163] 219 US 346 (1911) (discussed at notes 56–60). See also Richard M. Re, *Relative Standing*, 102 Georgetown L J 1191, 1232 (2014) ("[T]he Court has . . . insisted that there are limits on Congress's power to confer standing, and it is easy to see why. Unfettered authority to confer standing would empower the political branches to compel adjudication of controversies that are, as presented, poorly suited to judicial resolution. And courts have said for decades, even centuries, that effective judicial resolution of disputes is facilitated through adjudication focused by concrete adversity." (citing *Muskrat*)).

same things that had concerned them about advisory opinions—the possibility of courts being asked to adjudicate only "[t]he public's nonconcrete interest in the proper administration of the laws."[164]

And once courts have started invalidating such statutory rights, it is easy to see how they might keep going. The rule that all federal legal rights can be vindicated in federal court has been replaced with a judicial limitation on which legal rights are sufficiently real to be judicially enforced. Such judicial limitation is not inherently flawed, but the Court has not fully understood the problem it is trying to solve, and so it has not deployed a solution that is likely to solve it.

The concept of "concreteness" does not do much to resolve these problems. Nor does it help to rephrase that term, as *Spokeo* does, into a judicial inquiry into which injuries, including "intangible" ones, are nonetheless "real."[165] What makes some rights "real" enough to justify nominal damages, and others insufficiently real to justify the statutory damages available under the Fair Credit Reporting Act? What makes the word "Israel" on Menachem Zivotofsky's passport more concrete than the word "married" on Robins's Spokeo profile? What makes the zip code disclosed in *Hancock* less concrete than the internet cookie disclosed in *Nickelodeon*?

The way to make the concept of "intangible" yet "real" injury coherent is to say that only injuries recognized in some form by the common law will suffice. But this is a position that the Court has (rightly) rejected, and it is one that is not really reconciled to a post-*Lochner* world. The inquiry in *Spokeo* looks, at best, like an effort to identify the subset of statutory rights that vaguely resemble the common law. That inquiry is both indefinite, but more importantly, misguided. So while the doctrinal problem faced in *Spokeo* is a genuinely tricky one, the Court's attempted answer should be classified as a misstep.

IV. Justice Thomas's Alternative

One Justice on the *Spokeo* Court seemed to see the problem. Justice Thomas, who joined the majority opinion in full, wrote a

[164] *Lujan*, 504 US at 580 (Kennedy, J, concurring in part and concurring in the judgment in part).

[165] *Spokeo*, 136 S Ct at 1548–49. See also Re, 102 Georgetown L J at 1203 (cited in note 163) (arguing that because of the failure of the concept of adequate factual injury, "the Court has adopted a 'standard' for factual injury defined only by a list of synonymous adjectives").

concurring opinion that put forward a proposed rule that is both theoretically and historically consistent and that may provide a way to reconcile the tension between Proposition A and Proposition B. Justice Thomas's opinion built off of insightful articles by Andrew Hessick[166] and by Ann Woolhandler and Caleb Nelson.[167] While Justice Thomas's argument may need to be articulated more fully in the future, here are the essential parts:

The fundamental inquiry that standing derives from is who is a "proper party" to a given lawsuit. Having the so-called proper party is an independent requirement for judicial cognizance of a case.[168] Most importantly, the "proper party" for bringing a lawsuit depends very much on whether the suit is one to vindicate public rights or private rights. Public rights are owed "to the whole community, considered as a community, in its social aggregate capacity,"[169] such as "free navigation of waterways, passage on public highways, and general compliance with regulatory law."[170] Public rights can most paradigmatically be vindicated by the government itself.[171] But they can also be vindicated by private people if those people suffered "special damage" that distinguishes them from other members of the public.[172]

By contrast, private rights are those "belonging to individuals, considered as individuals,"[173] such as "rights of personal security (including security of reputation), property rights, and contract rights."[174] They can be vindicated by the holders of those private rights regardless of what kind of damage they had suffered. These include the

---

[166] Hessick, 93 Cornell L Rev at 275 (cited in note 12).

[167] Woolhandler and Nelson, 102 Mich L Rev at 689 (cited in note 8).

[168] Id at 695 ("The concept of proper parties is central to standing doctrine, and it may also infuse notions of a 'Case'"). The relationship of proper parties to Article III may also explain the constitutionalization of sovereign immunity. See Caleb Nelson, *Sovereign Immunity as a Doctrine of Personal Jurisdiction*, 115 Harv L Rev 1559, 1568–75 (2002). See also William Baude, *Sovereign Immunity and the Constitutional Text*, 103 Va L Rev 1 (2017).

[169] *Spokeo*, 136 S Ct at 1551 (Thomas, J, concurring) (quoting 4 William Blackstone, Commentaries at *5).

[170] *Spokeo*, 136 S Ct at 1551 (Thomas, J, concurring) (quoting Woolhander and Nelson, 102 Mich L Rev at 693 (cited in note 8)).

[171] Hessick, 93 Cornell L Rev at 278–279 (cited in note 12).

[172] Woolhandler and Nelson, 102 Mich L Rev at 701 (cited in note 8).

[173] *Spokeo*, 136 S Ct at 1551 (Thomas, J, concurring) (quoting 3 William Blackstone, Commentaries at *2).

[174] *Spokeo*, 136 S Ct at 1551 (Thomas, J, concurring) (citing 1 Blackstone at *130–*39 and Woolhander and Nelson, 102 Mich L Rev at 693 (cited in note 8)).

instances of nominal damages and trespass without injury discussed earlier.[175]

Put together, these two principles led Justice Thomas to the conclusion that Proposition A controlled in private rights cases, while Proposition B controlled in public rights cases:

> Congress can create new private rights and authorize private plaintiffs to sue based simply on the violation of those private rights. A plaintiff seeking to vindicate a statutorily created private right need not allege actual harm beyond the invasion of that private right. A plaintiff seeking to vindicate a public right embodied in a federal statute, however, must demonstrate that the violation of that public right has caused him a concrete, individual harm distinct from the general population. Thus, Congress cannot authorize private plaintiffs to enforce public rights in their own names, absent some showing that the plaintiff has suffered a concrete harm particular to him.[176]

This position has several virtues. It is consistent with the historical antecedents of standing doctrine, and also basically consistent with the Court's invocations of Propositions A and B. Under this theory, the Proposition A cases are generally correct because Congress had in those cases created a private right, which can be enforced by the holder of that right without anything more.[177] Meanwhile, *Lujan* and *Summers* and *Muskrat* and *Raines*—the Proposition B cases—are correct because they all involve the enforcement of a public right, namely, that of "general compliance with regulatory law."[178]

I am not certain that this position is sound, but it is plausible and generally consistent with history and doctrine, and it provides an actual attempt at a way forward. The historical categories of public and private rights, though not of crystalline purity, seem more workable and more apt than the Court's struggle to define some injuries as "real" and "concrete." By focusing the inquiry on the distinction between public and private rights, Justice Thomas helps us see that the question is not about whether the injury matches some platonic class of real injuries, but rather about whether Congress has

---

[175] See notes 12–15.

[176] *Spokeo*, 136 S Ct at 1553 (Thomas, J, concurring) (citations omitted).

[177] Justice Thomas joined Justice Scalia's dissent in *FEC v Akins*, 524 US 11, 30 (1998), which argued that the cause of action in that case should be narrowly construed to avoid rendering it unconstitutional. It is possible, but not certain, that the cause of action at issue in *Akins* could be seen as conferring a private right to information, rather than a public right.

[178] *Spokeo*, 136 S Ct at 1551 (Thomas, J, concurring) (quoting Woolhander & Nelson, 102 Mich L Rev at 693 (cited in note 8)).

given the right a particular *form*—a form that matches the judicial function in resolving it.

To be sure, Justice Thomas's position, and the scholarship on which he relied, does not fully resolve an important and hard question: Under what circumstances can Congress privatize a previously public right? When and how can Congress convert a legal duty that might traditionally have seemed public into a private one?[179] Answering this question will be important to know whether a new statutory right should be classed with the cases under Proposition A or Proposition B.

It seems to me that Justice Thomas's approach could yield at least two plausible answers to this question, one more restrictive of Congress's power and one more generous. Under the more restrictive approach, one might say that private rights must take a particular form. For instance, at one point Justice Thomas deployed a quotation from *Tennessee Electric Power v TVA*,[180] implying that a private right must have one of four specific forms.[181] It must be "'a legal right,—one of property, one arising out of contract, one protected against tortious invasion, or one founded on a statute which confers a privilege.'"[182]

These categories exclude the Proposition B cases. None of them were rights of property or contract. The "procedural right" at issue in *Lujan* and *Summers* was not a "privilege," at least if that term is used in the Hohfeldian sense of being "the opposite of a duty, and the correlative of a 'no-right.'"[183] It did not give its holders the privilege to do anything, other than sue to enforce the duty it imposed on the government.[184] Nor was it "protected from tortious invasion,"[185]

---

[179] Cf. William Baude and James Y. Stern, *The Positive Law Model of the Fourth Amendment*, 129 Harv L Rev 1821, 1880 (2016) (noting that "one of the great debates among legal theorists is over how to determine whether and upon whom a legal duty confers a legal right" and that it is "not yet resolved").

[180] 306 US 118 (1939).

[181] *Spokeo*, 136 S Ct at 1553 (Thomas, J, concurring).

[182] Id (quoting *Tennessee Electric*, 306 US at 137–38).

[183] Wesley Newcomb Hohfeld, *Some Fundamental Legal Conceptions as Applied in Judicial Reasoning*, 23 Yale L J 16, 32 (1913).

[184] This made it a "right in the strictest sense." Id at 30. See also id at 32 ("In other words, if X has a right against Y that he shall stay off the former's land, the correlative (and equivalent) is that Y is under a duty toward X to stay off the place").

[185] 306 US at 138.

because the government's violation of the right was not treated as a tort or subject to damages. The same seems even more clearly true of *Raines* and *Muskrat*.

Under this restrictive approach, however, rights like those at issue in *Spokeo* may well be validly created private rights, because they do seem to be "protected against tortious invasion."[186] Hence, Justice Thomas concluded that if the Fair Credit Reporting Act created "a private duty owed personally to Robins to protect *his* information," that was enough for standing, but not if it "vests any and all consumers with the power to police the 'reasonable procedures' of *Spokeo*, without more."[187]

There is also a more permissive version of Justice Thomas's approach, one that would not wed itself to particular Hohfeldian categories or the language of *Tennessee Electric*. Under this version, any legal duty may be said to create a private right so long as it is adequately personalized—owed to a specific person or group of persons rather than to the public at large.

There are parts of Justice Thomas's opinion that point to this more permissive formulation[188] and it would have the advantage of simplicity. It would not get bogged down in categories like "privilege" or "tortious invasion."[189] Indeed, this more permissive approach would look a great deal like what Judge O'Scannlain had written for the Ninth Circuit earlier in the *Spokeo* litigation: that a statutory right is an enforceable private right if it is "individualized rather than collective," and if the person suing is "among the injured."[190] In other words, Justice Thomas's concurrence not only suggests that the majority opinion in *Spokeo* was a misstep, but also suggests that a more principled and workable approach may have been lying in front of the Court all along.

---

[186] Id.

[187] *Spokeo*, 136 S Ct at 1554 (there was some statutory ambiguity on that point).

[188] Id (Thomas, J, concurring) (emphasizing the question of whether there was "a private duty owed personally to Robins").

[189] Id (quoting *Tennesse Electric*, 306 US at 137–38).

[190] *Robins v Spokeo, Inc.*, 742 F3d 409, 413–14 (9th Cir 2014).

GENEVIEVE LAKIER

REED v TOWN OF GILBERT, ARIZONA, AND THE RISE OF THE ANTICLASSIFICATORY FIRST AMENDMENT

The distinction between content-based and content-neutral regulations of speech is one of the most important in First Amendment law. For decades now, the Supreme Court has insisted that content-based laws—laws that restrict speech because of its ideas or messages or subject matter—are presumptively unconstitutional, and will be sustained only if they can satisfy strict scrutiny.[1] In contrast, content-neutral laws—laws that regulate speech for some reason other than its content—are reviewed under a lesser, and often quite deferential, standard.[2] Whether a law is found to be content-based or content-

Genevieve Lakier is Assistant Professor of Law, The University of Chicago Law School.

Author's note: This article benefited enormously from the comments of Amy J. Cohen, Aziz Huq, Richard McAdams, Geoffrey R. Stone, Louis Michael Seidman, David Strauss, Nelson Tebbe, and Laura Weinrib. I am also grateful for the feedback I received from participants in the Brooklyn Law School Faculty Workshop and the University of Chicago Law School Works in Progress Workshop. Excellent research assistance was provided by Lisa Frasco, Kathrine Gutierrez, Kevin Oliver, Jacob Walley, and Katie Ryan.

[1] See, for example, *United States v Playboy Entertainment Group, Inc.*, 529 US 803, 817 (2000); *R.A.V. v City of St. Paul, Minn.*, 505 US 377, 382 (1992).

[2] The standard articulation of this test can be found in *Ward v Rock Against Racism*, 491 US 781, 791 (1989) (requiring content-neutral speech regulations to be "narrowly tailored to serve a significant governmental interest, and [to] leave open ample alternative channels for communication of the information").

978-0-226-49084-7/2017/2016-0007$10.00

neutral therefore determines, in many cases, whether a First Amendment challenge to it succeeds.

Despite the importance of the distinction, the Court has had trouble settling on a single test of content-based lawmaking. Instead, it has vacillated between two different tests. In one line of cases, the Court has insisted that laws are content-based whenever they treat speakers differently because of the content of their speech—that is to say, whenever they employ explicit content distinctions. In another line of cases, the Court has instead insisted that laws are content-based only when they cannot be justified by a content-neutral purpose—that is to say, when the government cannot adequately demonstrate that the distinction the laws draw furthers some purpose other than to restrict speech because the government dislikes its content, or fears its communicative effects.

These two tests of content-based lawmaking are not merely different; in many cases, they lead to different results. Hence lower courts tasked with determining whether a given law is content-neutral or content-based have had to choose between two competing but incompatible lines of precedent. The result has been the creation of what commentators have described as a confused,[3] inconsistent,[4] and highly malleable body of law.[5]

Two terms ago, in *Reed v Town of Gilbert*,[6] the Court attempted to bring some clarity to this messy area of First Amendment jurisprudence when it held that laws that employ content distinctions are *always* content-based, regardless of the purposes they serve.[7] The Court acknowledged that in earlier cases it had looked at the government's purposes when deciding whether a given law was or was not content-based. It insisted, however, that those cases dealt only with regulations that did not treat speakers differently because of what they said—that did not make what it described as "obvious" or

---

[3] Leslie Gielow Jacobs, *Clarifying the Content-Based/Content Neutral and Content/Viewpoint Determinations*, 34 McGeorge L Rev 595, 602 (2003) ("[T]he Court has experienced increasing difficulty in making [content determinations], and in making them consistently.").

[4] Barry McDonald, *Speech and Distrust: Rethinking the Content Approach to Protecting Freedom of Expression*, 81 Notre Dame L Rev 1347, 1353 (2006).

[5] Dan V. Kozlowski, *Content and Viewpoint Discrimination: Malleable Terms Beget Malleable Doctrine*, 13 Communication L & Pol 131, 132–34 (2008).

[6] 135 S Ct 2218 (2015).

[7] Id at 2227.

"subtle" content distinctions.[8] The Court thus construed the test of content neutrality as a two-step inquiry in which courts first determine whether a law makes facial content distinctions, and second, if—but only if—it doesn't, do they look at the purposes that justify the law.[9]

By insisting that both the face of the law and the government's purposes have a role to play in the content-neutrality inquiry, the *Reed* Court managed to reconcile what up until then had appeared to be irreconcilable precedents. What this required, however, was the implicit overruling of the multiple decisions in which the Court did what the *Reed* majority said it had never done: namely, it held that a law that made facial content distinctions was content-neutral because it could be justified by reference to a content-neutral purpose.[10] And what it means, going forward, is that the government will have a much harder time defending facially content-based laws against constitutional challenges than it did in the past, when, notwithstanding the conflicting instructions they received from the Supreme Court, lower courts frequently held that laws that made facial content distinctions were content-neutral.

Reed thus represents an important change in First Amendment doctrine, and one that will in all likelihood have a significant impact in many areas of law. Indeed, we are already seeing evidence of *Reed*'s effects across the country, as courts apply strict scrutiny to—and strike down—laws that previously were, or likely would have been, upheld as content-neutral prior to *Reed*.[11] This may only be the tip of the iceberg. By insisting that strict scrutiny applies to all laws that treat speakers differently because of the content of their speech, *Reed* potentially imperils the hundreds, even perhaps thousands, of local, state, and federal laws that make subject matter or viewpoint distinctions.[12] The decision thus demonstrates once again the pro-

[8] Id.

[9] Id.

[10] See note 88, and accompanying text.

[11] See *Free Speech Coalition, Inc. v Attorney Gen. United States*, 825 F3d 149 (3rd Cir 2016); *Sarver v Chartier*, 813 F3d 891, 905–06 (9th Cir 2016); *Central Radio Co. v City of Norfolk*, 811 F3d 625, 631 (4th Cir 2016); *Norton v City of Springfield, Ill.*, 806 F3d 411 (7th Cir 2015).

[12] Laws that make facial content distinctions include local, state, and federal sign laws; laws that zone adult movie theaters and bookstores differently than other kinds of theaters and bookstores; laws that impose special tax burdens on lobbying and other expressive activities; campaign finance laws that distinguish between electioneering and nonelectioneering com-

nounced deregulatory tilt of the Roberts Court's First Amendment jurisprudence.[13]

This article examines the change that *Reed* makes to First Amendment doctrine, and its normative justifications. It does so by means of an analogy to the Court's equal protection jurisprudence, and specifically its case law dealing with race discrimination.

As the article demonstrates, the shift that *Reed* enacts in First Amendment law resembles in many respects the shift that occurred several decades ago in equal protection law, when the Court squarely embraced what scholars have described as an anticlassificatory test of race discrimination and insisted that all laws that employ racial distinctions are presumptively invalid, no matter the purposes the government invokes to justify them.[14] *Reed* insists, similarly, that all laws that employ content distinctions are presumptively invalid, no matter the purposes the government invokes to justify them. It announces what we might thus describe as an anticlassificatory test of content discrimination. In so doing, it makes it—in theory at least—as difficult for the government to defend facially content-based laws against constitutional challenge as it is to defend racially classificatory laws.

The question that *Reed* raises is whether it *should* be as difficult to defend facially content-based laws against constitutional challenge as it is to defend racially classificatory ones. Some scholars have argued that the answer to this question is an obvious and unqualified yes.[15] This article suggests that the answer is a good deal more complicated

---

munications; mail regulations that allow certain kinds of publications lower rates on their mail; and even portions of the Digital Copyright Millennium Act that prohibit the posting of certain kinds of information. See *Universal City Studios, Inc. v Corley*, 273 F3d 429, 447–55 (2d Cir 2001). This is by no means a complete list. For more discussion of some of the laws that *Reed* may affect, see Part II.B.

[13] For other perspectives on the Roberts Court's approach to the First Amendment, see Genevieve Lakier, *The Invention of Low-Value Speech*, 128 Harv L Rev 2166 (2016); Gregory P. Magarian, *Marrow of Tradition: The Roberts Court and Categorical First Amendment Speech Exclusions*, 56 Wm & Mary L Rev 1339 (2015); Erwin Chemerinsky, *The Roberts Court and Freedom of Speech*, 63 Fed Commun L J 579 (2011).

[14] Jack M. Balkin and Reva B. Siegel, *The American Civil Rights Tradition: Anticlassification or Antisubordination?*, 58 U Miami L Rev 9, 10 (2003) ("Roughly speaking, [the anticlassification] principle holds that the government may not classify people either overtly or surreptitiously on the basis of a forbidden category: for example, their race"). For more discussion, see notes 115–22 and accompanying text.

[15] See, for example, Seth F. Kreimer, *Good Enough for Government Work: Two Cheers for Content Neutrality*, 16 U Pa J Const L 1261, 1305 (2014); Chemerinsky, 63 Fed Commun L J at 59–61 (cited in note 13).

than that. This is because of the value that content distinctions possess, as regulatory tools.

In its equal protection cases, the Court has insisted that all laws that employ racial distinctions should be treated as presumptively invalid because these distinctions are not, in the vast majority of circumstances, relevant to the government's legitimate regulatory concerns. It is this fact, the Court has insisted, that allows courts to presume that when the government employs racial distinctions as regulatory tools, either prejudice or animus motivates its actions.

Content distinctions are not, however, usually irrelevant to the government's legitimate regulatory concerns. Instead, they play an important role in the regulation of both the public and private spheres. What this means is that the mere fact that a law employs content distinctions is not enough to create a presumption of bad intent. The consequence is that the *Reed* Court's embrace of an anticlassificatory test of content-based lawmaking is likely to result in the invalidation of a good many laws that are not in fact the product of a discriminatory purpose and that do not otherwise pose a significant threat to First Amendment interests. The costs of the *Reed* rule are likely, in other words, to be significant.

The fact that the test of content-based lawmaking announced in *Reed* is likely to result in the invalidation of a good number of laws that pose no apparent threat to any significant First Amendment interest suggest that it can be justified only if there is no other, less costly, means of protecting speakers against discrimination. It is by no means obvious, however, that there isn't. Indeed, in her concurring opinion in *Reed*, Justice Kagan suggested an alternative test of content-based lawmaking that may be superior to *Reed* in a variety of ways.

By exploring the connections between equal protection and free speech law, this article attempts to shed new light on familiar First Amendment questions. It proceeds in four parts. Part I examines the decades-long struggle on the Court between two competing approaches to the identification of content-based laws, and the significant shift *Reed* enacts in the doctrine. Part II explores *Reed*'s virtues as a test of content-based lawmaking. Part III explores its significant drawbacks by means of an analogy to the Equal Protection Clause. Part IV explores the alternative tests the Court could employ to identify content-based regulations of speech and suggests why these would be superior to the very broad anticlassificatory test that *Reed* announces.

I. Identifying Content Discrimination

The First Amendment guarantees expressive freedom—specifically, "the freedom of speech, and press."[16] For over seventy years, however, the Court has held that the First Amendment prohibits not only state actions that make it very difficult for individuals to express themselves but also regulations—even not very repressive ones—that "unfairly discriminate" among speakers based on the content of their speech.[17] It has interpreted the First Amendment, in other words, to guarantee not only expressive liberty but also expressive equality, of a sort.

The Court has read an antidiscrimination principle into the First Amendment because it has recognized that what freedom of speech requires is not only that individuals can speak but that they can do so in a public arena that is free from governmental manipulation and control.[18] It has accordingly interpreted the First Amendment to guarantee not only an individual right to speak but also the existence of a particular kind of social institution—what is commonly referred to today as the "marketplace of ideas."[19]

Laws that discriminate among speakers based on the content of their speech, the Court has argued, threaten the vitality and independence of this marketplace of ideas. They do so by giving a competitive advantage to ideas and messages the government likes.[20] They also, the Court has argued, undermine the "equality of status" of those who participate in public debate.[21] For these reasons, the Court has

---

[16] US Const, Amend I.

[17] The quote comes from *Cox v New Hampshire*, which is the first case I know of that explicitly recognizes the First Amendment antidiscrimination principle. 312 US 569, 576 (1941) (recognizing that municipalities have the "authority to control the use of [their] public streets for parades or processions" and to impose "time, place and manner" restrictions on those who wish to participate in parades, so long as they do so "without unfair discrimination").

[18] See, for example, *Cohen v California*, 403 US 15, 24–25 (1971) (arguing that the "constitutional right of free expression . . . is designed and intended to remove governmental restraints from the arena of public discussion"); *Roth v United States*, 354 US 476, 484 (1957) ("The protection given speech and press was fashioned to assure unfettered interchange of ideas for the bringing about of political and social changes desired by the people.").

[19] See generally Stanley Ingber, *The Marketplace of Ideas: A Legitimizing Myth*, 1984 Duke L J 1 (1984).

[20] *R.A.V.*, 505 US at 387 (content discrimination "raises the specter that the Government may effectively drive certain ideas or viewpoints from the marketplace"); *City of Ladue v Gilleo*, 512 US 43, 60 (1994) (O'Connor, J, concurring) (noting that "the free speech principle" makes it "improper [for the government to] attempt[] to value some forms of speech over others, or . . . to distort public debate").

[21] *Police Department of the City of Chicago v Mosley*, 408 US 92, 96 (1972).

insisted that "regulations that permit the Government to discriminate on the basis of the content of its message cannot be tolerated under the First Amendment."[22]

Ensuring that regulations that permit the government to engage in content discrimination *aren't* tolerated has proven to be no easy matter, however. This is in part a consequence of what the Court has interpreted the prohibition against discrimination to mean.

Even though the primary argument that the Court has relied upon to explain why discriminatory laws violate the First Amendment is a consequentialist one—namely, that laws of this sort pose a threat to the "robust [and] wide-open" debate the First Amendment is intended to guarantee[23]—the Court has unequivocally rejected the idea that laws might be considered discriminatory merely on the basis of their effects on the speech marketplace.[24] Instead, the Court has tended to equate discrimination with discriminatory purpose. The Court has not done so explicitly.[25] Nevertheless, it has, almost without exception, insisted that the evil the prohibition against content discrimination guards against are efforts by the government to "proscrib[e] speech, or . . . expressive conduct, because of disapproval of the ideas expressed," or to otherwise advance what Justice Scalia once described as "thought-control purposes."[26]

The Court has nevertheless expressed considerable skepticism about the ability of courts to accurately identify, in individual cases, when the government acts with bad purposes of this sort. It has in-

---

[22] *Regan v Time, Inc.*, 468 US 641, 648–49 (1984).

[23] *NY Times Co. v Sullivan*, 376 US 254, 270 (1964).

[24] *Ward*, 491 US at 791 ("A regulation that serves purposes unrelated to the content of expression is deemed neutral, even if it has an incidental effect on some speakers or messages but not others.").

[25] Elena Kagan, *Private Speech, Public Purpose: The Role of Governmental Motive in First Amendment Doctrine*, 63 U Chi L Rev 413, 428 (1996) (noting that the Court "has hesitated to discuss the [role that] illicit motive [plays in First Amendment law] in any detail or with any directness").

[26] *R.A.V.*, 505 US at 382; *Madsen v Women's Health Center, Inc.*, 512 US 753, 794–95 (1994). See also *Gilleo*, 512 US at 51 (arguing that regulations that treat some speakers differently from others threaten First Amendment interests because of the risk that they "may represent a governmental attempt to give one side of a debatable public question an advantage in expressing its views to the people . . . [or] to control . . . the search for political truth") (quotation marks omitted); id at 60 (O'Connor, J, concurring) (noting that "the free speech principle" makes it "improper [for the government to] attempt[] to value some forms of speech over others, or . . . to distort public debate"); *Arkansas Writers' Project, Inc. v Ragland*, 481 US 221, 228–29 (1987) (arguing that discriminatory taxes are prohibited by the

sisted that "[i]nquiries into congressional motives or purposes are a hazardous matter" and one that judges are ill-suited to perform.[27]

As a result, the Court has generally refused to engage in a direct analysis of discriminatory intent. Instead, it has attempted to identify discrimination indirectly, by analyzing the "fit" between the ends the government claims a particular law advances and the means chosen to advance those ends. It has insisted that laws that reveal a very poor fit between statutory means and ends should be struck down—even in cases where the poor fit results from the narrowness of the statutory prohibition, not its breadth.[28] Underinclusive speech regulations are considered as suspect as overinclusive speech regulations, the Court has explained, because, in both cases, what the poorness of the fit between the statute's means and ends produces is doubt about the credibility of the government's purported motivations.[29]

This indirect approach to the analysis of discrimination provides an elegant solution to the problems created by the fact-finding limitations of judges. It also has the benefit of making it difficult for the government to restrict speech even when its actions are not in fact motivated by dislike of the targeted speech but are instead merely the product of carelessness or laziness, or political expediency on the legislature's part.[30] This is because in all cases, what the government must demonstrate in order to justify the restriction of constitutionally protected speech is the existence of a substantial or, at least, a le-

First Amendment because they give the government "a powerful weapon against the taxpayer selected"). See also Kagan, 63 U Chi L Rev at 414 (cited in note 25) (arguing that "First Amendment law, as developed by the Supreme Court over the past several decades, has as its primary, though unstated, object the discovery of improper governmental motives"); Susan H. Williams, *Content Discrimination and the First Amendment*, 139 U Pa L Rev 615, 617 (1991) ("The Court . . . has interpreted content discrimination quite narrowly as involving a particular type of government purpose served by the regulation of speech.").

[27] *United States v O'Brien*, 391 US 367, 383–84 (1968).

[28] Cases in which the Court struck down laws that failed to apply broadly enough include *Florida Star v B.J.F.*, 491 US 524 (1989); *Carey v Brown*, 447 US 455, 465 (1980); *Mosley*, 408 US at 96.

[29] *Gilleo*, 512 US at 51–52 ("Exemptions from an otherwise legitimate regulation of a medium of speech . . . may diminish the credibility of the government's rationale for restricting speech in the first place. . . . [A]n exemption from an otherwise permissible regulation of speech may represent a governmental attempt to give one side of a debatable public question an advantage in expressing its views to the people.").

[30] Id at 51.

gitimate state interest—and the Court has made clear that administrative convenience does not qualify as an interest of this sort.[31]

The approach has a significant drawback, however. Because it operates prophylactically, it may be used to invalidate laws that are not in fact a product of discriminatory purpose, nor the consequence of legislative laziness or political self-interest. Depending on how tight a fit between means and ends is required, it may in fact make it extremely difficult for the government to ever justify regulating speech. This is a problem because, as the Court has long recognized, speech regulations can further important constitutional, as well as extraconstitutional, goals, by creating the conditions under which individuals can effectively utilize their free speech rights, and by protecting the "safety and convenience" of the people.[32] Even if the ability of the government to regulate is not entirely foreclosed, a very high fit requirement grants judges a great deal of power to second-guess legislative choices, and thus threatens what the Court has recognized in the post-*Lochner* era to be an important value: namely, the regulatory autonomy of the democratically elected legislature.[33]

The Court has been unwilling as a result to construe the First Amendment to require a very close fit between means and ends in *all* cases in which the government restricts protected expression. Instead, in most cases involving the regulation of speech, it requires only that the fit between statutory means and statutory ends be a reasonable

[31] *Mosley*, 408 US at 102 n 9; *Schneider v New Jersey, Town of Irvington*, 308 US 147, 151 (1939) ("Mere legislative preferences or beliefs respecting matters of public convenience may well support regulation directed at other personal activities, but be insufficient to justify such as diminishes the exercise of rights so vital to the maintenance of democratic institutions.").

[32] As the Court put it in *Cox*: "Civil liberties, as guaranteed by the Constitution, imply the existence of an organized society maintaining public order without which liberty itself would be lost in the excesses of unrestrained abuses. The authority of a municipality to impose regulations in order to assure the safety and convenience of the people in the use of public highways has never been regarded as inconsistent with civil liberties but rather as one of the means of safeguarding the good order upon which they ultimately depend." 312 US at 574. The suggestion here is that governmental regulation of the public sphere may not only be constitutional; it may be constitutionally required.

[33] See, for example, *United States v Albertini*, 472 US 675, 689 (1985) (arguing that the constitutionality of speech regulations "does not turn on a judge's agreement with the responsible decisionmaker concerning the most appropriate method for promoting significant government interests"); *Clark v Community for Creative Non-Violence*, 468 US 288, 299 (1984) (rejecting lower court decision striking down park service regulation preventing protestors from sleeping in two national parks because "[w]e do not believe . . . that [the First Amendment] assign[s] to the judiciary the authority to replace the Park Service as the manager of the Nation's parks or endow the judiciary with the competence to judge how much protection of park lands is wise and how that level of conservation is to be attained").

one. Hence, when the government regulates speech in limited or nonpublic forums—that is, in spaces and institutions that have not traditionally served as important sites for the public expression of ideas—the Court requires only that the restrictions the government imposes on expression are "reasonable in light of the purpose served by the forum."[34] What this means is that the government may not restrict speech because it dislikes its viewpoint or its ideas, but it may reserve the forum "for use by certain speakers, or for the discussion of certain subjects."[35] Similarly, when the government restricts speech by government employees, the Court has made clear that it need only show that the restriction serves a legitimate workplace goal and that the government's interest in regulating the speech outweighs the employee's interest in speaking.[36] The Court applies even more lenient review to the regulation of the private workplace.[37]

The Court applies more stringent scrutiny when the government regulates speech that takes place in the public forum—that is, on government property that has traditionally or by design been used for the public expression of ideas.[38] It also applies more stringent scrutiny when the government regulates speech on private property that addresses itself to the public sphere.[39] This is because it recognizes that the government has fewer legitimate reasons to regulate the public sphere than to regulate the private.[40] Hence, the risk that when it does regulate, it does so to achieve impermissible ends, is greater.

---

[34] *Cornelius v NAACP Legal Defense & Educational Fund, Inc.*, 473 US 788, 806 (1985).

[35] Id at 802 (citing *Perry Education Association v Perry Local Educators' Association*, 460 US 37, 45, 46 n 7 (1983)).

[36] *Garcetti v Ceballos*, 547 US 410, 418 (2006) (citing *Pickering v Board of Education of Township High School District 205, Will County, Ill.*, 391 US 563, 568 (1968)) (noting that, when a public employee speaks on matters of public concern, "[t]he question becomes whether the relevant government entity had an adequate justification for treating the employee differently from any other member of the general public").

[37] See, for example, Julius Getman, *Labor Law and Free Speech: The Curious Policy of Limited Expression*, 43 Md L Rev 4 (1984); James Q. Pope, *The Three-Systems Ladder of First Amendment Values: Two Rungs and a Black Hole*, 11 Hastings Const L Q 189 (1984); Robert Post, *Informed Consent to Abortion: A First Amendment Analysis of Compelled Physician Speech*, 2007 U Ill L Rev 939, 949 (2007); Terry Ann Halbert, *The First Amendment in the Workplace: An Analysis and Call for Reform*, 17 Seton Hall L Rev 42 (1987).

[38] *Perry Education Association*, 460 US at 45.

[39] See, for example, *Metromedia, Inc. v City of San Diego*, 453 US 490 (1981); *Erznoznik v City of Jacksonville*, 422 US 205, 211–12 (1975).

[40] Compare *Garcetti*, 547 US at 418 ("Government employers, like private employers, need a significant degree of control over their employees' words and actions; without it, there would be little chance for the efficient provision of public services.") and *Adderley v Fla*, 385

Even in such cases, however, the Court imposes only a relatively modest burden of justification when the government regulates speech in a content-neutral manner. In such cases, the Court requires only that the regulation "promotes a substantial government interest that would be achieved less effectively absent the regulation," that it does so by means that are neither significantly overbroad nor significantly underbroad, and that it leave open adequate alternative channels for those impacted by it to communicate.[41]

The Court imposes a much heavier burden of justification when the government engages in the content-based regulation of speech—at least high-value speech. For decades now, the Court has insisted that regulations that restrict high-value speech because of its content are "presumptively invalid" under the First Amendment.[42] As a result, they can be upheld only if the government can satisfy strict scrutiny by demonstrating that the regulation advances a compelling interest by the least restrictive means available.[43] This is a demanding standard; and one the government usually has trouble satisfying.[44]

The Court has explained that strict scrutiny is necessary because of the significant risk that content-based speech regulations either are the product of, or can be used to further, discriminatory purposes. As Justice Powell noted in *Consolidated Edison Co. of New York v Public Service Commission of New York*[45] in 1980: "[W]hen regulation is based on the content of speech, governmental action must be scrutinized more carefully [than in other cases] to ensure that communication has not been prohibited 'merely because public officials disapprove

US 39, 47 (1966) ("The State, no less than a private owner of property, has power to preserve the property under its control for the use to which it is lawfully dedicated.") with *Mosley*, 408 US at 96 ("[G]overnment may not grant the use of a forum to people whose views it finds acceptable, but deny use to those wishing to express less favored or more controversial views. And it may not select which issues are worth discussing or debating in public facilities. . . . Once a forum is opened up to assembly or speaking by some groups, government may not prohibit others from assembling or speaking on the basis of what they intend to say.").

[41] *Ward*, 491 US at 797–800.

[42] *Playboy*, 529 US at 817 (citing *R.A.V.*, 505 US at 382).

[43] *Playboy*, 529 US at 813.

[44] Kreimer, 16 U Pa J Const L at 1293 (cited in note 15). In a recent survey of content neutrality cases in the lower federal courts, Kreimer found that, at least in cases involving the regulation of public forums, content-based restrictions were struck down in 97 percent of the district court cases and 87 percent of court of appeals cases. Id. In contrast, he found that laws deemed content-neutral were struck down only 28 percent of the time in the district court cases and 56 percent of the time in the court of appeals. Id.

[45] 447 US 530 (1980).

the speaker's views.' "[46] The implication, of course, is that regulations that are not "based on the content of the speech" are subject to less careful scrutiny because they pose less of a risk that they were enacted "merely because public officials disapprove of the speakers' views."

By requiring a higher burden of justification in cases in which it is more likely that invidious purposes are at work and a lesser burden of justification in cases in which this is less likely the case, the Court has attempted to effectively enforce the prohibition against discriminatory speech regulations without unduly limiting the government's regulatory power. This is an obviously worthy goal. Nevertheless, it is one that has proven, in practice, extremely hard to implement, given serious and pervasive disagreement on the Court about how broadly the prophylactic instrument of strict scrutiny should apply.

A. THE FIGHT OVER THE MEANING OF CONTENT-BASED LAWMAKING

For decades now, scholars have complained about the "[p]rofound problems [that] plague the . . . use of the judicially created categories of content-neutral and content-based speech regulations and orders."[47] They have argued that the distinction between content-based and content-neutral laws that the cases draw is "inconsistent" and prone to manipulation.[48] They have blamed this on the results-oriented nature of the Court's jurisprudence and its theoretical incoherency.[49] In fact, much of the doctrinal inconsistency that scholars have identified can be blamed on the significant, and persistent, disagreement among members of the Court about how broadly the presumption against content-based lawmaking should apply.

Some on the Court have argued that the presumption should apply broadly: that strict scrutiny is the appropriate standard of review for all speech regulations that make regulatory distinctions that turn on

---

[46] Id at 536.

[47] Clay Calvert, *Free Speech and Content-Neutrality: Inconsistent Applications of an Increasingly Malleable Doctrine*, 29 McGeorge L Rev 69, 71 (1997).

[48] McDonald, 81 Notre Dame L Rev at 1353 (cited in note 4). See also Robert Post, *Recuperating First Amendment Doctrine*, 47 Stan L Rev 1249, 1265 (1995) ("Whatever the ultimate merits of a First Amendment focus on content neutrality, the Court's doctrinal elaboration of [it] has been haphazard, internally incoherent, and for these reasons inconsistent with any possible principled concern for content neutrality."); Williams, 139 U Pa L Rev at 616 (cited in note 26) ("The doctrinal web surrounding the free speech clause of the [F]irst [A]mendment is one of the most complicated and confusing in constitutional law.").

[49] McDonald, 81 Notre Dame L Rev at 1353 (cited in note 4).

the content of speech. This is because, they have argued, laws of this kind are more likely than other kinds of laws to be used for "thought-control purposes" given the power they give the government to target ideas or messages or topics it dislikes. Justice Scalia made this argument, for example, in his concurring and dissenting opinion in *Madsen v Women's Health Center*: "The danger of content-based statutory restrictions upon speech," Scalia wrote, "is that they may be designed and used *precisely* to suppress the ideas in question rather than to achieve any other proper governmental aim."[50] The fact that laws of this sort "lend [themselves] . . . readily to the targeted suppression of particular ideas . . . render[] [them] deserving of the high standard of strict scrutiny."[51]

Other members of the Court have argued for a narrower application of strict scrutiny. Justice Stevens, for example, argued that because there are many legitimate reasons why the government might want to distinguish between speakers based on the content of their speech, a rule that subjected all facially content-based laws to strict scrutiny would intrude too much on the government's legitimate regulatory powers.[52] He argued that strict scrutiny should therefore apply only when there was some reason to suspect that the government's motivations for acting were improper. This was always the case, Justice Stevens argued, when the purposes the government invoked to justify the law were constitutionally prohibited—such as, for example, when the government enacted a law in order "to curtail expression of a particular point of view on controversial issues of general interest."[53] In other cases, however, Stevens argued that strict scrutiny was only appropriate when there was some evidence that the "regulation [was] biased in favor of one point of view or another, or [provided the government] . . . a subtle method of regulating the controversial

---

[50] *Madsen*, 512 US at 792 (Scalia, J, concurring in part and dissenting in part).

[51] Id at 793–94 (emphasis omitted).

[52] See, for example, *R.A.V.*, 505 US at 420 (Stevens, J, concurring) (arguing that "[a]lthough the Court has, on occasion, declared that content-based regulations of speech are 'never permitted' . . . our decisions demonstrate that content-based distinctions . . . are an inevitable and indispensable aspect of a coherent understanding of the First Amendment"); *Consolidated Edison Co.*, 447 US at 545–46 (Stevens, J, concurring) ("There are . . . many situations in which the subject matter, or, indeed, even the point of view of the speaker, may provide a justification for a time, place, and manner regulation [of speech]. . . . As is true of many other aspects of liberty, some forms of orderly regulation actually promote freedom more than would a state of total anarchy.").

[53] *Consolidated Edison Co.*, 447 US at 546.

subjects that may be placed on the agenda for public debate[.]"[54] But the mere fact that a law made content-based distinctions did not, he insisted, mean that it should be treated as a presumptively invalid "content-based" regulation of speech.[55]

In different cases, these different points of view managed to persuade a shifting majority of the Court. The result was the creation of two distinct and inconsistent tests of content-based lawmaking.

In one line of cases, the Court employed the strict test of content-based lawmaking that Justice Scalia advocated. That is to say, it treated laws that made facial content distinctions as *necessarily* content-based. In *Burson v Freeman*,[56] for example, the Court concluded that a Tennessee law that prohibited election-related speech near polling places was content-based because "[w]hether individuals may exercise their free speech rights near polling places depends entirely on whether their speech is related to a political campaign."[57] In *Arkansas Writers' Project, Inc. v Ragland*, the Court similarly held that a state tax law that taxed magazines but exempted "religious, professional, trade and sports journals" from the tax was content-based because the law required state officials to "examine the content of the message . . . conveyed" by the magazine to determine whether it was subject to the tax.[58] And in *Simon & Schuster, Inc. v Members of New York State Crime Victims Board*,[59] the Court concluded that a New York law that prohibited convicted felons from making a profit off stories of their crimes was content-based because it was "directed only at works with a specified content."[60]

In another line of cases, the Court employed instead the more purpose-oriented test of content-based lawmaking that Justice Stevens championed. In this line of cases, the Court insisted that speech regulations were content-based when, but only when, they could

---

[54] *Metromedia, Inc.*, 453 US at 552 (Stevens, J, dissenting in part).

[55] *Consolidated Edison Co.*, 447 US at 545–46.

[56] 504 US 191 (1992).

[57] Id at 197.

[58] 481 US at 229–30.

[59] 502 US 105 (1991).

[60] Id at 116. Other cases in which the Court concluded that a law was content-based on the basis of an analysis of its text alone include *McCullen v Coakley*, 134 S Ct 2518, 2525 (2014); *Republican Party of Minnesota v White*, 536 US 765, 770 (2002); *Holder v Humanitarian Law Project*, 561 US 1, 27 (2010); *McIntyre v Ohio Elections Commission*, 514 US 334 (1995); *Leathers v Medlock*, 499 US 439, 449 (1991); *Regan*, 468 US at 648.

not be "justified without reference to the content of the speech they regulated."[61] Although, as we shall see later, what precisely this meant varied over time; in its most rigorous form, the Court interpreted this test to require it to first look at the purposes the government claimed the regulation furthered. If these purposes evinced a concern with the communicative effects of the speech—that is to say, if they evinced a concern with the effect of the expression of its ideas or messages on an audience—the Court concluded that the risk that the government was acting because it disliked the speech, or for some other impermissible reason, was sufficiently great to warrant strict scrutiny and accordingly deemed the law content-based.[62] If not, the Court examined whether there was evidence that the purposes the government invoked to justify the law were actually furthered by the distinctions it drew.[63] If there was, the Court treated the law as content-neutral; if not, it treated the law as content-based.[64]

Although these two lines of cases could easily be reconciled when it came to facially content-neutral laws—in such cases, the Court rather unproblematically applied the "justified without reference to the content of speech" test[65]—they could not be easily reconciled

[61] Cases stating this as the test of content discrimination include *Sorrell v IMS Health Inc.*, 564 US 552, 566 (2011); *Bartnicki v Vopper*, 532 US 514 (2001); *Hill*, 530 US 703; *Playboy*, 529 US 803; *City of Erie v Pap's A.M.*, 529 US 277, 294 (2000); *Madsen*, 512 US 753; *City of Cincinnati v Discovery Network, Inc.*, 507 US 410 (1993); *Ward*, 491 US 781; *Boos v Barry*, 485 US 312 (1988).

[62] In *Boos v Barry*, for example, the Court concluded that a DC law that prohibited the display of signs within 500 feet of foreign embassies that "tend[ed] to bring that foreign government into 'public odium'" was content-based not because it applied differently to speakers based on the messages they communicated but because the purpose the government invoked to justify "focuse[d] *only* on the content of the speech and the direct impact that speech has on its listeners" rather than on other, secondary effects, such as "congestion . . . [or] the need to protect the security of embassies." 485 US at 316, 321. See also *Playboy*, 529 US at 811 (holding that a law requiring cable providers to scramble channels dedicated to sexually oriented programming was content-based because "[t]he overriding justification for the regulation is concern for the effect of the subject matter on young viewers.").

[63] *Discovery Network*, 507 US at 42 (requiring the city to establish some empirical "basis" for the distinctions it drew).

[64] Id at 428 (concluding that "the absence of some basis for distinguishing between 'newspapers' and 'commercial handbills' that is relevant to an interest asserted by the city" meant that a law that distinguished between the two kinds of speech was not "justified without reference to the content . . ."). See also *Erznoznik*, 422 US at 214–15 (concluding that a regulation that prohibited the showing of nudity in places viewable from the public road could not be adequately justified by the city's interest in traffic safety given no evidence that speech involving nudity was more distracting to drivers than "a wide variety of other scenes in the customary screen diet, ranging from soap opera to violence") (quotation marks omitted).

[65] See, for example, *Bartnicki*, 532 US at 526; *Ward*, 491 US at 791; *Clark*, 468 US at 293.

when it came to facially content-based laws. Consider, for example, *City of Renton v Playtime Theatres, Inc.*,[66] a case in which the Court held that a zoning ordinance that prohibited adult movie theaters from locating within 1,000 feet of any residences, churches, parks, or schools was content-neutral even though the law identified adult movie theaters by reference to the content of the movies they exhibited.[67] The Court acknowledged that the law made distinctions based on the content of speech but nevertheless concluded that strict scrutiny was not the appropriate standard of review because the law "aimed not at the *content* of the films shown [by adult movie theaters] but rather at the *secondary effects* of such theaters on the surrounding community."[68] Because the purpose of the ordinance, the Court found, was to "prevent the crime, protect the city's retail trade, maintain property values, and generally protect and preserve the quality of the city's neighborhoods, . . . not to suppress the expression of unpopular views," and because the Court found that the city council had a reasonable basis for its beliefs that the speech it restricted differed in a relevant way from the speech it left unrestricted, the majority concluded that the ordinance was "completely consistent with our definition of content-neutral speech regulations as those that are *justified* without reference to the content of the regulated speech."[69]

Justice Brennan wrote an impassioned dissent in which he argued that, because the ordinance "selectively imposes limitations on the location of a movie theater based exclusively on the content of the films shown there," it could not be treated as a content-neutral regulation of speech.[70] And indeed, the holding in *Renton* is impossible to reconcile with the various precedents in which the Court had insisted that laws were content-based whenever their application depended upon "the nature of the message . . . conveyed" by the speech they regulated.[71]

---

[66] 475 US 41.

[67] Id at 47.

[68] Id (emphasis in original).

[69] Id at 48 (quotation marks omitted) (emphasis in original). See also id at 50–52 (noting detailed evidence of the harm of adult movie theaters that the City Council relied upon when it enacted the law).

[70] Id at 55 (Brennan, J, dissenting).

[71] *Regan*, 468 US at 648; see also *Carey*, 447 US at 462 (concluding that a law was content-based because "it is the content of the speech that determines whether it is within or without the statute's blunt prohibition").

Nevertheless, in subsequent cases, the Court continued to construe as content-neutral laws that made content distinctions on their face but that it found to be adequately justified by a content-neutral purpose.[72] In other cases, however, it continued to insist that laws were content-based if their application "depend[ed] on what [individuals] say."[73]

The persistence of these two distinct and inconsistent tests of content-based lawmaking in the Court's First Amendment cases created a very confusing and contentious body of law. As Seth Kreimer noted in 2014, members of the Supreme Court "regularly [fell] into acrimonious disputes" about whether laws were content-based or content-neutral—frequently because of disagreement about which test to apply—and a "similar perplexity . . . afflicted the lower courts."[74] Indeed, on multiple occasions, different courts—and sometimes different members of the same court—applied different tests of content-based lawmaking to reach opposite conclusions about the content neutrality, or lack thereof, of the same or very similar laws.[75] Even the Supreme Court acknowledged that "[d]eciding whether a particular

---

[72] See, for example, *Alameda Books*, 535 US at 431–32 (concluding that a law that prohibited the establishment of more than one adult bookstore or video arcade in the same building could be considered content-neutral); *Hill*, 530 US at 703–04 (concluding that law that prohibited "oral protest, education, or counseling" near the entrance to abortion clinics was content-neutral because it was not "adopted because of disagreement with the message [the speech it regulated conveys]"); *Taxpayers for Vincent*, 466 US at 793 n 1 (construing as content-neutral a law that prohibited the posting of any handbill or signs on public property, but exempted from the ban "metal plaque[s] or plate[s] . . . commemorating an historical, cultural, or artistic event, location or personality for which the Board of Public Works, with the approval of the Council, has granted a written permit").

[73] *Humanitarian Law Project*, 561 US at 27.

[74] Kreimer, 16 U Pa J Const L at 1269–70 (cited in note 15).

[75] Compare *Norton v City of Springfield, Ill.*, 768 F3d 713, 714 (7th Cir 2014) (holding that a city ordinance that prohibited panhandling—which it defined as "an oral request for an immediate donation of money"—was content-neutral because it did not target specific ideas or reflect governmental disapproval of a message), with *ACLU of Nev. v City of Las Vegas*, 466 F3d 784, 788, 796 (9th Cir 2006) (quotation marks omitted) (holding city policy that made it illegal "to ask, beg, solicit or plead . . . for the purpose of obtaining money" was content-based because "[u]nder the city's . . . policy, whether any particular [communication] falls within the ban is determined by the content of the [communication]"); compare *Reed v Town of Gilbert, Ariz.*, 707 F3d 1057, 1068 (9th Cir 2013) (concluding that the Gilbert sign code was a reasonable content-neutral regulation of speech that was "adequately justified without reference to the content of the regulated speech") with id at 1079 (Watford dissenting) (holding that the Gilbert sign code "violates the First and Fourteenth Amendments by drawing content-based distinctions among different categories of non-commercial speech").

regulation is content based or content neutral [was] not always a simple task."[76]

B. REED AND THE TURN AWAY FROM PURPOSES

The decision two terms ago in *Reed* can be understood as an attempt, by at least some members of the Court, to finally resolve the endemic confusion that has plagued the content-discrimination cases by asserting explicitly what no prior opinion had: namely, that all laws that employ content classifications trigger strict scrutiny, no matter what purposes the government invokes to justify them and no matter how innocuous they may seem.

The case involved a municipal sign ordinance promulgated by the small town of Gilbert, Arizona.[77] The ordinance imposed a general permit requirement on those who wished to erect signs within the city limits but it exempted twenty-three types of signs from the requirement, including "Temporary Directional Signs Relating to a Qualifying Event," "Political Signs," and "Ideological Signs."[78] To qualify for the exemption, a sign not only had to fall into one of the exempt categories; it also had to comply with the detailed restrictions the ordinance imposed on the display of each type of exempted sign. These restrictions varied in severity. To qualify as a Temporary Directional Sign Relating to a Qualifying Event, for example, a sign had to direct viewers to an event organized by a religious, charitable, or other nonprofit group, be no more than six square feet in size, and to be put up no more than twelve hours before and be taken down no more than one hour after the event it gave directions to ended.[79] In contrast, Political Signs (defined as "temporary sign[s] designed to influence the outcome of an election called by a public body") could be up to thirty-two square feet and could be displayed up to sixty days before a primary election, and up to fifteen days following a general election.[80]

The law treated speakers differently, in other words, based on the content of their speech. Nevertheless, both the district court and

---

[76] *Turner Broadcasting Systems, Inc. v FCC*, 512 US 622, 642 (1994).

[77] *Reed*, 135 S Ct at 2224.

[78] Id.

[79] Id at 2225.

[80] Id at 2224–25.

Ninth Circuit concluded that the law was a content-neutral regulation of speech because it could be justified without reference to the speech it regulated.[81]

Justice Thomas, writing for six members of the Court, rejected the lower courts' conclusion that the sign ordinance was content-neutral, as well the test of content discrimination they employed to reach this result. "Government regulation of speech is content based," he wrote, "if a law applies to particular speech because of the topic discussed or the idea or message expressed."[82] Therefore, because the Gilbert law applied different rules to signs depending on the topic or idea or message they expressed, the Court "ha[d] no need to consider the government's justifications or purposes . . . to determine whether it is subject to strict scrutiny."[83]

Thomas acknowledged that in earlier cases the Court had looked at the government's purposes to determine whether laws were content-based but insisted that these cases dealt with an entirely "separate and additional category of laws"—namely, laws that did not make subject matter or viewpoint-based distinctions on their face (that were, as he put it, "facially content neutral").[84] But laws that "appl[y] to particular speech because of the topic discussed or the idea or message expressed," Thomas insisted, are "subject to strict scrutiny regardless of the government's benign motive, content-neutral justification, or lack of 'animus toward the ideas contained' in the regulated speech."[85] Therefore the "crucial first step" courts have to employ when confronted with a First Amendment challenge to a law is to look at the face of the law and determine whether it makes either "subtle" or "obvious" content distinctions.[86] Only if the statute does not make these kinds of facial content distinctions, Thomas explained, should the court proceed to the second step of the analysis and look at the purposes the government invoked to justify the law.[87]

By insisting that the "justified without reference" test applied only to facially content-neutral laws, the opinion finally provided lower

[81] *Reed*, 707 F3d at 1069–72 (affirming 832 F Supp 2d 1070, 1078 (D Ariz 2011)).

[82] *Reed*, 135 S Ct at 2227.

[83] Id.

[84] Id.

[85] Id at 2228.

[86] Id at 2227.

[87] Id.

courts what they had been missing: namely, clear instructions on what to do when faced with facially content-based laws. What this required, however, was the implicit overruling of the multiple decisions in which the Court had done precisely what the *Reed* majority asserted it never had: namely, construed facially content-based laws as content-neutral because of the purposes that justified them.[88] What *Reed* means, going forward, is that it will be much more difficult than previously for the government to defend facially content-based regulations of speech against constitutional challenge.

The decision thus raises anew the question that has been simmering for more than three decades: namely, does *Reed*'s approach better advance First Amendment interests than the alternative, "justified without reference" standard? Answering this question turns out to be quite difficult. In Part II, I examine the advantages of the *Reed* approach, and I then turn in Part III to an examination of its costs.

II. Reed's Virtues

The case for the *Reed* test is an easy one to make. It is absolutely true, as Justice Scalia argued on multiple occasions, that laws that treat speakers differently because of the ideas or messages or subject matter of their speech "lend themselves" to invidious uses.[89] This is because content distinctions give the government the power to target *only* those specific ideas or messages or topics it dislikes. They thus lower the costs of repression, by making it possible for the government to repress only the speech of its enemies and not the speech of its friends.[90] They provide, in other words, an attractive vehicle for advancing constitutionally prohibited purposes.

---

[88] Besides *Renton*, decisions that fall into this category include *City of Los Angeles v Alameda Books, Inc.*, 535 US 425 (2002), *Hill v Colorado*, 530 US 703 (2000), and *Members of City Council of City of Los Angeles v Taxpayers for Vincent*, 466 US 789 (1984).

[89] *Hill*, 530 US at 743 (quoting *Madsen*, 512 US at 794) (Scalia, J, concurring in part and dissenting in part) ("'The vice of content-based legislation—what renders it deserving of the high standard of strict scrutiny—is not that it is always used for invidious, thought-control purposes, but that it lends itself to use for those purposes.' A restriction that operates only on speech that communicates a message of protest, education, or counseling presents exactly this risk.").

[90] Geoffrey R. Stone, *Content Regulation and the First Amendment*, 25 Wm & Mary L Rev 189, 230–31 (1983) ("[T]he probability that an improper motivation has tainted a decision to restrict expression is far greater when the restriction is directed at a particular idea, viewpoint, or item of information than when it is content-neutral . . . for government officials considering the adoption of such a restriction will almost invariably have their own opinions about the merits of the restricted speech . . .").

Certainly there are plenty of examples of facially content-based laws that have been used to repress speech because the government disliked it or feared its effect on an audience.[91] The history of speech regulation in the United States thus provides vivid testament to the dangers inherent in facially content-based lawmaking. And the willingness of courts to uphold, in various circumstances, laws that targeted the speech of communists, radicals, Jehovah's Witnesses, and other unpopular groups on what seem to us today to be reed-thin pretexts provide a good example of how easily judges can be persuaded to acquiesce in the repressive impulses of legislatures.[92]

The bright-line test of content-based lawmaking that *Reed* announced appears, at least at first glance, to provide a more effective means of constraining the repressive and censorial impulses of both legislators and judges than the alternative, more complicated justification test the *Reed* majority rejected, at least as applied to facially content-based laws. This is because, by making the statutory text the primary determinant of the level of scrutiny, it limits the ability of courts to afford stricter scrutiny to laws they dislike and lesser scrutiny to laws they like. It vests courts with less discretion than does a test that requires courts to evaluate whether the government's purposes are adequately justified before determining the standard of scrutiny that applies. As a result, it makes it harder for courts to ap-

[91] The complex network of oath laws and loyalty tests that emerged across the United States in the 1930s, 1940s, and 1950s and that played a tremendously important role in the distribution of welfare benefits and jobs during that period provides a good example of how viewpoint-based laws have been used in the past to stigmatize and marginalize unpopular speakers. See generally Ralph S. Brown Jr., *Loyalty and Security: Employment Tests in the United States* (1958). Laws that required teachers, doctors, civil servants, and the like to disavow radical political beliefs, or to submit to tests of their loyalty, were justified by the pressing needs of national security. In practice, however, they functioned equally well if not better to stigmatize those who, because of their sexuality, their political leanings, or their lifestyle, appeared to those who enforced these laws to be "un-American." See, for example, Daniel J. Solove, *Digital Dossiers and the Dissipation of Fourth Amendment Privacy*, 75 S Cal L Rev 1083, 1111 (2002). Content-based laws have also been used to suppress the speech of Jehovah's Witnesses, radical abolitionists, and socialists—to name only a few of the unpopular groups targeted by facially content-based laws. See generally Geoffrey R. Stone, *Perilous Times: Free Speech in Wartime: From the Sedition Act of 1798 to the War on Terrorism* (2005).

[92] For an excellent analysis of judges' willingness to "vastly exaggerate and react against the threats posed by disfavored groups," see Christina Wells, *Fear and Loathing in Constitutional Decision-Making*, 2005 Wisc L Rev 115, 119 (2005). See also Kreimer, 16 U Pa J Const L at 1309 (cited in note 15) ("A robust line of research demonstrates that decision makers are less willing to accord weight to free speech principles when they feel threatened by the ideology or actions of the groups at issue.").

ply a lower standard of scrutiny in cases in which they are sympathetic to the government.

Of course, no test is entirely foolproof. Judicial power carries with it inherent discretion, and the tiered system of scrutiny provides particular room for maneuver. As the Court's own cases reveal, what it means for a law to be narrowly tailored to further a compelling interest, or to serve a significant interest by reasonably tailored means, can vary considerably from case to case.[93] Furthermore, in *Reed*'s wake, courts retain considerable discretion to determine how broadly the decision applies, although this discretion may ultimately be limited by the articulation of clear rules.[94]

Nevertheless, it is not difficult to understand why a majority of the Court believed that a bright-line test of content-based lawmaking would provide better protection against judges' and legislators' worst impulses than the alternative. This is particularly the case given plenty of evidence that, prior to *Reed*, lower courts frequently applied the "justified without reference" test in a manner that was excessively deferential to government interests. Rather than requiring the government to provide evidence that the content distinctions it drew actually furthered the purposes it invoked to justify the law, courts frequently took the government's claims of statutory purpose at face value.

The lower court opinion in *Reed* provides a good example of how little evidence courts sometimes required to conclude that a law that made facial content distinctions was adequately justified by a content-neutral purpose. In her concurring opinion in *Reed*, Justice Kagan argued that the arguments the town of Gilbert provided to explain why directional signs were treated differently from political signs and ideological signs were so weak they couldn't pass the "laugh test," let alone strict or intermediate scrutiny.[95] The town failed entirely, for

---

[93] Compare, for example, the Court's very lenient application of strict scrutiny in *Burson v Freeman*, 504 US 191 (1992), with its very rigorous application of strict scrutiny in *Ashcroft v ACLU*, 535 US 564 (2002).

[94] Justice Thomas's opinion in *Reed* failed almost entirely to specify in what circumstances the decision applied. *Reed*, 135 S Ct at 2227 (noting simply that "[g]overnment regulation of speech is content based if a law applies to particular speech because of the topic discussed or the idea or message expressed" and that content-based regulations are "subject to strict scrutiny"). This has led to considerable debate among the lower courts about the scope of the rule and—for reasons I discuss below—has led some courts to read it quite narrowly. See generally Note, *Free Speech Doctrine After Reed v Town of Gilbert*, 129 Harv L Rev 1981, 1990–92 (2016) (noting that courts have distinguished *Reed* "up, down, and sideways.").

[95] *Reed*, 135 S Ct at 2239 (Kagan, J, concurring).

example, to explain why only four such signs could be placed on any given private property.[96] The only argument the town could come up with to explain why temporary directional signs had to be so much smaller than other signs was that they had "to direct travelers along a route."[97] But of course one would think precisely the opposite would be the case. Meanwhile the only argument the town provided to explain why directional signs had to be taken down within one hour after the event they advertised had concluded, but election-related signs could stay up for ten days after the election they advertised had concluded, and ideological signs never had to be taken down at all, was that "Ideological Signs and Political Signs . . . retain expressive value" even when they advertise a completed event and moreover "do not have the same potential to confuse travelers because [they do not provide] guidance to a specific location for a time-sensitive event."[98] It is far from clear, however, why a sign advertising a now-concluded religious meeting should prove any less expressively meaningful or more confusing than a sign advertising a now-concluded election. Nor did the town provide any evidence to back up its claim that directional signs had more potential to confuse travelers than other kinds of signs.[99]

Notwithstanding the problems with the arguments the town made to justify the law, both the district court and two panels of the Ninth Circuit held that the Gilbert sign ordinance was adequately justified by the town's interests in aesthetics and traffic safety. The lower courts were untroubled by the logical problems with the town's arguments that Kagan identified because they did not encounter them. Rather than asking the town to explain why it drew the distinctions it did, the lower courts asked only whether the restrictions the sign code imposed on directional signs could be plausibly justified by traffic safety and aesthetic concerns. The Ninth Circuit concluded, for example,

---

[96] Id.

[97] Oral Argument, *Reed v Town of Gilbert, Ariz.*, Docket No 13-502, *40 (US filed Jan 12, 2015) (available on Westlaw at 2015 WL 2399396).

[98] Brief for Respondents, *Reed v Town of Gilbert, Ariz.*, Docket No 13-502, *48–49 (US filed Nov 14, 2014) (available on Westlaw at 2014 WL 6466937).

[99] *Reed*, 135 S Ct at 2232 (Kagan, J, concurring) ("The Town similarly has not shown that limiting temporary directional signs is necessary to eliminate threats to traffic safety, but that limiting other types of signs is not. The Town has offered no reason to believe that directional signs pose a greater threat to safety than do ideological or political signs. If anything, a sharply worded ideological sign seems more likely to distract a driver than a sign directing the public to a nearby church meeting.").

that the size restrictions the law imposed on the display of temporary directional signs "actually advance[d]" the town's aesthetic and safety interests because they did "not appear substantially broader . . . than required to make sure the rights-of-way are not so thicketed with signs as to pose a safety hazard or create an aesthetic blight."[100] At no point, however, did the court require the town to explain why political and ideological signs—which were allowed to be considerably larger than directional signs—did not pose an equivalent threat to rights-of-way to cause the same problems.[101] Nor did it require the town to produce any empirical evidence that directional signs posed the problems it said they did.[102]

The Ninth Circuit failed to ask whether the distinctions the Sign Code drew were justified because it found that the signs that fell into each of the exempted categories were "not in competition" with one another and that "the erection of one type of temporary sign does not preclude the placement of another."[103] But this is to mistake the nature of the inquiry: what the analysis of the government's justifications for distinguishing between different kinds of speakers and different kinds of speech seeks to ensure is *not* that those engaged in direct competition in the marketplace of ideas are treated equally but instead that the government has legitimate reasons for acting as it does. The Ninth Circuit's application of the "justified without reference" test entirely failed to achieve this aim.

The Ninth Circuit opinion is a striking but by no means exceptionally egregious example of how leniently courts applied the "justified without reference" test in the years prior to the Court's decision in *Reed*. Courts engaged in a similarly cursory analysis of the government's justifications in many other cases. In *Thorburn v Austin*,[104] for example, the Eighth Circuit held that a local law that prohibited the targeted picketing of residences—and defined targeted picketing to mean picketing that was "directed towards a specific person or per-

---

[100] *Reed v Town of Gilbert, Ariz.*, 587 F3d 966, 980 (9th Cir 2009).

[101] Id.

[102] In a later opinion, the Ninth Circuit did analyze whether the distinction the code drew between commercial and noncommercial speech was adequately justified, but its analysis was again extremely cursory. *Reed*, 707 F3d at 1074 (noting that "courts generally defer to a city's determinations of size and duration").

[103] *Reed*, 707 F3d at 1075.

[104] 231 F3d 1114 (8th Cir 2000).

sons"—was content-neutral because the city's justification for the law (namely, that it protected residential privacy and tranquility) had "nothing to do with the content of the regulated speech."[105] The Court reached this conclusion even though the city provided no evidence that targeted picketing posed a greater threat to residential privacy and tranquility than other kinds of picketing, let alone evidence demonstrating that it posed a greater threat to residential privacy for reasons *other* than the presumably personal messages it conveyed.

Similarly, in *Norton v City of Springfield*,[106] the Seventh Circuit held that a city law that prohibited panhandling—which it defined as the oral request for an immediate donation of money—was content-neutral because it did not, on its face, distinguish between speakers based on their viewpoint or message.[107] In reaching this conclusion, the court presumed that the distinction the law drew between oral requests for the immediate donation of money and other kinds of oral requests was justified by the city's interest in protecting its residents against a particularly intrusive and disruptive kind of speech.[108] But neither the court, nor the city, pointed to any evidence that panhandling, as the city defined it, in fact posed any significant threat to the well-being of pedestrians in the downtown area, or any more threat than other kinds of speech.[109] Absent this kind of evidence, the court had no way of telling whether the city enacted the ordinance for the purposes it claimed or instead did so to suppress unpopular speech.

By accepting the government's justifications at face value, courts—in these and other cases—essentially allowed the government to determine, through artful pleading, the standard of review that applied to its speech regulations. The effect, as Mark Rienzi and Stuart Buck noted critically, was to make the "justified without reference"

[105] Id at 1117.

[106] 678 F3d 713.

[107] Id at 717.

[108] Id at 714.

[109] The closest the city's brief came to an assertion of this fact was its claim that solicitation "is unquestionably a particular form of speech that is disruptive of business." Brief of the Defendant-Appellee, *Norton v City of Springfield*, Docket No 13-3581, *11 (7th Cir filed Feb 11, 2014) (available on Westlaw at 2014 WL 688306). This assertion was unsupported by any evidence, however.

test "a shallow and easily evaded inquiry into whether the government [could] name just one neutral purpose served by the law."[110]

Given this shoddy record, one can well understand why, after decades of vacillation on the question of what makes a law content-based, the Court was no longer willing to put up with the "justified without reference" test, at least as applied to facially content-based laws. And to the extent the rule announced in *Reed* makes it harder for the government to "make an end run around the First Amendment" than was the case under the pre-*Reed* regime, the decision represents a doctrinal step forward.[111]

The benefits that *Reed* produces, however, come with serious costs. This is because, by requiring courts to treat *all* facially content-based laws as presumptively invalid—at least to the extent they regulate speech to which the presumption against content-based regulation applies—the decision will make it very difficult for the government to defend even entirely legitimate laws against constitutional challenge. This is because, although the Court has sometimes described the purpose of strict scrutiny to be the "smok[ing] out [of] illegitimate [government purposes]," in fact the prophylactic rule does much more than that.[112] By requiring the government to demonstrate a compelling and not just a legitimate purpose, and that the means it has chosen to achieve that end are the least restrictive possible, strict scrutiny makes it difficult to defend even laws that are not the product of a bad intent.[113] The result is that *Reed* may imperil many laws that employ content distinctions to achieve entirely legitimate aims. In

[110] Mark Rienzi and Stuart Buck, *Neutral No More: Secondary Effects Analysis and the Quiet Demise of the Content-Neutrality Test*, 82 Fordham L Rev 1187, 1191 (2013).

[111] Marcy Strauss, *From Witness to Riches: The Constitutionality of Restricting Witness Speech*, 38 Ariz L Rev 291 (1996).

[112] *Adarand Constructors, Inc. v Pena*, 515 US 200, 226 (1995) (quoting *City of Richmond v J. A. Croson Co.*, 488 US 469, 493 (1989) (plurality)).

[113] This is of course why Gerald Gunther famously quipped that strict scrutiny was "fatal in fact, if not in theory." Gerald Gunther, *Foreword: In Search of Evolving Doctrine on a Changing Court: A Model for a Newer Equal Protection*, 86 Harv L Rev 1, 8 (1972). Although later empirical work has suggested that strict scrutiny is *not* always fatal, Seth Kreimer's analysis of lower court decisions in content discrimination cases makes clear how frequently fatal it can be. Compare Adam Winkler, *Fatal in Theory and Strict in Fact: An Empirical Analysis of Strict Scrutiny in the Federal Courts*, 59 Vand L Rev 793, 815 (2006) (reporting reports of empirical study finding that courts applying strict scrutiny in First Amendment cases upheld the challenged law in 22 percent of cases) with Kreimer, 16 U Pa J Const L at 1293 (cited in note 15) (finding that, in cases involving the regulation of speech in public forums, laws subjected to strict scrutiny were struck down in 97 percent of district court cases and 87 percent of appellate cases).

this respect, *Reed* extends the prophylactic rule of strict scrutiny further than the Court in other contexts has been willing to go. The analogy to the law of race discrimination illuminates just how broad the *Reed* test truly is.

III. Reed's Vices

In insisting that all laws that employ either "obvious" or "subtle" content distinctions should be considered, for constitutional purposes, presumptively invalid and subject to strict scrutiny, the *Reed* majority articulated what we might call, borrowing from equal protection scholarship, an "anticlassificatory" test of content discrimination.

Equal protection scholars use the term "anticlassification" to refer to the view of the Equal Protection Clause that has been dominant on the Court since at least the early 1990s.[114] On this view, the government presumptively violates its obligation to provide equal protection of the law whenever it classifies individuals on the basis of a limited number of constitutionally "suspect" categories, such as race or nationality or alienage.[115] Or, at least, on this view, the government presumptively discriminates whenever it classifies individuals on the basis of a suspect category and the result is to burden or benefit those classified.[116] When the government acts in this way, proponents of this view of the Equal Protection Clause insist that its actions will be constitutional only if they satisfy strict scrutiny.[117]

---

[114] See, for example, Reva B. Siegel, *Equality Talk: Antisubordination and Anticlassification Values in Constitutional Struggles over Brown*, 117 Harv L Rev 1470, 1475–76 (2004); Balkin and Siegel, 58 U Miami L Rev at 9 (cited in note 14).

[115] The most succinct recent articulation of this view can be found in Chief Justice Roberts's assertion in his plurality opinion in *Parents Involved in Community Schools v Seattle School District Number 1* that "[t]he way to stop discrimination on the basis of race is to stop discriminating"—that is, making legal distinctions—"on the basis of race." 551 US 701, 747–48 (2007) (plurality). Although race remains the archetypal suspect category, the Court has recognized the existence of other suspect categories such as nationality and alienage. *Graham v Richardson*, 403 US 365, 371–72 (1971).

[116] Racial classifications that merely describe social reality—such as, for example, the racial classifications employed on the census—are not in fact usually reviewed under strict scrutiny. See Balkin and Siegel, 58 U Miami L Rev at 18 (cited in note 14) (noting that "courts seem to act on the belief that a group-based classification must inflict some dignitary or distributive harm to violate the anticlassification principle"); see also *Morales v Daley*, 116 F Supp 2d 801, 813–15 (S D Tex 2000) (declining to apply strict scrutiny to census policies that require the collection of individual racial as well as other demographic information because it is "differential treatment, not classification [per se], that implicates equal protection").

[117] *Adarand Constructors*, 515 US at 227.

Reed articulates an almost identical approach to the analysis of allegedly discriminatory speech regulations. It too insists that whenever the government classifies individuals on the basis of a constitutionally "suspect" category, and the result is to burden or benefit those so classified, it acts presumptively unconstitutionally.[118] The only real difference between the *Reed* test of content discrimination and the test of discrimination articulated in the Court's recent equal protection cases is the identity of the suspect categories. If, in the equal protection context, the categories that are considered suspect are racial categories or categories of national origin or alien status, the categories that *Reed* identifies as constitutionally suspect are instead content-based categories. Indeed, the first question that *Reed* requires courts to ask when confronted with an allegedly discriminatory content-based speech regulation is essentially the same question courts must ask when confronted with an allegedly discriminatory race-based regulation: does the law treat individuals differently on a constitutionally suspect basis?

Nor is it only in its first step that the *Reed* test mirrors contemporary equal protection doctrine. So too does its second step, which requires courts faced with a speech regulation that does not make a facial content distinction to determine whether the regulation was enacted in order to further illegitimate ends.[119] This is essentially the same inquiry that courts must engage in when faced with an equal protection challenge to a facially neutral law. This is the case even though, in First Amendment cases, it is the government that has the burden of demonstrating that a speech regulation is adequately justified by a legitimate purpose, and in equal protection cases, it is the litigant who bears the burden of establishing the existence of a discriminatory purpose.[120] In practice, this difference matters very little, given how easy it is for the government to establish that a facially

[118] Hence, the Court concluded that the Gilbert ordinance was facially content-based—and therefore subject to strict scrutiny—because it "treated [speakers] differently" based on nothing other than the content of their signs. *Reed*, 135 S Ct at 2227.

[119] Id ("[L]aws that cannot be justified without reference to the content of the regulated speech, or that were adopted by the government because of disagreement with the message [the speech] conveys, . . . like those that are content based on their face, must also satisfy strict scrutiny.") (quoting *Ward*, 491 US at 791) (quotation marks omitted).

[120] *Village of Arlington Heights v Metropolitan Housing Development Corp.*, 429 US 252, 264–66 (1977) (requiring "[p]roof of racially discriminatory intent or purpose . . . to show a violation of the Equal Protection Clause" in cases involving facially neutral laws).

neutral law is adequately justified and how difficult it is for litigants to establish a discriminatory purpose.[121] The result is that, after *Reed*, what will determine in the vast majority of both free speech and equal protection cases whether strict scrutiny applies is whether the challenged law employs a "suspect" classification on its face.

That *Reed* makes the rules that govern content-discrimination cases so similar to those that govern race-discrimination cases is not entirely surprising. There are, after all, deep continuities between First Amendment and equal protection law. In equal protection law, for example, as in free speech law, the Court has tended to equate discrimination with discriminatory purpose.[122] And in both bodies of law, the tiered system of scrutiny has come to serve essentially the same doctrinal function: by imposing very rigorous scrutiny on constitutionally "suspect" laws, it "ensure[s] that courts are most skeptical in cases in which it is highly predictable that illegitimate motives are at work" and less skeptical in other cases.[123]

Nor are these the only similarities between these two bodies of law. As in its First Amendment cases, the Court's equal protection cases have generated sharp disagreement among the Justices about how broadly strict scrutiny should apply. For a time, this disagreement produced the kind of vacillation in the Court's race discrimination cases that has characterized First Amendment doctrine. This is evident in the Court's decisions in the 1970s, 1980s, and 1990s addressing equal protection challenges to affirmative action programs and to other minority empowerment policies that classified individuals on the basis of race, but did so in order to integrate and equalize, rather than to segregate and divide. In some cases, the Court insisted that strict scrutiny was the appropriate standard of review in these cases; but in other cases the Court applied a less demanding standard because it found that the purposes that led the government to enact

[121] Reva Siegel, *Why Equal Protection No Longer Protects: The Evolving Forms of Status-Enforcing State Action*, 49 Stan L Rev 1111, 1136 (1997) (noting that the very high evidentiary standards required to establish discriminatory purpose "insulate[] many, if not most, forms of facially neutral state action from equal protection challenge").

[122] *McCleskey v Kemp*, 481 US 279, 292 (1987) ("[A] defendant who alleges an equal protection violation has the burden of proving the existence of purposeful discrimination."); *Washington v Davis*, 426 US 229, 240 (noting that it is a "basic equal protection principle that the invidious quality of a law claimed to be racially discriminatory must ultimately be traced to a racially discriminatory purpose") (quotation marks omitted).

[123] Cass R. Sunstein, *Foreword: Leaving Things Undecided*, 110 Harv L Rev 4, 78 (1996).

these programs were constitutionally legitimate.[124] In yet other cases, the Court failed to articulate a standard of scrutiny at all, because it could not agree on what standard should govern.[125]

In its equal protection cases, the Court struggled to decide, in other words, between an anticlassificatory approach and a more purpose-oriented approach to racial classifications—just as it struggled to decide, in its First Amendment jurisprudence, between an anticlassificatory and a more purpose-oriented test of content discrimination. In this respect, the histories of the two constitutional doctrines of discrimination are quite similar.

In other respects, however, the histories of the two doctrines of discrimination are quite dissimilar. In the Court's equal protection cases, after several decades of uncertainty and vacillation, the anticlassificatory view won the day. In 1995, in *Adarand Constructors, Inc. v Pena*,[126] for example, the Court unequivocally rejected the possibility that a benign governmental purpose could justify treating laws that classify on the basis of race as anything less than constitutionally suspect.[127] In subsequent cases, the Court has adhered to this position, despite persistent dissent.[128]

In the Court's First Amendment cases, in contrast, the struggle between the two tests of content discrimination continued for much longer. Justices who readily signed on to the anticlassificatory view of equal protection continued to join—and even to author—opinions in which the Court upheld as content-neutral laws that made content

[124] *Metro Broadcasting, Inc. v FCC*, 497 US 547, 564–65 (1990) (holding that "benign race-conscious measures mandated by Congress—even if . . . not 'remedial' in the sense of being designed to compensate victims of past governmental or societal discrimination—are constitutionally permissible to the extent that they serve important governmental objectives within the power of Congress and are substantially related to achievement of those objectives").

[125] *Wygant v Jackson Board of Education*, 476 US 267 (1986); *Regents of University of California v Bakke*, 438 US 265, 325 (1978).

[126] 515 US 200.

[127] *Adarand Constructors*, 515 US at 227.

[128] For recent critiques of the majority's anticlassificatory approach, see *Fisher v University of Texas at Austin*, 133 S Ct 2411, 2434 n 4 (2013) (quoting *Gratz v Bollinger*, 539 US 244, 301 (2003) (Ginsburg, J, dissenting) ("Actions designed to burden groups long denied full citizenship stature are not sensibly ranked with measures taken to hasten the day when entrenched discrimination and its aftereffects have been extirpated.")); *Parents Involved*, 551 US at 836–37 (Breyer, J, dissenting).

distinctions on their face.[129] The result was that, whereas the Court, by the mid-1990s, had firmly embraced the view that, to stop discriminating on the basis of race, government must stop classifying on the basis of race, the Court had not embraced the view that to stop discriminating on the basis of content, one must stop classifying on the basis of content.

It is *Reed* that brings the First Amendment doctrine of content discrimination and the Fourteenth Amendment doctrine of race discrimination into alignment. In so doing, it makes it as difficult, at least in theory, for the government to make content distinctions as racial distinctions.

It is not obvious, however, that the same rules that apply to all racially classificatory laws *should* apply to all laws that classify on the basis of content. This is because of what we might call the different ontological status of race and content in American constitutional law.

A. THE CONSTITUTIONAL IRRELEVANCE OF RACIAL DISTINCTIONS

It is a basic principle of equal protection law that racial distinctions are "in most circumstances irrelevant" to the government when it regulates.[130] This is what the Court asserted, in *Hirabayashi v United States* in 1943, to explain why "[d]istinctions between citizens solely because of their ancestry are by their very nature odious to a free people whose institutions are founded upon the doctrine of equal-

---

[129] This was true of Justice Powell, for example, who was a vigorous advocate for a purposive approach to First Amendment equality but an equally vigorous advocate of an anticlassifactory approach to the Equal Protection Clause. Compare *Bakke*, 438 US at 289–90 ("The guarantee of equal protection cannot mean one thing when applied to one individual and something else when applied to a person of another color. If both are not accorded the same protection, then it is not equal.") with *Young v American Mini Theatres, Inc.*, 427 US 50, 73–84 (1976) (Powell, J, concurring) (voting to uphold city zoning law that applied only to adult movie theaters because "[i]t is clear from both the chronology and from the facts that Detroit has not embarked on an effort to suppress free expression"). Justice Powell was not the only member of the Court, however, who showed much more distaste for laws that classified on the basis of race than they did for laws that classified on the basis of content. The same was also true of Justices Rehnquist, White, and O'Connor. Compare *Renton*, 475 US 41 (applying a purpose test of content discrimination) with *J. A. Croson Co.*, 488 US at 476 (plurality) (applying an anticlassificatory test of race discrimination) (plurality). Others on the Court, meanwhile, were strong proponents of anticlassification in the First Amendment context but strong critics of an anticlassificatory approach to equal protection. This was true, for example, of Justices Marshall and Brennan. Compare *Renton*, 475 US at 55–56 (Brennan, J, dissenting) with *J. A. Croson Co.*, 488 US at 528–30 (Marshall, J, dissenting).

[130] *Hirabayashi v United States*, 320 US 81, 100 (1943).

ity."[131] Since then, the Court has repeated that claim on multiple occasions, often without further elaboration or exploration.[132]

The claim is not a self-evident one, however. After all, we live in a racially stratified society, one in which racial and ethnic disparities are evident in almost all arenas of public and private life. Racial differences are closely correlated to where people live, their access to medical care, the likelihood that they will be victims of crime, and many other economic, social, and political differences.[133] There are consequently many reasons, we might think, why the government might want to take race into account when making regulatory policy that have nothing to do with prejudice or animus.

The Court has nevertheless refused to allow the government to take race into account, even in response to the obvious racial differences in the society it governs. It has made clear that, even when the government makes what appear to be rational racial distinctions—that is to say, when it treats individuals differently because of observable, even perhaps statistically significant, differences in the characteristics of different racial groups—its actions offend the Equal Protection Clause.[134]

The Court's refusal to allow the government to engage in what David Strauss has described as "rational discrimination" reflects its underlying belief that race is a social construct; or at least, that racial differences do not reveal anything about the individual's inherent "ability to perform or contribute to society."[135] Hence, the Court pre-

---

[131] Id.

[132] See, for example, *Parents Involved*, 551 US at 741; *Adarand Constructors*, 515 US at 214; *McLaughlin v Fla*, 379 US 184 (1964).

[133] See, for example, Sara Sternberg Greene, *Race Class, and Access to Civil Justice*, 101 Iowa L Rev 1263 (2016) (noting significant racial disparities in housing); Nicholas O. Stephanopoulos, *Race, Place, and Power*, 68 Stan L Rev 1323, 1357–59 (2016) (finding robust and stable differences in racial voting patterns); David R. Williams, *Race, Health, and Health Care*, 48 SLU L J 13, 15 (2003) (noting that "[r]acial and ethnic disparities are pervasive across a broad range of health outcomes and for multiple populations in the United States").

[134] David Strauss, *The Myth of Colorblindness*, 1986 Supreme Court Review 99, 111 (1986) ("[I]t is well established that the prohibition against discrimination established by *Brown* extends to what I have called rational discrimination. A court's decision to strike down rational discrimination would be constitutionally required."); compare *J.E.B. v Ala*, 511 US 127, 139 n 11 (1994) ("Even if a measure of truth can be found in some of the gender stereotypes . . . , that fact alone cannot support discrimination on the basis of gender in jury selection. We have made abundantly clear in past cases that gender classifications that rest on impermissible stereotypes violate the Equal Protection Clause, even when some statistical support can be conjured up for the generalization.").

[135] Strauss, 1986 Supreme Court Review at 108 (cited in note 134); *Frontiero v Richardson*, 411 US 677, 686 (1973) (plurality) (noting that racial differences, like sexual differences,

sumes that differences in the characteristics of different racial groups are not inherent but the product of centuries of racial subordination and inequality. They are the product of private biases, in other words, to which the government cannot give effect without risking reinforcing.[136]

As a result, the situations in which the government may constitutionally take racial differences into account are few and far between. The Court has acknowledged that the government can take race into account in order to promote diversity in the university setting, or to undo the effects of the government's own prior acts of discrimination.[137] But in the vast majority of cases, the Court has taken the view that government may not treat its citizens differently because of their race.[138] The consequence is a public sphere in which the *explicit* use of racial distinctions is extremely rare.

B. THE CONSTITUTIONAL RELEVANCE OF CONTENT DISTINCTIONS

The situation is very different when it comes to content distinctions. Unlike racial distinctions, content distinctions play a pervasive role in the regulation of both private and public life.

Consider, for example, the rules that govern the private workplace. Federal labor laws prohibit employers from engaging in certain kinds of speech during union election campaigns.[139] Title VII of the Civil Rights Act of 1964, as well as many state and local laws, prohibit the

---

"frequently bears no relation to [the individual's] ability to perform or contribute to society"). See also Michael J. Klarman, *An Interpretive History of Modern Equal Protection*, 90 Mich L Rev 213, 314 (1991) (arguing that the Court's affirmative action decisions reveal the belief of the majority of Justices on the Court that "race almost invariably should be irrelevant to governmental decisionmaking").

[136] *Palmore v Sidoti*, 466 US 429, 433 (1984) ("Private biases may be outside the reach of the law, but the law cannot, directly or indirectly, give them effect."). This helps explain why racial profiling is considered discriminatory, even when those who engage in it do so for the purpose of combating crime, not harming minorities. See Albert Alschuler, *Racial Profiling and the Constitution: The Scope of Equal Protection*, U Chi Legal F 163, 211 (2002) ("[T]reat[ing] race . . . as an indicator of criminality . . . [has the effect of] ratify[ing] and encourag[ing] the view that minorities are crime-prone [and] . . . is likely to encourage discrimination, not only in the administration of criminal justice, but throughout society.").

[137] *Parents Involved*, 551 US at 721–22.

[138] See, for example, *Johnson v California*, 543 US 499, 515–16 (2005) (Ginsburg, J, concurring).

[139] Getman, 43 Md L Rev at 5 (cited in note 37) (noting that federal labor regulations "regularly enforced by the courts of appeals, limit the campaign arguments, the method of delivery, and even the tone of rhetoric that an employer may use" during the course of union elections).

use of speech that creates a hostile work environment.[140] Health and safety regulations require employers to post signs containing certain kinds of information where their workers can see them.[141] Rules of professional conduct—rules that the government helps to enforce—govern what doctors and lawyers may say when talking to their clients, or when soliciting new work.[142]

All of these rules involve distinctions between certain kinds of speech and others—distinctions that ultimately depend on the content of the expression. What employers are prohibited from doing under federal labor law is expressing certain messages (such as, for example, that a union strike will cause the workplace to close).[143] What workers are prohibited from doing under Title VII is expressing certain kinds of messages (such as "you're a slut").[144] What doctors are prohibited from doing is giving their patients medically unsound advice.[145] What employers are required to do under a plethora of federal laws is conveying specific information to their workers.[146]

---

[140] Eugene Volokh, *Freedom of Speech and Workplace Harassment*, 39 UCLA L Rev 1791, 1799 (1992) (quotation marks omitted) ("Harassment, courts have held—whether it is harassment by speech or by nonspeech conduct—violates Title VII if it is sufficiently severe or pervasive to alter the conditions of [the victim's] employment and create an abusive working environment because of the worker's sex, race, religion, or national origin.").

[141] See, for example, 29 CFR § 516.4 ("Every employer employing any employees subject to the [Fair Labor Standard] Act's minimum wage provisions shall post and keep posted a notice explaining the Act, as prescribed by the Wage and Hour Division, in conspicuous places in every establishment where such employees are employed so as to permit them to observe readily a copy."); 29 CFR § 1903.2(a)(1) ("Each employer shall post and keep posted a notice or notices . . . informing employees of the protections and obligations provided for in the [Occupational Safety and Health] Act, and that for assistance and information, including copies of the Act and of specific safety and health standards, employees should contact the employer or the nearest office of the Department of Labor.").

[142] Post, 2007 U Ill L Rev at 949 (cited in note 37) (noting that "[w]hen a physician speaks to the public, his opinions cannot be censored and suppressed, even if they are at odds with preponderant opinion within the medical establishment. But when a physician speaks to a patient in the course of medical treatment, his opinions are normally regulated on the theory that they are inseparable from the practice of medicine."); Kathleen M. Sullivan, *The Intersection of Free Speech and the Legal Profession: Constraints on Lawyers' First Amendment Rights*, 67 Fordham L Rev 569, 569 (1998) ("Lawyers, as professionals, are subjected to speech restrictions that would not ordinarily apply to lay persons. These restrictions have been particularly prevalent in the areas of solicitation of clients, lawyer interaction with the media, and lawyer advertising.").

[143] *NLRB v Gissel Packing*, 395 US 575, 588–89.

[144] See, for example, *EEOC v Hacienda Hotel*, 881 F2d 1504, 1507 (9th Cir 1989).

[145] Post, 2007 U Ill L Rev at 949–50 (cited in note 37).

[146] See note 141.

Although some of these rules have proven to be more controversial than others, courts have recognized that the government has legitimate reasons to regulate speech in these ways.[147] They have recognized, for example, that the government can penalize harassing speech in order to ensure equality of access to the workplace,[148] that it can limit employer speech during union election campaigns in order to ensure that union elections are free and fair,[149] and that it can limit the speech of doctors and lawyers in order to promote the integrity of their professions and the well-being of their patients and clients.[150] The widespread recognition that content-based distinctions play an important role in the regulation of the workplace helps explain why the standard of means-end scrutiny that applies in work environments tends to be relatively lenient, and why the strong presumption against content-based regulation does not apply.

Even when it comes to the regulation of speech in the public sphere—to speech to which the presumption against content-based restrictions *does* apply—content distinctions play an important regulatory role. This is true even though the range of purposes that may legitimately motivate the government to employ content distinctions in the public sphere is more limited than when it regulates in the private sphere. This is because First Amendment doctrine recognizes

[147] There is a vigorous debate, for example, about whether the breadth of the prohibition against sexually harassing speech violates the First Amendment. See, for example, Volokh, 39 UCLA L Rev (cited in note 140); Cynthia L. Estlund, *Freedom of Expression in the Workplace and the Problem of Discriminatory Harassment*, 75 Tex L Rev 687 (1997). Even critics of the rules acknowledge, however, that some sexually harassing speech at work can be punished *because of its content*. Volokh, 39 UCLA L Rev at 1807 (cited in note 140) ("Many harassment cases involve truly harrowing abuse, abuse that can shut women and minorities out of the workplace almost as surely as would explicit discrimination in hiring.").

[148] See, for example, *Henson v City of Dundee*, 682 F2d 897, 902 (11th Cir 1982) (noting that "[s]exual harassment which creates a hostile or offensive environment for members of one sex is every bit the arbitrary barrier to sexual equality at the workplace that racial harassment is to racial equality").

[149] *Gissel Packing*, 395 US at 619 (holding that government may prohibit employers from communicating, even indirectly, a "threat of reprisal or force or promise of benefit," during the course of a union election, in order to protect economically dependent employees against employer coercion).

[150] *Planned Parenthood of Southeastern Pa v Casey*, 505 US 833, 838 (1992) (affirming state's right to compel physicians to provide specific information to their patients about abortion and holding more generally that "the physician's First Amendment rights not to speak are implicated only as part of the practice of medicine, which is licensed and regulated by the State"); *Ohralik v Ohio State Bar Association*, 436 US 447, 460 (1978) (upholding state professional rule prohibiting certain kinds of legal solicitation given the state's "general interest in protecting consumers and regulating commercial transactions" and its "special responsibility for maintaining standards among members of the licensed professions").

the distinction between what Immanuel Kant famously described as the "public" and the "private use of one's reason."[151] That is to say, it recognizes, or at least presumes, that speech that addresses itself to a public audience is especially important to the marketplace of ideas.[152] Thus, when the government regulates public speech, the constitutional constraints on its authority are much greater. In such cases, the government is barred not only from punishing speech because it dislikes it, as it is prohibited from doing when it regulates the private sphere,[153] but when it pursues legitimate ends via paternalistic means.[154] For example, in contrast to when the government regulates private speech, when the government regulates public speech, it may not limit the speech of the more powerful in order to protect the less powerful against indirect forms of threat and coercion. Instead, it may prohibit coercive speech only when it represents a "serious expression of an intent to commit an act of unlawful violence to a particular individual or group of individuals."[155] Nor may the government limit speech because it may persuade people to do bad things, or because it is offensive or threatening to the status quo, as it can when it regulates in the private sphere.[156]

---

[151] Immanuel Kant, *An Answer to the Question: What Is Enlightenment?*, in H. S. Reiss, ed, *Political Writings* 54, 55 (1991) ("[T]he public use of one's reason must be free at all times, and this alone can bring enlightenment to mankind. On the other hand, the private use of reason may frequently be narrowly restricted without especially hindering the progress of enlightenment. By 'public use of one's reason' I mean that use which a man, as *scholar*, makes of it before the reading public. I call 'private use' that use which a man makes of his reason in a civic post that has been entrusted to him.").

[152] This helps explain the persistent emphasis in the cases on *public speech*. See, for example, *Cohen*, 403 US at 24 (arguing that the "constitutional right of free expression . . . is designed and intended to remove governmental restraints from the arena of *public* discussion") (emphasis added); *Thornhill v Ala*, 310 US 88, 101–02 (1940) ("The freedom of speech and of the press guaranteed by the Constitution embraces at the least the liberty to discuss *publicly* and truthfully all matters of *public* concern without previous restraint or fear of subsequent punishment.") (emphasis added).

[153] See, for example, *Waters v Churchill*, 511 US 661, 675 (1994) (holding that the government has greater power to regulate speech when operating as a public employer because of its interest in "achieving its goals as effectively and efficiently as possible" but that it may not restrict speech that does not interfere with its legitimate workplace goals).

[154] Stone, 25 Wm & Mary L Rev at 212 (cited in note 90) ("The Court has long embraced an 'antipaternalistic' understanding of the [F]irst [A]mendment.").

[155] *Virginia v Black*, 538 US 343, 359 (2003).

[156] See, for example, *Waters*, 511 US at 672 (noting that while, when it comes to the regulation of public speech, "[t]he First Amendment demands a tolerance of verbal tumult, discord, and even offensive utterance, as necessary side effects of . . . the process of open debate, . . . a government employer may bar its employees from using . . . offensive utterance[s] to members of the public or to the people with whom they work"; and that "though a private

Even given these constraints, though, there are good reasons why the government might want to, and regularly does, make content distinctions when regulating the speech of public citizens. Consider, for example, privacy laws. Laws of this sort frequently prohibit the use or distribution—including the public use and distribution—of personally identifiable information.[157] They make, in other words, a content-based distinction between information that can be used to identify a person and information that cannot. We can well understand why the government might want to employ a distinction of this sort. This is because the unconstrained dissemination of such information poses a distinction threat to personal privacy.[158]

We cannot therefore presume that when the government distinguishes between these two kinds of information it does so in an attempt to "control the search for truth" or to "give one side on a debatable public question an advantage in expressing its views to the public." Nor is it necessarily acting paternalistically. In fact, it is highly unlikely that when the government regulates personal information its motive is to prevent people from being persuaded by "bad" speech to do bad things, or to shield them from offensive or unpleasant speech. The best explanation of these laws is that they represent an effort to protect individual autonomy, by allowing individuals to maintain some control over who knows what about them.[159]

---

person is perfectly free to uninhibitedly and robustly criticize a state governor's legislative program, we have never suggested that the Constitution bars the governor from firing a high-ranking deputy for doing the same thing") (quotation marks omitted); Post, 2007 U Ill L Rev at 977 (cited in note 37) ("[W]hen physicians address the general public, they are . . . free to express themselves as they wish, without the constraints of ordinary professional responsibility. But when physicians speak to us as our personal doctors, they must assume a fiduciary obligation faithfully and expertly to communicate the considered knowledge of the 'medical community.' ").

[157] See, for example, Health Insurance Portability and Accountability Act ("HIPAA") Privacy Rule, 45 CFR § 164.502 (imposing significant constraints on the use and dissemination of "individually identifiable health information"); Driver's Privacy Protection Act ("DDPA"), 18 USC § 2721 et seq (prohibiting individuals from knowingly obtaining or disclosing "personal information" from motor vehicle records); see generally Daniel J. Solove, *The Virtues of Knowing Less: Justifying Privacy Protections Against Disclosure*, 53 Duke L J 967, 971–73 (2003) (describing the many and varied state and federal laws that regulate the disclosure of personal information).

[158] As the Court has recognized, "[t]he capacity of technology to find and publish personal information . . . presents serious and unresolved issues with respect to personal privacy and the dignity it seeks to secure." *Sorrell*, 564 US at 579.

[159] The Court has recognized on multiple occasions the important First Amendment interests promoted by privacy laws. See, for example, *Bartnicki*, 532 US at 532–33 (noting

This is not to say that privacy laws pose no First Amendment problems. Like any regulations of speech, they can be employed for bad purposes. And when they deprive the press or other relevant actors of important information on matters of public concern, they can undermine the quality of public debate and thereby violate the First Amendment.[160] But there is nothing *inherently* problematic about privacy laws from a standpoint of discriminatory purpose—which is why courts have frequently upheld the constitutionality of such laws when they restrict speech that does not touch on "matters of public concern."[161]

The same is true of many other kinds of facially content-based regulations of public speech. Consider, for example, campaign finance laws. These frequently impose restrictions on electioneering speech that are not imposed on other kinds of speech.[162] This is a content distinction—what makes something electioneering speech is the fact that it refers to a candidate for elected office.[163] Yet the Court has recognized that the government has a compelling interest in regu-

---

that "[p]rivacy of communication is an important interest" and that "the fear of public disclosure of private conversations might well have a chilling effect on private speech"); *Griswold v Connecticut*, 381 US 479, 483 (1965) ("[T]he First Amendment has a penumbra where privacy is protected from governmental intrusion.").

[160] In such cases, the Court has not hesitated to strike laws of this kind down. See, for example, *Florida Star*, 491 US 524; *Smith v Daily Mail Publishing Co.*, 443 US 97 (1979).

[161] See, for example, *Dahlstrom v Sun-Times Media, LLC*, 777 F3d 937, 949 (7th Cir 2015) (upholding the DDPA against constitutional challenge on the grounds that the government has a "legitimate interest in preventing stalkers and criminals [from] acquir[ing] personal information from state DMVs") (quotations omitted); *Law School Admission Council, Inc. v State*, 222 Cal App 4th 1265, 1271–72 (2014), as modified (Feb 11, 2014) (reversing injunction against enforcement of California law that prohibited the LSAC from informing law schools that candidates received an accommodation when taking the LSAT); *Individual Reference Services Group, Inc. v FTC*, 145 F Supp 2d 6, 43–44 (DDC 2001), aff'd sub nom; *Trans Union LLC v FTC*, 295 F3d 42 (DC Cir 2002) (upholding constitutionality of regulation that requires banks to inform customers when using or disseminating their personally identifiable information).

[162] See, for example, 52 USC § 30104(f) (imposing detailed reporting requirements on anyone who "makes a disbursement for the direct costs of producing and airing electioneering communications in an aggregate amount in excess of $10,000 during any calendar year"); 52 USCA § 3012(a) (requiring electioneering communications to clearly state if funded and/or authorized by a political committee, or candidate, or by some other source).

[163] 11 CFR § 100.29 (defining electioneering communications as "any broadcast, cable, or satellite communication that: (1) [r]efers to a clearly identified candidate for Federal office; (2) [i]s publicly distributed within 60 days before a general election . . . ; or within 30 days before a primary or preference election [and] (3) [i]s targeted to the relevant electorate, in the case of a candidate for Senate or the House of Representatives").

lating electoral speech in order to preserve the integrity of the electoral process.[164]

Or consider the many laws that prohibit making false statements to government agents[165] or falsely claiming to be a government agent.[166] In distinguishing between true and false speech, these laws make an obvious content distinction. Nevertheless, it is easy to understand why the government might want to penalize false speech to and about government agents. This is because false speech creates harms that true speech does not: it undermines the integrity of government processes. It undermines the ability of law enforcement to effectively investigate crime, the ability of federal agents to distribute benefits in accordance with law, and the ability of the public to trust that government officials are who they say they are.[167]

---

[164] *Citizens United v Federal Election Commission*, 558 US 310, 370–71 (2010) ("With the advent of the Internet, prompt disclosure of expenditures can provide shareholders and citizens with the information needed to hold corporations and elected officials accountable for their positions and supporters. . . . This transparency enables the electorate to make informed decisions and give proper weight to different speakers and messages."); *Buckley v Valeo*, 424 US 1, 66–68 (1976) (noting that disclosure requirements "provide[] the electorate with information as to where political campaign money comes from . . . [and therefore aid] the voters in evaluating those who seek federal office . . . [,] deter actual corruption and avoid the appearance of corruption by exposing large contributions and expenditures to the light of publicity . . . [and provide] the data necessary to detect violations of [campaign finance laws]").

[165] See, for example, 18 USC § 1001 (making it a crime to knowingly and willfully "make[] any materially false, fictitious, or fraudulent statement or representation; or make[] or use[] any false writing or document . . . in any matter within the jurisdiction of the executive, legislative, or judicial branch of the Government of the United States"); Ala Code § 13A-10-9 (making it a crime to "knowingly make[] a false report . . . to law enforcement authorities of a crime or relating to a crime"); DC Code Ann § 5-117.05 (same); Fla Stat Ann § 817.49 (same). For a list of dozens of similar laws, see *United States v Gaudin*, 28 F3d 943, 961 nn 3 and 4 (9th Cir 1994) (Kozinski dissenting).

[166] 18 USC § 912 (criminalizing the actions of those who "falsely assume[] or pretend[] to be an officer or employee acting under the authority of the United States or any department, agency, or officer thereof, and acts as such"); 18 USC § 709 (prohibiting a speaker's unauthorized use of federal agencies' names in a manner reasonably calculated to convey the impression that the speaker's message was approved or endorsed by the agency).

[167] Courts have recognized as much. See, for example, *Bryson v United States*, 396 US 64, 70 (1969) (noting the "valid legislative interest in protecting the integrity of official inquiries"); *People v Morera-Munoz*, 210 Cal Rptr 3d 409, 420 (Ct App 2016) (holding that a state law that prohibited the making of false reports to police officers protected against "th[o]se falsities [that] have the potential to corrupt an official investigation"); *United States v Barnow*, 239 US 74, 78 (1915) ("In order that the vast and complicated operations of the government of the United States shall be carried on successfully and with a minimum of friction and obstruction, it is important . . . that a spirit of respect and good will for the government and its officers shall generally prevail. And what could more directly impair this spirit than to permit unauthorized and unscrupulous persons to go about the country falsely assuming, for fraudulent purposes, to be entitled to the respect and credit due to an officer of the government?").

These examples merely hint at the diverse range of contexts in which content distinctions help the government tailor its coercive force to the specific harms that different kinds of speech can create. Indeed, one can easily come up with many other examples of content distinctions that, until *Reed*, played a relatively unproblematic role in the regulation of the public sphere. Sign laws, for example, regularly distinguish between directional and nondirectional signs.[168] Federal aviation law requires pilots to ensure that passengers are provided specific safety information at the beginning of all flights.[169] Right-of-publicity laws impose penalties on those who misappropriate another person's name or likeness for their own economic benefit.[170] National security laws criminalize the distribution of material containing secret or classified information.[171]

The fact that content distinctions play such an important role in regulation reflects what we might call the different ontological status of content and racial distinctions in contemporary constitutional law. It reflects the fact that, in contrast to racial distinctions, the Court does *not* consider content distinctions to be merely social constructions—the product of unjust social forces, mystifications that hide from us our essential humanity. Instead, it recognizes that content distinctions sometimes reflect real differences in the characteristics of different kinds of speech.[172] Or at least, it recognizes this to be true of content distinctions *other* than those based on viewpoint.

---

[168] See, for example, Dover, Del Code of Ordinances, Pt II, App B, Art 5, § 4.5(F) (exempting directional signs from general licensing requirement provided such signs are no more than three square feet in size). City of Fort Worth Sign Ordinance, 6.403 (exempting from general permit requirement "[w]arning, security and directional signs for parking or vehicle access" as well as "informational, directional or traffic signs").

[169] 14 CFR § 136.7 (requiring pilots to ensure before takeoff that each passenger has been briefed on emergency and smoking regulations).

[170] See, for example, Cal Civ Code § 3344 ("Any person who knowingly uses another's name, voice, signature, photograph, or likeness, in any manner, on or in products, merchandise, or goods, or for purposes of advertising or selling, or soliciting purchases of, products, merchandise, goods or services, without such person's prior consent . . . shall be liable for any damages sustained by the person or persons injured as a result thereof."); Ohio Rev Code Ann § 2741.02 (prohibiting the use of "any aspect of an individual's persona for a commercial purpose" for a period of sixty years after their death).

[171] See, for example, 18 USC § 793; 18 USC § 798.

[172] This helps explain why content distinctions play such an important role in the doctrinal rules the Court applies in First Amendment cases. See Paul B. Stephan III, *The First Amendment and Content Discrimination*, 68 Va L Rev 203, 211–14 (1982).

The Court has not upheld an explicitly viewpoint-based regulation of public speech in almost thirty years.[173] One could thus interpret the Court's First Amendment jurisprudence as establishing the principle that viewpoint distinctions—like racial distinctions—are so rarely relevant to the government's legitimate aims that they are, for all intents and purposes, impermissible mechanisms of lawmaking.[174]

The same is not true, however, of other kinds of content distinctions, which the Court has, on many occasions, upheld. And certainly the Court has never suggested that, when making these kinds of content distinctions, the government may not rely upon generalizations about the characteristics of the different kinds of speech. It has instead insisted that when the government relies upon generalizations, they should be *accurate*.[175] The result is that there are many contexts in which the government can, and regularly does, take subject matter—and various other kinds of content—distinctions into account.

C. THE CONSEQUENCE OF THE DIFFERENCE BETWEEN CONTENT AND RACE

The fact that the government may employ content distinctions to further all sorts of ends but may not employ racial distinctions undermines the implicit analogy that *Reed* draws between the law of content discrimination and the law of race discrimination. This is because one of the primary justifications the Court has provided for treating all laws that employ racial classifications as suspect is that there are so few legitimate reasons for government to employ such

[173] The last case in which the Court upheld a viewpoint-based regulation of high-value speech was, as far as I can discern, *Meese v Keene*, 481 US 465 (1987) (upholding law imposing registration requirements on foreign agents who disseminate "political propaganda," defined to include material which "advocates, advises, instigates, or promotes any racial, social, political, or religious disorder, civil riot, or other conflict involving the use of force or violence"). Even still, the Court upheld the law as constitutional only after finding that it did not restrict any speech or impose any "burden on protected expression." Id at 480.

[174] Stone, 25 Wm & Mary L Rev at 200 (cited in note 90) (noting the Court's tendency to apply strict scrutiny even to modest viewpoint-based laws).

[175] See, for example, *Mosley*, 408 US at 100 (holding that city may not prohibit some types of pickets but not others unless it demonstrates "that [the] picketing [it prohibits] is clearly more disruptive than the picketing [it] already permits"); *Tinker v Des Moines Independent Community School District*, 393 US 503, 508–09 (1969) ("[I]n our system, undifferentiated fear or apprehension of disturbance is not enough to overcome the right to freedom of expression. . . . In order for the State in the person of school officials to justify prohibition of a particular expression of opinion, it must be able to show that its action was caused by something more than a mere desire to avoid the discomfort and unpleasantness that always accompany an unpopular viewpoint.").

distinctions, thus suggesting improper motivation when it does so. As Justice White explained in *Cleburne v Cleburne Texas Living Center*:[176]

> The general rule is that legislation is presumed to be valid and will be sustained if the classification drawn by the statute is rationally related to a legitimate state interest. . . . The general rule gives way, however, when a statute classifies by race, alienage, or national origin. These factors are so seldom relevant to the achievement of any legitimate state interest that laws grounded in such considerations are deemed to reflect prejudice and antipathy—a view that those in the burdened class are not as worthy or deserving as others.[177]

The irrelevance of racial distinctions is not the only justification the Court has provided for treating all racially classificatory laws as suspect. It has also argued that laws that employ racial distinctions are especially likely to be the product of invidious motivations, given the "long and tragic" history out of which they emerge.[178] It has also suggested that laws that employ racial distinctions are particularly problematic because they discriminate on the basis of an immutable characteristic—one for which the individual bears no responsibility.[179]

The Court has nevertheless made clear that, even if not a sufficient condition for suspect class status, the fact that race is "seldom relevant to the achievement of any legitimate state interest is a necessary condition for it." Conversely, the Court has made clear that classifications that do not share these characteristics need not be subjected to strict scrutiny. In *Cleburne*, for example, the Court explained that mental disability should not count as a suspect or even semisuspect classification for equal protection purposes because "legislation . . . singling out the retarded for special treatment reflects the real and undeniable dif-

[176] 473 US 432 (1985).

[177] Id at 440.

[178] See, for example, *Bakke*, 438 US at 303 ("[T]he perception of racial classifications as inherently odious stems from a lengthy and tragic history"); *Mass Board of Retirement v Murgia*, 427 US 307, 313 (1976) (denying suspect class status to the aged because "[w]hile the treatment of the aged in this Nation has not been wholly free of discrimination, such persons, unlike, say, those who have been discriminated against on the basis of race or national origin, have not experienced a history of purposeful unequal treatment") (quotation marks omitted).

[179] *Frontiero*, 411 US at 686 ("[S]ince sex, like race and national origin, is an immutable characteristic determined solely by the accident of birth, the imposition of special disabilities upon the members of a particular sex because of their sex would seem to violate the basic concept of our system that legal burdens should bear some relationship to individual responsibility.") (quotation marks omitted); *Fullilove v Klutznick*, 448 US 448, 525 (1980) (Stewart, J, dissenting) ("The color of a person's skin and the country of his origin are immutable facts that bear no relation to ability, disadvantage, moral culpability, or any other characteristics of constitutionally permissible interest to government.").

ferences between the retarded and others"—differences that were "not only legitimate but desirable" for the government to take into account.[180] Hence, the Court argued, to treat the mentally disabled as a suspect or semisuspect class would do more harm than good, because although "legislation designed to benefit, rather than disadvantage, the retarded would generally withstand examination under a test of heightened scrutiny . . . merely requiring the legislature to justify its efforts in these terms may lead it to refrain from acting at all."[181] And, indeed, the affirmative action cases provide a vivid illustration of how severe a constraint on government power the declaration of suspect class status can be.[182]

There is no reason to think that a similar concern with the constraining and even perhaps chilling effects of strict scrutiny should not apply in the First Amendment context as well. Here too, the Court has long recognized, as we saw in Part I, that the regulation of speech furthers important constitutional as well as extraconstitutional goals. For that reason, the Court should be as concerned about the costs of strict scrutiny in the First Amendment as in the equal protection context.

And yet, if the same concerns apply, the *Reed* test starts to look much less attractive. This is because, given the many legitimate reasons the government has to make content distinctions when it regulates speech, what *Reed* seems to require is the application of strict scrutiny to many laws that are not in fact the product of a discriminatory purpose. And given how difficult it is for the government to satisfy the demands of strict scrutiny, the likely result will be to invalidate many laws that are *not* discriminatory, as the Court understands the term.[183]

---

[180] *Cleburne*, 473 US at 444.

[181] Id.

[182] Siegel, 49 Stan L Rev at 1142 (1997) (cited in note 121) ("[T]oday, especially in the area of race, doctrines of heightened scrutiny are functioning primarily as a check on affirmative action programs."). See also David Schraub, *The Siren Song of Strict Scrutiny*, 84 UMKC L Rev 859 (2016) (arguing that supporters of gay rights should not push the Court for suspect class status because doing so would limit, rather than enhance, their ability to protect their interests in the political process).

[183] One could make the same argument about the use of strict scrutiny to review affirmative action laws. This is because the Court has recognized that, when the government acts to regulate admissions to universities, there are at least two legitimate, even "compelling," reasons why it might want to take race into account—namely, to promote diversity and remedy past racial discrimination. *Parents Involved*, 551 US at 721–22. In these cases, as well,

Nor can the *Reed* test easily by justified by recourse to a theory of discriminatory effect. Even if one rejected the focus on discriminatory purpose, and instead construed strict scrutiny as a defense against regulations that are particularly likely to disparately effect the expression of particular ideas or topics, *Reed* would still require applying strict scrutiny to many laws that do not pose a significant threat to First Amendment interests. This is because the presence or absence of content classifications is not a reliable predictor of a law's disparate effects. Some facially content-based laws may have a very modest impact on the ability of speakers to communicate.[184] Laws prohibiting the impersonation of government officers, for example, burden speech only minimally. They prevent speakers from falsely pretending to be government officials, but not from criticizing, condemning, or praising government officers.[185] As a result, they seem unlikely to have anything close to a significant disparate impact on the ability of different speakers to participate in the marketplace of ideas. The same is true of many other facially content-based laws.[186]

Other content-based distinctions, meanwhile, operate to *lessen* the disparate effects of a law, by exempting or partially exempting from its operation those who are most likely to be severely burdened by it.[187] The result is that many facially content-based laws are unlikely to have the kind of disparate effects that critics have argued First Amendment doctrine should take into account.[188]

---

the application of strict scrutiny may therefore result in the invalidation of many laws that are not in fact a product of impermissible purposes. The argument is somewhat weaker in the affirmative action context, however, given the smaller range of permissible purposes the Court has recognized racially classificatory laws can promote when compared to facially content-based speech regulations. Nevertheless, the same logic holds.

[184] See Stone, 25 Wm & Mary L Rev at 200 (cited in note 90) (noting that "not every law that restricts the communication of a particular idea, viewpoint, or item of information substantially prevents the message from being communicated" and that "[t]o the contrary, such restrictions are often limited in scope, restricting expression in only narrowly defined circumstances."). id at 219 (noting that the disparate effects of facially content-based laws is not necessarily greater than the disparate effects of facially content-neutral laws that impose only a modest burden on expression).

[185] 18 USC § 912.

[186] Stone, 25 Wm & Mary L Rev at 200–01 (cited in note 90) (canvasing other examples of facially content-based laws that have only a minimal impact on the speech marketplace).

[187] See notes 207–08, and accompanying text.

[188] Susan Williams has argued, for example, that the Court has understood the anti-discrimination principle too narrowly to adequately protect free speech interests and that laws that "reduc[e] the availability of [particular] point[s] of view in the marketplace" or that "remove[] certain symbols or symbolic activities from the range of expression available to

What this means is that *Reed* likely imperils many laws that pose no significant threat to First Amendment interests. This is certainly what Justice Kagan argued in her concurring opinion in *Reed*, which Justices Breyer and Ginsburg joined.[189] Contra the majority claim that strict scrutiny is the correct standard of review whenever the government employs regulatory distinctions that turn on the content of speech, Kagan argued that it is only when there is a "realistic possibility that [the] official suppression of ideas is afoot" that courts should—and had in the past—applied strict scrutiny.[190] By refusing to employ this "common sense" approach to the content-neutrality analysis, Kagan argued, the majority imperiled thousands of "eminently reasonable" sign laws for no good reason.[191]

There is some evidence already, just two years after the decision was handed down, that Justice Kagan was correct when she predicted that *Reed* would result in the invalidation of many "eminently reasonable" laws. Indeed, by focusing entirely on *Reed*'s impact on sign laws, Justice Kagan may have underestimated the impact of the decision. In *Reed*'s aftermath, lower courts have relied upon the decision to strike down not only sign laws[192] but also panhandling laws,[193]

---

speakers" should also be considered discriminatory. Williams, 139 U Pa L Rev at 620 (cited in note 26). While some facially content-based regulations of speech probably will have these effects, it is unlikely all, even most, will. Even when evaluated according to this more expansive conception of content discrimination, the *Reed* test is in some respects too broad and in other respects too narrow, as I argue in Part IV.

[189] *Reed*, 135 S Ct at 2236 (Kagan, J, concurring).

[190] Id at 2238–39.

[191] Id at 2239 ("As the years go by, courts will discover that thousands of towns have [content-based] ordinances, many of them entirely reasonable. And as the challenges to them mount, courts will have to invalidate one after the other. . . . And courts will strike down those democratically enacted local laws even though no one—certainly not the majority—has ever explained why the vindication of First Amendment values requires that result.").

[192] See, for example, *Central Radio Co. Inc. v City of Norfolk, Va*, 811 F3d 625, 629 (4th Cir 2016) (applying *Reed* to reverse earlier decision holding that sign code that applied to "any sign within the city which is visible from any street, sidewalk or public or private common open space" was content-neutral) (quotation marks omitted); *Citizens for Free Speech, LLC v County of Alameda*, 194 F Supp 3d 968, *3 (N D Cal 2016) (holding that sign code that exempted official public signs from its restrictions was content-based under *Reed* and striking it down on equal protection grounds); *Auspro Enterprises, LP v Tex. Department of Transportation*, 2016 WL 7187475, *13 (Tex App) (striking down as unconstitutional content-based regulations of speech sections of the Texas Highway Beautification Act); *Thomas v Schroer*, 127 F Supp 3d 864, 872–73 (W D Tenn 2015) (granting preliminary injunction to enjoin enforcement of Tennessee Billboard Act after finding that plaintiff had a strong likelihood of succeeding on the merits of a First Amendment challenge to the law).

[193] In *Norton v City of Springfield, Ill.*, for example, the Seventh Circuit reversed its previous decision upholding as content-neutral Springfield's antipanhandling law. 806 F3d 411, 413

election laws,[194] trademark laws,[195] and even state right-of-publicity statutes.[196]

In at least some of these cases, it is far from obvious what First Amendment interests have been vindicated. Consider, for example, two recent decisions in which courts applied *Reed* to strike down facially content-based regulations of speech.

1. *Billboard control.* The first case involved a constitutional challenge to the Texas Highway Beautification Act.[197] The Texas law was enacted in 1972 in response to the passage of the Federal Highway Beautification Act, which, in an effort to "protect the public investment in . . . highways, . . . promote the safety and recreational value of public travel, and . . . preserve natural beauty" required states to impose strict limits on what "advertising signs, displays, and devices" could be erected adjacent to its interstate highways or risk losing a substantial portion of their federal highway funding.[198] As required by the federal law, the Texas Highway Beautification Act prohibited the display, outside of urban areas, of any advertising signs or devices within 660 feet of the interstate highways.[199] Like the federal law, however, it carved out a limited number of exemptions from the general ban on advertising signs and devices. It exempted, for example, "directional [signs], including advertising pertaining to a natural wonder or a scenic or historic attraction"; "outdoor advertising for the sale or lease of the property on which it is located"; "outdoor advertising solely for activities conducted on the property on which it is located"; and "outdoor advertising erected on or before October 22, 1965, that [is] determine[d] to be a landmark of such historic or artistic significance that preservation is consistent with the purposes of [the act]."[200]

(7th Cir 2015), cert denied, 136 S Ct 1173 (2016). See also *Thayer v City of Worcester*, 144 F Supp 3d 218, 221 (D Mass 2015) (reaching the same result based on an application of the *Reed* test); *McLaughlin v City of Lowell*, 140 F Supp 3d 177 (D Mass 2015) (same); *Browne v City of Grand Junction*, 136 F Supp 3d 1276, 1280–82 (D Colo 2015) (same).

[194] *Rideout v Gardner*, 123 F Supp 3d 218 (D NH 2015); *Cahaly v Larosa*, 796 F3d 399, 402 (4th Cir 2015).

[195] *In re Tam*, 808 F3d 1321, 1356 (Fed Cir 2015), as corrected (Feb 11, 2016).

[196] *Sarver v Chartier*, 813 F3d 891, 905–06 (9th Cir 2016).

[197] *Auspro*, 2016 WL 7187475, at *5–6.

[198] 23 USCA § 131(a); 23 USCA § 131(b).

[199] Tex Transportation Code Ann § 391.031(a).

[200] Id at § 391.031(b).

The act distinguished between permitted and prohibited billboards by reference to their content. In a pre-*Reed* decision, the Texas Supreme Court upheld the law as a reasonable content-neutral regulation of speech because it found it was adequately justified by the government's legitimate interest in "stemming visual clutter on the landscape, . . . and promoting travel safety."[201]

Reed changed the rules of the game, however, and when a constitutional challenge to the Texas law was brought before the Texas Court of Appeals in 2016, it concluded that the law should now be considered a content-based regulation of speech to which strict scrutiny applied.[202] After a very cursory analysis of the relationship between the Highway Beautification Act's means and ends, the court found that the law could not satisfy strict scrutiny because the signs it exempted from its billboard ban were not categorically less ugly or less dangerous to the traveling public than the signs it banned.[203] The court therefore concluded that the act was therefore fatally underinclusive with respect to the goal of preventing visual clutter and enhancing traffic safety.[204]

This conclusion is understandable given the tight fit between statutory means and statutory ends that strict scrutiny requires. Indeed, the Court has held that a law fails strict scrutiny if it fails to restrict a significant amount of speech that threatens the same kind of harm as the speech it does restrict.[205] This is because, as noted in Part I, such underinclusiveness casts doubt on the legislature's purported motivations for the law.

In the context of the Texas Highway Beautification Act, though, the statutory exemptions *do not* cast doubt on the legislature's motivations. This is so because to the extent they privilege any particular type of speech it is speech about historically significant places located near the highway and speech advertising goods and services located

---

[201] *Texas Department of Transportation v Barber*, 111 SW3d 86, 100 (Tex 2003).

[202] *Auspro*, 2016 WL 7187475, at *6 ("Under *Reed*'s standard for content neutrality—which simply asks whether the law applies to particular speech because of the topic discussed or the idea or message expressed—the Texas Act's outdoor-advertising regulations are clearly content based.").

[203] Id.

[204] Id.

[205] See, for example, *Florida Star*, 491 US at 540; *Carey*, 447 US at 468.

adjacent to the highway (gas stations, as well as antique stores).[206] This is precisely the kind of speech the state would logically want to privilege if it was trying to promote the recreational value of public travel—which of course was exactly what Congress was trying to do when it passed the Highway Beautification Act, and what the Texas legislature claimed it was doing when it enacted the Texas Highway Beautification Act.[207]

Nor are there other reasons to be concerned about the law's effect on free speech. Its impact on the marketplace of ideas is unlikely to be significantly distorting. Although the act privileges speech about attractions and activities located near the highway, it does not privilege or burden any particular ideas or messages or topics. Directional markers can direct travelers to all kinds of places. Local advertising signs can advertise all kinds of goods. And the law defines advertising broadly to include noncommercial as well as commercial messages.[208] In fact, at least some of the statutory exemptions can reasonably be understood as efforts by Congress, and, by proxy, by the Texas legislature, to *lessen* the distorting effects of the act by exempting from its application those most likely to have no other feasible alternative than highway billboards to advertise their goods and services to the public: namely, those small businesses located along the side of the road.[209]

The most obvious reading of the law, in other words, is that it represents an effort to reconcile a number of important but competing interests: on the one hand, its aesthetic interest in the "natural

---

[206] See *State v Lauderdale, LP*, 2003 WL 1948903, at *1 (Tex App) (noting that to qualify as exempt under the Texas law, directional signs must provide "information useful to the traveler in locating [an] attraction or activity, such as mileage, route numbers, or exit numbers . . . cannot contain descriptive words or phrases or pictorial or photographic representations of the activity . . . and must meet the size and spacing requirements set forth in the statute.").

[207] Tex Transportation Code Ann § 391.002 (declaring the purposes of the law to be to "(1) promote the health, safety, welfare, morals, convenience, and enjoyment of the traveling public; and (2) protect the public investment in the interstate and primary systems").

[208] Tex Transportation Code Ann § 391.001 (defining "outdoor advertising" to mean "an[y] outdoor sign, display, light, device, figure, painting, drawing, message, plaque, poster, billboard, or other thing designed, intended, or used to advertise or inform"); *Barber*, 111 SW3d at 99 ("T[he] [Texas] Act defines 'outdoor advertising' broadly. It includes both commercial and noncommercial speech.").

[209] This is at least how courts have understood these exemptions. See *State v Lotze*, 593 P2d 811, 814 (Wash 1979), abrogated on other grounds by *Collier v City of Tacoma*, 854 P2d 1046 (Wash 1993) (interpreting the exemption in the Washington Highway Beautification Act as a legislative effort to ensure that those who owned property adjacent to the highway did not lose all means of advertising to the public); id at 815 (noting that "[a] total prohibition of on-premise business signs . . . may violate the First Amendment [by] deny[ing] the only available channel of communication to one trying to identify, rather than merely advertise his business or property").

beauty" of the landscape; on the other hand, its interest in the safety and convenience of the traveling public; and on the third hand, its interest in ensuring that the act does not deprive those who rely especially upon highway advertising to communicate information about their products, land, or services of what for them is an important means of communicating. This is the kind of reconciling of interests that legislatures are routinely allowed to do when they enact content-neutral laws.[210]

It is therefore not surprising that, when characterized as content-neutral, the Texas Highway Beautification Act was found to be sufficiently narrowly tailored to survive constitutional scrutiny but, when characterized as content-based, it was not. Indeed, it is difficult to see how any of the remaining forty-nine state highway beautification acts, or the federal law, will be able to survive strict scrutiny, given the stringent tailoring now required by *Reed*.[211] In fact, a Tennessee court recently issued an injunction against enforcement of the Tennessee Billboard Act after finding, on similar grounds as the Texas court, that the plaintiff had a strong likelihood of succeeding on his First Amendment challenge to the act.[212] It is nevertheless hard to see what First Amendment interests are promoted by requiring Congress and the states either to prohibit all highway billboards or to prohibit none of them. Yet this is what the Texas decision portends.

2. *Robocalls.* Consider now a second post-*Reed* case—this time involving a First Amendment challenge to South Carolina's antiro-

[210] See *Taxpayers for Vincent*, 466 US at 810–11 (concluding that a content-neutral law that prohibited the posting of all signs on public property was narrowly tailored to promote the city's aesthetic interests even though it failed to do anything about the aesthetic problems created by the posting of signs on private property because "[t]he private citizen's interest in controlling the use of his own property justifies the disparate treatment"); *Metromedia, Inc.*, 453 US at 510–12 (plurality) (upholding as content-neutral city ordinance that banned offsite advertising but not onsite advertising on the grounds that "the prohibition of offsite advertising is directly related to the stated objectives of traffic safety and esthetics" and "[t]his is not altered by the fact that the ordinance is underinclusive because it permits onsite advertising").

[211] The federal government was sufficiently worried about this possibility when *Reed* made its way to the Court that it filed an amicus brief in which it urged the Court to strike the Gilbert sign law down but not by applying so broad a test of content-based lawmaking that it would imperil the Federal Highway Beautification Act. See Brief for the United States as Amicus Curiae Supporting Petitioners, *Reed v Town of Gilbert, Ariz.*, Docket No 13-502, *8 (US filed Sept 22, 2014) (available on Westlaw at 2014 WL 472504) (arguing that the Court should apply intermediate scrutiny to strike down the Gilbert sign law but not "the more carefully calibrated Highway Beautification Act").

[212] *Schroer*, 127 F Supp 3d at 874–75 (finding that the Tennessee Billboard Act was content-based but unlikely to satisfy strict scrutiny because it was "hopelessly underinclusive").

bocall law.[213] The law prohibited the use of automatic dialing devices to make unsolicited phone calls ("robocalls") for commercial and some political purposes.[214] The law exempted from its general ban calls made to persons with whom the robocaller had an existing or previous business relationship but imposed numerous restrictions on those robocalls that were allowed.[215]

Robert Cahaly, a Republican political consultant, challenged the law on First Amendment grounds after he was charged with illegally making political robocalls in six South Carolina legislative districts in the weeks leading up to an election.[216] Invoking *Reed*, the Fourth Circuit invalidated the law as a content-based regulation of speech.[217] The court assumed, for purposes of argument, that the law furthered a compelling state interest—namely, it protected residential privacy and tranquility from the unwanted intrusion of unsolicited robocalls.[218] It nevertheless found that the law failed strict scrutiny because it was not the least restrictive means by which the state could have promoted this compelling interest. The court argued that, rather than banning only select robocalls, South Carolina could have protected residential privacy by imposing time-of-day limitations, requiring mandatory disclosure of the robocaller's identity, or creating a do-not-call list.[219]

This conclusion follows naturally from *Reed*. The least-restrictive-means requirement has been an integral part of the strict-scrutiny analysis for many decades;[220] it has been justified as yet another means by which courts ensure that the government's motivations are what it says they are.[221]

---

[213] *Cahaly*, 796 F3d 399.

[214] Id at 402.

[215] Id at 402–03 (quoting SC Code Ann § 16-17-446) (noting that the law required permitted robocalls to "disconnect immediately when the called party hangs up"; "[to be] made between 8:00 AM and 7:00 PM" and required those who made robocalls to disclose their identity and the purpose of the call to those they called).

[216] Id at 404.

[217] Id at 402.

[218] Id at 405.

[219] Id.

[220] *Playboy*, 529 US at 813; *Sable Communications of Cal, Inc. v FCC*, 492 US 115, 126 (1989).

[221] See Stone, 25 Wm & Mary L Rev at 231 (cited in note 90) (interpreting the requirement as a means of ensuring that "the government would have adopted the restriction even in the absence of improper motivation").

In this case, however, the fact that South Carolina did not employ what the court considered to be the least restrictive means available does not suggest that its motivations for enacting the antirobocall law were censorial. This is so because all of the supposed less restrictive alternatives have obvious and significant weaknesses. There is by now plenty of evidence that do-not-call lists provide relatively weak protection against the problem of robocalls.[222] Mandatory disclosure does little to prevent one of the problems associated with robocalls: namely, the annoying ringing of the telephone, particularly at dinnertime.[223] And, of course, time-of-day limitations preserve residential privacy only during certain times of the day.

One can therefore well understand why South Carolina might have chosen to address the problem of robocalls directly, by means of a ban on *some* robocalls. The problem of invasive robocalls exists almost entirely because of commercial telemarketers who, over the past three decades, have increasingly turned to inexpensive automated calling technology to reach consumers.[224] The result has been what some have described as an "epidemic" of robocalling.[225] As the FTC noted in 2013 testimony to the Senate, complaints about commercial robocalls increased from 63,000 per month in the fourth quarter of 2009 to 200,000 per month in the fourth quarter of 2012.[226]

---

[222] See Maria G. Hibbard, *Hanging Up Too Early: Remedies to Reduce Robocalls*, 5 Case W Reserve J L Tech & Internet 79, 79–80 (2014) ("Despite the prevalence of the National Do Not Call Registry, telemarketing still plagues millions of Americans. . . . Although the F[ederal] T[rade] C[omission]'s Do Not Call Registry, the national list of consumers who do not wish to receive telemarketing calls, has significantly reduced the number of unwanted telemarketing calls . . . from legitimate marketers who honor the system and recognize the importance of respecting consumer choice, illegitimate companies and telemarketers . . . continue to abuse the market with growing frequency.") (quotations omitted).

[223] The Minnesota Supreme Court put the point very nicely in *Humphrey v Casino Marketing Group, Inc.*, 491 NW2d 882 (Minn 1992). The Court wrote: "[T]he residential telephone is uniquely intrusive. The caller, who can convey messages which very young children can understand, is able to enter the home for expressive purposes without contending with such barriers as time or distance, doors or fences. . . . Moreover, the shrill and imperious ring of the telephone demands immediate attention. . . . Indeed, for the elderly or disabled, the note of urgency sounded by the ring of the telephone signals a journey which may subject the subscriber to the risk of injury. Unlike the radio or the television, whose delivery of speech, either commercial or noncommercial, depends on the listener's summons, the telephone summons the subscriber, depriving him or her of the ability to select the expression to which he or she will exposè herself or himself." Id at 888–89.

[224] Hibbard, 5 Case W Reserve J L Tech & Internet at 82–85 (cited in note 222).

[225] *Rage Against Robocalls*, Consumer Reports (July 28, 2015).

[226] Stopping Fraudulent Robocall Scams: Can More Be Done?, Hearing before the Subcommittee on Consumer Protection, Product Safety, and Insurance of the Senate Committee

There is also some evidence that consumers perceive commercial robocalls—robocalls made by telemarketers—as more invasive than robocalls made by schools, charitable organizations, and other nonprofit entities. Indeed, this is precisely what Congress found in 1991, when it enacted the federal antirobocall law, the Telephone Consumer Protection Act.[227]

By prohibiting commercial but not charitable robocalls—by making it illegal to use an automated dialing device to sell products but allowing it to be used to invite friends to a birthday party or to send out a weather forecast—South Carolina was not making an arbitrary, and therefore presumably invidious, distinction.[228] It was instead targeting the primary source of the evil it was trying to combat.

This is not to say that the South Carolina law was unproblematic. In addition to prohibiting commercial robocalls, it also prohibited some political robocalls.[229] The state was unable to provide any evidence to the court for why these kinds of robocalls posed a more serious threat to residential privacy than the nonprofit robocalls the law permitted.[230] In this respect, the law was, as the Fourth Circuit noted, overinclusive, insofar as it prohibited both speech the state had

---

on Commerce, Science, and Transportation, 113th Cong, 1st Sess 10 (2013) (testimony of Lois Greisman, Associate Director of the Division of Marketing Practices, FTC Bureau of Consumer Protection). See also Telephone Advertising Consumer Rights Act, HR Rep No 102-317, 102d Cong, 1st Sess 16 (1991) ("Complaint statistics show that unwanted commercial calls are a far bigger problem than unsolicited calls from political or charitable organizations.").

[227] Telephone Consumer Protection Act ("TCPA"), 47 USC § 227; HR Rep No 102-317 at 16 (cited in note 226) (noting that evidence gathered during drafting of the TCPA suggested that "[i]n addition to the relative low volume of non-commercial calls, . . . such calls are less intrusive to consumers because they are more expected" and concluding that "the two main sources of consumer problems—high volume of solicitations and unexpected solicitations—are not present in solicitations by nonprofit organizations").

[228] See Opening and Response Brief of Appellee/Cross-Appellant, *Canhaly v Larosa*, Docket No 14-1651(L), 14-1680, *35 (4th Cir filed Oct 21, 2014) (available on Westlaw at 2014 WL 5360252).

[229] The South Carolina Attorney General, clearly uncomfortable about the scope of the prohibition against political robocalls, wrote an opinion shortly before the incidents that led to Cahaly's arrest that interpreted the South Carolina law, despite its broad wording, to prohibit only those political robocalls that were most like commercial robocalls: namely, those that specifically advocated for a particular candidate. *Cahaly*, 796 F3d at 403–04. Survey and other election-related robocalls, the Attorney General indicated, were permitted by the South Carolina law. Id at 404.

[230] Id at 406.

reason to believe posed a particular threat to residential privacy and speech that didn't.[231]

Nothing in the Fourth Circuit opinion turned on the overinclusivity of the South Carolina law, however. It was its failure to employ the least restrictive means available to protecting residential privacy that doomed the law. This suggests that the Fourth Circuit would have struck down the law had South Carolina, like many states and the federal government, prohibited only unsolicited commercial robocalls. Yet it is not clear what First Amendment interests would be advanced by doing so. There is little reason to believe that these laws are the product of a discriminatory purpose. Nor is their impact on the marketplace of ideas likely to be significant. The South Carolina law, like the federal and many similar state antirobocall laws, do not prohibit phone calls; they merely prohibit automated phone calls.[232]

By raising the costs of making robocalls, these laws attempt to encourage those who use this device to be more selective in whom they call. Given pervasive consumer unhappiness with the problem of unwanted robocalls, this does not seem to be an unreasonable thing for the legislature to attempt to do. And yet, in the name of expressive equality, *Reed* imperils these, as well as other, antirobocall laws.

D. IMPLICATIONS

These examples demonstrate how difficult *Reed* makes it for the government to defend facially content-based laws against constitutional challenge, even when there are good reasons for the government to employ the content distinctions it did. They give some idea of why, although the ideal of the color-blind society has long been an aspirational trope (wrongly or rightly) in equal protection law, free speech law has never been organized around the ideal of a content-blind society. This is because what Paul Brest argued was true of racial classifications is absolutely not true of content classifications: namely, they do not "correlate[] so weakly with the legitimate characteristics for which [they] might be used as a proxy that . . . society loses little if they are presumptively forbidden."[233] Instead, the costs may be significant.

---

[231] Id.

[232] See, for example, 47 USC § 227; SC Code Ann § 16-17-446.

[233] Paul Brest, *Foreword: In Defense of the Antidiscrimination Principle*, 90 Harv L Rev 1, 11 (1976).

Of course, any system of prophylactic rules is likely to result in the invalidation of some laws that do not pose the problem the prophylaxis is designed to combat. That is the nature of prophylactic rules, and what makes them both useful and frequently controversial.[234] In this case, however, the number of false positives that *Reed* is likely to produce is higher than the Court has indicated, in its equal protection cases at least, it will ordinarily allow.

That it is willing to allow a significant number of entirely legitimate speech regulations to be invalidated under the *Reed* test presumably reflects the Court's view that there is no adequate alternative test of content-based lawmaking, given the very evident problems with the "justified without reference" test canvassed in Part II. This is not an unreasonable belief, but as the next part argues, it may be a mistaken one. This is because it is far from obvious that the problems with the justification test are an inevitable feature of the test, or evidence of lower courts' unwillingness to protect speech unless absolutely forced to do so by the Court. Instead, many of the problems with the justified test can be blamed on the Court itself. In this respect, *Reed* may be a case of chickens coming home to roost: the Court turning to an extremely broad test of content-based lawmaking in response to its own failure to interpret the more nuanced "justified without reference" test with rigor.

What this suggests is that, even if the test of content-based lawmaking that *Reed* announces is an improvement over what came before, it may nevertheless represent a second-best solution to the very serious problem of pretextual discrimination—and one that is likely to create significant doctrinal problems in the future.

IV. Alternatives and Implications

The fact that the anticlassificatory test of content-based lawmaking that *Reed* announces imposes such significant constraints on the government's legitimate regulatory authority suggests that the decision should be considered a good solution to the problem of pretextual discrimination only if there are no other, less restrictive but

[234] On this point, see David Strauss, *The Ubiquity of Prophylactic Rules*, 55 U Chi L Rev 190 (1988).

equally effective means of guarding against the repressive impulses of both judges and legislatures.

One might think, given the discussion of pre-*Reed* lower court opinions in Part II, that there isn't: that when provided with the more discretionary "justified without reference to content" test of content-based lawmaking, lower courts failed to interpret it in a way that vigorously enforced free speech values or protected speakers against pretextual discrimination. Given that record, one might argue that a highly formal, bright-line test like the one announced in *Reed* provides the only effective, if imperfect, means of enforcing the First Amendment's antidiscrimination principle.[235]

It is not obvious, however, that this is true. Although lower courts tended to apply the "justified without reference" test in the years prior to *Reed* in an overly lenient manner, there is no reason to assume that this leniency was due to the lower courts' refusal to vigorously enforce the speech-protective rules the Supreme Court handed them. To the contrary, in taking the government's claimed justifications at face value, the lower courts were simply following the Court's own example. Indeed, almost all of the problems with the lower courts' approach to the justification inquiry during this period can be traced to the Supreme Court itself.

A. THE DEVOLUTION OF THE JUSTIFICATION TEST

In *Police Department of the City of Chicago v Mosley*,[236] the Court first articulated the general framework for cases involving potentially discriminatory regulations of public speech. The case involved a Chicago ordinance that prohibited the picketing of city public schools while they were in session and for half an hour before and after school was in session but that made an exception for picketing that occurred outside schools involved in labor disputes.[237] The city interpreted the ordinance to ban all kinds of picketing outside schools (including

[235] Seth Kreimer has argued so much. In a pre-*Reed* article, he argued that the anticlassificatory test of content-based lawmaking articulated in cases such as *Arkansas Writers Project* and *Simon & Schuster* was superior to the alternative because, as a bright-line test, it generated results that were "less likely to be distorted by heuristics of fear and outrage" and therefore was "well adapted to counterbalance [the] predictable cognitive biases that warp [judicial] judgments." Kreimer, 16 U Pa J Const L at 1316, 1318 (cited in note 15).

[236] 408 US 92.

[237] Id at 102.

schools involved in labor disputes) *except* labor pickets.[238] The Court concluded that, construed as such, the ordinance violated both the Equal Protection Clause and the First Amendment because it restricted speech because of its content.[239]

The Court reached the conclusion that the ordinance was content-based because the city was unable to offer any legitimate reason for the distinction between labor and nonlabor picketing. The city argued, for example, that it prohibited picketing, except for labor pickets, near schools in order to prevent disruption of the educational experience. The Court rejected this argument because the government provided no evidence demonstrating that nonlabor pickets were more disruptive than labor pickets. "Although preventing school disruption is a city's legitimate concern," Justice Marshall noted, "Chicago itself has determined that peaceful labor picketing during school hours is not an undue interference with school. Therefore . . . Chicago may not maintain that other picketing disrupts the school unless that picketing is *clearly more disruptive* than the picketing Chicago already permits."[240]

Similarly, the Court rejected the government's claim that it exempted labor pickets from the law in order to avoid intruding on a sphere of activity normally governed by federal labor law.[241] It rejected this argument because it found that the city's desire to avoid the legal headaches caused by the potentially preemptive effect of federal labor law was insufficient to justify the labor exemption. "This attenuated interest," Marshall wrote, "at best a claim of small administrative convenience and perhaps merely a confession of legislative laziness, cannot justify the blanket permission given to labor picketing and the blanket prohibition applicable to others."[242]

Mosley established the principle that what is required to justify a speech regulation that involves "differential treatment" on the basis of content is clear evidence that the distinction actually furthers, or is likely to further, a significant governmental interest. In *Carey v*

---

[238] Id at 94 n 2 (noting that although "[b]y its terms, the statute exempts 'the peaceful picketing of any school involved in a labor dispute[,]' [i]t is undisputed that this exemption applies only to labor picketing of a school involved in a labor dispute.").

[239] Id at 92.

[240] Id at 212.

[241] Id at 102 n 9.

[242] Id.

Brown, eight years later, the Court reemphasized this point when it insisted, in the course of striking down a similar law, that "[w]hen government regulation discriminates among speech-related activities in a public forum . . . any distinctions it draws must be carefully scrutinized."[243]

In subsequent decisions, however, the Court failed to insist on clear evidence that the distinctions speech regulations drew actually furthered an "appropriate government interest." Instead, it interpreted the justification test to require only evidence showing that the government did not *intend* to repress ideas.

Renton provides perhaps the most egregious example of the Court's tendency, in these cases, to shy away from a rigorous application of *Mosley*. As noted earlier, *Renton* involved a First Amendment challenge to a local zoning ordinance that prohibited adult movie theaters from locating close to schools, churches, and other specified places.[244] The Ninth Circuit held that the zoning ordinance was unconstitutional because the city was unable to show that it actually furthered, or was likely to further, a substantial government interest.[245] To justify the law, the city relied almost entirely on studies of the secondary effects of adult movie theaters in other cities, of very different size and character.[246] The Ninth Circuit held that this was not adequate. "Renton has not studied the effects of adult theaters and applied any such findings to the particular problems or needs of Renton," the court wrote. "We do not say that Renton cannot use the experiences of other cities as part of the relevant evidence upon which to base its actions, but in this case those experiences simply are not sufficient to sustain Renton's burden of showing a significant governmental interest."[247]

The Supreme Court reversed this decision because it concluded that the city *was* entitled to rely upon the evidence compiled by other cities. "The First Amendment does not require a city," Justice Rehn-

---

[243] *Carey*, 447 US at 461–62.

[244] Id at 47.

[245] *Playtime Theaters, Inc. v City of Renton*, 748 F2d 527, 537 (9th Cir 1984).

[246] Renton relied, for example, upon studies conducted in Detroit, a much larger city and one in which the legislature had implemented a very different zoning law than that which Renton implemented. *Renton*, 475 US at 46 (noting that the Detroit law dispersed theaters, rather than concentrating them).

[247] 748 F2d at 536–37.

quist wrote, "before enacting such an ordinance, to conduct new studies or produce evidence independent of that already generated by other cities, so long as whatever evidence the city relies upon *is reasonably believed to be relevant* to the problem that the city addresses."[248] The Court held that any more rigorous standard would limit the ability of municipalities like Renton to adequately respond to novel social problems.[249] The result of the Court requiring (as Justice Kennedy later put it) only "very little evidence" to uphold facially content-based zoning laws was to make it easier for governments to pretextually justify discrimination.[250] *Renton*, in other words, "elevate[d] motive—which is easy for governments to fake and hard for courts to assess—over the more objective application and justification inquiries" the Court had previously used to deal with content-based discrimination.[251]

Renton was not the only Supreme Court opinion to embrace this approach. A few years later, in *Ward v Rock Against Racism*, the Court once again emphasized intent over evidence, albeit this time in a case involving a challenge to a facially content-neutral law. The case involved a regulation that required performers at a Central Park bandshell to use a sound amplification engineer provided by the city.[252] Rock Against Racism, a group that organized charity rock concerts in the bandshell, argued that the law was content-based because it privileged a particular conception of sound quality (the city's conception) and discriminated against its very different conception of what counted as quality sound. The Court rejected this argument because it found no evidence in the record that the city was attempting to impose a particular aesthetic ideal on performers. To the contrary, it found evidence that the city "require[d] its sound technician to defer to the wishes of event sponsors concerning sound mix."[253] More generally, the Court concluded that the regulation was content-

---

[248] *Renton*, 475 US at 51–52.

[249] Id at 52 ("The city must be allowed a reasonable opportunity to experiment with solutions to admittedly serious problems" (quoting *American Mini Theatres, Inc.*, 427 US at 71 (plurality)).

[250] *Alameda Books*, 535 US at 451 (Kennedy, J, concurring) ("[W]e have consistently held that a city must have latitude to experiment, at least at the outset, and that very little evidence is required.").

[251] Rienzi and Buck, 82 Fordham L Rev at 1200 (cited in note 110).

[252] *Ward*, 491 US at 787–88.

[253] Id at 792–93.

neutral because "the principal inquiry in determining content neutrality . . . is whether the government has adopted a regulation of speech because of disagreement with the message it conveys." In this case, the Court found that the city's principal justification for the regulation—namely, that it was intended to "control noise levels at bandshell events"—did not evince a desire to repress speech because the government disliked its message.

In reaching the conclusion that the sound regulation was adequately justified by a content-neutral purpose, the Court may have been correct. There was ample evidence that New York was not trying to repress the expression of messages or music it disliked, nor attempting to do anything other than what it said it was trying to do.[254] The Court's conclusion that the law was content-neutral did not rest on this evidence, however. Instead, the Court relied solely on the city's assertions of regulatory purpose—and the district court's finding that the city enforced the law with deference to the wishes of concert organizers.[255]

The opinion thus suggested that what the government had to show to establish the content neutrality of a speech regulation was *not* clear evidence that the speech it restricted differed in some relevant way from the speech it did not restrict, but merely the existence of some plausible, nondiscriminatory purpose it intended the regulation to further. This is certainly how lower courts subsequently interpreted the decision. The Eighth Circuit, for example, relied heavily on *Ward*'s "principal inquiry" language to justify its conclusion in *Thorburn* that, because the targeted picketing law was not intended to suppress any particular messages, but applied to all targeted picketing, it was content-neutral and subject only to intermediate scrutiny.[256]

---

[254] Prior to enacting the speech regulation, the city attempted on several occasions to achieve a less speech-restrictive solution to the problem of excessive noise at the bandshell, and specifically the noise problems generated by the respondent in the case. Id at 784–88 (noting the "numerous complaints about excessive sound amplification" the city received and its multiple efforts to negotiate a solution with Rock Against Racism).

[255] Id at 792.

[256] *Thorburn*, 231 F3d at 1117 ("Because the Lincoln ordinance regulates protected speech in a public forum, we first determine whether the ordinance is content-neutral or content-based in order to apply the appropriate level of scrutiny. The government cannot regulate speech because it disagrees with the message conveyed. . . . Lincoln does not disagree with a particular message; the ordinance applies equally to anyone engaged in focused picketing without regard to his message. Because Lincoln's justification for the ordinance is the protection of residential privacy and tranquility and has nothing to do with the content of the regulated speech, the ordinance is content-neutral.").

The Ninth Circuit also relied upon *Ward* to conclude that the Gilbert sign ordinance was content-neutral because it was not obviously motivated by animus.[257]

These opinions do not, in other words, demonstrate the unwillingness of lower courts to follow Supreme Court precedents. Rather, they demonstrate how inconsistent the Court has been in articulating the requirements of the justification test. They suggest, as a result, that the Court did not necessarily need to embrace the highly formalist test of content-based lawmaking that *Reed* announced in order to ensure that lower courts carefully evaluated potentially discriminatory speech regulations. Instead, the Court could merely have reaffirmed the rigorous standards that *Mosley* and other earlier cases insisted courts should apply when reviewing regulations of speech.

B. A MISSED OPPORTUNITY

Imagine an alternative universe in which, rather than denying that government purpose has any role to play in the content-neutrality inquiry, the Court in *Reed* had instead concluded that the Gilbert ordinance was unconstitutional because the town failed to present any clear evidence that the distinctions it drew actually furthered its legitimate interests in reducing traffic accidents and maintaining the municipality's aesthetic appeal. This is largely what Justice Kagan's concurring opinion concluded.[258]

Such an approach would have been superior to the approach taken in *Reed* in a number of ways. First, it would not have established a significantly overbroad rule. It would not, in other words, have required the application of strict scrutiny even in cases where the government has good reasons to employ the distinctions it employs.

Second, and as a consequence, it would not have created a situation in which courts would be encouraged to apply the test narrowly, or to dilute the meaning of strict scrutiny to uphold laws they perceived to be entirely reasonable but that *Reed* designated as content-based.

---

[257] *Reed*, 707 F3d at 1074–75.

[258] *Reed*, 135 S Ct at 2239 (Kagan, J, concurring) ("The absence of any sensible basis for [the distinctions between directional, ideological, and political signs] dooms the Town's ordinance under even the intermediate scrutiny that the Court typically applies to 'time, place, or manner' speech regulations. Accordingly, there is no need to decide in this case whether strict scrutiny applies to every sign ordinance in every town across this country containing a subject-matter exemption.").

Justice Breyer warned in his concurring opinion that the majority rule might lead courts to "water[] down the force of the presumption against constitutionality that 'strict scrutiny' normally carries with it," thereby "weaken[ing] the First Amendment's protection in instances where 'strict scrutiny' should apply in full force."[259] This is certainly a concern. But it is equally plausible that courts will simply apply the decision as narrowly as possible to avoid reaching unpalatable conclusions.

Indeed, there is already plenty of evidence that courts are construing *Reed* narrowly in order to avoid reaching undesirable results. For example, in cases involving the regulation of strip clubs and other forms of adult entertainment, courts have continued to apply the *Renton* test of content neutrality rather than the much stricter *Reed* test.[260] This is notwithstanding the fact that, as a judge on the First Circuit acknowledged recently, the two opinions are "logically irreconcilable."[261]

These decisions demonstrate how *Reed*'s potentially more radical implications may be domesticated by the lower courts. They also, however, complicate the argument that *Reed*, because it is a formal test, provides more reliable protection against discrimination than the "justified without reference" inquiry. They suggest that formalism is not necessarily the best way to combat judicial bias, particularly in cases where the formal rule strikes judges as unreasonable. This is particularly the case given the very complicated doctrinal structure of much of First Amendment law.[262] The proliferating array

---

[259] Id at 2235 (Brennan, J, concurring).

[260] See, for example, *Cricket Store 17, LLC v City of Columbia*, 2017 WL 360545 (4th Cir); *American Entertainers, LLC v City of Rocky Mount, NC*, 2016 WL 4728077, *11 (EDNC); *BBL, Inc. v City of Angola*, 809 F3d 317, 326 n 1 (7th Cir 2015) (refusing to apply *Reed* on the grounds that "[w]e don't think *Reed* upends established doctrine for evaluating regulation of businesses that offer sexually explicit entertainment, a category the Court has said occupies the outer fringes of First Amendment protection"). See also *Free Speech Coalition, Inc. v Attorney General United States*, 825 F3d 149, 161 n 8 (3d Cir 2016) (citation omitted) ("Although we do not reach the issue, we . . . [think] that it is doubtful that *Reed* has overturned the *Renton* secondary effects doctrine.").

[261] *Free Speech Coalition*, 825 F3d at 174 (Rendell dissenting).

[262] See, for example, Geoffrey R. Stone, *Free Speech in the Twenty-First Century: Ten Lessons from the Twentieth Century*, 36 Pepperdine L Rev 273, 274 (2009) (noting that First Amendment doctrine is "maddeningly complex"); Kagan, 63 U Chi L Rev at 515 (cited in note 25) (noting that the "technical, complex classificatory schemes of First Amendment law" have only become "more intricate [over time], as categories have multiplied, distinctions grown increasingly fine, and exceptions flourished and become categories of their own"); Williams, 139 U Pa L Rev at 616 (cited in note 26) ("The doctrinal web surrounding the free speech

of categorical distinctions that populate free speech doctrine make it quite easy for courts to distinguish *Reed* "up, down, and sideways."[263] The result may be to only intensify what is already a pronounced threat: namely, overarching doctrinal incoherency.[264] It also may inoculate from stringent constitutional scrutiny what are in fact very troubling laws, like the zoning laws at issue in *Renton*.

By not requiring courts to distinguish the decision away, a revitalized justification test might, ironically, have provided more protection to speakers targeted by certain kinds of facially content-based laws. It also would have altered the standards that apply to the review of facially content-neutral as well as to the review of facially content-based regulations.

One of the great disadvantages of anticlassificatory rules like the one announced in *Reed* is that they make the stringency of the constitutional analysis depend almost entirely on the presence of proscribed classifications. But the fact that a statute fails to employ suspect classifications does not, by any means, imply that it is not a tool of discriminatory aims. Although it may be the case, for reasons discussed in Part II, that statutes that classify on the basis of race, or content, or other suspect classifications are more likely than other kinds of laws to reflect a discriminatory purpose, facially neutral laws can also provide a perfectly serviceable tool for carrying out unlawful purposes. Scholars of the Equal Protection Clause have argued in fact that today it is *primarily* by means of facially neutral laws that race and gender biases continue to be given effect in American law.[265] The

---

clause of the first amendment is one of the most complicated and confusing areas in constitutional law.").

[263] Note, *Free Speech Doctrine After Reed v. Town of Gilbert*, 129 Harv L Rev 1981, 1990–1992 (2016) (documenting the various ways in which courts have distinguished *Reed*).

[264] Post, 47 Stan L Rev at 1275 (cited in note 48) (arguing that the "Court's First Amendment jurisprudence, which is a lively and growing area of constitutional law, dances now macabrely on the edge of complete doctrinal disintegration"); Paul Horwitz, *Universities as First Amendment Institutions: Some Easy Answers and Hard Questions*, 54 UCLA L Rev 1497, 1497 (2007) (noting "increasing sense" that First Amendment doctrine "has become incoherent").

[265] Siegel, 49 Stan L Rev at 1143 (cited in note 121) ("Today doctrines of heightened scrutiny function primarily to constrain legislatures from adopting policies designed to reduce race and gender stratification, while doctrines of discriminatory purpose offer only weak constraints on the forms of facially neutral state action that continue to perpetuate the racial and gender stratification of American society."); John Tyler Clemons, *Blind Injustice: The Supreme Court, Implicit Racial Bias, and the Racial Disparity in the Criminal Justice System*, 51 Am Crim L Rev 689, 700 (2014) (arguing that the facially neutral operation of the criminal justice system is pervaded by racial bias, both implicit and explicit).

Court's unwavering commitment to an anticlassificatory approach to equal protection, they argue, provides as a result extremely poor protection against the often subtle forms of discrimination that perpetuate racial and other kinds of inequality in contemporary society.[266]

The Court's embrace of an anticlassificatory approach to the First Amendment raises the same concern. As Timothy Zick has noted, facially neutral speech regulations—regulations that distinguish between speakers on the basis of their location, or the genre of their speech, or some other, noncontent features of that speech—can serve as "powerful weapon[s] of social and political control."[267] *Reed* certainly incentivizes legislators who want to discriminate to figure out a facially neutral means of doing so. And yet the decision does nothing to address the very palpable weaknesses with the justification test, as it presently exists.

Of course, nothing prevents the Court from making clear, in a future decision, that a law is not justified by a content-neutral purpose simply because the government says it is. The analogy to the equal protection cases suggests, however, that this is unlikely to occur. Scholars have complained for decades now about the weakness of the test of discrimination the Court has developed to smoke out discriminatory purpose in equal protection cases involving facially neutral laws, but to no avail.[268] This is not surprising if one understands the

---

[266] Siegel, 49 Stan L Rev at 1137 (cited in note 121) (arguing that "the empirical literature on racial bias suggests that . . . [given contemporary precedents], most race-dependent governmental decisionmaking will elude equal protection scrutiny"); Randall L. Kennedy, *McClesky v. Kemp: Race, Capital Punishment, and the Supreme Court*, 101 Harv L Rev 1388, 1419–20 (1988) (noting that, by requiring evidence of purposeful discrimination—at least in cases involving facially neutral laws—the Court has "articulate[d] a conception of discrimination that ignores the chameleonlike ability of prejudice to adapt unobtrusively to new surroundings and, further, to hide itself even from those firmly within its grip" and "manifest views attuned only to the most blatant deprivations of the equal protection of the laws").

[267] Timothy Zick, *Speech and Spatial Tactics*, 84 Tex L Rev 581, 582 (2006). Zick cites as an example the 25-block restricted zone that prohibited all protests within 25 blocks of the 1990 World Trade Organization meetings in Seattle. Id. These protests obviously impacted the ability of the antiglobalization protestors who gathered in Seattle to communicate their message. See *Menotti v City of Seattle*, 409 F3d 1113, 1173 (9th Cir 2005) (Paez, J, concurring and dissenting) (noting that the zone "confined all demonstrations to outside areas where the message the protestors sought to convey may never have reached the intended audience" and left "the WTO protestors . . . silenced and relegated to the sidelines"). Nevertheless, when faced with a First Amendment challenge to the ordinance creating the zone, the Ninth Circuit upheld it as content-neutral, after applying the deferential *Ward* test. *Menotti*, 409 F3d at 1129–30.

[268] See, for example, Charles R. Lawrence III, *The Id, the Ego, and Equal Protection: Reckoning with Unconscious Racism*, 39 Stan L Rev 317, 366–70 (1987); Michael J. Perry, *Modern*

Court's turn to an anticlassificatory test of race discrimination as motivated, at least in part, by its discomfort with vesting courts with the discretionary authority that a more vigorous purposive inquiry would require. In its equal protection jurisprudence, the Court has demonstrated a pronounced unwillingness to allow courts to strike down facially neutral laws absent extremely pronounced evidence of bad intent. There is no reason to believe its approach in First Amendment cases will be any different. The result is that *Reed* is likely to produce a test of content-based lawmaking that is both too broad and too narrow.

C. THE DRAWBACKS

This is not to say that a reinvigorated justification test would have no drawbacks. By requiring courts to determine in most cases whether there is sufficiently clear evidence to justify the differential treatment of speech, it would vest courts with considerably more discretion than they possess under *Reed.*

This discretion could be cabined somewhat by embedding within the test a much narrower anticlassificatory rule. In her concurring opinion, Justice Kagan argued that, although courts should only apply strict scrutiny to laws that make subject matter and other kinds of content distinctions when they raise the "realistic possibility that [the] official suppression of ideas is afoot," they should always apply strict scrutiny to laws that make viewpoint distinctions because laws of this sort always raise doubts about the government's motivations.[269]

This approach to the content discrimination inquiry would certainly not create the problems that the extension of strict scrutiny to subject matter-based and other kinds of content-based laws would, given how infrequently the government employs viewpoint distinctions when it regulates the public sphere, and how difficult it is to think of legitimate reasons why the government might wish to do so. It would also limit the range of cases in which courts would be required

---

Equal Protection: A Conceptualization and Appraisal, 79 Colum L Rev 1023, 1038–39 (1979); Alan David Freeman, *Legitimizing Racial Discrimination through Antidiscrimination Law: A Critical Review of Supreme Court Doctrine*, 62 Minn L Rev 1049, 1053–55 (1978).

[269] *Reed v Town of Gilbert, Ariz.*, 135 S Ct 2218, 2237 (2015) (Kagan, J, concurring).

to evaluate the evidentiary basis of the government's justifications in order to determine the standard of scrutiny that applies.

What a test that applied strict scrutiny to all laws that make viewpoint distinctions would require courts to do, however, is to identify when laws make a viewpoint as opposed to some other kind of content distinction. Given how blurry the line between subject matter and viewpoint distinctions frequently turns out to be, it is not at all clear how much in practice Justice Kagan's narrower anticlassificatory rule would actually constrain the discretion vested courts under the justification test.[270]

A revitalized justification test would constrain judicial discretion in another way, however: namely, by reminding courts of the fundamental constitutional values that motivate the doctrinal rules. Over seventy years ago, in *Schneider v State*, Justice Roberts asserted what remains today a fundamental principle of First Amendment law: namely, that although "[m]ere legislative preferences or beliefs respecting matters of public convenience may . . . support regulation directed at other personal activities, [they are] insufficient to justify such as diminishes the exercise of rights so vital to the maintenance of democratic institutions" as the rights protected by the First Amendment.[271] Hence, Justice Roberts concluded, "the delicate and difficult task falls upon the courts to weigh the circumstances and to appraise the substantiality of the reasons advanced in support of the regulation of the free enjoyment of the[se] rights."[272] A test of content-based lawmaking that required courts, in almost all cases, to evaluate the empirical evidence provided to justify restricting speech in order to determine the level of scrutiny that applies would operate as a continuing reminder of this central First Amendment norm.

---

[270] See Frederick Schauer, *Codifying the First Amendment: New York v. Ferber*, 1982 Supreme Court Review 285, 317 (1982) (expressing skepticism about the existence of a "clear line of demarcation between viewpoint and subject-matter discrimination"); Leslie Kendrick, *Content Discrimination Revisited*, 98 U Va L Rev 231, 243 (2012) (noting the many have argued "that viewpoint classifications are very difficult to distinguish, both descriptively and normatively, from subject-matter classifications."). Members of the Court have certainly disagreed, at times quite vigorously, about whether particular laws can be classified as viewpoint based. See, for example, *R.A.V. v City of St. Paul, Minn.*, 505 US 377, 391–92 (1992) (concluding that law that prohibits use of racially motivated fighting words makes a viewpoint-based distinction); id at 433 (Stevens J, dissenting) (rejecting the conclusion that the law makes a viewpoint-based distinction).

[271] *Schneider v State of New Jersey*, 308 US 147, 161 (1939).

[272] Id.

This may be, ultimately, the best way to guard against the repressive impulses of judges, given the inherent power of courts to make even bright-line tests fuzzy. Vincent Blasi has argued that "[i]t would be a mistake to assume that the strategy for protecting the central norms of the first amendment must emphasize the tactic of doctrinal compulsion—the fashioning of specific, highly protective tests that would bind lower courts and officials in times of stress."[273] This is because, Blasi argued, it is difficult to fashion any legal rule "with sufficient prescience and precision to achieve that type of behavioral effect to any great degree."[274] The complicated ways in which lower courts are already trying to limit the effects of the *Reed* decision provide a good illustration of Blasi's point.

In articulating what Justice Thomas described in his opinion in *Reed* as a "clear and firm" test of content-based lawmaking, the Court may have thus been attempting to guarantee a kind of predictability that no formal test can provide.[275] Meanwhile, it created a test that overly constrains the government's regulatory autonomy in some respects and provides, in other respects, insufficient protection to those targeted by facially neutral laws. Given these serious problems with the *Reed* test, it is hard to see why a revitalized justification test would have provided a worse solution to the problem of content discrimination than that which the *Reed* test provides—and in many respects it would have been far superior.

Of course, the *Reed* majority did not embrace Justice Kagan's alternative solution. *Reed* remains, for now at least, the law. The sheer breadth of the *Reed* test makes it likely, however, that Justice Kagan was correct when she predicted that its application would not be easy or without contestation: that litigants would continue to seek ways to narrow the test and that these efforts would continue to generate difficult questions about the scope and the meaning of the presumption against content-based lawmaking.[276] Despite its efforts to do so,

---

[273] Vincent Blasi, *The Pathological Perspective and the First Amendment*, 85 Colum L Rev 449, 467 (1985).

[274] Id.

[275] *Reed*, 135 S Ct at 2231.

[276] Id at 2239 (Kagan, J, concurring) ("I suspect this Court and others will regret the majority's insistence today on answering that question in the affirmative. As the years go by, courts will discover that thousands of towns have such ordinances, many of them 'entirely reasonable.' . . . And as the challenges to them mount, courts will have to invalidate one after the other. (This Court may soon find itself a veritable Supreme Board of Sign Review.)").

the *Reed* majority may not, in other words, have resolved the decades-long fight over the meaning of the First Amendment antidiscrimination principle. Going forward, it therefore behooves both scholars and courts to remember the costs, as well as the benefits, of an anti-classificatory approach.

NEAL DEVINS AND
LAWRENCE BAUM

SPLIT DEFINITIVE: HOW PARTY POLARIZATION TURNED THE SUPREME COURT INTO A PARTISAN COURT

Since 2010, when Elena Kagan replaced John Paul Stevens, all of the Republican-nominated Justices on the Supreme Court have been to the right of all of its Democratic-nominated Justices.[1] This pattern is widely recognized, but it is not well recognized that it is unique in the Court's history. Before 2010, the Court never had clear ideological blocs that coincided with party lines.

Today's partisan split, while unprecedented, is likely enduring. The very political changes that underlie the current split make it likely that, for the foreseeable future, a Court with five Democratic-nominated

Neal Devins is Sandra Day O'Connor Professor of Law and Professor of Government, William and Mary Law School; Lawrence Baum is Professor Emeritus of Political Science, Ohio State University.

AUTHORS' NOTE: Thanks to our research assistants Caitlin Cater, Peter Kyle, Barbara Marmet, and Amber Shepherd. Thanks also to participants at workshops at Cornell Law School, George Mason Law School, University of California-Berkeley Law School, and Vanderbilt Law School. Thanks too to Geof Stone for his thoughtful edits and to Josh Chafetz, Eric Clayes, Mike Dorf, Paul Edelman, Tara Grove, Peter Schuck, Mark Tushnet, and John Yoo for helpful comments.

[1] When classifying Justices as Democrats or Republicans we are referring to the party of the appointing president. We do so because presidential appointments of Justices are at the heart of our analysis of partisan polarization on the Court. As late as 1971, presidents would sometimes appoint Justices who were associated with a different political party than their own. For reasons detailed throughout this article, there is little prospect of cross-party appointments during the current era.

978-0-226-49084-7/2017/2016-0008$10.00

Justices would reach decisions quite different from those a Court with five Republican-nominated Justices would reach.[2] For this reason, presidential elections matter more for the Court than ever before.

Indeed, the Court was a focal point of the 2016 presidential campaign. Following the sudden death of Antonin Scalia, Democrats and Republicans divided over the propriety of President Obama's appointing a successor during an election year—exposing a deep, divisive gulf between the parties over the very issues that divide the Justices.[3] Democratic candidates Hillary Rodham Clinton and Bernie Sanders spoke both of President Obama's constitutional responsibility to fill the Scalia seat and of their having a "litmus test" for Supreme Court nominees to overturn what Sanders called the "disastrous" *Citizens United* ruling;[4] Republican candidates Donald Trump, Marco Rubio, Jeb Bush, and Ted Cruz backed Senate Republican efforts to block an Obama nominee, proclaimed the 2016 election a "referendum" on the Supreme Court, and spoke of the need for "future Supreme Court[s]" to undo the Roberts Court's decisions on the Affordable Care Act and same-sex marriage.[5] Correspondingly, after

---

[2] For a sampling of post-2010 5–4 decisions along party lines, see note 62.

[3] For discussions of the political import of Scalia's successor and the efforts of Republican Senators to block any Obama nominee to the Court, see *How Antonin Scalia Changed America*, Politico (Feb 14, 2016), archived at https://perma.cc/JP48-LREG; Michael D. Shear and Jennifer Steinhauer, *More Republicans Say They'll Block Supreme Court Nomination*, NY Times (Feb 15, 2016), archived at https://perma.cc/FPS9-SP23. Before Scalia's death, the Court was an emerging election issue; the advanced age of several Justices and the Court's politically charged docket contributed to its electoral significance. See Richard Wolf, *Aging Supreme Court Energizes Republicans More than Democrats in 2016 Race*, USA Today (Oct 25, 2015), archived at https://perma.cc/FC5A-F4SQ; Tony Mauro, *SCOTUS v. Presidential Race*, Natl L J (Jan 4, 2016), archived at https://perma.cc/HD9S-HFSX; Adam Liptak, *Supreme Court Takes on Politically Charged Cases*, NY Times (Oct 4, 2015), archived at https://perma.cc/VZ8D-4CTB.

[4] John Wagner and Anne Gearan, *Clinton, Sanders Agree on This Much in Colorado: GOP Shouldn't Wait on Scalia Replacement*, Wash Post (Feb 13, 2016), archived at https://perma.cc/M5DQ-QXNJ; Martea Gold and Anne Gearan, *Hillary Clinton's Litmus Test for Supreme Court Nominees: A Pledge to Overturn Citizens United*, Wash Post (May 14, 2015), archived at https://perma.cc/6U4S-NEWT (quoting Sanders). Clinton also spoke of having a "bunch of litmus tests," including gay rights and the Voting Rights Act. See Jonathan Easley, *Clinton: "I Have a Bunch of Litmus Tests" for Supreme Court Nominees*, The Hill (Feb 3, 2016), archived at https://perma.cc/VEZ8-FPW9.

[5] Jonathan Martin, *Republican Candidates Unite Against Obama Replacing Scalia*, NY Times (Feb 13, 2016), archived at https://perma.cc/BRA5-BV3D; Liz Fields, *Marco Rubio Says He Has a Plan to Make Gay Marriage Illegal Again*, Vice News (Dec 14, 2015), archived at https://perma.cc/H6ZR-TDKA (quoting Rubio); Bob Egelko, *Trump, Rubio Weigh in on Supreme Court Ahead of Debate*, San Francisco Chronicle (Dec 14, 2015), archived at https://perma.cc/HA2T-YFS3; Katie Zezima, *Ted Cruz Calls for Judicial Retention Elections of Supreme Court*

securing their party's nomination, Clinton and Trump continued to highlight the Republican-Democratic Supreme Court divide. They repeatedly called attention to the Court and, with it, party differences on gun control, immigration, health care, abortion, campaign finance, and voter identification laws.[6]

This article documents that today's Court is different from past Courts in the linkage between party and ideology. More important, it offers an explanation for this development. That explanation is based on the growth in polarization among political elites—polarization that has shaped the Court in multiple ways and that is likely to continue.

One key element of polarization is partisan sorting, in which conservatives increasingly migrate to the Republican Party and liberals to the Democratic Party. Among political elites, the ideological distance between Democrats and Republicans is perhaps greater today than at any other time in the nation's history.[7] Because of partisan sorting, the party leaders who participate in the selection of Justices and the pools of prospective nominees to the Court are more ideologically homogeneous.

A second key element of polarization is growing ideological consciousness among the selectors of Justices and the Justices themselves. Political elites have become more sharply divided into ideological

---

Justices, Wash Post (June 27, 2015), at https://www.washingtonpost.com/news/post-politics/wp/2015/06/27ted-cruz-calls-for-judicial-retention-elections-for-supreme-court-Justices/; Katie Zezima, *Cruz Wants to Make 2016 a Referendum on the Supreme Court: He's Already Done It*, Wash Post (Feb 15, 2016), at https://www.washingtonpost.com/news/post-politics/wp/2016/02/15/cruz-wants-to-make-2016-a-referendum-on-the-supreme-court-hes-already-done-it/?utm_term=.793513a5caad.

[6] For general discussions of differences in party platforms and campaigns, see Melanie Mason and Chris Megerian, *How the Democratic and Republican Party Platforms Stack Up on Climate Change, Iran, and More Key Issues*, LA Times (July 27, 2016), available at http://www.latimes.com/politics/la-na-pol-democrats-republicans-platforms-20160727-snap-htmlstory.html; Jonathan D. Salant, *10 Huge Differences Between Democratic and Republican Platforms*, nj.com (July 28, 2016), available at http://www.nj.com/politics/index.ssf/2016/07/dnc_2016_10_big_ways_the_democratic_platform_diffe.html; Richard Wolf, *Supreme Court Debate: Stark Contrasts Emerge Between Trump, Clinton*, USA Today (Oct 20, 2016), available at http://www.usatoday.com/story/news/politics/elections/2016/10/20/supreme-court-debate-clinton-trump-guns-abortion/92452362; Dahlia Lithwick and Mark Joseph Stern, *Who Will Protect the Constitution? Donald Trump vs. Hillary Clinton, Amendment by Amendment*, Slate (Oct 30, 2016), available at http://www.slate.com/articles/news_and_politics/jurisprudence/2016/10/who_will_protect_the_constitution_donald_trump_or_hillary_clinton.html.

[7] Measures of congressional voting patterns show that the ideological distance between Democrats and Republicans is greater today than at any other time in our nation's history (see fig. 3); see generally Daryl J. Levinson and Richard H. Pildes, *Separation of Parties, Not Powers*, 119 Harv L Rev 2311 (2006).

camps that view each other with hostility, a process that has been labeled *affective polarization*.[8] In part, this development is tied to the ideological sorting of Democrats and Republicans.[9] Affective polarization does not necessarily mean that conservatives and liberals are farther apart than they were in the past. Rather, it means that individuals are more conscious of being in an ideological camp that is opposed to the competing camp.

We analyze the impact of political polarization on the Court largely in terms of elite social networks. Polarization is reflected in the social networks that are critical to grooming and identifying appointees to the federal courts, including the Supreme Court.[10] It also pervades the social networks of which the Justices themselves are a part; conservative Republican-appointed Justices interact with elites who support conservative outcomes and liberal Democratic-appointed Justices interact with elites who support liberal outcomes.[11]

In highlighting the profound impact of party polarization on today's Court, we contrast the current period with earlier periods. Even a few decades ago, the world in which the Justices lived and worked was more homogeneous than it is today, with a center-left tilt among academic and media elites. This social environment probably helps to account for an apparent drift to the left by Republican-appointed Justices such as John Paul Stevens, David Souter, and especially Harry Blackmun.[12] Today, the elite world has become ideo-

---

[8] See Shanto Iyengar, Gaurav Sood, and Yphtach Lelkes, *Affect, Not Ideology: A Social Identity Perspective on Polarization*, 76 Pub Opinion Q 405, 406 (2012); Patrick R. Miller and Pamela Johnston Conover, *Red and Blue States of Mind: Partisan Hostility and Voting in the United States*, 68 Pol Research Q 225 (2015). Affective polarization is also seen in the increasing acrimony between members of opposition parties on talk shows and on the floor of Congress. See Danny Hayes, *The Words Hurt Model of Polarization*, Wash Post (Jan 6, 2013), archived at https://perma.cc/57YS-3GZ8.

[9] Cass R. Sunstein, *Partyism Now Trumps Racism*, Bloomberg View (Sept 22, 2014), archived at https://perma.cc/4CQW-FY9E.

[10] For an insightful treatment of efforts by the Reagan Justice Department to groom young conservatives for judgeships, see Steven Teles, *Transformative Bureaucracy: Reagan's Lawyers and the Dynamics of Political Investment*, 23 Studies in Am Pol Dev 61 (2009).

[11] On the importance of these social networks to judicial decision making, see Section IV.A. See generally Lawrence Baum, *Judges and Their Audiences: A Perspective on Judicial Behavior* (Princeton, 2006).

[12] See Lawrence Baum and Neal Devins, *Why the Supreme Court Cares about Elites and Not the American People*, 98 Georgetown L J 1515, 1574–79 (2010). To a degree, the appearance of a movement to the left by Justices such as Blackmun and Stevens is a product of the rightward movement of the Court as a whole with the appointments of new Justices. Indeed, Stevens and (to a lesser degree) Blackmun cited that rightward movement as the source of

logically polarized, so that Justices on both the left and right are part of social networks that reinforce conservatism for Republican-appointed Justices and liberalism for Democratic-appointed Justices. Of particular importance, conservative elites have consciously sought to overcome what they see as a liberal bias in the legal system, including the courts. That effort is reflected in the rise of the Federalist Society and the related establishment of a conservative legal network.[13]

Our analysis does not speak to how liberal a Court with a Democratic-appointed majority would be or how conservative a Court with a Republican-appointed majority would be, because a range of circumstances can affect the Court's ideological center of gravity.[14] But the changes in the Court that we describe have had a tendency to move it to the right, because Republican appointees on the whole are now more conservative than in the past while Democratic appointees as a group have not changed appreciably.[15] Our analysis shows that

their apparent change. Jeffrey Rosen, *Interview Transcript: Justice John Paul Stevens*, NY Times Magazine (April 12, 2010); Moyers & Company, *In Search of the Constitution: Mr. Justice Blackmun*, April 16, 1987, at http://billmoyers.com/content.mr-Justice-blackmun-supreme-court/. However, several appointees of Republican presidents who joined the Court between 1953 and 1990 showed a movement to the left during their Court tenure based on their votes on case outcomes even with controls for the voting of the same colleagues over time. Baum, *Judges and Their Audiences* at 148 (cited in note 11). Rates of agreement with the same opinions show a similar pattern. For instance, Blackmun agreed with Chief Justice Burger 23 percentage points more often than he agreed with Justice Brennan in the 1970–79 Terms but agreed with Brennan 12 percentage points more often than with Burger in the 1980–85 Terms; Stevens agreed with Brennan 1 percentage point more often than with Justice Rehnquist in the 1976–78 Terms and 14 percentage points more often in the 1979–85 Terms; Souter agreed with Justice Scalia 11 percentage points more often than with Stevens in the 1990–92 Terms but agreed with Stevens 21 percentage points more often than with Scalia in the 1993–2004 Terms. Agreement rates were calculated from data in *The Statistics*, Harv L Rev, published annually in the November issue.

[13] See Steven M. Teles, *The Rise of the Conservative Legal Movement: The Battle for Control of the Law* (Princeton, 2008); Amanda Hollis-Brusky, *Ideas with Consequences: The Federalist Society and the Conservative Counterrevolution* (Oxford, 2015).

[14] Today's Court does not have a sharper conservative-liberal divide than past Courts; what distinguishes it is that ideological divisions coincide with partisan divisions. On trends in ideological polarization, see Tom S. Clark, *Measuring Ideological Polarization on the United States Supreme Court*, 62 Pol Research Q 146 (2009); Donald Michael Gooch, *Ideological Polarization on the Supreme Court: Trends in the Court's Institutional Environment and Across Regimes, 1937–2008*, 43 Am Pol Research 999 (2015).

[15] In Part I, we highlight how it is that today's Democrats are all moderate liberals as compared to earlier Courts where there were strong liberal Democrats as well as more conservative Democrats. In Part II, we link this phenomenon to the appointment strategies of Democratic presidents. In so doing, we explain why Democrats on today's Court are about

the growing ideological gap between Democratic-appointed Justices and Republican-appointed Justices is largely attributable to the appointment of conservative Republican nominees.[16]

In this article we point to the ways that polarization in the larger world of political and social elites has reshaped the Court. But in doing so, we do not ignore the differences between the Court and the other branches.[17] For one thing, the Justices' partial insulation from partisan constituencies gives them more freedom to depart from the ideological positions that those constituencies subscribe to in particular cases, and their embrace of the norm of judicial independence enhances that freedom.[18] Further, the Justices' preference for consensus where it is possible reduces the impact of ideological divisions on some decisions.[19]

Finally, and perhaps most important, Justices decide cases in legal terms. As a result, ideological considerations often do not figure into the Court's decision making.[20] Then-Senator Barack Obama underlined this reality when he voted against confirmation of Chief Justice John Roberts not because of the "95 percent of the cases" that

---

equally liberal as those on earlier Courts but less ideologically diverse (see figs. 1 and 2). See also David Strauss, *The Last Liberal Justice?*, 21 Democracy 114 (2011) (noting that some liberals think there "have been no truly progressive Justices on the Court for many years"); Jeffrey Rosen, *What's a Liberal Justice Now?*, NY Times Magazine, MM50 (May 26, 2009) (noting differences between Warren-era liberalism and liberalism today).

[16] See Section IV.C.

[17] Thomas Keck has presented evidence that on four sets of controversial issues, voting differences between Republicans and Democrats in Congress are substantially greater than voting differences in the Supreme Court and the federal courts of appeals. Thomas Keck, *Judicial Politics in Polarized Times* 147–50 (Chicago, 2014).

[18] Justice Antonin Scalia, for example, took great pride in casting "liberal" votes on flag burning, search and seizure, and other issues because of his commitment to a set of interpretive principles that transcend ideology. See Margot Talbot, *Supreme Confidence*, New Yorker (Mar 28, 2005), archived at https://perma.cc/E7GC-HUMT. Correspondingly, to the extent that today's Justices have an incentive to demonstrate that partisanship does not impact their decision making, the partisan divide on today's Court may moderate Court decision making in ways that the earlier conservative-liberal divide did not moderate decision making. For a general treatment of this topic, see Lawrence S. Wrightsman, *The Psychology of the Supreme Court* 111–15 (Oxford, 2006).

[19] See Pamela C. Corley, Amy Steigerwalt, and Artemus Ward, *The Puzzle of Unanimity: Consensus on the United States Supreme Court* 161 (Stanford Law Books, 2013); Cass R. Sunstein, *Unanimity and Disagreement on the Supreme Court*, 100 Cornell L Rev 769 (2015).

[20] For a provocative study on how Roberts Court Justices are divided on methodological as well as ideological grounds (and how it is that methodological preferences sometimes prevail), see Joshua B. Fischman and Tonja Jacobi, *The Second Dimension of the Supreme Court*, 57 Wm & Mary L Rev 1671 (2016).

would be decided as a matter of law but because of the "5 percent of cases that are truly difficult."[21]

For those reasons, we do not expect the Justices *always* to cast votes that match their ideological and partisan affiliations. Chief Justice Roberts's votes in both the 2012 and 2015 Affordable Care Act decisions are prominent examples,[22] but these votes do not mean that the Chief Justice is a moderate or a liberal; he is clearly a conservative.[23] Likewise, just because the Justices sometimes issue unanimous opinions on issues that divide conservatives and liberals outside the Court does not mean that today's Court transcends partisan labels.[24] Republican-appointed Justices are conservative notwithstanding the fact that all nine Justices agreed that the police cannot search digital information on a cellphone without a warrant; correspondingly, Democratic-appointed Justices are liberal notwithstanding the Court's unanimous ruling that the Constitution excludes ministers from the protections of employment discrimination laws.[25]

---

[21] Nomination of John Roberts, 109th Cong, 1st Sess (Sept 22, 2005), in 151 Cong Rec 21032 (remarks of Senator Obama); Mark Tushnet, *In the Balance: Law and Politics on the Roberts Court* xiv (W. W. Norton, 2013) (expressing agreement with Obama).

[22] *National Federation of Independent Business v Sebelius*, 132 S Ct 2566 (2012); *King v Burwell*, 135 S Ct 2480 (2015). See David G. Savage, *Chief Justice Roberts Signals That Supreme Court Remains Independent*, LA Times A1 (June 30, 2012).

[23] See notes 252–57 and accompanying text. For identical reasons, Justices Stephen Breyer and Elena Kagan are clearly liberal notwithstanding the fact that they joined the Court's Republicans in finding the Affordable Care Act's Medicaid extension unconstitutional.

[24] See generally Sunstein, 100 Cornell L Rev (cited in note 19).

[25] *Riley v California*, 134 S Ct 2473 (2014) (cell phone searches); *Hosanna-Tabor Evangelical Lutheran Church & School v EEOC*, 132 S Ct 694 (2012) (recognizing ministerial exception to employment discrimination legislation). Moreover, the Court sometimes masks deep divisions among the Justices by issuing narrow unanimous or near-unanimous rulings that defer decision on deeply divisive issues. Examples include the Court's unanimous 2009 ruling in *Northwest Austin Municipal Utility District No. 1 v Holder*, 557 US 193 (2009) (deferring decision on the constitutionality of the preclearance requirements of the Voting Rights Act), the Court's 7–1 ruling in *Fisher v University of Texas*, 133 S Ct 2411 (2013) (deferring decision on University of Texas affirmative action program), and the Court's unanimous ruling in *Zubik v Burwell*, 136 S Ct 1557 (2016) (inviting the parties to resolve a dispute over contraceptive coverage in certain health plans). Some unanimous rulings feature sharp disagreements on doctrinal matters. Examples include *McCullen v Coakley*, 134 S Ct 2518 (2014) (allowable regulation of protest activities at abortion clinics), *NLRB v Noel Canning*, 134 S Ct 2250 (2014) (scope of presidential recess appointment power), and *Bond v United States*, 134 S Ct 2077 (2014) (reach of federal power to implement treaties through legislation). The proportion of unanimous decisions in recent terms is typically between 40 and 50 percent, and it was about two-thirds in the 2013 Term. See Statistics, SCOTUSblog, http://www.scotusblog.com/statistics/. This frequent agreement among the Justices underlines the difference between the Supreme Court and Congress noted in this paragraph.

This article is organized as follows: Part I documents that the contemporary Court is the first Court to be divided sharply along partisan lines by examining historical patterns of division on the Court. Part II examines the growth in polarization in government and in the broader political elite. It also points to the implications of that polarization for the Court.

The remainder of the article examines those implications in greater detail. Part III examines how polarization has affected the appointments of Supreme Court Justices. It emphasizes differences in the appointment strategies of Democratic and Republican presidents, differences that reflect the rise of the conservative legal movement and its impact on the grooming and identification of conservative nominees. It therefore explains why Republican appointees to the Court in the current era are distinctly more conservative as a group than their predecessors, while today's Democratic appointees are about as liberal as their predecessors.[26]

Part IV turns to sitting Justices. It uses social psychology to explain further why today's party polarization has resulted in partisan voting patterns by the Justices, focusing on the impact of elite social networks in judicial decision making. Here, too, we probe differences between the parties. During the 1960s through 1980s, the dominant legal elite culture pushed Republican-appointed Justices away from the right and toward the center-left. Today, however, Justices are less prone to drift and, with no post-1990 Republican-appointed Justice moving to the center-left, there has been a hardening of the right.

Part V briefly considers the ramifications of all this: why presidential elections matter more for the Court today than ever before; why the Court is likely to move more sharply to the right or left depending on whether there is a majority of Democratic or Republican appointees; and, correspondingly, why—after Justice Kennedy—there is not likely to be a "super-median" Justice[27] who sometimes sides with conservatives and other times with liberals in the Court's most divisive opinions.

Following Part V, we will consider how the nomination and confirmation of Neil Gorsuch reinforce our central claim.

---

[26] See figure 2 (comparing historic means of Democratic and Republican appointees).

[27] Lee Epstein and Tonja Jacobi, *Super Medians*, 61 Stan L Rev 37 (2008).

I. Party and Ideology in Supreme Court History

On the current Supreme Court, ideological lines coincide with party lines: since Elena Kagan succeeded John Paul Stevens in 2010, every Justice who was appointed by a Democratic president has had a more liberal voting record than every Republican appointee. In the 2010–15 Terms of the Court, the Justice appointed by a Democratic president who cast the highest proportion of conservative votes (43.5 percent) was Stephen Breyer; the Justice appointed by a Republican president who cast the lowest proportion of conservative votes (53.4 percent) was Anthony Kennedy.[28]

The coincidence of party and ideology on today's Court has been widely noted,[29] but the departure from traditional patterns on the Court is not as well recognized. This is the first period in which the Court has been sharply divided between substantial blocs of Justices from each of the two major political parties. To demonstrate this difference, we will analyze ideological differences among Justices over time. We divide our analysis into two periods: 1801–1937 and 1937–2016. During the first period,[30] we look principally to historical studies of the Court and our own analysis of dissenting opinions in landmark cases. For the 1937–2016 period, we look primarily to Martin-Quinn scores, which are available beginning with the 1937 Term, as measures of the Justices' ideological positions.[31]

---

[28] These percentages are based on analysis of data in the Supreme Court Database, http://scdb.wustl.edu/. We analyzed cases decided after oral argument (decision type = 1, 6, or 7). The criteria for coding votes as liberal or conservative are described at http://scdb.wustl.edu/documentation.php?var=decisionDirection.

A similar pattern exists for the Martin-Quinn scores, in which higher scores indicate greater conservatism. In the mean Martin-Quinn scores across the 2010–14 Terms, Justice Kennedy had the lowest score for a Republican at +0.07; Justice Breyer had the highest score for a Democrat at −1.41; the nine Justices' scores ranged from +3.14 to −2.34. See table 1 for a detailing of Justices' rankings by Martin-Quinn scores over time; for additional discussion of Martin-Quinn scores, see note 31.

[29] See, for example, Greg Stohr, *Roberts Supreme Court's Partisan Split Shows New Justices Are Predictable*, Bloomberg News (July 1, 2011), at http://www.bloomberg.com/news/2011-07-01/roberts-supreme-court-s-partisan-split-shows-new-Justices-are-predictable.html; Adam Liptak, *The Polarized Court*, NY Times, SR1 (May 11, 2014) (discussing, inter alia, findings in an earlier version of the study that is the basis of this article).

[30] We do not consider the 1789–1800 period, a time when the Court was headed by three different Chief Justices and issued very few opinions and when all the Justices were appointed by Federalist presidents.

[31] The Martin-Quinn scores are based on a transformation of the patterns of interagreement on votes among the Justices, without a priori labeling of their ideological direction and with a procedure that is designed to minimize the impact of random fluctuations in the Jus-

A. THE PERIOD BEFORE 1937

Throughout the period that ended in 1937, there is little evidence of partisan division within the Court. Indeed, it is difficult to trace patterns of division at all. Dissent was infrequent, and the Justices typically spoke with one voice (issuing unanimous opinions for the Court).[32] In part, this reflected the common practice of suppressing dissenting views in the Court's final votes on the merits.[33] Moreover, as in the federal courts of appeals today,[34] many of the mandatory cases that constituted a large share of the Court's docket until 1925

---

tices' voting from term to term that results from the specific mix of cases that the Court hears. The procedure was first set out in a 2002 article and is widely used in research on the Supreme Court. See Andrew D. Martin and Kevin M. Quinn, *Dynamic Ideal Point Estimation via Markov Chain Monte Carlo for the U.S. Supreme Court 1953–1999*, 10 Pol Analysis 134 (2002); Brandon Bartels, *The Constraining Capacity of Legal Doctrine on the U.S. Supreme Court*, 103 Am Pol Sci Rev 474 (2009); Lee Epstein and William M. Landes, *Was There Ever Such a Thing as Judicial Self-Restraint?*, 100 Cal L Rev 557 (2012); William M. Landes and Richard A. Posner, *Rational Judicial Behavior: A Statistical Study*, 1 J Legal Analysis 775 (2010). It should be noted that the Martin-Quinn scores are not fully linear, so that the distances between different pairs of Justices are not necessarily comparable. Daniel E. Ho and Kevin M. Quinn, *How Not to Lie with Judicial Votes: Misconceptions, Measurement, and Models*, 98 Cal L Rev 813, 846–47 (2010).

We use the Martin-Quinn scores rather than scores based on ideological coding of votes in the Supreme Court Database because they extend several terms further than the currently available data in the database (the 1937 Term rather than the 1946 Term) and because their properties make them somewhat better indicators of the Court's ideological lineup. A division at the 1937 Term is sensible for another reason: 1937 is considered the start of the modern Court. In 1937, the "old Court" acquiesced to the New Deal and Franklin Delano Roosevelt was able to appoint his first (out of eight) Supreme Court Justice. See William E. Leuchtenburg, *The Supreme Court Reborn: The Constitutional Revolution in the Age of Roosevelt* (Oxford, 1996). The year 1937 also corresponds to Congress's decision to grant the Court discretionary certiorari power in 1925, legislation that allowed the Court to assume a broader role expounding legal principles. See Tara Leigh Grove, *The Exceptions Clause as a Structural Safeguard*, 113 Colum L Rev 929, 931–32, 948–78 (2013). For other prominent academic studies that treat 1937 as the transformative year separating the old Court from the modern Court, see Bruce Ackerman, *We the People: Foundations* (Belknap, 1993); Thomas M. Keck, *The Most Activist Supreme Court in History* (Chicago, 2004).

[32] In the period from 1801 through 1938, at most there were four terms in one era (1836, 1845, 1852, 1854) in which more than 20 percent of the Court's decisions included dissenting opinions. Lee Epstein et al, *The Supreme Court Compendium: Data, Decisions and Developments* 227–30 (CQ Press, 4th ed 2007). See also Sunstein, 100 Cornell L Rev at 773–84 (cited in note 19).

[33] Alexander M. Bickel, *The Unpublished Opinions of Mr. Justice Brandeis: The Supreme Court at Work* (Harvard, 1957); Lee Epstein et al, *The Norm of Consensus on the U.S. Supreme Court*, 45 Am J Pol Sci 362 (2001); Robert Post, *The Supreme Court Opinion as Institutional Practice: Dissent, Legal Scholarship, and Decisionmaking in the Taft Court*, 85 Minn L Rev 1267, 1331–55 (2001).

[34] Harry T. Edwards and Michael A. Livermore, *Pitfalls of Empirical Studies That Attempt to Understand the Factors Affecting Appellate Decisionmaking*, 58 Duke L J 1895, 1950–58 (2009).

were "easy" and therefore unlikely to provoke disagreement among the Justices.

When the Justices did disagree, those disagreements did not tend to break along party lines.[35] One piece of evidence for the lack of polarization can be derived from a listing of the Court's most important decisions in the *Guide to the U.S. Supreme Court*.[36] Of the seventy-five most important decisions between 1790 and 1937 in which there were at least two dissenting votes, in only one were all of the Justices on one side appointed by presidents of one party and all of the Justices on the other side appointed by presidents of the other party.[37] Consider, for example, two of the most noteworthy cases from this period, *Dred Scott v Sandford* (1857) and *Lochner v New York* (1905). In *Dred Scott*, the two dissenters were the Whig-appointed Benjamin Curtis and the Democratic-appointed John McLean;[38] in *Lochner*, Justices appointed by both Democratic and Republican presidents were in both the majority and the dissent, and Justices

[35] Prior to 1910, there is little research that systematically analyzes disagreements among the Justices. The Legacy Supreme Court Database includes data on the Justices' votes in all decisions in the 1790–1945 Terms. From the late 1860s on, there were enough nonunanimous decisions to allow meaningful analysis of voting patterns. When the Justices' votes in the nonunanimous decisions are characterized in terms of the database coding of ideology, there were no terms between 1867 and 1909 in which there were at least two Justices appointed by presidents of each party and all the Justices from one party had more liberal records than all the Justices from the other party. This finding should not be given undue weight, because the numbers of nonunanimous decisions that could be coded as liberal or conservative were as low as nine or ten in some terms and because the definitions of liberal and conservative positions in the current era do not necessarily capture possible lines of division in the late nineteenth century. The database and its definitions of liberal and conservative positions are cited in note 28.

[36] David G. Savage, *Guide to the U.S. Supreme Court* 1276–94 (CQ Press, 5th ed 2010). The criteria for selection of important cases were not made explicit in the successive editions of the *Guide*, and there are biases and idiosyncrasies in that selection. Still, the list in the *Guide* is a good and substantial sampling of decisions that can be considered important, and it is unique in covering the full history of the Supreme Court. For evaluations of the list, see Saul Brenner, *Majority Opinion Assignment in Salient Cases on the U.S. Supreme Court: Are New Associate Justices Assigned Fewer Opinions?*, 22 Just Sys J 209, 212 n 4 (2001); Beverly Blair Cook, *Measuring the Significance of U.S. Supreme Court Decisions*, 55 J Pol 1127, 1132, 1136 (1993); Lee Epstein and Jeffrey A. Segal, *Measuring Issue Salience*, 44 Am J Pol Sci 66, 68–71 (2000).

[37] That decision was *United States v Texas*, 143 US 621 (1892). The dissenters were Democrats Melville Fuller and Lucius Lamar.

[38] 19 How 393 (1857). *Dred Scott* was hardly an anomaly. Even during Reconstruction (when the parties were highly polarized), Republicans and Democrats joined together to issue unanimous decisions on major postwar issues. See *Ex Parte McCardle*, 7 Wall 506 (1869); *Mississippi v Johnson*, 4 Wall 475 (1867).

John Harlan and Oliver Wendell Holmes broke ranks with the other Republican-appointed Justices in voting to uphold the challenged economic regulation.[39]

Quantitative analyses of the Justices' voting behavior are available for the full period beginning with the Court's 1910 Term.[40] Donald Carl Leavitt's study of the White Court (1910–21) used the Justices' votes to calculate scores on ideological scales for the 1910–15 and 1916–20 Terms. In neither period were the Court's Republican- and Democratic-appointed Justices separated from each other ideologically; most notably, Democratic president Woodrow Wilson's appointee James McReynolds (1914–41) took positions that were relatively and increasingly conservative.[41]

Eloise C. Snyder tracked agreements and disagreements among the Justices and used analysis of votes to identify what she called ideological "cliques" for each "natural Court"[42] from 1921 to 1937.[43] At no time were all the Justices appointed by Democratic presidents in separate cliques from all the Justices appointed by Republican presidents.[44] In cases dealing with New Deal programs that sharply

---

[39] 198 US 45 (1905). See also Owen M. Fiss, *Oliver Wendell Holmes Devise History of the United States Supreme Court: Troubled Beginnings of the Modern State, 1888–1910*, 35 (Cambridge, 1993) (concluding that there was no ideological divide between Democrats and Republicans of this period).

[40] These analyses begin with agreements and disagreements of the Justices in individual cases and use statistical techniques to place each Justice on a unidimensional scale for particular time periods. Although the votes used in these analyses are not labeled ideologically, the scales can be interpreted in ideological terms because patterns of agreement and disagreement tend to reflect a dominant ideological dimension. See Bernard Grofman and Timothy J. Brazill, *Identifying the Median Justice on the Supreme Court Through Multidimensional Scaling: Analysis of "Natural Courts" 1953–1991*, 113 Pub Choice 55 (2002).

[41] Donald Carl Leavitt, *Attitudes and Ideology on the White Supreme Court 1910–1920*, *186 (PhD dissertation, Michigan State University, 1970). Leavitt undertook several dimensional analyses of the Justices' votes; we relied primarily on the first principal axis loading in Q-analyses of votes. Another analysis of voting in the 1916–21 Terms found a similar pattern. Roger Handberg, *Decision-Making in a Natural Court, 1916–1921*, 4 Am Pol Q 357, 365 (1976). Chief Justice White might be classified as a Democrat because of his own party affiliation and his initial appointment by President Cleveland, or as a Republican because of his elevation to Chief Justice by President William Howard Taft. In Leavitt's analysis, White stood somewhat to the left among his colleagues in the 1910–15 Terms and somewhat to the right in the 1916–21 Terms.

[42] A natural Court is a period during which the Court's membership is unchanged.

[43] Eloise C. Snyder, *The Supreme Court as a Small Group*, 36 Soc Forces 232, 235 (1958). The Snyder study, based on a subset of cases, extended to 1953.

[44] The best known of the natural Courts in that period was the Court that sat in the 1932–36 Terms, the one that collectively came into severe conflict with President Franklin Roosevelt during his first term in office. That Court split along lines that cut across party.

divided the Court, the Court's two Democratic-appointed Justices (Louis Brandeis and James McReynolds) were in opposing camps and the Justices appointed by Republican presidents were also divided.[45]

Without question, then, Supreme Court decision making transcended party-line divisions throughout the 1801–1937 period. That is not to say that party identity was irrelevant to the Court's decision making;[46] presidents sometimes appointed Justices with an eye toward advancing their party's policy agenda.[47] Nonetheless, all available evidence suggests that the Court's decision making did not track party lines.

B. THE PERIOD SINCE 1937

For the period beginning with the 1937 Term, the Martin-Quinn scores can be used to trace the relationship between party and ideology by allowing us to array the Justices from left to right in each term of the Court. As these arrays show, before 2010 the Court never divided along strictly partisan lines. It came closest to a full split between Republican and Democratic appointees in the 1941–44 Terms. Seven of the nine Justices had been appointed by Democrat Franklin Roosevelt; Owen Roberts and Chief Justice Harlan Fiske Stone had been appointed by Republican Calvin Coolidge (although Stone had been elevated to Chief Justice by Roosevelt). Throughout that period, Roberts was the Court's most conservative Justice. In all but one of the four terms (and in 1945), Stone was more conservative than any of the Justices who had initially been appointed by Roosevelt. But the differences between him and the most conserva-

---

The well-known alignments of that period are documented in Snyder, 36 Soc Forces at 235 (cited in note 43), and C. Herman Pritchett, *The Roosevelt Court: A Study in Judicial Politics and Values 1937–1947*, 32, 34, 242 (Macmillan, 1948).

[45] See, for example, *National Labor Relations Board v Jones & Laughlin Steel Corp.*, 301 US 1 (1937) (upholding National Labor Relations Act of 1935); *United States v Butler*, 297 US 1 (1936) (declaring Agricultural Adjustment Act of 1933 unconstitutional); *Railroad Retirement Board v Alton Railroad Co.*, 295 US 330 (1935) (declaring Railroad Retirement Act of 1934 unconstitutional).

[46] For example, in the major cases that arose from secession and President Lincoln's policies during the Civil War, the Court's Republicans generally were more favorable to the Union's position than were its Democrats.

[47] One famous example is President U. S. Grant's appointment of two Supreme Court Justices (Joseph Bradley and William Strong) who supported Grant's view that paper money was constitutional. With the backing of Bradley and Strong, the Court in 1871 voted 5–4 to overturn an 1870 case that ruled that the federal government was without authority to issue paper money. *Knox v Lee*, 79 US 457 (1871) (overturning *Hepburn v Griswold*, 75 US 603 (1870)).

tive Roosevelt appointee in each of those terms, as measured by the Martin-Quinn scores, were small.[48]

Unlike today's partisan divide, there was widespread agreement among the Justices on issues that had previously divided the Court. Stone and Roberts, for example, joined the Court's Democratic-appointed Justices in *Wickard v Filburn*,[49] embracing an extraordinarily broad interpretation of Congress's Commerce Clause power. More telling, there was wide divergence among the Martin-Quinn scores of the seven Democratic-appointed Justices on the 1941–44 Court.[50] In particular, there were sharp conflicts over civil rights and civil liberties issues.[51] Furthermore, it was in the Stone Court, beginning in 1941, that dissenting votes and dissenting and concurring opinions began to proliferate.[52] In several landmark rulings involving the First Amendment rights of Jehovah's Witnesses, for example, the Court's Democratic-appointed Justices were bitterly divided.[53] Beyond disagreements over legal doctrine, enmity among the Roosevelt

---

[48] To the extent that the Court's ideological division in that period coincided with party lines, it should be noted that it is considerably more likely mathematically that these lines will coincide when only two Justices are from the minority party, and even more likely when there is one Justice from that party, than when the partisan division is 6–3 or 5–4. For example, the odds of two specific Justices out of nine randomly standing to the right of all their colleagues is 1 in 36; the odds of four out of nine is 1 in 126.

[49] 317 US 111 (1942). For an illuminating discussion of internal Court deliberations (revealing that Democrats such as Robert Jackson were especially concerned about the reach of the decision), see Barry Cushman, *Formalism and Realism in Commerce Clause Jurisprudence*, 67 U Chi L Rev 1089 (2000).

[50] The range of Martin-Quinn scores among the four Democrats in the 2010 Term was .678; in the 2011 Term, it was .947. In contrast, the ranges among the seven Democrats in the 1941–44 Terms were, successively, 3.489, 3.475, 3.349, and 3.095. Ranges of Martin-Quinn scores should be interpreted with caution, because the scores are not on a fully linear scale (see Ho and Quinn, 98 Cal L Rev at 846–47), but the differences are nonetheless striking.

[51] See generally, Leuchtenburg, *The Supreme Court Reborn* (cited in note 31) (noting divisions within New Deal Court on civil rights and liberties).

[52] See Thomas G. Walker, Lee Epstein, and William J. Dixon, *On the Mysterious Demise of Consensual Norms in the United States Supreme Court*, 50 J Pol 362 (1988).

[53] In *Murdoch v Pennsylvania*, 319 US 105 (1943), the Court struck down a city ordinance with licensing and tax requirements for door-to-door sales as applied to the activities of Jehovah's Witnesses. Id (overruling *Jones v Opelika*, 316 US 584 (1942)). The dissenters included not only Republican appointee Owen Roberts but also Roosevelt appointees Felix Frankfurter, Stanley Reed, and Robert Jackson. In *West Virginia State Board of Education v Barnette*, 319 US 624 (1943), the Court held that compulsory participation of public school students in flag salute ceremonies violated First Amendment Rights of Jehovah's Witnesses. Id (overruling *Minersville Sch. Dist. v Gobitis*, 310 US 586 (1940)). Democratic appointees Roberts, Frankfurter, and Reed dissented.

appointees reached a level that has had few if any parallels in the Court's history.[54]

The Warren Court illustrates the complicated relationship between party and ideology throughout this period. President Harry Truman's four appointees[55] all developed relatively conservative records on the Court, while Eisenhower appointees Earl Warren and William Brennan were distinctly more liberal. Correspondingly, in the decisions that sharply divided the Court, both majority and minority coalitions typically had representatives from both parties. In *Miranda v Arizona*,[56] for instance, the majority consisted of two Republican- and three Democratic-appointed Justices, while the dissenters included two Republican- and two Democratic-appointed Justices.[57]

The relationship between party and ideology remained complicated in the Burger and Rehnquist Courts. Based on the Martin-Quinn scores, Brennan was one of the two most liberal Justices in each of his last twenty terms on the Court, from 1970 to 1990. President Gerald Ford's appointee John Paul Stevens was to the left of the Court's center throughout his tenure from 1975 to 2010, and from 1991 to 2010 he was the most liberal Justice. President George H. W. Bush's appointee David Souter was at the center of the Court in the 1991 Term, his first year as a Justice, and to the left of center for the remainder of a tenure that ended in 2009. For his part, John Kennedy's appointee Byron White was near the Court's ideological center throughout his tenure on the Court from 1962 to 1993, and during the Burger and Rehnquist Courts he stood to the right of Brennan, Stevens, and (from the 1979 Term on) Harry Blackmun, a Richard Nixon appointee.

As in the period from 1790 to 1937, the lack of a partisan divide in the Court from 1938 to 2010 is underlined by the divisions of the

---

[54] See Noah Feldman, *Scorpions: The Battles and Triumphs of FDR's Great Supreme Court Justices* (Grand Central, 2010); H. N. Hirsch, *The Enigma of Felix Frankfurter* 127–200 (Basic Books, 1981).

[55] Those appointees were Chief Justice Fred Vinson (appointed in 1946), Harold Burton (1945), Tom Clark (1949), and Sherman Minton (1949).

[56] 384 US 436 (1966).

[57] Justices in the majority were Roosevelt appointees Hugo Black and William O. Douglas, Eisenhower appointees Earl Warren and William Brennan, and Johnson appointee Abe Fortas. The dissenters were Truman appointee Tom Clark, Kennedy appointee Byron White, and Eisenhower appointees John Harlan and Potter Stewart.

Justices in important cases.[58] Of the 322 cases in that period that the *Guide to the U.S. Supreme Court* lists as important and in which at least two Justices dissented,[59] only one case divided all the Court's Republican-appointed Justices from all of their Democratic-appointed colleagues (and that decision is itself ambiguous).[60] That is a remarkable record.

But even while the Court continued to be without a sharply partisan division, the conditions for such a division were developing through the appointment process. Byron White, appointed by President Kennedy in 1962, was the last moderate-to-conservative Democratic appointee. David Souter, appointed by George H. W. Bush in 1990, was the last moderate-to-liberal Republican appointee. We will discuss the changes in presidential appointment strategies in Part III. For now, we simply note that these changes created the preconditions for an ideological division on the Court that coincided with party.

We have described the partisan division between substantial blocs of Democratic- and Republican-appointed Justices that has existed since the beginning of the Court's 2010 Term, a division that stands in sharp contrast with earlier periods in the Court's history. Another indication of the distinctiveness of the current era is the number of important decisions in which the Justices lined up along party lines. As noted earlier, between 1790 and early 2010 there were only two decisions that the *Guide to the U.S. Supreme Court* designated as important and that had at least two dissenting votes in which the Justices divided along party lines, about one-half of one percent.[61] By contrast, among the cases decided by the Court in the 2010–14 Terms, seven decisions in which the Court divided 5–4 or (in one case) 5–3 along party lines are obvious candidates for inclusion in the *Guide*'s

---

[58] We will return to the period from 1969 to 1990 in Part IV to examine more closely the differences between the Court of that period and the current Court.

[59] Savage, *Guide to the U.S. Supreme Court* at 1294–1340 (cited in note 36). Savage's list of important cases terminates in the mid-2009 Term.

[60] That case was *Fed. Election Commission v National Conservative Political Action Comm.*, 470 US 480 (1985). Four Justices (two Democrats and two Republicans) wrote or joined dissenting opinions. Of those four, the Court's two Democrats (Byron White and Thurgood Marshall) dissented most fully from the Court's decision, and David G. Savage treats the Court's vote as 7–2. Savage, *Guide to the U.S. Supreme Court* at 1240 (cited in note 36).

[61] In that period, there were 397 important decisions on which there were at least two dissents. The *Guide*'s list of important decisions includes only part of the Court's 2009 Term.

list of important decisions.[62] During the Court's 2015 Term, the Justices split 4–4—most likely on partisan lines—in high-visibility cases on public sector unions and on President Obama's immigration directive.[63]

C. PARTISANSHIP AND IDEOLOGICAL CONFORMITY

Today's partisan divide manifests itself in other ways. Most striking, the groups of Justices appointed by Republican presidents and by Democratic presidents have each become more ideologically homogeneous. Moreover, each of the distinct groups of Justices lacks centrists, with the partial exception of Justice Kennedy. Instead, there is ideological conformity within each group, even as the groups have diverged over time.

The high level of homogeneity among Democratic- and among Republican-appointed Justices can be measured by the standard de-

---

[62] Those decisions are: *Burwell v Hobby Lobby Stores*, 134 S Ct 2751 (2014) (interpreting the Religious Freedom Restoration Act to protect closely held corporations from a mandate to include certain contraceptives in employee health plans); *McCutcheon v FEC*, 134 S Ct 1434 (2014) (striking down a federal statutory provision that put limit on an individual's total contributions to election candidates and candidate committees); *Shelby Cnty v Holder*, 133 S Ct 2612 (2013) (striking down Title IV of the Voting Rights Act); *Florence v Bd of Chosen Freeholders*, 132 S Ct 1510 (2012) (allowing routine strip-searches of arrestees at jails); *AT&T Mobility LLC v Concepcion*, 563 US 333 (2011) (disallowing state restrictions on contract provisions prohibiting class actions in arbitration); *Arizona Free Enterprise Club's Freedom Club PAC v Bennett*, 131 S Ct 2806 (2011) (striking down a state system of public funding for candidates for state offices); and *Chamber of Commerce v Whiting*, 131 S Ct 1968 (2011) (allowing sanctions on employers for hiring of undocumented aliens). In preparing this inventory of cases, we consulted with David Savage, author of the *Guide*.

[63] Those cases are *Friedrichs v California Teachers Association*, 136 S Ct 1083 (2016) (dividing 4–4 on whether mandatory fees to public sector unions violate free speech rights), and *United States v Texas*, 136 S Ct 2271 (2016) (dividing 4–4 on legality of 2014 Obama immigration directive). For news stories speculating that these 4–4 splits were a Democratic-Republican split, see Adam Liptak, *Victory for Unions as Supreme Court, Scalia Gone, Ties 4–4*, NY Times (March 29, 2016), available at http://www.nytimes.com/2016/03/30/us/politics/friedrichs-v-california-teachers-association-union-fees-supreme-court-ruling.html?_r=0; Robert Barnes, *Supreme Court Won't Revive Obama Plan to Shield Illegal Immigrants from Deportation*, Wash Post (June 23, 2016), available at https://www.washingtonpost.com/politics/supreme-court-wont-revive-obama-plan-to-shield-illegal-immigrants-from-deportation/2016/06/23/6cea5f1e-3950-11e6-9ccd-d6005beac8b3_story.html. In other high-profile cases (involving a religious liberty challenge to the Affordable Care Act and Article III standing limits on class action lawsuits), the Justices may well have masked partisan divisions by issuing ambiguous, inconclusive opinions. See Mark Joseph Stern, *SCOTUS Misses an Opportunity to Gut Class Actions and Consumer Privacy Laws*, Slate (May 16, 2016), available at http://www.slate.com/blogs/the_slatest/2016/05/16/spokeo_v_robins_spares_class_actions_and_consumer_privacy.html; Garrett Epps, *The U.S. Supreme Court's Nonsense Ruling in Zubik*, The Atlantic (May 16, 2016), available at http://www.theatlantic.com/politics/archive/2016/05/the-supreme-courts-non-sensical-ruling-in-zubik/482967/.

viations of the Justices' conservative votes within each group,[64] based on the coding of votes in the Supreme Court Database. The lower the standard deviation, the greater the ideological conformity within each group. The results are shown in figure 1, divided into subperiods that track changes in the Court's composition.

For the Court's Democratic-appointed Justices, the standard deviation was very high in the 1986–93 period because the only Democratic appointees in that period were the very liberal Thurgood Marshall and the moderate conservative Byron White.[65] In the longer period from 1994 through 2008, the two Democratic-appointed Justices were the like-minded Ruth Bader Ginsburg and Stephen Breyer, and the standard deviations were low. That remained true after Ginsburg and Breyer were joined by Sonia Sotomayor and Elena Kagan.

The change came later for the Court's Republican-appointed Justices. The standard deviation remained high as long as the relatively liberal John Paul Stevens and David Souter remained on the Court. After Souter retired at the end of the 2008 Term, though, the standard deviation fell by almost half; when Stevens retired after the 2009 Term, it again fell by half.[66] With a more homogeneous set of Republican-appointed Justices on the Court, the standard deviation has remained low ever since.

Similarly, as figure 2 shows, the Republican and Democratic appointees have separated from each other ideologically. The average difference between these two sets of Justices in the frequency with which they cast conservative votes has fluctuated considerably over time, but there was a general movement upward in the early 1990s and again in 2009 and 2010, as the Court's Republican and Democratic appointees became more ideologically distinct from each other. As in other analyses that we present, the percentages of conservative and liberal votes cast by a Justice or by a set of Justices can be

---

[64] The standard deviation measures how widely a range of scores deviates from the mean of those scores. For the formula, see, e.g., Hubert M. Blalock, Jr., *Social Statistics* 67 (McGraw-Hill, 1960). The standard deviation is useful for our purposes because it indicates the extent to which the Justices of one party vary in their ideological positions.

[65] There were no standard deviations for the 1991–93 Terms because there was only one Democrat on the Court; Marshall retired before the 1991 Term and White before the 1993 Term.

[66] When Stevens retired, it fell from 16.2 to 9.1 percent; when Souter retired, it fell to 4 percent.

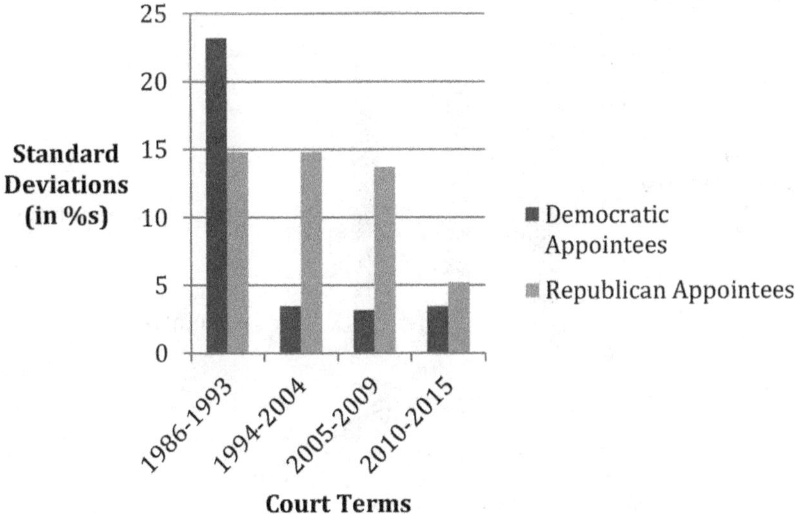

Figure 1. Mean standard deviations of percentages of conservative votes among Justices appointed by presidents from each party. The standard deviations shown for each period are the means of the standard deviations for individual Court terms during that period. The proportions of conservative votes are calculated from data in the Supreme Court Database, with votes that are not defined as either liberal or conservative excluded.

compared over time only with considerable caution, because those percentages are affected by the composition of the cases that the Court decides at any given time. For this reason, the data in figure 2 do not necessarily mean that Democratic-appointed Justices became slightly more conservative and Republican-appointed Justices became substantially more conservative across the periods shown.[67]

Does the growing ideological distance between these two groups of Justices mean that moderate Justices have disappeared from the Court? That question cannot be answered definitively, because there is no clear benchmark for moderation.[68] But it appears that Republican-

[67] Thus when the Court's membership is unchanged, term-by-term fluctuations in percentages of liberal and conservative decisions are likely to result primarily from changes in the composition of the Court's agenda. Fluctuations in the agenda have an even greater impact on the ideological direction of the small numbers of decisions in a given term that receive the greatest attention.

[68] For a recent academic treatment of this subject (measuring moderation by the number of swing Justices there are on the Court), see Brandon Bartels, *The Sources and Consequences of Polarization in the U.S. Supreme Court*, in James Thurber and Antoine Yoshinaka, eds, *American Gridlock* 171–200 (Cambridge, 2015).

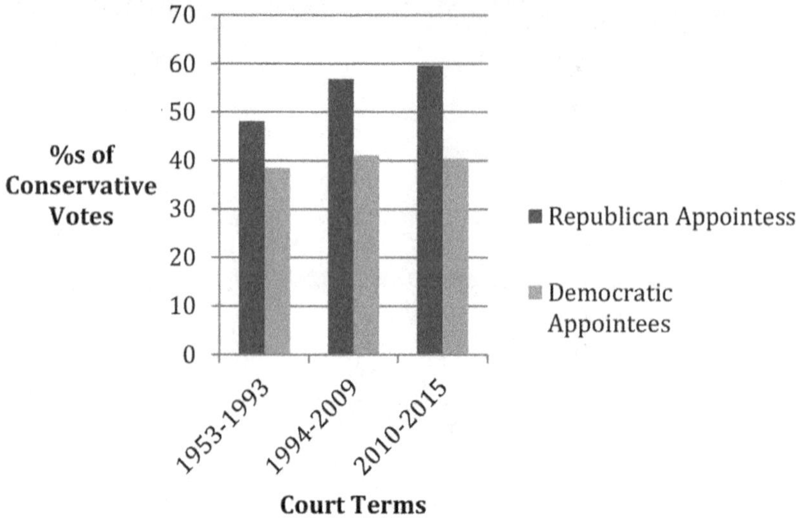

Figure 2. Mean percentage of conservative votes among Justices appointed by presidents from each party. As in figure 1, the proportions of conservative votes are calculated from data in the Supreme Court Database, with votes that are not defined as either liberal or conservative excluded. The percentages shown are the means of the mean percentages of conservative votes among a party group (for instance, all Democratic appointees). The periods coincide with the retirement of the last Democratic moderate (Byron White) in 1993 and last Republican moderate (John Paul Stevens) in 2010.

appointed Justices are more strongly conservative than the Court's Democratic-appointed Justices are liberal.[69] There are no strong liberals on today's Court; more telling, analyses by Lee Epstein, William Landes, and Richard Posner rank four Roberts Court Republican-appointed Justices as among the most conservative Justices ever to sit on the Court.[70] Finally, the evidence indicates that

[69] See Strauss, 21 Democracy at 114 (cited in note 15) (arguing that there are no strong liberals on today's Court); Lee Epstein, William M. Landes, and Richard A. Posner, *The Behavior of Federal Judges: A Theoretical and Empirical Study of Rational Choice* 108–09 (Harvard, 2013) (contending that today's Republican appointees are among the most conservative Justices ever to sit on Court).

[70] See id at table 3.2 (ranking—based on percentage of conservative votes cast—Roberts, Thomas, Alito, Scalia as among ten most conservative since 1937); Lee Epstein, William M. Landes, and Richard A. Posner, *Revisiting the Ideology Ranking of Supreme Court Justices*, 44 J Legal Stud S295, 313–14 (Thomas, Scalia, Alito among most conservative with respect to votes cast in cases covered by *New York Times* and Roberts among most conservative in cases decided 5–4). See also notes 142–52 and accompanying text (discussing Democratic appointments strategies).

the separation between Democratic- and Republican-appointed Justices is unique in the Court's history. In the parts that follow, we probe the reasons for this fundamental change in the Court.

II. Partisan Polarization in American Politics

Starting in the 1980s, there has been a substantial increase in partisan polarization in government and among political elites outside government.[71] As noted earlier, we focus on two overlapping forms of polarization. Through partisan sorting, ideological views and partisan identifications are more closely related than they were in the mid-twentieth century.[72] Through affective polarization, Democrats and Republicans increasingly see themselves as members of opposing teams and increasingly hold negative attitudes toward members of the other party.[73]

It is inevitable that the growth in political polarization in both of these senses would affect the Supreme Court, both directly and indirectly. In the first section of this part, we highlight the growth of polarization in government. In the second section we examine polarization in the larger elite world, including media outlets, the legal profession, and the academy.

A. Government

The growing ideological separation between the two parties is reflected in the federal government. Democratic and Republican

---

[71] For general treatment of the rise of polarization in Congress, among elites, and among media outlets, see Nolan M. McCarty, Keith T. Poole, and Howard Rosenthal, *Polarized America: The Dance of Ideology and Unequal Riches* (MIT, 2006); Cass R. Sunstein, *Republic.com 2.0* (Princeton, 2009); Earl Black and Merle Black, *Divided America: The Ferocious Power Struggle in American Politics* (Simon & Schuster, 2008); Sean M. Theriault, *Party Polarization in Congress* (Cambridge, 2008); Mark A. Graber, *The Coming Constitutional Yo-Yo? Elite Opinion, Polarization, and the Direction of Judicial Decision Making*, 56 Howard L J 661, 681–703 (2013); Geoffrey C. Layman et al, *Party Polarization in American Politics*, 8 Ann Rev Pol Sci 83 (2006).

In contrast with people in government and other political elites, the extent to which polarization has grown in the mass public is uncertain and a matter of debate. However, there is evidence of an increased level of affective polarization in the public as a whole. See Shanto Iyengar and Sean J. Westwood, *Fear and Loathing Across Party Lines: New Evidence on Group Polarization*, 59 Am J Pol Sci 690 (2015); Miller and Conover, 68 Pol Res Q at 225 (cited in note 8).

[72] See notes 74–82 and accompanying text.

[73] See notes 107–09 and accompanying text.

officials have grown more distinct from each other ideologically and more hostile to each other.

Because congressional behavior can be analyzed through voting patterns, the separation between the parties is especially clear in Congress.[74] Today, Republicans and Democrats in Congress are ideologically distinct, as measured by their votes. No Democrat in either the House or the Senate is more conservative than the most liberal Republican in the same chamber.[75] By 2009, the ideological distance between the Democratic and Republican parties was greater than it had been at any time since Reconstruction.[76] This trend is largely attributable to the rightward movement of the Republican Party.[77] By 2012, the growth of the Tea Party had pushed the divide even further (as relatively moderate senators such as Texas's Kay Bailey Hutchinson were replaced by strong conservatives like Ted Cruz).[78] In contrast, while the Democratic Party has become more liberal over time, the change has been less dramatic.[79] The dearth of members who can be characterized as moderates is one of the most striking features of today's Congress.[80] In 1980, moderates made up approximately 40 percent of Congress; today, moderates are nearly extinct, making up less than 5 percent of Congress.[81]

---

[74] On ramifications of partisanship in Congress, see Neal Devins, *Party Polarization and Congressional Committee Consideration of Constitutional Questions*, 105 Nw U L Rev 737, 753–59, 776–81 (2011). For related discussion of polarization's impact on state politics, see Neal Devins and Saikrishna Prakash, *50 States, 50 Attorneys General, 50 Approaches to the Duty to Defend*, 124 Yale L J 2100, 2150–54 (2015).

[75] Data on the ideological ordering of senators and House members are presented at *DW-NOMINATE Scores 1st to 113th Congresses*, Voteview.com, voteview.com/dwnl.htm.

[76] See *Party Polarization: 1879–2014*, at http://voteview.com/political_polarization_2014.htm. The widened ideological gap between Republicans and Democrats in Congress reflects multiple forces, including growing differences in the personal ideological positions of congressional Republicans and Democrats, increasingly extreme views of party activists who influence members' positions, and members' and leaders' interest in enhancing their party's power in government and in the country. For a discussion of how party efforts to amass power exacerbate polarization and produce more party-line voting, see Theriault, *Party Polarization in Congress* 177–80 (cited in note 71).

[77] See Matt Grossman and David A. Hopkins, *Asymmetric Politics* 253 (Oxford, 2016).

[78] See *"Common Space" DW-NOMINATE Scores with Bootstrapped Standard Errors (Joint House and Senate Scaling)*, at http://voteview.com/dwnomin_joint_house_and_senate.htm.

[79] Grossman and Hopkins, *Asymmetric Politics* at 253 (cited in note 77).

[80] See Richard L. Hasen, *End of the Dialogue? Political Polarization, the Supreme Court, and Congress*, 86 USC L Rev 205, 235–37 (2013).

[81] See *The Polarization of the Congressional Parties*, at http://voteview.com/political_polarization_2014.htm.

The ideological distance between the parties today presents a striking contrast to the Congresses of the Warren and Burger Court eras (1953–86). The rapid rise in partisan sorting began in the 1980s; starting in the 1990s, a surge of southern Republicans substantially propelled the polarization of the parties.[82]

These developments are illustrated in figure 3. The figure, developed by Keith Poole and Howard Rosenthal, employs a measure of the ideological positions of members of Congress to show the ideological distance between the two parties in the House and Senate over time.[83] The figure highlights the sharp increase in polarization that has occurred in recent decades. In contrast with the late nineteenth and early twentieth centuries, Congress from the 1920s to the 1970s featured relatively limited polarization between the parties. But that period was followed by a sharp increase, resulting in a Congress that is even more polarized now than the Congress of a century ago.

One area in which polarization in Congress and the executive branch has had a particularly powerful effect is in the process of nominating and confirming federal judges. As we will discuss in Part III, in recent decades presidents—especially Republican presidents—have increasingly chosen nominees who represent their party's ideological orientation. In the Senate, there has been a dramatic increase in the amount of time it takes to confirm lower-court judges and an equally dramatic decrease in the percentage of lower-court nominees whom the Judiciary Committee now approves.[84] Over the past two decades, and especially over the past ten years, the number of failed nominations has sharply increased and failed nominations for the courts of appeals typically lingered in the Senate for over a year.[85] It was this trend that spurred Senate Democrats in 2013 to invoke the so-called "nuclear option"—allowing for a simple up-or-down majority vote on presi-

---

[82] See Earl Black and Merle Black, *The Rise of Southern Republicans* (Harvard, 2003).

[83] Chart available at http://voteview.com/political_polarization_2014.htm.

[84] See Sarah A. Binder and Forrest Maltzman, *The Politics of Advice and Consent: Putting Judges on the Federal Bench*, in Lawrence C. Dodd and Bruce I. Oppenheimer, eds, *Congress Reconsidered* 265 (10th ed 2012); Roger H. Davidson and Walter J. Oleszek, *Congress and Its Members* 379–87 (CQ Press, 11th ed 2008).

[85] See Binder and Maltzman, *Congress Reconsidered* at 266–71 (cited in note 84).

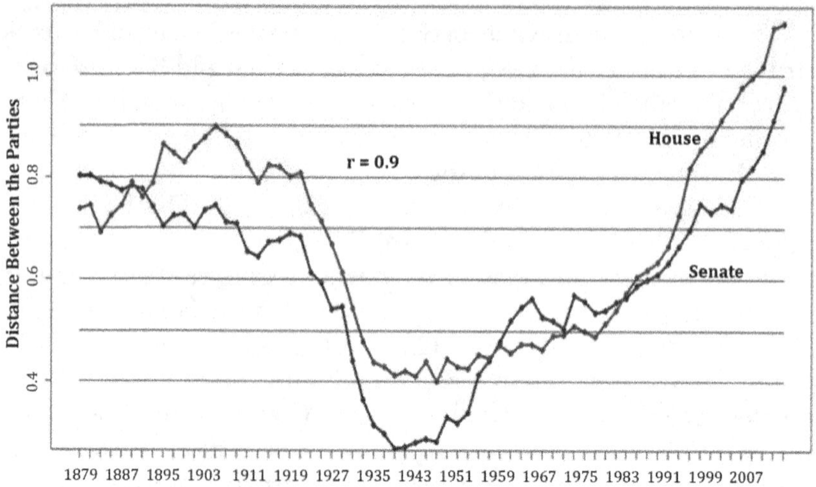

Figure 3. Party polarization, 1879–2014. Distance between the parties on the first (liberal–conservative) dimension. Source: Keith T. Poole and Howard Rosenthal, voteview blog.

dential nominations to lower courts, independent agencies, and executive branch positions.[86]

Senate voting on judicial nominees, especially Supreme Court nominees, has also become increasingly partisan.[87] Except for Clarence Thomas, the Justices on the Court today who were nominated prior to 2005 were all confirmed by unanimous or overwhelmingly positive votes.[88] Starting with John Roberts, however, nominees have received large numbers of negative votes from senators of the opposing party.[89]

---

[86] See Humberto Sanchez, *A Landmark Change to the Filibuster*, CQ Weekly Rpt, 1992 (Dec 2, 2013). For tables detailing a dramatic rise in filibusters tied to judicial and other executive branch nominations, see US Senate, Senate Action on Cloture Motions, archived at https://perma.cc/NR5X-4HW4; Sahi Kapur, *Charts: Why the Filibuster May Soon Be Dead*, Talking Points Memo (Nov 25, 2013, 6:00 a.m.), archived at https://perma.cc/WBR3-QM9K.

[87] See A. E. Dick Howard, *The Changing Face of the Supreme Court*, 101 Va L Rev 231, 292–315 (2015).

[88] Thomas was confirmed by a 52–48 vote. Stephen Breyer received nine negative votes, Ruth Bader Ginsburg three; Antonin Scalia and Anthony Kennedy were confirmed unanimously. See U. S. Senate, Supreme Court Nominations, Present–1789, archived at https://perma.cc/EV9N-GPZG.

[89] Consider, for example, then-Senator Barack Obama's statement (in explaining his no vote on Chief Justice Roberts) that he has "absolutely no doubt" that Roberts was qualified to sit on the Court but that he gave weight to the impact of a Justice's "deepest values" and "the depth and breadth" of a Justice's "empathy." See Nomination of John Roberts, 151 Cong Rec 21032 (cited in note 21).

Roberts, Samuel Alito, and Sonia Sotomayor all had the unanimous support of the president's party in Congress, and only one Democrat voted against Elena Kagan. Democrats split evenly in the Roberts confirmation vote; Alito, Sotomayor, Kagan, and Gorsuch were opposed by a majority of members of the opposition party.[90] It is difficult to imagine that a nominee like Ruth Bader Ginsburg could be confirmed today with only three negative votes, or that a nominee like Antonin Scalia could win unanimous approval; indeed, the extraordinary decision of Senate Republicans to block any consideration of President Obama's nomination of Merrick Garland to succeed Justice Scalia underscores how divisive and partisan Supreme Court confirmation battles have become.[91]

B. THE LARGER ELITE WORLD

Party polarization in government tracks a growing ideological divide among affluent, well-educated Democrats and Republicans. During the 1960s and 1970s, when both Republicans and Democrats occupied every ideological niche, Democratic and Republican elites tended to agree on some major issues, especially with respect to civil rights and civil liberties.[92] Today, however, Democratic and Republican elites are at opposite ends of the ideological spectrum in their policy positions. Indeed, Democratic elites are more liberal than other Democrats, and Republican elites are more conservative than other Republicans.[93]

The consequences of such elite polarization are profound. Although the potential impact of the views of the general public on the

---

[90] Hasen, 86 USC L Rev at 246–48 (cited in note 80). For this very reason, there is now widespread speculation that the Senate (if controlled by the opposition party) would not allow a vote on future Supreme Court nominations. See Linda Hirschman, *Why the Next Supreme Court Vacancy Will Favor Liberals No Matter Who Retires*, Wash Post (Dec 31, 2015), archived at https://perma.cc/G9DJ-L3AW.

[91] See Shear and Steinhauer, *More Republicans* (cited in note 3). See also Brent Martin, *Chief Justice Roberts: Scalia, Ginsburg Wouldn't be Confirmed Today*, Nebraska Radio Network (Sept 19, 2014), archived at https://perma.cc/RQ6Z-MRT4 (quoting Chief Justice Roberts 2014 comment that neither Ginsburg nor Scalia "would have a chance" of confirmation today).

[92] See Herbert McClosky, *Consensus and Ideology in American Politics*, 58 Am Pol Sci Rev 361 (1964); Peter Skerry, *The Class Conflict over Abortion*, 52 Pub Interest 69 (1978).

[93] See Graber, 56 Howard L J at 693–712 (cited in note 71) (discussing polling data); Geoffrey C. Layman and Thomas M. Carsey, *Party Polarization and "Conflict Extension" in the American Electorate*, 46 Am J Pol Sci 786, 789 (2002) (noting elite polarization with respect to "social welfare, racial, and cultural issues").

Supreme Court receives a great deal of attention,[94] elite values exert an even more powerful impact. Because the Justices are part of the elite sector of society, their own views tend to reflect elite attitudes.[95] During the 1960s, for example, Warren Court liberalism was fueled by elite support in both parties; today, the Roberts Court's sharp ideological divide is fueled by the partisan divide between elite Democrats and Republicans.[96]

During the Warren and Burger Court eras, Supreme Court decisions on race, religion, and other socially divisive issues tended to track elite views.[97] The Court's school prayer decisions of 1962 and 1963, for example, were widely unpopular with the mass public (85 percent disapproved in a 1964 survey), but elite support "for the Supreme Court's secularization project was clearly visible in the activities of law professors and deans [and] in the prominent newspaper editorials endorsing" the Court's decisions.[98] On issues involving free speech and equal protection, several studies pointed to a gap between elite and popular opinion. As one study concluded, "[s]ocial learning, insofar as it affects support for civil liberties, is likely to be greater among the influentials (that, is political elites) of the society than among the mass public."[99] Likewise, attitudes toward abortion in 1965–80 revealed a striking gap between elites and the mass public; indeed, "the best predictor of abortion attitudes" was level of education.[100]

Unlike elites during the Warren and Burger Court eras, today's elites, like Congress itself, are sharply divided along partisan lines.

---

[94] See, for example, Barry Friedman, *The Will of the People: How Public Opinion Has Influenced the Supreme Court and Shaped the Meaning of the Constitution* (Macmillan, 2009); and Richard L. Pildes, *Is the Supreme Court a "Majoritarian" Institution?*, 2010 Supreme Court Review 103.

[95] Baum and Devins, 98 Georgetown L J at 1537–46 (cited in note 12).

[96] We are not the first to make this point. See Graber, 56 Howard L J at 665 (cited in note 71).

[97] Baum and Devins, 98 Georgetown L J at 1570–74 (cited in note 12) (documenting that Supreme Court is more likely to adhere to views of individuals with postgraduate degrees than individuals with lower levels of education).

[98] John C. Jeffries, Jr. and James E. Ryan, *A Political History of the Establishment Clause*, 100 Mich L Rev 279, 325 (2001). For 1964 survey data, see Univ of Mich Survey Research Ctr, *American National Election Studies: 1964 Pre-Post Election Study* 13 (Sept–Nov 1964), archived at https://perma.cc/PDV8-Q8NR. The decisions were *Engel v Vitale*, 370 US 421 (1962); and *Abington School District v Schempp*, 374 US 203 (1963).

[99] Herbert McClosky and Alida Brill, *Dimensions of Tolerance: What Americans Believe About Civil Liberties* 233 (Russell Sage, 1983). See also McClosky, 58 Am Pol Sci Rev at 373 (cited in note 92) (noting that "political influentials" give "stronger approval" to "democratic ideas" than "ordinary voters"). For additional studies, see sources cited in Graber, 56 Howard L J at 686–87 (cited in note 71).

[100] Donald Granberg and Beth Wellman Granberg, *Abortion Attitudes, 1965–1980: Trends and Determinants*, 12 Family Planning Persp 250, 254 (1980).

Polling data make it clear that the opinions of Republicans and Democrats with high socioeconomic status and high levels of education diverge more than the opinions of the population as a whole. In turn, the political class is dominated by polarized elites and, as such, the "extremes are overrepresented in the political arena and the center underrepresented."[101]

This state of affairs is evident in 2005, 2011, and 2014 surveys by the Pew Research Group.[102] By correlating income and education to political beliefs, the Pew studies make clear that the most liberal Americans are affluent, well-educated Democrats and the most conservative Americans are affluent, well-educated Republicans.[103] These studies also highlight growing polarization among elites. Most significant (and tracking the hardening of the right on today's Supreme Court),[104] these studies identify dramatic changes among strong political conservatives since the 1980s. In the 1980s, conservatives divided between two groups: economic and social conservatives. By 2005, economic conservatives had adopted the cultural beliefs of social conservatives.[105] Liberal Democrats became even more liberal during this period. On same-sex marriage, abortion rights, and restrictions on civil liberties tied to the War on Terror, "[m]embers of the most affluent well educated group of Democrats tended to be far more liberal on all issues than members of other Democratic groups."[106]

At the same time, political competition has become more personalized and more bitter. Republicans and Democrats increasingly view each other negatively, see themselves in competition, and are "angry" when the other side wins a close election.[107] Moreover, voters now seek out information to back up preexisting policy preferences

[101] Morris P. Fiorina et al, *Culture War? The Myth of a Polarized America* 200 (Longman, 3d ed 2011).

[102] *The 2005 Political Typology*, Pew Research Center for the People and the Press (May 10, 2005), archived at https://perma.cc/SN5Z-8XU9; *Beyond Red vs. Blue: Political Typology*, Pew Research Center for the People and the Press (May 4, 2011), at http://www.people-press.org/files/legacy-pdf/Beyond-Red-vs-Blue-The-Political-Typology.pdf; *Beyond Red vs. Blue: The Political Typology*, Pew Research Center (June 26, 2014). The 2005 and 2011 polls are discussed in Graber, 56 Howard L J at 695–700 (cited in note 71).

[103] Pew, *2005 Political Topology* at 64–65 (cited in note 102); Pew, *Beyond Red v. Blue* (2011) at 105, 109, 111 (cited in note 102); Pew, *Beyond Red v. Blue* (2014) at 92, 99–102, 111–12 (cited in note 102).

[104] See Part IV.

[105] Pew, *2005 Political Topology* at 53 (cited in note 102).

[106] Graber, 56 Howard L J at 698 (cited in note 71).

[107] See Miller and Conover, 68 Pol Res Q at 232 (cited in note 8).

rather than to educate themselves.[108] The level of animosity along ideological lines is suggested by a 2014 survey that found that 23 percent of people with consistently liberal views would be unhappy if an immediate family member were to marry a Republican, and 30 percent of their conservative counterparts would be unhappy about a marriage to a Democrat.[109]

The growth in ideological and partisan polarization is reflected in today's news media. During the Warren and Burger Court eras, moderate-to-liberal network television and daily newspapers dominated public discourse.[110] As a response to a perceived liberal bias in the media, conservatives established their own informational infrastructure, which culminated with the establishment of the Fox News channel.[111] Liberal ideologues attempted to replicate this trend, though they were not as successful.[112] Over the past thirty years, the proliferation of cable television, the Internet, and the blogosphere has transformed the public discourse by producing major media outlets that are distinctly on the political left or right.[113] Surveys show that among people who are politically involved, liberals and conservatives have strong tendencies to select news sources whose political orientation is similar to their own.[114]

---

[108] See Ilya Somin, *Knowledge About Ignorance: New Directions in the Study of Political Information*, 18 Critical Rev 255, 260–62 (2006); Neal Devins, *The D'Oh! of Popular Constitutionalism*, 105 Mich L Rev 1333, 1340–46 (2007).

[109] *Political Polarization in the American Public* 48, Pew Research Center (June 12, 2014).

[110] See William Powers, *The Massless Media*, Atlantic (Jan/Feb 2005) at 124 ("[T]he political culture of the 1940s and 1950s discouraged extremism. . . . Politics hewed to the center, and the media both reflected and reinforced this tendency. . . . Th[e] establishment consensus exploded in the 1960s and 1970s, . . . but the mass media hung on for a few decades, a vestigial reminder of what had been."). For additional discussion, see notes 92–100 and accompanying text (examining how elite social networks favored liberal outcomes during 1969–90 era).

[111] Grossman and Hopkins, *Asymmetric Politics* at 147 (cited in note 77).

[112] Id at 152–53.

[113] See Richard A. Posner, *Bad News*, NY Times (July 31, G9 2005) ("The current tendency to political polarization in news reporting is thus a consequence of changes not in underlying political opinions, but in costs, specifically the falling cost of new entrants."). Polarization was also fueled by changes in federal regulatory policy, most notably the repeal of the Fairness Doctrine in 1987, and the related proliferation of conservative and liberal media outlets that allowed consumers to get their news and opinion programming from stations that reinforced preexisting ideological commitments. See Cass R. Sunstein, *Deliberative Trouble? Why Groups Go to Extremes*, 110 Yale L J 71, 101 (2000) (arguing that changes in the news media resulting from the repeal of Fairness "may create group polarization" as "all too many people might be exposed to louder echoes of their own voices").

[114] Markus Prior, *Medial and Political Polarization*, 16 Ann Rev Pol Sci 101 (2013); Amy Mitchell et al, *Political Polarization and Media Habits*, Pew Research Center (Oct 21, 2014), at

Analogous changes have occurred in the legal profession. In the 1960s and 1970s the elite segment of the legal profession, including bar groups like the American Bar Association, leaned to the left.[115] In response, conservatives in the profession sought to redress what they saw as an ideological imbalance.[116] One result was the establishment of public interest law firms representing conservative positions.[117] Another was the creation and growth of the Federalist Society, which originated as a reaction to the perceived liberal bias of elite law schools.[118] The Federalist Society serves as a reference group for conservative law students and lawyers, each with its own organizations and activities under the society's umbrella;[119] the American Constitution Society, created in response to the success of the Federalist Society, serves a similar though less critical function for liberals.[120]

These developments are reflected in the emergence of distinct career paths for conservatives and liberals in the elite segment of

---

http://www.journalism.org/2014/10/21/political-polarization-media-habits/. Due to this trend, conservative Republicans have become increasingly ideologically distinct from Democrats. See Grossman and Hopkins, *Asymmetric Politics* at 157 (cited in note 77).

[115] See Teles, *Conservative Legal Movement* at 41–59 (cited in note 13) (tracking rise of liberal legal establishment). Changes in the views of the elite segment of the legal profession were reflected in the shift of the American Bar Association from its traditional conservatism to a more liberal stance beginning in the 1960s. Id at 28–35. There was a similar leaning to the left in the news media that covered the Supreme Court. The most prominent Supreme Court reporters, such as Anthony Lewis and Linda Greenhouse of the *New York Times* and Nina Totenberg of National Public Radio, reported and assessed the Justices' positions primarily from a liberal perspective. Conservative complaints about the impact of a liberal elite sometimes singled out Greenhouse, and Thomas Sowell and Laurence Silberman popularized the term "Greenhouse effect" to refer to this impact. See Thomas Sowell, *Blackmun Plays to the Crowd*, St. Louis Post-Dispatch 7B (May 4, 1994); *Attacking Activism, Judge Names Names*, Legal Times 14–17 (June 22, 1992) (hereafter *Attacking Activism*) (reporting on speech by federal court of appeals Judge Laurence Silberman).

[116] See generally, Ann Southworth, *Lawyers of the Right: Professionalizing the Conservative Coalition* (Chicago, 2008); Teles, *Conservative Legal Movement* at 58–59, 135–80 (cited in note 13). For a discussion of the efforts of the Reagan administration to transform the legal profession by credentialing young conservative lawyers, see notes 170–76 and accompanying text (discussing Reagan administration efforts to groom conservatives who would later become federal court judges and Supreme Court Justices).

[117] See Southworth, *Lawyers of the Right* at 8–40 (cited in note 116).

[118] Michael Avery and Danielle McLaughlin, *The Federalist Society: How Conservatives Took the Law Back from Liberals* (Vanderbilt, 2013); Hollis-Brusky, *Ideas with Consequences* (cited in note 13).

[119] Hollis-Brusky, *Ideas with Consequences* at 13–15 (cited in note 13); descriptions of the sectors of the society for students and for practicing lawyers are at its website, http://www.fed-soc.org/.

[120] See Hollis-Brusky, *Ideas with Consequences* at 166–67 (cited in note 13).

the legal profession. Outstanding students at the most prestigious law schools increasingly move into clerkships with federal appellate judges who share their ideological orientations, and then into presidential administrations, law firms, and other institutions that also share their liberal or conservative views.[121]

Of course, Supreme Court Justices are part of the social and legal elite. They are "overwhelmingly upper-middle or upper-class and extremely well educated, usually at the nation's more elite universities."[122] The current Justices of the Supreme Court, as Judge Richard Posner has observed, are "sheltered, cosseted," and most of them "grew up in privileged circumstances and do not rub shoulders with hoi polloi."[123] All the Justices who sat on the Court from 2010 through 2016 attended Harvard or Yale law schools, nearly all came from well-to-do families, and those who did not (Thomas, Sotomayor) received million dollar plus advances for writing their autobiographies.[124] In Part IV, we explain the importance of elite social networks to Supreme Court decision making and to the growth in partisan polarization on the Court.

III. Explaining the Growth in Polarization: The Appointment Process

As we have suggested, the simultaneous growth of polarization on the Supreme Court and among elites in politics, the media, and the legal profession is not a coincidence; changes in the Court

---

[121] See William E. Nelson et al, *The Liberal Tradition of the Supreme Court Clerkship: Its Rise, Fall, and Reincarnation?*, 62 Vand L Rev 1749, 1775–91 (2009) (discussing both postclerk employment and the increasing polarization among Justices in selecting clerks who had previously worked for appeals court judges of the same political party). For additional discussion, see notes 258–61 and accompanying text.

[122] Michael J. Klarman, *What's So Great About Constitutionalism*, 93 Nw U L Rev 145, 189 (1998).

[123] Richard A. Posner, *How Judges Think* 306 (Harvard, 2008).

[124] Id; Howard, 101 Va L Rev at 251–52 (cited in note 87); Adam Liptak, *Sotomayor Got $1.175 Million for Memoir, Forms Reveal*, NY Times (May 27, 2011), archived at https://perma.cc/5EAE-SYWJ; Brent Kendall, *Sotomayor Got $1.175 Million Book Advance*, Wall St J (May 27, 2011 3:28 p.m.), archived at https://perma.cc/QF8Z-R2DH. When campaigning for president, Donald Trump issued a list of twenty-one potential Supreme Court nominees that seemed "a revolt against the elites." Adam Liptak, *Trump's Supreme Court List: Ivy League? Out. The Heartland? In*, NY Times (Nov 14, 2016), available at http://www.nytimes.com/2016/11/15/us/politics/trump-supreme-court-Justices.html?_r=0. Trump's list largely eschewed elites from the east or west coast as well as candidates who attended Harvard or Yale law schools. Id.

reflect changes in its political environment. In this part and in Part IV we probe the linkages between the two. In this part, we examine changes in the process of presidential appointment of Justices. In Part IV we examine changes in the social environments of the Justices.

The role of ideology in the appointment of Justices has grown in both Democratic and Republican administrations over the past few decades. But this growth has taken different forms in the two parties, and it has been more substantial on the Republican side due to the fact that Republicans have become more ideologically homogenous than Democrats.[125]

A. DEMOCRATIC PRESIDENTS

In nominating Supreme Court Justices, presidents consider much more than the "objective" qualifications of potential nominees, such as their legal abilities and their ethical behavior. Presidents also consider ideology, use of nominations as a reward for service to the president and the president's party, political benefits that may be gained through a nomination, and the nominee's prospects for confirmation.[126]

The relative weights given to policy and other considerations have varied considerably from president to president and even from nomination to nomination.[127] Over the Court's history, some presidents have given close attention to the policy preferences of at least some of their nominees,[128] but they were distinctly in the minority. Our historical analysis focuses on the period since the 1930s, which might be regarded as the beginning of the "modern" era of the Court.[129]

1. *From Roosevelt to Johnson.* Franklin Roosevelt (1933–45) gave a high priority to policy considerations in his Supreme Court appoint-

---

[125] Grossman and Hopkins, *Asymmetric Politics* (cited in note 77).

[126] Lawrence Baum, *The Supreme Court* 35–40 (CQ Press, 12th ed 2015).

[127] See generally, Henry J. Abraham, *Justices, Presidents, and Senators: A History of U.S. Supreme Court Appointments from Washington to Bush II* (Rowman and Littlefield, 2007).

[128] Presidents who seem to fit that description include Jefferson (see id at 70), Theodore Roosevelt (id at 124), and Taft (id at 131). The two appointments by Ulysses S. Grant to achieve reversal of the Court's first Legal Tender decision are another example of policy-oriented choices. Robert G. McCloskey and Sanford Levinson, *The American Supreme Court* 76 (Chicago, 2005). The decisions were *Hepburn v Griswold*, 8 Wall 603 (1870), and *Knox v Lee*, 12 Wall 457 (1871).

[129] McCloskey and Levinson, *The American Supreme Court* at 121–47 (cited in note 128).

ments. Specifically, he responded to Court rulings invalidating New Deal initiatives[130] by nominating Justices who seemed likely to support broad interpretations of federal power over the economy.[131] The Roosevelt appointees diverged considerably on civil liberties issues, however. This may be partially due to the fact that Roosevelt's Democratic Party largely rejected liberalism on civil liberties, as it would have likely alienated important voting blocs.[132] Further, in contrast with economic policy, civil liberties were only beginning to become prominent on the Court's agenda and, in any event, were not a priority for Roosevelt.[133]

Policy considerations were less important to the next three Democratic presidents, Harry Truman (1945–53), John Kennedy (1961–63), and Lyndon Johnson (1963–69). Although Roosevelt chose nominees primarily from his circle of personal and political acquaintances,[134] his Democratic successors gave even more weight to their personal and political ties with prospective nominees to the Court. Ideology clearly played a secondary role.

This was especially true of Truman, who gave particular emphasis to personal ties with nominees.[135] Because of his indifference to ideological considerations, the liberal Truman appointed four relatively conservative Justices to the Court.[136] Personal connections also

---

[130] Jeff Shesol, *Supreme Power: Franklin Roosevelt vs. The Supreme Court* (W. W. Norton, 2011).

[131] Leuchtenburg, *The Supreme Court Reborn* at 154 (cited in note 31).

[132] See Hans Noel, *Political Ideologies and Political Parties in America* 37 (Cambridge, 2013).

[133] See notes 51–53 and accompanying text (highlighting divergent views of Roosevelt appointees on civil liberties). See generally Pritchett, *The Roosevelt Court* (cited in note 44); C. Herman Pritchett, *Civil Liberties and the Vinson Court* (Chicago, 1954).

[134] "Nearly all of the Justices chosen by Presidents Franklin Roosevelt, Truman, Kennedy, and Johnson had at least a fairly confidential relationship with them prior to their appointment." Robert Scigliano, *The Supreme Court and the Presidency* 95 (Free Press, 1971).

[135] In one leading analysis of presidents' appointment strategies, the chapter on Truman is entitled "Truman Rewards Loyalty and Friendship." David Alistair Yalof, *Pursuit of Justices: Presidential Politics and the Selection of Supreme Court Nominees* 20–40 (Chicago, 1999). Truman was a party-centrist whose main concern was presiding over a factionalized Democratic Party. See Nelson Lichtenstein, *From Corporatism to Collective Bargaining: Organized Labor and the Eclipse of Social Democracy in the Postwar Era*, excerpted in Steve Fraser and Gary Gerstle, eds, *The Rise and Fall of the New Deal Order, 1930–1980*, 122–52 (Princeton, 1989).

[136] Based on the coding of votes in the Supreme Court Database (see note 28), all four Truman appointees ranked above the median among Justices serving in the 1937–2006 Terms for their proportions of conservative votes. With the exception of Clark, all were well above the median. Landes and Posner, 1 J Legal Analysis at 782–83 (cited in note 31). Among Justices who served in the 1946–85 Terms, the Truman appointees have similar rankings in civil liberties cases, with voting scores modified in an effort to take into account change in the

explain John F. Kennedy's appointments of Byron White and Arthur Goldberg. Both were members of his Cabinet, and Kennedy had long-standing ties with White. Indeed, White wrote the intelligence report on the sinking of a boat that Kennedy piloted during World War II.[137]

Lyndon Johnson also had close ties to Abe Fortas, whom he appointed to the Court in 1965 and unsuccessfully nominated for Chief Justice three years later, and to Homer Thornberry, whose 1968 nomination became moot when Fortas failed to win confirmation as Chief Justice. Both were personal friends of Johnson, and Fortas served Johnson as an informal but close advisor.[138] Thurgood Marshall, appointed to the Court in 1967, was Johnson's Solicitor General, and his appointment also reflected the political value of choosing the first African American Justice.

While Truman may have been indifferent to ideology in choosing nominees, Kennedy and Johnson were not. Kennedy, for example. considered elevating federal judge William Hastie to the Supreme Court; had Hastie been nominated and confirmed, he would have become the first African American Justice. But Kennedy chose not to make the nomination, and it appears that Hastie's relative moderation played a role in that decision.[139]

In general, though, these presidents did not emphasize ideology in their selection of Justices. There was therefore considerable room for variation in the ideological orientations of their nominees. Largely because the Democratic Party of that era included many conservative southerners, it was ideologically heterogeneous.[140] Although the Justices appointed by Democratic presidents from Roosevelt through Johnson tended on average to be fairly liberal, the relatively low priority that most of those presidents gave to ideology resulted in a set of Justices who were mixed in their ideological views.

---

composition of cases over time. Lawrence Baum, *Comparing the Policy Positions of Supreme Court Justices from Different Periods*, 42 Western Pol Q 509, 511 (1989).

[137] Henry J. Abraham, *Justices and Presidents* 275 (Rowman and Littlefield, 2d ed 1985).

[138] Laura Kalman, *Abe Fortas: A Biography* 199–227 (Yale, 1990).

[139] Sheldon Goldman, *Picking Federal Judges: Lower Court Selection from Roosevelt Through Reagan* 166 (Yale, 1999).

[140] See Stefanie A. Lindquist, David A. Yalof, and John A. Clark, *The Impact of Presidential Appointments to the U.S. Supreme Court: Cohesive and Divisive Voting within Presidential Blocs*, 53 Pol Res Q 795 (2000).

2. *Clinton and Obama.* Bill Clinton (1993–2001) and Barack Obama (2009–17) each made two appointments to the Supreme Court. The Clinton-Obama approach differed considerably from that of Truman, Kennedy, and Johnson. Clinton and Obama were careful to select nominees whose records gave strong evidence of liberalism. Clinton, for example, drew from "a pool of mostly liberal and Democratic candidates" and seriously considered liberal criticisms of Ginsburg's position on abortion.[141] Before choosing Sonia Sotomayor in 2009, Obama read long memoranda on the leading candidates and "kept asking for more original writings by the candidates."[142]

Nonetheless, ideology did not play a determinative role in the Clinton and Obama nominations. Instead, both presidents veered away from nominees whose strong liberalism would prompt confirmation battles and toward nominees who embraced the rhetoric of judicial restraint, had rich personal histories, and were perceived as relatively moderate in their views.[143] When nominating Merrick Garland to fill Antonin Scalia's seat, for example, Obama was well aware of Senate

---

[141] Yalof, *Pursuit of Justices* at 196 (cited in note 135). See also Jeffrey Toobin, *The Nine: Inside the Secret World of the Supreme Court* 70–71 (Anchor, 2007). At the same time, Clinton identified as a centrist "New Democrat," and disavowed several liberal positions. See Grossman and Hopkins, *Asymmetric Politics* at 225–26 (cited in note 77).

[142] Peter Baker and Adam Nagourney, *Tight Lid Defined Process in Selecting a New Justice*, NY Times at A17 (May 28, 2009).

[143] On Ginsburg, see Elizabeth Drew, *On the Edge: The Clinton Presidency* 217–18 (Touchstone, 1995); Toobin, *The Nine* at 70 (cited in note 141). Clinton also thought it important that Ginsburg was championed by Senator Daniel Patrick Moynihan (D-NY), who held considerable influence over proposed health care legislation. Id. On the unhappiness of some liberals about Breyer's appointment, see Jan Crawford Greenburg, *Supreme Conflict: The Inside Story of The Struggle for Control of The United States Supreme Court* 182 (Penguin, 2007). On Breyer's ties to influential Republicans, see Drew, *On the Edge* at 214. On Obama's appointments, see Peter A. Baker, *Favorites of Left Don't Make Obama's Court List*, NY Times at A12 (May 26, 2009), and Jeffrey Toobin, *Bench Press: Are Obama's Judges Really Liberal?*, New Yorker (Sept 21, 2009). More generally, Obama "paid less attention" to the opportunity to use judicial appointments to appoint young lawyers who "could make significant marks on the law" than did Ronald Reagan and his Republican successors. Jeffrey Toobin, *Obama's Unfinished Judicial Legacy*, New Yorker (July 31, 2012), available at http://www.newyorker.com/news/daily-comment/obamas-unfinished-judicial-legacy.

Scores developed by Jeffrey Segal and Albert Cover measure perceptions of Supreme Court nominees' ideological positions in newspaper editorials after their nominations. The scores range from 0.0 at the conservative end to 1.0 at the liberal end. The Segal-Cover scores for these four nominees underline the difference: .680 for Ginsburg, .475 for Breyer, .780 for Sotomayor, and .730 for Kagan. By contrast, Roberts's score was .120 and Alito's .100. See Jeffrey A. Segal and Albert D. Cover, *Ideological Values and the Votes of U.S. Supreme Court Justices*, 83 Am Pol Sci Rev 557 (1989). The scores can be found at http://www.stonybrook.edu/polsci/jsegal/.

Republican threats to derail any nomination.[144] Acknowledging that Garland was "just the right nominee during such a divisive time in our politics,"[145] Obama selected a sixty-three-year-old moderate-liberal who stood a better chance of confirmation than any other candidate.[146] Reflecting the tendency of Democrats to place interest group politics ahead of ideology,[147] Clinton and Obama also put substantial emphasis on racial and gender diversity in their judicial nominations, including Supreme Court appointments.[148] As Mark Tushnet has observed, "Democratic presidents tend to pursue a demographic strategy rather than an ideological one for Supreme Court nominations."[149]

One way to characterize the Clinton-Obama appointments is that, in comparison with the appointments of earlier Democratic administrations, the average ideological position has not changed a great deal, but the variation has been reduced. Unlike earlier Democrats (who appointed both strong liberals and conservatives), the Clinton-

[144] See Gregory Korte, *How Obama Picked Merrick Garland for Last Supreme Court Pick*, USA Today (March 17, 2016), available at http://www.usatoday.com/story/news/politics/2016/03/16/white-house-garland-obamas-first-choice-supreme-court/81866606/; Lawrence Baum and Neal Devins, *Ideological Imbalance: Why Democrats Usually Pick Moderate-Liberal Justices and Republicans Usually Pick Conservative Ones*, Slate (March 17, 2016), available at http://www.slate.com/articles/news_and_politics/jurisprudence/2016/03/democrats_always_pick_moderates_like_merrick_garland.html.

[145] Korte, *How Obama Picked Merrick Garland* (cited in note 144) (quoting Deputy White House Press Secretary Eric Schultz).

[146] See Adam Liptak, *Where Merrick Garland Stands: A Close Look at His Judicial Record*, NY Times (March 17, 2016), available at http://www.nytimes.com/2016/03/18/us/politics/merrick-garlands-record-and-style-hint-at-his-appeal.html; Matthew Yglesias, *The Real Reason President Obama Appointed Merrick Garland*, Vox (March 18, 2016), available at http://www.vox.com/2016/3/18/11261416/why-obama-picked-garland. For a similar assessment of why Hillary Clinton might have reappointed Garland, see Joan Biskupic, *Why Merrick Garland Should Keep Hoping*, CNN Politics (Oct 23, 2016), available at http://www.cnn.com/2016/10/23/politics/hillary-clinton-merrick-garland-supreme-court/.

[147] See Matt Grossman and David A. Hopkins, *Ideological Republican and Group Interest Democrats*, 13 Persp on Pol 119 (2015). Democrats are limited in their pursuit of ideology, in part, because Democrats are not dominated by a single interest group; instead, Democrats advance the interests of a pro-government coalition that includes interest groups interested in the environment, economic inequality, race, and much more. See id at 119–20, 134–35.

[148] See Jeffrey Toobin, *Obama's Unfinished Judicial Legacy*, New Yorker (July 31, 2012), available at http://www.newyorker.com/news/daily-comment/obamas-unfinished-judicial-legacy (noting that "half of [Obama's] successful nominees have been women (compared to twenty-three per cent for Bush II), and nineteen per cent have been African American (compared to seven per cent for Bush II)"); Sheldon Goldman and Matthew D. Saronson, *Clinton's Non-Traditional Judges: Creating a More Representative Branch*, 78 Judicature 68 (1994).

[149] Tushnet, *In the Balance* at 74 (cited in note 21).

Obama appointees were all moderate liberals. A measure of Justices' ideological positions by year that was devised by Michael Bailey confirms this conclusion.[150] His measure pertains to civil liberties cases and covers the period from 1951 to 2011. A score of 1.22 is the most conservative in a particular year for any Justice in his study, and −1.87 the most liberal.[151] For the Democratic appointees who served during the study period, the average of their mean scores across terms was −0.55 for the Obama and Clinton appointees and −0.24, a little less liberal, for the Justices appointed by the presidents from Roosevelt to Johnson. But the Clinton and Obama appointees were clustered together, with a standard deviation of only .09 in their scores;[152] in contrast, their predecessors had a standard deviation of 1.03. Of the thirteen pre-Clinton Democratic appointees, five were more liberal than any of the Clinton and Obama Justices, and eight were more conservative than any of them. Thus, the Obama and Clinton appointees have contributed to partisan polarization of the Court by standing on the liberal side of the ideological spectrum, but they have adhered to a position of moderate rather than strong liberalism. More to the point, recent Democratic appointees to the Court do not reflect the sharp leftward shift of Democratic elites discussed in Part II. Instead, because Clinton and Obama valued interest group politics as much as ideology, they did not appoint strong liberals to the Court. Indeed, none of their nominees was as liberal as William O. Douglas, Earl Warren, William J. Brennan, Abe Fortas, Arthur Goldberg, or Thurgood Marshall.

---

[150] The scores are compiled at http://faculty.georgetown.edu/baileyma/JOPIdealPointsJan 2013.htm. The method for creating them is discussed in Michael A. Bailey, *Is Today's Court the Most Conservative in Sixty Years? Challenges and Opportunities in Measuring Judicial Preferences*, 75 J Pol 821 (2013). Because these scores were compiled only through calendar year 2011, only two terms are available for Justice Sotomayor and one term for Justice Kagan, but the stability of their voting records relative to their colleagues since that time indicates that their scores over a more extended period would be similar.

[151] Calculations in this paragraph were prepared by the authors based on scores compiled by Bailey.

[152] Obama's March 2016 nomination of Merrick Garland conforms to this practice. See Baum and Devins, *Ideological Imbalance* (cited in note 144). For example, ideological measures of Garland locate him smack in the middle of Clinton-Obama Democratic appointees. See Adam Liptak and Alicia Palapiano, *How Clinton's or Trump's Nominees Could Affect the Balance of the Supreme Court*, NY Times (Sept 25, 2016), available at http://www.nytimes.com/interactive/2016/09/25/us/politics/how-clintons-or-trumps-nominees-could-affect-the-balance-of-the-supreme-court.html?_r=0.

B. REPUBLICAN PRESIDENTS

The changes in appointment strategies on the Republican side have been more dramatic. That difference reflects a more fundamental change in the role of ideology in the Republican Party.

1. *From Eisenhower to Ford.* In contrast with Democratic presidents during the period from the 1930s through the 1960s, Republicans Dwight Eisenhower and Gerald Ford focused neither on personal relationships with nominees nor on policy considerations. Eisenhower named Earl Warren Chief Justice in 1953 to pay back a political debt for crucial support that the Warren-led California delegation had provided to him at the 1952 Republican Party convention.[153] The choice of William Brennan in October 1956 was motivated primarily by the perceived electoral advantages of choosing a Catholic Democrat.[154]

Gerald Ford's appointment of John Paul Stevens in 1975 was unusual in that personal, political, and ideological considerations played essentially no role in his decision. Ford delegated the selection of a nominee to Attorney General Edward Levi, asking him to focus on the qualifications of prospective nominees. Ford's approach can be understood in part as a response to Watergate, and especially to abuses in the Justice Department.[155]

President Richard Nixon's approach was more ambiguous. When running for president in 1968, Nixon sharply criticized the decisions of the Warren Court.[156] Once in office, Nixon sought to woo con-

---

[153] Abraham, *Justices and Presidents* at 200–02 (cited in note 137); Yalof, *Pursuit of Justices* at 44–45 (cited in note 135).

[154] Christine L. Nemacheck, *Strategic Selection: Presidential Nomination of Supreme Court Justices from Herbert Hoover Through George W. Bush* 49 (Virginia, 2007); Abraham, *Justices and Presidents* at 208 (cited in note 137); Yalof, *Pursuit of Justices* at 55–56, 61 (cited in note 135). The Segal-Cover scores for Warren and Brennan were .750 and 1.000, respectively. Segal and Cover, 83 Am Pol Sci Rev (cited in note 143). Eisenhower's disappointment with Warren and Brennan led him to give attention to ideology in his second-term appointments of Charles Whittaker (1957) and Potter Stewart (1958), but even in those instances the policy preferences of prospective nominees were considered to only a limited degree. Yalof, *Pursuit of Justices* at 61–69 (cited in note 135).

[155] Yalof, *Pursuit of Justices* at 125–31 (cited in note 135); Abraham, *Justices, Presidents, and Senators* at 160–61 (cited in note 127). Levi and Stevens did have a long personal relationship, dating back to elementary school. George L. Priest and William Ranney Levi, *Justice Stevens, Edward Levi, and the Chicago School of Antitrust*, Nat'l L Rev (May 24, 2010), available at http://www.law.uchicago.edu/news/Justice-stevens-edward-levi-and-chicago-school-antitrust.

[156] Donald Grier Stephenson, Jr., *Campaigns and the Court: The U.S. Supreme Court in Presidential Elections* 179–82 (Columbia, 1999).

servatives to the Republican Party by emphasizing several policy concerns, including criminal justice and school busing, relating to the Court.[157] At the same time, though, Nixon was careful not to alienate northern moderates who were still important to the Republican Party. Nixon's Supreme Court appointments reflected those sometimes conflicting goals: he sought Justices with conservative positions on the issues that were politically important to him, but he sought "ideological conformity" only on criminal justice and busing, and he was not interested in appointing a "hardliner."[158] In other words, "politics far more than ideology drove all six of [Nixon's] choices for the Court."[159]

2. *From Reagan to George W. Bush*. The Reagan administration broke ranks with its predecessors by making ideological considerations "the most important criteria" in the screening of judicial candidates, seeking to reshape Supreme Court decision making by sponsoring "ardently conservative candidates to the high court."[160] Unlike Roosevelt, who focused specifically on economic regulation, and Nixon, who focused specifically on criminal justice and school busing, Reagan sought to fundamentally transform the role of the Supreme Court.[161] Ideology played a dominant role in his nominations of such conservative stalwarts as Antonin Scalia, Robert Bork, Douglas Ginsburg, and (as Chief Justice) William Rehnquist.[162]

---

[157] Kevin J. McMahon, *Nixon's Court: His Challenge to Judicial Liberalism and Its Political Consequences* (Chicago, 2011).

[158] Eric A. Posner, *Casual with the Court*, New Republic (Oct 24, 2011), at https://newrepublic.com/article/94516/nixons-court-kevin-mcmahon (reviewing McMahon, *Nixon's Court* (cited in note 157)).

[159] McMahon, *Nixon's Court* at 6 (cited in note 157). Nixon White House Counsel John Dean's account of the chaotic process through which several of the Nixon nominations were made also underlines the lack of a systematic effort to choose nominees on the basis of their policy positions. See John W. Dean, *The Rehnquist Choice: The Untold Story of the Nixon Appointment That Redefined the Supreme Court* (Free Press, 2002).

[160] Yalof, *Pursuit of Justices* at 134 (cited in note 135).

[161] See Keith E. Whittington, *Political Foundations of Judicial Supremacy: The Presidency, the Supreme Court, and Constitutional Leadership in U.S. History* 89 (Princeton, 2009). See also John C. Hughes, *The Federal Courts, Politics, and the Rule of Law* 74 (Harpercollins, 1995) (claiming that Reagan had been elected on a wave of conservative populism, and he "could not afford to be indifferent to the courts").

[162] See Yalof, *Pursuit of Justices* at 142–65 (cited in note 135). All four had markedly conservative records on the federal appellate courts. Reflecting perceptions of those records, the Segal-Cover scores (Segal and Cover, 83 Am Pol Sci Rev (cited in note 143)) for the four nominees were all below .100.

Ideology also played a central role in the appointment strategies of Republicans George H. W. Bush and George W. Bush. George H. W. Bush chose Clarence Thomas in part to maintain African American representation on the Court, but Thomas also had a very strong record of conservatism. By nominating John Roberts, Harriet Miers, and Samuel Alito in 2005, George W. Bush sought to select the "most conservative possible Supreme Court Justice."[163] More striking, he put the desires of conservative leaders ahead of his own preferences. In particular, well-placed staunch conservatives were able to secure the withdrawal of Harriet Miers[164]—even though she was a trusted personal and political associate of Bush[165] and someone the president thought was strongly conservative.[166] Staunch conservatives—especially those for whom abortion was a high priority—had already succeeded in preventing the nomination of Attorney General Alberto Gonzales, another close associate of the president, for the same seat on the Court.[167]

It is important to note, though, that ideology was not the only criterion that these Republican presidents took into account. In nominating Sandra Day O'Connor, Reagan honored a campaign pledge to nominate a woman,[168] and when nominating Anthony Kennedy in 1987 and David Souter in 1990, the Reagan and George H. W. Bush administrations went out of their way to avoid potentially bruising confirmation battles.[169]

---

[163] Toobin, *The Nine* at 345 (cited in note 141).

[164] See notes 185–90 and accompanying text.

[165] Before becoming White House counsel, Miers had served as Bush's personal attorney. See Toobin, *The Nine* at 286–87 (cited in note 141).

[166] For Bush, Miers was the perfect "stealth" candidate—like David Souter but without the risk. See Steve Holland, *Bush Defends Pick for Supreme Court*, Toronto Star at A11 (Oct 5, 2005) (quoting Bush as saying "there's not a lot of opinions for people to look at").

[167] Toobin, *The Nine* at 266–70 (cited in note 141). The importance of the abortion issue in the blocking of a Gonzales nomination and in Miers's nomination is discussed in Geoffrey R. Stone, *Sex and the Constitution* 423–24 (Liveright, 2017).

[168] Douglas E. Kneeland, *Reagan Pledges Women on Court; Carter Challenges Foe on Economy*, NY Times at A1 (Oct 15, 1980). On the array of considerations that may have affected the choice of O'Connor, see Nemacheck, *Strategic Selection* at 9–13 (cited in note 154).

[169] Although administration insiders thought Kennedy and Souter were solid conservatives, they were chosen over more conservative alternatives—and, in Kennedy's case, after two of those alternatives were nominated or announced as a nominee but not confirmed. See Yalof, *Pursuit of Justices* at 145–46, 164 (cited in note 135) (discussing Kennedy); James MacGregor Burns, *Packing the Court: The Rise of Judicial Power and the Coming Crisis of the Supreme Court* 217 (Penguin, 2009) (discussing Souter).

Despite these exceptions, the overall shift in emphasis in the appointment strategies of these three Republican presidents was largely the product of the political and judicial priorities of their administrations, priorities that were shaped in no small part by the emergence of a new conservative legal movement.

After Ronald Reagan took office in 1981, the Reagan Justice Department began grooming a cadre of well-credentialed conservative lawyers in an effort to transform both constitutional discourse and judicial decision making. Under the leadership of Attorney General Edwin Meese, the Department of Justice in Reagan's second term sought aggressively to advance conservative goals in the judiciary.[170] Recognizing that the "project of getting the Constitution right was more than just appointing judges, and that we had to have a rhetoric that was persuasive, and an analysis that became talked about by public intellectuals,"[171] Meese formally embraced the "Jurisprudence of Original Intention."[172] He gave speeches, organized seminars on originalism within the department, and directed his Office of Legal Policy to issue *Guidelines for Constitutional Litigation* to enable Justice Department attorneys to adhere to the principles of originalism in their legal analyses and arguments.[173] In these and other ways, Meese sought to "facilitate the orderly development of conservative legal ideals and their injection into the mainstream."[174]

Meese also sought to staff the Justice Department with young conservative lawyers—making "ideological commitment . . . a credential rather than a disqualification."[175] The recently established Federalist Society was an important component of this strategy, be-

---

[170] Meese became Attorney General in 1985. First-term Attorney General William French Smith also embraced conservative ideals but did not pursue long-term objectives. See William French Smith, *Urging Judicial Restraint*, 68 ABA J 59 (1982); Teles, *Transformative Bureaucracy* at 66–69 (cited in note 10).

[171] Teles, *Transformative Bureaucracy* at 76 (cited in note 10) (quoting Kenneth Cribb, who served as Counselor to the Attorney General).

[172] Attorney General Edwin Meese, Address Before the American Bar Association, *The Supreme Court of the United States: Bulwark of a Limited Constitution* (July 9, 1985), available at http://www.fed-soc.org/publications/detail/the-great-debate-attorney-general-ed-meese-iii-july-9-1985. See also Teles, *Transformative Bureaucracy* at 80–81 (cited in note 10) (noting that the "critical turning point in the development of originalism" was a lunch-time talk by then-D.C. Circuit Judge Antonin Scalia to DoJ political appointees).

[173] Teles, *Transformative Bureaucracy* at 75–82 (cited in note 10).

[174] Teles, *Conservative Legal Movement* at 136 (cited in note 13).

[175] Teles, *Transformative Bureaucracy* at 74 (cited in note 10).

cause it enabled Meese and others in the administration to identify promising candidates for positions both in the Department of Justice and on the courts. Meese hired the society's founders as special assistants and tapped Stephen Markman, who headed the Washington, D.C. chapter of the Federalist Society, to become the Assistant Attorney General in charge of judicial selection.[176]

The George H. W. Bush administration followed the Reagan administration's lead. The administration looked to Lee Liberman Otis, co-founder of the Federalist Society, to lead its judicial selection process.[177] Both administrations aimed to nominate conservative judges, and membership in the Federalist Society was a proxy for adherence to conservative ideology. Reagan made all three of the society's original faculty advisors federal court judges and nominated two of the three—Robert Bork and Antonin Scalia—to the Supreme Court.[178] Nine of President George H. W. Bush's fifty-five[179] nominees to the federal courts of appeals and the Supreme Court were Federalist Society members (including Clarence Thomas, Samuel Alito, and John Roberts).[180]

At the same time, the Reagan and George W. Bush administrations were limited in their ability to nominate reliable conservatives. They did not yet have a "farm team" of conservatives who had joined the Federalist Society as law students and cut their teeth either

---

[176] Id at 68, 74. The Federalist Society was established in 1982 by conservative Yale and University of Chicago law students who felt "alienated from the prevailing political orientation of their classmates and their schools." Avery and McLaughlin, *The Federalist Society* at 1 (cited in note 118). See also Southworth, *Lawyers of the Right* at 124–48 (cited in note 116).

[177] Teles, *Rise of the Conservative Legal Movement* (cited in note 13).

[178] Nancy Scherer and Banks Miller, *The Federalist Society's Influence on the Federal Judiciary*, 62 Pol Res Q 366, 367 (2009).

[179] George H. W. Bush nominated fifty-three individuals to U.S. Circuit Courts, see Denis Steven Rutkus et al, Cong Research Serv, RL31868, *U.S. Circuit and District Court Nominations by President George W. Bush During the 107th–109th Congresses* 30 (2007) (listing the number of U.S. Circuit Court nominees of recent presidents), and two individuals to the U.S. Supreme Court, see US Senate, Supreme Court Nominations, present–1789, available at http://www.senate.gov/pagelayout/reference/nominations/ Nominations.htm.

[180] Id. (Roberts's 1992 nomination was not acted on by the Senate. Alito was confirmed to the Third Circuit, Thomas to the D.C. Circuit and Supreme Court.) At the time of Roberts's 2005 nomination to the Supreme Court, there was some uncertainty about whether he had ever been an official member of the Federalist Society, and Roberts reported that he did not remember being a member. Charles Lane, *Federalist Affiliation Misstated; Roberts Does Not Belong to Group*, Wash Post at A16 (July 21, 2005); Charles Lane, *Roberts Listed in Federalist Society '97–98 Directory; Court Director; Court Said He Has No Memory of Membership*, Wash Post at A1 (July 25, 2005). But Roberts has had ties with the society since his Supreme Court appointment.

clerking for a conservative judge or working as a government attorney. As Reagan Justice Department official Richard Willard explained, "these were the days before the Federalist Society was really off the ground, so it was hard to find lawyers who had a conservative political outlook. At that time, the law schools and the professional associations were overwhelmingly liberal in their outlook, and so finding conservative lawyers who had the outlook, but also the professional competence, to do the job, was a challenge."[181]

By the time George W. Bush became president in 2001, though, the conservative legal movement dominated Department of Justice and judicial appointments. Not only did Federalist Society members play "key roles in selecting, vetting, and shepherding nominees through the confirmation process" during the George W. Bush administration, but legal positions in the administration were overwhelmingly filled by members of the Federalist Society.[182] The administration tapped Federalist Society members Brett Kavanaugh and Viet Dinh to be in charge of judicial selection.[183] By 2005, the "farm team" of credentialed conservatives included John Roberts and Samuel Alito, and approximately half of George W. Bush's appointees to the federal courts of appeals were members of the Federalist Society.[184]

The nomination and withdrawal of Supreme Court nominee Harriet Miers vividly illustrates both the power of the conservative legal movement and the depth of the current pool of potential conservative Supreme Court nominees. Determined "not to repeat his father's mistake with Souter," Bush had the backing of Leonard Leo, the executive vice president of the Federalist Society.[185] Nonetheless, the reaction to the Miers nomination from the conservative legal

---

[181] Quoted in Teles, *Transformative Bureaucracy* at 70–71 (cited in note 10). See also id at 73 (noting Kenneth Cribb's comment to Attorney General Meese that "there aren't enough gray haired people who agree with us" to staff critical positions).

[182] Hollis-Brusky, *Ideas with Consequences* at 154 (cited in note 13). According to Daniel Troy, Federalist Society member and Bush-appointed counsel to the FDA, "Everybody, I mean everybody who got a job who was a lawyer was involved with the Federalist Society. I mean everybody." Id (quoting Troy).

[183] Michael Avery and Danielle McLaughlin, *How Conservatives Captured the Law*, Chron Higher Educ (Apr 15, 2013).

[184] Id; Scherer and Miller, 62 Pol Res Q at 368 (cited in note 178) (noting that around two-thirds of Bush's first-term judicial nominees were Federalist Society members).

[185] Greenburg, *Supreme Conflict* at 265 (cited in note 143).

establishment was "immediate, harsh, and pointed."[186] Attacking her both for her lack of Federalist Society "credentials"[187] and for her ties to the American Bar Association (which conservatives had turned against as too liberal in its screening of judges),[188] conservatives demanded that Miers withdraw and be replaced by a nominee from the "deep farm team of superbly qualified and talented circuit court judges primed for this moment."[189] Twenty-four days after her nomination, with conservative criticism unabated, Miers withdrew. Her replacement was Samuel Alito—a Federalist Society member and the favorite of the very conservatives who had attacked Miers.[190]

With four Federalist Society members sitting on the Supreme Court from 2006 to 2016, there is little question that the society has become a "mediating institution" for legal conservatives, helping to maintain "channels of communication through which individuals and organizations can exercise political influence."[191] Indeed, when 2016 Republican presidential candidate Donald Trump sought to establish his bona fides with the conservative legal network, he consulted with Federalist Society leadership in assembling his lists of potential Su-

---

[186] Teles, *Conservative Legal Movement* at 1 (cited in note 13). See generally Greenburg, *Supreme Conflict* at 263–84 (cited in note 143).

[187] See Hollis-Brusky, *Ideas with Consequences* at 153 (cited in note 13) (quoting Federalist Society member Tony Cotto as saying "No Fed Society credentials, that's going to hurt you. It hurt Harriet [Miers] a lot. . . . We want credentials. We want to see you've spoken at Federalist Society conferences, we want to know you've been to dinners, gripping and grinning").

[188] On Miers's ties to the ABA, see *Miers v The Federalist Society*, Daily Kos (Oct 7, 2005, 2:53 p.m.), archived at http://www.dailykos.com/story/2005/10/07/155092/-Miers-v-The-Federalist-Society (quoting a post on the *Volokh Conspiracy* by Jim Lindgren). On conservative disapproval of the ABA (including the George W. Bush administration's refusal to seek ABA screening of judicial nominees), see Teles, *Conservative Legal Movement* at 167–73 (cited in note 13).

[189] Todd Zywicki, *A Great Mind*, 28 Legal Times (Oct 10, 2005), archived at https://perma.cc/LHK7-2JGB. See also Randy E. Barnett, *Cronyism*, Wall St J, A26 (Oct 5, 2005) (suggesting that Miers lacked "a firm grasp on constitutional text, history and principles" as well as the ability to "resist the severe pressure brought by Congress, by the executive branch, by state and local governments, and also by fellow Justices to exceed the Constitution's limits on government power"); Michael A. Fletcher and Charles Babington, *Miers, Under Fire from Right, Withdrawn as Court Nominee*, Wash Post (Oct 28, 2005), archived at https://perma.cc/X7MP-EMAW.

[190] See Greenburg, *Supreme Conflict* at 269–70 (cited in note 143) (recounting story of former Reagan official Mike Carvin's strong support of Alito and opposition to Miers); see also Peter Baker, *Alito Nomination Sets Stage for Ideological Battle*, Wash Post (Nov 1, 2005), archived at https://perma.cc/9D5E-92UA ("Conservative leaders who helped force Miers to pull out Thursday rejoiced at the selection, seeing in Alito the philosophical equivalent of Justice Antonin Scalia.").

[191] Southworth, *Lawyers of the Right* at 135, 141 (cited in note 116).

preme Court nominees.[192] And when the society held its annual National Lawyers Convention a week after the 2016 election, nine of the twenty-one judges on that list were among the speakers and "nearly all the others" were in attendance.[193] Today, membership in the Federalist Society is critical to the credentialing of conservative lawyers. Michael Greve put it this way: "[O]n the left there are a million ways of getting credentialed; on the political right there's only one way in these legal circles."[194]

IV. The Justices in Their Social Environments

In this part, we focus on the social environments of the Justices, that is, the individuals and groups with whom the Justices interact directly or indirectly and whose regard the Justices care about. We argue that a Justice's social environment can exert significant influence on his or her jurisprudence.

A. The Justices' Social Identities

In addition to the goal of making sound legal decisions, Supreme Court Justices have other interests and values that affect their judicial behavior.[195] Like other people, they have social identities,[196] and

---

[192] See Alan Rappeport and Charlie Savage, *Donald Trump Releases List of Possible Supreme Court Picks*, NY Times (May 18, 2016), available at http://www.nytimes.com/2016/05/19/us/politics/donald-trump-supreme-court-nominees.html?_r=0; Bob Woodward and Robert Costa, *In a Revealing Interview, Trump Predicts a Massive Recession but Intends to Eliminate the National Debt in 8 Years*, Wash Post (April 2, 2016), available at https://www.washingtonpost.com/politics/in-turmoil-or-triumph-donald-trump-stands-alone/2016/04/02/8c0619b6-f8d6-11e5-a3ce-f06b5ba21f33_story.html (quoting Trump as saying "I'm getting names, The Federalist people. Some very good people.").

[193] Richard Wolf, *Supreme Court Wannabes Audition*, USA Today (Nov 21, 2016), 5A.

[194] Quoted in Hollis-Brusky, *Ideas with Consequences* at 152 (cited in note 13). It is for this very reason that the Federalist Society can have a de facto monopoly on the credentialing of the right, whereas the American Constitution Society cannot occupy a similar role on the left. The liberal legal establishment is far too large for any one group to truly capture Democratic judicial appointments.

[195] Baum, *Judges and Their Audiences* at 1–24 (cited in note 11); Frederick Schauer, *Incentives, Reputation, and the Inglorious Determinants of Judicial Behavior*, 68 U Cin L Rev 615, 619–21 (2000). For this reason, we take issue with political science models that assume that the Justices are single minded in their pursuit of their preferred legal policy agenda. See Baum and Devins, 98 Georgetown L J at 1529–32 (cited in note 12) (discussing these political science models and our critique of them).

[196] On social identities generally, see Henry Tajfel, *Differentiation Between Social Groups: Studies in the Social Psychology of Intergroup Relations* (1978); Marilynn B. Brewer, *The Many Faces of Social Identity: Implications for Political Psychology*, 22 Pol Psychol 115 (2001).

they care about how they are regarded by people who are important to those identities. Family members, friendship networks, and other relationships that relate to Justices' social identities serve as reference groups.[197]

Indeed, people who are interested in becoming federal appellate judges are likely to be *more* interested in the esteem of others than are most other people.[198] Such individuals willingly accept reduced monetary compensation and constraints on their personal activities and behaviors in exchange for the power and esteem that attach to a position on the federal bench.[199] Moreover, the high level of public attention that Supreme Court Justices receive today heightens their incentive to attain positive reputations with those whose esteem they most care about. Certainly, today's Justices invest substantial energy in cultivating their image with outside audiences. In terms of the number of extrajudicial appearances and interviews Justices have per year, one study shows that, in the years since 1960, the nine current Justices are all in the top ten.[200] It is therefore reasonable to posit that a desire for the esteem of others affects the Justices' behavior as decision makers.

As some scholars have posited, some Justices seem to care a good deal about how they are regarded by the American people as a whole.[201] But Justices generally orient themselves more specifically toward the political, legal, and social elite groups to which they belong.[202] No doubt, the elite audiences that are particularly important to individual Justices differ, but the Justices' personal backgrounds

---

[197] Moreover, Supreme Court Justices are often associated with one or the other political party; many have worked for Democratic or Republican administrations and most have contributed to political parties. Correspondingly, recent social science evidence links partisanship to the composition of the federal bench, including the fact that most federal court of appeals judges contributed to political campaigns before their appointment. See Adam Bonica and Maya Sen, *The Politics of Selecting the Bench from the Bar: The Legal Profession and Partisan Incentives to Politicize the Judiciary* (Harv Kennedy School, Working Paper No RWP 15-001, 2015), archived at https://perma.cc/CS5V-2VCD.

[198] Baum and Devins, 98 Georgetown L J at 1532 (cited in note 12). Judges' interest in the esteem of other people is discussed in Thomas J. Miceli and Metin M. Cosgel, *Reputation and Judicial Decision-making*, 23 J Econ Behav & Org 31 (1994), and in Schauer, 68 U Cin L Rev at 625–31 (cited in note 195).

[199] See Baum and Devins, 98 Georgetown L J at 1532 (cited in note 12).

[200] See Richard L. Hasen, *Celebrity Justice: Supreme Court Edition* 9 (U.C. Irvine School of Law, Research Paper No 2015-61, 2016), archived at https://perma.cc/3CZG-ZLS3.

[201] Friedman, *The Will of the People* (cited in note 94); Jeffrey Rosen, *The Most Democratic Branch: How the Courts Serve America* (Oxford, 2006).

[202] Baum and Devins, 98 Georgetown L J (cited in note 12).

and positions make some audiences especially relevant. In particular, today's Justices are members of increasingly polarized elite social networks that help to create and reinforce their ideological commitments.[203] These competing networks have replaced the relatively consensual center-left social network that once helped shape the thinking of both Republican and Democratic appointees to the Court. In part because of this change, Justices appointed to the Court by Republican presidents since 1990 have been less likely to support liberal positions than pre-1990 Republican appointees. The change has had less impact on the Democratic side, because Justices appointed by Democratic appointees were part of social networks that leaned to the left even before the era of strong polarization.

B. REPUBLICAN APPOINTEES TO THE COURT: FROM THE 1950S TO THE 1990S

In their votes and opinions, several of the Republican appointees to the Supreme Court between 1950 and 1990 were more liberal than some Democratic appointees.[204] As noted in Part III, Republican presidents' appointment strategies help to explain this phenomenon.[205] But as early as the 1960s, when President Nixon complained about the liberalizing influence of the "Washington-Georgetown social set" on certain Justices,[206] some observers maintained that a milieu of people and groups that shared liberal values, especially on civil liberties issues, influenced the behavior of the Justices. This milieu included the American Bar Association, legal academics, Supreme Court reporters, and elite social circles in Washington, D.C.[207] According to this narrative, Justices who came to the Court as con-

---

[203] Justice Scalia described one result: "It's a nasty time. When I was first in Washington, and even in my early years on this Court, I used to go to a lot of dinner parties at which there were people from both sides. Democrats, Republicans. [*Washington Post* publisher] Katharine Graham used to have dinner parties that really were quite representative of Washington. It doesn't happen anymore." Jennifer Senior, *In Conversation: Antonin Scalia*, 22, 27 NY Mag (Oct 14, 2013).

[204] See Section I.B. For a discussion of conservative disappointment in such appointments, see Marc A. Thiessen, *Why Are Republicans So Awful at Picking Supreme Court Justices?*, Wash Post (July 2, 2012), archived at https://perma.cc/R52G-YHTM.

[205] See Section III.B.

[206] Richard Reeves, *President Nixon: Alone in the White House* at 338 (Simon & Schuster, 2001); John W. Dean, *The Rehnquist Choice* at 171 (Free Press, 2001).

[207] On the components of this milieu within the legal profession, see Teles, *Conservative Legal Movement* at 22–57 (cited in note 13).

servatives often moved to the left during their tenure on the Court in order to please this left-leaning audience.[208] Indeed, Justice Antonin Scalia adopted this narrative in his opinions, complaining of what he saw as his colleagues' undue responsiveness to the views of a liberal elite.[209]

To determine whether some Republican appointees actually moved to the left during their tenure on the Court, we begin by comparing the Justices' voting records from early in their tenure with their records in later years. Such comparisons are very difficult, because shifts in the Court's agenda can create an impression of ideological change (or, for that matter, an impression of stability) that is illusory.[210] But imperfect measures[211] do support claims of leftward movement by

---

[208] Economist and columnist Thomas Sowell and two conservative federal judges have posited that impact with particular clarity. Thomas Sowell, *Justice Kennedy Goes Soft on Crime*, Columbus Dispatch A11 (Aug 13, 2003); Sowell, *Blackmun Plays to the Crowd* at 7B (cited in note 115); *Attacking Activism* at 14 (cited in note 115); Robert H. Bork, *Again, a Struggle for the Soul of the Court*, NY Times A19 (July 8, 1992).

[209] *Romer v Evans*, 517 US 620, 636 (1996) (Scalia, J, dissenting); *United States v Virginia*, 518 US 515, 567 (1996) (Scalia, J, dissenting); *Lawrence v Texas*, 539 US 558, 602 (2003) (Scalia, J, dissenting); *Obergefell v Hodges*, 135 S Ct 2584, 2629 (2015) (Scalia, J, dissenting).

[210] See Kevin T. McGuire and James A. Stimson, *The Least Dangerous Branch Revisited: New Evidence on Supreme Court Responsiveness to Public Preferences*, 66 J Pol 1018, 1023–27 (2004).

[211] The measures employed for this discussion include the simple proportions of pro–civil liberties votes by Justices in their fifth through tenth terms, compared with their first and second terms, reported in Baum, *Judges and Their Audiences* at 147 (cited in note 11); the same proportions, but with an adjustment for change in the Court's agenda, reported in id at 148; and the simple proportions of pro–civil liberties votes in the fifth through tenth terms, compared with the first and second terms, in cases covered on the front page of the *New York Times*, reported in Baum and Devins, 98 Georgetown L J at 1577 (cited in note 12). The proportions of pro–civil liberties votes were calculated with use of the Supreme Court Database, described in note 28. Cases were defined as involving civil liberties if they fell within issue areas 1 through 6 in the Database, described at https://perma.cc/6FKS-BRPE.

The adjustment is described in Lawrence Baum, *Measuring Policy Change in the U.S. Supreme Court*, 82 Am Pol Sci Rev 905 (1988). That adjustment is clearly imperfect, in that it rests on an assumption that the average movement of the Justices between two terms is close to zero. However, it does provide a control for change in the composition of the Court's agenda that causes Justices' voting records to become more liberal or more conservative even if those Justices' actual ideological positions have not changed.

A second complication in tracking the Justices' voting records is that the definition of certain issue positions as conservative or liberal has an element of arbitrariness, because the positions that are considered to be conservative or liberal do not simply follow deductively from broad values. One result is that perceptions of the ideological sides on an issue (such as freedom of expression) sometimes change substantially over time. Lawrence Baum, *Ideology in the Supreme Court* (Princeton, 2017). The coding of Justices' votes in the Supreme Court Database has been criticized on the ground that it reflects coders' prior expectations about the Justices. Anna Harvey and Michael J. Woodruff, *Confirmation Bias in the United States Supreme Court Judicial Database*, 29 J Law, Econ & Org 414 (2013). For this reason, data on Justices' voting in table 1 and the tables that follow should be read with caution. At the same time, there is considerable consensus on the ideological direction of the competing positions on most issues, and in the

several Republican appointees with respect to civil liberties. Table 1 shows those measures for several Republican appointees from Earl Warren through David Souter.

This pattern of leftward movement might be idiosyncratic rather than a reflection of any systematic forces.[212] But it is a reasonable inference that these Justices, or at least some of them, were influenced by the elite groups with whom they interacted. As we saw in Section II.B, Republican and Democratic elites often favored liberal outcomes on civil liberties issues during this period.[213] Moreover, legal academia and the most prestigious sector of the mass media leaned to the left in these years.[214]

The impact of social environments seems most evident in the case of Justice Blackmun, whose substantial turn to the left was clearly reinforced by the approval of liberal audiences in the elite news media and other sectors.[215] Blackmun was unusually attentive to the mail he received relating to his work as a Justice,[216] and he was close to some reporters.[217] In public appearances before sympathetic audiences, he solicited and received positive responses to his decisions.[218]

Justice Kennedy also seems particularly concerned with his public persona. According to one of his law clerks, Justice Kennedy "would constantly refer to how it's going to be perceived, how it's going to

---

short term there is considerable stability in the understanding of which positions are liberal and which positions are conservative.

[212] On the role of chance in creating what appear to be meaningful patterns of behavior, see Carol Mock and Herbert F. Weisberg, *Political Innumeracy: Encounters with Coincidence, Improbability, and Chance*, 36 Am J Pol Sci 1023 (1992).

[213] See notes 97–100 and accompanying text.

[214] See notes 110 and 115 and accompanying text; see also Deborah Jones Merritt, *Research and Teaching on Law Faculties: An Empirical Exploration*, 73 Chi Kent L Rev 765, 780 n 54 (1998) (discussing left-leaning tendencies of legal academies); Stanley Rothman and S. Robert Lichter, *Personality, Ideology, and World View: A Comparison of Media and Business Elites*, 15 Brit J Pol Sci 29 (1985) (discussing liberal tendencies of journalists before the Internet age); and David H. Weaver and G. Cleveland Wilhoit, *The American Journalist: A Portrait of U.S. News People and Their Work* 25–32 (1991) (discussing the same tendencies).

[215] Baum, *Judges and Their Audiences* at 153–55 (cited in note 11).

[216] Linda Greenhouse, *Becoming Justice Blackmun: Harry Blackmun's Supreme Court Journey* 134, 242 (Times Books, 2005); Harold Hongju Koh, *A Tribute to Justice Harry A. Blackmun*, 108 Harv L Rev 20, 20 (1994).

[217] Richard Davis, *Decisions and Images: The Supreme Court and the Press* 106 (1994).

[218] Neil A. Lewis, *Blackmun on Search for the Center*, NY Times, A7 (Mar 8, 1986); Reynolds Holding, *Blackmun Says Court Direction Disappointing*, SF Chron, A12 (June 10, 1992).

Table 1

Change in Percentages of Liberal Votes in Civil Liberties Cases, Selected Republican Appointees, 1st–2nd Terms to 5th–10th Terms (Part 1)[a]

Justice	All Votes	All Votes, Adjusted[b]	Important Cases[c]
Earl Warren	+34.8	+38.9	+16.6
Potter Stewart	+13.0	+12.5	+6.6
Harry Blackmun	+6.9	+9.6	+15.1
Lewis Powell	+2.2	+7.9	+12.0
John Paul Stevens	+1.6	+4.4	+6.7
Sandra Day O'Connor	+1.4	−3.0	+14.3
Anthony Kennedy	+13.9	+1.6	+33.7
David Souter	+24.9	+25.7	+20.4

[a] Scores on the first two measures are taken from Baum, *Judges and Their Audiences* at 147–48 (cited in note 11); scores on the third measure are taken from Baum and Devins, 98 Georgetown L J at 1577 (cited in note 12).

[b] On this adjustment, see note 211.

[c] Cases are defined as important if the Court's decisions were reported the following day on the front page of the *New York Times*. This measure of case importance is described and examined in Epstein and Segal, 44 Am J Pol Sci (cited in note 36).

look."[219] On the day the Court reaffirmed *Roe* in *Planned Parenthood v Casey*,[220] he told a reporter that "[s]ometimes you don't know if you're Caesar about to cross the Rubicon or Captain Queeg cutting your own tow line."[221]

By the time of *Casey*, however, the dominance of left-leaning media and academic elites had begun to wane. Conservative media outlets started to permeate the American mainstream,[222] the conservative legal network was on the rise, and the very incentives that had once pushed Republican nominees to the left now pushed a new breed of Republican nominees to the right.

C. Republican Appointees: The Current Court

Aside from Justice Kennedy, the Republicans on the Roberts Court have remained steadfast in their conservatism: Justice Scalia

---

[219] Jeffrey Rosen, *The Agonizer*, New Yorker (Nov 11, 1996), 82, 86 (quoting an unnamed Supreme Court clerk).

[220] *Planned Parenthood v Casey*, 505 US 833 (1992).

[221] Terry Carter, *Crossing the Rubicon*, Cal Lawyer 39, 39–40 (quoting Justice Kennedy).

[222] Grossman and Hopkins, *Asymmetric Politics* at 150 (cited in note 77).

Table 2
Change in Percentages of Liberal Votes in Civil Liberties Cases, Selected Republican Appointees, 1st–2nd Terms to 5th–10th Terms (Part 2)[a]

Justice	All Votes	All Votes, Adjusted	Important Cases
Warren Burger	−4.4	−9.7	−10.0
William Rehnquist	−4.6	+2.1	−3.0
Antonin Scalia	−3.3	−16.1	−9.7
Clarence Thomas	−3.9	−3.3	−20.6
John Roberts	+13.2	+8.5	–
Samuel Alito	+5.2	+1.0	–

[a] See notes to table 1. No results are shown for important cases for Roberts and Alito because the list on which that analysis is based has not been updated since 2010.

served for close to thirty years before his death, Justice Thomas has served for more than twenty-five years, and Justice Alito and Chief Justice Roberts have served for more than a decade.[223] As table 2 shows, only Roberts has moved in a liberal direction by the measures reflected in the table. Table 3 details the proportions of liberal and conservative votes by the conservative Justices—showing both fluctuations over time and the substantial gap between all four of the strong conservatives and Justice Breyer, the most moderate of the Court's liberals.[224] Because voting records are affected by changes in the Court's agenda from term to term, a Justice's record relative to the records of her colleagues in each pair of terms provides a better sense of her ideological positions than do changes in her proportions of liberal and conservative votes over time.[225]

The primary reason for the difference between the voting behavior of these Republican appointees and several of their predecessors is the evolution of appointment strategies discussed earlier.[226] In Sec-

[223] This, of course, is not to suggest that conservative Justices vote as a bloc, consistently supporting conservative outcomes. There are important deviations, but these Justices generally back conservative outcomes.

[224] And while change in the Court's civil liberties agenda has resulted in some upward movement in their support for parties with civil liberties claims, the Court's four strong conservatives were relatively unfavorable to such claims—though with some important exceptions—throughout the 2005–15 Terms.

[225] See notes 210–11 and accompanying text.

[226] See Section III.B.

Table 3
Proportions of Liberal Votes in Civil Liberties Cases,
Roberts Court, Selected Justices (Part 1)

	Justice				
Terms[a]	Scalia	Thomas	Roberts	Alito	Breyer
2005–06	23.9	19.7	23.5	19.6	63.4
2007–08	27.9	18.6	31.4	26.7	61.2
2009–10	44.4	34.6	43.2	30.4	56.8
2011–12	32.9	25.0	32.9	21.3	53.9
2013–15	37.0	32.7	48.5	34.7	64.0

[a] Each entry refers to a pair of terms or, for 2013–15, three terms. Thus, "2005–06," for instance, includes the 2005 and 2006 Terms of the Court.

tion III.B, we explored the role of ideology in these appointments[227] and explained that these four appointees have social identities that are deeply rooted in the conservative legal movement.[228]

Once these Justices joined the Court, the conservative movement continued to serve as an important reference group for them. Unlike earlier periods (when elite social networks were dominated by liberals), conservative Justices on the Roberts Court had links with like-minded groups and individuals who supported and reinforced their conservative positions. In particular, as noted in Section II.B, changes in the news media, academia, and the legal profession led to the establishment of conservative elite social networks.[229]

In the case of Justice Thomas,[230] for example, the elite conservative sector provided personal support during his early years on the Court, when he felt beleaguered by the criticism he had received during his highly contentious confirmation hearings. In response, in the words of one reporter, Thomas "constructed a world apart from his critics."[231] He has appeared at law schools with relatively con-

[227] See notes 160–93 and accompanying text.

[228] See notes 170–94 and accompanying text (noting ties of these nominees to conservative movement); notes 185–90 and accompanying text (discussing disavowal of Miers by conservative legal movement).

[229] See notes 111–21 and accompanying text.

[230] This paragraph draws from Baum, *Judges and Their Audiences* at 132–35 (cited in note 11).

[231] Marc Fisher, *The Private World of Justice Thomas*, Wash Post at B1 (Sept 11, 1995).

servative orientations[232] and focused his attention on news media with a similar point of view.[233] He has maintained ties with conservative leaders and organizations like the Federalist Society,[234] and he has acknowledged that conservatives in the legal community serve as an important reference group for him.[235] It is noteworthy that when Thomas returned to Yale Law School in 2011, the two student groups with which he met were the Black Law Students Association and the law school's chapter of the Federalist Society.[236]

As an original leader of the Federalist Society,[237] Justice Scalia already had deep roots in the conservative segment of the legal elite by the time he became a Justice. Over the years, he made frequent appearances before groups with a conservative orientation. He was regularly honored by the Federalist Society[238] and participated frequently in the organization's events. In 2012 alone Scalia participated in at least five Federalist Society events.[239] In 2013 he traveled to Montana to speak at a lunch aimed at building support for creation of a state chapter of the society,[240] and in 2014 he journeyed to New York City to give a speech before a Federalist Society group.[241]

---

[232] As a few examples, Justice Thomas has recently appeared at Duke, see Duke Law School, *Justice Clarence Thomas Shares His Journey from the South to the Supreme Court* (Oct 25, 2013), archived at https://perma.cc/EKY3-ETAA, and Harvard, see Harvard Law School, *Justice Thomas Speaks at Harvard Law* (video) (Feb 11, 2013), archived at https://perma.cc/WKV3-LV47, and UVA, see University of Virginia School of Law, *U.S. Supreme Court Justice Thomas Visits UVA Law School* (Mar 13, 2012), archived at https://perma.cc/KBW9-XX2N.

[233] Lee Roderick, *Leading the Charge: Orrin Hatch and 20 Years of America* 369–70 (Gold Leaf, 1994).

[234] Baum, *Judges and Their Audiences* at 133–34 (cited in note 11).

[235] Clarence Thomas, *Address Before the Federalist Society at the 1999 National Lawyers Convention* (Nov 12, 1999), archived at https://perma.cc/9TWX-PU9D.

[236] Yale Law School, *Justice Clarence Thomas '74 Visits the Law School; Meets with Student Groups, Teaches Class* (Dec 14, 2011), archived at https://perma.cc/QU7X-TYXP.

[237] Teles, *Conservative Legal Movement* at 141–42 (cited in note 13); Joan Biskupic, *American Original: The Life and Constitution of Supreme Court Justice Antonin Scalia* 5 (Farrar, Straus and Giroux, 2009).

[238] Biskupic, *American Original* at 7 (cited in note 237).

[239] Antonin Scalia, *Financial Disclosure Report for Calendar Year 2012*, 3 (May 15, 2013), archived at https://perma.cc/PJL6-E7R4. The financial disclosure reports indicate reimbursed travel, so they do not include appearances in Washington, D.C.

[240] Laura Lundquist, *Supreme Court Justice Is Draw for Conservative Luncheon*, Bozeman Chron (Aug 19, 2013), archived at https://perma.cc/VR5D-6M2R.

[241] Antonin Scalia, *Financial Disclosure Report for Calendar Year 2014*, 3 (May 15, 2015), archived at https://perma.cc/N79M-USF3.

Among his other appearances that year was a speech before a group of Hollywood conservatives called the "Friends of Abe."[242] In 2011, he spoke to members of Congress about constitutional interpretation at an event organized by the Tea Party Caucus.[243]

As a judge on a federal court of appeals, Samuel Alito was "particularly active at Federalist Society national meetings."[244] He was strongly backed by conservative groups at the time of his nomination to the Supreme Court[245] and he has maintained his ties with conservative groups in the years since. Between 2010 and 2012, he appeared at three meetings of the Federalist Society outside Washington, D.C. and at the conservative Manhattan Institute.[246] In 2008, Alito was the keynote speaker at the annual dinner for the conservative magazine the *American Spectator*, and his remarks included distinctly partisan content. He also appeared at the magazine's annual dinner in 2010.[247] At a 2012 Federalist Society dinner, Alito took aim at both the Obama administration and critics of *Citizens United*, charging that critics of the decision were misleading the public and that the Obama Department of Justice was advancing a vision of society in which the "federal government towers over the people."[248] In 2014, Alito was again the featured speaker at the Federalist Society's annual dinner.[249] In 2016 Alito spoke at the society's annual meeting for lawyers, as did Justice Thomas. Alito described what

---

[242] Id. On the Friends of Abe, see Amy Fagan, *Hollywood's Conservative Underground*, Wash Times A1 (July 23, 2008).

[243] Bill Mears, *Justice Scalia Set to Address Tea Party Caucus on Capitol Hill*, CNN.com (Jan 21, 2011), archived at https://perma.cc/LK7W-ZQTA.

[244] Tushnet, *In the Balance* at 49 (cited in note 21).

[245] See note (discussing Alito's support from conservative groups).

[246] Samuel A. Alito, *Financial Disclosure Report for Calendar Year 2010*, 3 (May 12, 2011), archived at https://perma.cc/UN8S-ERNC; Samuel A. Alito, *Financial Disclosure Report for Calendar Year 2011*, 2–3 (Aug 13, 2012), archived at https://perma.cc/X932-ZALF. The Manhattan Institute for Public Policy describes its mission and activities at https://perma.cc/5R7M-KQ8R.

[247] Jeff Shesol, *Should Justices Keep Their Opinions to Themselves?*, NY Times A23 (June 29, 2011). The 2010 appearance featured a confrontation with a liberal blogger who challenged Alito's involvement in a fundraising dinner. Debra Cassens Weiss, *Blogger Loudly Questions Alito's Dinner Attendance, Tapes Irate Security Guard*, ABA J (Nov 11, 2010), archived at https://perma.cc/MGQ3-Z9PT.

[248] See Mark Sherman, *Samuel Alito, Supreme Court Justice, Takes on Citizens United Critics*, Huffington Post (Nov 17, 2012), archived at https://perma.cc/9LNE-9R6B.

[249] Shortly after that Federalist Society appearance, Linda Greenhouse wrote that Alito has a "base" in the conservative movement. Linda Greenhouse, *It's All Right with Sam*, NY Times (Jan 7, 2015), archived at https://perma.cc/F9TK-PBSK.

one publication called a "conservative agenda" for the Court.[250] For his part, Thomas referred to his friendship with Justice Scalia as a "band of brothers," and he urged his audience "to join this band of brothers."[251]

Chief Justice Roberts's record is more ambiguous than that of the Court's other conservatives.[252] On the whole, however, Roberts is clearly a conservative.[253] As table 3 shows, his record is much more conservative than that of Justice Breyer, the most moderate of the Court's liberal Justices.[254] Roberts's voting record is best explained by a more moderate set of conservative policy preferences and his strategic considerations as Chief Justice.[255] Although his ties to the conservative movement since he joined the judiciary have not been as dramatic as those of Alito, Scalia, and Thomas, he participated in the twenty-fifth anniversary celebration of the Federalist Society in

---

[250] Lawrence Hurley, *Alito Outlines Possible Conservative Agenda for U.S. High Court*, Reuters (Nov 17, 2016), http://www.reuters.com/article/us-usa-court-alito-idUSKBN13C2E7.

[251] Tony Mauro, *Justice Thomas to Fed Society: Scalia's Work Is "Prologue,"* Nat'l L J (Nov 18, 2016), http://www.nationallawjournal.com/id=1202772781445/Justice-Thomas-to-Fed-Society-Scalias-Work-Is-Prologue?slreturn=20161025123108.

[252] In one of the debates among the candidates for the 2016 Republican nomination for president, Ted Cruz referred to his support for Roberts's confirmation in 2005 as "a mistake," and even Jeb Bush hedged in his approval of his brother's nomination of Roberts. *CNN Reagan Library Debate: Later Debate Full Transcript*, CNN.com (Sept 16, 2015), archived at https://perma.cc/G78M-25UA. Donald Trump also attacked Roberts for writing an opinion catering to those inside the "beltway." See Egelko, *Trump, Rubio Weigh in on Supreme Court Ahead of Debate* (cited in note 5).

[253] Adam Liptak, *Chief Justice Amasses a Conservative Record, and Wrath from the Right*, NY Times A16 (Sept 29, 2015).

[254] Roberts's Martin-Quinn scores also highlight his relative conservativism, as does an ideological ranking devised by Judge Richard Posner and William Landes. See note 70 and accompanying text. Roberts's relatively high proportions of liberal votes in the 2013 and 2014 Terms, like the Court's relatively high proportions of liberal decisions in those terms, probably reflect the kinds of cases that the Court heard in those terms. See Brendan Nyhan, *Supreme Court: Liberal Draft v. Conservative Overreach*, NY Times (June 25, 2015), archived at https://perma.cc/E8GR-CQCX. See also Kevin T. McGuire et al, *Measuring Policy Content on the U.S. Supreme Court*, 71 J Pol 1305 (2009) (explaining how case selection skews ideological ranking of Justices by making courts appear more liberal or conservative).

[255] See Dan Balz, *Roberts Health Care Ruling Sends a Message to Politicians*, Wash Post (June 30, 2012), archived at https://perma.cc/6AQT-8RCF (discussing institutional concerns in Roberts ruling); Adam Liptak, *Angering Conservatives and Liberals, Chief Justice Roberts Defends Steady Restraint*, NY Times (June 26, 2015), archived at https://perma.cc/Z78C-YGX2 (discussing ways Roberts trades off ideology for the pursuit of institutional goals). For a general treatment of how institutional concerns, including the power to assign decisions, shape the decision making of Chief Justice Roberts, see Richard J. Lazarus, *Back to Business at the Supreme Court: The Administrative Side of Chief Justice Roberts*, 129 Harv L Rev F 33 (Nov 9, 2015), archived at https://perma.cc/7VL9-2U6S.

2007[256] and, following Justice Scalia's lead, he presented a featured lecture at the society's annual meeting that same year.[257]

Another measure of the allegiance of today's Republican-appointed Justices to the conservative legal network is their tendency to hire law clerks who share their ideological views.[258] Justices gave some weight to ideology in their selection of law clerks even before party polarization took hold, but that weight was limited. Reflecting the dominant ideology of the time, law clerks in that earlier era tended to be left-leaning, even if their Justice was not.[259] That is no longer true. Today, as measured by the lower-court judges from whom the Justices draw their clerks, the tendency of Justices to take ideology into account has become markedly stronger since the early 1990s, especially among conservative Justices.[260] Table 4 shows the Justices' hiring practices for the 2005–16 Terms, the first twelve terms of the Roberts Court. The differences between conservative and liberal Justices shown in table 4 are far greater than those that existed in the late 1970s and early 1980s.[261]

---

[256] Robert Barnes, *Federalists Relish Well-Placed Friends: President, Several Justices Help Celebrate Legal Society's 25 Years of Conservatism*, Wash Post A3 (Nov 16, 2007). Justice Thomas participated prominently in the 2013 annual convention of the Federalist Society, and Justices Scalia and Alito attended the convention. Ian Millhiser, *How Conservatives Abandoned Judicial Restraint, Took Over the Courts and Radically Transformed America*, ThinkProgress (Nov 19, 2013), archived at https://perma.cc/MP2Y-SJBD.

[257] *7th Annual Barbara K. Olson Memorial Lecture*, The Federalist Society (Nov 16, 2007), archived at https://perma.cc/7P2P-WNKH.

[258] Artemus Ward and Davis L. Weiden, *Sorcerers' Apprentices: 100 Years of Law Clerks at the United States Supreme Court* (New York University, 2006). Since the 1970s, when it became standard practice for Justices to select clerks who had served in lower courts, there has been a similar tendency for Justices to take clerks from judges on the same side of the ideological spectrum. See id at 83–84.

[259] Todd C. Peppers, *Courtiers of the Marble Palace: The Rise and Influence of the Supreme Court Law Clerk* 34–37 (Stanford Law and Politics, 2006).

[260] Corey Ditslear and Lawrence Baum, *Selection of Law Clerks and Polarization in the U.S. Supreme Court*, 63 J Pol 169 (2001); Lawrence Baum, *Hiring Supreme Court Law Clerks: Probing the Ideological Linkage Between Judges and Justices*, 98 Marq L Rev 333 (2014). See also Nelson et al, 62 Vand L Rev at 1775–80 (cited in note 121); Adam Liptak, *A Sign of Court's Polarization: Choice of Clerks*, NY Times A1 (Sept 7, 2010); Geoffrey R. Stone, *The Difference Between Conservative and Liberal Justices*, Huffington Post (Nov 2, 2013), archived at https://perma.cc/PTP5-RB39. As in the past, at least some Justices also take the ideological positions of prospective clerks themselves into account. Amy Bach, *Movin' on Up with the Federalist Society: How the Right Rears Its Young Lawyers*, Nation 11, 15 (Oct 1, 2001).

[261] In the 1975–80 Terms, the highest percentage of clerks drawn from Democratic-appointed judges was 68.2 (for Justice Marshall); the lowest proportion was 37.5 (for Justice Rehnquist). In the 1981–85 Terms, the highest proportion was 73.7 (for Justice Brennan); the lowest was 40.0 (for Rehnquist and Chief Justice Burger). Ditslear and Baum, 63 J Pol at 880 (cited in note 260). It is also noteworthy that clerks working for or slotted to work for Justice

Table 4
Proportion of Justices' Law Clerks Who Had Previously Served with a Republican-Appointed Lower-Court Judge, 2005–16 Terms[a]

Justice	Percentage
Thomas	97.9
Scalia	97.7
Alito	94.4
Roberts	80.9
Kennedy	79.2
Breyer	40.4
Stevens	40.0
Sotomayor	37.5
Kagan	32.1
Souter	25.0
Ginsburg	23.4

[a] These percentages were calculated from the information sheets compiled by the Court each term, *Law Clerks—October Term [various years]: Law Schools and Prior Clerkships;* for the 2016 term, the information is from David Lat, *Supreme Court Clerk Hiring Watch: The Official List, Above the Law* (July 22, 2016), abovethelaw.com/2016/07/supreme-court-clerk-hiring-watch-the-official-list-for-ot-2016/. Clerks who served with state judges or with the future Justice on a lower court and those who had no prior clerkships are not included. Where a clerk had multiple prior clerkships, the most recent clerkship was used; when the most recent clerkship could not be ascertained, a clerkship in a court of appeals was counted rather than one in a district court.

Unlike the 1950s through the 1990s, there is no longer a leftward pull on Republican appointees. Justices whose social identities were linked with conservatives and conservative groups prior to their appointments can now gain enthusiastic approval from conservative elites. Moreover, as demonstrated by their reactions to the 2012 and 2015 health care decisions and the 2015 decision on same-sex mar-

Antonin Scalia found homes with Republican Justices after Scalia's death. Scalia's 2015 Term clerks completed their clerkships with Justices Alito and Thomas; clerks hired by Scalia for the 2016 Term found positions with Justices Thomas, Alito, and Kennedy. Tony Mauro, *Future Scalia Clerks Find New Homes with Other Justices*, Natl L J (May 13, 2016), at http://www.nationallawjournal.com/id=1202757606269/Future-Scalia-Clerks-Find-New-Homes-With-Other-Justices; David Lat, *Supreme Court Hiring Watch*, *Above the Law* (July 28, 2016), at http://abovethelaw.com/2016/07/supreme-court-clerk-hiring-watch-a-look-at-october-term-2017/.

riage, conservative elites will sharply condemn any deviations from their own positions.[262]

D. DEMOCRATIC APPOINTEES

The increasing ideological distance between Democratic- and Republican-appointed Justices is largely a story of changes in the Republican Party. As a group, the Republican-appointed Justices have been appreciably more conservative than previous Republican nominees.[263] For their part, Democratic-appointed Justices are more homogeneous than before, but as a group they are not more liberal. Unlike previous Democratic appointees (some of whom were very liberal and others of whom were either moderate or conservative), all of today's Democratic-appointed Justices are moderate liberals.[264] As noted in Part III, the ideology of Supreme Court nominees has been more important to recent Republican presidents than to recent Democratic presidents.

The changing profile of Democratic nominees is tied to broader changes in the Democratic Party. Before the mid-1960s, the Democratic Party reflected an uneasy alliance between northern liberals and southern conservatives.[265] The ideologically mixed character of the Democratic Party at that time was reflected in Supreme Court nominations. In a later era, nominees who held views like those of Stanley Reed, Fred Vinson, Sherman Minton, and Tom Clark would have been Republicans rather than Democrats; perhaps the same is

---

[262] The decisions were, respectively, *National Federation of Independent Business v Sebelius* (note 22); *King v Burwell* (note 22); and *Obergefell v Hodges* (note 209). Examples of conservatives' responses to Justice Kennedy's decisive vote on *Obergefell* are Daniel Horowitz, *Justice Kennedy's Naked Politics and the Hypocrisy of the Court*, Conservative Review, July 6, 2015, at https://www.conservativereview.com/commentary/2015/07/Justice-kennendys-naked-politics-and-the-hypocrisy-of-the-court; and S. Ernie Walton, *Conservatives Should Attack Obergefell's Interpretive Method, Not Its Hijacking of the Democratic Process*, September 26, 2015, at https://papers.ssrn.com/sol3/papers.cfm?abstract_id=2667223. For conservative elite reaction to Chief Justice Roberts's votes in the Affordable Care Act decisions, see Adam Liptak, *Chief Justice John Roberts Amasses a Conservative Record, and Wrath from the Right*, NY Times (Sept 28, 2015), at http://www.nytimes.com/2015/09/29/us/politics/chief-Justice-john-roberts-amasses-conservative-record-and-the-rights-ire.html?_r=0; David G. Savage, *Chief Justice Roberts' Record Isn't Conservative Enough for Some Activists*, LA Times (Sept 25, 2015), at http://www.latimes.com/nation/la-na-roberts-conservative-backlash-20150924-story.html.

[263] See notes 69–70.

[264] See figure 1 and accompanying text. See note 152 and accompanying text.

[265] See Richard H. Pildes, *Why the Center Does Not Hold: The Causes of Hyperpolarized Democracy in America*, 99 Cal L Rev 273, 290 (2011).

true of Byron White.[266] Nor was there anything like a liberal legal establishment in that era. The leaders of the American Bar Association, for instance, tended to be relatively conservative until the 1960s.[267]

Steven Teles has described how this changed with the development of what he calls "the liberal legal network."[268] Following the social changes of the 1960s, the American Civil Liberties Union and the NAACP Legal Defense and Education Fund were joined by a set of new liberal public interest law firms. Legal academia took on a more liberal cast. Elite institutions, including the American Bar Association, also embraced more liberal positions. The civil libertarianism of the late Warren Court both reflected and contributed to these changes. The result was the creation of a liberal network in the elite segment of the legal profession, although that network was looser and more diverse in its thinking than the conservative network that developed later.[269]

The changes of the 1960s extended beyond the legal profession. The elite news media became more liberal, as did the "Washington-Georgetown social set" to which President Nixon referred.[270] The leftward shift of the Democratic Party in the 1960s and 1970s helped ensure that when Democratic presidents once again gained an opportunity to appoint Justices (beginning with Clinton in 1993), they would choose people who were at least moderately liberal. At the same time, the development of a liberal legal network created an elite audience for the Justices who supported liberal policy positions. Because there was no competing conservative legal network at that time, the growing liberalism of the elite world reinforced the liberalism of Democratic judicial appointees.

Since roughly 2000, the success of conservative legal organizations in shaping law and policy has made liberals more aware of the impact of elite networks. In particular, liberal lawyers and law professors perceived a need for an organization that would serve as a counter-

---

[266] See note 136 (discussing relative conservativism of the Truman nominees).

[267] Teles, *Conservative Legal Movement* at 28–29 (cited in note 13).

[268] Id at 22–57.

[269] David Fontana, *How Size Matters for Liberal and Conservative Constitutionalism* (unpublished manuscript) (on file with authors).

[270] See note 206.

weight to the Federalist Society.[271] The American Constitution Society (ACS), founded in 2001, is largely parallel to the Federalist Society in its activities and goals.[272] At the same time, though, no one group dominates the liberal legal network, and ideology plays a less overt role in Democratic appointments.[273] The lack of dominance for a single group reflects the multiplicity of organizations with a liberal orientation that have an interest in judicial appointments and policies.[274]

Nonetheless, Democratic-appointed Justices undoubtedly see themselves as members of a different team than their Republican counterparts.[275] The ACS accentuates and facilitates this divide. Justices Breyer, Ginsburg, and Sotomayor have all been keynote speakers at the ACS national convention.[276] In greeting a national student convention of the Federalist Society in 2005 when she was dean of the Harvard Law School, Elena Kagan declared that "I love the Federalist Society," but "You are *not* my people."[277] Moreover, all of the Democratic-appointed Justices in recent years have tended to appoint law clerks who have served with judges nominated by Democratic presidents, although the strength of that inclination varies considerably and is dwarfed by the tendency of the Republican-appointed Justices to rely on Republican-appointed lower court judges.[278]

---

[271] Crystal Nix Hines, *Young Liberal Law Group Is Expanding*, NY Times A17 (June 1, 2001).

[272] Alexander Wohl, *Liberalizing the Law*, The Nation 6 (June 16, 2003); Carol D. Leonnig, *Dancing? It's Good for the Constitution: Janet Reno and Friends Try an Unconservative Approach*, Wash Post C1 (Aug 4, 2003); Tresa Baldas, *Law School Turf War Ignites*, Natl L J 1, 12 (Apr 26, 2004).

[273] See notes 143–52 and accompanying text.

[274] See Fontana, *How Size Matters* (cited in note 269).

[275] See notes 101–09.

[276] Most recently, Ginsburg was the keynote speaker in 2015 and Sotomayor in 2014. See Adam Liptak, *Justices Get Out More, but Calendars Aren't Open to Just Anyone*, NY Times (June 1, 2015), archived at https://perma.cc/M9JM-6NTA. Breyer was also keynote speaker at the banquet of the ACS national conference in 2004, see *Justice Stephen Breyer at the 2004 Annual Convention*, American Constitution Society (July 25, 2005), archived at https://perma.cc/WGD9-9RP4, and Ginsburg spoke at the first national conference in 2003, "because the Society's mission is important to the health and welfare of our Nation," see Ruth Bader Ginsburg, Associate Justice, Supreme Court of the United States, *Remarks for the American Constitution Society: Looking Beyond Our Borders: The Value of a Comparative Perspective in Constitutional Adjudication* 1 (Aug 2, 2003), archived at https://perma.cc/UA8P-UNUG.

[277] Tushnet, *A Court Divided: The Rehnquist Court and the Future of Constitutional Law* 90 (Norton, 2005).

[278] See table 4.

Table 5
Percentage of Liberal Votes in Civil Liberties Cases,
Roberts Court, Selected Justices (Part 2)

	Justice					
Terms	Ginsburg	Breyer	Sotomayor	Kagan[a]	Kennedy	Alito
2005–06	66.2	63.4	–	–	35.2	19.6
2007–08	69.8	61.2	–	–	39.5	26.7
2009–10	60.5	56.8	63.8	64.3	46.9	30.4
2011–12	68.4	53.9	66.7	67.6	46.7	21.3
2013–15	63.4	64.0	71.0	62.6	50.5	34.7

[a] Kagan, whose tenure began with the 2010 Term, participated in only twenty-eight civil liberties decisions in that term.

Table 5 provides some perspective on the ideological positions of the current Court's Democratic appointees. All have been distinctly to the left of even the most liberal Republican-appointed Justice, Anthony Kennedy. The gap between them and the four more strongly conservative Republican-appointed Justices (represented in table 5 by Justice Alito) is even more substantial.

The convictions of Democratic-appointed Justices are undoubtedly strengthened by liberal elite networks. These networks still dominate the academy, lawyer groups, and much of the media.[279] As this part makes clear, the fact that there are substantial audiences on both the liberal and conservative sides reduces the possibility that Republican or Democratic appointees will move away from their parties' predominant positions during their tenure on the Court.

V. Conclusions

In the period that ended with Clarence Thomas's appointment to the Supreme Court in 1991, the role of the president's party affiliation in shaping the Court's ideology was surprisingly small by current standards. Republicans often appointed moderates and liberals; Democrats often appointed moderates and conservatives.

[279] See John O. McGinnis et al, *The Patterns and Implications of Political Contributions by Elite Law Faculty*, 93 Georgetown L J 1167 (2005) (noting the propensity of law professors to contribute to Democrats); Adam Bonica, Adam S. Chilton, and Maya Sen, *The Political Ideologies of American Lawyers*, J Legal Analysis (forthcoming), archived at https://perma.cc/URQ8-QWWL (asserting that law professors are at least as liberal as any other cohort of lawyers, including public defenders).

One vivid reflection of that pattern is evident in the frustration of conservatives with the failure of the Burger and Rehnquist Courts to turn as far to the right as they had hoped for after a string of eight consecutive Republican appointments to the Court.[280]

Things have changed, though. Starting with the Reagan administration, presidents have increasingly paid attention to ideology in Supreme Court appointments. Republicans, in particular, helped establish a conservative legal network to vet and groom candidates for judicial appointment. And following the retirements of moderate Republican-appointed Justices David Souter in 2009 and John Paul Stevens in 2010, the lines of ideological division on the Court have, for the first time, coincided with partisan division. Today, every Justice appointed by a Democratic president stands to the left of every Justice appointed by a Republican president, and this is not likely to change any time soon.

This development reflects fundamental changes in American politics. The growing ideological polarization of the parties at the elite level has given presidents stronger incentives to choose nominees whose ideological orientations match those of the president's own party. Elite polarization has also spurred the development of rival liberal and conservative social networks, and those networks have enhanced the president's ability to reliably identify predictably liberal or conservative nominees. Partisan polarization has affected the Justices as well, reducing the likelihood that they will stray from the ideological positions that brought them to the Court in the first place.

The most direct consequence of this change is that presidential elections mean even more for the direction of the Supreme Court than they did in the past. The sudden death of Antonin Scalia and the ensuing imbroglio over the nomination of Merrick Garland underscore this realty. More generally, although the timing of vacancies on the Court is usually uncertain, it has become more certain how presidents will fill them.[281] Because Justices today typically serve for

---

[280] See Vincent Blasi, ed, *The Burger Court: The Counter-Revolution That Wasn't* (1986); Craig Bradley, ed, *The Rehnquist Legacy* (Oxford, 2006); Robert F, Nagel, *Bowing to Precedent*, Weekly Standard (Apr 17, 2006), archived at https://perma.cc/MTY7-AKNN (noting failure of Rehnquist Court to overrule precedents on school prayer, abortion, and other divisive issues).

[281] We do not mean to suggest that a Republican president will never again appoint a liberal Justice or that a Democrat will never appoint a moderate or conservative Justice. Our point is that party polarization makes such an appointment unlikely.

longer periods than the Justices of earlier eras,[282] the impact of presidential elections on the Court's membership comes more slowly than in the past. But that impact is now more long-lasting.

Further, as the Court's Republican- and Democratic-appointed Justices become more distant from each other ideologically, the Court's policy direction will become more volatile. In times when the number of Justices appointed by presidents of each party is close to equal, a single appointment can produce a substantial shift in the balance on the Court and, thus, in its decisions. By the same token, it will be less common for a single Justice to play the role of a moderate who stands between the Court's conservative and liberal sides. Anthony Kennedy plays that role to some degree on today's Court.[283] No other Justice comes close to crossing party lines as frequently, and we doubt that future appointees will play such a role anytime soon.

The Senate Republicans' refusal to confirm Merrick Garland, combined with the election of Donald Trump in 2016, will have a profound impact on the balance and direction of the Court. As a candidate, Trump made clear his goal of appointing Justices who would take conservative positions on specific issues,[284] and the candidates on his lists of potential nominees are all strong conservatives.[285] Thus, if any of the three most senior Justices (Ginsburg, Kennedy, and Breyer) leaves the Court in the next four years, we can expect to see a sharp turn to the right, even relative to the Court before Justice Scalia's death. No longer will Anthony Kennedy be the "swing vote." Instead, it will likely be Chief Justice Roberts.[286] In that event, the Court will even more strongly reflect the partisan divide that is the central attribute of government and politics today. And presidential elections will matter more to the Supreme Court's decision making going forward than they have ever mattered in our nation's history.

On January 31, 2016, President Donald Trump nominated Judge Neil Gorsuch to fill the vacancy on the Supreme Court; on April 7, 2017, the Senate confirmed the nomination. The choice of Gorsuch

---

[282] Justin Crowe and Christopher F. Karpowitz, *Where Have You Gone, Sherman Minton? The Decline of the Short-Term Supreme Court Justice*, 5 Persp on Pol 425 (2007).

[283] See table 5; see also Epstein and Jacobi, 61 Stan L Rev (cited in note 27).

[284] See note 5.

[285] See note 192 and accompanying text.

[286] See Wolf, *Aging Supreme Court Energizes Republicans More Than Democrats* (cited in note 3). Justice Stephen Breyer will be 78. Id.

and the process by which he won confirmation underline the changes in the selection of Justices that we have described.

As we have discussed, the augmented list of twenty-one prospective nominees that Trump announced as a presidential candidate was created primarily by leaders of the Federalist Society.[287] Gorsuch had established strong conservative credentials through his clerkships for conservative judges, his service in the George W. Bush administration, his involvement in the Federalist Society, and his record as a court of appeals judge.[288] He also had the advantages of strong educational credentials, a reputation as a very able judge, and a relatively young age.

In the process that made Gorsuch a finalist for the nomination and ultimately the nominee, Leonard Leo of the Federalist Society played a central role.[289] An experienced participant in the selection of federal judges, Leo took a leave from the society to assist in the selection of the nominee (and later in his confirmation). From the perspective of the Federalist Society and other people and organizations in the conservative legal movement, all or nearly all the judges on the Trump list would have fit the desired mold rather well. But after a careful vetting process that included multiple interviews of leading candidates, Gorsuch's combination of strengths elevated him above all the other contenders.

In the polarized atmosphere of the confirmation process today, it was certain that nearly all Democratic senators would vote against confirming Gorsuch and equally certain that every Republican senator would vote for him. As we have discussed, judicial confirmation politics exemplify pervasive party polarization; today, the votes of Democratic and Republican Senators on Supreme Court nominees increasingly

[287] See note 192 and accompanying text. For a discussion of the Federalist Society's role in vetting Trump nominees, see Lawrence Baum and Neal Devins, *Federalist Court*, Slate (Jan 31, 2017), available at http://www.slate.com/articles/news_and_politics/jurisprudence/2017/01/how_the_federalist_society_became_the_de_facto_selector_of_republican_supreme.html.

[288] Dylan Matthews, *Neil Gorsuch, Donald Trump's Supreme Court Nominee, Explained*, Vox (March 20, 2017), available at http://www.vox.com/policy-and-politics/2017/1/31/14450024/neil-gorsuch-supreme-court.

[289] See Jeffrey Toobin, *The Conservative Pipeline to the Supreme Court*, New Yorker (April 17, 2017), available at http://www.newyorker.com/magazine/2017/04/17/the-conservative-pipeline-to-the-supreme-court; Eric Lipton and Jeremy W. Peters, *In Gorsuch, Conservative Activist Sees Test Case for Reshaping the Judiciary*, NY Times (March 18, 2017), available at https://www.nytimes.com/2017/03/18/us/politics/neil-gorsuch-supreme-court-conservatives.html.

fall along party lines.[290] Further, the refusal of the Republican Senate to hold hearings on President Obama's March 2016 nominee Merrick Garland ensured Democratic antipathy to any Trump nominee.

The hearings before the Judiciary Committee were uneventful, but even if there had been more fireworks, it is unlikely that the hearings would have changed many senatorial minds. The committee voted 11–9 across party lines, with Democratic Senators condemning a process whereby Merrick Garland never received a hearing.[291] Following this vote, Senate Democratic leadership backed a filibuster of the Gorsuch nomination; all but three of the Senate's forty-eight Democrats joined this effort. With no Republican Senators opposing Gorsuch, the Senate's Republican leadership invoked the "nuclear option" and the Senate voted 55 (52 Republicans and 3 Democrats) to 45 (all Democrats) to change Senate rules requiring sixty votes to end a filibuster.[292] By the same 55–45 margin, Gorsuch was confirmed.[293]

The nomination and confirmation of Gorsuch reinforce our central claims. Republican presidents emphasize ideology and look to the conservative legal network—especially the Federalist Society—when making Supreme Court nominations. In the Senate, Republicans and Democrats increasingly see judicial confirmation as a partisan affair, a perception that powerfully affects both votes on the confirmation of specific nominees and decisions about confirmation procedures—allowing consideration of nominees, eliminating the filibuster (which Democrats did for lower-court nominees in 2013). And even before

---

[290] See notes 89–90 and accompanying text. There has also been a marked increase in filibustering judicial nominees along party lines. See Allison Graves, *Did Senate Republicans Filibuster Obama Court Nominees More Than All Others Combined?*, Politifact (April 9, 2017), available at http://www.politifact.com/truth-o-meter/statements/2017/apr/09/ben-cardin/did-senate-republicans-filibuster-obama-court-nomi/.

[291] See Matt Flegenheimer, *Senate Judiciary Committee Approves Gorsuch in Party-Line Vote*, NY Times (April 3, 2017), available at http://www.politifact.com/truth-o-meter/statements/2017/apr/09/ben-cardin/did-senate-republicans-filibuster-obama-court-nomi/.

[292] See Ed O'Keefe and Sean Sullivan, *Senate Republicans Go "Nuclear," Pave the Way for Gorsuch Confirmation to Supreme Court*, Wash Post (April 6, 2017), available at https://www.washingtonpost.com/powerpost/senate-poised-for-historic-clash-over-supreme-court-nominee-neil-gorsuch/2017/04/06/40295376-1aba-11e7-855e-4824bbb5d748_story.html?utm_term=.ff405943c962.

[293] Ed O'Keefe and Robert Barnes, *Senate Confirms Neil Gorsuch to Supreme Court*, Wash Post (April 7, 2017), available at https://www.washingtonpost.com/powerpost/senate-set-to-confirm-neil-gorsuch-to-supreme-court/2017/04/07/da3cd738-1b89-11e7-9887-1a5314b56a08_story.html?utm_term=.3d3788f3d61f. One Democrat who voted for Gorsuch (Joe Manchin of West Virginia) voted against the change in Senate rules; one Democrat who voted for the "nuclear option" voted against Gorsuch (Michael Bennet of Colorado).

Neil Gorsuch had cast a vote on the Supreme Court, his conservative orientation and connections to the conservative legal network made it very likely that he will be more conservative than any of the Court's Democratic appointees. In all these ways, the Gorsuch confirmation will strengthen the partisan divide that now grips the Supreme Court.

BARRY CUSHMAN

INSIDE THE "CONSTITUTIONAL REVOLUTION" OF 1937

The nature and sources of the New Deal Constitutional Revolution are among the most discussed and debated subjects in constitutional historiography. Scholars have reached significantly divergent conclusions concerning how best to understand the meaning and the causes of constitutional decisions rendered by the Supreme Court under Chief Justice Charles Evans Hughes.[1] Though recent years have witnessed certain refinements in scholarly understandings of various dimensions of the phenomenon, the relevant documentary record seemed to have been rather thoroughly explored. Judicial opinions, case records and appellate briefs, congressional hearings and debates, scholarly and popular commentary, and the papers of the Justices all had been examined in considerable detail. Though further review of the papers of government lawyers promised to shed additional light on aspects of the period's legal and constitutional development, it appeared that the portion of the documentary rec-

Barry Cushman is John P. Murphy Foundation Professor of Law, University of Notre Dame.

Author's note: Thanks to Matthew Hofstedt, Devon Burge, Franz Jantzen, Lauren Morrell, Nikki Peronace, and Erin Huckle, all of the Office of the Curator of the Supreme Court of the United States, for their kind hospitality and splendid assistance with the Hughes Court docket books; to Margaret Adema for helpful research assistance; and to participants in the Notre Dame Law School Faculty Colloquium for valuable comments and conversation.

[1] For a survey and analysis of the scholarly literature, see Barry Cushman, *The Jurisprudence of the Hughes Court: The Recent Literature*, 89 Notre Dame L Rev 1929 (2014).

978-0-226-49084-7/2017/2016-0009$10.00

ord illuminating the intentional states of the Justices had been exhausted.

Recently, however, a remarkably instructive set of primary sources has become available. For many years, the docket books kept by a number of the Hughes Court Justices have been held by the Office of the Curator of the Supreme Court. Yet the existence of these docket books was not widely known, and access to them was highly restricted. In April of 2014, however, the Court adopted new guidelines designed to increase access to the docket books for researchers. These docket books supply a wealth of information concerning the internal deliberations of the Justices, much of which has been analyzed in detail elsewhere.[2] This article considers what the docket books can teach us about the cases comprising what some have called the "switch-in-time": *West Coast Hotel Co. v Parrish*,[3] which upheld Washington state's minimum-wage law for women and overruled *Adkins v Children's Hospital*;[4] the *Labor Board Cases*,[5] which upheld the constitutionality of the National Labor Relations Act;[6] and the *Social Security Cases*,[7] which upheld the constitutionality of provisions of the Social Security Act[8] establishing an old-age pension system and a federal-state cooperative plan of unemployment insurance, as well as corresponding state unemployment compensation statutes.

During the 1936 October Term, the Court's personnel consisted of Chief Justice Hughes and Associate Justices Willis Van Devanter, James Clark McReynolds, Louis D. Brandeis, George Sutherland, Pierce Butler, Harlan Fiske Stone, Owen J. Roberts, and Benjamin N. Cardozo. For the 1936 Term, the Office of the Curator's collection

---

[2] See Barry Cushman, *Vote Fluidity on the Hughes Court: The Critical Terms, 1934–1936*, 2017 U Ill L Rev 269 (2017); Barry Cushman, *The Hughes Court Docket Books: The Late Terms, 1937–1940*, 55 Am J Legal Hist 361 (2015); Barry Cushman, *The Hughes Court Docket Books: The Early Terms, 1929–1933*, 40 J S Ct Hist 103 (2015). See also Barry Cushman, *Inside the Taft Court: Lessons from the Docket Books*, 2015 Supreme Court Review 345 (2016).

[3] 300 US 379 (1937).

[4] 261 US 525 (1923) (invalidating District of Columbia's minimum-wage law for women).

[5] *Associated Press v National Labor Relations Board*, 301 US 103 (1937); *NLRB v Friedman-Harry Marks Clothing Co.*, 301 US 58 (1937); *NLRB v Fruehauf Trailer Co.*, 301 US 49 (1937); *NLRB v Jones & Laughlin Steel Corp.*, 301 US 1 (1937).

[6] 49 Stat 449 (1935).

[7] *Helvering v Davis*, 301 US 619 (1937); *Steward Machine Co. v Davis*, 301 US 548 (1937); *Carmichael v Southern Coal & Coke Co.*, 301 US 495 (1937); *Chamberlin v Andrews*, 299 US 515 (1936).

[8] 49 Stat 620 (1935).

contains the docket books of five of these Justices. Unfortunately, the docket books of Chief Justice Hughes and Justices Sutherland and Cardozo do not appear to have survived, and it seems that for the 1936 Term Justice McReynolds followed his regular practice of burning his docket book at the conclusion of each Term.[9] Though Van Devanter's docket book for the Term survives and contains entries for most of the cases decided by the Court that year, it contains no records of conference votes or conference discussion. As a consequence, it is of little use to the historical researcher.

The collection does, however, contain the Term's docket books kept by Justices Stone, Roberts, Brandeis, and Butler. The Stone docket book contains records of the conference votes in most cases, and occasionally some notes on the remarks made by colleagues during conference discussions. The Roberts docket book similarly contains records of the conference votes in most cases, along with an occasional but none-too-frequent note on conference discussions. Professor Paul Freund, who clerked for Justice Brandeis during the 1932 Term, reported that for most of his judicial career the Justice destroyed his docket books at the end of each Term.[10] Brandeis discontinued this practice toward the end of his tenure, however, and as a result the Curator's collection holds his docket book for the 1936 Term. Brandeis's docket book contains records of the conference votes in most cases, along with occasional notes on conference discussions. Regrettably, in some instances the Justice's notes on the conference discussion are obscured by a pasted-over, typed account of the ultimate disposition.

The Curator's collection also contains Justice Butler's docket book for the 1936 Term. Butler's docket book provides not only a record of conference votes, but also a remarkably rich set of notes on conference discussions. These notes corroborate numerous accounts of Hughes's conduct of the Court's conferences,[11] at which the Chief Justice would begin with a masterful presentation of the facts and

---

[9] Dennis J. Hutchinson and David J. Garrow, eds, *The Forgotten Memoir of John Knox* 84 (2002). The Office of the Curator does, however, contain McReynolds's docket book from the 1934 Term. It also houses Cardozo's docket book from the 1932 Term.

[10] Chief Justice William H. Rehnquist and Professor Paul A. Freund: "A 'Colloquy,'" Proceedings of the Forty-Ninth Judicial Conference of the District of Columbia Circuit (May 24, 1989), reprinted in 124 FRD 241, 347 (1988).

[11] See, for example, the discussion and sources collected in William G. Ross, *The Chief Justiceship of Charles Evans Hughes, 1930–41* at 219–21 (2007).

issues in each case and a statement of his own views of how those issues should be resolved. The Justices next would present their own views in descending order of seniority, and finally would cast their votes in ascending order of seniority, with Hughes voting last. Butler's notes therefore often consist principally of the Chief Justice's remarks, which help to compensate for the fact that Hughes's docket books and Court papers have not survived.[12]

Considered in concert with information previously known, the data revealed by these four docket books shed considerable new light on the nature of the Court's deliberations in each of these three sets of cases. Let us take up each of them in turn.

I. The Minimum-Wage Cases

In the June 1936 decision in *New York ex rel. Morehead v Tipaldo*, Justice Roberts voted with the Four Horsemen (Van Devanter, McReynolds, Sutherland, and Butler) to strike down New York's minimum-wage law for women. In the March 1937 decision in *West Coast Hotel Co. v Parrish*, by contrast, Roberts joined the four *Tipaldo* dissenters to uphold Washington state's minimum-wage law for women. This "switch" calls out for an explanation, and in 1945, the year of his retirement from the Court, Roberts supplied one at the request of Felix Frankfurter.[13] Roberts explained in his 1945 memorandum that the New York attorney general had not requested that the Court overrule *Adkins v Children's Hospital*, but that in *West Coast Hotel* "the authority of *Adkins* was definitely assailed and the Court was asked to reconsider and overrule it."[14] For many, the takeaway from the memorandum was that the fault for the result in *Tipaldo* lay not with the Court but instead with New York's timorous lawyers.

[12] With the exception of the McReynolds OT 1934 Docket Book, which was donated to the Curator's Office in the 1990s by a descendant of a law clerk, each of these docket books remained in the Supreme Court building after the respective Justice either retired or died while in office. It is not known why these volumes were retained, nor why not all of the sets of docket books are complete. In 1972 all of the "historic" docket books held in the Supreme Court building were boxed up by the Court's Marshal at the order of Chief Justice Warren Burger, and were later transferred to the Curator's Office. E-mail communication from Matthew Hofstedt, Associate Curator, Supreme Court of the United States, Aug 26, 2014.

[13] Frankfurter held the memorandum that Roberts produced at his request until Roberts's death in 1955, when he published it in the *University of Pennsylvania Law Review*. Felix Frankfurter, *Mr. Justice Roberts*, 104 U Pa L Rev 314, 314 (1955).

[14] Id at 314–15.

It was true that the New York attorney general had not asked the Justices to overrule *Adkins*. It also was true that in its opinion upholding the statute in *West Coast Hotel*, the Washington state supreme court had effectively declared that *Adkins* already had been overruled. As Chief Justice Hughes put it: "The state court has refused to regard the decision in the *Adkins* case as determinative and has pointed to our decisions both before and since that case as justifying its position."[15] It was true as well that counsel for the party *challenging* the Washington statute observed that "the issue before this Court is simply whether the *Adkins* case is to be reconsidered and reversed or whether its authority is to be sustained."[16] And because the Washington statute was substantially identical to the law struck down in *Adkins*, it is difficult to see how the Court could have affirmed the state court without overruling *Adkins*. But despite all of this, the fact that New York's lawyers had not requested that *Adkins* be overruled was not particularly helpful to Roberts's explanation. For there was no denying that neither the brief for the party *defending* the statute in *West Coast Hotel*, nor the amicus curiae brief filed by the attorneys for the state of Washington, had requested that *Adkins* be overruled.[17] In that respect, the litigation posture of *West Coast Hotel* was no different from that in *Tipaldo*.

Other evidence, however, suggests a different explanation. As I have noted, the Roberts memorandum is not without its difficulties, but some of the Justice's recollections point toward the understanding ultimately articulated by his later confidante, Felix Frankfurter. Roberts reported that at the conference at which certiorari was granted in *Tipaldo*, he told his colleagues that he "saw no reason to grant the writ unless the Court were prepared to re-examine and overrule the *Adkins* case."[18] This suggests that it was not Roberts's position that he would not confront the issue of *Adkins*'s continuing authority unless the state asked him to. This remark suggests instead that Roberts was prepared to consider the question of whether *Adkins* should be overruled, but that he would not join an opinion upholding the New York measure on the ground that it was distinguishable from the

---

[15] 300 US at 389.

[16] Appellant's answer to Brief of Amicus Curiae, *West Coast Hotel Co. v Parrish*, at 18.

[17] See Brief for the Appellee, *West Coast Hotel Co. v Parrish*; Brief of Amici Curiae, *West Coast Hotel Co. v Parrish*.

[18] Frankfurter, 104 U Pa L Rev at 314 (cited in note 13).

statute invalidated in *Adkins*. Roberts's memorandum recounts that he stated at the conference following the argument in *Tipaldo* that he was "unwilling to put a decision" on the ground for which New York had contended, namely, that the two statutes could be meaningfully distinguished.[19] But that was precisely the ground upon which Hughes planted his flag.[20] Hughes was famously averse to overruling precedents where he did not regard it as absolutely necessary, and he has been subject to criticism for the distinctions he sometimes fashioned in order to avoid such official disruptions to the Court's doctrine.[21] In his dissenting opinion in *Tipaldo*, Hughes insisted that the two statutes were distinguishable, and he therefore refused to entertain the question of whether *Adkins* should be overruled.[22] And though Brandeis, Stone, and Cardozo joined this opinion,[23] Hughes declined to join them in Stone's dissent calling for *Adkins* to be overruled.[24] This caused Stone to complain that it was "'a sad business to stand only on differences of the two statutes,'" and that he "could not

[19] Id. In an interview with Merlo J. Pusey, Roberts recalled: "'When the case came before the judicial conference, we discussed it thoroughly and decided simply to let the old precedent stand. New York had come down to the Court without challenging the old precedent, *Adkins v Children's Hospital*. I thought that was a dishonest argument. I wasn't going to vote . . . to indicate there was any distinction. I agreed to stand on what was done before.'" Quoted in Charles Leonard, *A Search for a Judicial Philosophy* 90 (1971).

[20] A line from Justice Sutherland's majority opinion in *Adkins* had stated that "a statute requiring the employer . . . to pay the value of services rendered, even to pay with fair relation to the extent of the benefit obtained from the service, would be understandable." 261 US at 559. The statute at issue in *Adkins*, by contrast, had "ignored" the "moral requirement implicit in every contract of employment, *viz.*, that the amount to be paid and the service to be rendered shall bear to each other some relation of just equivalence." Id at 558. Benjamin Cohen had seized on that language in drafting the New York statute, which required that employers pay a "fair wage" based on "the fair and reasonable value of the service rendered," and it was on this basis that the lawyers for New York had sought to distinguish *Adkins*. Though Hughes and the other dissenters found the distinction constitutionally significant, Sutherland and the other remaining members of the *Adkins* majority did not. See William Lasser, *Benjamin V. Cohen: Architect of the New Deal* 154–56 (2002).

[21] Paul A. Freund, *Charles Evans Hughes as Chief Justice*, 81 Harv L Rev 4, 35 (1967); Samuel Hendel, *Charles Evans Hughes and the Supreme Court* 279 (1951); Alpheus Thomas Mason, *Harlan Fiske Stone: Pillar of the Law* 796 (1956); F. D. G. Ribble, *The Constitutional Doctrines of Chief Justice Hughes*, 41 Colum L Rev 1190, 1210 (1941); Owen J. Roberts, *The Court and the Constitution* 18 (1951). Paul Freund once characterized a distinction drawn by Hughes as one that "could be remembered just long enough to be stated once." Freund, 81 Harv L Rev at 35.

[22] 298 US at 618–31 (Hughes, CJ, dissenting).

[23] Id at 631.

[24] Id at 631–36 (Stone, J, dissenting).

understand why 'the Chief Justice felt it necessary to so limit his opinion.'"[25]

Roberts was the author of the landmark due process decision in *Nebbia v New York*, which many observers believed had implicitly overruled *Adkins*.[26] Commentators therefore expressed considerable surprise when he joined the *Tipaldo* majority,[27] and a satisfied sense of resolution when he voted to uphold the Washington statute the following year.[28] In a letter to Paul Freund written in 1953, Frankfurter explained the reason for the *Tipaldo* hiccup on the road from *Nebbia* to *West Coast Hotel*. "The fact is that Roberts did not switch. He was prepared in *Tipaldo* to make a majority overruling *Adkins*. He was not prepared to distinguish *Adkins*. Because there was no majority for overrruling *Adkins* he was in the majority in the *Morehead* case. . . ."[29] Two years later, in the *University of Pennsylvania Law*

---

[25] Mason, *Harlan Fiske Stone: Pillar of the Law* at 423 (cited in note 21) (quoting Stone to Frankfurter, June 3, 1936).

[26] See Thomas C. Chapin, *Stare Decisis and Minimum Wages*, 9 U Colo L Rev 297, 306 (1937); Robert Hale, *Minimum Wages and the Constitution*, 36 Colum L Rev 629, 633 (1936); Morris Duane, *Government Regulation of Prices in Competitive Business*, 10 Temple L Rev 262, 264 (1936); John E. Hannigan, *Minimum Wage Legislation and Litigation*, 16 BU L Rev 845, 865 (1936); Hugh Willis, *Constitutional Law of the United States* 736 (1936); *Recent Cases*, 85 U Pa L Rev 109, 118 (1936); Thomas Raeburn White, *Constitutional Protection of Liberty of Contract: Does It Still Exist?*, 83 U Pa L Rev 425, 438, 440 (1935); Norman J. Macbeth, Jr., Note, *Present Status of the Adkins Case*, 24 Ky L J 59, 66 (1935); Note, *Nebbia v. People: A Milestone*, 82 U Pa L Rev 619, 619, 622 (1934); Francis W. Matthys, *Recent Decision*, 9 Notre Dame L Rev 468, 470 (1934); Alpheus Thomas Mason, *Labor, the Courts, and Section 7(a)*, 28 Am Pol Sci Rev 999, 1007–08 (1934); Joseph H. Mueller, Note, *Price Fixing*, 23 Ill Bar J 89, 91 (1934). See also *Nebbia*, 291 US at 555 (McReynolds, J, dissenting) ("The argument advanced here would support general prescription of prices for farm products, groceries, shoes, clothing, all the necessities of modern civilization, as well as labor, when some legislature finds and declares such action advisable and for the public good").

[27] See Olin Browder, Jr., Note, *Validity of New York Minimum Wage Law*, 25 Ill Bar J 75, 76 (1936); Louis H. Rubenstein, *The Minimum Wage Law*, 11 St John's L Rev 78, 82–83 (1936); Comment, 34 Mich L Rev 1180, 1187 (1936). See also *Tipaldo*, 298 US at 635–36 (Stone, J, dissenting) (arguing that *Nebbia* "should control the present case," is "irreconcilable with the decision and most that was said in the *Adkins* case," and has "left the Court free of [*Adkins*'s] restriction as a precedent. We should follow our decision in the *Nebbia* case").

[28] See Kurt Stern, Note, *Recent Interpretation by the Supreme Court of Liberty of Contract in Employment Cases*, 11 U Cin L Rev 82, 89 (1937); Paul Y. Davis, *The Washington Minimum Wage Decision*, 12 Ind L J 415, 417 (1937); Chapin, 9 U Colo L Rev at 306 (cited in note 26); Browder, Jr., 25 Ill Bar J at 286 (cited in note 27); Note, *Progress in the Minimum Wage Struggle*, 22 Iowa L Rev 565, 570–71 (1937).

[29] Felix Frankfurter to Paul Freund, microformed on Felix Frankfurter Papers, Harvard Law School Library, at Part III, Reel 15, quoted in Michael Ariens, *A Thrice-Told Tale, or Felix the Cat*, 107 Harv L Rev 620, 633 n 78 (1994). See also Arthur M. Schlesinger, Jr., *The Age of Roosevelt: The Politics of Upheaval* 479 (1960) ("Prepared to reverse *Adkins* but not to distinguish it, Roberts felt that existing alternatives left him no choice but to vote with those

Review, Frankfurter announced publicly that "when the *Tipaldo* case was before the Court in the spring of 1936," Roberts "was prepared to overrule the *Adkins* decision. Since a majority could not be had for overrruling it, he silently agreed with the Court in finding the New York statute under attack in the *Tipaldo* case not distinguishable from the statute which had been declared unconstitutional in the *Adkins* case."[30] In Frankfurter's accounting, Roberts had not believed that the Court could legitimately sustain the New York statute unless a majority of the Justices was prepared to overrule *Adkins*. Because there was not such a majority, he acquiesced in an opinion invalidating the statute on the authority of *Adkins*, just as Stone and *Adkins* dissenters Chief Justice William Howard Taft and Justices Oliver Wendell Holmes, Jr. and Edward Terry Sanford had in the 1920s—even when state attorneys had specifically requested that the Court overrule *Adkins*.[31]

This explanation suggested that the reason for the outcome in *Tipaldo* rested not with the litigation strategy of the New York attorney general, but instead with Hughes's refusal to confront the question of whether *Adkins* should be overruled. When Hughes got his "shot at redemption"[32] later that same year, however, he certainly made the most of it. Butler typically did not keep notes of remarks made during discussions concerning whether to grant certiorari or note probable jurisdiction, but when the Justices met on October 10, 1936 to decide whether to hear *West Coast Hotel*, he did. The case came up on appeal rather than on certiorari, so the issue was whether to note

who would strike down the New York law"); Thomas Reed Powell, *Vagaries and Varieties in Constitutional Interpretation* 81 n 89 (1956) ("Mr. Justice Roberts's position in the two cases can be harmonized as the view of one who was unable to distinguish the *Adkins* case but who would accept an opportunity to overrule it").

[30] Frankfurter, 104 U Pa L Rev at 314 (cited in note 13). Freund apparently concurred in this interpretation. See Freund, 81 Harv L Rev at 29–30 (cited in note 21).

[31] See *Donham v West-Nelson Mfg. Co.*, 273 US 657 (1927) (Taft, Holmes, Sanford, and Stone all concurring silently in affirming per curiam a decision invalidating Arkansas minimum-wage statute on authority of *Adkins*); *Murphy v Sardell*, 269 US 530 (1925) (Taft, Sanford, and Stone concurring silently in per curiam decision striking down Arizona's minimum-wage statute, and Holmes concurring only because he regarded himself as bound by the authority of *Adkins*). As Charles Curtis noted, "Roberts had done no more by joining with the ex-majority [in *Tipaldo*] than to follow [*Adkins*] as a precedent that was binding on him. No more, indeed, than Holmes himself had done, when he accepted *Adkins* in the two cases that had come up from Arizona and Arkansas shortly afterwards." Charles Curtis, *Lions Under the Throne: A Study of the Supreme Court* 163–64 (1947).

[32] Jeff Shesol, *Supreme Power: Franklin D. Roosevelt vs. the Supreme Court* 415 (2011).

probable jurisdiction. Appeals remained an area of the Court's nominally mandatory jurisdiction, but a 1936 treatise on the Court's jurisdiction that Hughes had commissioned two of his former clerks to prepare reminded its readers that the Court would not note probable jurisdiction unless the case presented a "substantial federal question."[33] The Court would reject a case where the federal question involved was "frivolous," or where the question was "deemed to be foreclosed by well settled principles enunciated in prior decisions."[34] As then-Professor Frankfurter and James Landis had put it in an article published in 1930, counsel were obliged to "persuade the Court that the record presents an issue that is not frivolous and is not settled by prior decisions."[35]

This was the question with which the Court was faced at the conference on probable jurisdiction that October. The principles articulated in *Adkins* would have appeared to be well settled. They had been affirmed in per curiam decisions in 1925 and again in 1927,[36] and had been vigorously championed by Butler's majority opinion in *Tipaldo* only four months earlier. Yet Butler records Hughes as presenting the case to the conference with the statement, "This case is under Adkins rather than Tipaldo."[37] *Tipaldo*, he appeared to assert, did not actually settle the precise principles set out in *Adkins*, because the statutes involved in the two cases had differed materially. Nevertheless, those principles had been settled in *Adkins* and the two per curiam decisions handed down shortly thereafter, and if they were to be affirmed again, *West Coast Hotel* might have been handled by a

---

[33] Reynolds Robertson and Francis R. Kirkham, *The Jurisdiction of the Supreme Court of the United States* 48 (1936).

[34] Id at 96.

[35] Felix Frankfurter and James M. Landis, *The Business of the Supreme Court at October Term, 1929*, 44 Harv L Rev 1, 12 (1930). The authors went on to observe, "[p]lainly the question of substantiality is neither rigid nor narrow. The play of discretion is inevitable. . . . To the extent that there are reasonable differences of opinion as to the solidity of a question presented for decision or the conclusiveness of prior rulings," the question of substantiality "operates to subject the obligatory jurisdiction of the Court to discretionary considerations not unlike those governing certiorari." Id at 12, 14. See Edward A. Hartnett, *Questioning Certiorari: Some Reflections Seventy-Five Years After the Judges' Bill*, 100 Colum L Rev 1643, 1708 (2000).

[36] See note 31.

[37] Butler OT 1936 Docket Book. Butler reports that Hughes "quoted words of the act." Some of the words in the next sentence unfortunately are difficult to make out, but it appears to read, "Adkins case distinguished because act of gross final [illegible]."

simple summary reversal. But the Court instead noted probable jurisdiction and set the case down for briefing and argument.[38]

At the December 19 conference after oral argument in *West Coast Hotel*, Hughes made clear why he had wanted to hear the case. Butler recorded the Chief as asking, "Can Adkins be distinguished." Hughes maintained that the argument in favor of the statute "that [the] Hotel [was a public] utility etc. [was] not good." It offered a "Possible but not satisfactory distinction" from *Adkins*. "Then" Hughes raised the question, "should Adkins be overruled." He indicated that he "Agreed with Taft's [dissenting] op[inion]" in *Adkins*. "J's opn has more weight now." Those challenging the statute had "not shown" that the "Reasonable value" of the employee's labor was "less than [a] living wage." In concluding his argument in favor of overruling *Adkins*, Hughes "Cited other instances of overruling."[39] Brandeis did not often take notes of remarks made during conference discussions, but on this occasion he wrote, "CJ thinks we should overrule Adkins Case."[40]

The public reaction to *Tipaldo* had been very unfavorable. Out of 344 newspaper editorials on the decision, only ten supported it. Some sixty of these publications, including some of the more conservative, called for a constitutional amendment to overturn it. Even Herbert Hoover stated in response to the decision that "something should be done to give back to the states the powers they thought they already had."[41] The Republican party's 1936 campaign platform included a plank favoring minimum wages for women and children, and the party's presidential candidate, Alf Landon, endorsed such legislation in his telegram to the convention accepting the party's nomination.[42] The public outcry following *Tipaldo* was

---

[38] Id.

[39] Id.

[40] Brandeis OT 1936 Docket Book. Each of the available docket books records both Hughes and Roberts as voting to affirm at the December 19 conference. Butler OT 1936 Docket Book; Roberts OT 1936 Docket Book ("Hold for Stone"); Brandeis OT 1936 Docket Book ("Hold for Justice Stone"). Stone was absent from the conference on account of a lengthy illness, but his docket book also records the vote as 4–4 on December 19 ("12/19/36 Hold for Stone"), with Stone's vote later entered by pencil. Stone OT 1936 Docket Book. The Roberts and Brandeis Docket Books show Stone returning to cast the deciding vote on February 6.

[41] Schlesinger, *The Age of Roosevelt* at 489 (cited in note 30).

[42] Kirk Porter and Donald Johnson, *National Party Platforms, 1840–1972* at 367 (1973); Curtis, *Lions Under the Throne* at 154 (cited in note 31); Paul L. Murphy, *The Constitution in Crisis Times, 1918–1969* at 151 & n 74 (1972).

simply of a different order than the criticism that had been leveled at the Court for earlier decisions invalidating New Deal measures.

Though Frankfurter maintained that Roberts had been prepared in *Tipaldo* to face squarely the issue of whether *Adkins* should be overruled, some scholars have suggested that it was the strength of the public reaction to *Tipaldo* that prompted Roberts to take that step in *West Coast Hotel*.[43] The docket books do not enable us to evaluate that hypothesis with respect to Roberts, but they do with respect to Hughes. At the October 10 conference on whether to note probable jurisdiction in *West Coast Hotel*, Butler records Hughes as saying, "Public mind much disturbed—Campaign."[44] The reference to "Campaign" is a bit obscure, but it presumably refers to the fact that both of the major political parties were exercised about the issue and critical of the *Tipaldo* decision. But there can be no doubt that the mention of the "disturbed" state of the "public mind" refers to the response to *Tipaldo*. None of the docket books records Hughes as raising such considerations during the deliberations on the merits in *West Coast Hotel*, nor have I seen in any of the docket books records of this sort of consideration being raised in any other case. Indeed, in view of Hughes's record in cases involving due process, it seems very likely that if he had confronted the question of whether *Adkins* should be overruled in the spring of 1936, he would have determined that it should. It did not take the reaction to *Tipaldo* to persuade Hughes that *Adkins* was wrong on the merits. But his remarks at the conference on probable jurisdiction suggest that that reaction may have played at least some role in his determination to confront the issue of *Adkins*'s continuing authority in *West Coast Hotel*.[45]

In any event, the docket books reveal that, whereas in *Tipaldo* Hughes refused to confront the question of whether *Adkins* should be overruled, in *West Coast Hotel* Hughes took the lead in urging his colleagues to confront and overrule that precedent. This may help to resolve a difficulty with the account that attempts to shift the blame for *Tipaldo* to the New York attorney general for failing to request

---

[43] Richard D. Friedman, *Switching Time and Other Thought Experiments: The Hughes Court and Constitutional Transformation*, 142 U Pa L Rev 1891, 1952 (1994); Edward A. Purcell, Jr., *Rethinking Constitutional Change*, 80 Va L Rev 277, 289–90 (1994); Merlo J. Pusey, *Justice Roberts' 1937 Turnaround*, 1983 YB Sup Ct Hist Soc 102, 106.

[44] Butler OT 1936 Docket Book.

[45] Accord, Merlo J. Pusey, *The Supreme Court Crisis* 51 (1937).

that the Court overrule *Adkins*. Several commentators who question that account have rightly observed that in 1938 Roberts voted in *Erie Railroad v Tompkins*[46] to overrule the nearly century-old precedent of *Swift v Tyson*[47] even though neither of the parties had challenged the vitality of that decision.[48] The docket book accounts in *West Coast Hotel*, however, suggest that *Erie* may support rather than impeach the claim that Roberts was consistent in these matters. For when Hughes presented *Erie* to the conference, he announced that, "If we wish to overrule *Swift v Tyson*, here is our opportunity."[49] Perhaps in part as a result of Hughes's leadership—which may have been prompted by his experience in *Tipaldo*—a majority to overrule *Swift* was assembled. In *Tipaldo*, by contrast, Hughes played an isolated, idiosyncratic role in the deliberations and did not take the lead in confronting *Adkins*. As a result, no majority to overrule that decision could be assembled. But in *West Coast Hotel*, even though none of the litigants had requested that *Adkins* be overruled, Hughes played the kind of leadership role that he would in *Erie*. The explanation for Roberts's "switch" in the minimum-wage cases thus would appear to lie not in the litigation strategies of the parties, but instead in the conduct of the Chief Justice.[50]

II. The Labor Board Cases

No less celebrated than *West Coast Hotel* were four sharply divided decisions in which the Court upheld the government in cases testing the constitutionality of the National Labor Relations Act

[46] 304 US 64 (1938).

[47] 41 US 1 (1842).

[48] See John W. Chambers, *The Big Switch: Justice Roberts and the Minimum-Wage Cases*, 10 Labor Hist 44, 66–67 (1969); Michael E. Parrish, *The Hughes Court, the Great Depression, and the Historians*, 40 Hist 286, 296 (1978); Purcell, 80 Va L Rev 277 at 289–90 (cited in note 43); Hendel, *Charles Evans Hughes and the Supreme Court* at 130 (cited in note 21).

[49] Merlo J. Pusey, *Charles Evans Hughes* 710 (1951).

[50] Because the conference vote in *West Coast Hotel* was taken six weeks before the President unveiled his Court-packing plan, which was a very closely guarded secret, it is widely agreed that the plan could not have been a causal factor in the Court's deliberations. See Barry Cushman, *Rethinking the New Court Deal* 18 (1998). It is also doubtful that Roosevelt's landslide victory in the 1936 election played any appreciable role. See id at 25–32. For reasons to doubt that public reaction to the Court's earlier decisions significantly affected Roberts's votes during the 1936 Term, see Cushman, 89 Notre Dame L Rev at 1984 (cited in note 1); Barry Cushman, *The Man on the Flying Trapeze*, 15 U Pa J Const L 183, 235–37 (2012).

(NLRA): *NLRB v Jones & Laughlin Steel Corp.*,[51] which upheld application of the act to a large steel manufacturer; *NLRB v Fruehauf Trailer Co.*,[52] upholding application of the act to a midsized company making trailers; *NLRB v Friedman-Harry Marks Clothing Co.*,[53] upholding application of the act to a small clothing manufacturer in Richmond, Virginia; and *Associated Press v National Labor Relations Board*,[54] upholding the act's application to a major wire service notwithstanding the company's First Amendment objections. Unfortunately, in all but the *Associated Press* case, the docket books are not very revealing about the conference deliberations. Brandeis did not record the vote in any of the cases.[55] Stone and Roberts recorded only that each vote was 5–4, with the Four Horsemen dissenting.[56] Butler recorded the vote in each case, as well as some remarks of Hughes concerning the *Jones & Laughlin* case. According to Butler's notes, Hughes stated: "Extensive operations. Aliqippa Local not I.C. [interstate commerce] normally under control of state. Power 'to protect' against direct burden."[57]

Butler preserved lengthy notes on the conference discussion in *Associated Press*, however, presumably in part because it appears to have been the one of the *Labor Board Cases* in which the Justices considered whether the NLRA was facially invalid.[58] After laying out some of the facts, Hughes posed the question, "Is it [the NLRA] void on its face?" In order to answer that question, he next "examined [the] Act," noting that it covered labor disputes that "affect 'Commerce,'" which section 6 of the act "defines classically." "But for this"—determining whether a labor dispute was one "'affecting com[merce]'"—Hughes continued, "ct. is to say what is permissible." This was because the statute "Refers to [the] constitutional range of power." The question was, "Is each legitimate?" To be such, the effect of the dispute "must be so 'immediate and direct' as to affect

[51] 301 US 1 (1937).

[52] 301 US 49 (1937).

[53] 301 US 58 (1937).

[54] 301 US 103 (1937).

[55] Brandeis OT 1936 Docket Book.

[56] Stone OT 1936 Docket Book; Roberts OT 1936 Docket Book.

[57] Butler OT 1936 Docket Book. Butler mistakenly recorded Hughes as voting with the Four Horsemen in *Fruehauf*.

[58] Butler OT 1936 Docket Book. In the published decisions that issue was analyzed and resolved in *NLRB v Jones & Laughlin Steel Corp.*, 301 US 1, 29–32 (1937).

com[merce]." The aim of the act, Hughes observed, was to "Protect employ[ee]s in bargaining." He then added that "'agencies and instrumentalities'" of commerce "are like the principal." Both were "interstate com[merce]." Thus, Hughes concluded, the act was "not void on [its] face."[59]

Hughes next asked, "Is A.P. engaged in i.c. [interstate commerce]?" Here Hughes "Referred to cases on trans[portation] unions [illegible] intelligence." He "Used illustration to show state law can not burden A.P. [pre]dominantly in i.c." "Then (passing A.P.['s] 5th Am. [objection])," Butler noted parenthetically, Hughes took up the question of "Freedom of Press." Here, he maintained, there was "no compulsion"—the requirement was "only to have representation." "Membership [in a union] does[n't] in itself interfere with freedom of Press," Hughes argued. AP's "Right of discharge must be saved except for membership." Hughes therefore concluded that the Circuit Court's decision upholding the act should be affirmed.[60]

Van Devanter spoke next, and he voiced disagreement neither with Hughes's analysis of the statute's facial validity, nor with his Commerce Clause analysis of the act as applied to the Associated Press (AP). Neither did he defend AP's Fifth Amendment objections to the statute. Instead, he argued that the Circuit Court should be "Reverse[d] solely on [the] ground of interference with freedom of [the] press." AP was in the business of "forming" and "shaping" the news, and in order to do so "impartially & fairly" it was under a "Duty" to have "unbiased employees." For this reason, Van Devanter argued, "A.P. can oppose unions." McReynolds agreed that the "Freedom [of the] Press [argument was] good." He also maintained that AP was "a partnership" and "can employ whom they please." Finally, Sutherland agreed that "A.P. can follow any policy it please."[61] So far as Butler's notes reveal, none of the Four Horsemen maintained that the AP was not engaged in interstate commerce. In the end, Sutherland's dissent for his fellow Horsemen confined itself to the First Amendment issue, expressly without meaning "thereby to record our assent to all that has been said with regard to other questions in the case."[62]

---

[59] Butler OT 1936 Docket Book.

[60] Id.

[61] Id.

[62] 301 US at 134 (Sutherland, J, dissenting).

Perhaps the most interesting fact that the docket books reveal about the conference on the *Labor Board Cases* is the date on which it took place. The cases were argued on February 9, 10, and 11—in the immediate wake of President Roosevelt's February 5 announcement of his Court-packing plan—and many scholars have contended that they were decided in the government's favor due to the pressure brought to bear by FDR's proposal.[63] In the ordinary course, the *Labor Board Cases* probably would have been discussed and voted on at the conference held on the Saturday following oral argument.[64] In this instance, that would have been February 13, still in the early days of the plan's life, when many of its proponents were most optimistic about its prospects for passage. The Justices did meet for conference on February 13, and they voted on at least six cases, including *Herndon v Lowry*[65] and *Hartford Steam Boiler, Inspection, & Ins. Co. v Harrison*.[66] But they did not discuss the *Labor Board Cases*. Nor did they discuss those cases on the following Saturday, February 20. Indeed, it does not appear that the Justices even met for conference on that day—the docket books contain no record for that date of any votes on or discussions of cases.[67] Instead, the conference at which the discussion and vote on the *Labor Board Cases* took place was held on Saturday, February 27.[68]

---

[63] Nelson L. Dawson, *Brandeis and the New Deal*, in Nelson L. Dawson, ed, *Brandeis and America* 152 (1989); Murphy, *The Constitution in Crisis Times* at 115, 153–54 (cited in note 42); Alpheus Thomas Mason, *The Supreme Court from Taft to Warren* vii, 122–24 (1968); Richard C. Cortner, *The Wagner Act Cases* 188 (1964); Alpheus Thomas Mason, *The Supreme Court: Palladium of Freedom* 137–38, 145–46 (1963); Alpheus Thomas Mason and William Beaney, *The Supreme Court in a Free Society* 95, 182, 184 (1959); Fred Rodell, *Nine Men* 247, 250 (1955); Carl B. Swisher, *American Constitutional Development* 944, 954 (2d ed 1954); Robert Stern, *The Commerce Clause and the National Economy, 1933–1946*, 59 Harv L Rev 645, 677 (1946); Benjamin F. Wright, *The Growth of American Constitutional Law* 200, 202, 225 (1942); Edward S. Corwin, *Court over Constitution* 127 (1938).

[64] Edwin McElwain, *The Business of the Supreme Court as Conducted by Chief Justice Hughes*, 63 Harv L Rev 5, 17 (1949) ("After argument, a case was always discussed and voted upon at the noon conference the following Saturday.").

[65] Butler OT 1936 Docket Book; Roberts OT 1936 Docket Book; Brandeis OT 1936 Docket Book.

[66] Roberts OT 1936 Docket Book; Brandeis OT 1936 Docket Book; Stone OT 1936 Docket Book. Other cases voted on in conference that day include No 494, *Swayne & Hoyt, Ltd. v US*; No 460, *Van Beeck v Sabine Towing Co.*; No 549, *Lawrence v Shaw*; and No 563, *Hoffman v Rauch*.

[67] Stone OT 1936 Docket Book; Butler OT 1936 Docket Book; Roberts OT 1936 Docket Book; Brandeis OT 1936 Docket Book.

[68] Butler OT 1936 Docket Book; Roberts OT 1936 Docket Book. Stone's docket book records the votes on pages dated February 13, but there are subsequent pages indicating that

The docket books do not disclose the reasons for the delay in the Court's deliberations, but the two weeks between February 13 and February 27 witnessed important developments in the fortunes of the Court-packing plan. By February 13 there were already significant reasons to doubt that the President's plan would be enacted by Congress. There was the nearly unanimous denunciation of the plan in the media.[69] There was the deluge of mail and telegram traffic into congressional offices that ran heavily against the plan.[70] There was the comparable flood of supportive correspondence addressed to the Justices.[71] There was the very public opposition of the Chairman of the House Judiciary Committee, Hatton Sumners of Texas.[72] There was the passage by the House on February 10 of a previously stalled judicial pension bill that opponents of the plan hoped would defuse the crisis by creating an attractive inducement to retirement for some of the elderly Justices.[73] There was the public opposition to the bill by every Republican member of the Senate, and by nearly twenty of their conservative Democratic colleagues.[74] And on Feb-

the conference votes were held on February 27. It appears that the person on Stone's staff in charge of preparing docket book pages before conferences entered the dates on which the cases ordinarily would have been taken up, and later prepared pages entering the dates on which the cases actually were taken up. Stone apparently simply recorded the conference votes on the former set of pages, and never transferred them to the latter. Stone did the same with two other cases that were argued during the week of February 8 but discussed at conference February 27, *Virginian Railway Co. v System Federation No. 40*, 300 US 515 (1937), and *Washington, Virginia, & Maryland Coach Co. v NLRB*, 301 US 142 (1937). Stone OT 1936 Docket Book.

[69] Shesol, *Supreme Power* at 301–05 (cited in note 32); Burt Solomon, *FDR v the Constitution: The Court-Packing Fight and the Triumph of Democracy* 110, 113–14 (2008); Robert Shogan, *Backlash: The Killing of the New Deal* 122 (2006); James T. Patterson, *Congressional Conservatism and the New Deal: The Growth of the Conservative Coalition in Congress, 1933–1939* at 87, 89–90 (1967); Pusey, *Charles Evans Hughes* at 753 (cited in note 49); Joseph Alsop and Turner Catledge, *The 168 Days* 71–72 (1938).

[70] Shesol, *Supreme Power* at 305–06 (cited in note 32); Solomon, *FDR v the Constitution* at 112–13 (cited in note 69); Shogan, *Backlash* at 123 (cited in note 69); Marian McKenna, *Franklin Roosevelt and the Great Constitutional War: The Court-Packing Crisis of 1937* at 303–04 (2002); Patterson, *Congressional Conservatism and the New Deal* at 87–88 (cited in note 69); Alsop and Catledge, *The 168 Days* at 71–72 (cited in note 69).

[71] Pusey, *Charles Evans Hughes* at 753–54 (cited in note 49).

[72] Shesol, *Supreme Power* at 343–44 (cited in note 32); McKenna, *Franklin Roosevelt and the Great Constitutional War* at 314–16 (cited in note 70); Shogan, *Backlash* at 121 (cited in note 69); Alsop and Catledge, *The 168 Days* at 67 (cited in note 69).

[73] Shesol, *Supreme Power* at 342–44 (cited in note 32); Solomon, *FDR v the Constitution* at 125–26 (cited in note 69); Shogan, *Backlash* at 82–84, 123–24 (cited in note 69); McKenna, *Franklin Roosevelt and the Great Constitutional War* at 266, 301–02, 317, 335–37 (cited in note 70); Alsop and Catledge, *The 168 Days* at 77 (cited in note 69).

[74] Alsop and Catledge, *The 168 Days* at 70–71, 88, 96 (cited in note 69).

ruary 13 came the announcement that liberal Democratic Senator Burton Wheeler of Montana would lead the fight in opposition to the President's bill.[75]

By February 13 Hughes and his colleagues were aware of two additional, highly salient pieces of information. First, they knew that the factual predicate for the President's proposal was vulnerable to challenge. In his message to Congress, Roosevelt had charged that the Court was failing to deliver "full justice" because it was "forced by the sheer necessity of keeping up with its business to decline, without even an explanation, to hear 87 percent of the cases presented to it by private litigants."[76] The appointment of additional Justices, Roosevelt contended, was necessary in order to relieve and eliminate this "congestion" on the Court's calendar by "supplement[ing] the work of older judges and accelerat[ing] the work of the court."[77] Brandeis, who as the Court's sole octogenarian was deeply offended by Roosevelt's claim that he and his elderly colleagues had been failing to discharge their duties with alacrity, later suggested to Wheeler that he solicit a letter from the Chief Justice answering the President's allegations. Hughes agreed to Wheeler's request,[78] and Wheeler read Hughes's letter to great effect when the opponents of the bill opened their testimony at the hearings before the Senate Judiciary Committee on March 22.

Hughes's letter reported that the Court was "fully abreast of its work," that there was "no congestion of cases upon our calendar," and that in fact "[t]his gratifying condition has obtained for several years. We have been able for several Terms to adjourn after disposing of all cases which are ready to be heard."[79] Responding to the charge that the Justices had declined to grant meritorious petitions for certiorari, Hughes insisted that the contrary was the case. The Court had been, if anything, too liberal in accepting cases for review. Indeed, many of the petitions denied had been so wholly lacking in merit that they

[75] Id at 101.

[76] 81 Cong Rec 878 (1937).

[77] Id.

[78] Leonard Baker, *Back to Back: The Duel Between FDR and the Supreme Court* 153–56 (1967); Burton K. Wheeler and Paul F. Healy, *Yankee from the West* 328–29 (1962); Alsop and Catledge, *The 168 Days* at 124–26 (cited in note 69).

[79] Reorganization of the Federal Judiciary, Hearings on S 1392 before the Senate Commission on the Judiciary, 75th Cong, 1st Sess 488 (1937).

ought never to have been presented for consideration.[80] Moreover, Hughes observed, an "increase in the number of Justices of the Supreme Court . . . would not promote the efficiency of the Court." Indeed, the Chief Justice maintained that "it would impair that efficiency so long as the Court acts as a unit. There would be more judges to hear, more judges to confer, more judges to discuss, more judges to be convinced and to decide. The present number of Justices is thought to be large enough so far as the prompt, adequate, and efficient conduct of the work of the Court is concerned."[81]

Robert Jackson later remarked that Hughes's letter "did more than any one thing to turn the tide in the Court struggle."[82] Shortly after Wheeler had read the letter before the Judiciary Committee, Vice-President John Nance Garner telephoned FDR at Warm Springs to tell him, "We're licked."[83] Though Hughes and his brethren could not be certain that they would have the opportunity to refute Roosevelt's charges in a public forum, they must have anticipated early on both the possibility and the likely effect.

The second salient fact about which the Justices had inside information by February 13 was the result in the pending minimum-wage case of *West Coast Hotel Co. v Parrish*. They knew that Hughes and Roberts had joined Brandeis and Cardozo in voting to uphold the law at the conference on December 19, and they knew that the ailing Stone, as expected, had returned to cast the deciding vote in favor of the statute at the conference on February 6.[84] In short, they already knew that the "self-inflicted wound"[85] of *Tipaldo*, which had so "disturbed" the "public mind," would soon be healed. Hughes also knew that he could control the timing of the decision's announcement. In fact, the Chief Justice delayed the delivery of the opinion for several weeks in order to avoid conveying the false impression that the Court had reversed course on the minimum-wage issue in response to the

[80] Id at 489.

[81] Id at 491.

[82] New York Times (June 24, 1943), quoted in Pusey, *Charles Evans Hughes* at 766 (cited in note 49).

[83] Baker, *Back to Back* at 159–60 (cited in note 78); Wheeler and Healy, *Yankee from the West* at 333 (cited in note 78).

[84] See note 40.

[85] Charles Evans Hughes, *The Supreme Court of the United States: Its Foundation, Methods, and Achievements: An Appraisal* 50 (1928).

Court-packing plan. He therefore held the opinion until the propitious date of March 29—exactly one week after Wheeler's dramatic reading of Hughes's letter at the Judiciary Committee hearings.[86]

Here again, the impact was significant. "[I]t was obvious," surmises Leonard Baker, "that the decision upholding the minimum wage would make it more difficult to push FDR's Court plan through the Senate."[87] "Particularly after the Roberts switch, there was no nationwide desire for altering the Court, and as a result, no great desire in Congress either."[88] James MacGregor Burns concluded that "[b]y April, the chances for the Court plan were almost nil."[89] The Justices certainly could have anticipated this public and congressional response to *West Coast Hotel*, and they knew the outcome of that decision long before they met to discuss the *Labor Board Cases*.

But if the Justices knew all of this by February 13, they had the opportunity to learn much more about the Court-packing plan's fortunes over the course of the two weeks following. Wheeler was able to recruit other liberal and progressive colleagues such as Gerald Nye and Lynn Frazier of North Dakota and Henrik Shipstead of Minnesota to the opposition.[90] By the middle of the month, regular Democrats Joseph C. O'Mahoney of Wyoming and Tom Connally of Texas had added their names to the ranks of the plan's opponents.[91] Many other Democratic senators remained conspicuously noncommittal.[92] Soon a group of eighteen Democratic senators opposed to the plan met for dinner at the home of Maryland Democrat Millard Tydings for the purpose of forming a steering committee to lead the opposition.[93] By February 15, Roosevelt's Secretary of the

---

[86] Pusey, *Charles Evans Hughes* at 757 (cited in note 49).

[87] Baker, *Back to Back* at 179 (cited in note 78).

[88] Id at 191.

[89] James Macgregor Burns, *Roosevelt: The Lion and the Fox* 303 (1956).

[90] Alsop and Catledge, *The 168 Days* at 103 (cited in note 69). See also Shesol, *Supreme Power* at 346 (cited in note 32).

[91] Alsop and Catledge, *The 168 Days* at 87–88 (cited in note 69).

[92] William E. Leuchtenburg, *Franklin D. Roosevelt's Supreme Court "Packing" Plan*, in Harold M. Hollingworth and William F. Holmes, eds, *Essays on the New Deal* 88 (1969); Leon Keyserling, *The Wagner Act: Its Origins and Current Significance*, 20 Geo Wash L Rev 199, 210–11 (1960).

[93] In addition to Senator Tydings, those present included Burton Wheeler of Montana, Walter George of Georgia, Fredrick Van Nuys of Indiana, Edward Burke of Nebraska, Peter Gerry of Rhode Island, Harry Byrd of Virginia, Josiah Bailey of North Carolina, Bennett Champ Clark of Missouri, Tom Connally of Texas, William King of Utah, Kenneth Mc-

Treasury Henry Morganthau gave the plan only a fifty-fifty chance of passage.[94]

Within a few days another ominous signal would emerge. The administration had planned to introduce the bill in the House, whose members were more dependent upon presidential favor owing to the necessity of standing for election every two years.[95] But Chairman Sumners had lined up a comfortable majority of the House Judiciary Committee in opposition to the bill, which meant that he could "keep the bill bottled up in his committee all summer."[96] The bill could be dislodged and brought to the floor only by a discharge petition signed by 218 members, or by suspension of the House Rules, which would require the support of two-thirds of the members.[97] Such strong-arm tactics appealed neither to Majority Leader Sam Rayburn, nor to Speaker William Bankhead,[98] who was already angry with the President for having excluded him from the discussions in which the Court-packing plan had been devised.[99] Both of these Democratic leaders believed that such tactics would seriously impair and possibly destroy the bill's chances of passage by the Senate, and would produce so much ill will in the House that the bill's enactment by that body would be unlikely even if the measure survived the Senate gauntlet. After strenuous efforts at persuasion, they ultimately prevailed upon Roosevelt to introduce the bill first in the Senate. The formal announcement of this decision came on February 18.[100] And as everyone recognized, even were the bill to survive the Senate, upon its return

---

Kellar of Tennessee, and Royal Copeland of New York. See Alsop and Catledge, *The 168 Days* at 103–04 (cited in note 69); Baker, *Back to Back* at 97–99 (cited in note 78); Wheeler and Healy, *Yankee from the West* at 322 (cited in note 78); Pusey, *Charles Evans Hughes* at 754 (cited in note 49).

[94] McKenna, *Franklin Roosevelt and the Great Constitutional War* at 330 (cited in note 70).

[95] Shogan, *Backlash* at 24 (cited in note 69); McKenna, *Franklin Roosevelt and the Great Constitutional War* at 314, 317 (cited in note 70).

[96] Shogan, *Backlash* at 24 (cited in note 69).

[97] McKenna, *Franklin Roosevelt and the Great Constitutional War* at 316 (cited in note 70).

[98] Id; Alsop and Catledge, *The 168 Days* at 88–89 (cited in note 69).

[99] McKenna, *Franklin Roosevelt and the Great Constitutional War* at 293 (cited in note 70). Professor McKenna reports that "Bankhead and Rayburn listened patiently, but they then told FDR that they would have nothing to do with his proposal [to pry the bill out of Committee with a discharge petition]. Rayburn was furious at this attempt 'to make the House do the administration's dirty work,' as he put it, and in a needless battle." Id at 453.

[100] Shesol, *Supreme Power* at 344–45 (cited in note 32); McKenna, *Franklin Roosevelt and the Great Constitutional War* at 316 (cited in note 70).

to the House it would still face the same obstacles that concerned Bankhead and Rayburn.

Meanwhile, congressional Democrats seeking some sort of compromise proposal found the President intransigent on every front.[101] On February 20th, for example, a delegation headed by Vice-President John Nance Garner, Senate Majority Leader Joseph Robinson, and Senate Judiciary Committee Chairman Henry Fountain Ashurst urged Roosevelt to agree to a compromise measure involving the addition to the Court of only two or three Justices, rather than the six contemplated by the President's proposal. FDR responded to this entreaty by "laugh[ing] in their faces."[102] This refusal to compromise, which was manifested very early in the struggle and persisted into June, was not unfounded in reason. For as internal Justice Department documents reveal, Roosevelt and others were well aware that any plan promising fewer than six additional appointments would not have achieved the objective of a "dependable" Court that could be relied upon to uphold New Deal legislation. A compromise on the number of additional Justices simply was not in the cards.[103]

By late February the relentless, highly organized, and well-informed lobbying efforts of the opposition senators[104] had given them ever greater reason for confidence. On February 26, Senator Arthur Capper of Kansas wrote to William Allen White, "I think the Roosevelt program in its present form is blocked. I feel quite certain that we have enough votes to upset him."[105] Leonard Baker reports that in late February, an agent of the opposition informed Chief Justice Hughes that thirty-seven senators were "hostile" to the bill and twenty more were "doubtful."[106] Under the Senate rules in force at the time, only thirty-three votes were necessary to prevent cloture of floor debate.[107] The opposition had begun by this time to formulate plans

---

[101] Shesol, *Supreme Power* at 345–48 (cited in note 32).

[102] Solomon, *FDR v the Constitution* at 126–27 (cited in note 69); Alsop and Catledge, *The 168 Days* at 178 (cited in note 69).

[103] See Barry Cushman, *Court-Packing and Compromise*, 29 Const Comm 1 (2013).

[104] Shesol, *Supreme Power* at 355–56 (cited in note 32); Alsop and Catledge, *The 168 Days* at 186–87 (cited in note 69).

[105] Senator Arthur Capper to William Allen White, Feb 26, 1937, Box 186, William Allen White MSS, Manuscript Division, Library of Congress, quoted in Baker, *Back to Back* at 192 (cited in note 78).

[106] Baker, *Back to Back* at 93–94 (cited in note 78).

[107] Solomon, *FDR v the Constitution* at 220 (cited in note 69); Baker, *Back to Back* at 233 (cited in note 78).

for a filibuster of the bill,[108] and Hughes was informed that they had the votes necessary to sustain it. At about the same time, a Democratic member of the opposition informed Idaho Republican Senator William Borah—who was a leader in the movement to filibuster the bill as well as an old friend of Van Devanter's who helped to orchestrate the Justice's May 18 retirement announcement—that there were forty-two senators opposed to the President's plan.[109] As a prominent Republican wrote not long after the Court's conference on the *Labor Board Cases*, "unless there is a change of attitude caused by the tremendous propaganda of the Administration, there are enough senators pledged to speak against the President's proposal to prevent a vote upon it."[110]

To be sure, there were those—including most conspicuously Roosevelt himself—who continued in the face of these developments to believe that the bill ultimately would achieve passage. Moreover, we do not know how many of the Justices were made aware of this information, nor to what extent, if at all, it may have influenced their deliberations. But the postponement of the conference on the *Labor Board Cases* to February 27 certainly made it possible for the Justices to learn things about the political landscape confronting the Court-packing plan that they could not have known had they taken the cases up at conference only two weeks earlier.

III. The Social Security Cases

The first of the *Social Security Cases* to reach the Court was *Chamberlin v Andrews*,[111] which concerned the constitutionality of New York State's unemployment compensation statute. That act imposed a flat tax of 3 percent on the payrolls of all industrial enterprises employing four or more persons, with the proceeds held by a common fund for the relief of the unemployed. Chamberlin alleged that the tax was for the private purpose of benefiting a particular class rather than

---

[108] Patterson, *Congressional Conservatism and the New Deal* at 94–95 (cited in note 69); Baker, *Back to Back* at 151–52 (cited in note 78); Walter F. Murphy, *Congress and the Court* 59 (1962).

[109] McKenna, *Franklin Roosevelt and the Great Constitutional War* at 341 (cited in note 70); Ronald L. Feinman, *Twilight of Progressivism* 128 (1981); Pusey, *Charles Evans Hughes* at 760 (cited in note 49); Alsop and Catledge, *The 168 Days* at 206 (cited in note 69).

[110] Baker, *Back to Back* at 151 (cited in note 78).

[111] 299 US 515 (1936).

for a public purpose, and that it violated due process and denied equal protection because it required employers who had not laid off any of their employees "to contribute to a fund to help those who have lost positions in failing or bankrupt businesses."[112] A divided New York Court of Appeals had held that the tax was imposed for the legitimate public purpose of relieving unemployment, and that the classification was reasonable and not arbitrary.[113]

Hughes presented the case to the conference on November 21. He noted that the "Reply brief admits unemployment a matter of public concern. Means this fund for a public purpose—Separate 'fund' not uncon. feature. Has element of 'relief'. Need not consider whether it will 'prevent' unemployment. [New York] C[ourt] of A[ppeals] calls it a 'tax'—But says whether is not a tax or a police power tax is not controlling. I think it a 'tax.'" Having concluded that the tax was for a public purpose, Hughes next turned to the question of equal protection, asking, "May employers be singled out to bear whole burden—little discretion—Is it 'clear & hostile.'" He then ran through a list of hypothetical taxes that might single out certain elements of the population to bear their burdens. "Might all be put on real estate." "Could be income tax alone—Occupation tax—Production tax—if in Okla on oil." Hughes then noted that "this is not a tax on property," but instead on "payrolls." At this point he invoked the authority of *"Mountain Timber" Co. v State of Washington*.[114] That decision had upheld a state workmen's compensation statute that grouped industries into classes based upon the hazardousness of their work, and required employers in each such class to pay a flat percentage of their payrolls into a fund to be used to compensate employees in that class suffering workplace injuries. Hughes continued, observing that there was "no 'clear and hostile' discrimination" involved in the "Flat tax" "On employers." The state "Could do that for any purpose." Finally, the Chief Justice addressed the issue of the tax's "flat rate without regard to hazard." He noted that the "Difficulties to classify intersese" had been "emphasized," and concluded that a "Means test [was] not necessary its allowance is small."[115]

---

[112] *Chamberlin v Andrews*, 271 NY 1, 10 (1936).

[113] Id.

[114] 243 US 219 (1917).

[115] Butler OT 1936 Docket Book.

Van Devanter and McReynolds had dissented without opinion in *Mountain Timber*,[116] so it was not surprising that they took a different view. Van Devanter argued that New York's unemployment compensation law was "In respect of beneficiaries arbitrary" and "Unequal," and McReynolds indicated his agreement with this assessment. Sutherland added that he believed that the law was "bad because of flat rate on all." Brandeis conceded that the New York law was a "bad act," but insisted that it was "within power." He observed that the "Wisconsin act [was] much better."[117] That act also created a common unemployment compensation fund, but established within it individual reserve accounts for each employer. Employers were required to pay into the fund only if they did not maintain their employment rolls intact, and then only to the extent that they laid off their employees. Moreover, the funds in each account were to be used only to compensate that employer's own former employees.[118] Brandeis's expression of his admiration for the Wisconsin act was no mere random display of erudition. The statute had been drafted by his son-in-law, Paul Raushenbush, and was based on a memorandum that Brandeis himself had prepared in 1911.[119]

The conference vote in *Chamberlin* was evenly divided at 4–4, with the Four Horsemen opposing Hughes, Brandeis, Roberts, and Cardozo. The ailing Stone was absent from the conference, however,[120] so the decision of the New York Court of Appeals upholding the statute was affirmed by an equally divided Court.[121] It would not be long, however, before a full Court would hear and decide *Carmichael v Southern Coal & Coke Co.*,[122] which considered the question of the constitutionality of Alabama's unemployment compensation act. The Alabama statute was substantially similar to New York's, and as the vote in *Chamberlin* had anticipated, the Court sustained it by a

---

[116] 243 US at 246.

[117] Butler OT 1936 Docket Book.

[118] See *Carmichael v Southern Coal & Coke Co.*, 301 US 495, 530–31 (Sutherland, J, dissenting).

[119] Bruce A. Murphy, *The Brandeis/Frankfurter Connection* 93–96 (1982).

[120] Butler OT 1936 Docket Book; Roberts OT 1936 Docket Book; Brandeis OT 1936 Docket Book; Stone OT 1936 Docket Book.

[121] 299 US 515.

[122] 301 US 495.

vote of 5–4. The April 17 conference vote was the same.[123] In his presentation to his colleagues, Hughes noted that the Alabama statute was "like [the] N.Y. Act" upheld in *Chamberlin*. It was "not essentially dif[ferent]." The Chief's presentation of the case largely recounted the decision of the Alabama Supreme Court, but he appeared to agree with that court that the excise was for a "public purpose." Van Devanter agreed that the excise was for a "public purpose," but argued that it was "clearly arbitrary" and denied due process and equal protection "because" it provided "no classification" among employers. Instead, it simply created a "Hodge podge."[124] Butler records no further conference remarks, but Brandeis may again have mentioned the Wisconsin act. For Sutherland's dissenting opinion for himself, Van Devanter, and Butler, while echoing the due process and equal protection objections to the Alabama act's pooling feature that Van Devanter had raised at conference, praised the Wisconsin statute as "so fair, reasonable and just as to make plain its constitutional validity."[125]

Steward Machine Co. v Davis[126] upheld Title IX of the Social Security Act, which imposed a federal payroll tax on employers, payable to the U.S. Treasury, and then provided a credit of up to 90% against the tax for moneys paid into a qualifying state unemployment compensation fund.[127] The statute's tax-and-credit scheme emulated a comparable arrangement that the Court had sustained unanimously in the 1927 decision of *Florida v Mellon*.[128] There Congress had provided a credit against the federal estate tax for inheritance taxes paid to the decedent's state government. In 1933 Brandeis had suggested to his son-in-law, Paul Raushenbush, that a federal-state cooperative unemployment insurance program could be structured in the same way. Just as the credit for state death taxes left the states free to enact such taxes without fear of disadvantaging their residents, so the credit against the federal tax imposed by the Social Security Act might encourage states to establish programs of unemployment insurance

[123] Stone OT 1936 Docket Book; Butler OT 1936 Docket Book; Roberts OT 1936 Docket Book; Brandeis OT 1936 Docket Book.

[124] Butler OT 1936 Docket Book.

[125] 301 US at 531 (Sutherland, J, dissenting).

[126] 301 US 548 (1937).

[127] Id at 574–76.

[128] 273 US 12 (1927).

without fear of placing their employers at a competitive disadvantage with employers in other states.[129]

At the conference following oral argument in *Steward Machine*, the vote to uphold the statute was 5–2, with McReynolds and Butler dissenting and Van Devanter and Sutherland passing.[130] Butler records Hughes as opening the conference by asking, "What is quality of exaction is it a tax—permitted by const.?—coercing states or territories in its control. Proceeds not earmarked may be used for any pub[lic] purpose." The value of Brandeis's insightful counsel was confirmed when Hughes continued, "90% cr sustained by Fla v. Mellon—may be 225,000,000 = After the credit $22,000,000 will remain—Power not affected by credit. Fits like a glove. 'Mere fact of credit' does not detract." Hughes next asked, "Is this 'tax & credit' an invasion of state authority. State loses unless it pays." Here again the Chief's answer was simple: "Fla v. Mellon."[131]

Hughes then turned to the recent precedent of *United States v Butler*,[132] in which the Court had invalidated the 1933 Agricultural Adjustment Act's (AAA)[133] use of the fiscal powers to induce farmers to reduce their output. That act had imposed an excise on the processors of agricultural commodities, the proceeds of which were dedicated to benefit payments made to individual farmers who contracted with the federal government to curtail their production of specified commodities. The receiver of an insolvent textile mill successfully

---

[129] For details on Brandeis's involvement in the planning, drafting, and passage of the unemployment compensation provisions of the Social Security Act, see Joseph P. Lash, *Dealers and Dreamers* 244–45 (1988); Philippa Strum, *Louis D. Brandeis: Justice for the People* 386–87 (1984); Lewis J. Paper, *Brandeis* 354–57 (1983); Murphy, *The Brandeis/Frankfurter Connection* at 165–77 (cited in note 119); Melvin I. Urofsky, *A Mind of One Piece: Brandeis and American Reform* 131 (1971); David J. Danelski, *The Propriety of Brandeis' Extrajudicial Conduct*, in Dawson, ed, *Brandeis and America* at 11, 26–27 (cited in note 63); Dawson, *Brandeis and the New Deal* at 38, 48 (cited in note 63); Thomas H. Eliot, *The Advent of Social Security*, in Katie Louchheim, ed, *The Making of the New Deal* 150, 159, 160–61 (1983); Paul Freund, *Mr. Justice Brandeis*, in Allison Dunham and Philip B. Kurland, eds, *Mr. Justice* 177, 190 (1964); 5 *Letters of Louis D. Brandeis* 520, 523, 526–27 (Melvin I. Urovsky and David W. Levy, eds, 1978); Franklin D. Roosevelt to Felix Frankfurter, June 11, 1934, in *Roosevelt and Frankfurter: Their Correspondence, 1928–1945* at 122–23 (Max Freedman, annot, 1968); Tom Corcoran and Ben Cohen to FF, June 18, 1934, id at 123–26.

[130] Stone OT 1936 Docket Book; Butler OT 1936 Docket Book; Roberts OT 1936 Docket Book; Brandeis OT 1936 Docket Book. Stone records the conference as taking place on April 10, but both Butler and Roberts record it as occurring on April 17.

[131] Butler OT 1936 Docket Book.

[132] 297 US 1 (1936).

[133] 48 Stat 31 (1933).

challenged the excise, with the Court holding by a vote of 6–3 that the exaction was invalid because the revenue it generated was devoted to effectuating a federal program regulating agricultural production and thereby intruding on the legislative domains of the states.

Many scholars have argued that *Steward Machine* and *Helvering v Davis* implicitly repudiated *Butler*,[134] but the Chief Justice and his colleagues did not see it that way. In the "Butler Case," Hughes observed, "AAA individuals induced to make contracts. Majority thought coercive." But here, he argued, "The state has agreed. It is sovereign & can agree = state is helped." At this point in his notes Justice Butler interjected his own thoughts in brackets: "[But may state agree vs. power to deal with matters reserved to states?]." Butler's record of Hughes's remarks concludes with what appears to be another question: "are particular conditions fair offer of cooperation."[135]

It was Van Devanter's turn to speak next, but the most senior Associate Justice kept his own counsel and passed. McReynolds similarly withheld his views. Brandeis next stated that "This legislation is opposite to invasion of state power." The last Justice on whose remarks Butler took notes was Sutherland, whom he records as saying that he "Agrees with most of 1 [Hughes]. State is free." For this proposition Sutherland relied on a bit of his own handiwork, "Mass v. Mellon."[136] In the 1923 case of *Massachusetts v Mellon*,[137] Sutherland had written for a unanimous Court upholding the Sheppard-Towner Maternity Act of 1921.[138] That act created a federal grant-in-aid program under which Congress appropriated funds to be disbursed to

---

[134] Robert McCloskey, *The American Supreme Court* 118, 123 (4th ed 2005); Melvin I. Urofsky and Paul Finkelman, 2 *A March of Liberty* 695 (2002); William E. Leuchtenburg, *The Supreme Court Reborn* 142, 219 (1995); Alfred H. Kelley, Winfred Harbison, and Herman Belz, 2 *The American Constitution: Its Origins and Development* 488–89 (7th ed 1991); David P. Currie, *The Constitution in the Supreme Court: The Second Century* 238 (1990); Wright, *The Growth of American Constitutional Law* at 205 (cited in note 63); Mason and Beaney, *The Supreme Court in a Free Society* at 147–48 (cited in note 63); Bernard Schwartz, *The Supreme Court: Constitutional Revolution in Retrospect* 22 (1957); Rodell, *Nine Men* at 250 (cited in note 63); Samuel J. Konefsky, *Chief Justice Stone and the Supreme Court* 118–19 (1945); Edward S. Corwin, *Constitutional Revolution, Ltd.* 71 (1941); Alsop and Catledge, *The 168 Days* at 143 (cited in note 69). A few scholars have contended that the decisions were in fact consistent. See, for example, Pusey, *Charles Evans Hughes* at 760 (cited in note 49).

[135] Butler OT 1936 Docket Book.

[136] Id.

[137] 262 US 447 (1923).

[138] 44 Stat 224 (1921).

states that established qualifying programs for the promotion of maternal and infant health. Massachusetts had contended "that the statute constitutes an attempt to legislate outside the powers granted to Congress by the Constitution and within the field of local powers exclusively reserved to the states"; "that the ulterior purpose of Congress thereby was to induce the states to yield a portion of their sovereign rights"; and that "there is imposed upon the states an illegal and unconstitutional option either to yield to the federal government a part of their reserved rights or lose their share of the moneys appropriated."[139] Sutherland had answered that "the powers of the state are not invaded, since the statute imposes no obligation but simply extends an option which the state is free to accept or reject."[140] "Nor does the statute require the states to do or to yield anything. If Congress enacted it with the ulterior purpose of tempting them to yield, that purpose may be effectively frustrated by the simple expedient of not yielding."[141] Yet Sutherland concluded his discussion of *Steward Machine* with remarks suggesting that he remained troubled by at least one of the act's features: "Am not sure does not invade power. State may not surrender or give US any part of its sovereignty."[142]

Cardozo's opinion for the majority largely tracked the presentation that Hughes had made at conference. The tax was a valid excise,[143] and the excise in combination with the credit was "not void as involving the coercion of the States in contravention of the Tenth Amendment or of restrictions implicit in our federal form of government."[144] Indeed, the state of Alabama did not "offer a suggestion that in passing the unemployment law she was affected by duress. For all that appears she is satisfied with her choice, and would be sorely disappointed if it were now to be annulled."[145] Cardozo explained that "*Florida v. Mellon* supplies us with a precedent, if precedent be needed,"[146] and in the same paragraph he also cited *Massachusetts v*

[139] 262 US at 482.

[140] Id at 480.

[141] Id at 482.

[142] Butler OT 1936 Docket Book.

[143] 301 US at 578–83.

[144] Id at 585.

[145] Id at 589 (citations omitted).

[146] Id at 589.

Mellon as a supportive decision.[147] The majority concluded that the statute did "not call for a surrender by the states of powers essential to their quasi-sovereign existence."[148]

Cardozo distinguished *Butler* on four grounds. First, unlike the processing tax imposed by the AAA, which the *Butler* majority had held was not a true tax, the proceeds of the payroll tax were not "earmarked for a special group." Second, unlike the AAA's regulation of agricultural production without the consent of the state in which it was conducted, "[t]he unemployment compensation law which is a condition of the credit has had the approval of the state and could not be a law without it." Third, the state under the Social Security Act, unlike the farmer under the AAA, was not bound to "an irrevocable agreement, for the state at its pleasure may repeal its unemployment law, terminate the credit, and place itself where it was before the credit was accepted." And fourth, unlike the "coercive contracts" under the AAA, which the *Butler* majority had held were "unlawful in their aim and oppressive in their consequences," the condition of the tax credit available under the Social Security Act was "not directed to the attainment of an unlawful end, but to an end, the relief of unemployment, for which nation and state may lawfully cooperate."[149]

As they had at conference, McReynolds and Butler dissented. In an opinion consisting principally of quotations from President Franklin Pierce's 1854 message vetoing a congressional bill granting lands to the states for the support of the indigent insane,[150] McReynolds insisted that the challenged portion of the act "unduly interferes with the orderly government of the State by her own people and otherwise offends the Federal Constitution."[151] Butler similarly objected that "in principle and as applied to bring about and to gain control over state unemployment compensation, the statutory scheme is repugnant to the Tenth Amendment."[152]

> The Constitution grants to the United States no power to pay unemployed persons or to require the states to enact laws or to raise or disburse money

---

[147] Id at 592.

[148] Id at 593.

[149] Id at 592–93 (citations omitted).

[150] Id at 600–09 (McReynolds, J, dissenting).

[151] Id at 598 (McReynolds, J, dissenting).

[152] Id at 616 (Butler, J, dissenting).

> for that purpose. The provisions in question, if not amounting to coercion in a legal sense, are manifestly designed and intended directly to affect state action in the respects specified. And, if valid as so employed, this "tax and credit" device may be made effective to enable federal authorities to induce, if not indeed to compel, state enactments for any purpose within the realm of state power and generally to control state administration of state laws.[153]

"The terms of the measure make it clear," Butler concluded, "that the tax and credit device was intended to enable federal officers virtually to control the exertion of powers of the states in a field in which they alone have jurisdiction and from which the United States is by the Constitution excluded."[154]

Sutherland's separate dissenting opinion, in which he was joined by Van Devanter, faithfully reprised the comments he had made at conference. "With most of what is said in the opinion just handed down," wrote the author of *Massachusetts v Mellon* and *Florida v Mellon*, "I concur."[155]

> I agree that the pay roll tax levied is an excise within the power of Congress; that the devotion of not more than 90 per cent. of it to the credit of employers in states which require the payment of a similar tax under so-called unemployment-tax laws is not an unconstitutional use of the proceeds of the federal tax; that the provision making the adoption by the state of an unemployment law of a specified character a condition precedent to the credit of the tax does not render the law invalid. I agree that the states are not coerced by the federal legislation into adopting unemployment legislation. The provisions of the federal law may operate to induce the state to pass an employment law if it regards such action to be in its interest. But that is not coercion. If the act stopped here, I should accept the conclusion of the court that the legislation is not unconstitutional.[156]

But as he had signaled at the conference, he could not overcome his doubts about the act's provision requiring payment of the proceeds of state taxes into the federal treasury, to be withdrawn only for unemployment compensation payments made through state agencies approved by a federal board.[157] These "administrative provisions of the act," Sutherland maintained, "invade the governmental administrative powers of the several states reserved by the Tenth Amend-

---

[153] Id at 616–17 (Butler, J, dissenting).

[154] Id at 618 (Butler, J, dissenting).

[155] Id at 609 (Sutherland, J, dissenting).

[156] Id at 609–10 (Sutherland, J, dissenting).

[157] Id at 612–13 (Sutherland, J, dissenting).

ment."[158] Therefore, he concluded, "the congressional act contemplates a surrender by the state to the federal government" of "state governmental power to administer its own unemployment law" and "the state payroll-tax funds which it has collected for the purposes of that law."[159]

The last of the *Social Security Cases* was *Helvering v Davis*,[160] which challenged the old-age pension provisions of the statute. Title VIII of the statute imposed payroll taxes on employers and employees; Title II made provision for the payment of old age benefits. As with the taxes imposed by Title IX of the act, the taxes imposed by Title VIII were paid directly into the treasury, and were "not earmarked in any way."[161] Title II created an account in the treasury to be known as the "Old-Age Reserve Account" from which future old age benefits were to be paid, but the act made no appropriation to fund that account. A shareholder of a Massachusetts corporation brought suit to restrain the company from paying the taxes and making the payroll deductions required by the act. The company indicated that it intended to comply with the act's requirements unless it were restrained by an injunction. The Commissioner of Internal Revenue intervened, and argued that the shareholder had no standing to challenge the validity of the act's tax on employees. The District Court agreed that the tax on employees was not properly at issue, and upheld the tax on employers. The First Circuit, however, held that Title II constituted an invasion of powers reserved to the states by the Tenth Amendment, and that the invalidity of the expenditures to be made under Title II was fatal to the taxes imposed by Title VIII. On certiorari, the government waived its defense that the legal remedy was adequate, so as to bring the case within equity and secure a ruling on the merits.[162]

The threshold question for the Court was whether there was jurisdiction in equity to entertain the suit for an injunction. Cardozo's opinion for the majority questioned whether the directors had violated any duty by resolving to pay the taxes, and also whether the

[158] Id at 610 (Sutherland, J, dissenting).

[159] Id at 611 (Sutherland, J, dissenting).

[160] 301 US 619 (1937).

[161] Id at 635.

[162] Id at 635–39.

shareholder had "standing to challenge that resolve in the absence of an adequate showing of irreparable injury." The question was further complicated, Cardozo suggested, by "the acquiescence of the company in the equitable remedy" imposed below, and by the government's waiver of its defense to equitable jurisdiction. Cardozo concluded that "in a controversy such as this a court must refuse to give equitable relief when a cause of action in equity is neither pleaded nor proved," and therefore that the shareholder's suit for an injunction "should be dismissed upon that ground." Brandeis, Stone, and Roberts agreed with this position, but a majority of their colleagues "reached a different conclusion," apparently because the company and the government had not challenged the equitable remedy "at every stage of the proceeding."[163]

This division over the jurisdictional issue had been at the center of the conference discussion. Indeed, from Butler's notes it appears that Brandeis, Stone, and Roberts spoke only to the issue of jurisdiction in equity. Brandeis remarked that he "Can't see the propriety of passing on quest[ion]" of the act's "validity" in this case. "Our obligation," he concluded, "is not to." Stone added that he "doubts Jur[isdiction]—parties can't by waiver give Jur[isdiction]—must be finding that directors have not violated their duty. Not 'entirely clear' as to compelling. Can't get to this [illegible]." Roberts is recorded only as agreeing with Brandeis and Stone that there was "no Jur[isdiction]." Cardozo added that there was "no cause of action—Directors have no[t] exceeded power as the Company owes tax—US indemnifies Co for tax on employers."[164]

The vote on the question of jurisdiction was 5–4, with Hughes and the Four Horsemen prepared to decide the merits.[165] Among those in the majority on the jurisdictional question, only Hughes appears to have spoken to the issue at conference. As to the "Standing of Davis to sue," Hughes noted that "Both [parties] say there can be waiver [of the defense of an adequate remedy at law] and was," citing "Pollock Case." The reference was to *Pollock v Farmer's Loan & Trust Co.*,[166]

[163] Id at 639–40.

[164] Butler OT 1936 Docket Book.

[165] Stone OT 1936 Docket Book; Butler OT 1936 Docket Book; Roberts OT 1936 Docket Book. In Brandeis OT 1936 Docket Book, the vote is obscured by a paste-over.

[166] 157 US 429 (1895).

where the Court held that it had jurisdiction to entertain a suit in equity where the defendant had waived the defense of adequate remedy at law.[167] The *Davis* case was "Clearly analogous," Hughes argued. The Chief Justice invoked his own opinion in "Henrietta Mills [v Rutherford] 281 [US 121 (1930)]," which had held that the Court was without equitable jurisdiction to entertain a suit to enjoin collection of a state tax because the complaining party had an adequate remedy at law. In the final paragraph of that opinion, Hughes had written that "unless the case is one where the objection [that the plaintiff had an adequate remedy at law] may be treated as waived by the party entitled to raise it, the prohibition is not to be disregarded. There was no waiver in the present case, and, as the petitioner had an adequate remedy at law, the district court could not properly entertain the suit."[168] *Henrietta Mills*, Hughes maintained in the *Davis* conference, "held remedy at law qu[estion] is wh[ether] equity is needed? Can def[initely] by waiver compel court to go on in equity. One 'variant.'" Hughes focused on the "wages of employees," noting that an "employee in Mass[achusetts] can compel full payment of wages," as there was "No plain clear adequate rem[edy] at law as to wages." Hughes urged that the Court "Should not overrule" *Pollock* and *Henrietta Mills* on this point, and should hold that the Court had "jurisdiction" "in equity."[169]

On the merits, the Court upheld the tax on employers and the provisions of Title II by a vote of 7–2, with only McReynolds and Butler noting dissents. Cardozo's opinion held that the provisions of Title II were expenditures in aid of the general welfare, and that there was therefore "no occasion to inquire whether Title VIII would

[167] "The jurisdiction of a court of equity to prevent any threatened breach of trust in the misapplication or diversion of the funds of a corporation by illegal payments out of its capital or profits has been frequently sustained . . . this bill proceeds on the ground that the defendants would be guilty of such breach of trust or duty in voluntarily making returns for the imposition of, and paying, an unconstitutional tax; and also on allegations of threatened multiplicity of suits and irreparable injury.

"The objection of adequate remedy at law was not raised below, nor is it now raised by appellees, if it could be entertained at all at this stage of the proceedings; and, so far as it was within the power of the government to do so, the question of jurisdiction, for the purposes of the case, was explicitly waived on the argument. The relief sought was in respect of voluntary action by the defendant company, and not in respect of the assessment and collection themselves. Under these circumstances, we should not be justified in declining to proceed to judgment upon the merits." Id at 553–54.

[168] 281 US at 128 (citations omitted).

[169] Butler OT 1936 Docket Book.

have to fall if Title II were set at naught."[170] The vote on the merits had been the same at conference.[171] After discussing the jurisdictional question, Hughes began by pointing out that Title VIII imposed its tax on "all employers" rather than only on those having a certain number of employees, making the question of its constitutionality "easier [than Section] 901," the taxing provision of Title IX upheld in *Steward Machine*. The "Only possible question" was thus the " 'way in wh[ich] [the tax was] laid'—purpose for which laid." "As to [the] purpose," it was for "old age benefits." There were "No provisions for using [the proceeds of the tax imposed by] Title VIII for [payment of the benefits payable under] Title II." The proceeds of the tax were "no[t] earmarked," and it would be "Extraordinary to draw inferences for supposed relation." Title VIII imposed a "mere excise on payroll."[172]

Van Devanter then followed, saying that he was "Not sure [whether] Title II & Title VIII [were] not so distinct" as Hughes had made them out to be, but that he believed that the "Tax [was] valid." McReynolds indicated his preference to affirm the First Circuit, and Brandeis is recorded as speaking only to the jurisdictional issue. Sutherland spoke next, agreeing with Hughes that the tax was a valid excise. The "Tax and purpose," he observed, "appear on face of act." He disagreed with Hughes's effort to dissociate Titles VIII and II, maintaining that "They are tied in as in Butler." But that was of no consequence, because here, unlike in *Butler*, the "purpose is within power Congress." These titles were "free from [the] object[ions] in other cases" like *Steward Machine*, because here there was "no interfere[nce] with [the] power of the state. Congress," he concluded, "can 'appropriate' for the old." Justice Butler then signaled his view that the Circuit Court should be affirmed, after which Stone and Roberts spoke only to the jurisdictional question. Cardozo then took up the jurisdictional question as well, but added that "On [the] merits" he was "with 1 [Hughes]" and "also [with] 5 [Sutherland]."[173]

---

[170] 301 US at 640–45.

[171] Stone OT 1936 Docket Book; Butler OT 1936 Docket Book; Roberts OT 1936 Docket Book. In Brandeis OT 1936 Docket Book, the vote is obscured by a paste-over, but one can see that Hughes and Van Devanter voted to reverse and that McReynolds voted to affirm.

[172] Butler OT 1936 Docket Book.

[173] Id.

One feature of this exchange is worthy of brief remark. After Hughes, Van Devanter, and Sutherland had spoken, it would have been clear to Stone, Roberts, and Cardozo—all of whom had been in the *Steward Machine* majority—that if the Court were to reach the merits, there would be a majority to uphold the act. It would have been a simple matter for them to voice agreement with Hughes and Sutherland on both the jurisdictional issue and the merits. Yet Butler records both Stone and Roberts, like Brandeis, as saying only that the case should be dismissed on jurisdictional grounds, and Cardozo stood with them on this point both at conference and in his opinion for the Court. Even when they were faced with the question of the constitutional validity of a massive new social program in the midst of a "constitutional crisis," Butler's conference notes depict these men as conscientiously focused on the particular features of the specific litigation before them, and as thinking and speaking about that litigation in very professional, lawyerly terms.[174]

Finally, it bears emphasis that Butler's notes of the conferences on *Steward Machine* and *Davis* reinforce what was said in the published opinions: that the Justices in the majority did not believe that they were in any way retreating from the positions that they had taken in *United States v Butler*. In *Steward Machine*, Hughes and Sutherland agreed that, unlike the farmers who had entered into acreage-reduction contracts under the AAA, the states enacting qualifying programs of unemployment compensation had acted freely and were not coerced. In *Davis*, Hughes saw the fact that the proceeds of the payroll tax were not earmarked as distinguishing the Social Security Act from the AAA. And both Hughes and Van Devanter appear to have agreed with Sutherland that the benefit payments authorized by Title II, unlike those made under the AAA, were for a public

[174] The image of careful and thorough deliberation that emerges from the docket book notes on the conferences in the *Social Security Cases* stands in sharp contrast with other depictions of the conference under Hughes as rushed and truncated. See, for example, Memorandum Re: No 401, *United States v Butler*, Feb 4, 1936, Box 62, Harlan Fiske Stone MSS, Manuscript Division, Library of Congress (complaining of the conference in *United States v Butler* that "the main question in the case was decided practically without discussion"); Mason, *Harlan Fiske Stone: Pillar of the Law* at 790 (cited in note 21) (quoting Stone writing to John Bassett Moore in 1932 that he had "no hesitation in saying that I think discussion of our cases should be much fuller and freer"); Andrew Kaufman, *Cardozo* 480 (1993) (Cardozo writing shortly after joining the Court in 1932, "there is nothing like the genuine debate—the painstaking and willing interchange of views that gave my old court [the New York Court of Appeals] whatever strength it had").

purpose within the power of Congress. Where others have seen a new doctrinal departure, these Justices saw doctrinal continuity.[175]

IV. Conclusion

The Hughes Court docket books thus shed valuable new light on each of the major sets of cases decided during the 1936 Term. For the minimum-wages cases, the docket books help us to reconstruct an account of the Court's deliberations highlighting three salient features. First, that the failure to assemble a majority to sustain the New York minimum-wage statute in *Tipaldo* was attributable to Hughes's extreme reluctance to overrule a precedent and his insistence on distinguishing the statute invalidated in *Adkins*, coupled with Roberts's insistence that there was no constitutionally significant distinction to be drawn and that the New York law could not be upheld unless there were a majority prepared to overrule *Adkins*. Second, that even though the Court was not asked to overrule *Adkins* in *West Coast Hotel*, Hughes's leadership in persuading his colleagues to confront and abandon that precedent made it possible to assemble a majority to uphold the Washington statute. And third, that the

[175] The docket book depictions of the deliberations in the *Social Security Cases* thus complement the analysis recently provided by Michele Landis Dauber, *The Sympathetic State: Disaster Relief and the Origins of the American Welfare State* 176–84 (2013). For contemporary commentary viewing the *Social Security Cases* as consistent with antecedent fiscal power precedents, see, for example, Paul Huser, Comment, *Constitutional Law—Validity of Social Security Taxes*, 16 Tex L Rev 224, 225 (1938) (distinguishing the taxes imposed in *Steward Machine* and *Butler* on the ground that the former tax, unlike the latter, was "not earmarked for any particular purpose nor set aside to be used to pay the benefits provided for by the Act, but may be used to pay the general costs of the Federal Government, as is the case generally with any internal revenue collections"); Recent Decision, *Constitutional Law—Scope of the National Spending Power—Validity of Federal Old-Age Benefit Appropriations under Social Security Act*, 37 Colum L Rev 1206, 1208 (1937) ("In basing its decision [in *Helvering*] on the general welfare clause, the Court established as a rule of law the Hamiltonian conception of the spending power, which it had already adopted in *dicta* in the A.A.A. case"); Elbert R. Gilliom, Comment, *The Federal-State System of Unemployment Compensation Under the Social Security Act*, 35 Mich L Rev 1306, 1311–13 (1937) (detailing the manner in which the act's unemployment compensation provisions were drafted so as to avoid constitutional pitfalls, and concluding that "the Court in [*Steward Machine*] properly distinguished the invalid AAA processing tax on the ground that since the proceeds were earmarked for the benefit of individual farmers complying with prescribed conditions, the latter was not a true tax, but part of a scheme to regulate agricultural production without the consent of the state affected"); Roger Sherman Hoar, Note, *Constitutional Law—By-Products of the Social Security Decisions*, 21 Marq L Rev 215, 215 (1937) ("Economists and experts on constitutional law were not surprised at the two unemployment compensation opinions of the United States Supreme Court rendered on May 24, 1937, for it had been expected that both the Alabama unemployment compensation law and Title IX of the Social Security Act would be sustained by a narrow margin").

uproar of popular disapproval that followed in the wake of the *Tipaldo* decision played a role in persuading Hughes that *West Coast Hotel* presented a substantial federal question meriting a notation of probable jurisdiction.

Though the docket books do not shed much new light on the doctrinal dimensions of the Court's deliberations in the *Labor Board Cases*, they do reveal that Hughes delayed the conference discussion and initial voting on those cases for two weeks, making it possible for the Justices to acquire and digest information about the Court-packing plan's prospects that would have been unavailable to them had the conference been held according to the Court's ordinary course of business.

These revelations speak principally to questions of causation. What can be said of the claim that the Justices wrought a "Constitutional Revolution" in the spring of 1937? Let us take each of the principal sets of cases in turn. To be sure, *West Coast Hotel* overruled *Adkins v Children's Hospital*, eliminating that strand of substantive due process from the Court's jurisprudence. But a few observations help to place the significance of that event in proper perspective. First, several of the principal precedents comprising *Lochner*-era substantive due process had been retired well before the spring of 1937. Constitutional restrictions on maximum-hours legislation were effectively discarded in 1917, when the Court upheld a working-hours limitation of general applicability in *Bunting v Oregon*.[176] Though *Lochner* would be cited as a live authority in *Adkins* six years later,[177] never again would it be relied upon to invalidate legislation prescribing maximum hours of work. As far as such legislation was concerned, Chief Justice William Howard Taft was accurate in his view that *Bunting* had overruled *Lochner* sub silentio.[178] Similarly, in 1930, the Court upheld provisions of the Railway Labor Act of 1926 that protected the rights of railway employees to organize and bargain collectively, and affirmed a lower court order requiring a railroad to reinstate employees it had discharged for engaging in lawful union activities.[179] This effectively overruled the 1908 decision of *Adair v*

[176] 243 US 426 (1917).

[177] 261 US at 545, 548–50.

[178] *Adkins v Children's Hospital*, 261 US at 563–64 (Taft, CJ, dissenting).

[179] *Texas & N.O. R. Co. v Brotherhood of Ry. & Steamship Clerks*, 281 US 548 (1930).

United States,[180] which had invalidated on due process grounds a federal statute prohibiting railroad companies from "unjustly discriminat[ing] against any employee because of his union membership,"[181] and thereby removed due process obstacles to national collective bargaining legislation. And in the 1934 decision of *Nebbia v New York*, the Justices abandoned a long line of decisions restricting price regulation to a narrow category of businesses "affected with a public interest."[182] By the time that *West Coast Hotel* was handed down, much of the "revolution" in due process jurisprudence already had occurred.

Second, the centrality of *Adkins* to *Lochner*-era substantive due process is easily exaggerated. When Oregon's minimum-wage statute for women was challenged before the Court in 1917,[183] there were five Justices who believed it was constitutional. However, one of these, Justice Brandeis, had served as counsel to the state in the lower court proceedings before his appointment to the Court, and therefore had to recuse himself from participation on appeal. As a result, the Oregon Supreme Court's judgment upholding the statute was affirmed by an equally divided Court. This saved the statute from invalidation, but had no precedential effect.[184] By the time *Adkins* reached the Court six years later, the tribunal had undergone significant changes in personnel, and a new, bare majority to strike down the District of Columbia's statute was unconstrained by any prior decision on the issue.[185] When one member of that majority, Justice Joseph McKenna, was replaced by Stone in 1925, there were again five Justices who believed that *Adkins* had been wrongly decided. Indeed, internal Court documents previously unavailable to the public reveal that the authority of *Adkins* appears to have survived challenges in 1925 and 1927 only because four of these Justices

---

[180] 208 US 161 (1908). See also *Coppage v Kansas*, 236 US 1 (1915) (invalidating on due process grounds a state statute prohibiting employers from requiring employees to sign contracts promising not to join a union).

[181] 30 Stat 424, 428 (1898).

[182] 291 US 502 (1934).

[183] *Stettler v O'Hara*, 243 US 629 (1917).

[184] See Alexander Bickel and Benno C. Schmidt, *The Judiciary and Responsible Government, 1910–1921* at 592–603 (1984).

[185] See Thomas Reed Powell, *The Judiciality of Minimum Wage Legislation*, 37 Harv L Rev 545, 547–52 (1924) (surmising that there was a Court majority for sustaining minimum-wage legislation until June of 1922, and that the appeal in *Adkins* might have been heard and an opinion upholding the statute rendered had the Court of Appeals of the District of Columbia not ordered rehearing and reargument after its initial decision upholding the measure).

felt bound by stare decisis to uphold the recent precedent.[186] After *Nebbia* was decided in 1934, many commentators expressed the view that a majority of the Justices was poised to overrule *Adkins*,[187] which again survived in 1936 for the reasons discussed above. Many Justices who were invested in other strands of substantive due process were fully prepared to uphold minimum-wage legislation. There were several occasions during the so-called *Lochner* era when such legislation might have been sustained, and the fact that the prohibition on minimum-wage laws was adopted and perpetuated was the consequence only of these fortuitous vicissitudes.[188]

Third, and relatedly, the abandonment of that prohibition in *West Coast Hotel* did not signal a desertion of the larger enterprise of economic substantive due process. For the remainder of their judicial careers, Hughes and Roberts continued to cast votes to invalidate economic regulations on the ground that they deprived the regulated parties of property without due process of law,[189] denied them the equal protection of the laws[190] or the privileges or immunities of citizenship,[191] or took their property without just compensation.[192]

---

[186] See Cushman, 2015 Supreme Court Review at 381–83 (cited in note 2).

[187] See note 26. At least one commentator detected such a majority in 1931, when the Court upheld a statute regulating the commissions paid to agents selling fire insurance in *O'Gorman & Yong v Hartford Fire Ins. Co.*, 282 US 251 (1931). See Comment, 45 Harv L Rev 643, 644 (1931). See also Norman J. Macbeth, Jr., *Present Status of the Adkins Case*, 24 Ky L J 59, 64–65 (1935).

[188] See Powell, 37 Harv L Rev at 547–50 (cited in note 185) (concluding that thirty-five of forty-five judges and Justices hearing challenges to minimum-wage laws up to 1924 had voted to uphold the statutes).

[189] See *R.R. Comm'n of Tex. v Rowan & Nichols Oil Co.*, 310 US 573, 577 (1940) (Roberts and Hughes dissenting from opinion holding that oil proration order of Texas Railroad Commission did not deprive the company of its property without due process); *United States v Rock-Royal Co-op, Inc.*, 307 US 533, 583–87 (1939) (Roberts and Hughes dissenting from opinion upholding against a due process challenge an order issued by the Secretary of Agriculture pursuant to the Agricultural Marketing Agreement Act of 1937). See also *Thompson v Consolidated Gas Utilities Corp.*, 300 US 55 (1937) (Hughes and Roberts join opinion invalidating gas proration order of Texas Railroad commission on the ground that it deprived the company of its property without due process).

[190] See *Charleston Fed. Savings & Loan Association v Alderson*, 324 US 182, 192–93 (1945) (Roberts, J, dissenting from opinion upholding tax assessments against equal protection challenge); *Hartford Steam Boiler Inspection & Ins. Co. v Harrison*, 301 US 459 (1937) (Hughes, CJ, joining opinion invalidating Georgia statute imposing differing regulations on stock and mutual insurance companies).

[191] See *Madden v Kentucky*, 309 US 83, 93–94 (1940) (Roberts, J, dissenting from opinion upholding state tax against equal protection and privileges or immunities challenges).

[192] See *United States v Willow Power Co.*, 324 US 499, 511–15 (1945) (Roberts and Stone, dissenting from opinion holding that government action reducing the flow of water available to an electrical power plant did not constitute a taking requiring compensation under the

Their views on these matters no longer prevailed, but only because Roosevelt's replacement of their former colleagues with Justices who rejected such doctrinal commitments had relegated them to the Court's minority. Had Hughes and Roberts had their way, however, vestiges of economic substantive due process and its allied doctrines would have remained.

With respect to the *Labor Board Cases*, three principal points should be borne in mind. First, though many scholars[193] and some contemporary federal judges[194] have understood those decisions as marking reversals or substantial departures from the Court's established Commerce Clause precedents, many contemporary observers saw the opinions in those cases as fully consistent with prevailing doctrine. Those taking such a view included Solicitor General Stanley Reed;[195] Charles Fahy, the General Counsel to the NLRB who approved and oversaw the agency's litigation strategy;[196] many com-

Fifth Amendment); *United States v Commodore Park, Inc.*, 324 US 386, 393 (1945) (Roberts, J, dissenting from opinion holding that the Fifth Amendment did not require compensation of riparian landowner whose property was reduced in market value but not invaded by government dredging operation).

[193] See, for example, Murphy, *The Constitution in Crisis Times* at 153–54 (cited in note 42); William H. Swindler, 2 *Court and Constitution in the Twentieth Century* 99–100, 137 (1969); Leuchtenburg, *Franklin D. Roosevelt's Supreme Court "Packing" Plan* at 94 (cited in note 92); Cortner, *The Wagner Act Cases* at vi, 176–77, 188 (cited in note 63); Murphy, *Congress and the Court* at 65 (cited in note 108); Robert McCloskey, *The American Supreme Court* 176–77, 224 (1960); Schwartz, *The Supreme Court: Constitutional Revolution in Retrospect* at 16, 35 (cited in note 134); Mason, *Harlan Fiske Stone: Pillar of the Law* at 455, 458 (cited in note 21); Rodell, *Nine Men* at 249–50 (cited in note 63); Wright, *The Growth of American Constitutional Law* at 179, 222 (cited in note 63); Robert H. Jackson, *The Struggle for Judicial Supremacy* 191–92, 218, 235 (1941); Corwin, *Constitutional Revolution, Ltd.* at 53, 72 (cited in note 134); Corwin, *Court over Constitution* at 156 n 60 (cited in note 63); Alsop and Catledge, *The 168 Days* at 143, 146 (cited in note 69).

[194] In the wake of the *Labor Board Cases*, the following decisions either explicitly stated or implicitly suggested that *Carter v Carter Coal Co.*, 298 US 238 (1936), had been thereby overruled: *Humble Oil & Refining Co. v NLRB*, 113 F2d 85, 88–89 (5th Cir 1940); *NLRB v Crowe Coal Co.*, 104 F2d 633, 637–39 (8th Cir 1939); *NLRB v Kentucky Fire Brick Co.*, 99 F2d 89, 91–92 (6th Cir 1938); *NLRB v Carlisle Lumber Co.*, 94 F2d 138, 144 (9th Cir 1937); *NLRB v Santa Cruz Fruit Packing Co.*, 91 F2d 790, 792–93 (9th Cir 1937); *Edwards v United States*, 91 F2d 767, 780 (9th Cir 1937); *Divine v Levy*, 39 F Supp 44, 48 (WD La 1941).

[195] Stanley Reed, *Memorandum for the Attorney General*, Apr 22, 1937, National Archives, Washington, DC, Dept of Justice 114-115-2, quoted in Leuchtenburg, *Franklin D. Roosevelt's Supreme Court "Packing" Plan* at 318–19 (cited in note 92) ("I do not see any clear inconsistency between Wagner on the one hand and the Guffey or N.R.A. decision on the other. The Wagner decision is based on the right to remedy situations which obstruct or tend to obstruct interstate commerce. The Guffey and Poultry Code were aimed directly at wages, hours and labor conditions").

[196] Charles Fahy, *Notes on Developments in Constitutional Law, 1936–1949*, 38 Georgetown L J 1, 11 (1949) ("My own view was at the time and is now that the *Labor Board Cases* con-

mentators in the law review literature;[197] and several lower federal court judges appointed by presidents of both political parties.[198] Second, between 1938 and 1940 the Court's commerce power decisions proceeded along rather conventional lines of doctrinal analysis pertaining to federal legislative jurisdiction over interstate marketing and transportation. Doctrinal innovation was not necessary to

---

stituted no departure from the past, unless the very recent past, and that indeed they were distinguishable from the *Carter Coal* case. The principles laid down in earlier cases, cited and quoted in detail in the *Labor Board Cases*, seemed directly applicable"). See also Peter Irons, *The New Deal Lawyers* 252–53, 258 (1982) (Fahy was confident that the superior draftsmanship of the NLRA would meet with the approval of Hughes and Roberts and that they would vote to uphold the statute, and "encouraged his staff to prepare their arguments on the assumption that an unfavorable decision in *Carter* would not invalidate the Wagner Act"); Leonard, *A Search for a Judicial Philosophy* at 243 (cited in note 19) (quoting Fahy as stating in a 1963 interview that "the Wagner Act should have been sustained on the basis of precedents . . . and I am not inclined to attribute the fact that it was sustained to anything but that it was believed to be constitutional").

[197] The following publications viewed the *Labor Board* decisions as resting on the established doctrine, which had formed the basis of the NLRB's legal strategy, that Congress could regulate intrastate activities situated in a "stream," "flow," or "current" of interstate commerce: Donald R. Harter, Note, *Constitutional Law: A Survey of Recent Decisions on the Commerce Clause*, 26 Cornell L Q 464, 466–67 (1941); Walter L. Daykin, *Interstate Commerce as Defined in the National Labor Relations Act*, 19 BU L Rev 586, 598 (1939); Paul H. Douglas and Joseph Hackman, *The Fair Labor Standards Act of 1938 I*, 53 Pol Sci Q 491, 493 (1938); Note, *Interstate Commerce: Jurisdiction of the National Labor Relations Board*, 26 Cal L Rev 273, 274 (1938); P. N. Cooper, Comment, *Constitutional Law—Interstate Commerce—National Labor Relations (Wagner) Act*, 11 S Cal L Rev 240, 250–52 (1938); Burton A. Finberg, Note, 17 BU L Rev 710, 721 (1937); Warren Woods and Altha Connor Wheatley, *The Wagner Act Decisions—A Charter of Liberty for Labor?*, 5 Geo Wash L Rev 846, 853–54 (1937); Jane Alvies, *The Commerce Power—From Gibbons v Ogden to the Wagner Act Cases*, 3 Ohio St L J 307, 307–08 (1937). Others, while not using the terms "stream," "flow," or "current," nevertheless emphasized the importance of the interstate transits of materials and products both to and from the plants in question. See John J. Trenam, Note, *Commerce Power Since the Schechter Case*, 31 Georgetown L J 201, 205 (1943); D. J. Farage, *That Which "Directly" Affects Interstate Commerce*, 42 Dickinson L Rev 1, 8–9 (1937). Scholars taking such views therefore doubted that *A. L. A. Schechter Poultry Corp. v United States*, 295 US 495 (1935), or *Carter* had been overruled. See, for example, Alvies, 3 Ohio St L J at 309, 319–20; Joseph H. Mueller, *Businesses Subject to the National Labor Relations Act*, 35 Mich L Rev 1286, 1297–98 (1937); Note, *Constitutional Law—Interstate Commerce—Constitutionality of National Labor Relations Act as Applied to Manufacturing*, 6 Brooklyn L Rev 467, 469 (1937). See also Lloyd Garrison, *Government and Labor: The Latest Phase*, 37 Colum L Rev 897, 898–99 (1937); Mason, *Harlan Fiske Stone: Pillar of the Law* at 553 (cited in note 21).

[198] See *United States v Wrightwood Dairy Co.*, 123 F2d 100, 103 (7th Cir 1941) (*Schechter* still good law); *United States v Adler's Creamery, Inc.*, 107 F2d 987, 989 (2d Cir 1939) (*Schechter* and *Carter* still good law); *Moore v Chicago Mercantile Exchange*, 90 F2d 735, 736–40 (7th Cir 1937) (*Schechter* and *Carter* still good law); *United States v Barr & Bloomfield Shoe Mfg. Co.*, 35 F Supp 75, 77–78 (Dist NH 1940) (*Schechter* and *Carter* still good law); *United States v F. W. Darby Lumber Co.*, 32 F Supp 734 (SD Ga 1940) (holding that commerce power did not reach intrastate activities of production for interstate commerce); *Bagby v Cleveland Wrecking Co.*, 28 F Supp 271, 272 (WD Ky 1939) (*Schechter* and *Carter* still good law); *Currin v Wallace*, 19 F Supp 211, 217 (ED NC 1937) (*Carter* still good law).

sustain the statutes challenged before the Court in those years.[199] And third, when Congress asserted genuinely novel claims of regulatory authority over manufacturing and agriculture with the Fair Labor Standards Act (FLSA)[200] and the 1941 amendments[201] to the Agricultural Adjustment Act of 1938,[202] several of the Justices did not regard the *Labor Board* decisions as providing adequate constitutional foundation for those measures. Instead, they genuinely struggled with the Commerce Clause issues that those statutes raised. It was only with difficulty and reluctance that Hughes, the author of the *Labor Board* opinions, ultimately joined Stone's opinion upholding congressional power to regulate the wages and hours of factory employees engaged in "production for interstate commerce" in *United States v Darby Lumber Co.*[203] And even a Court now dominated by Roosevelt appointees required reargument and a good deal of soul searching before a majority could be assembled to uphold federal regulation of the growth of wheat for home consumption on Roscoe Filburn's farm.[204] *Darby* (1941) cited the *Labor Board Cases* only once in passing;[205] *Wickard v Filburn* (1942) did not cite them at all.[206] The Justices of the early 1940s treated the *Labor Board Cases* not as a germinal manifesto on the scope of federal power, but instead as yesterday's news.

Finally, the docket books provide extensive documentation of the Court's deliberations in the *Social Security Cases*. Here we see the Justices speaking for themselves and only to one another, almost certainly without expectation that the contents of their discussion ever would be disclosed to the public. Justice Butler's notes of the conference reveal that the jurists did not regard their decisions upholding the federal statute as repudiating the positions that they had taken in *United States v Butler*, nor as in any other way marking a new departure in the constitutional law governing congressional fiscal powers.

[199] For a detailed examination of these decisions, see Cushman, *Rethinking the New Court Deal* at 182–207 (cited in note 50).

[200] 52 Stat 1060 (1938).

[201] 55 Stat 203 (1941).

[202] 52 Stat 31 (1938).

[203] See Cushman, *Rethinking the New Court Deal* at 208–09 (cited in note 50).

[204] See id at 212–24.

[205] 312 US 100, 119 (1941).

[206] 317 US 111 (1942).

Both Van Devanter and Sutherland were in the majority in *Helvering v Davis*, and both their comments at conference and their published dissent in *Steward Machine* make clear their agreement with the majority's resolution of the fiscal power issues that the case presented. The majority applied standard taxing and spending power doctrine in utterly conventional ways. From the perspective of the seven Justices of the majority, so far as the fiscal powers were concerned, there simply was no "constitutional revolution" to explain.

There can be no doubt that the period between the Wall Street crash of 1929 and the Allied victory in World War II witnessed significant transformations in American constitutional law. Congressional power under the Commerce Clause became virtually plenary, executive authority was significantly enhanced, the remnants of economic substantive due process were retired, dormant Commerce Clause restraints on states and localities were relaxed, and the Court became more ardent in the defense of civil rights and civil liberties. None of this can be gainsaid. But thanks in part to the revelations discovered in the newly available Hughes Court docket books, the long-standing claim that the nation underwent a "Constitutional Revolution" in the spring of 1937 appears exceedingly weak indeed.